Lecture Notes in Artificial Intelligence   3257

Edited by J. G. Carbonell and J. Siekmann

Subseries of Lecture Notes in Computer Science

Enrico Motta   Nigel Shadbolt
Arthur Stutt   Nick Gibbins (Eds.)

Engineering Knowledge
in the Age
of the Semantic Web

14th International Conference, EKAW 2004
Whittlebury Hall, UK, October 5-8, 2004
Proceedings

 Springer

Series Editors

Jaime G. Carbonell, Carnegie Mellon University, Pittsburgh, PA, USA
Jörg Siekmann, University of Saarland, Saarbrücken, Germany

Volume Editors

Enrico Motta
Arthur Stutt
The Open University, Knowledge Media Institute
Walton Hall, Milton Keynes, MK7 6AA, UK
E-mail: {e.motta, a.stutt}@open.ac.uk

Nigel Shadbolt
Nick Gibbins
University of Southampton, School of Electronics and Computer Science
Highfield, Southampton, SO17 1BJ, UK
E-mail: {nrs, nmg}@ecs.soton.ac.uk

Library of Congress Control Number: 2004112955

CR Subject Classification (1998): I.2, H.4, H.3, J.1, C.2

ISSN 0302-9743
ISBN 3-540-23340-7 Springer Berlin Heidelberg New York

Springer is a part of Springer Science+Business Media

springeronline.com

© Springer-Verlag Berlin Heidelberg 2004
Printed in Germany

Typesetting: Camera-ready by author, data conversion by Scientific Publishing Services, Chennai, India
Printed on acid-free paper   SPIN: 11329886   06/3142   5 4 3 2 1 0

Preface

The central themes of the 14th International Conference on Knowledge Engineering and Knowledge Management (EKAW 2004) were ontological engineering and the Semantic Web. These provide the key foundational and delivery mechanisms for building open, Web-based knowledge services. However, consistent with the tradition of EKAW conferences, EKAW 2004 was concerned with all aspects of eliciting, acquiring, modelling and managing knowledge, and its role in the construction of knowledge-intensive systems. Indeed a key aspect of the Knowledge Acquisition Workshops (KAWs) held in the US, Europe and Asia over the past 20 years has been the emphasis on 'holistic' knowledge engineering, addressing problem solving, usability, socio-technological factors and knowledge modelling, rather than simply analyzing and designing symbol-level inferential mechanisms. The papers included in this volume are thus drawn from a variety of research areas both at the cutting edge of research in ontologies and the Semantic Web and in the more traditionally grounded areas of knowledge engineering.

A Semantic Web service can be seen as the addition of semantic technologies to Web services to produce Web-accessible services that can be described using appropriate ontologies, reasoned about and combined automatically. Since Web services can be seen as Web-accessible computational objects, much of the work in this area is also concerned with problem-solving methods (PSMs). Over the past 20 years the EKAW community has been at the forefront of research on PSMs and it remains the case that this event is one of the few places in which the reasoning structures that will make up knowledge services are discussed in depth. Ontologies may well be the current buzzword, but knowledge engineers know only too well that without PSMs or some other means of modelling inferential structures, we will never move beyond simple indexing and service discovery systems.

Thus, these proceedings show that research on PSMs is still going strong and PSM technology has much to offer both 'traditional KA' as well as research on the Semantic Web and on Semantic Web services. Van Harmelen et al. show how composite Web service configuration can be seen as an instance of the parametric design PSM. Svatek et al. discuss how PSMs can be deployed to describe deductive Web mining applications. Stojanovic uses the cover-and-differentiate PSM to model the reasoning patterns of a generic e-shop agent. López Cobo et al. present a notification agent in the financial domain, which is implemented using Semantic Web services. Johnston and Kushmerick present an algorithm for Web service data integration. Di Sciascio et al. show how request and offer descriptions can be reconciled.

We can also see several experiments in creating semantic applications. These applications range from semantic portals, through medical applications to applications that use ontologies to establish trust in social networks and extend the possibilities of e-learning.

Contreras presents an overview of a semantic portal currently operational at a Spanish current affairs institute. Lei et al. present OntoWeaver-S, an ontology-based infrastructure for building knowledge portals, which is integrated with a comprehensive Web service platform. This is the first example of an ontology-based modelling methodology to address the issue of providing remote Web services for knowledge portals. Tamma et al. describe a system that combines a number of technologies to search for digital content on the Semantic Web. Stuckenschmidt presents a system that combines thesaurus-based search and topic-based exploration for large information spaces.

Some of the earliest expert systems were concerned with the medical domain so it's good to see that this area of research is still very important to researchers in knowledge technologies. Hu et al. use DAML+OIL to model instances of breast cancer patient records while Dieng-Kuntz et al. model cooperative diagnosis using a medical ontology derived from a medical database and natural-language processing of a textual corpus.

In more explicitly Semantic Web-oriented work, Golbeck and Hendler show how it is possible to calculate reputation ratings to establish trust in a Web node. Stutt and Motta propose a vision of how current online learning environments can be extended through ontologically based learning services.

One of the fundamental problems that needs to be solved if the Semantic Web is to become a reality concerns ontologies. Knowledge engineers invented these as the key enabling technology to support knowledge sharing and reuse, and ontologies have gone on to become the defining property of the Semantic Web. Without an ontology, an application is just another Web application. Thus, at this conference we see several technical papers on issues such as ontological mapping and translation, ontology maintenance, and ontology representations and methodologies.

Papers on the technical aspects of ontologies include those by Herre et al. and van Elst and Kiesel on ontology mapping. Given the heterogeneous nature of the ontology representations to be found on the Web, it is vitally important that we find ways of integrating the knowledge to be found in distributed knowledge bases. One way of doing this is to map between terms in different knowledge bases. Corcho and Gómez-Pérez approach the problem from a different perspective, showing how it is possible to translate from one ontology to another.

If we are going to have large, distributed knowledge bases or populated ontologies that are able to change as knowledge changes, we need some means of maintaining these ontologies. Valarakos shows how an incremental ontology maintenance methodology coupled with ontology learning can lead to better results overall, while Baumeister et al. provide a framework for the automatic restructuring of knowledge bases.

One of the problems of deploying ontologies on the Web is in choosing the notation to use from those available. Wang et al. discuss their experience of teaching OWL-

DL, while Guizzardi et al. provide an ontological analysis of the commonly used UML representation. Van Acker et al. present a Web-based tool for the development of representations of innovation environments. Kitamura and Mizoguchi discuss a methodology for capturing functional knowledge.

We can't have knowledge-based applications (and knowledge services are knowledge intensive by definition) without knowledge, and knowledge needs to be acquired. Thus, true to the name of our conference, we have a range of papers on knowledge acquisition. These range from papers on technical solutions, through acquisition from multiple experts, to tools for KA and KA for specialist applications.

More-traditional knowledge acquisition papers include Pacheco et al.'s work on a knowledge authoring system that uses graphical assembly to capture different kinds of rules and relations. Bekmann and Hoffmann present a novel incremental knowledge acquisition approach to the introduction of domain knowledge in adapting probabilistic search algorithms. Tecuci et al. show how a knowledge base can be built from the knowledge of multiple experts. Helsper et al. discuss methods for acquiring the probabilities needed to build Bayesian networks in the domain of neonatology. Suryanto and Compton show how machine learning can be used to generalize from knowledge to produce new predicates that reduce knowledge acquisition. Molina and Blasco describe a document-oriented KA tool for modelling of emergency management in the domain of hydrology. Finally Simpson et al. discuss an environment for knowledge acquisition for AI planning in the hiking domain.

The EKAW series of workshops started in 1987 to provide a forum for researchers interested in the acquisition, modelling and engineering of knowledge. Seventeen years later this event is still going strong, and indeed the original motivation (engineering knowledge for use in intelligent applications) is of course more pressing today than it was 17 years ago. The dramatic growth of the Web and the rise of the knowledge economy makes knowledge-based decision making under uncertainty the key skill needed to deal with complexity. Thus, EKAW is even more important and topical now than it was when it was launched. At the same time the World Wide Web provides an infrastructure capable of realizing the ambitions and aspirations of our field. The goal ultimately is to offer up both services and content in the right form, at the right time to those agents (human and artificial) that need them.

We would like to acknowledge the sterling work of the members of the Programme Committee in reviewing and commenting on, in some heroic cases, up to eight papers. Special thanks also go to Jane Whild at the Open University and Susan Davies at the University of Southampton without whose organizational skills this conference would still be a gleam in the organizers' eyes. The other members of the local organization committee also deserve our gratitude for dealing with a variety of academic and support tasks. They include John Domingue, Martin Dzbor, Harriett Cornish and Damian Dadswell at the Open University and Kieron O'Hara at the University of Southampton (although we ought to point out that Kieron did not really have that much to do ...).

Finally we are also grateful to our sponsors, the Engineering and Physical Sciences Research Council (UK), the Advanced Knowledge Technologies (AKT) project, the KnowledgeWeb Network of Excellence, the British Computer Society, the Open University and the University of Southampton, for ensuring the financial viability of the event.

July 2004

Enrico Motta
Nigel Shadbolt
Arthur Stutt
Nick Gibbins

Organization

Conference Chairs

Enrico Motta   Open University (UK)
Nigel Shadbolt   University of Southampton (UK)

Workshop and Tutorials Chair

John Domingue   Open University (UK)

Poster Session Chair

Nick Gibbins   University of Southampton (UK)

Technology Demonstrations Chair

Martin Dzbor   Open University (UK)

Programme Committee

Stuart Aitken	University of Edinburgh (UK)
Hans Akkermans	Free University Amsterdam (Netherlands)
Nathalie Aussenac-Gilles	IRIT-CNRS Toulouse (France)
Richard Benjamins	iSOCO (Spain)
Brigitte Biébow	Université Paris-Nord (France)
Joost Breuker	University of Amsterdam (Netherlands)
Fabio Ciravegna	University of Sheffield (UK)
Olivier Corby	INRIA Sophia-Antipolis (France)
Paul Compton	University of New South Wales (Australia)
Monica Crubézy	Stanford University (USA)
Srinandan Dasmahapatra	University of Southampton (UK)
Ying Ding	University of Innsbruck (Austria)
Rose Dieng-Kuntz	INRIA Sophia-Antipolis (France)
John Domingue	Open University (UK)
Jérôme Euzenat	INRIA Rhône-Alpes (France)
Dieter Fensel	University of Innsbruck (Austria)
Mariano Fernández-López	Universidad Politécnica de Madrid (Spain)
Aldo Gangemi	ISTC-CNR (Italy)
John Gennari	University of Washington (USA)

Yolanda Gil	ISI University of Southern California (USA)
Asunción Gómez-Pérez	Universidad Politécnica de Madrid (Spain)
Nicola Guarino	ISTC-CNR (Italy)
Udo Hahn	Universitaet Freiburg (Germany)
Catholinj Jonker	Free University of Amsterdam (Netherlands)
Rob Kremer	University of Calgary (Canada)
Riichiro Mizoguchi	Osaka University (Japan)
Martin Molina González	Universidad Politécnica de Madrid (Spain)
Hiroshi Motoda	Osaka University (Japan)
Mark Musen	Stanford University (USA)
Kieron O'Hara	University of Southampton (UK)
Daniel E. O'Leary	University of Southern California (USA)
Bijan Parsia	University of Maryland (USA)
Enric Plaza i Cervera	Spanish Scientific Research Council, CSIC (Spain)
Alun Preece	University of Aberdeen (UK)
Ulrich Reimer	University of Konstanz (Germany)
Chantal Reynaud	University of Paris-Sud (France)
François Rousselot	ERIC-LIIA ENSAIS University of Strasbourg (France)
Marie-Christine Rousset	University of Paris-Sud (France)
Guus Schreiber	Free University of Amsterdam (Netherlands)
Derek Sleeman	University of Aberdeen (UK)
Steffen Staab	University of Karlsruhe (Germany)
Heiner Stuckenschmidt	Free University of Amsterdam (Netherlands)
Rudi Studer	University of Karlsruhe (Germany)
Arthur Stutt	Open University (UK)
York Sure	University of Karlsruhe (Germany)
Annette ten Teije	Free University of Amsterdam (Netherlands)
Frank Van Harmelen	Free University of Amsterdam (Netherlands)
Bob Wielinga	University of Amsterdam (Netherlands)
Mike Wooldridge	University of Liverpool (UK)
Zdenek Zdrahal	Open University (UK)

Additional Reviewers

Harith Alani	University of Southampton (UK)
Jesus Barrasa	Universidad Politécnica de Madrid (Spain)
Christopher Brewster	University of Sheffield (UK)
Liliana Cabral	Open University (UK)
Sam Chapman	University of Sheffield (UK)
Oscar Corcho	Universidad Politécnica de Madrid (Spain)
Jos de Bruijn	University of Innsbruck (Austria)

Gary Wills	University of Southampton (UK)
Lai Xu	Free University of Amsterdam (Netherlands)
Pinar Yolum	Free University of Amsterdam (Netherlands)
Valentin Zacharias	University of Karlsruhe (Germany)
Anna V. Zhdanova	University of Innsbruck (Austria)

Local Organization Committee

Damian Dadswell	Open University (UK)
Susan Davies	University of Southampton (UK)
John Domingue	Open University (UK)
Martin Dzbor	Open University (UK)
Nick Gibbins	University of Southampton (UK)
Enrico Motta	Open University (UK)
Kieron O'Hara	University of Southampton (UK)
Nigel Shadbolt	University of Southampton (UK)
Arthur Stutt	Open University (UK)
Jane Whild	Open University (UK)

Table of Contents

Ontology Maintenance

Applications to Medicine

Portals

Knowledge Acquisition

Web Services and Problem Solving Methods

Search, Browsing and Knowledge Acquisition

Short Papers

The Theory of Top-Level Ontological Mappings and Its Application to Clinical Trial Protocols

Barbara Heller[*], Heinrich Herre[#], and Kristin Lippoldt[*]

Onto-Med Research Group
[*]Institute for Medical Informatics, Statistics and Epidemiology (IMISE),
[#]Department of Formal Concepts, Institute for Informatics (IfI),
University of Leipzig, Germany
Liebigstrasse 27, 04103 Leipzig, Germany
Phone: +49 (0)341 9716104, Fax: +49 (0)341 9716130
herre@informatik.uni-leipzig.de
{barbara.heller, kristin.lippoldt}@onto-med.uni-leipzig.de

Abstract. In the present paper we expound a methodology for the development of terminology systems and the construction of semantically founded knowledge systems. This method is based on ontological mappings using reference top-level ontologies, and is inspired by rigorous logico-philosophical principles. We outline a framework consisting of a system of formal tools designed to support the development of data dictionaries, taxonomies and knowledge systems. The core-module of this system named *Onto-Builder* is an internet-based software application for building context-sensitive data dictionaries. To ensure the broad acceptance of context-dependent descriptions within a diverse group of domain experts, a multistage quality assurance cycle has been established. Ontological mappings based on top-level ontologies are the foundation of a further module of the system, which assists the construction of knowledge systems out of terminology systems. The framework is intended to be applied to the medical domain, in particular to the field of clinical trials.

1 Introduction

In achieving good medical care, quality assurance has become increasingly important in the last few years. This is particularly the case in the area of clinical research, where national and international projects have been undertaken to develop strict guidelines for carrying out clinical trials. The high level of documentation, which such guidelines require, however, is time-consuming and can result in enormous human resource expenditures. In part, this is due to the absence of standardized clinical trial protocols and corresponding CRFs[1]. Another factor is the unavailability of explicit definitions of the medical concepts used in these documents. This is particularly troublesome in multidisciplinary areas of medicine such as oncology, where cooperating experts often interpret medical data differently, each according to

---

[1] A Case Report Form (CRF) is a printed, optical or electronic document designed to record all of the protocol required information to be the reported to the sponsor on each trial subjects. [1]

E. Motta et al. (Eds.): EKAW 2004, LNAI 3257, pp. 1–14, 2004.

his or her individual area of expertise. These multiple interpretations or views often result in the ambiguous, misleading, or incorrect use of concepts in clinical trial protocols, CRFs, and other trial documentation, especially during the preparation of consecutive clinical trial protocols. This in turn can lead to misinterpretations of medical facts and incorrect diagnoses, diminishing the overall quality of health care in general and clinical research in particular.

To address these problems, software applications have been developed in recent years to support diagnostic and therapeutic guidelines [2] as well as the documentation and management process of clinical trials, e.g., eClinical Trial[®]2. Such systems do not currently support context-dependent definition variants for concepts, however, which are particularly useful in large, multidisciplinary projects such as clinical trials, which involve multiple users with diverse backgrounds, specializations and levels of expertise.

As discussed above, it is precisely under these conditions where a single concept can have different meanings for different users as a function of the specific context in which a concept is viewed. Against this background, our approach is focused on the development and implementation of a computer-based framework for a standardized medical terminology with the following aims:

– Reusability of precise definitions of medical concepts to optimize the development of clinical trial protocols and CRFs as well as to achieve better comparability of clinical trial results.
– Availability of a consistent concept base, which supports the harmonization of clinical trial databases as well as the interchange between clinical trial management software and local clinical information systems.
– Availability of a domain-specific ontology for clinical trials, which is based on a top-level ontology and executable on the computer.

The remainder of our paper is structured as follows. In the following section we review three medical terminology systems – SNOMED, UMLS and GALEN – and situate our proposal in the context of current research in terminology management. Section 3 describes the data dictionary model, introduces our software system *Onto-Builder* [3, 4], and discusses the quality assurance cycle. In section 4 the theory of ontological mappings, which are based on top-level ontologies, is expounded; the underlying formal principles are presented in some detail. The discussion on the chosen method and the outlook for further work in the area of ontological research are provided in the last two sections.

2 Terminology Systems

The different terminology systems can be distinguished into nomenclatures, classification systems and data dictionaries. These systems are based on different architectures and methods for the representation of concepts. In the sequel we restrict to the medical domain, which is sufficiently rich to present all types of terminology systems. The following authors [5, 6] [7, 8] [9] give a summary of different medical terminology systems and discuss the features of these systems with regard to

---

[2] http://www.ert.com/products/eresearch_network.htm

requirements for concept taxonomies. For our objective to construct an ontologically founded context-sensitive data dictionary - in the first step it was necessary to analyze medical terminology systems with regard to reusability for the construction of a context-sensitive data dictionary model. Therefore we analyzed medical terminology systems among other things concerning their context representation methods and their relation to top-level ontologies. In the following we give a short summary of our evaluation results concerning the context representation and concentrating on the most relevant terminology systems.

Within <u>SNOMED CT</u> [10] contexts are defined as "information that fundamentally changes the type of thing it is associated with". An example for a context is <family history of> because it changes e.g., the type of the concept <myocardial infarction> which is a heart disease to the new concept <family history of myocardial infarction> which is not a heart disease.

<u>UMLS</u> [11] integrates concepts and concept names (terms) from many controlled vocabularies and classification systems using a uniform representation structure with 134 different semantic types. In UMLS the context-dependency of concepts is not explicitly elaborated. UMLS uses contexts only to describe structural features of sources, e.g., the use of siblings and multiple hierarchical positions of concepts.

In <u>GALEN</u> [12] the entity-types modality and role can be interpreted as context-representing entities. An example for modality is <FamilyHistory> whereas in combination with the concept <Diabetes> the new concept <FamilyHistory of Diabetes> can be derived. Examples for role are <Steroid which playsRole HormoneRole> or <playsRole Drug-Role>. These examples describe the contexts <drug>, <hormone> which by implication are given by the denotations of the corresponding roles but can be derived explicitly.

In addition, the multi-axial classification of concepts can be considered as a representation form for contexts in which the root of a classification axis would correspond to a context; whereas a multiple assignment of concepts to super ordinate concepts does not have influence on its attributes/relations.

Our terminology systems analysis has shown that the underlying models of SNOMED, UMLS, GALEN do not fit our requirements with regard to a context-dependent description of concepts. To achieve our goal, namely the definition of a semantically founded and context-dependent data dictionary, we have conceived a terminology model of our own.

3 Terminology Building and Knowledge Acquisition

Our approach aims, in the first step, at the construction of context-sensitive data dictionaries. The innovation of this approach lies in the ontological foundation of the underlying terminology model for basic and domain-specific concepts and relations. The terminology framework is partly based on a generic, domain-independent top-level ontology, described in [13] [14].

The *Onto-Builder* [3] is the core-module of our general framework; it is an internet-based software application, which we have developed as a first prototype for the construction of terminology systems. The *Onto-Builder* offers the possibility to represent natural-language, as well as semi-formal concept descriptions. An ontologically founded frame-work [13] [14] is made available by basic and domain-specific entities for the representation of semi-formal concept descriptions. These concept descriptions are created according to our terminological guidelines [4] which contain lexical and semantic rules for defining medical concepts and relations.

Another module of the system assists the extraction of formal knowledge from several sources; it is intended, in particular, to support the translation of terminology systems and taxonomies into ontologically founded formal *knowledge systems*. Here we use the newly developed theory of ontological mappings, which is based on top-level ontologies. The resulting formal knowledge base is equipped with deductive machinery, which allows for intelligent queries and automatic problem solving abilities.

3.1 Model of the Data Dictionary

The model of the data dictionary is based on the following main entities: concept, denotation, description, context and relation, which are described below.

Concept, Denotation, and Term: A concept is an abstract unit of meaning which is constructed over a set of common qualities [15] and which can also describe a cognitive entity (e.g., feeling, compliance, idea, thought). A denotation or term consists of one or several words and is the linguistic representation of a concept. In our approach two pairs of opposing concepts are distinguished: generic/domain-specific (e.g., <disorder>/<disease>) and primitive/derived concepts (e.g., <therapy>/<supportive therapy>). A concept is called generic if it has the same general meaning in different domains (e.g., the concept <disorder> has the general meaning that something is deficient or has a defect, independently of the domain in which the concept <disorder> is used). The general meaning of a concept is derived of its domain-independent qualities/properties (e.g., in case of <disorder> the property <cause of disorder> is a general property).

Contrary to this, a domain-specific concept has a concrete meaning only in the domain affiliated to it, (e.g., the concept <disease> only has a meaning in the domain of <living beings> and not in the domain <computer science>). Primitive concepts are concepts which do not reference other concepts and therefore cannot be expressed on the basis of other concepts. In contrast to this, derived concepts reference other concepts. Further ontological categories are discussed in [13].

Description: The description of a concept contains information about its meaning with respect to its qualities, its relations to other concepts, statements about its use, etc. The representation method can be natural-language, semi-formal (e.g., attributes, relations, and rules) or formal (axioms).

Context: With regard to the various discussions on the notion of context, e.g., in [16] we give here the following preliminary definition: A context is a coherent frame of circumstances and situations on the basis of which concepts must be understood.

As in the case of *concepts*, we similarly distinguish between generic and domain-specific contexts. A context is generic if concepts which have general properties/qualities are available in it (e.g., a generic context is <process> which contains the concept <process course> with among others the generic property

`<process duration>`). Contrary to this, a domain-specific context includes concepts whose qualities/properties and their corresponding values specifically apply to this context (e.g., a domain-specific context is `<disease>` which contains the concept `<course of a disease>` with among others the domain-specific property `<course expression>` and the values `<chronic>` or `<acute>`.

Relation: according to [14] relations are defined as entities which glue together the things of the world. We distinguish between three classes of relations: basic, domain-specific and terminological relations. Our method handles at the present stage 11 basic relations (e.g., `<instantiation>`, `<membership>`, `<part-of>`, `<inherence>`, `<association`, `<denotation>`, `<ontical connectedness>`). These relations are defined and available in our representation language GOL[3] [14]. Examples for domain-specific relations are: `<treatedBy>`, `<SideEffectOf>` as well as for terminological relations: `<synonymy>`, `<homonymy>`, `<polysemy>`.

The basic entities and relations of the data dictionary model are represented in figure 1. The syntax of the model in figure 1 follows the UML[4] syntax, whereas rectangles represent classes (here: entities), rhombus n-ary associations (here: relations) and lines represent relations between the entities.

In our model one `Concept` can be assigned to many `Description/Context` pairs `[1..n]` and one `Context` can be assigned to many `Concept/Description` pairs `[1..n]`. A `Concept` can be defined only by one `Description` in one `Context`. Different `descriptions` for a `concept` apply in different `contexts`. The relation between `Description`, `Concept` and `Context` is expressed by the ternary association `ConceptDescriptionContext` which satisfies the above mentioned constraints. The entity `Denotation` describes `Concepts` and `Contexts` via the association *denotes*. The dependency (here: *dependentOn*) between `Denotation` and `Context` means that `Denotation` of a `Concept` can be dependent of the corresponding `Context`. If a `Concept` is not yet assigned to a `Context`, a default `Denotation` is given.

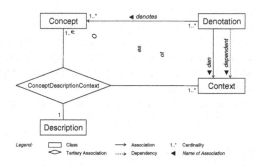

Fig. 1. Excerpt of the data dictionary model

---

[3] General Ontological Language is a formal framework for building ontologies. GOL is being developed by the Onto-Med research group at the University of Leipzig [http://www.onto-med.de].
[4] Unified Modeling Language [17].

The next two examples show context-dependent descriptions with regard to different granularities on the one hand, and to status and process-oriented aspects on the other.

Example 1: Remission of a tumor

```
<concept>: remission
  <context>: hematology
    <denotation>: hematological remission
      <description>: There are no signs of diseases using examination
      methods which identify variances on the cellular level.
  <context>: cytology
    <denotation>: cytological remission
      <description>: There are no signs of diseases [...] variances on
      the chromosomal level.
```

The difference between the two concept descriptions in example 1 is seen in the different granularity levels (here: the cellular and chromosomal level).

Example 2: Staging

```
<concept>: staging
  <context>: (status(documentation-results))
    <denotation>: staging
      <description>: Examination results of obligate examinations:
      anamnesis, clinical and laboratory examinations, gastroscopy, etc.
      <source>: CRF of RICOVER-60 Protocol [18]
  <context>: process
    <denotation>: staging
      <description>: Detection of the anatomic extent of the tumor, both
      in its primary location and in metastatic sites through
      exploratory surgery or biopsy and assignment to the TNM
      classification stages ...
      <source>: definition derived from [19]
```

Example 2 shows the interpretation of a concept description according to the contexts <status> (here: <documentation-results>) and <process>. It shows also the difference between generic and domain-specific descriptions of the very same concept (here: <staging>). In our example, the process-oriented description is generic for the oncological area, the status-oriented description is specific only for one disease (here: Aggressive Non-Hodgkin's Lymphoma) [18]. Different relations are valid in the various contexts (e.g., in the context (<status>(<documentation-results>)) the relation <has ExaminationResult> is valid and in the context <process> the relation <hasMethod> is valid).

3.2 Quality Assurance Cycle

The quality assurance cycle guarantees the broad acceptance of context-dependent descriptions within a group of domain experts. This cycle is based on five user roles, which are dependent on the following aspects: function, organization, experience, qualification, and language. A personal profile is derived from the information about the respective aspects for every user (e.g., person A has the following profile <function>: editor, <organization>: EORTC, <experience>: expert in medicine, <qualification>: principle investigator, <language>: English). According to this user profile, person A is authorized to work on difficult descriptions of medical concepts in the context of clinical trials within the consensus process of the EORTC (European Organization for Research and Treatment of Cancer). To reach a consensus, a workflow with integrated iterative steps has been established. According to the complexity of the concept descriptions, these steps can be modified dynamically with regard to multiple checks of concept descriptions and different user roles. The result of the whole quality assurance cycle is expected to be a consistent and accepted terminological basis. Real consistency cannot be guaranteed; so methods must be developed for consistency checks. In case no consensus can be found, the terminological basis will be tested against our ontological framework.

4 Ontological Mappings Based on Top-Level Ontologies

In this section we describe and discuss some formal basic principles, which are important for the task of constructing a knowledge base out from a terminology system. The ontological mappings, which are introduced and considered in the sequel, are centered on a top-level ontology TO. Hence, the implementation of ontological mappings according to our approach presupposes some fixed top-level ontology. The research group Onto-Med is developing a top-level ontology which is called GFO (General Formal Ontology) and which is part of the GOL-project of the University of Leipzig [13], [14]. The module of the *Onto-Builder*, which supports knowledge extraction, is based on the top-level ontology GFO.

4.1 Formal Principles

We expound in more detail the construction of a formal knowledge bases assisted and supported by top-level reference ontologies. Generally, a formal ontology $Ont = (L, V, Ax(V))$ consists of a structured vocabulary V, called ontological signature, which contains symbols denoting categories, individuals, and relations between categories or between their instances, and a set of axioms $Ax(V)$ which are expressions of the formal language L. The set $Ax(V)$ of axioms captures the meaning of the symbols of V implicitly. A definitional extension $Ont^d = (L, V \cup C(DF), Ax(V) \cup DF)$ of Ont is given by a set DF of explicit definitions over the signature V and a new set $C(DF)$ symbols introduced by the definitions. Every explicit definition has the form $t := e(V)$, where $e(V)$ is an expression of L using only symbols from V (hence the symbol t does not occur in e(V)).

A terminology system TS may be considered as a system $TS = (Tm, Rel, Def)$ consisting of a set Tm of terms which denote concepts, a set Rel of relation symbols denoting relations between concepts or instances, and a function Def associating to every term t of Tm a definition $Def(t)$ in natural or a semi-formal language which describes the meaning of the concept which is denoted by the term t.

An *ontological mapping* M of TS into Ont is given by a pair $M = (tr, DF)$ consisting of a definitional extension Ont^d of Ont by (the set of definitions) DF and function tr which satisfies the following condition:

For every term $t \in Tm$ the function tr determines an expression $tr(Def(t))$ of the extended language $L(V \cup C(DF))$ such that $Def(t)$ and $tr(Def(t))$ are semantically equivalent with respect to the knowledge base $Ax(Ont) \cup DF$.

Then the set $OntMap(TS) = Ax(V) \cup DF \cup \{tr(Def(t)) : t \in Tm\}$ is a formal knowledge base which captures the meaning of TS.

The notion of *semantical equivalence with respect to a knowledge base* is used here informally because a strict formal semantics for natural language sentences does not yet exist; the notion has to be read "the meaning of the natural language (or semi-formal) sentence $Def(t)$ is equivalent to the meaning of the expression $tr(Def(t))$.

An expression e is considered as ontologically founded on an ontology Ont if it is expressed in some definitional extension Ont^d of Ont. Hence, an ontological mapping of a terminology system TS associates to every term of TS an equivalent formal description which is based on a formal ontology Ont. Ontological mappings can be used as a formal framework for schema matching, which is a basic problem in many database application domains, compare [20]. An advanced elaboration of this theory, which is being investigated by the Onto-Med group, will be presented in [21].

We now consider the fine structure of an ontological mapping based on a top-level ontology TO. A definition D of a concept C of a terminology system is – usually – given as a natural language expression $e(C_1,..,C_n, R_1,..., R_m)$ which includes concepts $C_1,...,C_n$ and relations $R_1,..., R_m$. The concepts $C_1,..,C_n$ and relations $R_1,..., R_m$ are in turn defined by other (natural language) expressions based on additional concepts and relations. In order to avoid this infinite regress we select a certain number of concepts $D_1,..,D_k$ and relations $S_1,...,S_l$ – which arise from e – as primitive. An embedding of $\{D_1,...,D_k\}$ into TO is a function emb which associates to every concept D_i a category $emb(D_i) = F_i$ of TO which subsumes D_i, i.e. every instance of D_i is an instance of $emb(D_i)$. The problem, then, is to find a logical expression e_1 based on $\{F_1,...,F_k\}$ and the relations of TO which is equivalent to the initial expression e; such an expression is called a *local ontological mapping based on TO*. An ontological mapping based on TO, then, is a complete system of local ontological mappings covering all terms of the source system TS. It may be expected that – in general – the system TO is too weak to provide such ontological mappings. For this reason TO has to be extended to a suitable system TO_1 by adding further categories and relations, and axioms about them. TO_1 should satisfy certain conditions of naturalness, minimality (the principle of Occam's razor), and modularity. The construction of ontological mappings includes three main tasks:

1. Construction of a set *PCR* of primitive concepts and relations out from the set $\{Def(t) : t \in Tm\}$ (*problem of primitive base*)
2. Construction of an extension TO_1 of TO by adding new categories *Cat* and relations *Rel* and a set of new axioms. $Ax(Cat \cup Rel)$ (*axiomatizability problem*)
3. Construction of equivalent expressions for $Def(t) \cup PCR$ on the base of TO_1 (*definability problem*).

A developed theory of ontological mappings based on top-level ontologies is in preparation and will be expounded in [21].

4.2 The Basic Modularization

In analysing a natural language text T one should satisfy the following basic modularity principle: Firstly, we construct a primitive base PCR for the set CR of concepts and relations which are associated to T; usually, PCR is a proper subset of CR. Note that PCR is not uniquely determined. The explicit knowledge contained in T should be then represented as the union of two disjoint modules:

1. a set $Ax(PCR)$ of axioms about the concepts and relations of PCR
2. a set of explicit definitions $Def(CR - PCR)$ of the non-primitive concepts and relations which are contained in $CR - PCR$.

The knowledge associated to T and with respect to the selection PCR and CR, denoted by $KB(T,PCR)$, is defined by $KB(T) = Ax(PCR) \cup Def(CR - PCR)$.

The difficult task is to find the set $Ax(PCR)$ und to select PCR. If we do not introduce axioms about PCR, i.e. if $Ax(PCR)$ is empty, then the knowledge system $KB(T)$ becomes trivial. This phenomenon is sometimes overlooked in the field of knowledge engineering.

4.3 Example

To illustrate some aspects of ontological mappings we consider the following short example. We focus on the first reduction step of selecting a set of primitive domain-specific concepts. Therefore we will give a preliminary definition of primitive domain concepts.

Definition: A set of concepts C is called primitive concept base for a class DOM of domains (of the same granularity) iff every concept $d \in C$ is generic with respect to all domains from DOM and if there does not exist a concept $d \in C$ which is derivable from the set of concepts $C - \{d\}$ on the same granularity level.

Application
Tissue in the medical sense is to be seen as contained in a primitive domain-specific concept base because its meaning and interpretation is the same in different medical domains (e.g. pathology, endocrinology). The domain-specific concept tissue can be interpreted as a "part of an organism consisting of an aggregate of cells having a similar structure and function"[5]. Normally the concept tissue can be partly derived from the more granular concept cell. In our approach the derivation of concepts is limited to concepts of the same level of granularity and therefore the concept tissue is not derivable from the concept cell. In contrast to tissue the concept fatty tissue should not be considered as a primitive concept. It has the same meaning in different contexts but can be derived directly from the concept tissue and the concept fatty on the same granularity level. Further examples for primitive domain-specific concepts are body, cell, organ, tumour, disease, therapy. To give an example for the main ideas of a local ontological mapping ontological sketched above we consider the

---

[5] [http://www.hyperdictionary.com/]

concept C	organ system
and its	
definition D	A group of organs, vessels, glands, other tissues, and/or pathways which work together to perform a body function within a multicellular organism.

In the first step we analyze the natural language definition D with regard to the concepts and relations it includes. These concepts and relations must be classified in primitive and derived concepts and relations. In the given definition the following concepts should be included, among others, in a primitive domain-specific concept base: organ, vessel, gland, tissue, organism. For further analysis let us consider the primitive concept tissue and focus on its structural aspects. The concept tissue has to be classified within the top-level ontology GFO as physical endurant. This assignment is part of the ontological embedding of the base of primitive concepts into the hierarchy of categories of GFO i.e. (tissue is-a substance).

Further steps of the construction of an ontological mapping have to take into consideration suitable extensions of GFO to finally achieve formal expressions (in the framework of GOL) which are semantically equivalent to the concepts included in the primitive concept base C.

5 Comparison with Other Approaches

We suppose that a *semantic translation* maps knowledge formulated in a source language to some equivalent expression in a target language. This very broad understanding comprises *knowledge extraction* on the basis of natural language texts as well as translations between formal languages. It is common in both cases that the semantics is to be preserved by the transformation. *Ontological mappings* in the sense of the current papers are semantic translations, which are based on top-level ontologies. The meaning of the term *ontology mapping* differs from the meaning of our ontological mappings; ontology mappings are semantic translations between formal knowledge bases (which in many cases are called ontologies).

In the present scientific landscape, two types of tasks (knowledge capturing/extraction vs. ontology mapping) are rather separated. Ontology-related communities in computer science usually deal with translations of knowledge expressed in formal languages, e.g. translations between ontologies based on description logics as is popular in the Semantic Web area.

The problem of how to integrate several formal ontologies in order to use them in combination has been recognized in a number of fields. As a result, a number of approaches ranging from theory-oriented works to implemented tools have been developed. Recently, some overviews of approaches and problems were published [22] [23]; cf. also section 3.6 of [24] and related works discussed in [25]. Schema matching in the database area is frequently considered a similar task, and it is reviewed in [20]. Therefore, we refrain from giving an extensive comparison of single publications. Some of the major works as regards appearance in the literature are FCA-Merge [26], OntoMorph [27], Chimaera [28] and the tools of the PROMPT suite [25], which is developed at Stanford University.

Note that all of these works have not solved the need for a terminological standardization. This is still one problem of the emergent area of ontology mapping. This can also be recognized by the collections of terms presented in [22] [23].

Apart from considering several ontologies in one language, one may want to combine ontologies, which are stated in different languages. Another task, which is closely related to this type of ontology integration problem, is that of comparing formalisms themselves. [29] presents an attempt of a unifying approach. This is also important because each formalism contains itself certain basic ontological assumptions.

The second task from above, i.e. knowledge capturing/extraction, often refers to either knowledge acquisition or fields like natural language processing or computer linguistics. Knowledge acquisition pursues the development of methodologies for human users. In contrast, linguistic-related approaches employ a variety of methods for automated text understanding, from purely statistical approaches to machine learning, which is rooted more deeply in computer science.

One of the closer relationships to the field of ontology with respect to automation arises by WordNet [30]. WordNet is a linguistic resource with explicit semantic relationships connecting its synsets, which can roughly be understood as concepts. It has been used directly as an "ontology", which is debatable, and it has been related to a formal ontology (cf. [31]). Together with sample text corpora tagged with WordNet synsets such an alignment may allow for an improved automated formalization of natural language texts.

We may summarize that ontological mappings as introduced in the current paper can be understood as semantic translations which are centered around top-level ontologies. The target language is always a formal language in which the top-level ontology and its extensions are formalized. Hence, almost all of the mentioned approaches can be interpreted as special cases of ontological mappings.

6 Results and Conclusions

The software tool *Onto-Builder* is the core module of our general framework and has been developed as a first prototype to construct terminology systems. In 2002, the *Onto-Builder* was introduced in the *Competence Network Malignant Lymphoma* and in the *Coordination Centers for Clinical Trials, Cologne* and *Leipzig,* Germany.

Initially a multilingual data dictionary was constructed for the area of clinical trials. In the present version it includes approximately 13 contexts, 1000 domain-specific concepts and 2500 concept descriptions. The evaluation of the data dictionary in the medical research networks has shown that it can be efficiently adapted to different medical domains (here: malignant lymphoma, cardiovascular diseases). The experience gained has shown that explicit concept descriptions are of great use for applications in the domain of clinical trials, e.g., by saving time and improving quality assurance. By integrating medical experts into the development process, a high degree of acceptance of the concept definitions in the data dictionary was reached using the quality assurance cycle.

The explicit separation between the entity types concept, context and relation within our terminology framework permits a high degree of flexibility with regard to extendibility and adaptability. The concept descriptions existing in the first version of the data dictionary still allow for slightly different interpretations despite the assignment of concepts to contexts. This is due to the absence of a completed domain-specific ontology on the basis of which clear descriptions (statements) can be made about the concepts, as well as the absence of an ontological mapping method. In our opinion a clear context-dependent concept definition can be reached if the definition is available in a semi-formal representation language and if this language is based on the basic- and domain-specific entities of the ontological framework. On the way to a representation of concept descriptions which is semi-formal and based on ontologies, we have to be concerned following problems:

- Finding an adequate degree of ontological mapping to make applicability possible.
- Finding clear criteria for the distinction between primitive and derived concepts as well as between general and domain-specific concepts.
- Finding solutions for linguistic problems (e.g., handling of synonyms, homonyms, polysems).
- Finding an intermediate representation level of semantics, which is able to close the gap between natural-language representations and formal ontological propositions while remaining consistent with the top-level ontology of our ontological framework.

If we overcome these problems we will achieve a deeper semantic foundation of concept descriptions in contexts. Our data dictionary is merely a concept base for clinical trials at the present stage and not yet a fully developed and formalized domain ontology. The reason for this lies in the problem of the ontological mapping of natural-language concept definitions via a semi-formal definition to formal propositions based on the built-in top-level ontology. Ontological mapping is a current research topic in the science of *Formal and Applied Ontology*. Against this background in the present paper we discussed the following fundamental issues of ontological mapping:

- Formal principles and ontological mapping tasks
- Basic modularization of knowledge systems.

Future work consists in the further development of the theory of ontological mappings, in the explicit representation of semi-formal descriptions for domain-specific concepts as well as in the expansion of the theoretical framework by further basic categories (e.g., situations, views, qualities).

Acknowledgements

We want to thank our medical experts of the *Competence Network Malignant Lymphoma* and the *Coordination Centers for Clinical Trials*, *Cologne* and *Leipzig* for their support in creating and analyzing medical concepts. Many thanks to the members and the Ph.D. students in the Onto-Med research group for fruitful discussions and implementing software modules for the *Onto-Builder*. In particular we thank Frank Loebe for providing his analysis results concerning the comparison to other approaches (chapter 5).

References

[1] ICH. ICH Harmonised Tripartite Guideline: Guideline for Good Clinical Practice (GCP) E6: International Conference on Harmonisation of Technical Requirements for Registration of Pharmaceuticals for Human Use; May 1996.

[2] Heller B, Löffler M, Musen M, and Stefanelli M, eds. Computer-Based Support for Clinical Guidelines and Protocols. Amsterdam/Berlin/Oxford: IOS Press; 2001.

[3] Heller B, Lippoldt K, and Kuehn K. Onto-Builder - A Tool for Building Data Dictionaries. Onto-Med Report. Leipzig: Forschungsgruppe Ontologies in Medicine, Universität Leipzig; 2003. Report No. 3.

[4] Heller B, Lippoldt K, and Kuehn K. Guideline for Creating Medical Terms. Onto-Med Report. Leipzig: Research Group Ontologies in Medicine, University of Leipzig; 2003. Report No. 4.

[5] Campbell JR, Carpenter P, Sneiderman C, Cohn S, Chute CG, and Warren J. Phase II evaluation of clinical coding schemes: completeness, taxonomy, mapping, definitions, and clarity. *Journal of American Medical Association* 1997; 4:238-251.

[6] Cimino JJ. Desiderata for Controlled Medical Vocabularies in the Twenty-First Century. *Methods of Information in Medicine* 1998; 37(4-5):394-403.

[7] Rector AL. Clinical Terminology: Why Is it so Hard? *Methods of Information in Medicine* 1999; 38:239-252.

[8] de Keizer NF, Abu-Hanna A, and Zwetsloot-Schonk JHM. Understanding terminological systems. I: Terminology and typology. *Methods of Information in Medicine* 2000; 39(1):16-21.

[9] de Keizer NF, and Abu-Hanna A. Understanding terminological systems. II: Experience with conceptual and formal representation of structure. *Methods of Information in Medicine* 2000; 39(1):22-29.

[10] SNOMED. SNOMED® Clinical Terms Content Specification.: College of American Pathologists; 2001. Report No. DRAFT version 004.

[11] NLM. *UMLS Knowledge Sources*. 14 ed: National Library of Medicine (NLM); 2003.

[12] Rogers JE, and Rector AL. Extended Core model for representation of the Common Reference Model for procedures. Manchester, UK: OpenGALEN; 1999.

[13] Heller B, and Herre H. Ontological Categories in GOL. *Axiomathes* 2004; 14(1):57-76.

[14] [14]Heller B, and Herre H. Formal Ontology and Principles of GOL. Onto-Med Report. Leipzig: Research Group Ontologies in Medicine, University of Leipzig; 2003. Report No. 1.

[15] Deutsches Institut für Normung e.V. *DIN 2342 Teil 1: Begriffe der Terminologielehre*. Berlin: Deutsches Institut für Normung e.V.; 10/1992.

[16] Bouquet P, Ghidini C, Giunchiglia F, and Blanzieri E. Theories and uses of context in knowledge representation and reasoning. In: Journal of Pragmatics: Elsevier Science; 2003: p. 455-484.

[17] Booch G, Jacobson I, and Rumbaugh J. *The Unified Modeling Language User Guide*. Amsterdam: Addison-Wesley; 1999.

[18] Pfreundschuh M. Randomised Study Comparing 6 and 8 Cycles of Chemotherapy with CHOP at 14-day Intervals, both with or without the Monoclonal anti-CD20 Antibody Rituximab in Patients aged 61 to 80 Years with Aggressive Non-Hodgkin's Lymphoma. RICOVER-60: German High-grade Non-Hodgkin's Lymphoma Study Group; 1999.

[19] Braunwald E, Isselbacher KJ, Petersdorf RG, Wilson JD, Martin JB, and Fauci AS, eds. Harrison's Principles of Internal Medicine. 11 ed. New York: McGraw-Hill Book Company; 1987.

[20] Rahm E, and Bernstein PA. A survey of approaches to automatic schema matching. *The Very Large Databases Journal* 2001; 10(4):334-350.

[21] Heller B, Herre H, and Loebe F. Ontological Reductions Based on Top-Level Ontologies. forthcoming.

[22] Kalfoglou Y, and Schorlemmer M. Ontology mapping: the state of the art. *The Knowledge Engineering Review* 2003; 18(1):1-31.

[23] Klein M. Combining and relating ontologies: an analysis of problems and solutions. In: Workshop on Ontologies and Information Sharing, IJCAI'01; 2001; Seattle, USA; 2001.

[24] Gómez-Pérez A, Fernández-López M, and Corcho O. *Ontological Engineering: with examples from the areas of Knowledge Management, e-Commerce and the Semantic Web.* Berlin: Springer; 2004.

[25] Musen MA, and Noy NF. The PROMPT suite: interactive tools for ontology merging and mapping. *International Journal of Human-Computer Studies* 2003; 59(6):983-1024.

[26] Stumme G, and Maedche A. FCA-MERGE: Bottom-Up Merging of Ontologies. In: Nebel B, ed. Proceedings of the Seventeenth International Joint Conference on Artificial Intelligence (IJCAI 2001); 2001 Aug, 4-10; Seattle, Washington, USA: Morgan Kaufmann; 2001. p. 225-234.

[27] Chalupsky H. OntoMorph: A Translation System for Symbolic Knowledge. In: Proceedings of 7th International Conference on Knowledge Representation and Reasoning (KR2000); 2000; Breckenridge; 2000. p. 471-482.

[28] McGuinness DL, Fikes R, Rice J, and Wilder S. An Environment for Merging and Testing Large Ontologies. In: Cohn AG, Giunchiglia F, Selman B, eds. Proceedings of the 7th International Conference on Knowledge Representation and Reasoning (KR2000); 2000 April 11-15; Breckenridge, Colorado, USA: Morgan Kaufmann; 2000. p. 483-493.

[29] Flouris G, Plexousakis D, and Antoniou G. On a Unifying Framework for Comparing Knowledge Representation Schemes. In: Bry F, Lutz C, Sattler U, Schoop M, eds. Proceedings of the 10th International Workshop on Knowledge Representation meets Databases (KRDB 2003); 2003 September 15-16; Hamburg, Germany: Technical University of Aachen (RWTH); 2003.

[30] Fellbaum C, ed. WordNet: An Electronic Lexical Database. Language, Speech and Communication Series. Cambridge (Mass.): MIT Press; 1998.

[31] Gangemi A, Navigli R, and Velardi P. The OntoWordNet Project: extension and axiomatization of conceptual relations in WordNet. In; 2003 Nov 3-7; Catania, Italy; 2003. p. 820-838.

Generating and Integrating Evidence
for Ontology Mappings

Ludger van Elst and Malte Kiesel

German Research Center for Artificial Intelligence
– Knowledge Management Department –
{elst,kiesel}@dfki.uni-kl.de

Abstract. For more than a decade, ontologies have been proposed as a means to enable sharing and reuse of knowledge. While originally relatively narrow information landscapes have been in mind (e.g., knowledge sharing between a few expert systems) the application areas proposed nowadays (e.g., organizational knowledge management or the Semantic Web) are rather broad and open.

From abstract considerations about the distributed nature of knowledge as well as from observation of actual (human) ontology negotiation processes it seems clear that *globally* agreed-upon conceptualizations are probably not obtainable. Therefore, ontology matching and mapping procedures play an essential role in more open information landscapes.

In this paper, we present a framework that collects and integrates heuristic *evidence* for ontology mappings, allows a knowledge engineer to browse a space of (assessed) mapping candidates in order to select adequate candidates and then leverage them to a level of formal statements for ontology merging. A simple example session shows the intended handling of the prototype and demonstrates strengths and weaknesses of particular sources of matching evidence.

1 Motivation

Within the *sharing and reuse effort*, ontologies have been widely proposed as a means to alleviate model mismatches at the knowledge level [17]. The scenarios envisioned more than a decade ago were relatively narrow: Knowledge sharing between a few expert systems on the one hand and reuse of knowledge models by a couple of system engineers on the other. Nowadays, ontologies are proposed for much broader and more open information landscapes, e.g., as backbone technology for organizational knowledge management (KM) systems [1] or even as silver bullet in e-commerce applications and for the semantic web [10]. While already much research has been carried out in the areas of ontology representation, acquisition and inferencing, the broadening of the scope of ontology technology leads to (at least) two additional challenges:

1. *Involvement of end users* in ontology–related processes: While with the "expert system scenario" mainly knowledge engineers were the contributors and costumers of ontologies, in the broader application areas often also end users have to understand them (at least at a certain level of abstraction, e.g., in the case of web portals) or even are a valuable source for their maintenance (e.g., KM in product development).

E. Motta et al. (Eds.): EKAW 2004, LNAI 3257, pp. 15–29, 2004.

2. *Scaling–up* the idea of ontologies: From the viewpoint of the topology of communication, the "shared conceptualization approach" tries to reduce the exponentially growing number of one-to-one mappings between models by introducing the ontology as a "hub" or mediator, resulting in a star–shaped topology. However, in more open worlds a centralized "knowledge topology" is hardly reachable. While having OWL as a W3C recommendation[1] is a significant achievement with respect to a *representation* ontology for the semantic web, for conceptual as well as for pragmatic reasons it is unlikely that we will see a similarly high agreement on specific domain ontologies[2]. Consequently, the question of mediating between several domain ontologies will become more and more important.

Although we will concentrate on the latter topic we believe that for a viable approach to ontologies in more open information landscapes, in the long term both issues have to be tackled in an integrated manner[3].

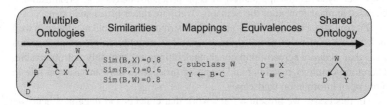

Fig. 1. Examplary Operation Points in the "Ontology Matching Continuum"

Ontology matchings can be seen as statements about relationships between elements (e.g., concepts) of two or more ontologies. Figure 1 exemplifies that these statements can occur on various levels of formalization: *Similarities* are relatively informal as the semantics of this relation is typically ill–defined or application specific (see, e.g., the discussion about similarity and utility in case-based reasoning [3]). *Mappings* can take various forms, from more heuristics-like to formally grounded ones (e.g., "class C is a subclass of class W", or "concept Y is a combination of the concepts B and C"). *Equivalences* state that (parts of) the ontologies indeed intend to express the same conceptualizations. The ultimate result of ontology matching may be a *shared ontology* that comprises the conceptualizations captured by the input ontologies.

Ontology matching procedures perform transitions along this continuum, from heterogeneous ontologies to shared conceptualizations. More logics-oriented approaches, for example, try to formally infer mappings from the input ontologies. It is well known that such a semantic unification is a complex, highly knowledge–intensive task that is in general not solvable (see [23] for recent results in this area). While these approaches have the attractiveness of being logically sound, they are quite heavy–weight and—even more important—rely on some common vocabulary in the definitions of the input ontologies. This pre–requisite might be satisfied relatively easily on closed–world scenarios

---

[1] see http://www.w3.org/News/2004#item14

[2] For an extended discussion on the distributed nature of knowledge, see, e.g., [8].

[3] With the notion of *ontological societies* we have made a first step into that direction [6, 21].

(e.g., schema matching in federated databases), but it is a serious problem in the case of more open information landscapes (like the semantic web and organizational knowledge management) with their continuously evolving domain ontologies.

The approach presented in this paper therefore abandons the path of formally sound reasoning for matching ontologies and instead establishes a framework that collects and integrates heuristic *evidence* for ontology mappings. As the sources of evidence are various forms of similarities in the input ontologies, the framework comprises the whole range depicted in Figure 1. The prototypical implementation computes these evidences and allows a knowledge engineer to browse a space of (assessed) mapping candidates in order to select adequate candidates and then leverage them to a level of formal statements for ontology merging.

The remainder of this paper is organized as follows: Section 2 gives an overview of the framework and its algorithmic basics. In section 3, we describe a prototypical implementation of the framework on top of the Protégé ontology environment. A simple example session shows the intended handling of the tool and demonstrates strengths and weaknesses of particular sources of matching evidence. Finally, we summarize the basic features of the approach and give a brief outlook on future work.

2   An Evidence-Based Framework for Ontology Mapping

The main task in merging ontologies is to identify relationships between elements of the input ontologies, most basically between the ontologies' classes. These relationships are necessary to determine which actions to perform in order to create a merged ontology (see Figure 2). As already stated above, in this paper we will not *formally infer* class relationships, but *gather evidence* for such relationships. In the literature, ontology merging operations are mainly based on two sources of evidence:

- *Term–based evidence* considers similarities in the the textual description (i.e., the "name") of concepts in the source ontologies. Examples are the Chimaera ontology environment [15, 14] and Protégé's PROMPT tab [18].
- *Topology–based evidence* considers the structure of the source ontologies, e.g., by determining similarities of the graphs representing concepts and their relationships, as done by the Similarity Flooding algorithm [16].

The charm of term–based evidence is that a variety of well–understood algorithms for the determination of string similarities makes this approach easy to implement. However, all precision and recall problems known from string–based information retrieval (e.g., due to synonyms or homonyms) directly apply here. Therefore, thesauri or lexica are sometimes incorporated as additional background knowledge to alleviate these problems.

Most methods that focus on topology–based evidence are, strictly speaking, hybrid: Approaches using formal logic apply matching and unification procedures that rely on some common vocabulary (i.e., they rely basically on term identity); the similarity flooding algorithm presented in [16] is hybrid as it derives its initial activation values from term similarities.

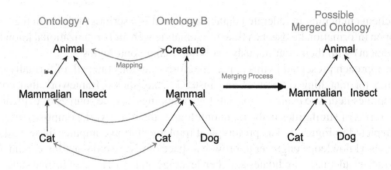

Fig. 2. Merging Ontologies

A third source of evidence for detecting ontology mappings are similarities in the *instances*. Two basic forms of underlying heuristics for instance–based mapping are

- "IF the instances of class A in ontology O_1 are very similar to the instances of class B in O_2 THEN suggest $A \approx B$", and
- "IF the instances of class A in ontology O_1 are classified as class B instances with respect to O_2 THEN suggest $A \subseteq B$".

The keys to these heuristics are obviously the definition of *instance similarity* and the *classifier*, respectively, without presupposing a shared terminology. How can we determine the similarity of instance a, formulated in terms of ontology O_1, and instance b, formulated in terms of ontology O_2? How can we classify instance a, formulated with the O_1 vocabulary, with respect to O_2? In general, we here face the same mapping and matching problems on the instance level that we actually wanted to solve on the ontology level. A first idea would be to step another level down and determine local similarities on the basic datatypes (e.g., number or string similarity) of properties. However, it is very unlikely that these basic property similarities really contain enough knowledge to reflect semantical similarity of the instances. Is an object o_1 that has a slot foo_1 with a value of 50 really similar to an object o_2 with a foo_2 slot value of 51? Without any additional knowledge this similarity would look rather random.

Fortunately, we are in the position that in many application areas envisioned in the semantic web and in organizational knowledge management, we actually can rely on better similarity and classifier functions. In these scenarios, domain ontologies are often not primarily used to manage "real" instances with the proper is-a semantics ("Allan is-a researcher"), but to *annotate* (text) documents or parts of them for better retrieval ("This document is about ontology mapping, semantic web, and knowledge management"). On these text documents we can, from experiences in information retrieval (e.g., [2]), rightly expect to obtain the required classification and similarity functions that also capture some semantics of the "instances". So, the above sketched heuristics for instance–based mappings can be re-formulated as

- "IF the documents annotated with concept A (of ontology O_1) are very similar to the documents annotated with concept B (of O_2) THEN suggest $A \approx B$".

  This similarity can for example be defined as vector similarity (typically the cosine measure) in a vector space model as is often used in document retrieval [20, 2].

– "IF the documents annotated with concept A (of ontology O_1) are classified as class B documents in O_2 THEN suggest $A \subseteq B$".

Such text classifiers can be automatically learned from the example documents that are annoted with B and than easily be applied to previously unknown documents, e.g., those documents that are annoted with A.

Examples for instance–based ontology mapping in document–centered applications can be found in [5, 13, 19]. For an overview of some merging tools and algorithms along with the kind of information they exploit, see table 1.

Table 1. Comparison of Ontology Merging Approaches

Reference	Term	Topology	Instance
COMA [4]	x	x[4]	
Chimaera [14]	x		
CAIMAN [13]		x[5]	x
Similarity Flooding [16]	x[6]	x	
PROMPT [18]	x		

The three basic sources of evidence, *term–based*, *topology–based*, and *instance–based* are of course not completely independent; certainty coming from one of the sources may reinforce or eliminate other evidence, and approval of instance– or term–based mapping evidence, for example, has direct impact on the topology. Which of the sources is to most adequate seems highly dependant on the input ontologies (and instances). This fact and the awareness that, by now, we just gather evidence, but not construct mappings, leads to the following two additional elements of the framework:

– *Evidence Integration*: The goal of this step is to generate a comprehensive view on the various interacting and potentially conflicting evidences. Possible integration techniques range from relatively light–weight voting procedures, like they are often used in classification tasks (e.g., Borda Count or Highest–Rank) [11], to more heavy–weight approaches like logic–based formalisms for evidences. An example for the latter is the Dempster–Shafer theory of evidence that also explicitly handles the absence of evidence (for an overview see [12]). A middle course would be to use global similarity measures known from case–based reasoning. [9] presented this approach for alignment of OWL-lite ontologies. COMA [4] is a system that also allows for combining different matchers for database schemas.
– *User Interaction*: It is unlikely that there is only one "true" solution to the problem of mapping ontologies. Every ontology is founded on design decisions. Therefore, incorporating a knowledge engineer's feedback is reasonable to catch an adequate representation bias (or: the right ontological commitment) in the merged ontology. Conceiving ontology merging as transitions in a continuum as described in section 1 suggests to have this interaction right at the interfaces of these transitions. This means the user decides if and when an integrated evidence for a relation between elements of the input ontologies is really leveraged to a mapping (which then may influence other evidences again) and how the mappings are used for an actual merger.

Figure 3 gives an overview of the framework for evidence–based ontology merging described in this section. One of its main features is that the conceptually quite different sources of evidence are also separated in the framework. The only point where combination of the approaches takes place is when combining the results of evidence generation algorithms. Thereby, one can on the one hand estimate the usefulness of the separate algorithms without any interference caused by the early combination of the approaches, and, on the other hand, more easily tune the overall system to the characteristics of particular input ontologies. Moreover, our approach emphasizes the need for user feedback, incorporating and enhancing its match proposals with every match the user confirms or rejects. If, for example, the user confirms that two classes match, the algorithm considers it more likely that subclasses of these two classes match, too.

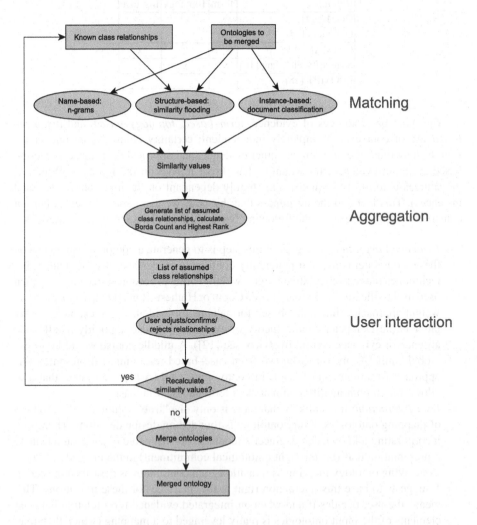

Fig. 3. Framework for Evidence-based Ontology Merging

In the next section, we describe a prototype implementation of the proposed framework. This implementation is realized as a plug-in for the Protégé ontology engineering environment.

3   PHASE: A Prototypical Implementation of the Merging Framework

The prototype presented in this section implements the general framework described in section 3. It is realized on three building blocks:

1. The *Protégé[7] ontology environment* is used for the representation of the source and result ontologies as well as for representing the mappings.
2. The *PROMPT tab [18]* is a tool for ontology merging and alignment with Protégé. As it already supports the main methodology and interaction cycle of framework, we used it as a backbone for our implementation.
3. The classification and document similarity procedures for the instance–based matching were realized on top of the *NextBot engine* that is the core of ProFiler, a commercial tool for information organization and retrieval by brainbot technolgies AG[8].

3.1   Basic Algorithms

In the following, we briefly sketch how the elements of the framework were instantiated. As we were mainly interested in the integration of the various sources of evidence we did not concentrate much on the optimization of the basic evidence generators.

Term-Based Matching. From the many well–known algorithms for determining string similarities we chose the n–gram approach to replace to original substring matcher in PROMPT. n-grams compute the similarity of two strings by comparing all substrings of length n. The degree of fitness of a particular match candidate is determined by the number of n-grams it matches. A threshold for the minimal n-gram similarity leads to *match pairs*, tuples of matching classes and a respective confidence value.

Structure-Based Matching. A structure-based algorithm that is already used in the area of databases for schema mapping is Similarity Flooding [16]. Similarity Flooding is a generic approach for determining matching nodes in graphs, taking two graphs as input and returning a set of match pairs with corresponding similarity values. The main part of Similarity Flooding is execution of a fixpoint calculation. In the original approach, Similarity Flooding uses a set of similarity values obtained by string comparison of the classes' names as an initial value of the similarity vector. However, as we do not want to mix name-based and structure-based approaches, we use a canonical vector for initialization. Also, the initialization vector is used to inject knowledge of user-confirmed matches. Match pairs which have been confirmed by the user get a higher

---

[7] http://protege.stanford.edu
[8] http://brainbot.com

initial similarity value than pairs which have not been confirmed. Accordingly, potential match pairs which the user rejected get an initial similarity value of zero.

Instance-Based Matching. Instance-based matching exploits similarities of the *instances* associated with the ontologies' classes. For example, instances of the class "car" can be named "VW Beetle", "Porsche 911", and so on, and it is likely that in another ontology that features the class "automobile" similar instances can be found. In our prototype, we do not compare "real" instances of the ontologies, but use text or HTML documents that are annotated with the concepts of the ontologies. Thereby, the documents define a kind of "semantic context" of the concepts. The commercial NextBot engine that was used for document classification and document similarities is based on the *vector space model* [20] and standard information retrieval methods [2] (mainly the TF–IDF weighting schema and the cosine similarity measure). This engine can automatically learn text classifiers with respect to a concept taxonomy. Input for the learning algorithm are *examples* that explicitly relate documents to one ore more concepts. Additionally, we use a simple algorithm for determining class similarities shown in figure 4. Again, *examples* of a class are documents that are a priori used for learning the classifier for a class in the vector space model. *Soft matches* are a document's (previously unknown) matches to other classes. These are automatically determined by applying the learned document classifier. So, the algorithm takes as input the examples, the (automatically learned) soft matches and their resemblance values (i.e., the strength of a soft match) and delivers pairwise similarities of classes that belong to different ontologies[9]. Basically, the algorithm aggregates all evidence that the example documents e_i for a class c of ontology O_1 also belong to class d of ontology O_2 and delivers this aggregate as $similarity(c, d)$.

```
for every class c in ontology O_n
    i = 0, s = {}
    for every example e of class c
        i = i + 1
        for every soft match m of example e
            if m.class is not in O_n /* no mappings within one ontology */
                inc(similarity(c, m.class), m.resemblanceValue)
                s = s ∪ m.class
    for every class d in s
        similarity(c, d) = similarity(c, d)/i
```

Fig. 4. Algorithm for Instance–based Evidence Generation

Detecting Different Kinds of Relationships. In many ontology merging approaches, detection and handling of relationships is limited to one-to-one matchings with "is-equal" semantics. This means that merging algorithms only search for direct semantic correspondence of classes of the ontologies to merge. However, due to the semantics of the subclass relation that is typically defined as set inclusion, subclasses and super-classes can be discovered by the instance-based matcher. If many instances of class a

---

[9] For convenience reasons, *one* NextBot engine is used to store all input ontologies. This accounts for the test into which ontology a soft match points (see Figure 4).

in ontology O_1 match class b in ontology O_2, but only few instances of class b match class a, it is likely class b represents a superclass of class a. Also, name-based matchers can be used for discovering evidence for subclass/superclass relationships as the names of subclasses often include the name of their respective superclass. However, as the classes reside in separate ontologies that probably use varying diction, discovery of subclass/superclass relationships using name-based approaches needs sophisticated synonym handling. Therefore, name-based discovery of subclass and superclass relationships is not used in our approach.

Handling Confirmed Matches. As knowledge of confirmed or rejected matches shall be incorporated in subsequent matching steps, we need to find a way to feed this knowledge into the matching process. The structure–based matching algorithm, Similarity Flooding, offers a way to achieve this by adjusting the algorithm's initial similarity vector according to the confirmed or rejected matches. However, while handling of confirmed "is-equal" matches is straightforward this way, handling of confirmed subclass or superclass matches is more difficult. In order to represent these matchings, we create *virtual classes* in the ontologies (see figure 5). Now, we can set the initial similarity value of the virtual class and the respective subclass to a higher value than normal, causing the Similarity Flooding matching algorithm to use the subclass relationship for improving its matching results by a certain degree.

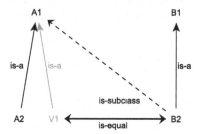

Fig. 5. Handling confirmed subclasses

Superclass relationships are handled accordingly. Note, that confirmed "is-equal" matches take precedence over subclass and superclass relationships of the same classes when building the initial similarity vector of Similarity Flooding.

Aggregation of Match Results. Typically, the output of the matching algorithms is ambiguous. Term–based matchers for example may conclude that class "University" from ontology A matches class "University" from ontology B while a structure-based matcher does not assign a high similarity value to this pair, perhaps because when taking the ontologies' structures into consideration it becomes clear that class "University" of ontology A means a set of buildings while in the context of ontology B, the class "University" denotes an organizational structure.

We apply a modified Borda Count method for combining matcher results using *rankings*. In the following, we will briefly explain the approach (for an overview see

[11]): A *ranking* is a list of match pairs, ordered by similarity value. Aggregation based on rankings is not affected by problems with different scales of the similarity values. Rankings are common scales for the matchers, regardless of the algorithms the matchers use or the scale of the similarity values the matchers return. The Borda Count method uses the rankings of match pairs computed by the matchers as input and outputs an real number (score) associated with every match pair as output. The real number can be used to construct a combined ranking of match pairs. Basically, the Borda Count for a match pair is the sum of the number of pairs ranked below it by each matcher. In order to account for ties in the input rankings, we group all pairs with the same similarity values on one rank when constructing the input rankings. In order to compensate for the fact that now each matcher's ranking probably has a different number of ranks, we assign a ranking score to each rank. The ranking score is $1 - (rank - 1)/(ranks - 1)$. For each pair, we sum up its ranking scores as each pair gets a separate score for each matcher. The pairs, ordered by summed-up ranking scores, represent the resulting aggregated ranking.

3.2   The PHASE Tab

The PROMPT tab [18] is an extension to Protégé and allows to manage multiple ontologies. Specifically, it provides means to compare and merge ontologies, extracts parts of an ontology and to move frames between including projects. PROMPT's merging part tries to identify semantically corresponding classes solely by using a simple term–based matcher. The PHASE tab depicted in figure 6 builds on PROMPT by replacing the original term—based matching algorithm by the evidence generation algorithms described above.

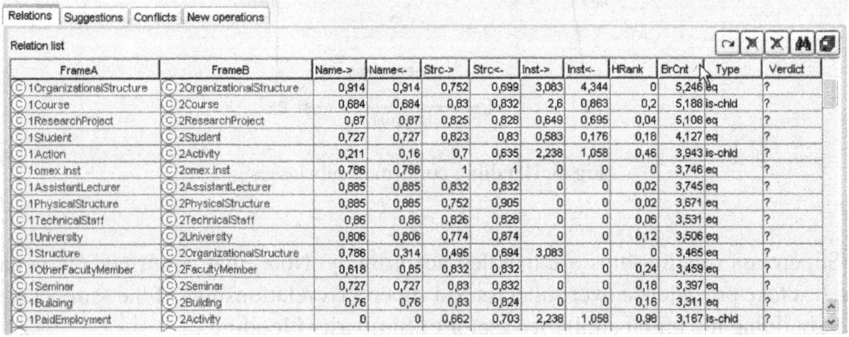

	FrameA	FrameB	Name->	Name<-	Strc->	Strc<-	Inst->	Inst<-	HRank	BrCnt	Type	Verdict
C	1OrganizationalStructure	2OrganizationalStructure	0,914	0,914	0,752	0,699	3,083	4,344	0	5,246	eq	?
C	1Course	2Course	0,684	0,684	0,83	0,832	2,6	0,863	0,2	5,188	is-chld	?
C	1ResearchProject	2ResearchProject	0,87	0,87	0,825	0,828	0,649	0,695	0,04	5,108	eq	?
C	1Student	2Student	0,727	0,727	0,823	0,83	0,583	0,176	0,18	4,127	eq	?
C	1Action	2Activity	0,211	0,16	0,7	0,635	2,238	1,058	0,46	3,943	is-chld	?
C	1omex.inst	2omex.inst	0,786	0,786	1	1	0	0	0	3,746	eq	?
C	1AssistantLecturer	2AssistantLecturer	0,885	0,885	0,832	0,832	0	0	0,02	3,745	eq	?
C	1PhysicalStructure	2PhysicalStructure	0,885	0,885	0,752	0,905	0	0	0,02	3,671	is-chld	?
C	1TechnicalStaff	2TechnicalStaff	0,86	0,86	0,826	0,828	0	0	0,06	3,531	eq	?
C	1University	2University	0,806	0,806	0,774	0,874	0	0	0,12	3,506	eq	?
C	1Structure	2OrganizationalStructure	0,786	0,314	0,495	0,694	3,083	0	0	3,485	eq	?
C	1OtherFacultyMember	2FacultyMember	0,618	0,85	0,832	0,832	0	0	0,24	3,459	eq	?
C	1Seminar	2Seminar	0,727	0,727	0,83	0,832	0	0	0,18	3,397	eq	?
C	1Building	2Building	0,76	0,76	0,83	0,824	0	0	0,16	3,311	eq	?
C	1PaidEmployment	2Activity	0	0	0,662	0,703	2,238	1,058	0,98	3,167	is-chld	?

Fig. 6. The PHASE Tab

As we want to differentiate between matching evidence the matching algorithms gather and the actions that may result from them, a new subtab is present in the PHASE tab that does not exist in PROMPT (see figure 6). The tab is named "relations". Its content is a list of (probably) matching classes. Along with the two classes' names, the similarity values for the three sources of evidence are shown. Also, the (modified) Borda Count value is shown. There is a column that shows the assumed relationship type (equal/subclass/superclass) between the classes which the user may change in case the estimate is wrong. Finally, there is a "verdict" column in which the user can confirm or reject the respective class pair.

3.3   An Example Session

Having described the software environment, we will go through an example merging session, outlining the typical steps necessary for merging ontologies and following the general framework depicted in Figure 3. We try to merge two ontologies that model data from the domain of science and teaching. These ontologies have been constructed in order to meet certain requirements that enable us to show strengths and weaknesses of the algorithm. Part of the ontologies we try to merge are depicted in figure 7. The ontologies each consist of about 30 classes.

Note that while both ontologies are roughly similar, there are also small differences that render most approaches that are solely based on one aspect (be it the classes names or the ontology structure) ineffective. As a start, many class names do not match directly. Also, the ontologies' structure is not identical. Some classes cannot be matched at all. Instances are not shown in the figure. The instances are HTML documents taken from the " 4 Universities Data Set"[10].

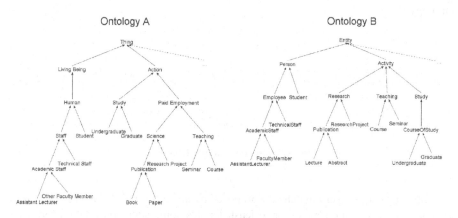

Fig. 7. Example Ontologies

In figure 6, the initial list of proposed matches can be seen, sorted using the modified Borda Count. The user should now confirm or reject matches. When assigning verdicts, it is important to verify that the proposed relationship types are correct or, if this is not the case, to select the proper relationship type. This is especially true if we confirm a match.

After having assigned verdicts to a number of matches, the user can decide to let the structural similarity values get recalculated using the new information.

---

[10] http://www-2.cs.cmu.edu/afs/cs.cmu.edu/project/theo-20/www/data/

Generally, discovering matching classes is done using the following steps:

- Browse/sort the relation list in order to find matches. At the beginning, using the Borda Count for sorting is most promising. Later, sorting by single matcher's values should be considered, too.
- Confirm or reject a number of match pairs. Adjust relationship types if necessary.
- Let the PHASE tab recalculate the structure-based similarity.
- Repeat until no more matches remain.

Then, the list of confirmed matches can be used for building a list of merging actions to perform. From then on, everything works as known from PROMPT.

As seen in figure 8, *structure–based matching* smoothly works where the other matchers cease to work. Neither the name-based matcher nor the instance–based matcher (due to lack of instances for the respective classes) can match "Human" and "Person" or "Science" and "Research". However, as can be seen in figure 7, the ontologies' topology in the vicinity of these classes is very similar. The structure-based matcher discovers this. Note that at the time the structure-based matcher computed the values shown in the figure, the user already confirmed some other matches, contributing to the structure–based matcher's accuracy. Also note that there is no matching class for "Room" in ontology B.

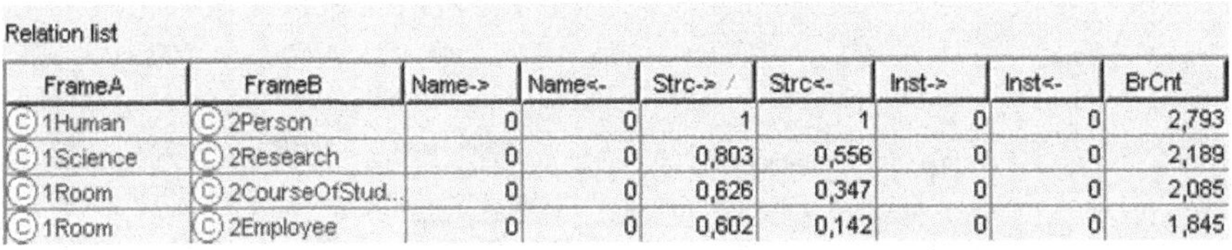

Relation list

FrameA	FrameB	Name->	Name<-	Strc->	Strc<-	Inst->	Inst<-	BrCnt
(C) 1Human	(C) 2Person	0	0	1	1	0	0	2,793
(C) 1Science	(C) 2Research	0	0	0,803	0,556	0	0	2,189
(C) 1Room	(C) 2CourseOfStud...	0	0	0,626	0,347	0	0	2,085
(C) 1Room	(C) 2Employee	0	0	0,602	0,142	0	0	1,845

Fig. 8. Structure-based Matcher

Not surprisingly, every match pair proposed by *instance–based matching* (see figure 9) represents a semantic match or at least denotes some semantic relationship. This probably looks even better when using corpora including more documents, as the zero values shown in the right instance–based similarity column are due to missing example documents for the respective classes.

4 Summary and Outlook

In this paper, we presented a framework that collects and integrates heuristic *evidence* for ontology mappings, allows a knowledge engineer to browse a space of (assessed) mapping candidates in order to select adequate candidates and then leverage them to a level of formal statements for ontology merging. The framework employs three basic sources of evidence for ontology mappings, namely *term–based*, *topology–based*, and *instance–based* evidence. In the prototypical implementation that is based on Protégé

Relation list

FrameA	FrameB	Inst->	Inst<-	Name->	Name<-	Strc->	Strc<-	BrCnt
(C)1OrganizationalStruc..	(C)2OrganizationalStruct..	3,083	4,344	0,914	0,914	0,765	0,438	5,263
(C)1Structure	(C)2OrganizationalStruct..	3,083	0	0,786	0,314	0,57	0,845	4,035
(C)1Course	(C)2Activity	2,845	0,717	0	0	0,749	0,066	2,805
(C)1Teaching	(C)2Activity	2,845	0	0	0	0,766	0,423	2,293
(C)1Course	(C)2Course	2,6	0,863	0,684	0,684	0,832	0,829	5,237
(C)1Teaching	(C)2Course	2,6	0	0	0	0,12	0,746	2,052
(C)1Action	(C)2Activity	2,238	1,058	0,211	0,16	0,669	0,533	4,119
(C)1PaidEmployment	(C)2Activity	2,238	1,058	0	0	0,628	0,898	3,631
(C)1PaidEmployment	(C)2Course	1,846	0,992	0	0	0,052	0,83	2,914
(C)1Action	(C)2Course	1,846	0,992	0	0	0,087	0,776	2,93

Fig. 9. Instance-based Matcher

and the PROMPT tab, we use a rather simple voting schema for the aggregation of evidence, the so–called Borda Count.

Further work will comprise

- *more flexible aggregation of evidence*, e.g., by using logic–based evidence integration and by adaptive aggregations functions whose parameters may be learned,
- *support for other types of relationships*, e.g., by additional heuristics for the instance–based evidence generation, and
- *richer mapping languages* that also allow for mapping composed concepts.

In addition to a more systematical evaluation of the ontology evidence framework, we also aim at an integration with the concept of ontology societies [5], leading to a comprehensive view on *ontology negotiation* which integrates both, the knowledge formalization aspect and the social aspect that are contained in the definition of ontologies as "explicit, shared conceptualizations". We think that such a comprehensive view on ontologies really makes them adequate tools for handling knowledge in today's open information landscapes.

Acknowledgement. The work described here has been supported by the German Ministry for Research under grant 01 IW 901 FRODO and 01 IW C01 EPOS. We thank brainbot technology AG for providing us with the NextBot engine and Björn Endres for implementing the JAVA API for the engine. We also thank the anonymous reviewers for their valuable feedback.

References

1. A. Abecker and L. van Elst. Ontologies for knowledge management. In *[22]*, pages 435–454. Springer, 2004.
2. R. Baeza-Yates and B. Ribeiro-Neto. *Modern Information Retrieval*. Addison Wesley, New York, 1999.
3. R. Bergmann, M. M. Richter, S. Schmitt, A. Stahl, and I. Vollrath. Utility-oriented matching: A new research direction for case-based reasoning. In S. Schmitt, I. Vollrath, and U. Reimer, editors, *Proceedings of the 9th German Workshop on Case-Based Reasoning*, 2001.

4. H. H. Do and E. Rahm. COMA — A system for flexible combination of schema matching approaches. In Philip A. Bernstein et al., editors, *VLDP 2002: proceedings of the Twenty-Eighth International Conference on Very Large Data Bases, Hong Kong SAR, China, 20–23 August 2002*, pages 610–621, Los Altos, CA 94022, USA, 2002. Morgan Kaufmann Publishers.

5. L. van Elst and A. Abecker. Negotiating domain ontologies in distributed organizational memories. In Paolo Bouquet, editor, *Meaning Negotiation (MeaN-02). Technical Report WS-02-09*, pages 32–35. AAAI Press, 2002.

6. L. van Elst and A. Abecker. Ontologies for information management: Balancing formality, stability, and sharing scope. *Expert Systems with Applications*, 23(4):357–366, November 2002.

7. L. van Elst, V. Dignum, and A. Abecker, editors. *Agent Mediated Knowledge Management, International Symposium AMKM 2003, Stanford, CA, USA, March 24-26, 2003, Revised and Invited Papers*, volume 2926 of *LNAI*. Springer, 2004.

8. L. van Elst, V. Dignum, and A. Abecker. Towards agent-mediated knowledge management. In *[7]*, pages 1–31, 2004.

9. J. Euzenat and P. Valtchev. An integrative proximity measure for ontology alignment. In A. Doan, A. Halevy, and N. Noy, editors, *Proceedings of the 1st Intl. Workshop on Semantic Integration*, volume 82 of *CEUR*, 2003.

10. D. Fensel. *Ontologies: A Silver Bullet for Knowledge Management and Electronic Commerce.* Springer, 2001.

11. T.K. Ho. *A Theory of Multiple Classifier Systems And Its Application to Visual Word Recognition.* PhD thesis, State University of New York at Buffalo, 1992.

12. J. Kohlhas and P.A. Monney. References theory of evidence – a survey of its mathematical foundations, applications and foundational aspects. *ZOR – Mathematical Methods of Operations Research*, 39:35–68, 1994.

13. M.S. Lacher and G. Groh. Faciliating the exchange of explicit knowledge through ontology mappings. In I. Russell and J. Kolen, editors, *Fourteenth International FLAIRS conference*, pages 305–309, 2001.

14. D.L. McGuinness, R. Fikes, J. Rice, and S. Wilder. The chimaera ontology environment. In *Proc. of the 17th National Conf. on Artificial Intelligence (AAAI 2000)*, Austin, Texas, 2000.

15. D.L. McGuinness, R. Fikes, J. Rice, and S. Wilder. An environment for merging and testing large ontologies. In *Proc. of the Seventh Int. Conf. on Principles of Knowledge Representation and Reasoning (KR2000)*, Breckenridge, Colorado, USA, 2000.

16. S. Melnik, H. Garcia-Molina, and E. Rahm. Similarity Flooding: A Versatile Graph Matching Algorithm and ist Application to Schema Matching. In *Proceedings 18th ICDE*, San Jose, CA, February 2002.

17. R. Neches, R. Fikes, T. Finin, Th. Gruber, R. Patil, T. Senator, and W.R. Swartout. Enabling technology for knowledge sharing. *AI Magazine*, 12(3):36–56, 1991.

18. N. Fridman Noy and M. Musen. PROMPT: Algorithm and tool for automated ontology merging and alignment. In *Proceedings of the 7th Conference on Artificial Intelligence (AAAI-00) and of the 12th Conference on Innovative Applications of Artificial Intelligence (IAAI-00)*, pages 450–455, Menlo Park, CA, July 30– 3 2000. AAAI Press.

19. S. Prasad, Y. Peng, and T. Finin. A tool for mapping between two ontologies using explicit information. In Paolo Bouquet, editor, *Meaning Negotiation – Papers from the AAAI Workshop*, volume WS–02–09 of *Technical Report*. AAAI, 2002.

20. G. Salton. *Automatic information organization and retrieval.* McGraw Hill, New York, 1968.

21. M. Schaaf and L. van Elst. An approach to cooperating organizational memories based on semantic negotiation and unification. In *AAAI-2002 Workshop on Meaning Negotiation, Technical Report WS-02-09*, pages 13–16. AAAI Press, 2002.
22. S. Staab and R. Studer. *Handbook on Ontologies*. International Handbooks on Information Systems. Springer Verlag, Heidelberg, 2004.
23. H. Wache. *Semantische Mediation für heterogene Informationsquellen*. Akademische Verlagsgesellschaft Aka GmbH, Berlin, 2003.

Ontology Translation Approaches for Interoperability: A Case Study with Protégé-2000 and WebODE

Oscar Corcho and Asunción Gómez-Pérez

Ontological Engineering Group. Departamento de Inteligencia Artificial.
Facultad de Informática. Universidad Politécnica de Madrid. Campus de
Montegancedo, s/n. 28660 Boadilla del Monte. Madrid (Spain)
{ocorcho,asun}@fi.upm.es

Abstract. We describe four ontology translation approaches that can be used to exchange ontologies between ontology tools and/or ontology languages. These approaches are analysed with regard to two main features: how they preserve the ontology semantics after the translation process (aka semantic or consequence preservation) and how they allow final users and ontology-based applications to understand the resulting ontology in the target format (aka pragmatic preservation). These approaches are illustrated with practical examples that show how they can be applied to achieve interoperability between the ontology tools Protégé-2000 and WebODE.

1 Introduction

In Computer Science, the term 'interoperability' is defined as the ability to transmit data and exchange information between systems whilst allowing each system to process information independently [18]. If we refer to ontology tools and languages, the term 'interoperability' can be defined as their ability to exchange ontologies without losing knowledge, in such a way that users of the target format (be them human users or applications) can understand correctly the ontology transformed. This complex transformation process is usually known as ontology translation [14].

The ontology translation problem appears when we decide to reuse an ontology (or part of an ontology) using a tool or language that is different from those ones in which the ontology is available. If we force each ontology developer or integrator, individually, to commit to the task of translating and incorporating ontologies to their systems, they will need both a lot of effort and a lot of time to achieve their objectives. Some of the reasons for the high effort needed are:

- The ontology developer may not know the language or tool where the ontology is available.
- The ontology developer may not know in depth the knowledge representation paradigm underlying the language or tool.
- The ontology developer may not be able to translate the ontology to another language or tool without losing knowledge.

E. Motta et al. (Eds.): EKAW 2004, LNAI 3257, pp. 30–46, 2004.
© Springer-Verlag Berlin Heidelberg 2004

Ontology reuse will be highly boosted if we provide ontology translation services among languages and/or tools. In fact, ontology tools provide export and import services to and from ontology and general-purpose languages and tools, and there are also translation systems between ontology languages, as shown in [12].

However, there are not deep studies about the quality of the translations performed by ontology translation services. Only a few works ([2], [23]) point out some of the problems that appear in ontology translations. Neither are there characterisations of the approaches followed by current translation technology and their impact in knowledge preservation. For instance, the results obtained in the interoperability experiment proposed at the ISWC'03 workshop on Evaluation of Ontology Tools[1] showed that the fact that two tools provide export and import services to and from a common language does not mean that they actually interoperate.

In this paper we propose a characterisation of ontology translation approaches, focusing on the following two aspects: (1) how these approaches can overcome the differences between the knowledge models of the source and target formats without losing semantics in the transformation, and (2) how these approaches allow end users and ontology-based applications to understand the ontology transformed, what can be considered as an important part of pragmatic or interpretation preservation[2].

To better show and compare these approaches, we have implemented several ontology translation systems between the ontology tools Protégé-2000 [20] and WebODE [1]. The objectives of having translators between both tools are manifold:

On the one hand, WebODE ontology developers and applications will benefit from the use of Protégé-2000 services not offered by the WebODE workbench: ontology merge with PROMPT, advanced instance edition with Protégé-2000 forms, ontology visualisation with Jambalaya, etc. On the other hand, Protégé-2000 ontology developers and applications will benefit from the use of WebODE services: ontology documentation using Methontology's intermediate representations, Semantic Web portal automatic generation with ODESeW, Semantic Web services development with ODESWS, etc.

Furthermore, new ontology services can be developed jointly in the future. For instance, one of the translators from WebODE to Protégé-2000 has been used to export the top level ontology of universals used by the WebODE ODEClean service [10], which supports class taxonomy evaluation with the OntoClean method [15], hence reducing the effort to create the OntoClean plug-in for Protégé-2000.

This paper is organised as follows: Section 2 presents a brief overview of the knowledge models of Protégé-2000 and WebODE, so that the examples shown in later sections can be better understood. Section 3 analyses four groups of ontology translation approaches, focusing on semantic and pragmatic preservation. For each group we show examples of ontology translation systems between Protégé-2000 and

---

[1] EON2003 (http://km.aifb.uni-karlsruhe.de/ws/eon2003).
[2] We use the term "pragmatics" as proposed by [19], with regard to the relationship between signs and their interpreters.

WebODE, with the travel ontology developed for the ontology modelling experiment proposed in the EKAW'02 workshop on Evaluation of Ontology Tools[3]. Finally, section 4 presents some conclusions and future work.

2 Protégé-2000 and WebODE Knowledge Models

We start describing the ***Protégé-2000 standard knowledge model*** [20], based on the frame-based knowledge model defined by the OKBC protocol [6], combined with first order logic constraints. It contains the following ontology components:

- **Classes** represent entities of the domain. They can be *concrete* or *abstract*, that is, they can have direct instances or not respectively. *Slot constraints* can be attached to the class, and determine constraints on the slot values of the class instances.
- The taxonomic relation **subclass-of** can be defined between classes, allowing multiple classifications. The relation **subslot-of** can be defined between slots.
- **Slots** represent interactions between domain objects or characteristics of class instances. They have *value types*, *minimum* and *maximum cardinalities*, *minimum* and *maximum values* in case of numeric slots, *default values*, *template values*, *constraints* and the *inverse slot*. Slots are defined independently of the classes to which they are attached, and can be attached in two different ways:
  - **Template slots**. They describe properties of the instances of the class to which they are attached or interactions between instances of the class and instances of other classes. They are inherited by the subclasses and instances of the class, where they can be constrained and/or take values.
  - **Own slots**. They describe properties of the class itself or interactions between the class and other classes, taking some values in the class. These values are not inherited by its subclasses nor by its instances. The template slots of a class become own slots in its instances.
- **Facets** define slot constraints. The features of slots defined before (value types, minimum and maximum cardinalities, etc.) are built-in facets in the Protégé-2000 knowledge model. However, new facets can be defined for them.
- **Instances** of classes define individuals in the domain. They contain own slots (which are the template slots of the classes from which they are instances) with their corresponding values. In Protégé-2000 instances belong only to one class.
- **Constraints** are first order logic sentences used to check constraints in the ontology. They are created with PAL (Protégé Axiom Language), which is a superset of first order logic.

One of the main features of the Protégé-2000 knowledge model is that it allows defining **metaclasses**, classes that act as templates for creating other classes. In fact, metaclasses are used to define the own slots of classes in an ontology. Own slots are defined as template slots in the metaclass, and later the classes that are instances of the metaclass inherit the slots as own slots.

---

[3] EON2002 (http://km.aifb.uni-karlsruhe.de/eon2002).

The **WebODE knowledge model** [7] is also based on a combination of frames and first order logic axioms, and contains the following ontology components:

- **Concepts** represent entities of the domain. They can have *synonyms* and *abbreviations*, and may contain *attributes*. Attributes are similar to slots in Protégé-2000, though in WebODE they cannot be defined independently from a concept but always attached to it. There are two types of attributes:
  - o **Class attributes** specify characteristics of the concept. They have a *value type* or *range*, which can be a basic data type (String, Integer, Float, etc.) or any XML Schema datatype [3]; *minimum* and *maximum cardinality*, which constrain the number of values that the attribute may have; and *value(s)*. Numeric class attributes can have a *measurement unit* and *precision*.
  - o **Instance attributes** describe properties of the instances of the concept to which they are attached. Hence their value may be different for each concept instance. They have the same facets than class attributes and two additional ones, *minimum value* and *maximum value*, used in numeric attributes. Values inserted for instance attributes are interpreted as explicit values for them.
- **Concept groups** are sets of disjoint concepts, that is, concepts that cannot share subconcepts nor instances. They are used to create disjoint and exhaustive concept partitions. A concept can belong to several concept groups.
- **Built-in relations** are predefined relations in the WebODE's knowledge model. They are divided into three groups: taxonomy relations between concepts (*subclass-of*, *not-subclass-of*), taxonomy relations between groups and concepts (*disjoint-decomposition*, *exhaustive-decomposition*, and *partition*), and mereology relations between concepts (*transitive-part-of*, *intransitive-part-of*).
- **Binary ad-hoc relations** between concepts are characterized by their *name*, the *origin* (source) and *destination* (target) concepts, and their *cardinality*, which establishes the number of destination terms of each origin term through the relation. Cardinality can be restricted to 1 (only one destination term) or N (any number of destination terms). Optionally, we can provide their *algebraic properties*. Ad-hoc relations are similar to Protégé-2000 slots whose value type is a class instance.
- **Constants** are components that have always the same value and can be used in any expression. They have a *value type*, *value* and *measurement unit*.
- **Axioms** and **rules** define *formal expressions* in first order logic.
- **Properties** are used to describe algebraic properties of ad-hoc relations. They are divided in two groups: *built-in properties* (reflexive, irreflexive, symmetric, asymmetric, antisymmetric and transitive), and *ad-hoc user-defined properties*.
- **Imported terms** are components from other ontologies that are included in another ontology. They are described by their *URI*.

Besides, the WebODE's knowledge model supports **instance sets**, which make possible to populate a conceptual model for different applications or scenarios, maintaining independent instantiations of the same conceptual model.

In summary, the knowledge models of both tools are based on a combination of frames and first order logic. In both of them we can represent classes, organized in class taxonomies where multiple classifications are allowed, ad hoc relations between classes, instances and first order logic axioms. However, there are also important differences between them, related to the types of slots that can be defined for classes, the types of relations that can be used to define class taxonomies, etc.

Figure 1 shows an informal comparison of both knowledge models. The components in the intersection of the Venn diagrams are those that can be expressed in both tools (although they usually differ in the term used to refer to them, for instance, the term "class" in Protégé is equivalent to the term "concept" in WebODE). The components outside the intersection are those with no direct representation in the other knowledge model, although they may be represented using other modelling primitives (e.g., the "subslot-of" relationship in Protégé-2000 can be represented as a first order logic axiom in WebODE).

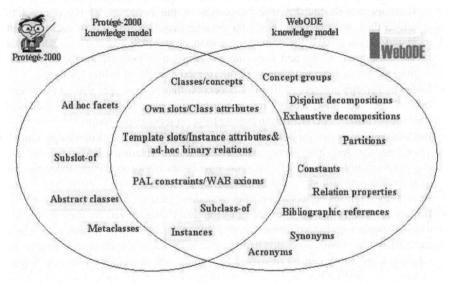

Fig. 1. Informal comparison of the knowledge models of Protégé-2000 and WebODE

3   A Classification of Ontology Translation Approaches

In this section we classify four approaches for ontology translation, according to their features with respect to their semantic and pragmatic preservation properties:

- Does the approach overcome the differences between the knowledge models of the source and target formats without losing knowledge in the transformation? This feature is specially important in cyclic transformations, where we should have exactly the same ontology when transformed back into the original tool.
- Are end users and ontology-based applications able to understand the ontology transformed, as if it was developed with the target ontology tool or language?

We will identify which of the current ontology translation systems have been developed according to each of these approaches, and we will present examples about ontology exchange between the ontology tools WebODE and Protégé-2000.

3.1   Indirect Translation, by Means of a Common Interchange Language

In the beginning of the 1990s, KIF (Knowledge Interchange Format) [11] was created for exchanging knowledge between heterogeneous knowledge representation systems. The objective of this standardization effort was to reduce the number of translators needed to achieve interoperability among a heterogeneous group of formats (from $O(n^2)$ to $O(n)$ translators for a number n of formats). The translation process only consists in exporting an ontology from the source format to the exchange language and importing the code obtained to the target format.

Recently, the World Wide Web Consortium (W3C) has proposed three language recommendations, namely RDF [17] and RDF Schema [5], whose combination is usually known as RDF(S), and OWL [9]. These languages have been created with the purpose of becoming widely used for representing knowledge in the Semantic Web. Consequently, they can be also considered as potential common exchange languages, although this is not their main objective.

Ontology tools like the Ontolingua Server and OntoSaurus are able to import from and export to KIF, and WebOnto is able to export to Ontolingua (which in its turn can be transformed directly to KIF by the Ontolingua Server). With regard to the W3C languages, [12] show that most of the existing ontology tools are able to import from and export to RDF(S) and OWL. However, this does not mean that they can really interoperate. We have already mentioned some of the results obtained in the EON2003 workshop, where this type of interoperability was experimented. The main reasons for the lack of interoperability are:

- Common interchange formats normally allow representing the same knowledge in many different ways. Hence, translations to and from interlinguas are usually written with regard to a specific format, making knowledge exchange difficult.
- Interoperability with interlinguas has been only proved with the same origin and target formats, but not between different source and target formats.
- In the case of RDF(S) and OWL, their standard knowledge models are not expressive enough to represent most of the knowledge that can be represented with other ontology languages and tools. However, their knowledge models can be extended to represent other pieces of knowledge, by means of metaclasses.

Therefore, **knowledge is not usually preserved** in the transformation and the resulting ontologies in the target format **are not always easy to understand**, since they incorporate expressions related to the source format. For further examples of these interoperability problems, we recommend [22], [2], [16], and [8].

Example: Achieving Interoperability Between WebODE and Protégé-2000 Using RDF(S) and OWL as Common Interchange Formats. Protégé-2000 and WebODE are able to export to and import from different ontology languages, such as RDF(S), and OWL, and to and from other formats that are not specific for ontology implementation, such as XML [4] and UML. For the last two ones, these tools are not able to exchange ontologies, since they use different tag sets (the case of XML) and different types of application-specific UML. Hence we will consider only the indirect translation with RDF(S) and OWL.

Figure 2 shows an example of the result of transforming an ontology from WebODE into Protégé-2000, using RDF(S) as a common interlingua. The classes and their slots (be them originally WebODE instance attributes or ad-hoc relations), and the class taxonomy are preserved. However, some knowledge is lost in this transformation. For instance, the standard knowledge model of RDF(S) does not allow specifying the cardinalities of attributes (called properties in this language).Therefore, if we transform an ontology from WebODE into RDF(S), and from RDF(S) into Protégé-2000, the information regarding cardinality restrictions is lost (the default cardinality restrictions in Protégé-2000 are 0 for minimum cardinality and multiple for maximum cardinality).

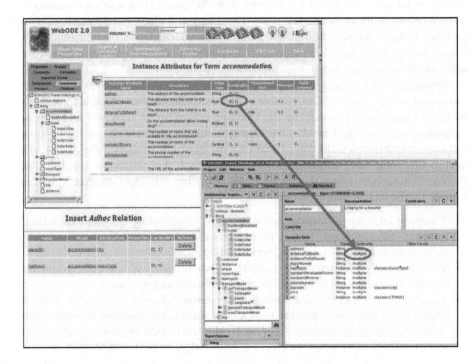

Fig. 2. Result of the transformation of the EON2003 travel ontology from WebODE to Protégé-2000, with RDF(S) as a common interchange format

Other knowledge that cannot be expressed in the standard knowledge model of RDF(S) is the disjoint and exhaustive knowledge in class taxonomies, formal axioms, bibliographic references to ontology components, etc.

The previous problem appears because the WebODE export service to RDF(S) does not export the knowledge that cannot be represented in the standard knowledge model of RDF(S). In order to avoid these knowledge losses in the export process, the metaclass facilities of RDF(S) could have been used to represent the knowledge model of WebODE. In fact, this is exactly what the Protégé-2000 RDF Storage backend does [21] when storing Protégé-2000 ontologies in RDF(S): it creates metaclasses for some of the components of the Protégé knowledge model that have not a direct translation into the standard knowledge model of RDF(S).

However, all this extra knowledge added to the standard knowledge model of RDF(S) cannot be usually imported into other RDF-aware tools different than Protégé-2000. They will only "understand" and import those parts of the ontology that are implemented with the standard RDF(S) knowledge model.

3.2 Direct Transformation Restricted to the Standard Knowledge Model of the Target Format

Transformations in this group consist in identifying the mappings between the standard knowledge models of the source and target formats, and executing these mappings. The knowledge components of the source format that have not a direct correspondance in the target format are not transformed, even in the case that the target format does provide means for extending its standard knowledge model.

This type of transformation is mainly driven by the objective of making **the transformed ontology easily understood by users and applications** aware of the target format. This is the reason why the standard knowledge model of the target format is not extended. As a consequence of this decision, **some knowledge is usually lost in the transformation**. This occurs when the standard knowledge model of the target format does not include the source one, that is, when the target format does not express all the knowledge that can be represented in the source format.

In this group of transformations we can include most of the ontology translation systems currently available in ontology tools: the WebODE import and export services from and to RDF(S), DAML+OIL, OWL, CARIN, FLogic, and UML; the OntoEdit import and export services from and to RDF(S), DAML+OIL, and FLogic. KAON import and export services to RDF(S), etc.

Example: Achieving Interoperability Between WebODE and Protégé-2000 by Direct Translation Restricted to the Target Format Standard Knowledge Model. With this transformation approach, we transform all the components from the WebODE domain ontology that have a direct representation in Protégé-2000. For example, WebODE concepts can be transformed into Protégé-2000 classes, WebODE instance attributes and ad hoc relations into Protégé-2000 slots, WebODE class attributes into Protégé-2000 own slots (with the use of some metaclasses), WebODE axioms to PAL constraints, etc. Not only this one-to-one transformations will be done, but also more complex ones, such as transforming WebODE partitions as Protégé-2000 class taxonomies creating *subclass-of* relationships between the classes in the partition and the superclass, declaring the superclass of the partition as abstract, and creating PAL constraints that ensure the disjointness between classes.

Some knowledge is lost in the transformation, such as algebraic properties of relations, synonyms and acronyms, bibliographic references, etc.

Figure 3 shows the result of transforming the travel ontology to Protégé-2000 following this proposal. The figure shows that the concepts *hotel1Star*, *hotel2Star*, *hotel3Star*, *hotel4Star* and *hotel5Star*, which form a partition of the class *hotel* in WebODE, are transformed into Protégé classes that are subclasses of the class *hotel*, and have constraints to ensure that they are disjoint with the other ones in the partition. Besides, the class *hotel* is defined as an abstract class in Protégé-2000, that is, it cannot have direct instances. It also shows that the metaclass *hotelTypes* has been created. This metaclass has the template slot *numberOfStars* attached, which is converted to an own slot in the classes *hotel1Star*, *hotel2Star*, etc.

The inverse transformation, that is, from Protégé-2000 to WebODE, is similar. It consists in determining the direct correspondances between the knowledge models of Protégé-2000 and WebODE (already identified previously) and performing the transformations of only those components that have such a direct correspondence.

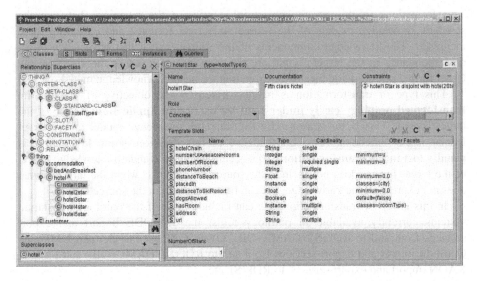

Fig. 3. Result of the transformation of the EON2003 travel ontology from WebODE to Protégé-2000, using only the standard knowledge model of Protégé-2000

3.3   Direct Transformation by Instantiation of the Source Format KR Ontology in the Target Format

Transformations in this group are performed following two steps. The first step consists in creating the KR ontology of the source format in the target one, with the standard knowledge modelling components of the target format. Basically, it consists in developing that KR ontology as if it was a domain ontology of the target format. Once that this KR ontology has been created, the second step of the translation process consists in instantiating it according to the contents of the ontology to be transformed. For instance, a concept in the source format is transformed into an instance of the class *Concept* in the target format; an instance in the source format is transformed into an instance of the class *Instance* in the target format, and is connected to one or several instances of the class *Concept* by means of the relation *isInstanceOf*, etc.

In summary, the only translation decisions taken into account in this transformation are related to how to transform the source ontology components to instances of the KR ontology created in the target format. That is, no real translation decisions are performed and the transformation process is extremely simple. The main advantage of this transformation proposal is that it is fairly easy to implement, since we do not have to use different ontology components in the target tool but only change the underlying format of the original ontology.

With regard to the two aspects that we are analysing for each approach, we must take into account that if the source KR ontology is correctly modelled in the target format, **the knowledge represented in the original ontology is preserved**. However, end users and applications will **not be able to understand correctly the ontology transformed**, since the components that represent domain knowledge (basically instances of concepts and of relations) are mixed with the components that represent the KR ontology of the source format.

In this group we can include some import and export formats of ontology tools, such as the WebODE import and export services from and to Prolog, XML and Java, the import and export services of OntoEdit from and to OXML, the ones between Protégé-2000 and XML, and XML Schema, etc. These languages are used mainly as a syntax for exchanging ontologies, but not as knowledge representation languages with their characteristics.

Example: Achieving Interoperability Between WebODE and Protégé-2000 by Instantiating the WebODE Knowledge Model in Protégé-2000. As described above, with this approach we follow a two-step process: (1) create the WebODE KR ontology in Protégé-2000; (2) transform all the components of the WebODE domain ontology according to that KR ontology, that is, instantiate the WebODE KR ontology with the knowledge from the source domain ontology.

The WebODE KR ontology contains 14 classes, which represent the ontology components of the WebODE knowledge model (*:WebODEComponent, :Concept, :Attribute, :InstanceAttribute,* etc.), and 36 slots, which represent the relationships between the previous components: *:name, :documentation, :hasAttribute, :hasDomain, :hasRange, :datatype, :maxCardinality,* etc. The ontology also contains 32 PAL constraints that model restrictions of the WebODE knowledge model.

Figure 4 shows a screenshot of the class taxonomy of the WebODE KR ontology modelled in Protégé-2000. It also shows the details of the It shows also the concept *accommodation*, with its documentation, the classes of which it is a subclass, the synonyms, etc. This concept is transformed into Protégé-2000 as an instance of the class *:Concept* in Protégé-2000.

To transform the ontology back to WebODE, the translation decisions are also easy to implement. They only consist in converting the instances of each class in this ontology to the corresponding component in WebODE.

The inverse case (translating from Protégé-2000 to WebODE, and then back to Protégé-2000) is similar to this one: we create the Protégé-2000 KR ontology in WebODE and transform all the components of the Protégé-2000 ontology according to it. To achieve complete interoperability between WebODE and Protégé-2000 in both directions we need four translation systems: two for the cycle WebODE-Protégé-2000-WebODE, and another two for Protégé-2000-WebODE-Protégé-2000.

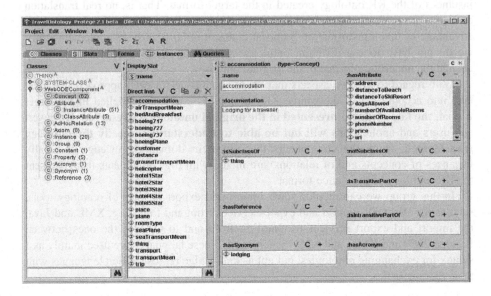

Fig. 4. Result of the transformation of the EON2003 Travel ontology from WebODE to Protégé-2000 as an instantiation of the WebODE KR ontology

3.4   Direct Transformation by an Extension of the Standard Knowledge Model of the Target Format

This group of transformations propose to transform as much knowledge as possible using the components of the target format's standard knowledge model (as described in section 3.2), so that **the knowledge transformed can be easily understood** and dealt with by human users and applications. Besides, it proposes **to preserve the knowledge that has not been transformed**, so that they can be recovered in case that the ontology is transformed back to the original format (as described in section 3.3). This proposal avoids mixing the domain ontology components transformed with the knowledge modelling components used for knowledge preservation.

To achieve this twofold objective, this approach proposes to implement part of the source format's KR ontology in the target format, by means of meta-knowledge (which is usually expressed with metaclasses, annotation properties, etc.). The KR ontology implemented contains only the ontology components that cannot be represented directly in the standard knowledge model of the target format, so that they are only used in case that some knowledge of the original ontology cannot be directly transformed to the target format. In summary, following this approach the translation of an ontology consists in performing the following steps:

- Create part of the KR ontology of the source format in the target format, by means of meta-knowledge, so as to represent the knowledge modelling components of the source format that have not a direct correspondence with the knowledge modelling components of the target format. Meta-knowledge can be represented by means of metaclasses, annotations, structured natural language documentations, etc.
- Whenever there is a direct correspondence between the source format's ontology components and the target format's ones, transform the component of the original ontology to its corresponding components in the target format.
- Transform all the knowledge that was not transformed previously, according to the partial KR ontology created in the first step.

To use this approach, the target format must allow representing fragments of KR ontologies in such a way that the domain ontology components transformed are not mixed with the knowledge modelling components used for knowledge preservation.

Inside this group we can include the Protégé-2000 backend for RDF(S), where specific pieces of knowledge of the Protégé-2000 knowledge model are exported to that language [21], the Protégé-2000 plug-in for OWL, which extends the Protégé-2000 standard knowledge model with OWL-specific features, and the current WebODE import and export services to Protégé-2000.

Example: Achieving Interoperability Between WebODE and Protégé-2000 by an Extension of the Protégé-2000 Standard Knowledge Model. As described above, this approach consists first in creating part of the WebODE KR ontology in Protégé-2000 by extending the Protégé-2000 standard metamodel.

This KR ontology contains six metaclasses (*:WebODEConcept*, *:WebODESlot*, *:WebODEAttribute*, *:WebODEAdHocRelation*, *:WebODEPredefinedSlots*, and *:WebODEPredefinedFacet*), three subclasses of the class *:PAL-CONSTRAINT* (*:WebODEDisjointConstraint*, *:WebODEPropertyConstraint*, and *:WebODEAxiom*), and five subclasses of the class *:THING* (*:WebODEReference*, *:WebODESynonym*, *:WebODEAbbreviation*, *:WebODEConstant*, and *:WebODEProperty*).

Figure 5 shows the details of the metaclass *:WebODEConcept*, which extends the metaclass *:STANDARD-CLASS*, used by default for creating Protégé-2000 classes. The extension consists in adding new WebODE-specific slots to store information about classes such transitive and intransitive parts of, not subclass of, and bibliographic references, abbreviations, and synonyms.

Two other slots are attached to this metaclass, so as to recover the original ontology in cyclic transformations: the original URI and name of the WebODE concept, since the class name may have suffered transformations in the translation process. The rest reuses the standard slots for standard classes in Protégé-2000.

Once this ontology has been generated, all the WebODE ontology components that have a direct representation in the standard knowledge model of Protégé-2000 are transformed. Then, the rest of the WebODE ontology components that have not a direct representation in the previous knowledge model are transformed. This transformation consists in creating instances of the WebODE KR ontology described above, hence preserving the knowledge that could have been lost in the translation when the ontology is transformed back to WebODE.

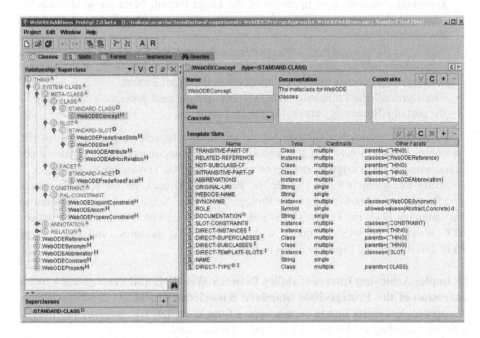

Fig. 5. WebODE KR ontology defined as an extension of the Protégé-2000 standard knowledge model

Figure 6 shows a screenshot of the travel ontology translated using this approach. The metaclass :*WebODEConcept* has a subclass *hotelTypes*, used as the metaclass for the classes *hotel1Star*, *hotel2Star*, *hotel3Star*, *hotel4Star*, and *hotel5Star*, since they all have an own slot *numberOfStars* whose value is 1, 2, 3, 4, and 5, respectively. The rest of classes in this ontology are instances of the metaclass :*WebODEConcept*.

In contrast with the solution presented in the previous section, the classes and class taxonomy of the ontology can be easily seen and understood. The figure shows the details of the class *hotel1Star*, with its template slots and the own slot *numberOfStars*, which come from the instance attribute and class attribute definition of WebODE. There are also other own slots that do not usually appear in Protégé-2000 ontologies: :*ORIGINAL-URI*, :*WEBODE-NAME*, :*SYNONYMS*, :*ABBREVIATIONS*, etc. These slots are used to include the extra knowledge from WebODE, as discussed above.

The main drawback of this approach is that an end-user who is not acquainted with the knowledge model of WebODE will not be able to understand what the terms :*WebODEReference*, :*WebODESynonym*, etc., mean, since this solution is merging the modeling of the domain ontology with the modeling of the KR ontology. We need a last step in this process, to ensure that the new components related to the WebODE KR ontology are not shown to Protégé-2000 users.

If we use the Protégé-2000 hiding-class functionality and remove some components from the forms showed to users, end users do not need to know anything about how to model ontologies with WebODE and can use the ontology using the common modeling conventions provided by Protégé-2000. In the transformation back to WebODE, this hidden knowledge is transformed without problems.

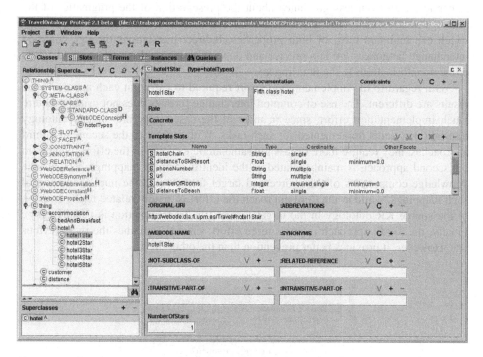

Fig. 6. Result of transforming the EON2003 Travel ontology from WebODE to Protégé-2000 with the Protégé-2000 standard knowledge model and part of the WebODE KR ontology

This proposal meets the two objectives of semantic and pragmatic preservation: it maintains all the knowledge in the transformation and allows end users and applications to understand easily the resulting ontology.

A similar approach can be applied to transform ontologies from Protégé-2000 into WebODE: the new components are not shown to WebODE users since they are instances of the WebODE KR ontology and are not accessed directly from the resulting ontology. However, they are also available for performing the transformation back to Protégé-2000.

3.5 Conclusion and Future Work

Figure 7 compares the four approaches presented in this paper according to the two criteria used in our description. The horizontal axis represents the amount of knowledge preserved in the transformation (semantic preservation), while the vertical axis represents the legibility preserved in the transformation (pragmatic preservation). We do not aim at providing quantitative measures about these amounts, but we just provide approximate qualitative measures for them. Besides, not all the source and target format pairs behave in the same way with respect to this preservation.

As shown in the figure, the second and third approaches have extremely different behaviours. The former is devoted to preserve pragmatics, with no guarantees about the semantics of the knowledge transformed; the latter is devoted to preserve semantics, with even less guarantee about the preservation of the pragmatics of the ontology transformed. The most interesting approach seems to be the fourth one, which can maintain most of both properties. Indirect translations through common interchange languages are less precise and depend on the quality and standardization of the transformations to the interlingua.

With regard to the implementation effort required to carry out each approach, the results are different. The use of common interchange formats does not usually require much implementation effort, since in most of the cases there are already ontology translation systems implemented for such tasks. With respect to the second and third approaches, they require more or less the same amount of effort: the effort required in the second approach is mainly related to the identification of mappings between the knowledge components of the source and target formats and the implementation of such mappings, while in the third approach the effort is mainly related to the creation of the source KR ontology in the target format (the transformation is usually easy). Finally, the fourth approach requires more effort, since it combines the two previous one. However, it provides better prevention than the other ones.

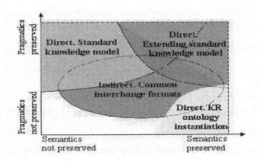

Fig. 7. Comparison of transformation approaches according to their preservation properties

Our future work will be devoted to exploring other possibilities of interoperability between formats that do not rely on translating all the components of the ontology each time that we need an ontology in a specific format. Ontologies can evolve in their source and target formats, due to reengineering processes [13], and in the case that we are reusing an ontology that has evolved in its original format and in its target format, it could be interesting to import only the ontology components that have changed, and to apply ontology merge techniques in order to detect which are the changes that affect the reengineered ontology.

Acknowledgements

This work is supported by the IST project Esperonto (IST-2001-34373).

References

1. Arpírez JC, Corcho O, Fernández-López M, Gómez-Pérez A (2003) *WebODE in a nutshell.* AI Magazine 24(3):37-48
2. Barley M, Clark P, Williamson K, Woods S (1997) *The neutral representation project.* In: Farquhar A, Grüninger M (eds) AAAI-97 Spring Symposium on Ontological Engineering, Stanford, California. AAAI Press
3. Biron PV, Malhotra A (2001) *XML Schema Part 2: Datatypes.* W3C Recommendation. http://www.w3.org/TR/xmlschema-2/
4. Bray T, Paoli J, Sperberg-McQueen CM, Maler E (2000) *Extensible Markup Language (XML) 1.0.* W3C Recommendation. http://www.w3.org/TR/REC-xml
5. Brickley D, Guha RV (2004) *RDF Vocabulary Description Language 1.0: RDF Schema.* W3C Recommendation. http://www.w3.org/TR/PR-rdf-schema
6. Chaudhri VK, Farquhar A, Fikes R, Karp PD, Rice JP (1998) *Open Knowledge Base Connectivity 2.0.3.* Technical Report. http://www.ai.sri.com/~okbc/okbc-2-0-3.pdf
7. Corcho O, Fernández-López M, Gómez-Pérez A, Vicente O (2002) *WebODE: an Integrated Workbench for Ontology Representation, Reasoning and Exchange.* In: Benjamins R, Gómez-Pérez A (eds) 13 International Conference on Knowledge Representation and Knowledge Management (EKAW2002). Sigüenza, Spain.
8. Corcho O, Gómez-Pérez A, Guerrero-Rodríguez DJ, Pérez-Rey D, Ruiz-Cristina A, Sastre-Toral T, Suárez-Figueroa MC (2003c) *Evaluation experiment of ontology tools' interoperability with the WebODE ontology engineering workbench.* In: Sure Y, Corcho O, Angele J (eds) ISWC2003 Workshop on Evaluation of Ontology Tools (EON2003). Sanibel Island, Florida. CEUR Workshop Proceedings 87. (*http://CEUR-WS.org/Vol-87/*)
9. Dean M, Schreiber G (2004) *OWL Web Ontology Language Reference.* W3C Recommendation. *http://www.w3.org/TR/owl-ref/*
10. Fernández-López M, Gómez-Pérez A (2002) *The integration of OntoClean in WebODE.* In: Angele J, Sure Y (eds) EKAW'02 Workshop on Evaluation of Ontology-based Tools (EON2002), Sigüenza, Spain. CEUR Workshop Proceedings 62:38–52. Amsterdam, The Netherlands. *http://CEUR-WS.org/Vol-62/*
11. Genesereth MR, Fikes RE (1992) *Knowledge Interchange Format. Version 3.0. Reference Manual.* Technical Report Logic-92-1. Computer Science Department. Stanford University, California, *http://meta2.stanford.edu/kif/Hypertext/kif-manual.html*
12. Gómez-Pérez A, Fernández-López M, Corcho O (2003) *Ontological Engineering.* Springer-Verlag. London, UK
13. Gómez-Pérez A, Rojas MD (2000) *Ontological Reengineering and Reuse.* In: Dieng R, Corby O (eds) 12 International Conference in Knowledge Engineering and Knowledge Management (EKAW'00). Juan-Les-Pins, France. Springer-Verlag, Lecture Notes in Artificial Intelligence (LNAI) 1937, Berlin, Germany, pp 139–156

14. Gruber TR (1993) *A translation approach to portable ontology specification*. Knowledge Acquisition 5(2):199–220
15. Guarino N, Welty C (2000) *A Formal Ontology of Properties*. In: Dieng R, Corby O (eds) 12 International Conference in Knowledge Engineering and Knowledge Management (EKAW'00). Juan-Les-Pins, France. (Lecture Notes in Artificial Intelligence LNAI 1937) Springer-Verlag, Berlin, Germany, pp 97–112
16. Isaac A, Troncy R, Malaise V (2003) *Using XSLT for Interoperability: DOE and The Travelling Domain Experiment*. In: Sure Y, Corcho O, Angele J (eds) ISWC2003 Workshop on Evaluation of Ontology Tools (EON2003). Sanibel Island, Florida. CEUR Workshop Proceedings 87. (http://CEUR-WS.org/Vol-87/), pp 92-102
17. Lassila O, Swick R (1999) Resource Description Framework (RDF) Model and Syntax Specification. W3C Recommendation. http://www.w3.org/TR/REC-rdf-syntax/
18. Merriam-Webster online. http://www.m-w.com/home.htm
19. Morris C (1938) *Foundations of the Theory of Signs*, in Carnap R et al (eds.) International Encyclopedia of Unified Science, 2:1, Chicago: The University of Chicago Press.
20. Noy NF, Fergerson RW, Musen MA (2000). *The knowledge model of Protege-2000: Combining interoperability and flexibility*. In: Dieng R, Corby O (eds) 12 International Conference in Knowledge Engineering and Knowledge Management (EKAW'00). Juan-Les-Pins, France. Springer-Verlag, LNAI 1937, Berlin, Germany.
21. Noy NF, Sintek M, Decker S, Crubézy M, Fergerson RW, Musen MA (2001) *Creating Semantic Web Contents with Protégé-2000*. IEEE Intelligent Systems and their applications. March/April. pp:60-71.
22. Raschid L, Vidal ME (1996) *A KIF for Multiple F-Logic databases*, Technical report, Institute for Advanced Computer Studies University of Maryland
23. Valente A, Russ T, MacGregor R, Swartout W (1999) *Building and (Re)Using an Ontology of Air Campaign Planning*. IEEE Intelligent Systems & their applications 14(1):27–36

On the Foundations of UML as an Ontology Representation Language

Giancarlo Guizzardi[1], Gerd Wagner[2], and Heinrich Herre[3]

[1]Centre for Telematics and Information Technology,
University of Twente, Enschede, The Netherlands
guizzard@cs.utwente.nl
[2]Eindhoven Univ. of Technology, Faculty of Technology Management,
G.Wagner@tm.tue.nl
[3]Institut fur Informatik, University of Leipzig and
Ontologies in Medicine Research Group (OntoMed)
herre@informatik.uni-leipzig.de

Abstract. There is a growing interest in the use of UML class diagrams as a modeling language to represent domain ontologies. In a series of papers [1,2] we have been using the General Ontological Language (GOL) and its underlying foundational ontology, proposed in [3,4], to evaluate the ontological correctness of a conceptual UML class model and to develop guidelines for how the constructs of the UML should be used in conceptual modeling and ontology representation. This paper can be seen as a continuation of this work, in which we focus on analyzing the UML metaconcepts of classes, attributes, data types and associations from an ontological point of view.

1 Introduction

The Unified Modeling Language (UML) is a language initially proposed as a unification of several different visual notations and modeling techniques used for systems design [5]. UML is now a *de facto* standard for modeling computational systems, and has recently been proposed that the language should be also used as an Ontology Representation Language [6]. A more explicit statement of interest on applying UML for ontology representation is made by the OMG Ontology Metamodel Definition Request for Proposals [7].

While modeling languages such as UML are evaluated on the basis of their successful use in information systems development, ontology specification languages and their underlying upper level ontologies have to be rooted in principled philosophical theories about what kinds of things exist and what their basic relationships with each other are. We believe that defining UML constructs only in terms of its mathematical semantics, although essential, is not sufficient to make it a suitable ontology representation language. We claim that, in order to model reality, a modeling language should be founded on formal upper-level ontologies, i.e it should have both formal and ontological semantics.

In a series of papers (e.g., [1,2]), we have used philosophical and psychological well-founded theories to evaluate the ontological correctness of UML conceptual models, and to develop methodological tools (language extensions, guidelines, profiles and design patterns) that assign principled ontological semantics to UML model-

E. Motta et al. (Eds.): EKAW 2004, LNAI 3257, pp. 47–62, 2004.

ing constructs. In [1], we focus on the analysis of the representation of *part-whole* (*mereological*) relations in UML and propose necessary extensions to the language to represent ontologically distinct sorts of parthood. While in [2], we present a theory of universals, which are then used to propose a *UML profile* representing different types of classifiers. This paper is a continuation of this work, focusing on the most basic ontology representation constructs, namely *classes, attributes, data types* and *associations*. Our main objective is to use a philosophically sound foundational ontology to provide: (i) an interpretation of UML constructs in terms of ontological categories and relations; (ii) principles for how these constructs should be used for ontology representation; (iii) guidelines to evaluate the ontological correctness of a conceptual UML class model representing a domain ontology.

The remaining of this article is structured as follows: section 2 presents a selection of concepts from a foundational ontology that form the theoretical basis of the analysis conducted in this paper. The theory is further used in section 3 to examine the UML metaconcepts of class, attributes, data type and associations from an ontological point of view. Section 4 provides some final considerations.

2 Background: Ontological Categories

Figure 1 depicts some of the basic elements of the foundational ontology, which will be referenced throughout this work. This ontology represents a version of the General Formal Ontology (GFO) underlying the language GOL as presented in [3,4]. The General Ontology Language (GOL) and GFO are under development as part of the OntoMed (Ontologies in Medicine) Research Group at the University of Leipzig. The GOL project was launched in 1999 as a collaborative effort between philosophers, linguists and other cognitive scientists and computer and information scientists with the aim to, on one hand, construct a formal framework for building models and representing complex structures of the world, and, on the other hand, at the development and implementation of domain-specific ontologies in several fields, especially medical sciences. GFO has been proven insightful in providing a principled foundation for analyzing and extending conceptual modeling and ontology representation languages and constructs [1,8].

Due to our objectives in the scope of this paper, we focus our discussion on a limited subset of the categories comprising GFO, which are briefly explained in the following subsections. For a complete and detailed presentation of GOL and GFO, one should refer to [3,4]. For a comparison between GFO and other upper-level ontologies, such as the IEEE Standard Upper Ontology, KIF, Sowa, Russel and Norvig and LADSEB (that can be considered a preliminary version of DOLCE [10]), one should refer to [3].

2.1 Sets and Urelements

A fundamental distinction in this ontology is between the categories of urelements and sets. We assume the existence of both urelements and sets in the world. Urelements are entities which are not sets. They form an ultimate layer of entities without any

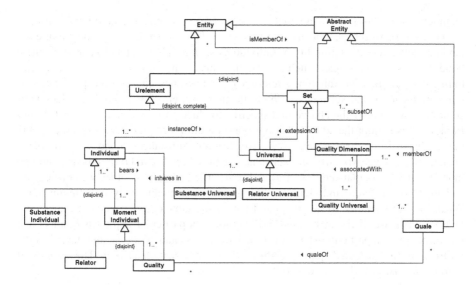

Fig. 1. Taxonomy of a fragment of GFO as a UML/MOF metamodel

set-theoretical structure in their build-up. Neither the membership relation nor the subset relation can unfold the internal structure of urelements. In GFO, urelements are classified into two disjoint categories of individuals and universals. Individuals are further classified in substance and moments.

2.2 Substance

Substances are individuals that can exist by themselves; this implies that a Substances is existentially independent from other individuals. Existential independence was introduced by E. Husserl: An individual A is existentially independent from an individual B if and only if it is logically possible for A to exist even if B does not exists. Examples of Substances include ordinary mesoscopic objects such as a dog, a house, a hammer, a car, Alan Turing and The Rolling Stones but also the so-called Fiat Objects [11] such as the North-Sea and its proper-parts, postal districts and a non-smoking area of a restaurant.

2.3 Moment

The word *Moment* is derived from the german *Momente* in the writings of Husserl and it denotes, in general terms, what is sometimes named *trope, abstract particular*, or *individualized property*. Therefore, in the scope of this work, the word bears no relation to the notion of time instant in ordinary parlance. *Moments* are individuals, which can only exist in other individuals (in the way in which, for example an electrical charge can exist only in some conductor). In other words, we can say that moments are *existentially dependent* on other individuals. The category of moments includes: (i) *qualities*: moments that are dependent on one single individual (an individual color or weight, an electric charge); (ii) *relators* (or relational moments): existentially dependent on a plurality of individuals such as a kiss, a handshake, a covalent bond, but also social objects such as a flight connection, a purchase order and a commitment or claim. The inherence relation *i* – sometimes called ontic predication – glues moments to the substances which are their bearers. For example it glues your smile to your face, or the charge in a specific conductor to the conductor itself. In our framework we adopt the so-called adopt non-migration principle [3]: it is not possible that an intrinsic moment *m* inheres in two different substances *a* and *b*. As a consequence, if we have two particular substances *a* (a red apple) and *b* (a red car), and two moments m_1 (particular redness of *a*) and m_2 (particular redness of *b*), we consider m_1 and m_2 to be different individuals, although perhaps qualitatively indistinguishable. What does it mean then to say that *a* and *b* have the same color? In conformance with DOLCE [10], we distinguish between the color of a particular apple (its quality) and its 'value' (e.g., a particular shade of red). The latter is named *quale*, and describes the position of an individual quality within a certain *quality dimension*. The notions of *quality dimension* is discussed as follows.

2.4   Quale, Quality Dimension and Quality Domain

An attempt to model the relation between qualities and their representation in human cognitive structures is presented in the theory of conceptual spaces developed by the Swedish philosopher and cognitive scientist Peter Gardenfors [9]. The theory is based on the notion of *quality dimension*. The idea is that for each perceivable or conceivable quality type there is an associated quality dimension in human cognition. For example, *height* and *mass* are associated with one-dimensional structures with a zero point isomorphic to the half-line of nonnegative numbers. Other qualities, such as color and taste, are represented by several dimensions. For instance, taste can be represented as tetrahedron space comprising the dimensions of saline, sweet, bitter and sour.

Gardenfors distinguishes between *integral* and *separable* quality dimensions: *"certain quality dimensions are integral in the sense that one cannot assign an object a value on one dimension without giving it a value on the other. For example, an object cannot be given a hue without giving it a brightness value...Dimensions that are not integral are said to be separable, as for example the size and hue dimensions."* [9, p. 24]. He then defines a *quality domain* as *"a set of integral dimensions that are separable from all other dimensions"* [9, p. 26]. Finally, he defends the idea that quality domains are endowed with certain structures (topological or ordering structures) that constrain the relations between its constituting dimensions. In his framework, the perception or conception of a quality individual can be represented as a point a in a quality domain. In accordance with DOLCE [10], this point is named here a *quale*.

An example of a quality domain is the set of integral dimensions related to color perception. A color quality *c* of an apple *a* takes its value (quale) in a three-dimensional color domain constituted of the dimensions hue, saturation and brightness. Figure 2 depicts the geometric space generated by the three quality dimensions that form this domain. One should notice that this structure constraints the relation between some of these dimensions. In particular, saturation and brightness are not totally independent, since the possible variation of saturation decreases as brightness approaches the extreme points of black and white, i.e., for almost black or almost white, there can be very little variation in saturation.

The position defended here is that the notion of a quality domain (and the constraints relating different quality dimensions captured in its structure) can provide a sound basis for the domain ontology representations of the corresponding quality universal, constraining the possible values that its attributes can assume. This point is discussed and illustrated in section 3.2. We adopt here as a quality domain any collection of integral quality dimensions regardless if these dimensions are physically, theoretically or socially motivated.

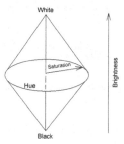

Fig. 2. The quality dimensions of hue, saturation and brightness forming the color splinter [9]

Gardenfors also advocates that, from a metaphysical point of view, quality dimensions and the relations between them as well as quality domains are *"theoretical entities that can be used to explain and predict various empirical phenomena concerning concept formation"* [9, p. 31], i.e., abstract entities. For the purpose of this article we also take qualia to be abstract entities and represent quality dimensions as sets of *qualia* (see fig. 1). For instance, the *mass* dimension can be represented as a subset the set of Real numbers (respecting the same axiomatization) and the *hue* dimension can be represented as an enumeration of color qualia augmented with a set of formal relations between its member qualia (e.g. *complementaryOf* and *closeTo*). A quality domain is thus defined as a subset of the cross-product between its constituent integral quality dimensions (e.g. ColorDomain $\subset$ HueDimension $\times$ SaturationDimension $\times$ BrightnessDimension). The formation rule for the tuples that are members of a quality domain must obey the constraints that relate its quality dimensions.

We adopt here the formal relations *assoc(x,y)*, with the meaning "quality dimension x is associated with quality universal y, and, *ql(x,y)* that represents that relation between a quality individual y and its quale x. Among others, the following axiom is stipulated for these relations: if x is the quale of y then x must be a member of the quality dimension associated with the universal of which y is an instance or, formally, $\forall x,y\ ql(x,y) \rightarrow \exists z\ (y::z) \land \exists w\ assoc(w,z) \land (x \in w)$.

In sum, if we have two particular substances a (a red apple) and b (a red car), and two moments m_1 (particular redness of a) and m_2 (particular redness of b). When saying that a and b have the same color, we mean that their individual color qualities

m_1 and m_2 are different, however, they can both be mapped to same point in the color quality domain, i.e., they have the same quale. The relation between a substance, one of its qualities and the associated quale is illustrated in figure 3.

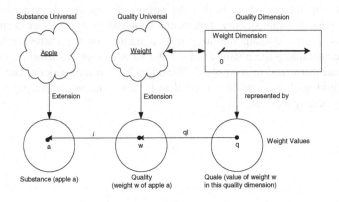

Fig. 3. Substances, qualities and qualia

2.5 Universals

A universal is a space-time independent pattern of features, which can be realized in a number of different individuals. Every individual instantiate at least one universal. Consequently, we account for the existence of Substantial Universals, Quality Universals, Relational Universals and so forth.

We use the symbol :: to denote the instantiation relation, a basic formal relation defined to hold between individuals (first argument) and universals (second argument). Hence, when writing x::U we mean that x is an instance of U or that x has the property of being a U. For example, x can be a molecule of DNA and u a pattern of features shared by all exactly similar molecules, where the notion of exact similarity is determined by the granularity and point of view of genetic science.

In this article, two universals which of particular interest are **quality universals**, such as color and weight, and **relational universals**, such as flight connection ('…is connected with…') or purchase ('…purchases…from…'). Every universal has an intension which, in our approach, is captured by means of an axiomatic specification, i.e. a set of axioms that may involve a number of other universals representing its essential properties. A particular form of such a specification of a universal U, called elementary specification, consists of a number of universals $U_1,...,U_n$ and corresponding functional relations $R_1, ...,R_n$ which attach instances from the U_i to instances of U, expressed by the following axiom:

$$\forall a \ (a::U \rightarrow \exists e_1...\exists e_n \bigwedge_{i \leq n} (e_i ::U_i \wedge R_i(a,e_i)))$$

The universals $U_1,...,U_n$ used in an elementary specification are called features. A special case of an elementary specification is a quality specification where $U_1,...,U_n$

are quality universals, the instances of U are substances and R_i represents the formal inherence relation i.

2.6 Relations and Relators

Relations are entities which glue together other entities. We divide relations into two broad categories, called *material* and *formal*. Formal relations hold between two or more entities directly without any further intervening individual. Examples of formal relations are: 5 *is greater than* 3, this day is *part-of* this month, and N *is subset of* Q but also the relations of instantiation (::), inherence (i), quale of a quality (*ql*), *assoc*, *dependence*, among others. In principle, the category of formal relations includes those relations that form the mathematical superstructure of our framework [1,3]. However, we also classify as formal those domain relations that exhibit similar characteristics, i.e. those relations of comparison such as *is taller than*, *is older than*, *know more greek than*. As pointed out in [12], the entities which are immediate relata of such relations are not substances but moments. For instance, the relation *heavier-than* between two atoms is a formal relation which holds directly as soon as the relata (atoms) are given. The truth-value of a predicate representing this relation depends solely the atomic number (intrinsic moment) of each atom and the material content of *heavier-than* is as it were distributed between the two relata.

Material relations, conversely, have material structure on their own and include examples such as kisses, conversations, fights and commitments. The relata of a material relation are mediated by individuals which are called *relators*. Relators are individuals with the power of connecting entities; a flight connection, for example, is a relator that connects airports, an enrollment a relator that connects a student with an educational institution. For the purpose of this article we define a relator simply as an *individual* r which is one-sidedly existentially dependent on two or more individuals x and y, discrete from r and from each other; r is said to *relate* x to y [12]. The notion of relators is supported in several works in the philosophical literature [4,8,12] and, the position advocated here is that, relators play an important role in answering questions of the sort: what does it mean say that John is married to Mary? Why is it true to say that Bill works for Company X but not for Company Y?

A relator universal is a universal whose instances are relators. If r connects the entities $a_1,...,a_n$, then this yields a new individual which is denoted by $\langle r: a_1,...,a_n \rangle$. Individuals of this latter sort are called material facts. For every relator universals R there exists a set of facts, denoted by *facts*(R), which is defined by the instances of R and their corresponding arguments. We assume the axiom that for every relator universal R there is a factual universal F(R) whose extension equals the set *facts*(R). The factual universal F(R) is the basis for the material relation R(F) whose instances are n-tuples of entities.

In general, a relation universal R(F) can thus be defined as follows. Let $\phi(a_1,...,a_n)$ denote a condition on the individuals $a_1,...,a_n$

$$[a_1...a_n]: R(F)\ (U_1...U_n) \leftrightarrow \bigwedge_{i \le n} aj::Ui \wedge \phi\ (a_1...a_n)$$

A relation is called *material* if there is a relator universal R such that the condition ϕ is obtained from R as follows: $\phi(a_1...a_n) \leftrightarrow \exists k\ (k::R \wedge \langle k:a_1...a_n \rangle::F(R))$.

Otherwise, R(F) is a formal relation whose instances are formal facts of the form $\langle R(F){:}a,b\rangle$.

Example: Let *Conn* be binary relator universal whose instances are individual flight connections. Then we may form a factual universal $F_{Conn} = F(Conn)$ having the meaning "An airport X is connected to a airport Y" whose instances are all facts of the form $\langle c{:}\ a,b\rangle$ where c is an individual flight connection and a,b are individual airports. A relation universal $R_{connected\text{-}to} = R(F_{Conn})$ is defined as such that its instances are pairs of the form [a,b].

3 Ontological Foundations for UML Class Diagrams

In the sequel, we refer to the *OMG UML Superstructure Specification 2.0* [5], when quoting text in italics. For simplicity, we write *UML-ontology* when we mean domain ontology in the form of a *UML class model*. Whenever the context is clear, we omit the name space prefix UML and simply say 'object', 'class', etc., instead of 'UML object', 'UML class', etc.

3.1 Classes and Objects

In the UML specification, *"an object represents a particular instance of a class. It has identity and attribute values."* While in the UML objects are instances of classes, individuals are instances of universals in GFO. A *"Class describes a set of Objects sharing a collection of Features, including Operations, Attributes and Methods, that are common to the set of Objects."* [p. 2-26] *"The model is concerned with describing the intension of the class, that is, the rules that define it. The run-time execution provides its extension, that is, its instances."* [p. 3-35]

We may observe a direct correspondence between universals and classes of a certain kind, as stated in the following principle:

Principle 1: In a *UML-ontology*, any universal U of the domain may be represented as a concrete class C_U. Conversely, for all concrete classes (of a *UML-ontology*) whose instances are basic objects or links (representing individuals), there must be a corresponding universal in the domain.

In a *UML-ontology*, any individual of the domain that is an instance of a universal may be represented as an object (or link) of the class representing the universal. For every universal *U* there is a set *Ext(U)*, called its extension, containing all instances of *U* as elements. Even if two universals U_1 and U_2 have identical extensions ($Ext(U_1) = Ext(U_2)$), they are considered as different universals. As a consequence, we can account for concomitant (co-extensional) universals, such as fluid and viscous and living and mortal but, which clearly have different intentions.

Most classes in a *UML-ontology* represent Substance Universals. This is due to the fact that Substantials are prior to Moments not only from an existential but also from an identification point of view. For example, Schneider [13] claims that moments (tropes) are *identificationally dependent* on substances (objects), i.e., while the latter can be 'single out on their own', in order to identify a moment m of substantial s, one has to identify s first.

The substances (belonging to the realm of concrete reality) that we talk and think about can be classified in all kinds of ways. We can sort things by color (e.g. creating the class of red things) or by shape (e.g. the class of things with circular form) or by (clusters of) properties that define classes of things such as the classes of elephants, oak trees, cars, europeans and students. One important question that arises at this point is: if things can be classified in a multitude of ways how do we create the conceptual categories used in cognition and language? Can we provide methodological guidelines that assist an ontology designer in evaluating modeling alternatives?

The development of a theory of substance universals that addresses these questions, due to its importance and complexity, cannot be dealt in here and deserves a paper on its own. In [2], we present a philosophically and psychologically well-founded formal theory of substance universals for conceptual modeling which is used to propose: (a) a profile for UML whose elements represent finer-grained distinctions between different types of substance universals; (b) a set of constraints defining the admissible relations between these elements. The categories in this profile provide a foundation for a number of modeling primitives that, albeit often used, are commonly defined in an ad hoc manner in the practice of conceptual modeling and knowledge representation (e.g. kind, phase or state, role, mixin). In the remaining of this paper, non-stereotyped classes that appear in the models represent substance universals.

3.2 Attributes and Data Types

Suppose that we have an extension of the situation illustrated in figure 3, i.e. a substantial universal *Apple* whose elementary specification contains the features *Weight* and *Color*. Thus, for an instance a of Apple there are instances c of the quality universal color and w of weight both inhering in a. The intention of this universal could be represented by the following quality specification: $\forall a$ (a::**Apple** $\rightarrow$ $\exists c \exists w$ (c::**Color** $\land i(c,a)) \land$ (w::**Weight** $\land i(w,a)))$.

Associated with w there is a quale q denoting a particular weight value, i.e. a point in the weight quality dimension such that $ql(q,w)$ holds. We assume the weight quality domain to be a one-dimensional structures isomorphic to the half-line of nonnegative numbers represented by the set **WeightValue**. The mapping between a substance a and its weight quale can be represented by the following function *weight_in_grams*: Ext(Apple) $\rightarrow$ **WeightValue** such that *weight_in_grams* $(x) = \{y \in$ **WeightValue** $|$ $\exists z::$**Weight** $i(z,x) \land ql(y,z)\}$.

In general, let U be a substance or quality universal and Q be a quality universal. Let E be a quality specification capturing the intention of universal U: $\forall x$ (x::U $\rightarrow \exists y$ (y::Q $\land i(c,a)))$. If D is a quality dimension associated with Q, we can define the function $f:$Ext(U) $\rightarrow$ D (named an *attribute function*) for S such that for every x::U we have that $f(x) = \{y \mid \exists z::Q \ i(z,x) \land ql(y,z)\}$. Analogous attribute functions can be defined for every quality universal Q_i in a quality specification of universal U'.

In the simplest case, quality universals appearing in the quality specification of U can be represented in a *UML-ontology* via their corresponding *attribute functions* and associated *quality dimensions* in the following manner:

Principle 2: Every attribute function associated to the elementary specification of the universal U may be represented as an attribute of the class C_U (representation of the universal U) in a *UML-ontology*; every quality dimension which is the co-domain of one these functions may be represented as data types of the corresponding attributes in this *UML-ontology*.

In UML, *"a data type is a special kind of classifier, similar to a class, whose instances are values (not objects)...A value does not have an identity, so two occurrences of the same value cannot be differentiated"* [5, p. 95]. A direct representation of Apple's elementary specification in UML according to principle 2 maps the attribute function **weight_in_grams:Ext(Apple)→WeightValue** to an attribute weight_in_grams with data type WeightValue in class Apple (figure 4(a) and 4(b)).

In order to model the relation between the quality c (color) and its quale, there are other issues to be considered. As previously mentioned, the quality dimension associated with the Color universal is a three-dimension splinter (fig. 2) composed of quality dimensions hue, saturation and brightness. In DOLCE, these dimensions are considered to be indirect qualities, i.e., there are quality individuals h, s, b instances of quality universals Hue, Saturation and Brightness, respectively, that inhere in the color quality c (which in turn inheres in substance a). For this reason h, s, b are named indirect qualities of a. The intention of the universal Color could then be represented by the following specification: ∀c (c::Color → ∃h∃s∃b (h::Hue ∧ i(h,c)) ∧(s::Saturation ∧ i(s,c)) ∧(b::Brightness ∧ i(b,c))).

In this case, we can derive the following attribute functions from the features in this specification: (a) **hue: Ext(Color) → HueValue**; (b) **saturation: Ext(Color) → SaturationValue**; (c) **brightness: Ext(Color) → BrightnessValue**. Together these functions map each quality of a color *c* to its corresponding quality dimension. One possibility for modeling this situation is a direct application of principle 2 to the Color universal quality specification. In this alternative, depicted in figure 4(a), the class Color directly represents the quality universal color and, its attributes the attribute functions *hue, saturation* and *brightness*.

Another modeling alternative is to use the UML construct of a data type to represent a quality domain and its constituent quality dimensions (figure 4(b)). In this case, first we define for the universal Apple an attribute function *color*: **Ext(Apple) → HueValue × SaturationValue × BrightnessValue** such that *color*(x) = {<y,z,w> ∈ **HueValue × SaturationValue × BrightnessValue** | ∃c::Color i(c,x) ∧ (y = hue(c)) ∧ (z = saturation(c)) ∧ (w = brightness(c))}.

In figure 4(b), the data type fields *hue, staturation, brightness* do not represent attribute functions but values (qualia) that form the data type tuple so that the "instances"(members) of ColorValue are tuples ⟨x,y,z⟩ where x ∈ HueValue, y ∈ SaturationValue and z ∈ BrightnessValue (and it is unfortunate, in this sense, that UML uses the same notation for both). The *navigable end name* **color** in the association between Apple and ColorValue represents the attribute function **color** described above. *Navigable end names* are a suitable alternative mechanism for representing attribute functions since in UML they are semantically equivalent to attributes [5,p. 82].

One should notice that these two forms of representation do not convey the same information (a fact which we highlight by the use of different stereotypes): in figure

4(a), color objects are one-sidedly existentially dependent on the individuals they are related to via the *inheres in* relation. These objects are *bonafide* individuals with a definite numerical identity. In figure 4(b), contrariwise, the members of the Color-Value are *pure values* that represent points in a quality domain. These values can qualify a number of different objects but they exist independently of them in the sense that a color tuple is a part of quality domain even if no object "has that color". Both representations are warranted, in the sense that ontologically consistent interpretations can be found in both cases and, which alternative shall be pragmatically more suitable is a matter of empirical investigation.

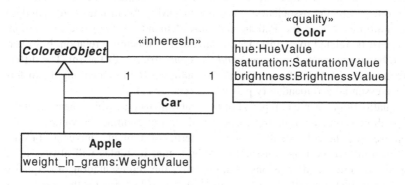

Fig. 4(a). Representing Quality Universals and indirect qualities

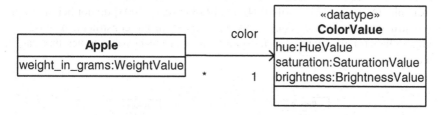

Fig. 4(b). Representing Qualia in a multi-dimensional quality domain

Notwithstanding, we believe that some guidelines could be anticipated. In situations in which the qualities of a quality all take their values (qualia) in a single quality domain (e.g. color), the latter alternative should be preferred due to its compatibility with the modeling tradition in conceptual modeling and knowledge representation. However, there are cases in which we want to directly represent the quality associated with a substance, not its qualia. An example of such a situation is depicted in Figure 5, which models the relation between a Hospital, its Patients, and a number of symptoms reported by these patients. Suppose an individual patient John is suffering from headache and influenza. John's headache and influenza are qualities inhering in John. Even if another patient, for example Paul, has a headache that is qualitatively indistinguishable from that of his, John's headache and Paul's headache are two different individuals. Moreover, instances of Symptoms can have qualities themselves (such as duration and intensity) and can participate in relations of, for example, causation or precedence. In figure 6, the quality universal Symptom is represented by a class construct decorated with the «quality» stereotype. The formal relation between Symptom and Patient is mapped to the *inherence* relation in the instance level, representing the existential dependence of a Symptom on a Patient. In other words, for an instance *s* of Symptom there must be a specific instance *p* of Patient associated with *s*, and in every situation that *s* exists *p* must exist and the inherence relation between the two must hold. One should notice that this formal relation has a semantics which is outside the usual interpretation of the association construct in UML. According to its standard usage, the multiplicity 1 in the Patient end only demands that, in every situation, symptom *s* must be related to *an* instance of Patient. The inherence relation, however, requires *s* to be always related to the *one and the same instance* of Patient. The difference between these two sorts of requirements is analogous to those marking the difference between essential and mandatory part-whole relations [1].

Finally, quality domains are composed of integral dimensions, which means that the value of one dimension cannot be represented without representing the values of others. By representing the color quality domain in terms of a quality universal (or data type) we can reinforce (via its constructor method) that its tuples will always have values for all the integral dimensions. Additionally, the representation of a quality domain should account not only for its quality dimensions but also for the constraints on the relation between them imposed by its structure. To mention another example, consider the Gregorian calendar as a quality domain (composed of the linear quality dimensions days, months and years) in which date qualities can be represented. It is clear that the value of one dimension constrains the value of the others in a way that, for example, the points [31-April-2004] and [29-February-2003] do not belong to this quality structure. Once more constraints represented on the constructor method of a «quality» class (or data type) can be used to restrict the possible tuples that can be instantiated.

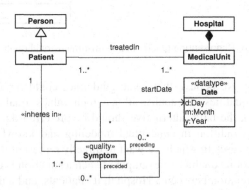

Fig. 5. Representing Quality Universals and Formal Relational Universals

In the sequel, we observe the following principle between quality domains and their representation in terms of data types:

Principle 3: Every quality dimension D associated to a quality universal Q may be represented as a data type DT in a *UML-ontology*; A set of integral dimension D_1... D_n (represented by data types DT_1... DT_n) constituting a quality domain QD can be grouped in data type W representing QD. In this case, every quality dimension D_i of QD may be represented by a field of W of type DT_i. Moreover, the relations between the dimensions D_i of QD may be represented by constraints relating the attributes of data type W.

3.3 Associations

In the UML, the ER concept of a relationship type is called association. "An association defines a semantic relationship between classifiers. *The instances of an association are a set of tuples relating instances of the classifiers.... An instance of an association is a link, which is a tuple of instances drawn from the corresponding classifiers*". The OMG UML Specification is somehow ambiguous in defining associations. An association is primarily considered to be a 'connection', but, in certain cases (whenever it has 'class-like properties'), an association may be a class: "An association class is an association that is also a class. It not only connects a set of classifiers but also defines a set of features that belong to the relationship itself and not any of the classifiers."

An association A between the classes C_1,...,C_n of a UML-ontology can be understood in our framework as a relation (relational universal) R between the corresponding universals U_1,...,U_n whose extension consists of all tuples corresponding to the links of A. In figure 5, an example of a formal relation is *precedence*. Precedence is a partial order relation between symptoms that depends only on the starting moment of each of them. The relation *treatedIn* between *Patient* and *MedicalUni*, contrariwise, requires the existence of a third entity, namely a *Treatment* process, in order for the relation to hold. This latter case can be modeled in our framework as follows: Let *treatedIn* be a binary material association corresponding to a relator universal *Treatment* whose instances are individual treatment processes. These individual *treatment* processes connect two individuals: a *patient*, say *John*, and a *MedicalUnit*, say *TraumaUnit#1*. Thus, **[John, TraumaUnit#1]:$R_{treatedIn}$(Person, MedicalUnit)**. Since *John::Person* and *TraumaUnit#1::MedicalUnit*, and there is a specific treatment process *t::Treatment* we have the fact: **⟨t:John,TraumaUnit#1⟩**.

We obtain the definition for the tuple $[a_1,a_2]$ being a link of the association *treatedIn* between *Person* and *MedicalUnit*: **$[a_1,a_2]:R_{treatedIn}$(Person, MedicalUnit) ↔ a_1::Person ∧ a_2::MedicalUnit ∧ ∃t(t::Treatment ∧ ⟨t:a_1,a_2⟩::F(Treatment))**.

We can now state the following principles regarding the representation of formal and material relations in a *UML-ontology*:

Principle 4: In a *UML-ontology*, any formal relation universal R_F of the domain may be represented as a standard association whose links represent the tuples in the extension of R_F. Conversely, a material relation R_M of the domain may be represented in a

UML-ontology by representing the *relator universal* associated with the relation as an association class.

There is a specific practical problem concerning the representation of *material relations* as standard associations that supports the modeling choice represented in this principle. This problem, pointed by Bock and Odell in [14], is caused by the fact that the standard notation collapses two different types of *multiplicity constraints*. Let us take, for instance, the association *treatedIn* depicted in figure 6. The model states that each Patient can be treated in one-to-many Medical Units and that each medical unit can treat one-to-many patients. However, this statement is ambiguous since many different interpretations can be given to it, including the following: (i) a patient is related to only one treatment to which participate possibly several medical units; (ii) a patient can be related to several treatments to which only one single unit participates; (iii) a patient can be related to several treatments to which possibly several medical units participate; (iv) several patients can be related to a treatment to which several medical units participate, and a single patient can be related to several treatments. The cardinality constraint that indicates how many patients (or medical units) can be related to one instance of Treatment is named *single-tuple* cardinality constraints. *Multiple-tuple* cardinality constraints restrict the number of treatments a patient (or medical unit) can be related to. By modeling the relator universal *Treatment* as an association class one can explicit represent both types of constraints. A version of figure 5 adopting this principle is presented in figure 6.

This problem is specific to material relations. Extensional formal relations are sets of tuples, i.e. an instance of the relation is itself a tuple with predefined arity. In formal relations, cardinality constraints are always unambiguously interpreted as being *multiple-tuple* (since there is no point in specifying single-tuple cardinality constraints for a relation with predefined arity). Hence, formal relations can be suitably represented as standard UML associations. One should notice that the relations between Patient and Treatment, and Medical Unit and Treatment are formal relations between universals (*inheres in*). This is important to block the infinite regress that arises if material relations are required to relate these entities.

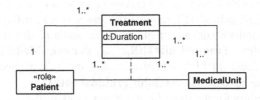

Fig. 6. Representing Material Relational Universals

In the same way as qualities, relators can have their own inhering moments (e.g. Duration, as a quality associated to the universal Treatment, in fig. 6) or they can be used as a foundation for other relations such as, for instance, a relator universal *Invoice* whose instances connect particular Treatments and Payers.

4 Final Considerations

The development of a well-grounded, axiomatized upper level ontology is an important step towards the definition of real-world semantics for ontology representation diagrammatic languages. In this paper, we use the General Formalized Ontology underlying the language GOL to evaluate the ontological correctness of UML as an ontology representation language, and to develop guidelines that assign well-defined ontological semantics to UML constructs. In particular, we focus on the ontology representation most basic primitives: class, attribute, data types and association.

However, despite the importance of these modeling constructs, there is still a deficiency of methodological support for helping the user of the language deciding how to model the elements of a given domain. For example, as reported in [15], the same real-world phenomena (e.g. Marriage) can sometimes be modeled as a class, a relation or an attribute. This situation is made worse by the fact that there is not in the literature a shared agreement on the ontological meaning of these constructs. To cite one example: in a series of papers (e.g. [15,16]) the proponents of the BWW (Bunge-Wand-Weber) approach claim that universals whose instances are properties (moments) should not be modeled as classes in a conceptual model of the domain. This claim is contested by Veres and Hitchman in [17] who employ Jakendoff's Semantic Structures [18] as well as empirical results from modeling sections with practioneers. In this paper, by presenting a principled interpretation for what an association is supposed to denote, we show that representing relational moments as classes is not only ontologically correct but also beneficial from a practical point of view.

In sum, the work presented here is part of larger effort that aims at developing: (i) a formal ontological framework that can be used as a system of domain-independent meta-level categories to provide ontological semantics for ontology representation languages [3,4]; (ii) a set of well-founded methodological tools (language extensions, guidelines, profiles and design patterns) that contribute to the discipline of ontological engineering [1,2].

References

1. Guizzardi, G., Herre, H., Wagner G.: Towards Ontological Foundations for UML Conceptual Models. 1st International Conference on Ontologies Databases and Applications of Semantics (ODBASE), USA, 2002.
2. Guizzardi, G., Wagner G., Guarino, N., van Sinderen, M. An Ontologically well-Founded Profile for UML Conceptual Models, 16th International Conference on Advanced Information Systems Engineering (CAiSE), Latvia, 2004.
3. Degen, W., Heller B., Herre H., Smith, B.: GOL: Towards an axiomatized upper level ontology. 2nd International Conference of Formal Ontologies and Information Systems (FOIS'01), USA, 2001.
4. Heller, B., Herre, H. Ontological Categories in GOL. Axiomathes 14: 71-90 Kluwer Academic Publishers, 2004.
5. Object Management Group, UML 2.0 Superstructure Specification, Doc.# ptc/03-08-02, Aug. 2003.

6. Cranefield, S., Purvis M.: UML as an ontology modelling language, Proceedings of the Workshop on Intelligent Information Integration, 16th International Joint Conference on Artificial Intelligence (IJCAI-99), Germany, 1999.
7. Object Management Group, Ontology Definition Metamodel Request for Proposals, OMG Document: ad/2003-03-40, 2003.
8. Loebe, F. An Analysis of Roles: Towards Ontology-Based Modelling, Diploma Thesis, Institute for Medical Informatics, Statistics and Epidemiology (IMISE), University of Leipzig, 2003.
9. Gärdenfors, P. Conceptual Spaces: the Geometry of Thought. MIT Press, USA, 2000.
10. Masolo, C.; Borgo, S.; Gangemi, A.; Guarino, N.; Oltramari, A.; Ontology Library, WonderWeb Deliverable D18, 2003.
11. Smith, B., Fiat Objects, 11th European Conference on Artificial Intelligence, The Netherlands, 1994.
12. Smith, B.; Mulligan, K.; A Relational Theory of the Act, Topoi (5/2), 115-30,1986.
13. Schneider, L., Designing Foundational Ontologies: The Object-Centered High-Level Reference Ontology OCHRE as a Case Study, 22th International Conference on Conceptual Modeling (ER), USA, 2003.
14. Bock, C.; Odell, J., A More Complete Model of Relations and Their Implementation Part I: Relations as Object Types, Journal Of Object-Oriented Programming Vol 10, No 3. June 1997.
15. Wand. Y.; Storey, V.C.; Weber, R.; An Ontological Analysis of the Relationship Construct in Conceptual Modeling, ACM Transactions on Database Systems, Vol.24, No.4, Dec.1999.
16. Evermann, J. and Wand, Y. Towards ontologically based semantics for UML constructs. In H. Kunii, S. Jajodia, and A. Solvberg, editors, Proceedings of the 20th International Conference on Conceptual Modeling (ER), Japan, 2001.
17. Veres, C.; Hitchman, S, Using Psychology to Understand Conceptual Modeling, 10th European Conference on Information Systems (ECIS 2002), Poland.
18. Jakendoff, R.S. Semantic Structures, Current Studies in Linguistics, MIT Press, 1990.

OWL Pizzas:
Practical Experience of Teaching OWL-DL: Common Errors and Common Patterns

Alan Rector[1], Nick Drummond[1], Matthew Horridge[1], Jeremy Rogers[1],
Holger Knublauch[2], Robert Stevens[1], Hai Wang[1], and Chris Wroe[1]

[1] Department of Computer Science, University of Manchester,
Manchester M13 9PL, UK
{rector, ndrummond, mhorridge, jrogers, stevensr, hwang,
wroec}@cs.man.ac.uk
[2] Stanford Medical Informatics, Stanford University,
Stanford, CA, USA 94305-5479
holger@smi.stanford.edu

Abstract. Understanding the logical meaning of any description logic or similar formalism is difficult for most people, and OWL-DL is no exception. This paper presents the most common difficulties encountered by newcomers to the language, that have been observed during the course of more than a dozen workshops, tutorials and modules about OWL-DL and it's predecessor languages. It emphasises understanding the exact meaning of OWL expressions – proving that understanding by paraphrasing them in pedantic but explicit language. It addresses, specifically, the confusion which OWL's open world assumption presents to users accustomed to closed world systems such as databases, logic programming and frame languages. Our experience has had a major influence in formulating the requirements for a new set of user interfaces for OWL the first of which are now available as prototypes. A summary of the guidelines and paraphrases and examples of the new interface are provided. The example ontologies are available online.

1 Introduction

1.1 Background

Most people find it difficult to understand the logical meaning and potential inferences statements in description logics, including OWL-DL. While there are several initial guides to ontologies available, e.g. [15, 6, 2, 7] and numerous works on ontological principles, e.g. [3, 4, 14], there is little guidance on how to use OWL-DL or related description logic formalism so as to make effective use of their classifiers (aka "reasoners") and even less on the pitfalls involved in their use. Likewise, few example ontologies on the web make extensive use of inference.

Over the past five years the authors have presented a series of tutorials, workshops and post-graduate modules, teaching people to use OWL-DL and its predecessors effectively. The purpose of this paper is to systematise the knowledge gained about new users' difficulties in understanding OWL, to present examples which address those misunderstandings and patterns which avoid them.

E. Motta et al. (Eds.): EKAW 2004, LNAI 3257, pp. 63–81, 2004.

The most common problems which we address are:

1. Failure to make all information explicit - assuming that information implicit in names is "represented" and available to the classifier.
2. Mistaken use of universal rather than existential restrictions as the default
3. Open world reasoning
4. The effect of range and domain constraints as axioms

To this we can add the additional problems posed by:

1. Trivial satisfiability of universal restrictions – that "only" (allValuesFrom) does not imply "some" (someValuesFrom).
2. The difference between defined and primitive classes and the mechanics of converting one to the other.
3. Errors in understanding common logical constructs.
4. Expecting classes to be disjoint by default.
5. The difficulty of understanding subclass axioms used for implication.

(Note that this paper only concerns issues in defining OWL classes, since this is the strength of OWL-DL and most existing classifiers deal with individuals incompletely or not at all.)

Our experience to date has been with the first generation of tools for OWL-DL and its predecessors, OilEd[1][1], and with even earlier tools from *Open*GALEN [11][2]. The requirements for the new tools being developed in the Protégé-OWL-CO-ODE environment[3] [5] collaboratively by the authors have been informed by this experience.

Ontologies corresponding to the paper can be found at http://www.co-ode.org/ontologies. All tools are available at the URLs for the projects given in the footnotes.

1.2 The Tutorials: Pizza, Manchester House Style, and "What Does it Mean"

We have used many example ontologies over the years - vehicles, IKEA catalogues, the University department and course, biomedical examples – but for Western audiences pizzas have proven most successful.[4] They are familiar; they are fun; they are fundamentally compositional. They are concrete and physical; real pizza menus are readily available; and they avoid thorny ontological issues involved in abstract notions such as "ideas", "causation", "agency", etc. Nonetheless, they are rich enough to illustrate key issues. Constructing correct definitions of pizzas from a menu and for a "vegetarian pizza" so that the correct pizzas are classified as "vegetarian" turns out to be a surprisingly challenging exercise.

The style presented here is unashamedly the *Manchester House Style* – what we consider good practice. We do not claim that it is the only way to model in OWL-DL,

---

[1] http://oiled.man.ac.uk

[2] http://www.opengalen.org

[3] http://protege.Stanford.edu → plugins → backends → OWL; http://www.co-ode.org

[4] For some non-western audiences, alternatives are required but are outside the scope of this paper.

but we do claim that it is one proven, effective way. The central feature of the style is "normalisation" described in detail in [10]. Note that a slightly simplified form of the OWL abstract syntax [8] is used in this paper which uses "and" and "or" rather than "intersectionOf" and "unionOf", as this corresponds more closely to what actually appears in both OilEd and the Protégé -OWL-CO-ODE interfaces.

2   The Basics

Before discussing the serious difficulties encountered by newcomers, it is helpful to introduce the pizza example and some basics - the notion of disjointness of classes, the function of the classifier in testing consistency, the basic notion of descriptions and existential graphs, and the first conventions for paraphrasing OWL. (The full set of conventions for paraphrasing appears at the end of the paper in Table 1).

2.1   Subsumption, Disjointness and the Classifier

A simple taxonomy of pizza toppings is shown in Figure 1. The first question for a newcomer to OWL is "What does such a hierarchy actually mean?" By contrast to frame systems, subsumption in OWL means necessary implication, so the hierarchy means that "All Pepperoni is Meat", that "All Meat is a Pizza topping", etc.[5]

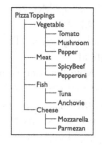

Does this mean that Meat and Fish and Vegetables etc. are all different? Can there be anything that is both Meat and Vegetable? Users of many other formalisms would naturally assume that they were different, at least unless they had an explicit common child.

Fig. 1. Pizza hierarchy (Revised disjoint)

However, in OWL, classes are overlapping until disjointness axioms are entered. This can be illustrated using a procedure that also demonstrates the role of the classifier in checking the consistency of the ontology.

First, a class MeatyVegetable is created that is a subclass of both Meat and Vegetable. This means that all MeatyVegetable are kinds of Meat and also kinds of Vegetable. The classifier is then run first without the disjointness axioms between Meat and Vegetable and then after they have been inserted. Without the disjointness axioms, running the classifier produces no change. However, when the disjointness axioms are added, MeatyVegetable is marked in red in the Protégé-OWL interface, indicating that it is inconsistent or "unsatisfiable". In Protégé -OWL-CO-ODE a note that it has been found unsatisfiable also appears in the list of changes, and a warning is issued during classification.

That the notion of a "meaty vegetable" should be inconsistent conforms with users' intuitions from the names of the classes. However, it is critical to understand that this

---

[5] One must immediately add something like "for purposes of this ontology." (It would be better to add a suffix Topping everywhere, and we normally do so in ontologies, but for this paper it leads to long expressions which tend not to fit on a single line.)

implicit information in their names is unavailable to the classifier. Meat and Vegetable are only recognised by the classifier as disjoint if the disjointness axioms are entered explicitly.

One of the most common errors in building ontologies in OWL has been to omit the disjointness axioms. To help users manage disjointness axioms, the Protégé -OWL-CO-ODE interface makes entering them easy by providing a single button to add or remove disjointness axioms amongst all siblings of a given parent[6] (See Figure 18).

2.2   Properties and Existential Restrictions

The purpose, however, of OWL is not just to create a concept hierarchy but to describe and define concepts. Therefore we want to 'build' some pizzas. Figure 2 gives a description of the concept – MargheritaPizza[7] – from a Pizza menu as typically constructed by students early on in the course.

The first problem for students is to understand exactly what the description in Figure 2 means. That all MargheritaPizza have Mozzarella and Tomato? That any pizzas having Mozzarella and Tomato are MargheritaPizza? That MargheritaPizza has Mozzarella and Tomato and nothing else? The paraphrase makes the meaning absolutely clear. The italicised words – "*amongst other things*" and "*some*" - are critical.

Note that one of the most common errors made by newcomers to OWL is to use universal (allValuesFrom) rather than existential (someValuesFrom) as the default qualifier. This error is pernicious because the results often appear to work initially with the problems only becoming evident later in the course of developing the ontology. (See also Section 5.3). In teaching we go to great effort to ensure that existential someValuesFrom restrictions are used as the default from the beginning, both through the order of presentation and through the software used, where someValuesFrom is always the default (See also section 5.1).

OWL:
Class (MargheritaPizza partial
  Pizza
    restriction (hasTopping someValuesFrom Mozzarella)
    restriction (hasTopping someValuesFrom Tomato))
Paraphrase:
Margherita pizzas have, *amongst other things*, *some* mozzarella topping and also *some* tomato topping.

Fig. 2. Description and paraphrase of a Margherita Pizza

---

[6] In OilEd, by contrast, disjointness axioms have to be entered on a separate tab.
[7] Margherita Pizzas are listed on the menu has having cheese and tomato toppings

3   Definitions and the Open World Assumption

3.1   Defined Classes: "Conceptual Lego"

"Primitive" and "defined"classes is one of the major novelties of OWL and Understanding the difference between them is one of the major stumbling blocks for newcomers.

Many potential users are familiar with either frame systems such as Protégé or object oriented programming and analysis and UML. In both formalisms, things can be described by necessary conditions but not as defined classes with sufficiency conditions. However, in OWL, new concepts can be built up from existing concepts by fitting them together in definitions like blocks of Lego. More formally, OWL allows concepts to be defined by sets of necessary and sufficient conditions as shown in Figure 3. We refer to classes for which there are only necessary conditions – marked by the keyword "partial"[8] in the abstract syntax – as "primitive" classes, harking back to an older terminology. Classes for which there is at least one set of necessary and sufficient conditions – marked in the abstract syntax by the keyword "complete" – are referred to as as "defined".[9]

OWL:
Class(CheeseyPizza complete
  Pizza
    restriction (hasTopping someValuesFrom Cheese))
Paraphrase:
A cheesey pizza is *any* pizza that has, *amongst other things*, *some* cheese topping.

Fig. 3. Initial definition of cheesey pizza

In the paraphrase the meaning of definitions is emphasized by the italicized "*any*" – i.e. any pizza that satisfies these conditions will be classified as a "cheesey pizza".

In our experience, the most common accidental error in implementing OWL ontologies is to fail to make a set of restrictions a definition - i.e. to fail to make the definition "complete" rather than "partial", or "necessary and sufficient" rather than just "necessary". It is critical to understand that, in general, nothing will be inferred to be subsumed under a primitive class by the classifier. For example in (Figure 3), if "complete" is replaced by "partial", then nothing will appear under CheesyPizza.

The first thing, therefore, to check when things fail to be classified under a concept, is whether or not the description of the concept is "defined" or "primitive". In OilEd, a small button in the upper right hand corner of the screen, is used to toggle from "partial"

---

[8] OWL descriptions are sometimes known as "partial definitions" and the keyword "partial", appears in OWL syntax and in OilEd. This usage is seriously misleading and the term "partial definition" a misnomer. Many of the restrictions on primitive, or indeed defined, classes are necessary implications and take no part in any set of necessary and sufficient conditions - i.e. in definitions - "partial" or otherwise.

[9] It is also possible to make the distinction using the difference between "SubClassOf" and "EquivalentClasses", but we usually postpone that discussion until the basics are understood.

to "complete" and is set to "partial" by default (Figure 4). A major goal for the the new Protégé -OWL-CO-ODE interface has been to make the distinction between primitive and defined classes clearer (See Figure 18).

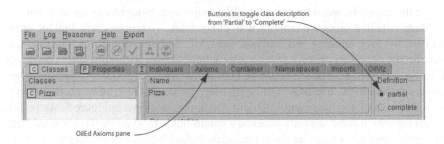

Fig. 4. OilED sets "partial" by default

3.2   Open World Reasoning: Vegetarian Pizzas

The biggest single hurdle to understanding OWL and Description Logics is the use of Open World Reasoning. Almost certainly, all systems that newcomers to OWL will have encountered previously use closed world reasoning with "negation as failure" – i.e. if something cannot be found, it is assumed to be absent, *e.g.* databases, logic programming, constraint languages in frame systems, etc. By contrast, OWL uses open world reasoning with negation as unsatisfiability - *i.e.* something is false only if it can be proved to contradict other information in the ontology.

This point is dramatically made by attempting to define a VegetarianPizza. Expressing the negation is a problem in itself that is discussed under section 5 "Logical Issues". However, even once a correct logical definition is formulated as in Figure 5, there are surprises.

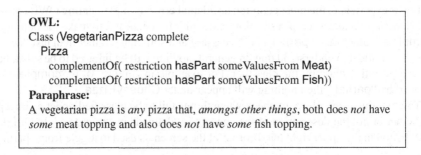

Fig. 5. Correct definitions of Vegetarian Pizza

Given the definitions so far, MargheritaPizza does not classify as VegetarianPizza. There is nothing in their definition that makes it contradictory to add meat or fish toppings. For example the MeatyMargherita pizza defined in Figure 6 is consistent and classifies under MargheritaPizza.

OWL:
Class (MeatyMargheritaPizza complete
  Pizza
    restriction (hasTopping someValuesFrom Tomato)
    restriction (hasTopping someValuesFrom Mozzarella)
    restriction (hasTopping someValuesFrom SpicyBeef))
Paraphrase:
A meaty margherita pizza is *any* pizza which, *amongst other things*, has *some* tomato topping and also *some* mozzarella topping and also *some* spicy beef topping.

Fig. 6. Definition of a "meaty margherita pizza" which is consistent and will be classified under Margherita pizza even though it has a meat topping

That the definition of MargheritaPizza was inadequate should be clear from the paraphrases in Figures 2 and 6. The rules for paraphrasing require adding "*amongst other things*" and "*any*" specifically so as to capture the open world assumption implicit in all OWL expressions. Clearly, the paraphrase does not correspond to what most restaurant customers would understand from the menu – that a Margherita pizza is a pizza that has mozzarella and tomato toppings and only those toppings. This intuitive understanding is captured formally in the OWL definition in Figure 7. The final restriction is known as a "closure restriction" or "closure axiom" because it closes off the possibility of further additions for a given property. "allValuesFrom" is paraphrased as "*only*", because to say that *all* values come from a given class is the same as saying that values may *only* come from that class.

OWL:
Class(MargheritaPizza complete
  Pizza
    restriction (hasTopping someValuesFrom Tomato)
    restriction (hasTopping someValuesFrom Mozzarella)
    restriction (hasTopping allValuesFrom (Tomato or Mozzarella)))
Paraphrase:
A margherita pizza is *any* pizza which, *amongst other things*, has *some* tomato topping and also *some* mozzarella toppings and also has *only* mozzarella *and/or* tomato toppings.

Fig. 7. Correct version of definition of Margherita pizza with closure restriction

The phrase "*amongst other things*" in the paraphrase still allows space for a MargheritaPizza to have restrictions involving properties other than hasTopping - *e.g.* to represent that it is stale, overcooked, chopped into pieces etc. Anything except a margherita pizza with additional toppings.

3.3 Which Classes Should be Defined? Which Primitive? How to Decide?

A common question from newcomers to OWL is how they should decide which classes to define. The choice of the "skeleton taxonomies" of primitive concepts is a key part of the method of "untangling" discussed in Section 6.2 and in more detail in [13, 12]. However, we suggest three basic heuristics:

- Pragmatic: Do you want things to be classified under the given class automatically?
- Do you want to commit to a definition now? You can always return to the item and change it from primitive to defined later. In fact this is a key part of the methodology we advocate.
- Philosophical. Can you define it completely? There are many things which are "natural kinds" [9] which are virtually impossible to define completely, at least outside a highly technical context - e.g. people, kinds of animals, universities, languages, etc. These are usually best left primitive and merely described. Definition of natural kinds usually turn out to be long and incomplete. Therefore a useful heuristic is that if the definition is getting long or controversial, consider leaving the class as primitive.

4 Domain and Range Constraints and Other Axioms

4.1 Subclass (Implication) Axioms

OWL allows general expressions to be used in axioms. Like domain and range constraints, axioms are global and do not necessarily appear near the classes affected. On the one hand, the notion that "B is a subclass of A" means "B implies A" emphasizes the meaning of subsumption. On the other, it seems an odd way to express implication, if that is really what is intended. Hence care is required with the paraphrase and improved user interfaces for axioms for Protégé -OWL-CO-ODE are under development.

4.2 Domain and Range Constraints are Axioms

Where most users encounter axioms is in domain and range constrains. In most languages domain and range constraints on properties are simply checked and generate errors if violated. In OWL they are axioms and are used in reasoning, with potentially far-reaching and unexpected effects. They may cause a class to be unsatisfiable or they may cause a class to be "coerced" to be subsumed by another class unexpectedly. For example, if we set the domain of hasTopping to be Pizza, it is the same as entering the axiom in Figure 8.

If we then add a Choc-icecream as shown in Figure 9 there are two possibilities. If Pizza and Icecream are not disjoint[10], then Choc-icecream will be classified as a kind of Pizza. If, on the other hand, Icecream is disjoint from Pizza, then Choc-icecream will be unsatisfiable. In either case, the reason for the classifier's action is nowhere to be seen in the definition of Choc-icecream, Icecream or Pizza. It must be searched for in the domain restriction on hasTopping. In a large and complex ontology this can be difficult.

---

[10] assusming Choc-icecream is subsumed by Icecream

Domain constraint
hasTopping domain Pizza
Equivalent axiom
SubClassOf(restriction (hasTopping someValuesFrom owl:Thing) Pizza)
Paraphrase:
Having a topping *imples* being Pizza.

Fig. 8. An axiom stating the domain of hasTopping is Pizza

OWL:
Class (Choc-icecream partial
    restriction(hasTopping someValuesFrom Chocolate))
Paraphrase:
All Choc-icecream have *some* Chocolate topping.

Fig. 9. Description of Choc-icecream

After problems with open world reasoning, difficulties with domain and range constraints are the largest single source of errors and difficulty in our experience with new users of OWL. Furthermore, checking domain and range constraints is more complicated than in other languages, because a class may not satisfy a constraint prior to classification may be inferred by the classifier to do so. Usually, but not always, such behaviour is unintended and indicates an error. Current developments on the Protégé -OWL-CO-ODE tools include options to warn of easily recognised situations in which classification is likely to be affected by domain or range constraints.

5   Common Logical Issues

Most people learning to use OWL have little or no background in formal logic. In so far as possible, we limit what needs to be known. However, there are a series of issues which users find difficult and cause them to make errors:

1. "Only" (allValuesFrom) does not imply "some" (someValuesFrom).
2. Difference between the linguistic and logical usage of "and" and "or" often cause confusion.
3. Class definitions involving only allValuesFrom can be trivially satisfiable; this is usually the result of error but is easy to miss.
4. It is easy to confuse the representation of "some not" and "not some".

Each issue will be discussed in turn, although confusion over one is often compounded by confusion over another, particularly with respect to issues 1) and 2).

5.1 "Only" Does not Imply "Some": Universal (allValuesFrom) Restrictions can be Satisfied Trivially

The definition for an "EmptyPizza" (Figure 10) satisfies the definition for a Vegetarian pizza - it does not have any Meat or Fish toppings.

OWL:
Class (EmptyPizza partial
  Pizza
    complementOf (restriction (hasToppings someValuesFrom owl:Thing)))
Paraphrase:
An empty pizza is *any* pizza which, *amongst other things*, does *not* have anything as topping.

Fig. 10. Definitions of an EmptyPizza

There is nothing inconsistent about a restriction that includes allValuesFrom owl:Nothing. It just means that, for the property in question, no values are allowed. Therefore, universal (allValuesFrom) restrictions can be "trivially satisfied" – *i.e.* satisfied by the trivial case in which there is no value at all for the property in question. The only way a universal (allValuesFrom) restriction can be made inconsistent is by there being some, *i.e.* at least one, value which contradicts it.

Note that by contrast, a restriction equivalent to someValuesFrom owl:Nothing is always inconsistent since the definition of owl:Nothing is that no value can be from owl:Nothing.

5.2 Linguistic vs Logical Use 'and' and 'or'

In common linguistic usage, "and" and "or" do not correspond consistently to logical conjunction and disjunction respectively. This is a common problem familiar to everyone who uses query languages, the more advanced features of search engines or to anyone who programs. "Find all of the Pizzas containing Fish and Meat " is ambiguous as to whether the request is for pizzas containing both Fish and Meat or either Fish or Meat. In other contexts we disambiguate the expression to use disjunction for "and". In response to instruction to "Find all the meat pizzas and fish pizzas and mark them as spoilt", most people would look for all pizzas which contained either meat or fish. Common though this problem is, it often causes confusion in those learning OWL. Definitions such as the first one in Figure 11 are not uncommon.

5.3 Trivially Satisfiable Class Definitions Are Easy to Miss

Since owl:Nothing is equivalent to any contradiction, confusion over "and" and "or" can lead to definitions which are consistent but only trivially satisfiable. Since they are not flagged as unsatisfiable, such errors often go undetected for some time. Consider the definitions in Figure 11 which are not uncommon in new users' exercises. After running the classifier, newusers are surprised to find ProteinLoversPizza classified under VegetarianPizza as well as under MeatyPizza.

The rules for paraphrasing are designed to minimize these errors. If "A and B" is paraphrased to "both A and also B"[11] and "A or B" is paraphrased to "A and/or B", the confusion is reduced.

The frequency with which we have encountered these errors in practical workshops and modules has motivated debugging options which:

- Check at classification time for universal restrictions with unsatisfiable fillers
- Indicate all unsatisfiable fillers in red in the restriction definition pane even if the restriction, taken as a whole, is satisfiable[12].

OWL:
Class (ProteinLoversPizza complete
  Pizza
    restriction(hasTopping allValuesFrom (Meat and Fish)))
Paraphrase:
A ProteinLoversPizza is *any* Pizza that, *amongst other things*, has *only* topping that are *both* meat *and* also fish.

OWL:
Class (MeatyPizza complete
  Pizza
    restriction(hasTopping allValuesFrom Meat))
Paraphrase:
A MeatyPizza is *any* pizza which, *amongst other things*, has *only* toppings that are Meat.

Fig. 11. Incorrect definition of ProteinLoversPizza which is trivially satisfiable and hence classifies under both MeatyPizza and VegetarianPizza

5.4 Confusion of "some not" and "not some"

It is not uncommon for students to form definitions such as those in Figure 12. Many pizzas classify under VegetarianPizza_wrong since most contain some topping which is not Fish and also contain something which is not Meat. The paraphrase makes the error in the placement of the negation clear. One of the requirements for tools remains to making negation of restrictions as easy as negation of their fillers.

5.5 The Benefits of Clear Definition - "What Does it Mean: To be a Pizza?"

Up to this point we have put no restriction on what counts as a Pizza. Do all pizzas have to have a base? toppings? Is a pizza base without a topping a Pizza? Is anything with a PizzaBase and PizzaToppings a Pizza? Can we completely define a Pizza?

---

[11] We have even had suggestions for the stronger "simultaneously A and also B"

[12] The second is still in development at time of writing.

OWL:
Class(VegetarianPizzaV4_wrong complete
   Pizza
      restriction(hasTopping someValuesFrom not **Meat**)
      restriction(hasTopping someValuesFrom not **Fish**)
Paraphrase:
A vegetarian pizza is *any* pizza which, *amongst other things*, both has *some*
topping which is *not* meat and also has *some* topping which is *not* fish.

Fig. 12. Incorrect definition of vegetarian pizza confusing "some not ..." with "not some ..."

There is no one right answer to these questions; they depend on our conceptualization of Pizzas. However, most users are reluctant to regard a bare base, or a pizza without a base,as a pizza. So the most common outcome is that shown in Figure 13.

Note that if this definition is used, then the ProteinLoversPizza in Figure 11 is unsatisfiable, because the restriction that all pizzas must have a topping contradicts *restriction*(hasTopping *allValuesFrom* (**Meat** *and* **Fish**). Entering definitions and early helps catch errors due to restrictions that would otherwise be trivially satisfiable.

OWL:
Class (**Pizza** partial
   restriction(hasBase someValuesFrom **PizzaBase**)
   restriction(hasTopping someValuesFrom **PizzaTopping**))
Paraphrase:
All pizzas, *amongst other things*, both have *some* base that is a Pizza base and
also have *some* topping that is a Pizza topping.

Fig. 13. Description (partial definition) of a pizza

6   Patterns: Values, Value Types, and "Untangling"

6.1   Values and Value Types

The examples to this point have dealt with what various authors call "first class entities", "independent entities", or "sortals" [4, 16], and what we prefer to call "Self-Standing entities" [10] and the relations between them. These correspond roughly to nouns and verbs in ordinary language. However there are many modifiers or "refiners" - roughly adjectives and adverbs in ordinary language - to account for. In object oriented design these are often represented as "attributes" that are entirely internal to objects (as indicated by their appearing inside the box in UML diagrams). It comes as a surprise to many newcomers to OWL that there is no corresponding distinction between "relation" and "attribute" in the formalism itself. The distinction is left to ontological patterns.

The requirements pattern for values and value types are that: [13]

1. There should be a functional property for each value type.
2. The values for each value type should be disjoint - it should not be possible for something to be Bland and also Hot.
3. The possible values for the value type are exhaustive - so that if we choose to say that the values for Spiciness are Bland, Mild, Medium, and Hot, then those are the only values.

Meeting these requirements requires a sequence of six operations:

1. Create a functional property, e.g. hasSpiciness
2. Create a subclass of value type, e.g. SpicinessValueType
3. Create the individual values as subclass of the value type, e.g. Bland, Mild, Medium, Hot
4. Make the values disjoint using a disjoint axiom
5. Make the values exhaustive by creating a subclass "covering" axiom, e.g. SpicinessVT subclass-of Bland or Mild or Medium or Hot
6. Set the range of the hasSpiciness property to the spiciness value type SpicinessValueType

Students have little trouble understanding these operations in principle, but the number of steps leaves many opportunities for mistakes in practice. One of the first requirements for the Protégé -OWL-CO-ODE interface was that it take users through the steps semi-automatically via a "wizard".

6.2 "Untangling"

The Ontology in Figure 1 is not, in fact, usually the first that students produce. Rather, most students initially produce something more like that shown in Figure 14.

We advocate a policy in which primitives form a skeleton of pure trees, *i.e.* have exactly one primitive parent. When multiple hierarchies appear in first drafts of the primitive hierarchy, as with SpicyTopping above, they must be *untangled – i.e.* an explicit characteristic found to differentiate the child concepts from all but one of the primitive parents. There are many advantages to this policy, which corresponds closely to traditional Aristotelian

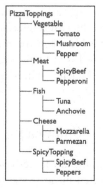

Fig. 14. Tangled First Draft Pizza hierarchy

notions of "differentia", but the overwhelming practical engineering advantage is that it makes it possible to make ontology more modular [10] because the hierarchy of primitives can be split into disjoint branches at any point.

---

[13] Some may question that we represent values as classes rather than individuals. On philosophical grounds, there is an argument to be made for either choice. However, existing reasoners for OWL cannot deal with the all required reasoning using individuals. Therefore, representing values as classes the only practical alternative. (We would also advocate the use of classes on philosophical grounds, but that is an argument for another paper.)

"Untangling" can involve either ordinary relations or value types, but is most simply illustrated with value types. Consider the above SpicenessVT along with an analogously defined FatcontentVT, with values LowFat, MediumFat, HighFat.

It is then only necessary to assign the correct values to the various ingredients and to replace any primitives such as SpicyTopping with a corresponding defined class Spicy-Topping. A visualisation of the pre-classification hierarchy, which is a strict tree, and the post classification polyhierarchy including LowFatTopping are shown in Figure 15.

Again, the mechanics can be tedious, so an extension of the value type wizard is being developed to guide users through the process and to warn of possible errors. In ontologies of any size, it is rare that the classifier does not infer new subsumptions missed by students when they created the hierarchy manually.

6.3   Converting Primitive Classes to Defined Classes

There is an unexpected complication to the above scenario. In the course of untangling, primitive classes are reformulated as defined classes. However, there may be restrictions in the description[14] of the primitive class that do not form part of its new definition but remain merely necessary implications. For example, the ontology might have contained a restriction that hot ingredients were unsuitable for children as shown in Figure 16. Clearly this restriction is not part of the necessary and sufficient conditions defining SpicyTopping, rather it is a further necessary condition to be inferred whenever something is found to be a SpicyTopping.

Such residual necessary implications must be converted to subclass axioms, as shown in Figure 16, which requires significant syntactic change. These changes are reflected in the OilEd interface, where subclass axioms are entered on a separate "tab" and not visible when the main class definition tab is selected. A major goal of the Protégé - OWL-CO-ODE interface has been to make this transition easy by placing necessary and sufficient conditions and necessary conditions in adjacent subpanes and allowing drag and drop/cut and paste operations between them (See Figure 18).

7   Summary

Using any logic-based ontology language presents new users with significant problems, often made worse by details of the language and user interface. The open world assumption and the representation of domain and range constraints as logical axioms run counter to most new users' experience.

In this paper we have described errors commonly made in a series of workshops, tutorials, and teaching modules. A prime goal is to help users understand the precise meaning of OWL-DL through questions and paraphrases. It is a difficult task in natural language generation to specify the paraphrases completely, but the basic forms are summarized in Table 1 with their rationale, and the examples throughout the paper should make their usage clear. A brief summary of guidelines for avoiding the most common pitfalls in building ontologies in OWL-DL are given in Figure 17.

---

[14] For this reason we dislike the use of the phrase "partial definition" and prefer the term "description".

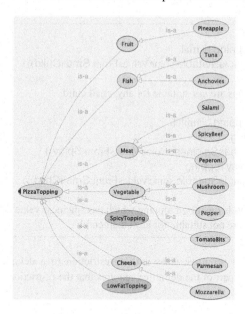

(a) Initial hierarchy

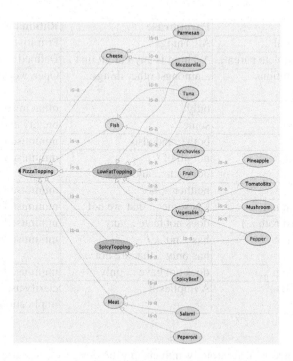

(b) Classified hierarchy

Fig. 15. Pizza hierarchy

> **OWL:**
> Class (SpicyTopping partial
>   not (restriction(isSuitable someValuesFrom SmallChild)))
> **Paraphrase:**
> All SpicyToppings are *not* suitable for any small child.
> **OWL:**
> Class (SpicyTopping complete
>   PizzaTopping
>   restriction(hasSpiciness someValuesFrom Spicy))
> SubclassOf (SpicyTopping
>   not (restriction(isSuitable someValuesFrom SmallChild)))
> **Paraphrase:**
> A SpicyTopping is *any* pizza topping which has spiciness value Spicy; all
> Spicy toppings are not suitable for any small child.

Fig. 16. Conversion of a primitive class with a restriction to a defined class in which the restriction does not form part of the definition requires that the restriction be reformulated as an axiom

Table 1. Summary of paraphrases. Examples in Figures throughout paper

OWL definition	Paraphrase	Rationale
Class(Thing partial ...	All Things ...	Primitive vs Defined
Class(Thing complete parent...	A Thing is any Parent that ...	Defined vs Primitive
(add to all descriptions and definitions)	...amongst other things...	Open world hypothesis
allValuesFrom	only	often misunderstood
someValuesFrom	some	brevity and clarity
and	both... and also	minimise logic errors
not(... and ...)	not all of / not both ... and also	minimise logic errors
not (... or ...)	neither ... nor ...	minimise logic errors
someValuesFrom not	has some ... that are not ...	minimise logic errors
not (someValuesFrom ...)	does not have ... any	minimise logic errors
AllValuesFrom not	has ...no ... / has only ...that are not ...	minimise logic errors
not (allValuesFrom ...)	does not have ... only	minimise logic errors
SubclassOf(A , B)	A implies B	clarify use of subclass for implication

This experience is also strongly influencing the design of new user interfaces. A screen shot of the basic Protege-OWL class screen is shown in Figure 18. Preliminary experience is encouraging, but to what extent these new features reduce new users' confusion remains to be proven in practice.

1. Always paraphrase a description or definition before encoding it in OWL, and record the paraphrase in the comment area of the interface.
2. Make all primitives disjoint - which requires that primitives form trees
3. Use *someValuesFrom* as the default qualifier in restrictions
4. Be careful to make defined classes defined – the default is primitive. The classifier will place nothing under a primitive class (except in the presence of axioms /domain/range constraints)
5. Remember the open world assumption. Insert closure restrictions if that is what you mean.
6. Be careful with domain and range constraints. Check them carefully if classification does not work as expected.
7. Be careful about the use of "and" and "or"(*intersectionOf, unionOf*)
8. To spot trivially satisfiable restrictions early, always have an existential (*someValuesFrom*) restriction corresponding to every universal (*allValues-For*) restriction, either in the class or one of its*superclasses* (unless you specifically intend the class to be trivially satisfiable).
9. Run the classifier frequently; spot errors early

Fig. 17. Brief summary of guidelines

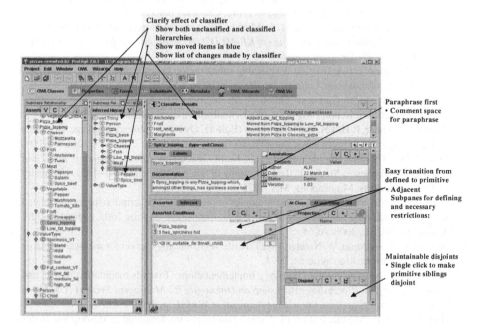

Fig. 18. Main pane of new Protégé-OWL-CO-ODE Interface indicating how requirements identified are met

Acknowledgements

This work was supported in part by the CO-ODE project funded by the UK Joint Information Services Committee and the HyOntUse Project (GR/S44686) funded by the UK Engineering and Physical Science Research Council and by 21XS067A from the National Cancer Institute. Special thanks to all at Stanford Medical Informatics for their continued collaboration and comments and to the other members of the ontologies and metadata group at Manchester for their contributions and critiques.

References

1. S. Bechhofer, I. Horrocks, C. Goble, and R. Stevens. Oiled: a reason-able ontology editor for the semantic web. In *Proceedings of KI2001, Joint German/Austrian conference on Artificial Intelligence*, Lecture Notes in Computer Science, pages 396–408. Springer-Verlag.
2. R.J. Brachman, D.L. McGuinness, P.F. Patel-Schneider, L.A. Resnick, and A. Borgida. Living with classic: When and how to use a kl-one-like language. In John Sowa, editor, *Principles of Semantic Networks: Explorations in the representation of knowledge*, pages 401–456. Morgan Kaufmann, San Mateo, CA, 1991. Good overview. Particularly good straw man section on the arbitrariness of class-instance division.
3. N. Guarino. Understanding, building and using ontologies. *International Journal of Human Computer Studies*, 46:293–310, 1997.
4. N. Guarino and C. Welty. Towards a methodology for ontology-based model engineering. In *ECOOP-2000 Workshop on Model Engineering*, Cannes, France, 2000.
5. H. Knublauch and O. Dameron a M. A. Musen. Weaving the biomedical semanticweb with the protégé owl plugin. In *Proceedings of KR-MED2004: International Workshop on Formal Biomedical Knowledge Representation*.
6. D.L. McGuinness and A. Borgida. Explaining subsumption in description logics. In *International Joint Conference on Artificial Intelligence (IJCAI-95)*, pages 816–821, 1995.
7. N. F. Noy and D.L. McGuinness. Ontology development 101: A guide to creating your first ontology. Technical Report SMI-2001-0880, Stanford Medical Informatics, 2001.
8. P. Patel-Schneider, P. Hayes, and I. Horrocks (Editor). Owl web ontology language semantics and abstract syntax. http://www.w3.org/TR/2004/REC-owl-semantics-20040210/, Feb, 2004.
9. H. Putnam. The meaning of 'meaning. In Keith Gunderson, editor, *Language, Mind and Knowledge*, Minnesota Studies in the Philosophy of Science VII, pages 131–193z. University of Minnesota Press, Minneapolis, MN, 1975.
10. A. Rector. Modularisation of domain ontologies implemented in description logics and related formalisms including owl. In John Genari, editor, *Knowledge Capture 2003*, pages 121–128, Sanibel Island, FL, 2003. ACM.
11. A. Rector, W. Solomon, W. Nowlan, and T. Rush. A terminology server for medical language and medical information systems, 1994.
12. A. L. Rector. Normalisation of ontology implementations: Towards modularity, re-use, and maintainability. In *Proceedings Workshop on Ontologies for Multiagent Systems (OMAS) in conjunction with European Knowledge Acquisition Workshop*, 2002.
13. Alan L. Rector. Modularisation of domain ontologies implemented in description logics and related formalisms including owl. In *Proceedings of the international conference on Knowledge capture*, pages 121–128. ACM Press, 2003.

14. S. Staab and A. Maedche. Ontology engineering beyond the modeling of concepts and relations. In R.V. Benjamins, A. Gomez-Perez, N. Guarino, and M. Uschold, editors, *ECAI 2000. 14th European Conference on Artificial Intelligence; Workshop on Applications of Ontologies and Problem-Solving Methods*, 2000.
15. M. Uschold and M. Gruninger. Ontologies: principles, methods and applications. *Knowledge Engineering Review*, 11(2), 1996.
16. C. Welty and N. Guarino. Supporting ontological analysis of taxonomic relationships. *Data and Knowledge Engineering*, 39(1):51–74, 2001.

Using a Novel ORM-Based Ontology Modelling Method to Build an Experimental Innovation Router

Peter Spyns, Sven Van Acker, Marleen Wynants, Mustafa Jarrar,
and Andriy Lisovoy

Vrije Universiteit Brussel – STAR Lab,
Pleinlaan 2, Gebouw G-10, B-1050 Brussel, Belgium
{firstname.lastname}@vub.ac.be
http://www.starlab.vub.ac.be

Abstract. Specific tools help to increase the effectiveness of a shortened innovation cycle. The paper presents a web based tool for the creation of a scenario
of what an innovation environment looks like, by enabling enriched queries and
by allowing the identification of specific innovation gurus and key role institutions. The tool relies on an ontology-based knowledge representation that has
been built using a recently adapted conceptual modelling methodology.

1 Introduction

Since the studies of Schumpeter[1] (e.g., [27]), (technological) innovation has been recognised as a crucial part of a company's assets. As a consequence, companies try to
set up processes to manage and stimulate innovation activities: internal R&D teams
define, select, develop, test and exploit innovative ideas that should lead to a next
generation of services and products. In essence, innovation has to do with knowledge
about technology, and business and production processes. Innovation is the result of a
mutual influence, difficult to capture and model, between science, industry and the
market. The government is another important actor who tries to stimulate innovation
via its policies (e.g. regarding science, (higher) education, SME programs etc.).

In the economic rat-race, the "time to market" and life span of a product have drastically been reduced, implying that the span of an innovation cycle in its turn has to be
shortened, while facing tighter budget constraints. Cumulative cash flow diagrams
(see e.g., [34]) get "squeezed". Specific tools to manage the innovation cycle help to
increase the effectiveness of a shortened innovation cycle. It would be essential to
align the functionality of these supporting tools technologies with the needs of knowledge users in a variety of industries including business and professional services, engineering, information technology, manufacturing, health care, publishing, etc [2].

---

[1] Actually, Karl Marx was the first classical economist who extensively studied innovation
(Capital, Vol. 1, 1867, especially Chapter 13) [remark from an anonymous reviewer].

[2] The project maintains a web site at http://www.innovanet.eu.com where systematic innovation
related information and resources may be found. The members of the consortium are: Inmark
Estudios y Estrategias S.A. (Spain), BioVista (Greece), FhG – IPSI (Germany), VUB STAR
Lab (Belgium), PIRA International UK (UK), ITC-IRST (Italy) and Bit Media e-Learning
Solution (Austria).

E. Motta et al. (Eds.): EKAW 2004, LNAI 3257, pp. 82–98, 2004.

2 Objectives

The main goal of the "Innovanet" project (EU 5FP IST 2001-38422 [3]) was to prepare a <u>strategic roadmap</u> on the possible 'systematisation' of the process of innovation and scientific discovery. It aims at a better understanding of where and how creativity and innovation come into play and of the kinds of software environments and IT technologies that could promote their emergence in research and industrial environments. One of the tasks of the *VUB STAR Lab* team consisted of building an ontology-based knowledge representation to organise data related to innovation processes in a manageable fashion. In addition, a web-based tool (called Innovation Router [4]) should enable the creation of a scenario of what an innovation environment looks like, by enabling enriched queries. The Innovation Router has to allow the identification of specific innovation gurus and key-role institutions. An adaptation of an existing conceptual modelling methodology (developed for the Flemish IWT GBOU 2001 #010069 "OntoBasis" project [5]) [30] has been used to create the innovation ontology.

This paper is organised as follows: after an overview of the material (section 3) and a summary of the modelling methodology (section 4.1) used to create the innovation ontology (section 4.2), the results (section 5) are discussed. In particular, two use cases for the Innovation Router are presented, one on searching for competent staff (section 5.2.1) and one on looking for patents (section 5.2.2). Related work is compared in section 6. Plans for future work (section 7) are given before a conclusion (section 8) ends the paper.

3 Material

The Innovation Router structures the relevant material of FP4 and FP5 from the Cordis[6] database, European patent applications and scientific literature. The data provided within the framework of the Innovanet project was limited geographically, at the level of disciplines and technologies with regard to defined activities and their actors. The results of a bibliometric analysis performed on the raw data [7] were stored in separate databases according to the data's provenance. These databases were, depending on the respective sources, of different data quality, contained redundant information, and had incomplete descriptions of database attributes. All these databases have been grouped in a single MS Access database that contains:

- 403 scientific papers
- 2.212 European patent applications

---

[3] The Innovanet project was a roadmap project that lasted from 01/11/2002 until 31/11/2003.

[4] A name « Router » symbolises that innovation information is intelligently guided or « routed » to a (human) user. On purpose we avoided to call it a portal as a portal involves many more things – e.g. see [28].

[5] See http://wise.vub.ac.be/ontobasis for more information.

[6] http://www.cordis.lu

[7] The analysis has been done by partner Clemens Wildhalm (Bit Media e-Learning Solution).

- 849 FP4 projects
- 3130 FP5 projects
- 867 Keywords (only for articles) [8]
- 6374 Phrases (articles, patents, proposals) [9]
- 24 Research Areas (only for proposals)

4 Methods

Due the amount, variety and complexity of innovation processes and their related data, precise and unambiguous semantics of the data were lacking. In order to enhance the potentialities of unambiguous data exchange and future exploitation activities, "an innovation ontology" was created. In current computer science parlance, an ontology [9], [1], [11] is understood as a vocabulary with semantically precise and formally defined terms that stand for concepts and their relationships of an application domain. VUB STAR Lab has adapted an ontology modelling methodology based on an existing conceptual schema modelling methodology [21] called Object Role Modelling (ORM [12]) – see section 4.1. The innovation application ontology has been created according to this methodology and served as a reference for the data model of the Innovation Router and as the underlying conceptual model of the web-based interface – see section 4.2.

4.1 Defining an Ontology Modelling Methodology

The ORM conceptual modelling methodology has been selected because of its strong foundation in natural language, which it inherited from its predecessor method called "a Natural Information Analysis Method" (NIAM) [35]. The latter was developed in the 1980s as a methodology to model databases. It introduced the distinction between a lexical (label) and non-lexical (thing) modelling objects, and supported subclassing and an extensive set of declarable integrity constraint types. While not an actual natural language-based approach with tools, NIAM did support the negotiation and agreement process to arrive at information requirement specifications. These took the form of conceptual semantic networks, or verbalisations of them, that were readable by non-computer experts and yet could be readily transformed into database designs [10]. Initially, ORM as such has been used before by the authors when creating ontologies (e.g., [16]), but the need occurred to have the methodology evolve into a "genuine" ontology modelling method. In this section, we summarise the results (section 4.1.1) and discuss some major differences with the original NIAM/ORM methods (sections 4.1.2 & 4.1.3).

---

[8] Unfortunately the data is rather of low quality.
[9] A phrase is a group of one to five words. Also here, the quality is rather low.
[10] We refer the interested reader to [12] and [35] for more details.

4.1.1 Modelling Steps

The seven basic steps of Halpin [12] were maintained but should be applied in a partially redefined way. An additional step (step 3: grounding the vocabulary) has been added. During this step, terms belonging to an application domain are explicitly attributed a meaning (be it still intuitively by a gloss and in principle irrespective of specific application requirements at hand) by creating a new concept with a corresponding unique definition for it or by associating the term to an existing concept and its definition. This is needed to reach an agreement on meaning prior to its sharing. This step is typical of and essential for ontologies.

The division of the steps into two parts corresponds to the double articulation of a DOGMA ontology, i.e. a clear separation between the lexon base and the commitment layer [29] [11]. The commitment layer "houses" the attribution of formal characteristics of use (constraints – e.g. cardinality) to a selection of concepts linked with terms (lexons from the ontology base) belonging to an external application (i.e. ontologically committing these terms).

1. Part I: conceptualise the domain
   1. verbalise information examples as elementary facts
   2. create the lexons (for a context and a language)
   3. ground the terms and roles constituting the lexons
2. Part II: add the constraints
   1. uniqueness
   2. mandatoriness
   3. subset, equality, exclusion and subtyping
   4. occurrence frequency and ring constraints
   5. final consistency checks

4.1.2 Modelling Constituents

According to Halpin, a conceptual schema of a database consists of three main constituents [12:p.31]:

- *basic fact types*: the kinds of primitive sentences or facts
- *constraints*: the restrictions that apply to the fact types
- *derivation rules*: rules, functions or operators (including mathematical calculation or logical inference) to derive new facts from other facts.

Basic facts are asserted concerning an application domain. A (binary) fact states that a specific object is related in a particular way (plays a specific role) with another object. Objects can be entities or values. A unary fact asserts that an object plays one role. The concrete factual information is represented in an "information template". It consists of a combination of entity types (in NIAM: non lexical object type or NoLOT), values types (in NIAM: lexical object type or LOT) and predicates. A predicate combining an entity type with a value type is called the reference mode (in

---

[11] Due to space restrictions, we cannot elaborate on DOGMA (Developing Ontology Guided Mediation for Agents). We refer the interested reader to the publication section of our website: http://www.starlab.vub.ac.be .

NIAM: bridge type). A predicate combining two (or more) entity types is called a fact type (in NIAM: idea type).

Translated in terms of the DOGMA initiative, it means that the *basic fact types* belong to the ontology base and the *constraints* belong to the commitment layer. The *derivation rules* are actually not considered as part of the actual ontology, in opposition to what other ontology researchers often claim. The derivation rules are situated in the application domain realm. Basically, inference rules use (e.g., as the signature of a first order language) the vocabulary as it has been defined and constrained in the ontology. Further research needs to be done on how to model these derivation rules.

4.1.3 Referencing

Referencing in an ORM conceptual data model happens by means of a *bridge type* (using the NIAM terminology) between a LOT (in ORM: entity type) and a NoLOT (in ORM: value type). E.g., a person is identified by his first name. The actual values (or strings) for the first names are stored in the database (e.g., table 'Person' with a column label 'firstname') [object level]. As ontologies, in principle, are not concerned with instances (=data) but with meta-data (concept labels), referencing can only be done when an application has adopted a commitment (via lexical mapping rules).

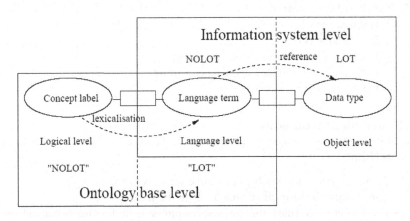

Fig. 1. three layer reference scheme (reproduced from [3])

Databases that use different terms for the same notion can share data if the meaning of the local database vocabulary (table and column labels) is mapped to the meaning of the corresponding term in the ontology vocabulary (the latter being precisely defined). A reference scheme (linking a notion to a data type – see Fig. 1) will now have three levels: a LOT that refers to a NoLOT (both belong to the conceptual data model of the information system) which in turn is linked to a centrally defined concept label – the latter two belonging to the ontology base level. At the time of modelling an ontology, the instance population is not always available. Reference schemas are thus no primary concern for an ontology modeller (but rather for an application developer). It implies that only NoLOTs can be used in an ontology (see Fig. 1).

LOTs only appear in an additional application layer, especially when vocabulary of legacy systems are associated with existing domain concepts [3].

In case a database model has been designed on basis of an ontology, it would be natural to see that the ontology terms are used inside of the conceptual data model (cf. global as view). It means that two levels of the reference scheme (concept label and DB NoLOT) are collapsed and that the terms play a double role (the middle part of Fig. 1 disappears). The inverse scenario is to create an application ontology [11:p.1], by extracting an ontology from a conceptual data model and defining the semantics of its terms that are promoted to concept labels (cf. local as view – e.g., [19] & [32]). An application ontology can subsequently be merged with more general domain ontologies and/or other application ontologies.

Even in the ontology literature, authors do not always make a clear distinction between a global concept and a local conceptual database model term (the latter in many cases expressed in the local natural language). In particular, application ontologies are a dubious case: terms of the conceptual scheme of a database are often treated as concept labels but without an accompanying specification of their meaning (gloss or dictionary style definition), a shared and agreed meaning cannot be reached. A term on it own is not sufficient. And as for ease of reading and simplicity, many knowledge engineers label concepts by means of a (representative) natural language term the result being that the (global) conceptual and (local) language or application levels become quickly mixed up, which can be harmful when aligning and merging ontologies.

4.2 Creating an Application Ontology for Innovation

A data model is "tuned" towards a specific application, and therefore has less or no needs for explicit semantics (since sharing is not required). A conceptual data model is a "parsimonious" model, i.e., only distinctions relevant for that particular application are considered. An ontology is a "fat model" as it is to be shared across many applications, therefore needing a larger coverage and higher granularity. An application ontology, since it is directly derived from a conceptual model, is rather to be considered as a parsimonious model.

With an eye on timely realising the Innovation Router, we choose to create a slightly extended application ontology. Relevant properties and relationships of the entities were extracted from the input databases. Additional concepts and relationships were added to extend the original ontology mainly to enhance its genericity and re-usability.

In the next section, we will illustrate the first part of the new methodology or the conceptualisation of the domain. Adding the constraints is quite straightforward for knowledge engineers familiar with ORM/NIAM. The reason for not discussing the second part is due to space limitations. In addition, there is point in explaining this for an application ontology, as the semantic restrictions simply correspond with the restrictions on the conceptual schema. Upgrading a conceptual schema to an application ontology consists in providing the semantics for the labels used in the schema. And in this particular case, the schema was simple and the restrictions were rather basic.

- [step 1] On basis of the relational schema of the various databases, the entities, relationships and their properties have been verbalised: *people are involved in projects, a person covers a scientific topic, a person works for an organisation, ...* [12] . These sentences can no longer be split into smaller units of information (i.e. elementary facts). They can be derived from tables like (expressed as relations) *Employs(Project, Person)* and *Expertise(Person, Skills, Institute)* respectively.

- [step 2] The elementary facts expressed in a restricted form of natural language are transformed into formally defined lexons that can be read from both sides:

$$<(\gamma, \lambda): \text{head-term, role, co-role, tail-term}> \tag{1}$$

The λ is a label that indicates the language, and the context identifier, γ, groups lexons that are intuitively "related" in an intended conceptualisation of a domain. See [3] for details on the most recent formalisation of a lexon.
e.g.,:

    <(innovation, English-UK): person, works_on, involves, project>
    <(innovation, English-UK): person, works_for, employs, organisation>
    <(innovation, English-UK): person, has_expertise_in, is_covered_by, topic>

- [step 3] The constituents of the lexons are associated with word sense definitions and concepts (potentially newly created) [13]. It is natural to use existing resources, such as WordNet [21]. Other potential resources are CYC [17], DOLCE [8], EuroWordNet [36], or UMLS [14] for the medical domain. WordNet contains synsets and definitions of what a term means. A disadvantage is that WordNet covers mostly non-technical vocabulary. Therefore, the modeller, with the collaboration of a terminologist or lexicographer, will have to come up with definitions for technical terms. We recommend doing it in the same style as WordNet [14]:

Terms:
- *person*: **person#1**
  individual, someone, somebody, mortal, human, soul -- (a human being; "there was too much for one person to do") [sense 1 of 3]]
- *organisation*: **organisation#1**
  (a group of people who work together) [sense 1 of 3]
- *topic*: **topic#2**
  topic, subject, issue, matter -- (some situation or event that is thought about; "he kept drifting off the topic"; "he had been thinking about the subject for several years"; "it is a matter for the police") [sense 2 of 2]

---

[12] Due to confidentiality agreements amongst the consortium partners, the entire ontology is currently still confidential. Only short excerpts will be provided for illustrative purposes.

[13] See Nirenburg [24] for a discussion on language neutrality vs. language independence of word senses.

[14] http://www.cogsci.princeton.edu/cgi-bin/webwn

- *project*: **project#2**
  project, projection -- (a planned undertaking) [sense 2 of 2]
- *expertise*: **expertise#1**
  expertness, expertise -- (skillfulness by virtue of possessing special knowledge) [sense 1 of 1]

Roles:

- *works_for*: **work#2(v)**
  work, do work -- (be employed; "Is your husband working again?"; "My wife
  never worked"; "Do you want to work after the age of 60?"; "She never did
  any work because she inherited a lot of money"; "She works as a waitress to
  put herself through college") [sense 2 of 27 as a verb]
- *employs*: **employ#2(v)**
  hire, engage, employ -- (engage or hire for work; "They hired two new secre-
  taries in the department"; "How many people has she employed?") [sense 2 of
  2 as a verb]
- *covers*: **cover#5(v)**
  cover, treat, handle, plow, deal, address -- (deal with verbally or in some form
  of artistic expression; "This book deals with incest"; "The course covered all
  of Western Civilization"; "The new book treats the history of China") [sense 5
  of 26 as a verb]
- *works_on*: **work_on#1**
  work at, work on -- (to exert effort in order to do, make, or perform something; "the child worked at the multiplication table until she had it down cold")
  [sense 1 of 2]
- *involves*: **involve#2**
  involve -- (engage as a participant; "Don't involve me in your family affairs!")
  [sense 2 of 7]

A lexon is thus an intermediary step towards a language independent conceptualisation of a domain. Note that no formal axiomatisation is done. In WordNet all entries
are linked to an internal upper ontology of which the semantics are currently under
revision [8]. Reasoning components (in our vision relegated outside the ontology [15])
can make use of these axioms.

Once the ontology was finalised, a new unified database schema has been created
using the English terms associated with the ontology concepts. It was, practically
speaking, not possible to define a mediator for the original subsystems on the one
hand, while it was more practical to have an integrated database (albeit with duplicated data) on the other. As a side effect, the quality of the data has been drastically
improved. A lot of manual and semi-automated cleaning had to be performed to stan-
dardise the entries of specific table-fields, e.g., the column containing the contact
names of CORDIS-FP4 proposals, which had an empty entry, or a name as an entry or
a entry of the form "name: *<name>   Tel: <tel>   Fax: <fax>*, etc... Some cells con-

---

[15] Interesting within this perspective is the remark that only 2 out of 22 industrial ontologies
surveyed « had clear inference requirements for which knowledge-based systems technology
is necessary » [5: p.79].

tained multiple data elements, e.g. inventors, within a single field that were separated by different delimiters.

One of the results from the EU OntoWeb thematic network, for which VUB STAR Lab was co-responsible in implementing an ontology based semantic web portal and graphical user interface (GUI) [25], was a generic data model to store the ontology and its instances. This data model has been used for the Innovation Router. It allows transparent retrieval of Innovation Router data. E.g., relationships of a concept instance can be retrieved in a single pass. It guarantees a minimum of maintenance at the data and database levels if extensions or modifications of the ontology are needed.

5   Results

In this section, a general overview of the Innovation Router (section 5.1) is presented followed by a discussion of two potential use cases: one on scientific headhunting (section 5.2.1) and one on patent (opportunities) detection (section 5.2.2).

5.1 Overview

We decided to separate the classification of *topics* from their related *activities* such as persons involved, registered patents, articles published, and project proposals being made. The topics are the research areas defined in the project proposals, keywords extracted from the scientific publications, and phrases [9] extracted from the project proposals, patent applications and scientific publications [16].

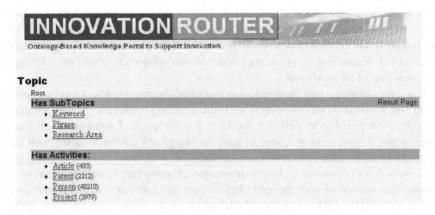

Fig. 2. Innovation Router starting page

---

[16] The extraction activities have been performed by Bit Media e-Learning Solution (Austria).

When one enters the site (see Fig. 2), the focus is on the *Root* topic. At this level, one can see all structuring mechanisms in parallel at the *Topics*-section. The *Activities*-section indicates all activities related to the current topic. Next to every activity, a number indicates the amount of all registered activities. Browsing through the structuring mechanisms is possible by clicking a *SubTopic* of the current topic, until no deeper levels of structuring are encountered. The *Activities*-section changes dynamically according to the selected topic. By clicking on an activity, a browseable result page is generated, containing all elements of the selected activity, similar to a result page generated by a web search engine. Each element is provided with a short description. Clicking on the elements header will display a full description on an individual page. This full detailed page contains besides the description of the element, all relations of this element with elements of the same or other activities. E.g., an article could be written by several authors who are included in the *Person* activity (inter-activity relationship).

5.2 Use Cases

The innovation ontology tells us what kind of things are available in this restricted domain of innovation, how they can be interrelated and what they mean. So first there is the informational need: because the ontology is a structured conceptual model of the innovation vertical domain, it supports parametric search and navigation using product and service knowledge by prospective innovators to discover what to use and to determine their chances and shortcomings. In addition, the ontology maps to the quickly changing data of the competitors. It models not only the product and service knowledge but also knowledge about the end users. By using user personalisation, queries could be customised to the user's experience and status – see e.g. [2]. In the following sections, we present two potential cases of how innovation preparing activities could happen within an enterprise.

5.2.1 Scientific Headhunting

One of the competitions between enterprises is the competition for talents. More and more enterprises are aware that high-level talents should be introduced through professional channels, which target the demand of enterprises and find the talents that they need in a timely manner. Recruitment agencies are adopting competency standards, used to classify the acquired competencies of the jobseekers and the required competencies of vacant jobs. Using the data and knowledge within the Innovation Router, we complement the traditional competency-based database search with a thematic search. The thematic search identifies individuals and provides details of and references to their involvement in the aforementioned projects, patent applications and articles, indicating the individual's professional expertise area(s) – see Fig. 3. Currently, considering the nature of the available data within the Innovation Router, thematic search results will be limited to scientific headhunting purposes only.

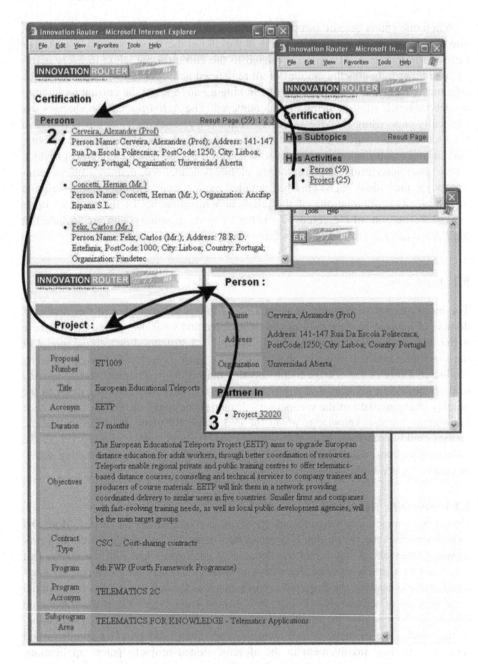

Fig. 3. Performing a thematic search on "certification" returns 59 persons of which one is selected for further reviewing of his contact information as well his professional involvement in various projects, patent applications and articles

5.2.2 Patent Detection

A patent is a right, granted by the government, that excludes others from making, using, or selling the invention covered in the claims of the patent [17]. A patent offers a legal ground for stimulating innovation, where the patentee acquires the right to forbid others to exploit his or her protected invention without permission. Nowadays, patents have become the primary intellectual property asset that companies rely upon to protect their innovations and to maintain competitive advantage by hampering the activities of current and future competitors [22].

Enterprises and individuals require efficient and effective tools and methodologies to identify existing patents and to screen patent opportunities [23]. Within the Innovation Router, we developed a service that contributes to the process of investigating research or business areas in order to identify patent opportunities. Given two themes, besides displaying activities proper to each theme individually, this service calculates the activities overlap between both themes – see Fig. 4. Focusing on the patent-overlap, we are able to present all patent activities which are related to or dependent

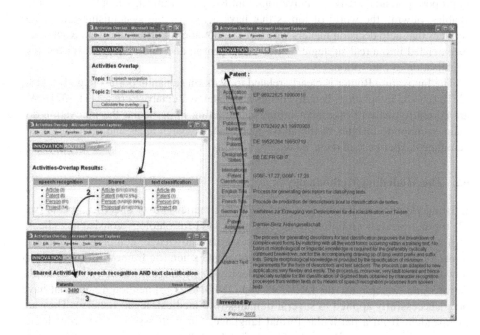

Fig. 4. Given two distinct themes, *"speech recognition"* and *"text classification"*, the service displays the activities of both themes individually and calculates the activities overlap between both themes. If overlapping activities do occur, the service allows individual selection of these activities in order to perform a detailed analysis of each item

---

[17] http://www.european-patent-office.org

on both themes. Two themes producing low patent-overlap are potential candidates of technologies, business/research areas, features... to be combined for investigation of novel patent opportunities.

6 Discussion and Related Work

6.1 The Router

The Innovation Router proved the strategic role it could play as part of an innovation process in linking the materials collected for surveys and state-of-the-art studies, in sharing knowledge and emerging insights after confronting the database with enriched queries. While the data available within the framework of the Innovanet project was limited in quantity, it is representative enough to define a preliminary model of innovation or scientific discovery – e.g., to find out who's who and who is doing what – to describe an innovation engineering environment and validate it, to predict trends and to propose potential areas of innovation to an R&D department. An optimised Router enables viewing the world of topics that have activities and systemising innovation services that help decision makers who direct innovation. Furthermore, the Router can be extended into a real strategic tool or instrument in any future research for the systematisation of innovation.

The Innovation Router is clearly related to work on semantic portals (e.g., [4], [18], [25]), schema integration, heterogeneous and federated databases (e.g., [1], [37]). We are currently unaware of similar initiatives targeting in particular the innovation domain, combining insights of the above mentioned research areas and building on accumulated experience in these fields.

6.2 The Modelling Methodology

Existing research methodologies and industry practices cover specific aspects (see [7] for an overview on ontology development; [11] for ontology consistency checking). Currently there hardly exist, at least to our knowledge, comprehensive cookbooks or methodologies (based on one formal and scientific framework) that covers how to actually create from scratch and deploy a *multilingual* ontology-based application. One example are the ONIONS and ONIONS-II [8] methodologies that have been successfully applied to several domains (bio-medical, legal, fishery). They are independent from a particular formal language, but both assume first-order logic, some classification service, and a foundational ontology as a unifying paradigm. Although they are not yet completely engineered, they contain nearly complete guidelines on how to start from scratch and/or to reuse existing sources. Many existing ontology engineering methods build on the CommonKADS [26] knowledge engineering methodology (e.g., [33]) and/or are based on questionnaires for typical expert knowledge elicitation [13]. Others, e.g., Methontology [6], try to encompass the entire knowledge life cycle, but do not provide detailed but generic guidelines (cook book style) on how to construct a domain ontology, as is the case with the adapted ORM/NIAM method.

7 Future Work

More efforts have to be spent on the GUI and human computer interface (HCI) aspects of the Router: e.g., a better visualisation of the search results, more flexible ways of navigation. Some (rather trivial) tweaking of the data needs to be done as well (e.g. formatting). A first step would be to migrate the data and ontology to the OntoWeb semantic portal to benefit from a more flexible and richer GUI. Additional user tests should be performed in order to specify innovation services based on innovation detection patterns. These could be implemented as (semantic) web services. E.g., it will be interesting to discover overlapping activities or expertise between research areas and implement this specific search as a built-in service available to software agents. On the modelling part, the methodology must be applied to other domains, in other circumstances, for other aims, and with a specific eye on the collaborative aspects.

8 Conclusion

The Innovation Router can be perceived as a fundamental element in any strategic innovative thinking. Its inherent innovative characteristic consists of further developing and exploiting recent work on ontologies, thereby offering a multi-dimensional perspective on the relationships between elements of the innovation processes. The parallel representation of data is a powerful means for decision-makers to identify advantages, follow-up actions, gaps and needs. Within the development of the strategic roadmap for the Innovanet project, this Innovation Router was a model or a proof-of-concept. In future applications, this Router can be a stepping stone for the implementation of semantic innovation-related web services, seen its facility to accept enriched queries.

Acknowledgment

This research has mainly been financed by the Innovanet project (EU FP5 IST 2001-38422). Some parts of this research have been funded by the Flemish IWT GBOU 2001 #010069 "OntoBasis" and the Belgian FWO G.0229.03 "BonaTema" projects. The Technology Transfer Centre Leoben, the Austrian project PROVISO, and Johan Hagman of the EU DG INFSO E2 unit are all gratefully acknowledged for providing access to patent data, FP4 and FP5 project information. We also like to thank our colleagues of the consortium for their fruitful collaboration in this project.

References

1. Bergamaschi S., Castano S., Vincini M. & Beneventano D., (2001), Semantic integration of heterogeneous information sources, Data & Knowlegde Engineering 36 (3): 215 – 249.
2. De Bo J., Jarrar M., Majer B. & Meersman R., (2002), Ontology-based author profiling of documents. In, Catizone, R., (ed.), Workshop Proceedings Event Modeling for Multilingual Document Linking (LREC2002 Workshop), pp. 23 – 38, Paris.
3. De Bo J. & Spyns P., (2003), Creating a "DOGMAtic" multilingual ontology infrastructure to support a semantic portal. In R. Meersman, Z. Tari et al., (eds.), *On the Move to Meaningful Internet Systems 2003: OTM 2003 Workshops*, LNCS 2889, page 253 – 266, Springer.
4. Dhraief H., Nejdl W., Wolf B. & Wolpers W., (2001), Open Learning Repositories and Metadata Modeling, In, Proc. of the 1st International Semantic Web Working Symposium (SWWS01), pp. 495 – 514.
5. Ellman J., (2004), Corporate Ontologies as Information Interfaces, IEEE Intelligent Systems jan-feb 2004: 79.
6. Fernández M., Gómez-Pérez A., & Juristo N., (1996), Methontology: From Ontological Art Towards Ontological Engineering, In Workshop on Ontological Engineering (ECAI 96), pp. 41 – 51.
7. Fernández-López M., Gómez-Pérez A., Euzenat J., Gangemi A., Kalfoglou Y., Pisanelli D., Schorlemmer M., Steve G., Stojanovic L., Stumme G., & Sure Y., (2002), A survey on methodologies for developing, maintaining, integrating, evaluating and reengineering ontologies, OntoWeb deliverable #D1.4, Madrid.
8. Gangemi A., Guarino N., Masolo C., Oltramari A., & Schneider L., (2003), Sweetening Ontologies with DOLCE. Proceedings of EKAW 2002. Siguenza, Spain.
9. Gruber T., (1995), Towards Principles for the Design of Ontologies Used for Knowledge Sharing, International Journal of Human-Computer studies, 43 (5/6): 907 – 928.
10. Guarino N. & Giaretta P., (1995), Ontologies and Knowledge Bases: Towards a Terminological Clarification, In, Mars N. (ed.), Towards Very Large Knowledge Bases: Knowledge Building and Knowledge Sharing, IOS Press, Amsterdam, pp 25 – 32.
11. Guarino N., (1998), Formal Ontologies and Information Systems, In, Guarino N. (ed.), Proceedings of FOIS98, IOS Press, pp. 3 – 15..
12. Halpin T., (2001), Information Modeling and Relational Databases: from conceptual analysis to logical design, Morgan-Kaufmann, San Francisco.
13. Hameed A., Sleeman D. & Preece A., (2002), OntoManager: A workbench Environment to facilitate Ontology Management and Interoperability, In, Sure Y. & Angele J. (eds.), (2002), Proceedings of the OntoWeb-SIG3 Workshop at the 13th International Conference on Knowledge Engineering and Knowledge Management EKAW 2002.
14. Humphreys B. & Lindberg D., (1999), The Unified Medical Language System Project: a distributed experiment, In, Lun K.C. (ed.), Improving access to biomedical information, Proceedings of MEDINFO92, Elsevier Science Publishers, pp. 1496 – 1500.
15. Jarrar M, Demey J., & Meersman R., (2003), On Reusing Conceptual Data Modeling for Ontology Engineering, Journal on Data Semantics, 1 (1): 185 – 207 [LNCS 2800, Springer].
16. Jarrar M., Verlinden R. & Meersman R., (2003), Ontology-based Consumer Complaint Management. In, R. Meersman, Z. Tari et al., (eds.), On the Move to Meaningful Internet Systems 2003: OTM 2003 Workshops, LNCS 2889, Springer Verlag, pp. 594 – 606.

17. Lenat, D, (1995), CYC: A large-scale investment in knowledge infrastructure. Communications of the ACM, 38(11), 33 – 48.
18. Maedche A., Staab S., Studer R., Sure Y. & Volz R., (2002), SEAL - tying up information integration and web site management by ontologies, IEEE Data Engineering Bulletin, 25 (1): 10 – 17.
19. Meersman R., (2001), Ontologies and Databases: More than a Fleeting Resemblance, In, d'Atri A. and Missikoff M. (eds), OES/SEO 2001 Rome Workshop, Luiss Publications.
20. Meersman R., (2002), Semantic Web and Ontologies: Playtime or Business at the Last Frontier in Computing ?, In, NSF-EU Workshop on Database and Information Systems Research for Semantic Web and Enterprises, pp.61 – 67.
21. Miller G., (1995), WordNet: a lexical database for English, Communications of the ACM 38 (11): 39 – 41.
22. Mogee M.E., (1997), Patents and technology intelligence. In, Ashton W. & Klavans R., (eds.), Technical Intelligence for Business: Keeping Abreast of Science & Technology, Battelle Press, Washington, D.C.
23. Mogee M.E., (1997), Patent analysis methods in support of licensing. Technology Transfer Society Proceedings of the 1997 Annual Meeting.
24. Nirenburg S. & Raskin V., (2001), Ontological Semantics, Formal Ontology and Ambiguity, In, Proc. of the 2nd International Conference on Formal Ontology in Information Systems, ACM Press, pp. 151 – 162.
25. Oberle D. & Spyns P., (2003), OntoWeb – Knowledge Portal, In, Staab S. & Studer R., (eds.), Handbook on Ontologies, International Handbooks on Information Systems, Springer Verlag, pp. 521 – 540.
26. Schreiber A., Akkermans J., Anjewierden A., De Hoog R., Shadbolt N., Van De Velde W., & Wielinga B., (2000), Knowledge Engineering and Management: The CommonKADS Methodology, MIT Press.
27. Schumpeter J., (1942), Capitalism, socialism and democracy, New York, Harper and Row.
28. Spyns P., Oberle D., Volz R., Zheng J., Jarrar M., Sure Y., Studer R., Meersman R., (2002), OntoWeb - a Semantic Web Community Portal, In, Karagiannis D., & Reimer U. (eds.), Proceedings of the Fourth International Conference on Practical Aspects of Knowledge Management (PAKM02), LNAI 2569, Springer Verlag, pp. 189 – 200.
29. Spyns P., Meersman R. & Jarrar M., (2002), Data modelling versus Ontology engineering, In, Sheth A. & Meersman R. (eds.), SIGMOD Record Special Issue 31 (4): 12 – 17.
30. Spyns P., (2004), Methods to be used in ontology engineering. OntoBasis Deliverable #D1.6, STAR Lab, Brussel.
31. Staab S. & Studer R., (2003), Handbook on Ontologies, International Handbook on Information Systems, Springer Verlag.
32. Stojanovic L., Stojanovic N. & Volz R., (2002), Migrating data-intensive Web Sites into the Semantic Web, in Proc. of the ACM Symposium on Applied Computing (SAC 2002), ACM Press, New York, pp.1100 – 1107
33. Sure Y., (2003), Methodology, Tools & Case Studies for Ontology based Knowledge Management, PhD thesis, AIFB Karlsruhe.
34. Twiss B., (1992), Managing Technological Innovation, London, Pitman Publishers.
35. Verheyen G. & van Bekkum P., (1982), NIAM, aN Information Analysis Method". In, Olle T., Sol H. & Verrijn-Stuart A., (eds), IFIP Conference on Comparative Review of Information Systems Methodologies, Noord-Holland.

36. Vossen P. (ed.), (1998), EuroWordNet: A Multilingual Database with Lexical Semantic Networks, Kluwer Academic Publishers, Dordrecht.
37. Wiederhold G., (1994), Interoperation, Mediation, and Ontologies, In, Proceedings International Symposium on Fifth Generation Computer Systems (FGCS94), Workshop on Heterogeneous Cooperative Knowledge Bases, vol. W3, ICOT, Tokyo, pp. 33 – 48.

Ontology-Based Functional-Knowledge Modeling Methodology and Its Deployment

Yoshinobu Kitamura and Riichiro Mizoguchi

The Institute of Scientific and Industrial Research, Osaka University
8-1, Mihogaka, Ibaraki, Osaka 567-0047, Japan
{kita,miz}@ei.sanken.osaka-u.ac.jp

Abstract. Functionality is one of the key concepts in understanding an artifact and in engineering domain knowledge. Although the importance of sharing of engineering knowledge in industry has been widely recognized, from our experience with collaborative research with a production company, industrial engineers have had difficulty in sharing engineering knowledge including functionality. To promote the sharing of the engineering knowledge from the viewpoint of functionality, we have established an ontology-based knowledge modeling methodology for functional knowledge, which has been successfully deployed in a production company. It consists of two ontologies to capture functionality and the specifications for modeling processes. This paper summarizes these ontologies and its deployment, and discusses the modeling process based on the ontologies, which includes detailed modeling steps, types of functional knowledge, and ontological guidelines.

1 Introduction

Understanding an artifact is a major part of domain knowledge. Functionality is one of the key concepts in understanding an artifact. While there is no common understanding of what a function is [1-4], people share the idea that functional knowledge is tightly related to design intention. In contrast to objective data about an artifact such as dimension, shape and structure, recognition of functionality is dependent on systems, environments or situations in which they are embedded. A function of a device explains what users can get using it in an environment (effects or worth of the artifact). A function of a component embedded in a system explains why the component exists in the system and how it contributes to achieving the system's whole-function. In the problem of design and manufacturing, such functional knowledge represents designer's intention (so-called design rationale (DR)). It plays a crucial role in engineering tasks such as designing and trouble shooting by engineers [1-5] as well as understanding artifacts by users.

The importance of the knowledge management (KM) of engineering knowledge in industry is widely recognized. The recent CAD systems and computer network technologies enable engineers to share *the objective data* of an artifact such as shape so-called Product Data Management (PDM). The current KM technology relies mainly on searching documents by keywords. From our experience with collaborative research with a production company, however, industrial engineers have had difficulty

E. Motta et al. (Eds.): EKAW 2004, LNAI 3257, pp. 99–115, 2004.

in sharing the engineering knowledge among them for long years. They have been regularly writing various kinds of technical reports for each of the jobs such as design review and maintenance. Such documents include real "know-how" in order to keep qualities and avoid troubles. Nevertheless, few of them are retrieved (and reused) by other engineers using the search technologies, because many of these documents are specific to each product from own viewpoint of each engineer. One of its reasons is the lack of semantic constraints (or guidelines) on document contents. We argue that ontologies of functionality can provide semantic constraints/guidelines on knowledge-contents as we will discuss its needs in the next section.

To promote the sharing of the engineering knowledge of artifacts from the viewpoint of functionality, our goal here is to establish an ontology-based knowledge modeling methodology for functional knowledge. We have developed two ontologies to capture functionality, i.e., the extended device ontology [6] for capturing the target world and the functional concept ontology [7] for rich generic functions of components. In addition to these ontologies, *specification on the knowledge-modeling process* plays a crucial role in the practice of knowledge management. It includes steps for knowledge authoring, the types of functional knowledge to be modeled in each step, and ontological guidelines. The modeling methodology has been successfully deployed in a production company [8]. In the deployment, it has been understood that such specification is one of its success factors.

This paper discusses the ontology-based modeling methodology for functional engineering knowledge. We overview the ontologies and its deployment in industry as a success story of Ontological Engineering. In Ontological Engineering research, how to use ontologies in real situations in industry is an important issue as well as theory, methodology and tools. The main topic of this paper is the specification on the modeling processes and guidelines based on the ontologies. The specification has been used in the deployment but has not been reported yet. Although we have reported the contents of ontologies in [6,7] and the deployment in [8], we summarize them from the viewpoint of knowledge modeling.

This paper is organized as follows. The next section discusses the needs of ontologies for functionality. Section 3 provides an overview of the ontologies for capturing functionalities. Section 4 discusses the modeling process based on these ontologies. Section 5 presents its successful deployment with our analysis of the success factors. Section 6 discusses related work, limitations, and application domains for our ontologies. Section 7 concludes the paper.

2   Needs of Ontologies for Functionality

A great deal of work on domain ontologies in the engineering domain has been done [9-11]. These, however, have mainly been concerned not with teleological functionality but objective structures and behaviors. On the other hand, although a great deal of research on the functionality of engineering products has been conducted in engineering design research [3,5,12,13], functional representation research [1,2,4,15-21], and value engineering [22], there have been few ontological considerations [4,23,24].

We think there is a considerable gap between such theoretical research and practice in industry. Here, we present two examples that demonstrate the difficulty in functional knowledge modeling and then the needs of ontologies. Firstly, functionality in Value Engineering is represented in "verb+noun" style [22] and on the basis of this, one might describe "to weld metals" is a function of a manufacturing machine as a keyword for its document. However, "to weld metals" implies both the metals are joined and their parts are fused. From the viewpoint of functionality in manufacturing, joining is only the goal the designer intends to attain, while the fusion can be regarded as a characteristic of "how to achieve that goal". In fact, the same goal, "to join", can be achieved in different ways (e.g., using nuts & bolts) without the fusion. When a designer looks for different ways to achieve a goal function by specifying the function as a keyword, his/her capturing it as "to join" instead of "to weld" enables him/her to find "nuts & bolts" as a possible alternative to "welding". This example demonstrates the importance of the concept of functionality in reusable functional knowledge.

The well-known systematic design methodology in [5], on the other hand, includes hierarchical structures of functionality based on input-output relations (so-called functional decomposition). However, this is not easy to describe such functional models. For the same welding machine, one might describe "to put objects together", "to make an arc", and "to leave them" as sub-functions (decomposed micro-functions) of the goal function "to join". These sub-functions certainly describe decomposition of the input-output relation. However, there is an implicit intermediate function "to heat objects" between "to make an arc" and the goal function. In fact, "to heat objects" can be achieved by "to make current flow" instead of "to make an arc". This second example demonstrates the importance of practical specifications for functional decomposition, in addition to standard specifications as decomposition of input-output.

These suggest the necessity for practical specifications for the content of functional knowledge and of how to describe it. The former can be specified as ontologies, i.e., "explicit specifications of conceptualization" [25]. Ontologies can provide fundamental concepts for capturing the target world in a consistent way and a vocabulary to describe the knowledge. The latter means specifications for modeling processes, which include steps for knowledge authoring and ontological guidelines. Ontologies specify the results of knowledge modeling and thus need detailed modeling steps, which are theoretically justified by the ontologies. We developed the two ontologies to specify knowledge content and the functional-knowledge modeling process.

3   Ontologies to Capture Functionality

Fig. 1 outlines our framework for functional modeling based on the ontologies. It has two levels, i.e., the behavioral and the functional ('a' axis). The extended device ontology [6] provides fundamental concepts such as "**device**" mainly for the behavioral level. (Terms in bold letters are defined in the ontology). The functional concept ontology [7] provides a vocabulary for describing the functional-level model and maps between behaviors and functions.

At the behavioral level, the model is objective without the designers' intentions. It consists of **devices**, **connections** between devices ('b' axis), **assembly** (or aggregation) relations of devices ('c' axis), and **behaviors** of entities. The "behavior" of a device is defined as the objective interpretation of its input-output relation considering it as a black box. Each device is connected to another through its input or output **ports**.

A device plays a role as an **agent** (or actor) that changes the states of what is input (called **operand**, i.e., what is being processed by the device) such as fluid, energy, motion, force, and information. The input-output relation of the behavior is, more precisely, the difference between the states of the operand at the input port and that at the output port (called **IO-State**). A device can be a mechanical element, a mechanical pair, a component, an assembly, or a system.

Fig. 2 shows definitions of such concepts in the extended device ontology in an ontology editor of an environment for building/using ontology named Hozo [26]. The ontology editor basically supports frame-based representation with slots. Concepts are represented as frames (denoted by nodes in Fig. 2) with slots (right-angled link) and the *is-a* relations among concepts (straight link with "is-a"). Concepts are categorized into the *wholeness* concepts composed of part concepts (shown in the left pane in the screen snapshot in Fig. 2) and the *relation* concepts between the concepts (the right pane). A wholeness concept has slots of *part* concepts (*part-of* relation denoted by right-angled link with "p/o") and slots of attributes ("a/o"). A relation concept has slots of *participant* concepts (*participate-in* relation. denoted by "p/i") and the attribute-slots. One of the features of Hozo is theoretical treatment of *role* concepts with slots. By role we mean here such a concept that an entity plays in a specific context and cannot be defined without mentioning external concepts [26], which is similar to the definitions in the literature [27,28]. For example, a man (class constraint for role) can play "husband role" (*role* concept) in a "marriage" relation (role context), who is called "husband" (*role holder*). It can be defined as that the "marriage" relation concept has two *participate-in* slots; i.e., the "husband" slot ("man" as a class constraint, "husband-role" as a role concept and "husband" as a role-holder) and the "wife" slot ("woman", "wife-role" and "wife", respectively). These roles can be defined also with part-of relation of the "married couple" which is a *wholeness concept* corresponding to the "marriage relation". For details of Hozo, see [26].

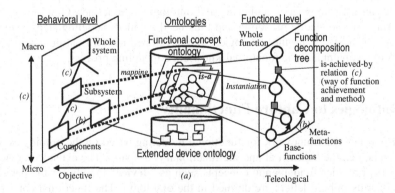

Fig. 1. Structure of a Functional Model

In the definition of the extended device ontology in Fig. 2, the **device** concept is defined as a *role-holder* in **behavioral-relation** between two **physical-entities** (Note that we assume this concept is a sub-class of more generic concept in an upper ontology). One of them plays the "agent" role, which is called **device**. It operates the other entity (**operand** which is another *role-holder*) and changes its physical attributes. The physical-entity as an operand has **IO-States**, which represents values of **physical-attribute**s at a port of a device. The pairs of IO-States at input ports of a device and those at output ports of the same device are defined as **behavior**. A physical-entity has a set of kinds (denoted by #) of physical-attributes (i.e., not instances of physical-attributes but pointers to the class) for description of qualitative relations between the physical-attributes.

We extended the conventional device-centered ontologies (e.g., in [9,11,23]) originating from systems dynamics theory by redefining the concepts of behavior, **conduit**, and **medium**. We categorized the meanings of behavior into four types [6]. The definition above (called B1 behaviour) is distinguished from the other three for capturing functionality. A **conduit** (e.g., a pipe and a shaft) is defined as a special device that transmits an operand without any change in an ideal situation. A **medium** (e.g., steam for heat energy) is something that holds an operand and enables it to flow between devices. In Fig. 2, **medium** is defined as a role-holder which carries another physical-entity(operand) in **carrying-relation**. The refined definition enables us to cope with mechanical domains that seemingly do not fit device ontology [29].

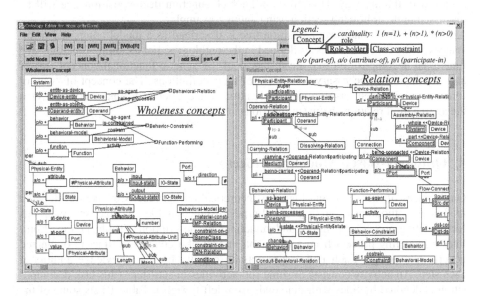

Fig. 2. Portion of the extended device ontology defined using Hozo

The functional level represents the "teleological" description of a system with the designer's intention. We define a "**function**" of a device as a conceptualization of the teleological interpretation of its "behavior" with the intended goal [7]. We have defined about 220 generic functions such as "to give energy" and "to split things" (called functional concepts) in the functional concept ontology. The definition is in terms of FTs (Functional Toppings), which represent information about the teleological interpretation of (mapping to) a behavior according to the designers' intentions.

The vertical axis denoted 'c' at the functional level in Fig. 1 represents aggregation (or decomposition) of functions, that is, a sequence of micro(sub)-functions achieves

a macro(whole)-function, which we call the "is-achieved-by" (a kind of *part-of*) relation. It corresponds to function decomposition [5], whole-part relation [19] and
"degree of complexity" [3]. In addition to such a description of "how to achieve the
function" (we call a *method*), the concept "*way of function achievement*" represents
the conceptualization of background knowledge for function decomposition such as
physical principles, which represents "why the sequence of micro-functions can
achieve the macro-function". The conceptualization of the *way* concept helps us
distinguish "how to achieve and why" (way) from "what is intended to be achieved"
(function). For example, the example of "to weld" in Section 2 can be described as *fusion way* of the *joining function*. The fusion way has specific characteristics of the
output that the operands are fused and they are hard to be separated. Although a functional concept "to join" loses some amount of information of "to weld", what is loses
goes to the characteristics of the fusion way. As a total, functional concepts are
successfully made very generic without any loss of information. In the fusion way, the
joining function (a macro-function) can be achieved by three micro-functions; "make
distance between operands zero", "melt parts of them" and "solidify them". The heat-
ing function in Section 2 is the sub-function of the melting function and can be
achieved in the arc way. How to describe such function decomposition tree will be
discussed in the following section using another example.

In Hozo, a functional decomposition tree is described as a model composed of instances of the functional classes defined in the ontologies. For example, functions in a
functional decomposition tree are instances of the generic functional-concept classes
and should satisfy necessary conditions of their definitions. The concept of "way of
function achievement" is defined as a relation concept between functions. It governs
the aggregation relations between functions.

4   Ontology-Based Modeling Process

On the basis of these two ontologies as theoretical background, we have developed a
modeling methodology that consists of types of functional knowledge, specifications
for modeling processes (Fig. 3), and guidelines for descriptions (Table 1). Fig. 3 outlines a modeling process from a functional model of a concrete artifact to organized
generic knowledge. Each node represents an activity by the knowledge authors at
each step. An activity consists of some sub-activities in sub-steps (this task decomposition is denoted by lines with diamonds from left to right). Table 1 lists some of the
guidelines for describing the function decomposition tree based on the ontologies.
Here, we use a production machine called a wire-saw as an example, which is shown
in Fig. 4. This is adapted from the deployment discussed in Section 5. It is designed to
slice semiconductor ingots with friction by moving wires. We extended the rough
steps reported in [30] and clarified the guidelines.

4.1 Clarifying System

The first step (#1 in Fig. 3) involves analyzing the system to be described and clarify-
ing it. The first sub-step (#1-1) involves determining the boundaries for the model,

i.e., criteria for judging whether a thing (a component etc.) will be modeled or not. If not, it will be treated as an external factor to the modeled system. The boundaries are spatial and temporal. The temporal boundary is important to distinguish the design process, manufacturing process, and product functioning process as shown in the guidelines F2 in Table 1.

The second sub-step (#1-2) is to identify physical things participating in the process (called participants) in the boundaries and then assign a role to each of them according to the extended device ontology discussed in Section 3 and guidelines F2, F3, and S3. Because decomposition has not yet been done at this point, the major (larger grain-sized) components (devices) are identified. In the wire-saw example in Fig. 4, the major components include the motor and the roller. The ingot is obviously an operand. However, the wire can be a problem in that it can be considered an *agent* (to exert force on ingots), an *operand* (to be moved by roller), or a *conduit* (to transmit tension). According to the semantic constraints in the extended device ontology, one possible consistent role-assignment is to decompose the wire into two parts, a working wire as an agent and a transmitting wire as both a medium and a conduit. The extension of the device ontology accepts the last situation.

4.2 Describing Function Decomposition Tree

The second step (#2) is to describe the *function decomposition tree* of the target system (denoted (a) in Fig. 3) at the functional level in Fig. 1. It consists of a macro-

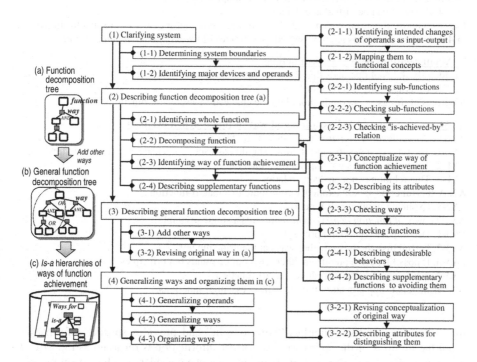

Fig. 3. Modeling Process of Functional-Design Knowledge

function, sub(micro)-functions, relations between sub-functions, and *ways of function achievement*. Figure 4 shows (a) the initial model and (b) the revised one for the function decomposition tree of the wire-saw.

(1) Identifying Whole Function

The first sub-step (#2-1) is to "identify the whole function" of the system according to F1-F4. Here, *"the way of function achievement"* discussed in the previous section plays an important role. In the example, the whole function is not "to slice" but "to

Table 1. Guidelines for function decomposition tree

F. About functions and behaviors
F1. A function represents "what to achieve" only and does not imply "how to achieve".
  F1-1. A device is a black-box. The inside is not shown at a level.
F2. A function represents (a teleological interpretation of) changes in physical things within the system boundary.
F2-1. Do not describe the designer's activities.
F2-2. Distinguish product's functions, manufacturing processes, and recycling activities.
F2-3. Determine a system boundary with a pre- and post-process.
F3. Agent of functions should be a "device" in the physical world.
F3-1. A human operator can be regarded as a "device".
F3-2. Designers and manufacturer should be distinguished.
F3-3. Sizes of devices decrease in function decomposition.
F3-4. A device can be virtual and dynamic.
F4. Decompose functions which imply kinds of operands and/or degrees of results for functions.
  F4-1. Such implications are represented as attributes of *ways of function achievement*

S: About relations between sub-functions
S1. Identify states of operands that flow sub-functions.
S2. Time passes along this relation.
S3. Roles of things as operands should not be changed in a series of functions.

A: About "is-achieved-by" relation and way of function achievement
A1. The "is-achieve-by" relation represents aggregation
  A1-1. The total changes in sub-functions should correspond to changes in the whole function.
  A1-2. This relation does not imply a time interval.
  A1-3. This relation is not an "is-a" relation.
A2. A sub-function should explicitly contribute to a macro-function.
  A2-1. Explicate implicit sub-functions.
A3. The *way of function achievement* represents a single principle.
  A3-1. Decompose compound principles
  A3-2. Distinguish them from other ways at the principle level.
  A3-3. If possible, conceptualize neither tools nor operands but principles
  A3-4. A way should refer to a direct macro-function.
A4. Distinguish supplementary functions from essential functions.

split", because "to slice" implies "how to split" and provides specific information about the thinness of the split part. The former information is regarded as the *way of function achievement*. The goal of slicing here can be considered to be "to split a part from the target operand (i.e. ingot)". It makes it possible to select other *ways* instead of "slicing" in the design. In reality, slicing with wire is not single *way of function achievement* but a composite as will be discussed later.

The latter information (i.e., thinness), on the other hand, is regarded as the quantitative degree of a function. Each *way of function achievement* has specific value of attributes like it. Then, such information can be used as conditions to select the *way* from all available *ways of function achievement*.

(2) Decomposing Functions

The second sub-step (#2-2) involves decomposing the whole function (generally, a macro-function) into sub (micro)-functions that can achieve the macro-function. When one regards it as a design activity, it corresponds to function decomposition [5]. After the modeler has tried to identify the sub-functions (step #2-2-1), important steps are to check the relations among sub-functions (as step #2-2-2) according to the S1-S3 guidelines and to check the relations between sub-functions and the whole-functions (as step #2-2-3) according to the A1-A4 guidelines.

As we can see from Fig. 4(a), one might describe "to move table to wire" and "to move wire" as sub-functions. However, against A2, why these two sub-functions can perform the whole function is not clear. Moreover, against S2, it is unclear which operands flow between the two sub-functions. One reason is that there is a missing sub-function, "to exert vertical force to ingot and wire". The original sub-function "to move table to wire" contributes to the vertical-force sub-function. The other missing sub-functions are found in the next sub-step.

(3) Describing Ways of Function Achievement

The third sub-step (#2-3) involves describing the *ways of function achievement*. The modelers identify a physical principle that can achieve the whole(macro-) function and conceptualize it (#2-3-1). Then, the attributes of the *way* are described (#2-3-2). Next, such descriptions are checked according to A3 (#2-3-3). As a result of identify-

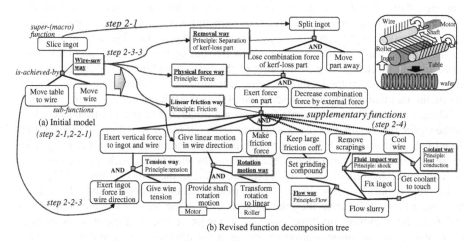

Fig. 4. A function decomposition tree of a wire-saw for slicing ingots (portion)

ing the *way*, the functions are sometimes changed (#2-3-4). To further decompose sub-functions, steps #2-2 and #2-3 are done recursively.

In the wire-saw example, the *wire-saw way* does not involve a single *way* but a composite of three *ways*, i.e., the removal way of splitting, the physical force way of losing combinatorial force of a part (kerf loss, i.e., the part lost by cutting), and the linear friction way of exerting force. Splitting is achieved in two sub-functions; losing the combinatorial force of the kerf-loss and moving it away. This *way* to achieve the function is conceptualized as the removal way based on separating the kerf loss part.

(4) Describing Supplementary Functions

The last sub-step (#2-4) involves adding *supplementary functions* that are not essential but provide additional effects to improve efficiency and/or to prevent faults. In other words, we recommend describing essential sub-functions only until this step, because this clarifies the principles for achievement. In this paper, we have omitted this aspect but it is reported in another [31].

4.3 Describing General Function Decomposition Tree

A *general function decomposition tree* (b) includes possible alternatives to achieving functions in an OR relationship. In the first sub-step (#3-1), the function decomposition tree described in the previous step (#2) is expanded by adding other *ways of function achievement* for each function decomposition. Then, the *way of function achievement* in the original function decomposition tree are revised by comparing with principles for the other *ways* (#3-2). This step can be omitted.

4.4 Generalizing Ways of Function Achievement

A concrete *way* in a (general) function decomposition tree can be generalized into a generic way in steps #4-1 and #4-2. Generic *ways* are called functional way knowledge and they consist of a macro-function, a set of sub (micro)-functions, temporal and causal constraints among sub-functions, principles of achievement, conditions for use of the way (e.g., the specific class of operands (e.g., solid objects) which can be changed in the way), and quantitative characteristics of the *way* (e.g., accuracy, cost, time, amount of change (e.g., limitation of thinness for splitting)). Although this includes a description of the method to achieve functions, we called it the "*way*", focusing on the fact that it includes a description of the principles of achievement.

Then, *ways* to achieve the same function are organized in *is-a* relations according to their principles (called an *is-a hierarchy of ways of function achievement* (c) in Fig. 3 and Fig. 5) in step #4-3. We distinguish the organization as an *is-a* hierarchy from the other derivative organizations depending on the viewpoint. Such ad-hoc trees can be reorganized by a functional-way server according to the given viewpoint [32].

Figure 5 details *is-a* hierarchies of *ways* to achieve split functions and others. They have been generalized from the specific *ways* used in the wire-saw example in Fig. 4 and from other cutting machines such as water-jet cutting and electrolysis cutting. Conventional organization of *ways* of cutting in a textbook of the field relies on "what is used for" against guideline A3-3. Figure 5 shows explicit differences between the wire-saw and other cutting devices. The wire-saw uses the three *ways* marked with asterisks. Moreover, *ways* of exerting force can also be used in other appliances, e.g., washing machines. In a screw-type washing machine, for example, dirt is separated from cloth by random frictional force caused by the rotating screw. This kind of knowledge is general and can be applied to different domains.

4.5 Types of Knowledge

Note that these types of trees concerning functions (Fig. 3) are different. Function decomposition tree (a) represents *is-achieved-by* (a kind of *part-of*) relations among functions. The *is-a* hierarchies of ways (c) represent an abstraction of the key information about how to achieve the function, while the *is-a* hierarchies in the functional concept ontology represent abstractions of functions themselves, i.e., the goals that are achieved. Moreover, there are a huge numbers of ways for a function in nature, while the numbers of functional concepts are small.

The modeling process discussed in this section is used to describe functional knowledge from the bottom-up from scratch. When the general functional way knowledge is available, the modeler can use this to describe the function decomposition tree and/or add a new way of function achievement to an existing general function decomposition tree or an existing *is-a* hierarchy. Moreover, the steps; #2-1 and #2-2 can be done in reverse, i.e., from micro-functions to macro-functions from the bottom up. The functions of components can be aggregated into macro-functions. In reality, both directions are mixed in the modeling process.

5 Deployment

The ontology-based modeling methodology discussed thus far has been deployed since May, 2001 at the plant and production systems engineering division of Sumitomo Electric Industries, Ltd. (hereinafter referred to as SEI) [8]. A knowledge management software named SOFAST has been developed based on part of the

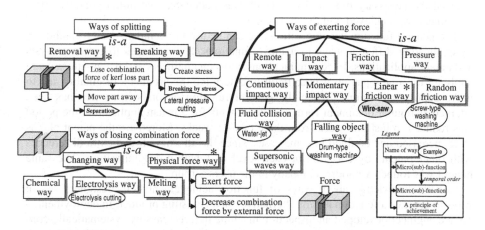

Fig. 5. Example of organizing generic ways of function achievement in *is-a* hierarchies

methodology and then deployed since December, 2002. Currently about 50 people in three factories use SOFAST in their daily tasks. The targets are manufacturing equipment mainly used in semiconductor manufacturing processes including the wire-saw shown in Figure 4, a wafer polisher, an optical fiber connector adjusting machine, and inspection machines. SOFAST has been used by 13 other companies since April, 2003 some of which use it in actual work. The followings summarize some of usages and effects in the deployment.

SOFAST is designed to support the description of functional knowledge and sharing the knowledge in an intra-network. It consists of client software and knowledge repositories. Using the client software, a user can describe function decomposition trees through a graphical user-interface and store them in the repository. Then, all users can search *ways of function achievement* in the repository to achieve the function of interest by specifying a goal function.

One of use of the function decomposition tree is to clarify functional knowledge, which is implicitly possessed by each engineer, and share it with other engineers. The experiential evaluation by Sumitomo's engineers was unanimously positive. Writing a function decomposition tree according to the methodology gives designers the chance to reflect on good stimuli, which leads them to an in-depth understanding of the equipment. This is because such a function decomposition tree shows the designer's intentions on how to achieve the goal function and justify design decisions, which are not included in the structural or behavioral models.

Such a deep understanding contributes to redesigning and solving problems with the equipment. For example, an engineer was not able to reduce the time a machine requires to polish semiconductor wafers after four months of investigation by adjusting the known working parameters. He consequently described its function decomposition tree, by referring to that of the wire-saw in Fig. 4. Although these two devices have the different main functions, he found the shared function "to maintain a large friction coefficient" and its sub-function "to place diamond powder between wafers and the table". As a result, he became aware of an implicit function and its parameters for placing more diamond powder to obtain a high friction coefficient. Eventually, he reduced the necessary time to 76%, which was better than the initial goal. This improvement was achieved within three weeks.

The general function decomposition tree can be used to compare design candidates by explicating different ways to achieve functions. It contributes to patent analysis and patent applications. In communications between engineers and patent attorneys in applying for a new patent, it is difficult to determine the product's originality and to make appropriate claims. When the general function decomposition tree has been adopted as regular document format of documents for a patent application, the period was reduced to just one week from three or four weeks. Moreover, the patent claims were increased and doubled in some cases, since the attorneys found extra differences with other patents by checking at each level of function decomposition. The same benefit was found by another company in the users' group.

Generic knowledge about ways of function achievement help designers search ways to achieve a function and/or alternatives in an existing product. In deployment, a novice engineer developed an inspection machine in three days by systematically consulting generic ways of shedding light in the knowledge repository of SOFAST. Such development usually requires experts two weeks.

The success factors for deployment can be summarized as (1) clear discrimination between function (goal) and way (how to achieve the goal) and (2) clear discrimination among the *is-a* relation of functions, that of ways, and the *is-achieved-by* (a kind of *part-of*) relations of functions. The modeling steps and guidelines based on these discriminations provide hints to users to interpret how a device works consistently.

6 Related Work and Discussion

The target knowledge of this research is functionality of physical artifacts. It is "domain" knowledge of design problem-solving or diagnosis. It is different from "task" knowledge of designing or diagnosing, which is activity of human or automated problem-solvers. In the task ontology research, generic tasks and generic problem-solving methods (PSMs) are proposed (e.g., [33]). If one ignores the difference between domain and task, the generic tasks and the generic methods are similar to our generic functions and generic ways of function achievement, respectively. We focus on structuring knowledge about how to achieve functions (activities in domain world). We conceptualize the principle behind the sequence of activities (called *method* in both researches) as the *way of function achievement*. It helps us organize them in *is-a* hierarchies, though PSMs for a specific task are usually not organized well. Moreover, we distinguish function at the teleological level from behaviors at the objective level.

Behavior of artifacts in our work is a kind of "process" by which we intuitively mean a sequence of state changes over time. We concentrate on *physical* process which represents temporal changes of physical quantities as we discuss in the following paragraphs. On generic "process", extensive research has been done. The process specification language (PSL) [34] defines "activity" as a basic concept and temporal relationships between them. Although it has the theory on sub-activities, it includes neither the concept of *way* nor generic activities. *Formal ontologies* for processes have been investigated (e.g., [35]). The MIT process handbook treats business activities [36]. It includes taxonomy of basic business activities. Some activities such as "buy in a store" in specialization of activities, however, imply "how to achieve" like "welding" in Section 2. It obstructs organizing "how to achieve" (the way of function achievement in our methodology) separately from specialization of activity itself.

The *is-achieved-by* relation in our work is a kind of the *parthood* relation between functions. Parthood has been extensively investigated in the *formal ontology* research. For example, DOLCE ontology includes formal specifications of *parthood* (and other fundamental concepts) [37].

A great deal of work on domain ontologies in the engineering domain has been done [4,10,11,23,24]. We concentrated on "ontology as meta-knowledge", which provides knowledge authors with constraints and guidelines on capturing the target world, though pioneering work [10] in ontological research and extensive work in semantic web research aimed at "ontology for agent communication" that contributes interpretabilities among agents. Borst et al. proposed PhysSys ontology as a sophisticated lattice for ontologies for the engineering domain [11]. Although their's did not include ontology for functionality, we focus on this. Ontological consideration on functionality can be found in the literature [4,23,24]. Chandrasekaran and Josephson identified a device-centric function and an environment-centric function [4]. Our definition of function is device-centric.

Our main point was to clarify several relationships related to functionality, i.e.,

(A)   The teleological interpretation of behavior as a function (axis (a) in Fig. 1),
(B)   The *is-a* hierarchy of functions,
(C)   The *is-achieved-by* (part-of) relations among functions (axis (c) in Fig. 1, Fig. 3(a), Fig. 3(b), and Fig. 4),
(D)   The *is-a* hierarchy of *ways of function achievement* (Fig. 3(c) and Fig. 5)

The relationship between function and behavior in (A) is similar to "means and ends" [19], the F-B relationship [20], and "aims-means" (including design requirements as well) [3]. On the other hand, papers such as [21] define that "behavior" is how to achieve a function (C) where distinction between behavior and function is relative. De Kleer defines function as a causal pattern between variables [15]. We identified operational primitives as FTs to represent intentions and then gave them operational definitions. Many "verb+noun"-style functional representations (as in Value Engineering [22]) lack such operationality. The recent efforts toward a standard taxonomy for engineering functions by the NIST Design Repository Project [14] are well established; however, they lack an operational relationship with behaviors and ontological specifications.

Concerning the *is-a* hierarchy of functions (B), the few (4-16) generally-valid functions [5] are too abstract to describe details of designer's intentions. The hierarchy of "degree of abstraction" [3] for functions represents the specialization of functions with additional conditions. These conditions, however, sometimes include a specific *way of function achievement* such as "transportation by sea" [3] in the same manner as "welding" discussed in Section 2. We separated their conditions for specialization into specific attributes for the *way of function achievement*. Our functional concept ontology includes the functions proposed by Keuneke [17] and similar functions in flow-based functional modeling [18,19].

The ways of function achievement in (C) and (D) is similar to the "means" [12,13]. However, they treated a product-specific model [12] or generic knowledge without explicit organization [13]. We investigated how to organize conceptualized generic ways of achieving functions in (D). Similar ideas on generic patterns to achieve functions are discussed in the literature [16,20,21]. As well as functional decomposition, the design prototypes [16] include structural decomposition and the function prototype [20] has physical feathers. Our description of *ways* tries to maximize generality by pointing out partial (and abstract) information on structure and behavior. Generic patterns or so-called design catalogs (e.g., in [5]) mainly concentrate on mechanical pairs. Generic teleological mechanisms (GTM) are modified in design based on analogy [21]. In our approach based on a limited set of functional concepts, the ways of function achievement are organized in *is-a* hierarchies (D). Designers can explore them on several abstract levels explicitly.

The TRIZ (TIPS) theory provides some patterns (or strategies) for inventions based on contradiction between two physical quantities [38]. We did not concentrate on design strategies but on the modeling schema. The TRIZ theory also pays attention to physical principles (effects), although we established a clear relationship between physical principles and functional structures.

Limitations with Ontologies and Application Domain
We cannot claim the completeness of concepts in our functional concept ontology. We applied the ontologies to modeling power plants, chemical plants and appliances as well as manufacturing machines. The models include changes in thermal energy, flow rate, ingredients of fluids, and force and motion of objects [7]. The current functional concept ontology can describe simple mechanical products, although it does not cover static force balancing and complex mechanical phenomena based on the shapes of objects.

7 Summary

An ontology-based knowledge modeling methodology was reported. It is domain-specific but is basically applicable to a great deal of knowledge about artifacts from the important viewpoint of functionality. It has been deployed successfully in industry. This paper discussed the detailed modeling process from specific models to generic knowledge in *is-a* hierarchies. The modeling steps and the guidelines based on ontologies help knowledge authors describe sharable knowledge clearly.

Our ontologies are operationally defined in an ontology editor as shown in Section 3. Using the editor, when a knowledge author describes a model or generic knowledge, the editor can check models against constraints defined in the ontologies (see [32] for detail). However, the current SOFAST software does not support such ontological constraints. Such functionality is being planned.

Acknowledgements. The authors would like to thank Tomonobu Takahashi, Kouji Kozaki, Yusuke Koji and Mariko Yoshikawa for their contributions. Special thanks go to Dr. Masayoshi Fuse, Mr. Masakazu Kashiwase and Mr. Shuji Shinoki of Sumitomo Electric Industries Ltd., for their cooperation in deploying our methodology in production systems.

References

1. Umeda, Y., Tomiyama, T.: Functional Reasoning in Design. IEEE Expert (1997) 42-48
2. Chittaro, L., Kumar, A.N.: Reasoning about Function and its Applications to Engineering. Artificial Intelligence in Engineering, 12 (1998) 331-336
3. Hubka, V., Eder, W.E.: Theory of Technical Systems. Springer-Verlag; Berlin (1998)
4. Chandrasekaran, B., Josephson, J.R.: Function in Device Representation, Engineering with Computers 16(3/4) (2000) 162-177
5. Pahl, G., Beitz, W.: Engineering design - a systematic approach. The Design Council (1988)
6. Kitamura, Y., Mizoguchi, R.: Ontology-based systematization of functional knowledge. Journal of Engineering Design, to appear (2004)
7. Kitamura, Y., Sano, T., Namba, K., Mizoguchi, R.: A Functional Concept Ontology and its Application to Automatic Identification of Functional Structures. Advanced Engineering Informatics, 16(2) (2002) 145-163

8. Kitamura, Y., Kashiwase, M., Fuse, M., Mizoguchi R.: Deployment of an Ontological Framework of Functional Design Knowledge. Advanced Engineering Informatics, to appear (2004)

9. De Kleer, J., Brown, J.S.: A Qualitative Physics based on Confluences. Artificial Intelligence, 24 (1984) 7-283

10. Cutkosky, M.R., et al.: PACT: An Experiment in Integrating Concurrent Engineering Systems. Computer (1993) 28-37

11. Borst, P., Akkermans, H., Top, J.: Engineering Ontologies. Int'l Journal of Human-Computer Studies, 46 (2/3) (1997) 365-406

12. Malmqvist, J.: Improved Function-Means Trees by Inclusion of Design History Information. Journal of Engineering Design, 8 (2) (1997) 107-117

13. Bracewell, R.H., Wallace, K.M.: Designing a Representation to Support Function-Means based Synthesis of Mechanical Design Solutions. In Proc. of the International Conference on Engineering Design (ICED) 01 (2001)

14. Hirtz, J., Stone, R.B., McAdams, D.A., Szykman, S., Wood, K.L.: A Functional Basis for Engineering Design: Reconciling and Evolving Previous Efforts. Research in Engineering Design, 13 (2002) 65-82

15. De Kleer, J.: How Circuits Work. Artificial Intelligence, 24 (1984) 205-280

16. Gero, J.S.: Design Prototypes: A Knowledge Representation Schema for Design. AI Magazine, 11(4) (1990) 26-36

17. Keuneke, A.M.: A Device Representation: the Significance of Functional Knowledge. IEEE Expert, 24 (1991) 22-25

18. Chittaro, L., Guida, G., Tasso, C., Toppano, E.: Functional and Teleological Knowledge in the Multi-Modeling Approach for Reasoning about Physical Systems: A Case Study in Diagnosis. IEEE Transactions on Systems, Man, and Cybernetics, 23(6) (1993) 1718-1751

19. Lind, M.: Modeling Goals and Functions of Complex Industrial Plants. Applied artificial intelligence, 8 (1994) 259-283

20. Umeda, Y, Ishii, M., Yoshioka, M., Shimomura, Y., Tomiyama, T.: Supporting conceptual design based on the function-behavior-state modeler. Artificial Intelligence for Engineering Design, Analysis and Manufacturing 10 (1996) 275-288

21. Bhatta, S.R., Goel, A.K.: A Functional Theory of Design Patterns. In Proc. of IJCAI-97 (1997) 294-300

22. Miles, L.D.: Techniques of value analysis and engineering. McGraw-Hill (1961)

23. Kumar, A.N., Upadhyaya, S.J.: Component-Ontological Representation of Function for Reasoning about Devices. Artificial Intelligence in Engineering 12 (1998) 399-415

24. Salustri, F.A.: Ontological Commitments in Knowledge-based Design Software: A Progress Report. In Proc. of the 3rd IFIP WG 5.2 Workshop on Knowledge Intensive CAD (1998) 31-51.

25. Gruber, T.: A Translation approach to portable ontologies. Knowledge Acquisition, 5(2) (1993) 199-220

26. Kozaki, K., Kitamura, Y., Ikeda, M., and Mizoguchi R.: Hozo: An Environment for Building/Using Ontologies based on a Fundamental Consideration of "Role" and "Relationship", Proc. of EKAW2002 (2002) 213-218

27. Sowa, J. F.: Knowledge Representation: Logical, Philosophical, and Computational Foundations. Brooks Cole (2000)

28. Masolo, C., Vieu, L., Bottazzi, E., Catenacci, C., Ferrario, R., Gangemi, A., Guarino, N.: Social Roles and their Descriptions, In Proc. of KR 2004 (2004)

29. Mortensen, N. H.: Function Concepts for Machine Parts - Contribution to a Part Design Theory, Proc. of ICED 99, 2 (1999) 841-846

30. Kitamura, Y., Mizoguchi, R.: Organizing Knowledge about Functional Decomposition. In Proc. of ICED 03, 2003
31. Koji, Y., Kitamura, Y., Mizoguchi, R.: Towards Modeling Design Rationale of Supplementary Functions in Conceptual Design. In Proc. of TMCE 2004 (2004) 117-130
32. Kitamura, Y., Mizoguchi, R.: Ontology-based description of functional design knowledge and its use in a functional way server. Expert Systems with Application 24 (2003)153-166.
33. Schreiber, G., Akkermans, H., Anjewierden, A., de Hoog, R., Shadbolt, N., Van de Velde, W. and Wielinga, B.: Knowledge Engineering and Management - The Common-KADS Methodology, The MIT Press, Cambridge, MA (2000)
34. ISO TC184/SC4/JWG8, Process Specification Language, Part 1, 11 and 12, http://www.tc184-sc4.org/SC4_Open/SC4_Work_Products_Documents/PSL_(18629)/ (2003)
35. Menzel, C., Gruninger, M., A Formal Foundation for Process Modeling, Formal Ontology in Information Systems; Collected Papers from the Second Int'l Conf. (2001) 256-269
36. Herman, G. A., Malone, T. W.: What is in the process handbook?, Organizing Business Knowledge: The MIT Process Handbook, MIT Press (2003) 221-258
37. Masolo, C., Borgo, S., Gangemi, A., Guarino, N., Oltramari, A., Schneider, L.: The WonderWeb Library of Foundational Ontologies, WonderWeb Deliverable D17 (2002)
38. Sushkov, V.V., Mars, N.J.I., Wognum, P.M.: Introduction to TIPS: a Theory for Creative Design. Artificial Intelligence in Engineering 9 (1995) 177-189

Accuracy of Metrics for Inferring Trust and Reputation in Semantic Web-Based Social Networks

Jennifer Golbeck and James Hendler

University of Maryland, College Park,
MIND Lab, 8400 Baltimore Ave.,
College Park, Maryland 20740
{golbeck, hendler}@cs.umd.edu

Abstract. While most research on the topic of trust on the semantic web has focused largely on digital signatures, certificates, and authentication, more social notions of trust which are reputation-based are starting to gain attention. In this paper, we describe an algorithm for generating locally-calculated reputation ratings from a Semantic Web Social Network. We present mathematical and experimental results that show the effectiveness of this algorithm to accurately infer the reputation of a node. We then describe TrustMail, an application that uses the network for rating email.

1 Introduction

On the hypertext web, any person is allowed to make any statement with no requirements about its accuracy or truthfulness. When reading a web page, humans make many judgments based on the appearance of the page and the source of the information. Although someone could lie about their sources, it is relatively easy to generate at least some information about the source. On the Semantic Web, content is a series of statements that cannot be judged by appearance or professionalism. Since the underlying philosophy of the Semantic Web is to allow a computer to take distributed statements about the same resource and aggregate them, the source of information becomes removed one step from the presentation. The word "Trust" has come to have several definitions on the Semantic Web. Much research has focused on authentication of resources, including work on digital signatures and public keys. This provides confidence in the source or author of a statement, which is very important, but trust in this sense ignores the credibility issue. Confirming the source of a statement does not have any explicit implication about the quality of the statement.

Reputation is more a social notion of trust. In our lives, we each maintain a set of reputations for people we know. When we need to work with a new, unknown person, we can ask people with whom we already have relationships for information about that person. Based on the information we gather, we form an opinion about the reputation of the new person. This system works well, even though there are a lot of people in the world, because communities tend to be highly interconnected, and the number of steps between any two people tends to be rather small. This is known as

E. Motta et al. (Eds.): EKAW 2004, LNAI 3257, pp. 116–131, 2004.

the Small World effect, and it has been shown to be true for a variety of social and web-based systems [1,4,21,22].

Trust and reputation can be expressed on the semantic web using ontologies that provide a method for describing entities and the trust relationships between them. These ontological foundations allow for trust to be expressed in people, statements, or the content of information sources. They also facilitate expressing different trust relationships with respect to different topics. To make use of these ratings, the proper subset of entities and relationships are extracted and metrics to infer relationships are used on this set.

This work is motivated by the sudden explosion of social network data on the web. The Friend of a Friend (FOAF) project now comprises millions of files. We have created a trust extension to FOAF that allows people to create ratings for one another. This project, located at http://trust.mindswap.org/, provides tools and support for producing trust data that can be linked to an aggregator. The site also has a set of methods that provide data about the network and an interface for making trust inferences between two individuals. In two months, the network has grown to nearly 1,300 users (see figure 1) and they were used as the foundation for applying these metrics to the email application in section 5.

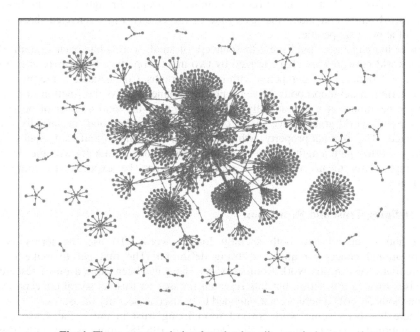

Fig. 1. The trust network developed at http://trust.mindswap.org/

For methods that use the network to be successful, metrics over it must be accurate. In this paper, we present an algorithm for aggregating and inferring reputation ratings on the Semantic Web. We show mathematically and through experiments that this algorithm gives very accurate inferences, even in the face of high uncertainty. In section 5, we discuss applications that we have developed using this reputation system, and then present more areas where such an analysis can be useful.

2 Background and Related Work

This research covers several spaces of research that typically has involved different communities. Because of that, the following sections are broken up by subfield.

2.1 Small World Networks and Power Law Distributions

The concept of small world networks and the notion of six degrees of separation – the idea that any two people in the world are connected through only six intermediate people – began with Stanley Milgram's seminal work, "The Small World Problem" [21] in 1967. He distributed letters to strangers in the Midwest, with the instruction that they pass the letters to friends with the ultimate goal of the letter reaching a specific person in Boston. Based on the number of people through whom the letters traveled, Milgram concluded that everyone in the county was connected through a chain of at most six people.

Since his paper was published, the concept of small worlds has been formalized. Small world networks are characterized by two main properties. First, there is a high degree of "connectance" compared with random graphs. Connectance is the property of clustering in neighborhoods. Given a node n, connectance is the fraction of edges between neighbors of n that actually exist compared to the total number of possible edges. Small world graphs have strong connectance; neighborhoods are usually very connected. The second property, which is computationally significant, states the average shortest path length between two nodes grows logarithmically with the size of the graph. This means that many computations can be expected to complete efficiently.

2.2 Defining Trust and Reputation

Trust and reputation are both socially loaded words. To use the terms as a computational concepts requires a strong definition. The first cut to make is to differentiate trust in this work from security. There has been quite a bit of research that uses trust in this sense, but this research focuses on trust as social concept, and the methods described here are not intended to be used as security measures.

There has been some work toward formalizing trust in the social sense as a computational concept. The work by Deutsch in 1962[8] contains a widely used definition. He states that trusting behavior occurs when a person encounters a situation where he or she perceives an ambiguous path, the result of which can be good or bad, and the occurrence of the good or bad result is contingent on the action of another person. Additionally, the negative impact of the bad result is greater than the positive impact of the good result, so the person is motivated to make the correct choice. If this person chooses to go down the path, the person has made a trusting choice – the belief that the outcome will be good lies in the fact that the other person on whom the outcome depends is trusted to do the right thing.

Marsh[marsh94] addressed the issue of formalizing trust as a computational concept in his PhD dissertation. His model is complex and based on social and psychological factors. This work is widely cited, but the model is highly theoretical and often considered too difficult to practically implement. In this work, where trust will sometimes be derived implicitly, and, in the most expressive cases, be indicated with a numerical value, psychological factors cannot be considered.

In this work, trust is treated as a measure of uncertainty in a person or resource. Specifically, given an ambiguous path as described above, having trust in a person is defined as a measure of the confidence that the person will take the action that leads to the positive result. Reputation is synonymous with the measure of that trust.

2.3 Trust and Reputation on the Web

The issue of trust and reputation on the web has been around since the web itself began. How users could have trust in websites has taken many forms. In an unpublished masters thesis [9], Dudek studied user trust in e-commerce systems, and found that it closely related to the aesthetics of the site. More formal methods for rating the reputation of a site or of a user are also common. The eBay rating system tries to use customers positive and negative feedback ratings as a measure of a seller's reputation. Epinions, a consumer reviews website, also allows customers to rate the transactions with sellers, and maintains a more explicit trust rating system. The Epinions dataset is commonly used in the study of trust on the web. The PageRank algorithm, used by the Google search engine, also is a trust metric of sorts. It uses the number of links coming into a particular page as votes for that site. This rating, combined with other text processing, is used to score results. The PageRank algorithm is so effective at rating the relevance of pages, that its results are commonly used as a control for testing the effectiveness of trust metrics.

Explicitly creating networks and analyzing them to form opinions about the reputation of content and users has been an issue gaining more attention over the last few years, particularly with the advent of the semantic web. Unlike the hypertext web, where users had to maintain any reputation information in HTML pages, or in the backend database of a website, the semantic web is designed to let users make explicit statements about any resource, and maintain that data themselves in an open, distributed way.

The algorithms and applications presented in this work are designed to be used with semantic web based social networks, founded on the Friend-Of-A-Friend (FOAF) vocabulary[10,11]. The FOAF project defines a mechanism for describing people, and who they know. We extend that ontology by adding binary trust relations (trusts and distrusts). This work focuses on social networks, and the trust between people, but semantic trust relationships have been researched in several other contexts.

Gil and Ratnakar addressed the issue of trusting content and information sources [12]. They describe an approach to derive assessments about information sources based on individual feedback about the sources. As users add annotations, they can include measures of Credibility and Reliability about a statement, which are later averaged and presented to the viewer. Using the TRELLIS system, users can view information, annotations (including averages of credibility, reliability, and other ratings), and then make an analysis.

In the peer to peer context, the EigenTrust system [15] (based on PageRank) effectively computes global trust values for peers, based on their previous behavior. Individuals with poor performance will receive correspondingly low trust ratings. Their system was shown to be highly resistant to attack.

Raph Levin's Advogato project [19] also calculates a global reputation for individuals in the network, but from the perspective of designated *seeds* (authoritative nodes). His metric composes assertions from members to determine membership within a group. The Advogato website at http://advogato.org, for example, certifies users at three levels – apprentice, journeyer, and master. Access to post and edit website information is controlled by these certifications. Like EigenTrust, the Advogato metric is quite attack resistant. By identifying individual nodes as "bad" and finding any nodes that certify the "bad" nodes, the metric cuts out an unreliable portion of the network. Calculations are based primarily on the good nodes, so the network as a whole remains secure.

Less centralized metrics are presented in work by Richardson, et al. [28]. That metric uses a local system for inferring reputations or trust relationships from a network. Richardson's work, like EigenTrust, presents a probabilistic interpretation of global belief combinations. The effectiveness of the system was shown in context with Epinions and BibServ.

3   The Reputation Inference Algorithm

3.1   Terms and Background

Different systems have used various ranges for trust and reputation ratings, including a three tiered system [20], a 1-9 rating system [13], and a continuous scale in the range [0,1] [28]. This work uses a {1,-1} scale where 1 indicates trustworthiness, and -1 indicates untrustworthiness. This simple binary scale makes it easier to develop a theoretical understanding of the behavior of trust metrics.

If two nodes, say node A and node C, do not have a direct edge connecting them, the network can be used to generate an *inferred reputation rating* (see figure 2). If node A knows node B, and node B knows node C, then A can use the path to compose the inferred rating for C. The algorithm for inferring this value forms the basis of any trust or reputation system.

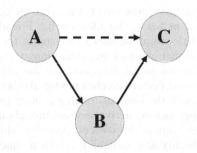

Fig. 2. A reputation inference from node A to node C, can be made by following the path through node B

In real situations, people make evaluations of others based on local views of the world. To form an opinion about an unknown person, we turn to people we know and ask about the unknown person's reputation; in most cases, we do not rely on some centralized authority that determines the reputation each person deserves. One of the fundamental characteristics of this algorithm is that it is a purely local analysis. To infer a reputation rating starting at node A, the algorithm begins with A's neighbors and expands out. This means that node A may infer that node C has a very good reputation, while node D infers a poor reputation for node C. The difference will arise from the reputation ratings given along the paths from A to C and from D to C.

3.2   The Reputation Inference Algorithm

When performing an inference, the *sink* (*s*) is the node for which a rating is desired, and the *source* (*i*) is the node for whom the rating will be made. In this metric, the source polls each of the neighbors to which it has given a positive reputation rating. Neighbors with negative ratings are ignored, since their reputation means that they give unreliable information. Each of the source's trusted neighbors will return their rating for the sink. The source will then average these ratings and round the final value (i.e. a value between 0.5 and 1 rounds to a 1, while anything under 0.5 rounds down to 0). This rounded value is the inferred reputation rating from source to sink.

```
getRating(source, sink)
    numberOfNeighborsWithRatings = 0;
    sumOfRatings=0;

mark source seen
if sink is a direct neighbor of source
    source's rating of sink= rating(source, sink)
else
    for each n  adjacent to source
        if n is unseen and rating(source,n)>0
            if  n has no ratingOfSink
                mark n seen
                inferredRating = getRating(n,sink)
                if inferredRating >= 0
                    sumOfRatings   +=inferredRating
                    n's rating of sink = inferredRating
                    numberOfNeighborsWithRatings++
                mark n unseen
            else
                if n's rating of sink >= 0
                    sumOfRatings+=n's rating of sink
                    numberOfNeighborsWithRatings++

    if numberOfNeighborsWithRatings > 0
        source's rating of sink=

round(sumOfRatings/numberOfNeighborsWithRatings)

        else
            source's rating of sink = -1
    return source's rating of sink
```

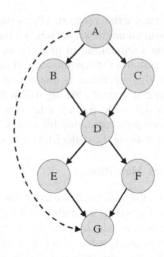

Fig. 3. An illustration of how nodes are used in the inference from node A to node G

Each of the source's neighbors will use this same process to come up with their reputation ratings for the sink– if there is a direct edge connecting them to the sink, the value of that edge is used; otherwise, the value is inferred. As shown in Figure 3, if a node is encountered in two paths from source to sink, it is considered in each path. Node B and C will both return ratings calculated through D. When a reputation rating from D is first requested, D will average the ratings from E and F. The value is then cached at D, so that the second time D's reputation rating is needed, no calculations are necessary.

Our system uses only 0 and 1 as reputation values. A value in the range [0,1] could be used, but the rounding in the algorithm will transform all of the values to 0 or 1 one iteration up from the nodes adjacent to the sink. Because of this, when a node polls its neighbors, it is essentially taking a majority vote. If half or more neighbors say that the sink has a good reputation, the average works out to be half or more, which rounds up 1.

3.3 Accuracy of Inferences

The quality of an inference can be measured by how accurate it is. Accuracy can be measured by choosing a source and sink that are connected, so the accrual rating that the source gives the sink is known. This edge from the source to the sink can be removed, and then the metric can be applied to infer a rating. Comparing the inferred rating to the actual rating will measure the accuracy of the metric. If the inferred values frequently match the actual values, the metric can be called highly accurate.

Accuracy will decrease when nodes along the path from source to sink return ratings different from the source's actual rating. Some of these differences will come from nodes with which the source would normally agree. Call these "good" nodes. Inaccuracy can also arise when nodes in the path occur that the source normally would disagree with. Call these "bad" nodes. The classification of "good" or "bad" will vary for each node, depending on which node is the source.

In reality, nodes will not be so easily categorized as "good" or "bad". However, the distinction makes this analysis clearer and does not diminish the quality of the results.

Bad nodes, which will produce many more inaccurate ratings than good nodes, are the largest threat to the quality of inferences in the network. At what points will results deteriorate? We will consider the worst case where "bad" nodes are always incorrect with their reputation ratings – they will always give the opposite rating that the source would give.

With this algorithm, the inference is accurate if a majority of the nodes return correct ratings. Since the bad nodes are always incorrect, the accuracy of the good nodes must compensate. Let b be the percentage of bad nodes in the network. Then g, the percentage of good nodes, is equal to $1-b$. Let p_a be the accuracy of the good nodes – how often the reputation ratings they give a node are consistent with what the source would give the node. To obtain a correct inference from a majority vote, we need

$$g * p_a \geq 0.5 \tag{1}$$

Let $a = g * p_a$. For a given graph with n nodes, the probability that the majority of the nodes will correctly rate the sink is given by the following formula:

$$\sum_{i=\lceil \frac{n}{2} \rceil}^{n} \binom{n}{i} a^i (1-a)^{n-i} \tag{2}$$

When $a \geq 0.5$, the probability that our inference is correct increases as the graph size increases.

$$\lim_{n \to \infty} \sum_{i=\lceil \frac{n}{2} \rceil}^{n} \binom{n}{i} a^i (1-a)^{n-i} \to 1 \tag{3}$$

The central limit theorem shows that for $a > 0.5$, the limit of the sum goes to 1 as the number of nodes goes to infinity. More specifically, if nodes are accurate at least half of the time, the probability that the summation will be 0.5 or greater increases as the population size increases. This is a critical point. As long as $g * p_a$ is greater than half, we can expect to have a highly accurate inference.

The formula above only gives the probability for the base level: nodes directly adjacent to the sink. As the algorithm moves up from the immediate neighbors of the sink toward the source, a will vary from node to node, but it will increase at each level. Figure 4 illustrates this point where the network starts with all good nodes, accurate in 70% of their classifications. After moving up three levels from the sink, the accuracy of the inference will be approximately 96%.

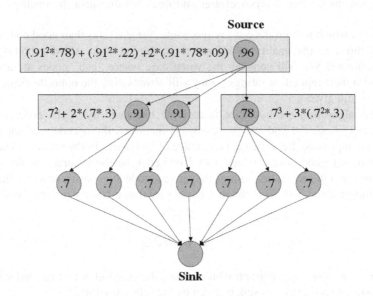

Fig. 4. This figure shows a simple network and demonstrates the increasing probability of accuracy. Beginning with a uniform accuracy of 0.7, the probability of properly classifying the sink increases as we move up the search tree from sink to source. After only three levels, this source has a 96% chance of properly classifying the sink

4 Experiments

The literature has demonstrated that both social and web-based systems exhibit small world behavior [4,6,7,18,22,24,29]. Because semantic reputation networks are essentially social networks that should have the small world properties, we used this model to automatically generate sample networks that were representative of what will occur in this domain. We used the ß-graph model [31] to generate small world graphs. Our main results are on graphs with 400 nodes, but similar results were achieved for graphs with 1000 nodes.

To test the effectiveness of this algorithm, we generated a series of small world graphs where one node was chosen as the source. We generated trust ratings from that source to every other node in the network for reference. To preserve the small world properties of the network, those ratings were not maintained as edges. A sink was randomly chosen in the graph and a rating from source to sink was inferred. The

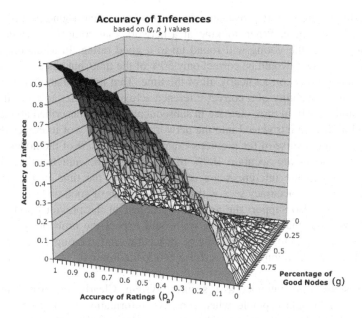

Fig. 5. A surface map illustration how the accuracy of inferences changes with respect to changes in g and p_a

accuracy of that inference was determined by whether or not it matched the source's rating. For each edge in the graph, a reputation rating was assigned. To make this a worst case analysis, every bad node (nodes that the sink rated a "0") rated each neighbor opposite of how the source rated it. This makes the bad nodes' ratings inaccurate 100% of the time. For the good nodes, ratings are correctly generated with probability p_a.

There are two variables in the network – percentage of good nodes, g, and the accuracy, p_a, of good nodes. If either variable were equal to 0, *every* inference would be inaccurate, so we did not include the 0 value for either variable in our experiments. Starting at 0.025 and using increments of 0.025, there are 1,600 pairs (g, p_a). For each pair we generated 1,000 small-world graphs with 400 nodes, and one inference was made and checked for accuracy on each graph. This created a smooth picture of the surface of the space.

As figure 5 shows, the accuracy of inferences remains very high, even as the accuracy of the initial ratings decreases. With no malicious nodes, inferences are 90% accurate for p_a as low as 65%. When attackers make up 10% of the population, inferences still remain over 90% accurate with p_a down to 0.75. With a population made up of 90% or more good nodes, the inferences actually remain more than 60% accurate, even when the initial ratings are below 40% accurate. Though initially this Seems to contradict the result presented in the previous section – the inaccuracy should actually grow as it propagates up the network – the rounding gives us one additional benefit here. When looking at a network that comprises primarily good nodes, any ties in the voting will round up to a good rating. In a random network, rounding up from 0.5 would be correct only 50% of the time, but since most nodes are good, rounding up is correct nearly all of the time. That means that after one level of inference, the probability of a correct inference actually increases to more than 50%. This probability will, in turn, increase in subsequent layers as described above.

As bad nodes are introduced into the network, the accuracy of inference drops off. For example, the inverse of the previous example – when 67% of the nodes are good, but the good nodes are accurate 100% of the time – does not translate to a high inference. Though the inferences are accurate 75% of the time in this case, it is nowhere close to the accuracy seen with the high number of good nodes.

These results also support the analysis described in the previous section and in Figure 4. Without that improvement, we would expect the probability of accurate inferences to be equal to the probability of an accurate initial rating – the variable a as presented above. As Figure 6 shows, for $p_a > 0.5$, the inferred value is always greater than a.

This system is *not* intended as a security system. Clearly, the error rates in this system would be unacceptable when sensitive information needs to be protected. However, its use as a system to make recommendations about the reputation of an information source is much better than most other recommendation systems [30]. In the recommendation context, our inferences are very accurate even in the face of exceptionally high uncertainty.

5 TrustMail: An Application

An ongoing project that has used these methods of reputation analysis is TrustMail [13]. TrustMail is an email client that looks up the mail sender in the reputation network and provides an inline rating for each email message. TrustMail can be configured to show trust levels for the mail sender either on a general level or with respect to a certain topic. Unlike spam filters that indicate which messages to ignore, reputation ratings in TrustMail can also tell users which messages are important to read.

Consider the case of two research groups working on a project together. The professors that head each group know one another, and each professor knows the students in her own group. However, neither is familiar with the students from the other group. If, as part of the project, a student sends an email to the other group's professor, how will the professor know that the message is from someone worth paying attention to? Since the name is unfamiliar, the message is not distinguishable from other, not-so-important mail in the inbox. This scenario is exactly the type of situation that TrustMail improves upon. The professors need only to rate their own students and the other professor. Since the reputation algorithm looks for *paths* in the

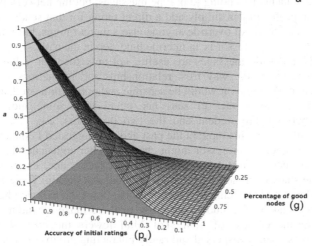

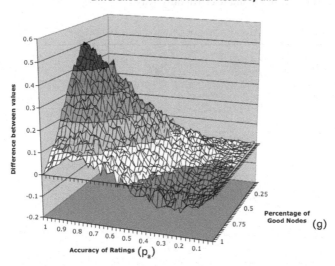

Fig. 6. The top surface chart shows the value of a ($g*p_a$), and the lower surface shows the difference between the inferred accuracy and the value predicted by a. Positive values indicate when the inferred value was higher than a, and negative values show when the inferred value was lower than a

graph (and not just direct edges), there will be a path from the professor one research group to students in the other through the direct professor to professor link. Thus, even though the student and professor have never met or exchanged correspondence, the student gets a high rating because of the intermediate relationship. If it turns out that one of the students is sending junk type messages, but the network is producing a high rating, the professor can simply add a direct rating for that sender, downgrading the reputation. That will not override anyone else's direct ratings, but will be factored into ratings where the professor is an intermediate step in the path.

The ratings alongside messages are useful, not only for their value, but because they basically replicate the way trust relationships and reputations work in social settings. For example, today, it would be sensible and polite for a student emailing a professor she has never met to start her email with some indication of the relationships between the student and the two professors, e.g., "My advisor has collaborated with you on this topic in the past and she suggested I contact you." Upon receiving such a note, the professor might check with her colleague that the student's claims were correct, or just take those claims at face value, extending trust and attention to the student on the basis of the presumed relationship. The effort needed to verify the student by phone, email, or even walking down the hall weighed against the possible harm of taking the student seriously tends to make extending trust blindly worthwhile. In the context of mail, TrustMail lowers the cost of sharing trust judgments across widely dispersed and rarely interacting groups of people. It does so by gathering machine readably encoded assertions about people and their trustworthiness, reasoning about those assertions, and then presenting those augmented assertions in an end user friendly way.

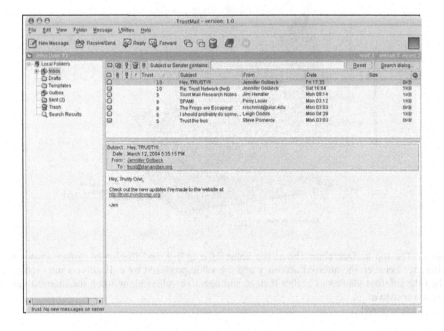

Fig. 7. The TrustMail Interface

6 Future Work

We have quite a bit of work in progress to extend the results presented here. The Trust Project, at http://trust.mindswap.org, provides a trust ontology that does not use the {-1.1} scale discussed here. Since users generally want a broader range of values, we provide a rating system from 1-10. Analyzing metrics for a range of values requires a variation on the theoretical approach described in this work. We adopted a weighted-average algorithm [14] and our early results show high accuracy, similar to the results here, with inferred values averaging within 1.16 of the actual value on the 1-10 scale. We plan continue work in this space by creating a strong theoretical connection between the results presented in this paper and the results on a continuous scale, and refining the algorithms.

One of the practical limitations of this work and the Trust Project is that they require explicit trust ratings to infer a trust rating. The data available for explicit trust networks is very limited, while the FOAF project's simple social network (people connected only by a "knows" relationship) has millions of people. We are currently developing an implicit trust metric that will make reputation recommendations based on the likelihood that two individuals may be connected. This implicit metric will open trust analysis to a much wider space of data. A longer-term project will integrate the implicit metric with explicit trust metrics to use both datasets together.

Acknowledgements

This work was supported in part by grants from DARPA, ARL, NSF, NIST, CTC Corp., Fujitsu Laboratories of America, NTT, and Lockheed Martin Advanced Technology Laboratories. The applications described in this paper are available from the Trust Project within the Maryland Information and Network Dynamics Semantic Web Agents Project at http://trust.mindswap.org/.

References

1. Adamic, L., "The Small World Web". *Proceedings of ECDL*, pages 443-- 452, 1999.
2. Adding SVG Paths to Co-Depiction RDF, http://Jibbering.com/svg/codepiction.html
3. The Advogato Website: http://www.advogato.org
4. Albert, R., Jeong, H. AND Barabasi, A.-L. "Diameter of the world-wide web." *Nature* **401**, 130–131, 1999.
5. Bharat, K and M.R. Henzinger. "Improved algorithms for topic distillation in a hyperlinked environment," *Proc. ACM SIGIR,* 1998.
6. Brin, S and L. Page, "The anatomy of a large-scale hypertextual Web search engine," *Proc. 7th WWW Conf.,* 1998.

7. Broder, R Kumar, F. Maghoul, P. Raghavan, S. Rajagopalan, R. Stata, A. Tomkins, and J. Wiener. "Graph structure in the web." *Proc. 9th International World Wide Web Conference*, 2000.

8. Deutsch, Morton. 1962. "Cooperation and Trust. Some Theoretical Notes." in Jones, M.R. (ed) *Nebraska Symposium on Motivation*. Nebraska University Press.

9. Dudek, C. (2003). "Visual Appeal and the Formation of Trust in E-commerce Web Sites." Unpublished Masters Thesis, Carleton University, Ottawa, Canada.

10. Dumbill, Ed, "XML Watch: Finding friends with XML and RDF." IBM Developer Works, http://www-106.ibm.com/developerworks/xml/library/x-foaf.html, June 2002.

11. FOAFBot: IRC Community Support Agent: http://usefulinc.com/foaf/foafbot

12. Gil, Yolanda and Varun Ratnakar, "Trusting Information Sources One Citizen at a Time," *Proceedings of the First International Semantic Web Conference (ISWC)*, Sardinia, Italy, June 2002.

13. Golbeck, Jennifer, Bijan Parsia, James Hendler, "Trust Networks on the Semantic Web," *Proceedings of Cooperative Intelligent Agents 2003*, August 27-29, Helsinki, Finland.

14. Golbeck, Jennifer, James Hendler "Reputation Network Analysis for Email Filtering." *Proceedings of the First Conference on Email and Anti-Spam*, July 30-13, 2004, Mountain View, California.

15. Kamvar, Sepandar D. Mario T. Schlosser, Hector Garcia-Molina, "The EigenTrust Algorithm for Reputation Management in P2P Networks", *Proceedings of the 12th International World Wide Web Conference*, May 20-24, 2003, Budapest, Hungary.

16. Kleczkowski, A. and Grenfell, B. T. "Mean-fieldtype equations for spread of epidemics: The 'small-world' model." *Physica A* **274**, 355–360, 1999.

17. Kleinberg, J, "Authoritative sources in a hyperlinked environment," *Journal of the ACM*, 1999.

18. Kumar, Ravi, Prabhakar Raghavan, Sridhar Rajagopalan, D. Sivakumar, Andrew Tomkins, and Eli Upfal. "The web as a graph". *Proceedings of the Nineteenth ACM SIGMOD-SIGACT-SIGART Symposium on Principles of Database Systems*, May 15-17, 2000.

19. Labalme, Fen, Kevin Burton, "Enhancing the Internet with Reputations: An OpenPrivacy Whitepaper," http://www.openprivacy.org/papers/200103-white.html, March 2001.

20. Levin, Raph and Alexander Aiken. "Attack resistant trust metrics for public key certification." *7th USENIX Security Symposium*, San Antonio, Texas, January 1998.

21. Milgram, S. "The small world problem." *Psychology Today* **2**, 60–67, 1967.

22. Moore, C. and Newman, M. E. J. "Epidemics and percolation in small-world networks." *Physical Review E* **61**, 5678–5682, 2000.

23. Mutton, Paul and Jennifer Golbeck, "Visualization of Semantic Metadata and Ontologies," *Proceedings of Information Visualization 2003*, July 16-18, 2003, London, UK.

24. Newman, Mark, "Models of the small world", *J. Stat. Phys.* 101, 819-841 (2000).

25. Open Privacy Initiative: http://www.openprivacy.org/

26. RDFWeb: FOAF: 'the friend of a friend vocabulary', http://rdfweb.org/foaf/

27. RDFWeb: Co-depiction Photo Meta Data: http://rdfweb.org/2002/01/photo/

28. Richardson, Matthew, Rakesh Agrawal, Pedro Domingos. "Trust Management for the Semantic Web," *Proceedings of the Second International Semantic Web Conference*, 2003. Sanibel Island, Florida.

29. Spertus, E, "ParaSite: Mining structural information on the Web," *Proc. 6th WWW Conf.,* 1997.
30. Swearingen, Kristen and R. Sinha. "Beyond algorithms: An HCI perspective on recommender systems," *ACM SIGIR 2001 Workshop on Recommender Systems*, New Orleans, LA, 2001.
31. Watts, D. Small Worlds: The Dynamics of Networks between Order and Randomness. Princeton, NJ: Princeton University Press, 1999.

Semantic Webs for Learning:
A Vision and Its Realization

Arthur Stutt and Enrico Motta

Knowledge Media Institute,
Open University, UK
{a.stutt,e.motta}@open.ac.uk

Abstract. Augmenting web pages with semantic contents, i.e., building a 'Semantic Web', promises a number of benefits for web users in general and learners in particular. Semantic technologies will make it possible to reason about the Web as if it was one extended knowledge base, thus offering increased precision when accessing information and the ability to locate information distributed across different web pages. Moreover, it will become possible to develop a range of educational semantic web services, such as interpretation or sense-making, structure-visualization, support for argumentation, novel forms of content customization, novel mechanisms for aggregating learning material, and so on. In this paper we provide a framework to show how Semantic Browsers which use ontologies to identity important concepts in a document as a means of providing access to associated educational services can be used in conjunction with Knowledge Charts (ontologically permeated representations of a community's knowledge) in a process we call Knowledge Navigation as an important new resource for learning.

1 Introduction

Augmenting web pages with semantic contents, i.e., building a 'Semantic Web', promises a number of benefits for web users in general and learners in particular. Semantic technologies will make it possible to reason about the Web as if it was one extended knowledge base, thus offering increased precision when accessing information and the ability to locate information distributed across different web pages. Moreover, it will become possible to develop a range of additional educational semantic web services, such as interpretation or sense-making, structure-visualization, support for argumentation, novel forms of content customization, novel mechanisms for aggregating learning material, and so on.

In this paper we provide a framework to show how semantic web technology can be harnessed to provide a much richer 'web experience' than that currently provided by web browsers and static web pages. In particular the ideas presented in these scenarios will be grounded on some of the work currently being carried out at the Knowledge Media Institute on semantic web browsing and on new forms of scholarly publishing.

E. Motta et al. (Eds.): EKAW 2004, LNAI 3257, pp. 132–143, 2004.

Of course, the semantic web, like any other attempt at formalizing knowledge, carries a risk: to simplify what is complex, to impoverish what is rich. For this reason it is important not to lose focus of what the technology should be about: it should support users in making connections, engaging in critical analysis, locating the right knowledge and navigating and making sense of alternative teaching narratives. If used correctly, this technology could provide a quantum leap in the level of support available to students.

1.1 The Semantic Web and Learning

If current research is successful there will be a plethora of e-learning platforms making use of a varied menu of reusable educational material or learning objects. For the learner, the Semantic Web will, in addition, offer rich seams of diverse learning resources over and above the course materials (or learning objects) specified by course designers. The annotation registries which provide access to marked up resources will make it possible for more focused, in some cases ontologically-guided (or semantic) search, to take place. This much is already in development. But we can go much further. Semantic Learning Webs (we believe there will never be a singular Learning Web) depend on four things: annotated educational resources, a means of reasoning about these, a means of retrieving the most suitable and a range of associated services. One important class of tool here is the Semantic Browser which uses ontologies to identity important concepts in a document and to provide access, via services, to relevant material.

1.2 Knowledge Charts, Navigation, Neighbourhoods

Briefly put, Knowledge Neighbourhoods are locations on the Web where communities collaborate to create and use representations of their knowledge - Knowledge Charts. These are browsed - in a process we call Knowledge Navigation - using Semantic Browsers. They are constructed, communally, using Semantic Constructors. Knowledge Charts are thus ontologically permeated representations of a community's knowledge or point of view.

In the rest of this paper we will say more about the notions of Semantic Browsers/Constructors, Knowledge Navigation and Knowledge Neighbourhoods. We will also examine the current state of the technologies needed to produce these, suggest ways in which they can be extended and combined and illustrate how they will act together to provide Semantic Learning Webs.

Before we do so we will say a bit about the pedagogic and practical needs of learners as they seek to interpret, and navigate through, the future Web. We will end with a brief discussion of how, armed with these new semantic tools, learners may be capable of becoming robustly critical thinkers, able not only to move easily through the surfeit of information sources but also to examine and critically assess the varied religious, scientific, economic, ethical and political claims and counter-claims which will find fertile ground on the Web.

2 Learning and Cognition

At a cognitive level students need environments which are congruent with what goes on in learning. We can distil learner needs into three categories: structure, relatedness and interpretation.

Structure. As Laurillard indicates [6], one central component of learning is coming to see structure. As the Web grows this ability will become even more important. Unless the learner can find a way to successfully navigate through and filter out irrelevancy, it will be more or less impossible to make use of the rich resources available on the web. In our view there are two main structures which can be used here and both of them can be aided by the use of ontologies: argumentation/debate, and narrative. Debate here includes the various scientific controversies which arise about notions such as continental drift, GM technology, global warming. These controversies are in themselves multi-dimensional since they often have ethical and economic/political aspects as well as scientific. Narrative here includes the historical account of how ideas change and evolve as well as the 'stories' we tell as a means of making sense of something (e.g., the story of the rise and fall of working class politics in the UK).

Relatedness. Part at least of the importance of structure is that it is a means of seeing something (a theory, concept, equation) as a whole. Equally important are the relations which link these to other ideas and theories. Both relate to Laurillard's discussion [6] of the need for the integration of parts.

Interpretation. The learner needs to be able to take a piece of learning material and situate it in a multidimensional space which includes at least: the social, economic and political context (an obvious example here is the GM debate); its place in the meta-narrative of advancement a science tells itself (e.g., Newton supersedes Copernicus, Quantum Physics finesses Newton); and, its role in an ongoing debate or conversation among academic stakeholders (e.g., the discovery of Archaeopteryx and the more recent Chinese feathered dinosaurs supports the notion that birds are dinosaur descendants).

In what follows we develop a vision of the use of the Semantic Web where:

- Learning is contextualized to specific locations in the Semantic Web (i.e., it is community related rather than generic);
- The structure of pieces of knowledge is given by Knowledge Charts and their Navigation tools;
- The charts represent structures (such as narratives, and arguments) using ontologies and provide access to them using graphical representations;
- Relatedness is given by these charts and by the links they provide to further learning resources;
- Interpretation is facilitated by the contextual knowledge these charts provide.

3   What Current Research on the Semantic Web and eLearning Offers: Getting Away from the Obsession with Learning Objects

Without going into a great deal of detail we can describe current research on learning and the (semantic) web as being centrally concerned with so-called Learning Objects (i.e., separable units of educational material which can be combined and reused in a variety of contexts). Central to their reusability are the descriptions which their designers provide using a variety of metadata schemes. Currently there are a number of standards in this area (see, for example, [1]) but it is likely that this number will be reduced with some standards combining and others being discarded as commercial and other pressures come into play.

Another development has been the growth in educational repositories and peer-to-peer networks for sharing these. One example here is the Edutella network [13].

At the same time as the means of sharing these objects has developed, work has also proceeded on adding detail to the metadata schemes in order that particular learning goals, object sequences, roles and activities (in short, a pedagogy) can be specified (see, for example, work on the Educational Modelling Language [4], [5]).

Most of this work has been accomplished without the use of explicitly semantic technologies. However, a natural development of the repositories and networks is the notion of ontology-based brokerages which match learners with learning materials [1] and course construction tools [15] which attempt to automatically combine learning objects into "courses" or sequences of objects.

More recently we have seen the development of educational semantic web services. An example here is the Smart Space for Learning approach using the Elena mediation infrastructure [14]. The services here range from assessment, to short lectures, courses and degree programmes.

There are two main points here. Firstly, the Semantic Web technologies depend for their success on the viability of the strategy of depending on reusable learning components, on the possibility of capturing the characteristics of these in formal descriptions using metadata schemes, on the widespread acceptance of these schemes and, finally and most importantly, on the likelihood that there will be enough incentive for learning object providers or others to annotate their products with the accepted metadata.

Secondly, while, Nejdl and his colleagues have advanced the notion of Educational Web Services, these are still based largely on learning objects. To this extent, their project may fail if learning objects fail to live up to their promise. However, it seems that their architecture may be generic enough to make use of any properly annotated World Wide Web content. Unlike Nejdl and colleagues, we envisage a form of educational service which can only be provided by the Semantic Web. For example it is possible to foresee a service which automatically re-creates the chain of reasoning used in discovering, say, the cause of the SARS outbreak, using unannotated Web pages.

However, our main problem with the learning object approach is that it seems to entail what we might call a Fordist model of education where the design process is seen as an assembly line with learning objects as the standardized components allowing mass production. This is a view of the Semantic web which limits the ways in which knowledge technologies can be deployed. We should be going beyond the static web with its Learning Objects, Portals, Pages, and Databases to a flexible, multi-layered, multiple-viewpoint, reasoning-oriented approach.

While much effort has been expended on learning objects and learning object repositories, from the Semantic Web perspective, the ontological commitments of the various contending metadata schemes are limited. In essence the metadata is intended to describe a learning object in sufficient detail for a human or other agent to be able to select it as appropriate in some learning context.

What we lack are any tags which can be used to indicate to a learner how the learning object may be contextualized. That is to say that there are no ontological relations in the learning object description which can indicate how an object should be interpreted, or how it fits into the central debates in the field. Faced with the current state of affairs a learner can successfully navigate the space of possible learning objects but cannot navigate the space composed of the far more important structures of relations which knit topics, concepts, examples and so on into the fabric of the disciplinary field.

For example in Earth/Climate Science there is much controversy about the notion of global warming. While most scientists accept that global warming is a reality and that it is caused by increased anthropogenic CO_2 emissions (e.g., the Intergovernmental Panel on Climate Change) there are others who either dispute the cause, the extent or reality of global warming. For instance Lomborg [8] has cast doubt on the quality of the IPCC models and has suggested that the costs of limiting CO_2 emissions far outweigh the benefits. In turn others have disputed the case Lomborg makes.

4 A Scenario

In the following scenario we explore the possible affordances of a Semantic Learning Web. The scenario is intended to give a more concrete form to our vision of a future learning environment based on Knowledge Charts, Knowledge Navigation, Knowledge Neighbourhoods and Semantic Browsing. It is important to emphasize that, while this scenario is visionary, many of the details are derived from ongoing work on the modelling of argumentation and semantic browsing. See the section on Realizing the Vision below for more details of this work.

We can imagine that our learner is reading a web page/document/learning object on climate change as part of some course on environmental studies. While some mention is made of alternative and competing viewpoints, this is not dealt with fully in the text. As she reads, our semantic system – let's call it SWEL for Semantic Web E-Learning - indicates portions of the text which it can assist with. In this case it can offer a way into the scientific debate/controversy about global warming and/or explain the scientific concepts involved.

The learner opts to access the scientific controversy. SWEL provides a graphical interface to the principal components of this debate. Figure 1 shows two levels of Knowledge Chart. Level 1 shows the structure of an argument linking CO_2 rise to climate change. Level 2 shows part of the ongoing scientific controversy about this linkage. Figures 2 and 3 show Lomborg's argument in slightly more detail.

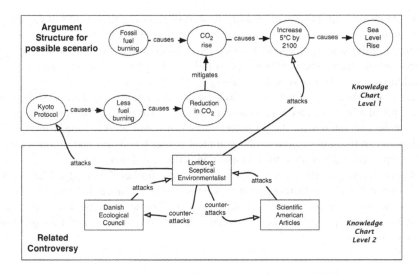

Fig. 1. A web of argumentation related to Global Warming

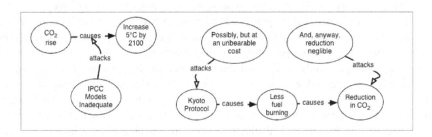

Fig. 2. Lomborg's arguments

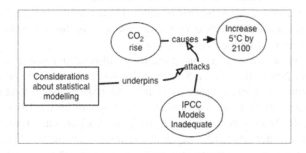

Fig. 3. Lomborg's arguments in more detail

The learner clicks on the "Lomborg Sceptical Environmentalist" node. This opens up to provide a more detailed version of Lomborg's argument. Basically Lomborg makes two points: (a) that the models used in the IPCC's calculations about the effects of CO_2 emissions are inadequate and (b) the cost of reducing the world's emissions by the negligible amount Kyoto would attain far outweighs the benefits.

Since Lomborg's argument about models is based on a view of what statistical models can do, the learner can now opt to follow a link to either a description of statistical models or a deeper view of Lomborg's argument here.

And so on. At each point in the debate model, the learner can access the original documents of which the model is a summary. In order for these to be of maximum use they can be annotated with the argument steps illustrated above using, for example, highlighting in the same colour as the graphical model for claims and grounds and so on. It is up to the learner how much annotation is displayed at any point.

Of course, any new document or Chart could have further Knowledge Charts associated with it which the learner can pursue in turn. For instance, Lomborg might appeal to various economic models in his reasoning. The learner could now decide to follow up links to pages or other Knowledge Charts on classical and ecology-based economic models.

5   Navigation of Knowledge Charts Using Semantic Browsers

As we have said, we envisage a new type or set of types of learning object (we call them Knowledge Charts) whose purpose is to provide pathways through controversies and narratives, and other structures such as analogies and expositions of scientific principles. Indeed, given the prevalence of documents filled with domain content, the system we envisage stands or falls on the existence of these meta-models. A whole new discipline concerned with the production of Knowledge Charts may spring up though it is more likely that they will be crafted by members of a particular learning community. Knowledge Charts (such as the several levels of argumentation and scientific controversy in Figures 1-3) differ from standard learning objects in that: they are built using ontologies, they include both content, annotation and associated graphical representations, they have a taxonomy, and, they are used both for navigation (viewed hypertextually) and interpretation (viewed conceptually). Knowledge Charts will probably be pre-constructed in the first instance. However, given the number of possible meta-learning objects for any course component, it is likely that we will have to find a means of automating their construction.

In order for the scenario to become a reality we also need a system which can perform Knowledge Navigation (i.e., a Semantic Browser). We can rely on our Semantic Browser to identify important concepts in learning objects using domain ontologies without demanding explicit annotation (although this will be used if available). The various traversals (from text to Chart, from Chart to Chart and from Chart to new material) require either explicitly expressed relations among the Charts (or Chart components) or depend on inferencing made possible by the domain and structure ontologies. For example, the system could have a set of rules which allow linkages from argument nodes (where theories are used to warrant particular claims) to Charts which represent the theory.

Note that while the illustrations given above in Figure 1 may indicate that Knowledge Charts are fixed, this is not so. Knowledge Charts reflect the points of view of an individual, a group or a community and as this knowledge may change it will be necessary for the individual or community to update their Knowledge Charts.

6 Knowledge Neighbourhoods

A Knowledge Neighbourhood can be viewed as a location in cyberspace where learners can congregate into groups or larger communities with the goal of acquiring knowledge about some topic. Knowledge Neighbourhoods are locations for possibly many virtual learning communities. Communities tend to be organized around their interest in particular topics which may range from something as wide-ranging as particle physics to something as specific as the use of mythology in Ovid. Communities are composed of a variety of members who fulfil different roles and enter into a variety of relations with each other. Members can belong to more than one community or group. For example a member may act as a leader in a particular community and have relations such as *sets-the-agenda-for* to other members. These roles and relations may change over time.

These semantic neighbourhoods for learning combine community support with educational semantic web services and are operationalized by providing portals though which their members interact. Underlying this are mappings from what is known about communities to services they provide.

The semantic web can support these communities in a variety of ways. Firstly, by providing ontologies for communities, community structures, roles, relations, spaces, topics, tasks, practices and so on, they can provide an accepted lingua franca for the community as a whole. And, since these neighbourhoods are relatively circumscribed, there will be fewer problems in formulating, negotiating and accepting these ontologies than if we attempted to provide global ontologies. Secondly, the semantic web community can provide a range of semantic web services which ensure that the community is built, maintained and flourishes. Specific services can assist with community tasks, such as intelligent search for topic-related information.

Knowledge important to the community will be annotated with ontologies relevant to the community. As we said in our introduction, it is unlikely that these ontologies will be generic - that in fact there will be a single Semantic Web for Learning. It is more likely that the Semantic Web for Learning, like Ancient Greece or Medieval Italy, will be composed of loosely related Knowledge Neighbourhoods.

7 Realizing the Vision: Technologies Available Now and Needed for SWEL

While the complete framework for Knowledge Navigation does not yet exist, enough of the necessary components are available for us to be confident that it could be available within the next few years.

Domain Ontologies. Both the ontologies and the means of representing them are already available. For instance, work is ongoing to devise a detailed ontology for the climate change domain.

Semantic Web Services for Learning. We need to do empirical research on the kinds of services learners require as well as on the tools we should provide for community construction of these. Currently we are considering services such as the following: Discovery Services, Summarization, Citation-makers, Interpretation, Structure visualization, Argumentation support, Argumentation discovery.

Service Infrastructure. The Knowledge Media Institute is one of the few research bodies involved in work on semantic web services (where an agent or service can reason about appropriate services and retrieve and configure these). The IRS-II infrastructure [9] provides service designers with the means of registering their services both in conventional and semantic registries. It also provides an environment for creating applications configured out of a number of these more primitive services. Currently, the demonstration system can schedule operations abroad for patients with arthritis and who need urgent hip replacement surgery, using primitive services such as hospital availability checkers and currency converters.

Ontologies for Argumentation-Based Knowledge Charts. There is already extensive support for scholarly argumentation in the ScholOnto project [2]. The ScholOnto project is developing an ontology-based digital library server to support scholarly interpretation and discourse with a rich set of relations (such as agrees with, is evidence for and so on) among papers.

Other Types of Knowledge Charts. There is embryonic support for representing and capturing narratives in the CIPHER project [10] which aims to support the exploration of national and regional heritage. This is accomplished by supporting online Cultural Heritage Forums (CHFs) where a community focussed on a specific theme or interest can browse or construct narratives relating to the theme or interest. For example, a CHF supports a community interested in communicating/recording narrative accounts of relevant experiences at Bletchley Park in Milton Keynes, UK where the Enigma encryption machine was deciphered during the Second World War.

Repositories for Structures/Charts. The ScholOnto tool provides the basis for a Knowledge Chart repository.

A Semantic Browser. This is perhaps the most important element in the idea of successful Knowledge Navigation. Our thinking here has been extensively influenced by the ongoing experiments with the Magpie semantic browser [3] in the Knowledge Media Institute. While Magpie can be used as a generic semantic web browser, it originated, in part, as a means of assisting in sense-making for participants in the Climateprediction.net experiment. This experiment, like the Seti@home project, makes use of the distributed computing resources of thousands of home computers, in this case, to run different versions of a climate model. Magpie provides access (via a contextual menu) to complementary sources of knowledge which can be used in contextualizing and interpreting the knowledge in a Web page. This is done by automatically associating a semantic layer to a Web page. This layer depends on one of a number of ontologies which the user can select. When an ontology is selected, the user can also decide which classes are to be highlighted on the Web page. Clicking on a highlighted item (i.e., an instance of a class from the selected ontology) gives access to a number of semantic services. For instance an ontology might contain the class 'Project'. Clicking on an instance of this class would provide access to Project details, Research Areas, Publications, Resulting Technologies, Members, Shared Research Areas and project Web Page. In the Climateprediction.net project access is to material which will help to make sense of statistical analyses of complex climate models as well as to the rich literature on climate modelling and climate change.

While Magpie is already capable of semantic browsing (linking from salient concepts to auxiliary material via services) it is currently unable to perform the sorts of complex linkages that would be required for Knowledge Navigation. We need extensions to enable it to link from text to Knowledge Charts, from Knowledge Chart to Knowledge Chart and from Knowledge Chart to alternative web documents. We also need extensions to its concept recognition abilities. Currently it is able to recognize only instances of concepts which are contained in its knowledge base. For example that ScholOnto is a project. There are already plans to make use of Human Language Technology, and in particular, information extraction tools, as a means of automatically identifying instances. This would ensure that textual items such as phrases referring to a project as well as texts in languages other than English would be identified as concept instances.

Note that Magpie does not require annotation of the Web page it operates on since it uses the ontology to pick out concepts to highlight. There is no reason why a full-scale Semantic Browser for Knowledge Charts should not make use of metadata when it is available.

The Semantic Writer/Constructor. This component of our system will assist in the creation of Knowledge Charts. Its main role is in providing the environment for learners and/or their teachers (and communities more generally) to construct, collaboratively, new Knowledge Charts which can represent the point of view of the community, the group of learners, the tutor or the individual learner. As well as assisting in the construction of Knowledge Charts the Semantic Constructor should be able to do all that is necessary to publish these (e.g., notify the registry, or reformat in RDFS). New work just started on Magpie will result in a system which can use information extraction to identify instances. This can also be used to create mark-up within documents thus providing a basis for the Semantic Construction of Knowledge Charts. This means that the extended Magpie will act as both Semantic Browser and Semantic Constructor.

Automated Construction of Knowledge Charts. As we said above, Knowledge Chart construction is the other side of the coin from Semantic Browsing, and an important activity for learning communities. However, some automated assistance in this will be needed. While there is ongoing work on the use of Human Language Technologies such as information extraction to identify concept instances in a text [16] more is needed for the identification of concepts from argumentation, narrative and other structural ontologies. Web resources could, but need not be, annotated with concepts from the various structural ontologies.

8 Related Work

One approach to e-learning, which has much in common with our notion of Knowledge Charts and their Navigation, has been developed at the Royal Institute for Technology (KTH) in Sweden by Naeve and colleagues. Their Gardens of Knowledge [11] are learning environments which can be used to explore networks of ideas. They are also developing [12] the idea of the Conceptual Web as a layer above the Semantic Web intended to make it more accessible to humans using graphical context maps which include concepts and relations among concepts. Conzilla is a concept browser which allows the user to navigate through a space of context maps to access associated content.

While the idea of graphical representations of domain concepts and their navigation are similar, our approach concentrates more on the elaboration of a typology of high level representations (of arguments, stories and so on) which can be used for navigation and sense-making. In addition, our Knowledge Charts are embedded in the social context of Knowledge Neighbourhoods and our Knowledge Navigation is performed by a tool - the Semantic Browser - which can make the necessary mappings from learning objects to learning objects as well as provide a range of ontologically-directed, community-oriented services such as automated argument construction. We also envisage another tool - a Semantic Writer/Constructor - which can construct or assist in the construction of Knowledge Charts.

9   Conclusion - Learning Webs and Critical Thinkers

The Web presents both challenges (e.g., the danger of information overload) and opportunities (e.g., the wealth of competing viewpoints). The Semantic Web (or Webs) will provide yet more opportunities for learning in the form of greater access to a multiplicity of diverse learning objects. It can also, as we have suggested, provide the means for learners to navigate through the plethora of sources, find help in their interpretation of material by contextualizing it to debates and narratives, and actively enter into these debates or construct these stories as members of living online communities of learners.

If we are to avoid the reductionism inherent in learning objects and related approaches and to support users in making connections, in engaging in critical analysis, in locating the right knowledge and in making sense of pedagogic narratives, we must provide a means of traversing the various links possible from web document to web document by means of Knowledge Charts which express the associated debates, narratives, and so on. By providing this in combination with a means of learner participation in these debates, using Knowledge Neighbourhoods, the learner becomes, not a passive recipient of knowledge, but the sort of critical thinker able to deal with the complexity of the material available in any future knowledge based society.

References

1. Anido, L. E., Fernández, M.J., Caeiro, M., Santos, J.M., Rodríguez, J.S., Llamas, M.: Educational metadata and brokerage for learning resources. Computers & Education Volume 38, Issue 4, (2002) 351-374
2. Buckingham Shum, S., Motta, E., Domingue, J.: ScholOnto: An Ontology-Based Digital Library Server for Research Documents and Discourse. International Journal on Digital Libraries 3 (3) (2000) 237-248

3   Dzbor, M., Domingue, J. B., Motta, E.: Magpie - towards a semantic web browser, In: Proc. Of the 2nd Intl. Semantic Web Conference, October 2003, Florida US (2003)

4. Koper, R.: From Change to Renewal: Educational Technology Foundations of Electronic Environments. Educational Technology Expertise Center, Open University of the Netherlands. (2000) Available from: eml.ou.nl/introduction/docs/ koper-inaugural-address.pdf

5. Koper, R.: Modeling Units of Study from a Pedagogical Perspective: The Pedagogical Meta-Model Behind EML. Educational Technology Expertise Center, Open University of the Netherlands. (2001) Available from: eml.ou.nl/introduction/docs/ped-metamodel.pdf

6. Laurillard, D.: Rethinking University Teaching: A Conversational Framework for the Effective Use of Learning Technologies. 2nd Edition. RoutledgeFarmer, London (2002)

7. Li, G., Uren, V., Motta, E., Buckingham Shum, S., Domingue, J.: ClaiMaker: Weaving a Semantic Web of Research Papers. 1st Int. Semantic web Conference (ISWC 2002), Sardinia (2002)

8. Lomborg, B.:The Skeptical Environmentalist. Cambridge: Cambridge UP, Cambridge (2001)

9. Motta, E., Domingue, J., Cabral, L., Gaspari, M.: IRS-II: A Framework and Infrastructure for Semantic Web Services. 2nd International Semantic Web Conference (ISWC2003) 20-23 October 2003, Sundial Resort, Sanibel Island, Florida, USA (2003)

10. Mulholland, P., Zdrahal, Z. Collins, T.: CIPHER: Enabling Communities of Interest to Promote Heritage of European Regions. Cultivate Interactive, issue 8, 15 November 2002. (2002) Available from: http://www.cultivate-int.org/issue8/cipher/

11. Naeve, A.: The Garden of Knowledge as a Knowledge Manifold - a Conceptual Framework for Computer Supported Subjective Education, CID-17, TRITA-NA-D9708, Department of Numerical Analysis and Computer Science, KTH, Stockholm (2002)

12. Naeve, A., Nilsson, M., Palmér, M.: E-Learning in the Semantic Age. Proc. 2nd European Web-based Learning Environments Conference (WBLE 2001), Lund, Sweden (2001)

13. Nejdl, W., Wolf, B., Qu, C., Decker, S. Sintek. M., Naeve, A., Nilsson, M., Palmér, M., Risch, T.: EDUTELLA: A P2P Networking Infrastructure Based on RDF. Proceedings Eleventh International World Wide Web Conference WWW2002, May 2002 (2002)

14. Simon, B., Miklós, Z., Nejdl, W., Sintek, M., Salvachua, J.: Smart Space for Learning: A Mediation Infrastructure for Learning Services. Proceedings of the 12th World Wide Web Conference, May, 2003 (2003)

15. Stojanovic, L., Staab, S and Studer, R.: ELearning Based on the Semantic Web. Proceedings WebNet2001, Orlando, Florida, USA, 2001 (2001)

16. Vargas-Vera, M., Motta, E. Domingue, J., Lanzoni, M., Stutt, A., Ciravegna, F.: MnM: Ontology Driven Semi-Automatic and Automatic Support for Semantic Markup. In: ed. Gomez-Perez, A. Proc. 13th International Conference on Knowledge Engineering and Management (EKAW 2002), Springer Verlag, Berlin (2002)

Enhancing Ontological Knowledge Through Ontology Population and Enrichment

Alexandros G. Valarakos[1,2], Georgios Paliouras[1],
Vangelis Karkaletsis[1], and George Vouros[2]

[1] Software and Knowledge Engineering,
Laboratory Institute of Informatics and Telecommunications,
National Centre for Scientific Research "Demokritos",
153 10 Ag. Paraskevi, Athens, Greece
{alexv, paliourg, vangelis}@iit.demokritos.gr
[2] Department of Information and Telecommunication Systems Engineering,
School of Sciences, University of the Aegean,
83200, Karlovassi, Samos, Greece
georgev@aegean.gr

Abstract. Ontologies are widely used for capturing and organizing knowledge of a particular domain of interest. This knowledge is usually evolvable and therefore an ontology maintenance process is required to keep the ontological knowledge up-to-date. We proposed an incremental ontology maintenance methodology which exploits ontology population and enrichment methods to enhance the knowledge captured by the instances of the ontology and their various lexicalizations. Furthermore, we employ ontology learning techniques to alleviate as much as possible the intervention of human into the proposed methodology. We conducted experiments using the CROSSMARC ontology as a case study evaluating the methodology and its partial methods. The methodology performed well enhancing the ontological knowledge to 96.5% from only 50%.

1 Introduction

The World Wide Web is the richest repository of information, whose semantics are oriented to humans rather than to machines. The enrichment of the Web with semantic annotations (metadata) is fundamental for the accomplishment of the Semantic Web [1], and is currently performed manually [2] or semi-automatically [3] [4] [5]. Semantic annotations associate information with specific entities within the domain of interest, aiming to facilitate a semantic-based interpretation of content by restricting their formal models of interpretation through ontologies. Domain entities are represented as instances of concepts in ontologies. A domain ontology captures knowledge in a static way, as it is a snapshot of knowledge concerning a specific domain from a particular point of view (conceptualization), in a specific time-period.

On the other hand, ontologies have the potential to organize and centralize knowledge in a formal, machine and human understandable way, making themselves an essential component to many knowledge-intensive services. However,

E. Motta et al. (Eds.): EKAW 2004, LNAI 3257, pp. 144–156, 2004.

due to changes concerning knowledge-related requirements and depending on the evolutionary tendencies of the domain of interest, a domain ontology might contain incomplete or out-of-date knowledge regarding its instances. For example, an ontology that has been constructed for the domain "laptop descriptions" last year will miss the latest processor types used in laptops. Moreover, the ignorance that an instance can appear with different surface appearances (lexicalizations) limits the knowledge of a domain captured in an ontology. For example, the ignorance that the instance 'Intel Pentium 3' can also appear as 'P III' or 'Pent. 3' is a serious knowledge leak for the modelling of the "laptop descriptions" domain. Thus, the maintenance of its captured knowledge is crucial for the performance of the application that uses it. Maintaining ontological knowledge through population and enrichment is a time-consuming, error prone and labor-intensive task when performed manually. Ontology learning can facilitate the ontology population and enrichment process by using machine learning methods to obtain knowledge from data.

In the context of ontology maintenance we employ ontology population and enrichment methods to enhance the knowledge captured in a domain ontology. We focus on the maintenance of the ontological instances and their various lexicalizations. We identify new instances for concepts of a domain ontology and add them into it (ontology population method). Moreover, we acquire a non-taxonomic relationship between instances (ontology enrichment method) that captures their different lexicalizations avoiding the existence of duplicate ontological instances. The latter is a problem that has not been given sufficient attention [6]. We integrate those methods in a proposed incremental methodology, which comprises the ontology population and enrichment methods aiming at the enhancement of the knowledge contained into the ontology concerning its ontological instances and their different lexicalizations. Furthermore, we employ machine learning methods for alleviating as much as possible the role of human into the ontology maintenance process.

In the next section we give information concerning the ontology of the information integration system CROSSMARC[1], which we used for our experiments for describing a case study. Then we present our incremental ontology population and enrichment methodology in section 3. Section 4 describes the experimental results on the population and enrichment of the domain ontology concerning laptop descriptions. Finally, we present the related work in section 5 and we conclude in section 6.

2   The CROSSMARC Ontology

The ontology that was used in our case study describes laptop products and has been manually constructed using the Protege-based[2] management system

---

[1] CROSSMARC is an R&D project under the IST Programme of the European Union (IST-2000-25366). http://www.iit.demokritos.gr/skel/crossmarc

[2] Protege Web Site: http://protege.stanford.edu/

developed in the context of the CROSSMARC project and will be public available at the CROSSMARC web site. The ontology was implemented in an xml dialect and consists of 'part-of ' relationship, which link the main concept, namely laptop, to its parts (e.g. processor, manufacturer, screen, price etc.) Additionally, there is a 'has attribute' property for each concept which links it either to another concepts (e.g. concept 'processor' has attribute 'processor name') which its range could be a string or a numeric data-type followed by its measurement unit (e.g. the concept 'Hard Disk' has attribute 'capacity' which its value is defined by an integer datatype followed by a measurement unit-the literal "G.B."). Also, there are constraints on the range of numerical data-types which are defined by a minimum and maximum value. Moreover, there is an 'instance-of' relationship that denotes the instances of the concepts, e.g. 'IBM' and 'Toshiba' instantiate the concept 'Manufacturer Name'. Furthermore, a lexical 'synonymy[3]' relationship associates the appropriate different surface appearances of an instance.

3   Knowledge Enhancement: Methodology

As we have already pointed out, in the context of our ontology maintenance methodology, we focus on the increase of ontological knowledge concerning the instances that exists in a domain of interest and of their lexical synonyms (different lexicalizations of an instance). Thus, we have to accomplish two subtasks: firstly to populate the ontology with new instances, and secondly, to acquire lexical synonymy relationships between the different lexicalizations of an instance. We employ an ontology population and enrichment method to deal with the first and second subtask, respectively.

The key idea is that we can keep the ontology instances and their lexical appearances up-to-date in a semi-automatic way, by periodically re-training an information extraction system using a corpus that contains the target knowledge and have been partially annotated (scattered annotations) using the already known instances captured in the ontology. The corpus is constructed gradually to secure the existence of new instances and their lexical synonyms, depending on the rate of domain instances' updates i.e. the ratio of the new instances to the already known that exist in the corpus for a specific time interval. The instances already in the ontology, as well as their lexical synonyms are used for annotating corpus' documents employing domain specific disambiguation methods in order to provide semantically consistent annotations (semantic consistency problem) i.e. according to our ontology the string 'Intel Pentium' is annotated only if it refers to processor name and not to something other e.g. company name. These scattered annotations constitute the training dataset that will be used for training the information extraction system.

---

[3] The meaning of this word is overridden; it refers mainly to the surface appearance of an instance rather to its meaning

3.1   Incremental Ontology Population and Enrichment

The incremental ontology population and enrichment methodology proposed, iterates through four stages:

1. Ontology-based Semantic Annotation. The instances of the domain ontology are used to semantically annotate a domain-specific corpus in an automatic way. In this stage disambiguation techniques are used exploiting knowledge captured in the domain ontology.
2. Knowledge Discovery. An information extraction module is employed in this stage to locate new ontological instances. The module is trained, using machine learning methods, on the annotated corpus of the previous stage.
3. Knowledge Refinement. A compression-based clustering algorithm is employed in this stage for identifying lexicographic variants of each instance supporting the ontology enrichment.
4. Validation and Insertion. A domain expert validates the candidate instances that have been added in the ontology.

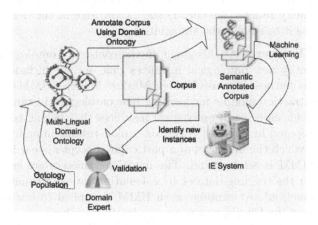

Fig. 1. Overall Method for Ontology Maintenance

Figure 1 depicts the above methodology which is presented in more detail in the following subsections.

Ontology-Based Semantic Annotation. The aim of this stage is to annotate a corpus with existing concept instances. This instance-based method differs from the semi-automated semantic annotation that has been proposed in the literature, as it intends to automatically annotate a document with metadata derived explicitly from the ontology at hand. Other methods (appear in section 5) can be characterized as concept-based as they intend to annotate all the potential instances that can be found in a corpus and belong to a particular concept. These methods usually exploit context-typed information using information extraction methods. Obviously, the instance-based semantic annotation is faster as it does not need to identify new instances but requires disambiguation techniques as the latter does as well. On its own, this method is sufficient when our knowledge about a domain is closed or when we are interested only in the known concept instances.

The semantic annotation of the corpus is currently performed by a string matching technique that is biased to select the maximum spanning annotated lexical expression for each instance. One problem with this method is the identification of properties, whose range of values is a numerical datatype followed by the corresponding measurement unit, e.g. dates, age, capacity. For example, the numeric string "32" could be an instance of ram memory or hard disk capacity. Those ambiguities are resolved by the exploitation of the measurement units e.g. if the "32" is being followed by the string "kb" then it is a ram memory's instance and if is being followed by the string "GB" then it is an instance of the hard disk capacity. Beyond exploiting measurement units (this knowledge is encoded in our ontology), properties are also identified by special rules that enhance string matching techniques by using again knowledge encoded in the ontology, such as the valid range of values that a property can take. For example, RAM capacity values range in a set that is different from the one that the Hard disk capacity ranges. We encode such knowledge in the definition of the concept and use it to resolve the ambiguities.

Knowledge Discovery. At this stage, in the context of ontology population, we aim to identify new ontological instances that are not included in the ontology. For this purpose, we use Hidden Markov Models (HMMs) to train an information extraction module for locating new ontological instances. We train a single HMM for each set of ontological instances that belong to a particular concept, as proposed in [7] and [8]. HMMs exploit tokens, intending to capture the context in which the instances of a particular concept appear in. The structure of each HMM is set by hand. The model parameters are estimated in a single pass over the training dataset by calculating ratios of counts (maximum likelihood estimation). At runtime, each HMM is applied to one document in the corpus, using the Viterbi procedure to identify matches.

The first stage of instance-based annotation provides training examples to the HMM. This ontology-driven machine learning approach differs from the classical supervised methods as it does not use human-provided training examples but examples provided by the domain ontology. After the training phase, the trained information extraction module is capable of recognizing new ontological instances for the concepts on which it has been trained. The extracted ontological instances constitute the set of candidate instances that will be validated by the domain expert in order to be inserted into the ontology.

Knowledge Refinement. This stage aims to reduce the amount of work required by the domain expert, by identifying different lexicalizations of the same ontological instance. For example, the processor name 'Pentium 2' can be written differently as 'Pentium II', 'p2', 'P II' or 'Intel Pentium 2'.

The identification of different lexicalizations of existing instances is performed by a novel compression-based clustering algorithm, named COCLU [9].This algorithm is based on the assumption that different lexicalizations of an instance use a common set of 'core' characters. Therefore, lexicalizations that are 'close' to this set are potential alternative appearances of the same instance, while those that are 'far' from this set are potentially related to a different instance.

COCLU is a partition-based clustering algorithm which divides the data into several subsets and searches the space of possible subsets using a greedy heuristic. Each cluster is represented by a model, rather than by the collection of data assigned to it. The cluster's model is realized by a corresponding Huffman tree which is incrementally constructed, as the algorithm dynamically generates and updates the clusters by processing one string (instance's lexicalization) at a time. The algorithm employs a new score function that measures the compactness and homogeneity of a cluster. This score function is defined as the difference of the summed length of the coded string tokens that are members of the cluster, and the length of the same cluster updated with the candidate string. The score function groups together strings that contain the same set of frequent letters according to the model of a cluster.

The use of COCLU is two-fold. Firstly, it can be used as a classifier which assigns a candidate string to the appropriate cluster-concept. A cluster is defined by an ontological instance and its synonyms. This scenario takes place when we want to discover synonyms only for the existing ontological instances. Additionally, COCLU can be used for discovering new clusters-concepts beyond those denoted by the existing ontological instances. In this way, COCLU can discover new instances in an unsupervised way.

Validation and Insertion. At this stage a domain expert should validate the candidate ontological instances as well as their synonyms that have been added to the ontology. At the end of this phase the method starts again from the first stage until no more changes are possible.

4   Experimental Results

We evaluated the performance of the incremental ontology population and enrichment methododology presented in section 3 on the laptop domain of the CROSSMARC project. Our intention is to evaluate the proposed method in acquiring all the knowledge that exists in the given corpus. We conducted experiments concerning the instance and concept-based semantic annotation as well as their combination to prove that is possible the innovative approach of training an information system exploiting the instances of a domain ontology, the knowledge captured in the ontology and a given domain-specific corpus, using automatically produced training examples. Moreover, the combination of the two methods (concept-based and instance-based) is possible to provide as with the appropriate knowledge. We also evaluated the COCLU algorithm in discovering instances that participate in the lexical synonymy relationship. Furthermore, we measured the performance of the method in discovering new ontological instances in its incremental mode.

The CROSSMARC laptop ontology covers all four languages examined in the project. However, we concentrated in the English instantiation, which consists of 119 instances. The corpus for English consists of 100 Web pages containing laptops' descriptions and is public available. The corpus processing was done using the text engineering platform Ellogon [10]. The proposed method requires the pre-processing of the corpus only from a tokenizer which identifies text tokens (e.g., words, symbols, etc.) in the Web pages and characterizes them according to a token-type tag set which encodes graphological information (e.g. the token is an English upper case word).

4.1 Knowledge Discovery

In order to investigate the tolerance of the method to the number of examples available for training the HMM, we performed three separate annotations of the training corpus using 75%, 50% and 25% of the initial ontology, respectively. These subsets represent the portion of the ontological knowledge that already exists in the corpus, as the corpus is constructed gradually. Therefore, the remaining documents in the corpus contain concept instances and their lexical synonyms that should be acquired. These subsets were constructed based on the evolution of the instances in time, thus simulating the real use of the methodology. For instance, in the laptop domain, 'Pentium' is a predecessor of 'Pentium 3'. Thus "Pentium" was selected to participate in the 25% of the initial ontology.

Applying the proposed methodology, we:

- annotated the corpus using the ontology
- used the annotated corpus to train the HMMs and
- applied the trained HMMs on the corpus to discover new ontological instances.

In case that annotations comprise inexact matches, the more precise ontology-based annotation was preferred over the HMM annotation. For example, when the same offset has been annotated by the HMM-based and ontology-based method the one that dominates and remains is the ontology-based method. The same happens when we have overlapping annotation offset between these methods.

The performance of the HMM-based and ontology-based annotation method as well as their combination was evaluated separately using the precision and recall measures. Table 1 shows average results for 5 concepts chosen from CROSS-MARC ontology and for an ontology size of 75%, 50% and 25%, respectively. We have chosen only the concepts for which new instances came out in a short period of time. The first row shows the results of applying the ontology-based method using the initial ontology. The second row shows the results of the trained HMM and the last row shows the results of their combination. It is worth noting that these results are limited to the first iteration of the methodology and at least one occurrence of an instance or a lexical synonym in the corpus is enough to indicate its successful discovery-annotation. However, the different sizes of the ontology used simulate, in a way, the iteration.

Examining the annotation using the original ontology, precision (P) was perfect, as expected. On the other hand, recall (R) was directly affected by the

Table 1. Semantic annotation results in the first iteration

Ontology	75%		50%		25%	
Method	P	R	P	R	P	R
Ontology-based	100	66.1	100	50	100	24.5
HMM-based	69.2	65.5	62.3	44.7	68	26.3
Combination	74	76	67	57.4	71.3	33.1

coverage of the ontology. The precision of the HMM-based annotation varied between 62.3% and 69.2%, while its recall was comparable to that of the ontology. However, the combination of the two methods performed better in terms of recall, as the HMMs provided new instances not included in the ontology. Furthermore, the precision of the combined approach was higher than that of the HMM-based annotation. Thus, the combination of the two methods seems like a viable approach to generating potential new instances for the ontology.

4.2   Knowledge Refinement

Table 2 measures the ability of COCLU to find lexical variations of correct concept instances. The grouping of instances can be considered to be classes whose members are different lexicalizations of an instance, hence are linked with the synonymy relationship. The experimental approach is similar to that presented above, i.e., we hide a number of randomly selected synonyms that are being linked with the instances of the selected concepts of the ontology and ask CO-CLU to classify them. The accuracy of the algorithm decreases as the number of hidden synonyms increases. However, it is encouraging that cluster's size can be further reduced to almost half of it without any loss in accuracy.

Table 2. Instance matching results for COCLU

Instance Reduction (%)	Correct	Accuracy (%)
90	3	100
80	11	100
70	15	100
60	19	100
50	23	95.6
40	29	96.5
30	34	94.1

We have also measured COCLU's ability to discover new ontological instances beyond the existing ones. These new ontological instances constitute new classes (herein they are named clusters) that their members have significantly different lexicalizations of the concept instances. To evaluate this method we hid incrementally from one to all clusters that have been constructed manually in the target ontology, measuring the algorithm's ability to discover the hidden clusters. We explored all possible combinations of hidden clusters. In all trials,

COCLU has re-generated all the hidden clusters. However, it was consistently splitting two of the clusters into smaller sub-clusters. In standard information retrieval terms, the recall of the algorithm was 100%, as it managed to generate all the required clusters, while its precision was 75%.

4.3   Method in Incremental Mode

In this experiment, we evaluated the improvement of the results as the methodology is iteratively applied (incremental mode) to the same corpus. Again we used 25%, 50% and 75% of the instances that exist in the target ontology as a starting point. Table 3 provides the results obtained by the experiment. Each row denotes the percentage of the initial concept instances used. Columns provide the number of the initial and target instances, as well as the number of instances annotated by the initial ontology (0th iteration) and by the system in each subsequent iteration. We do not count the multiple occurrences of an instance in the corpus but only one occurrence is enough to characterize the successful discovery of an instance. Also, it is worth noting that the method locates all the instances that are able to be discovered until the 2nd iteration. After this iteration no further improvement is noticed.

Table 3. Evaluation of the overall method

Initial Ontology	Initial Instances	Target Instances	0-th Iteration	1-st Iteration	2-nd Iteration	Final Coverage
25%	15	58	23	7	3	82.7%
50%	28	58	20	5	3	96.5%
75%	40	58	14	3	0	98.7%

The number of iterations required to retrieve most of the instances depends on the size of the initial concept instances, but is generally small. Starting with only 50% of the target instances the method succeeds to populate the ontology increasing its coverage from 48.3% to the 96.5% of the target instances in 2 iterations. It is worth noticing that a study on the evolution rate of a domain can indicate us with the exact time period in which the proposed methodology should be applied for keeping up-to-date the ontological knowledge. If the ontology contains at least the 50% of the instances that exist in the corpus, the methodology secures 96.5% coverage of the knowledge contained in the corpus.

5   Related Work

Ontology population can be characterized as the evolution of semantic lexicon learning task [11] [12] as the main difference between them is the formalism of the resource (dictionary of words with semantic category labels or an ontology) that accumulates the instances and will be populated with new one. The richer representation power of an ontology can bootstrap the task of learning exploiting knowledge encoded in it. This happens at the semantic annotation stage of our methodology.

The task of semantically annotating a corpus from several resources (ontologies, thesaurus, semantic lexicons or combination of them) has been researched by many works. As stated in section 3.1.1 we discriminates this task into concept and instance based approaches. The latter one concerns the recognition of all the instances that exist in the ontology and appear in the corpus [13]. A more sophisticated extension of this method usually uses disambiguation techniques to support the correct attribution of an instance sense according to the ontology used and the context in which the instance occurs [14]. The concept based approach, aims to discover new instances beyond those exist in the ontology, employing information extraction techniques [15] [16]. This approach is one step before be characterized as ontology population approach. Its missing part is the insertion of new concept instances under the appropriate concept of the ontology.

Various approaches based on information extraction methods have already been used for ontology population. Most of them uses information extraction systems to locate (mark up) the concept instances relying on manually annotated corpus [3]. Some of them face the semantic consistency problem allowing the human to evaluate the training examples that will later feed the information extraction system [17]. In contrast to Ciravegnia's work, our work relies entirely on the automatic creation of the training corpus exploiting the ontology-based annotation method which uses the knowledge encoded in the ontology when semantic ambiguities rise. Furthermore, we deal with the identification of typographic variations of an instance and their population. Those typographic variations are used in the semantic annotation stage as constitute part of our ontological knowledge. In [5] the problem is posed as a named entity recognition problem that uses linguistic analysis processes and manual crafted rules for identifying instances in documents. Although, this work intend to identify domain-independent name entities, the use of manual crafted rules are biased by the format of the documents. Moreover, all these approaches pre-process the corpus with various linguistic processes (e.g. part-of-speech tagging, morphological analysis, chunking etc.) whereas our approach uses only a tokenizer, hence it is faster.

The problem of the existence of instances that refer to the same entity is dealt in [18] using heuristic comparison rules. The same problem is being met in the database community as the existence of duplicate records [19] and in the Natural Language Processing community as the name matching problem [20]. We deal with this problem developing a machine learning algorithm named CO-CLU which exploits character typed information supporting a particular lexical synonymy relationship that is being implicitly used by many applications.

6 Conclusions

We have presented an incremental methodology for ontology maintenance, exploiting ontology population and enrichment techniques. Following the objective of CROSSMARC project for quick adaptation to new domains and languages we devised a methodology for efficient maintenance of the CROSSMARC ontology. This is crucial in the context of CROSSMARC, as the ontology has a key role in the functions of most of CROSSMARC components.

The proposed methodology uses the ontology for automatically annotating a domain specific corpus exploiting disambiguation methods which use domain specific knowledge encoded in the ontology. The annotated corpus is then used to train an information extraction system. The trained system identifies new candidate instances which are processed by a compression-based algorithm in order to discover lexical synonyms among them. Finally the candidate instances and the proposed lexical synonyms are validated by a domain expert. The method iterates until no new instances are being found.

We conducted experiments using the ontology and the corpus of a CROSS-MARC domain (laptops' descriptions) in one of the project languages (English). We evaluated each stage of the proposed methodology separately as well as the overall methodology. The initial results obtained are encouraging. The coverage of the ontology increased to 96.5% starting from a coverage of only 50%. Also, the clustering algorithm COCLU performed quite well assigning with 95.6% success a candidate instance to the correct cluster indicating the new instance that participates in the lexical synonymy relationship. It also managed to discover new pair of instances that are associated with the lexical synonymy relationship.

Concluding, the combination of the ontology-based method with the HMM-based annotation method gave very good results on a corpus of web pages with semi-structured content exploiting only token type information. Also, the incremental mode of the method indicates that the 50% of the instances that exists in the corpus is adequate enough for acquiring the 96.5% of the total instances.

In addition to the need for further experimentation of the proposed method, we plan to do large-scale experiments. The disambiguation technique used in our approach, which is driven by the measurement units, proved to work well but further research on this direction should be done for establishing this approach reliable enough. Also, we plan to investigate the discovery of instances realizing other types of synonymy relationships by extending the COCLU algorithm to identify them. Furthermore, we plan to support the semi-automatic maintenance of ontologies implemented in OWL, providing a platform that will centralize all these supportive tools.

References

1. Berners-Lee, T., Hendler, J., Lassila, O.: The semantic web. (Scientific American)
2. Kahan, J., Koivunen, M., Prud'Hommeaux, E., Swick, R.: An open rdf infrastructure for shared web annotations. In: The WWW10 Conference, Hong Kong (May 1-5, 2001)

3. Vargas-Vera, M., J., E.M., Domingue, Lanzoni, M., Stutt, A., Ciravegna, F.: Mnm: Ontology driven semi-automatic support for semantic markup. In: EKAW conference. (2002)
4. Vargas-Vera, M., Motta, E., Domingue, J., Shum, B.S., Lanzoni, M.: Knowledge extraction by using an ontology-based annotation tool. In: K-CAP. (2001)
5. Popov, B., Kiryakov, A., Kirilov, A., Manov, D., Ognyanoff, D., Goranov, M.: Kim - semantic annotation platform. In: The 2nd International Semantic Web Conference (ISWC2003). Volume 2870 of LNAI., Springer Verlag (2003)
6. Harith, A., Kim, S., Millard, D.E., Weal, M.J., Hall, W., Lewis, P.H., Shadbolt, N.R.: Automatic ontology-based knowledge extraction and tailored biography generation from the web. IEEE Intelligent Systems 18 (2003)
7. Freitag, D., McCallum, A.K.: Information extraction using hmms and shrinkage. In: Workshop on Machine Learning for Information Extraction (AAAI-99). (1999) 31–36
8. Seymore, K., McCallum, A.K., Rosenfeld, R.: Learning hidden markov model structure for information extraction. Journal of Intelligent Information Systems 8 (1999) 5–28
9. Valarakos, A., Paliouras, G., Karkaletsis, V., Vouros, G.: A name matching algorithm for supporting ontology enrichment. In: Proceedings of SETN. Volume 3025 of LNAI., Samos-Greece, Springer Verlag (May 2004)
10. Petasis, G., Karkaletsis, V., Spyropoulos, C.D.: Cross-lingual information extraction from web pages: the use of a general-purpose text engineering platform. In: Proceedings of the RANLP'2003 International Conference, Borovets, Bulgaria (2003)
11. Riloff, E., Jones, R.: Learning dictionaries for information extraction. In: Proceedings of the Sixteenth National Conference on Artificial Intelligence (AAAI-99). (1999)
12. Phillips, W., Riloff, E.: Exploiting strong syntactic heuristics and co-training to learn semantic lexicons. In: Proceedings of the 2002 Conference on Empirical Methods in Natural Language Processing (EMNLP 2002). (2002)
13. Volk, M., Ripplinger, B., Vintar, S., Buitelaar, P., Raileanu, D., Sacaleanu, B.: Semantic annotation for concept-based cross-language medical information retrieval. International Journal of Medical Informatics 67 (December 2002)
14. Dill, S., Eiron, N., Gibson, D., Gruhl, D., Guha, R., Jhingran, A., Kanungo, T., Rajagopalan, S., Tomkins, A., Tomlin, J.A., Zien, Y.: Semtag and seeker: Bootstrapping the semantic web via automated semantic anotation. In: The 12th International World Wide Web Conference (WWW2003), Budapest, Hungary (20-24 May, 2003)
15. Valarakos, A., Sigletos, G., Karkaletsis, V., Paliouras, G.: A methodology for semantically annotating a corpus using a domain ontology and machine learning. In: RANLP International Conference. (2003)
16. Dingli, A., Ciravegnia, F., Wilks, Y.: Automatic semantic annotation using unsupervised information extraction and integration. In: Workshop on Knowledge Markup and Semantic Annotation (KCAP). (2003)
17. Brewster, C., Ciravegna, F., Wilks, Y.: User-centred ontology learning for knowledge management. In: 7th International Conference on Applications of Natural Language to Information Systems. Volume 2253 of Lecture Notes in Computer Science., Springer Verlag (2002)

18. Alani, H., Kim, S., Millard, D.E., Weal, M.J., Hall, W., Lewis, P.H., Shadbolt, N.: Web based knowledge extraction and consolidation for automatic ontology instantiation. In: Workshop on Knowledge Markup and Semantic Annotation (K-Cap'03), Sanibel Island, Florida, USA (2003)
19. Cohen, W., Ravikumar, P., Fienberg, S.: A comparison of string distance metrics for name-matching tasks. In: Proceedings of IIWeb Workshop. (2003)
20. Bontcheva, K., Dimitrov, M., Maynard, D., Tablan, V., Cunningham, H.: Shallow methods for named entity co-reference resolution. In: Proceedings of TALN, Nancy (24-27 June, 2002)

Refactoring Methods for Knowledge Bases

Joachim Baumeister, Frank Puppe, and Dietmar Seipel

Department of Computer Science,
University of Würzburg, 97074 Würzburg, Germany
Phone: +49 931 888-6740, Fax: +49 931 888-6732
{baumeister, puppe, seipel}@informatik.uni-wuerzburg.de

Abstract. The manual development of large knowledge systems is a difficult and error-prone task. In order to facilitate extensions to an existing knowledge base the structural design of the implemented knowledge needs to be improved from time to time. However, experts are often deterred even from important design improvements since some restructurings are too complex to handle.

In this paper, we introduce a framework that allows for automated refactorings. Refactoring methods are well-defined and are executed in a semi-automated way. In this manner, the developer is supported during the process of restructuring of even large knowledge bases. Refactoring methods are usually applied to improve the design of the knowledge base; in this paper, we sketch some design anomalies that identify poor design of the knowledge base.

1 Introduction

Although knowledge systems have been established in many domains over the last years, the development and maintenance of such systems is still a costly and time-consuming task. Large knowledge systems are commonly build in a manual way, i.e., domain specialists are modeling the knowledge bases by hand and formalize the knowledge using specialized tools. Also the maintenance and extension of the knowledge bases is usually done by the specialists themselves.

In the last years we have gained experience in projects with building large diagnostic knowledge systems, mainly in the medical domain. For example, the HEPATOCONSULT system [4] is a publicly available consultation and documentation system for the diagnosis of liver diseases. A subsystem of HEPATOCONSULT is the SONOCONSULT system [10], which is in routine use in the DRK-hospital in Berlin/Köpenick, Germany. The practical installation of further systems, such as the ECHODOC system [13] (formerly QUALITEE), in a hospital environment is currently implemented.

An important aspect of knowledge system development is the continuous adaptation and extension of already deployed knowledge bases. Often, these modifications consider the improvement of the knowledge base design, i.e., the simplification and generalization of certain aspects of the available knowledge. However, changing existing and often large knowledge bases is not a simple problem, since unstructured modifications can cause unexpected deficiencies and errors.

E. Motta et al. (Eds.): EKAW 2004, LNAI 3257, pp. 157–171, 2004.

1.1   Refactoring, Restructuring and Refinement

We present refactoring methods for the save modification of diagnostic knowledge bases. Such restructurings are initiated by the domain specialist in order to improve the design of the knowledge base. The main focus of the presented approach is the improvement of the knowledge base design. Since even simple changes of knowledge objects can imply subsequent and complex adaptations of the remaining knowledge base the domain specialist should be supported by specialized tools.

The introduction of such restructurings for a step-wise and algorithmic modification of the knowledge base was inspired by *refactoring methods* introduced for software engineering [5, 14]. Here, refactoring considers the improvement of existing software code without changing the external behavior of the program. The implementation of refactorings is quite risky, especially for large systems. Therefore, refactoring methods are strongly connected with appropriate test methods. However, when performing a refactoring method the accompanying tests (e.g., unit tests) need to be adapted, and this is mostly done manually. In contrast to software engineering we can see that refactoring methods for knowledge bases often take advantage of the declarative nature of knowledge and test knowledge, respectively. Thus, refactoring methods for knowledge systems often can propagate their changes to the corresponding test knowledge, e.g., by modifying the respective objects in test cases.

The work on refactoring methods for knowledge bases is related to the concept of *KA scripts* of Gil and Tallis [7]. KA scripts and refactoring methods are both designed for supporting the knowledge engineer with complex changes of the knowledge. However, refactoring methods are focussing on improving the design of the knowledge base, whereas KA scripts mainly try to assist the user during extensions of knowledge bases. Thus, the application of refactoring methods is driven by detected design anomalies, whereas KA scripts try to provide methods for preserving a usable state of the knowledge after a manual modification of the knowledge base.

The refinement of the knowledge base performed by restructuring methods differs from *refinement techniques*, e.g., described by Boswell and Craw [3] or Knauf et al. [12]. Thus, refactoring is usually not applied for improving the accuracy of the system, but for improving the design of the knowledge base. Especially for this reason a refactoring method is currently applied manually, while supported by automated adaptations of attached knowledge. In ontological engineering [8] the problem of restructuring ontologies has been also recognized. For example, Góméz-Pérez and Rojas-Amaya [9] describe an approach for reengineering ontologies for reuse that consists of the three activities *reverse engineering*, *restructuring*, and *forward engineering*. Although no procedural methods were given for implementing the restructuring activity some typical concepts for refactoring the design of an ontology with a subsequent validation were discussed.

1.2   Basic Definitions

We consider the refactoring of diagnostic knowledge bases using instances of the domain ontology as given in the following.

Let Ω_Q be the universe set of all *questions* available in the application domain. The type of a question $q \in \Omega_Q$ depends on the domain $dom(q)$, i.e. the range of values for the answers to the question q. The value range can define

- numerical values for reals or integers,
- symbolic values with either one-choice or multiple-choice answers, and
- arbitrary content for text answers.

The assignment of a value $v \in dom(q)$ to a question $q \in \Omega_Q$ is called a *finding*, and we define $\Omega_{\mathcal{F}}$ to be the set of all possible findings in the given problem domain; a finding $f \in \Omega_{\mathcal{F}}$ is denoted by $q\!:\!v$. Each finding f is defined as a possible input of a diagnostic knowledge system. Questions concerning specific areas of the application domain are grouped into question sets. A *question set* Q contains a list of questions that are semantically related, i.e. $Q \subseteq \Omega_Q$.

A *diagnosis* is representing a possible output of a diagnostic knowledge system. We define $\Omega_{\mathcal{D}}$ to be the universe of all possible diagnoses for a given problem domain. With respect to a given problem a diagnosis $d \in \Omega_{\mathcal{D}}$ is assigned to a symbolic state $dom(d) = \{not\ probable,\ unclear,\ suggested,\ probable\}$.

A *case* is defined as a tuple $c = (\mathcal{F}_c, \mathcal{D}_c)$, where $\mathcal{F}_c \subset \Omega_{\mathcal{F}}$ is a set of findings given as input to the case. Often $\mathcal{F}_c$ is also called the set of *observed findings* for the given case. The set $\mathcal{D}_c \subseteq \Omega_{\mathcal{D}}$ contains the diagnoses describing the solution of the case c. The set of all possible cases for a given problem domain is denoted by Ω_C. We call a collection of cases $CB \subseteq \Omega_C$ a *case base*.

A *rule* $r = cond(r) \rightarrow action(r)$ consists of a rule condition $cond(r)$ containing disjunctions, conjunctions, and/or negations of arbitrary findings $F \in \Omega_{\mathcal{F}}$ or assigned diagnosis states, and a rule action $action(r)$, that is executed if the rule condition evaluates to true in a given case. The rule is called an *abstraction rule*, if the action assigns a value $v \in dom(q)$ to a question $q \in \Omega_Q$. Alternatively, an action $d\!:\!s$ of a *scoring rule* can assign a certainty score s to a given diagnosis $d \in \Omega_{\mathcal{D}}$. The dialog of the system, i.e., presenting questions and question sets to the user, is controlled by *indication rules*; such rules indicate a list of questions or a list of question sets in their rule action. We define $\Omega_{\mathcal{R}}$ to be the universe of all possible rules for a given universe of diagnoses $\Omega_{\mathcal{D}}$ and a given universe of questions Ω_Q; we call $\mathcal{R} \subseteq \Omega_{\mathcal{R}}$ a *rule base*.

2   A Framework for Refactoring Methods

When a knowledge system is build in an evolutionary way the design of the knowledge base needs to be improved by refactorings from time to time. The refactoring is motivated by the fact that the knowledge base is extended incrementally and consequently the knowledge design becomes messy. Furthermore, the use of the knowledge system in a real life environment can reveal overdetailed or unused knowledge objects, such as unneeded diagnoses or questions that are never answered. However, since the modification of (large) knowledge bases can be a difficult and error-prone task it is suggestive to propose structured approaches for such modifications.

It is worth mentioning, that refactoring methods differ from ordinary knowledge modifications: Refactoring methods provide an exact procedure describing the particular modification of the knowledge base, and they include all possible consequences for connected knowledge elements. For example, with the modification of a knowledge object the required adaptations and possible conflicts for the implemented knowledge are described. With the adaptation of such knowledge also the adjustment of the accompanying test knowledge is discussed.

Furthermore, refactoring methods differ from ordinary modifications with respect to their tight connection with automated test methods. For an automated application of tests the expected result of a test needs to be known beforehand. A commonly used automated test method is *empirical testing*, i.e., running a collection of previously solved cases and comparing the stored solution with the result derived by the knowledge system. There exist further tests that could be executed without any additional test knowledge like cases, e.g., anomaly testing [15]. The general procedure for the application of refactoring methods is as follows:

1. The actual refactoring is motivated by the detection of a design anomaly, or by a complex extension of the knowledge base.
2. An appropriate refactoring method is selected for the task.
3. An automated test suite is used for inspecting the valid behavior of the knowledge base. A refactoring cannot be applied, if the tests uncover an invalid behavior.
4. The refactoring method is performed with respect to the mechanics given in the methods description.
5. After the successful application of the method the test suite is again used for validating the behavior of the knowledge base. The method can only applied successfully if no errors have occurred.

In the context of this paper we consider rules and cases as possible representations for diagnostic knowledge. It is worth noticing, that case-based knowledge is not only suitable for diagnostic reasoning, but can be also used as test knowledge, e.g. by the application of empirical testing. In the next section we sketch some situations that typically point to design anomalies in the knowledge base. Based on such anomalies the knowledge base can be refactored in order to improve the design.

3   Design Anomalies in Knowledge Bases

With the manual construction of knowledge systems the design of the knowledge base often becomes complex over the time. For example, the level of detail for some findings turns out to be too specialized or findings/diagnoses are contained in the knowledge base, but are actually not used. Since refactorings are applied in order to simplify knowledge design it is important to discuss some typical examples of bad knowledge design. Such *design anomalies* are related to the classical definition of anomalies, e.g. described for rule bases by Preece and Shinghal [15]. Here, the knowledge base is checked for containing redundant, ambivalent or circular rules. According to Preece and Shinghal anomalies are not errors but are symptoms for probable errors in a knowledge base. Analogously, Iglezakis et al. [11, 18] introduced quality measures for the detection of design anomalies for case-based knowledge. In the context of this paper we focus on areas in the knowledge base that are mainly responsible for worsening the knowledge design. The understandability and maintainability of the system can be improved by modifying these areas, which we call *design anomalies*. In software engineering research design anomalies are often identified as *bad smells* in software code as described by Fowler [5];

we have adapted the concept of bad smells to knowledge design, and synonymously use the terms bad smell and design anomaly.

Although no exact metrics can be given for identifying such smells we want to introduce some situations in which a bad smell is probable. We do not give an exhaustive list of design anomalies but sketch some typical settings that are *smelly*.

Lazy Knowledge Object. The use of the implemented knowledge objects like findings and diagnoses is an important issue for the design of knowledge systems. If the finding or diagnosis is never used or used very infrequently in the real life environment, then the deletion of the object should be considered in order to simplify the knowledge design; fewer objects included in the knowledge base improve its simplicity. In such a case the methods REMOVEDIAGNOSIS and REMOVEQUESTION are appropriate refactorings. However, such an anomaly should be considered very carefully: of course, detected diagnoses or questions that are used very infrequently but can be used functionally in the problem domain, usually should not be removed from the knowledge base. Nevertheless, the detection of a lazy object can identify abandoned entities that have no more a functional meaning in the present version of the system, and can be therefore deleted without reducing the derivational power of the system.

Overdetailed Question. For a choice question the range of possible values may be too detailed in the used application. For example, the developer of the system has defined the five values in

$dom(temperature) = \{very\ low, low, normal, high, very\ high\}$

for a question *temperature*. During the following development of the knowledge base it turns out that a less detailed value range with only three possibilities is more suitable, e.g., *low*, *normal*, and *high*. In such cases, the method COARSENVALUERANGE can be used. Alternatively, the level of detail can be reduced by converting a question with a numerical domain into a choice question with a discrete and ordered value range; then, the refactoring method TRANSFORMNUMINTOOC is appropriate.

Lengthy Dialog. If the end user has to enter the findings manually, then the dialog efficiency of the knowledge system is an important issue to consider. Lengthy dialogs with many unnecessary questions are often perceived to be annoying and can critically affect the practical success of the implemented system. If the dialog turns out to be too long and too verbose for the end users, then the method EXTRACTABSTRACTION can be used to replace a list of original questions by a single, semantically equivalent and abstracted question. Alternatively, the method EXTRACTQUESTIONSET can be used to divide a large question set into a list of smaller questionnaires. Further modifications can improve the dialog capabilities by omitting extracted question sets that are perceived to be irrelevant.

Finding Clump. The rules defining the diagnostic knowledge for particular diagnoses frequently contain the same collection of findings. The design of the rule base may be simplified, if this *clump of findings* is substituted by a single finding representing an abstraction of the jointly occurring findings, i.e., using the EXTRACTABSTRACTION method. Then, complex rule conditions can be simplified by replacing the finding clump with the abstraction finding. However, the finding clump is very difficult to eliminate if the combined occurrence of the findings mean a disproportionate confirmation or disconfirmation of a diagnosis. It is very difficult, to map such reenforcing observations to a single abstraction, automatically.

Besides the bad smells mentioned above there exist various others mainly depending on the actual knowledge representation. For detecting some of the sketched design anomalies we can provide simple tests, e.g., using a sufficiently large case base with real life cases lazy objects can be easily identified by counting their occurrences in the cases. A question can be assumed to be overdetailed, if there exist similar rules, i.e., rules with equivalent rule action that only differ in assigned question values contained in the rule condition. In the following section we introduce the refactoring methods COARSENVALUERANGE and EXTRACTQUESTIONSET in detail and briefly describe other methods related to the described design anomalies.

4   A Catalog of Refactoring Methods

Refactoring methods are defined in a template-like from in order to allow for a convenient and simple application. Each refactoring method is described by the following seven elements.

Name	A short and meaningful name is chosen in order to simplify the identification of the particular methods. The names are used to build a vocabulary of refactoring methods.
Summary	A description of the method summarizing the functionality of the refactoring method.
Motivation	A collection of situations in which this refactoring method should be applied, e.g. referring to design anomalies.
Consequences	A report of experienced conflicts and restrictions, when applying this refactoring method. Additionally, hints are given as work-arounds in the case of a conflict.
Mechanics	A description of the actual refactoring method in an algorithmic and step-wise style.
Example	A simple example is given depicting the application of the refactoring method.
Related methods	An enumeration of related (e.g. inverse) refactoring methods.

Using this framework we can define a catalog of refactoring methods describing the particular modifications of a knowledge base in more detail. The developer can decide about an appropriate refactoring by simply browsing the catalog and retrieving the possible conflicts given in the consequences section.

The consequences of each refactoring strongly depends on the applied knowledge representation. In the context of this paper we only consider rule-based and case-based knowledge as possible representations; in [1] we also discussed the consequences for further types of knowledge, e.g. causal set-covering models. In the following, we provide (shortened) catalog entries of the methods CoarsenValueRange and ExtractQuestionSet.

CoarsenValueRange

Reduce the size of the value range of a choice question in order to scale down the granularity – interactive tool support can be provided.

Motivation

Often domain experts start implementing the ontological knowledge with choice questions providing detailed value ranges. During ongoing development the value range of some questions turns out to be unnecessarily precise, e.g. an overdetailed question. Furthermore, a smaller value range may simplify the dialog for the end-users, e.g. a lengthy dialog.

Consequences

Let $q \in \Omega_Q$ be the selected choice question with value range $dom(q)$. For the execution of the method the developer has to specify a transformation function $t : dom(q) \rightarrow dom'(q)$, which maps the values of the original value range to the values of the reduced value range.

Redundancies and conflicts can be caused due to the mapping to a smaller value range. The applied knowledge, i.e. the rule base $\mathcal{R}$ and case base CB, is investigated in oder to detect conflicts. The following conflicts can arise:

Rule-Based Knowledge

Creation of identical sub-conditions:

Due to the refactoring two rules with identical sub-conditions can be created.

Choice question, *or* condition

For choice questions the rule condition can contain an *or* condition of two equivalent sub-conditions that were originally referring to different choice values and have been mapped to the same value. One of the two equivalent sub-conditions can be deleted automatically in order to remove this redundancy.

Multiple-choice question, *and* condition

If the refactored question is a multiple-choice question, then the rule condition can contain an *and* condition of two equivalent sub-conditions targeting the same transformed choice value. This redundancy can be automatically removed by deleting one of the equivalent sub-conditions.

Creation of identical conditions:
The refactoring method modified two rules so that their conditions are equal. This can cause ambivalent and redundant rules.

Redundant rules

If all rules with identical rule condition contain an equal rule action, then all except one rule can be deleted automatically.

Ambivalent rules

The refactoring method can cause a conflict by creating ambivalent rules, i.e., rules with equal rule condition but different rule action.

Abstraction rules: A different value of the same question is derived by two rules with the same condition. The rules are presented to the user in order to resolve this conflict by manual adaptation.

Scoring rules: There exist two rules with identical rule condition, that derive a (different) state for a single diagnosis. By default, the rules are replaced with a newly created scoring rule with the same rule condition and a score aggregated from the original scores. However, the aggregated rule is presented to the user for a subsequent adaptation.

Case-Based Knowledge

Similarity knowledge needs to be adapted according to the transformation function. Refactored cases can cause redundant and ambivalent cases.

Identical cases

If two cases $c, c' \in CB$ have an identical set of findings and an equal set of diagnoses, i.e., $\mathcal{F}_c = \mathcal{F}_{c'}$ and $\mathcal{D}_c = \mathcal{D}_{c'}$, then by default the cases remain in the case base, and the developer has to decide manually about a possible deletion.

Ambivalent cases

If two cases $c, c' \in CB$ have an identical set of findings but a different set of diagnoses, i.e., $\mathcal{F}_c = \mathcal{F}_{c'}$ and $\mathcal{D}_c \neq \mathcal{D}_{c'}$, then by default the cases remain in the case base. However, for specialized case bases, e.g., defining test cases, ambivalence denotes a semantic contradiction, and therefore this conflict can require the method to be canceled.

Mechanics

The refactoring method is performed by the following procedure:
1. Apply the test suite to the knowledge system and abort, if errors are reported.
2. Select the choice question $q \in \Omega_Q$ for which the value range $dom(q)$ should be reduced; define a new value range $dom'(q)$ for q; $|dom'(q)| < |dom(q)|$.
3. Define a transformation function $t : dom(q) \rightarrow dom'(q)$, which maps the original values $v \in dom(q)$ to the new values $v' \in dom'(q)$. Usually, $dom'(q) \subset dom(q)$ and $t(v) = v$ for all $v \in dom'(q)$.
4. Adapt the available test knowledge with respect to the new value range $dom'(q)$, e.g., modify test cases containing findings $q{:}v$.

5. Modify the knowledge attached to question q according to the transformation function t. During the mapping of the values of q check for conflicts as described in the *Consequences* section.
6. Apply the test suite to the refactored knowledge system and cancel the refactoring method, if errors are reported; alternatively start a debug session.

Example

The one-choice question *"temperature"* (*temp*) with the value range

$$dom(temp) = \{very\ low,\ low,\ normal,\ high,\ very\ high\}$$

is too detailed and should be simplified by the value range

$$dom'(temp) = \{low,\ normal,\ high\}\,.$$

The developer defines a transformation function t given by the following table:

$dom(temp)$	$dom'(temp)$
very low	*low*
low	*low*
normal	*normal*
high	*high*
very high	*high*

Originally, the following rules connected with the question *temp* are contained in the knowledge base (with diagnosis *"infection"* and question set QS):

$$r_1 : temp{:}high \lor temp{:}very\ high \rightarrow infection{:}s_{suggested}$$
$$r_2 : temp{:}high \rightarrow indicate(QS)$$
$$r_3 : temp{:}very\ high \rightarrow indicate(QS)$$

After the application of the refactoring method we obtain the following rules:

$$r_1' : temp{:}high \lor temp{:}high \rightarrow infection{:}s_{suggested}$$
$$r_2' : temp{:}high \rightarrow indicate(QS)$$
$$r_3' : temp{:}high \rightarrow indicate(QS)$$

The rule r_1' contains a redundant sub-condition and is further reduced. Since the rule r_2' and r_3' are equal we also remove rule r_3'. We obtain the following final rules:

$$r_1'' : temp{:}high \rightarrow infection{:}s_{suggested}$$
$$r_2'' : temp{:}high \rightarrow indicate(QS)$$

Related Methods

n/a

EXTRACTQUESTIONSET

An existing question set is divided into two question sets by extracting a collection of questions from the original question set into a newly created question set – automated tool support can be provided.

Motivation

The number of questions contained in one question set may accumulate during the continuous development of the ontological knowledge. In order to facilitate a more compact and meaningful representation of the available questions large question sets can be partitioned into smaller chunks containing semantically related questions. If the *lengthy dialog* smell is detected, then this method is often applied as a first step. In subsequent steps the rules indicating the extracted question sets are modified in order to provide an optimized and reduced dialog.

Consequences

The behavior of the implemented dialog is affected, since extracted questions are not indicated any more. Let $Q = \{q_1, \ldots, q_n\}$ be the original question set with $q_i \in \Omega_Q$, and $Q' = \{q_k, \ldots, q_m\}$ be the questions extracted from Q, i.e., $Q' \subseteq Q$.

Indication Rules

During the execution of the refactoring method we need to consider all indication rules targeting the question set Q. All rules indicating Q are modified so that they are also indicating the extracted question set Q'. Here, the order of indication is an important aspect: If the first question of the extraction set is the first question of the original question set Q, i.e., $q_k = q_1$, then we indicate Q' before Q; otherwise, Q is indicated before Q'. With this procedure the original indication sequence often can be preserved.

If follow-up questions $q \in Q$ are extracted without their parent question, then indication rules targeting q are modified so that they are indicating the extracted question set Q'.

Mechanics

The refactoring method is performed by the following procedure:

1. Apply the test suite to the knowledge system and abort, if errors are reported. Especially, consider the test knowledge for the dialog behavior.
2. Select the question set Q and define the question set $Q' = \{q_k, \ldots, q_m\}$ with $q_i \in Q$ to be extracted.
3. Create a new question set Q' at the position after the question set Q.
4. Move questions $\{q_k, \ldots, q_m\}$ to the question set Q'.
5. Modify indication rules that target the original question set Q and follow-up questions contained in Q (see *Consequences* section).

6. Apply the test suite to the refactored knowledge system and cancel the restructuring method, if errors are reported; alternatively start a debug session. Especially, consider the test knowledge for the dialog behavior.

Example

The question set "*lab tests*" (*labtest*) with questions "*red blood cell*" (*rbc*), "*white blood cell*" (*wbc*), "*lt1*", and "*lt2*" should be simplified;

$$labtest = \{\, rbc, wbc, lt1, lt2 \,\} \,.$$

The questions "*rbc*" and "*wbc*" should be extracted to a new question set considering the blood parameters (*bp*). The following rule is contained in the knowledge base

$$r_1 = cond(r_1) \rightarrow indicate(labtest) \,.$$

With the transformation we obtain the question sets $labtest = \{\, lt1, lt2 \,\}$ and $bp = \{\, rbc, wbc \,\}$, and the rule is modified as follows

$$r_1' = cond(r_1) \rightarrow indicate(bp, labtest) \,.$$

The generated question set is indicated before the original question set because the first question of "*labtest*", i.e. the question "*rbc*", is extracted to "*bp*".

Related Methods

COMPOSEQUESTIONSETS (inverse).

Further Refactoring Methods

We briefly sketch the following refactoring methods REMOVEDIAGNOSIS, REMOVEQUESTION, TRANSFORMNUMINTOOC, and EXTRACTABSTRACTION.

REMOVEDIAGNOSIS *and* REMOVEQUESTION. These methods are executed if the corresponding diagnosis or question was detected as a lazy object. However, simply deleting the object can cause conflicts within the related knowledge. For example, if the object is contained in a rule condition, then the developer has to decide (e.g., by a default value) whether to delete the entire rule or only the affected sub-conditions. Furthermore, the deletion of the objects can cause deficiencies, such as ambivalent or redundant cases. Default settings can support the developer by removing deficient cases automatically.

TRANSFORMNUMINTOOC. This refactoring method converts a numerical question into an one-choice question, and is only applicable if the numerical value range can be disjointly partitioned given the available knowledge for the numerical question. Otherwise, the method is aborted. The generated partitions are mapped to choice values. Consequently, the generated value range is an ordered sequence. Notice, that often a post-processing of the generated partitions is reasonable, e.g., by defining a more coarse value range. Rule conditions containing the numerical questions are mapped to a choice value according to the disjunctive partition. Analogously, findings contained in cases are mapped to a choice finding. With a given definition of the partition this method can be fully automated.

EXTRACTABSTRACTION. A conjunction F of findings can be aggregated into an abstract finding f using the EXTRACTABSTRACTION refactoring method:

1. A new rule is created: the rule action is f, and the rule condition is given by F.
2. All rules using F in their rule condition are modified such that the modified rule condition contains f instead.

Case-based knowledge is not changed by the EXTRACTABSTRACTION method by default, i.e., the aggregated findings are not replaced with the abstract finding f. More generally, we can introduce rules of the form

$$r = q_1{:}X_1 \wedge \ldots \wedge q_n{:}X_n \rightarrow q{:}(X_1, \ldots, X_n),$$

where the X_i are variable symbols which can be instantiated by values $v_i \in dom(q_i)$, for refactoring several rules at the same time. If a rule condition contains a conjunction $F = q_1{:}v_1 \wedge \ldots \wedge q_n{:}v_n$ which is an instance of the condition of r, then we can replace it by the corresponding instance $f = q{:}(v_1, \ldots, v_n)$ of the action of r. Observe that the domain of the new abstract question q is the cross product of the domains of the original questions: $dom(q) = dom(q_1) \times \ldots \times dom(q_n)$. In many cases a subsequent editing of the modified rules r and the abstract question q by the user is necessary. E.g., using COARSENVALUERANGE we can condense the cross product to a simpler domain.

5   Automated Refactorings with d3web.KnowME

The system d3web.KnowME is a highly integrated workbench for the development of diagnostic knowledge systems. d3web.KnowME is the successor of the knowledge acquisition tool of D3 [16], which has been successfully applied in many medical, technical, and other domains. The workbench offers visual editors for implementing various types of knowledge, e.g., heuristic rules, case-based knowledge, and model-based approaches. Furthermore, the development process is supported by an automated test tool and a (preliminary) refactoring browser. The significance of combining refactoring methods with automated tests during the development of knowledge systems was discussed in [2]. The implementation of the test tool provides advanced methods for the identification of bad smells, e.g. lazy knowledge objects or integrity tests for detecting anomalies in knowledge. Furthermore, the correctness of the knowledge can be validated by, e.g., empirical testing and unit cases. The refactoring browser is under development, and currently only offers simple methods for the extraction/composition of question sets and for the modification of the type of questions, e.g. transforming a multiple-choice question into a set of semantically equivalent yes/no questions. A further extension of the browser by more sophisticated methods, that consider an interactive resolution of generated conflicts, is planned and will be available in the near future. A recent version of the d3web system can be downloaded at `http://www.d3web.de`.

6 Conclusion

We have introduced a structured approach for the automated modification of diagnostic knowledge systems. Refactoring methods are very useful for changing the design of (large) knowledge bases. When compared to refinement techniques the main goal of the presented methods is not the improvement of the system's accuracy, but the design of the implemented knowledge. Such refactorings of the knowledge are commonly initiated by the developer and are motivated by design anomalies detected in the design of the knowledge base. Furthermore, the knowledge is often restructured in order to facilitate a simplified extension of the knowledge base in a subsequent step.

In large knowledge systems design changes are complex and error–prone. For this reason, developers commonly avoid even important changes. We propose to use automated tools for these tasks but claim that structural approaches for the modification of knowledge are a necessary requirement for the application of automated tools. Thus, a method can be supported by interactive wizards that perform the implied adaptations.

The *automatization* of the refactoring and consequent adaptations allows for the accomplishment of even complex changes of a knowledge base, that were very difficult to perform manually in the past. For example, the reduction of a symbolic value range (performed by the method COARSENVALUERANGE) can imply the change of hundreds of rules and thousands of test cases if applied to a real world knowledge base. Hence, such modifications were not performed in the past, even if indicated by experience gained by a real world application of the system.

Due to the limited space a comprehensive catalog of typical refactorings could not be given in this paper; only two refactorings methods were described and some others were sketched. In [1] more methods are introduced in detail and in conjunction with the implications for rule-based, case-based, and set-covering knowledge. Furthermore, appropriate test methods for the refactoring methods are discussed.

We have described refactoring methods that consider the modification of small spots of the knowledge base. In the future we are planning to work on larger methods, i.e., *big refactorings*, that are applied in order to modify the entire design of the knowledge base. A promising motivation for big refactorings is the integration of *knowledge formalization patterns*. The idea of knowledge formalization patterns [17] is comparable to design patterns [6] known from software engineering, by providing a guideline for the developers on how to formalize and structure their knowledge. Appropriate refactoring methods can support the developer in modifying an existing knowledge base so that it complies with the specification of a pattern.

Since the definition and implementation of new refactoring methods is a complex task, we are developing methods for specifying refactorings in a declarative way. For this purpose we use a semi-structured knowledge representation based on XML, and we apply logic-based methods for managing and updating. The proposed approach was already applied for querying and visualizing knowledge bases, and presented in [19]. Such visualization techniques are especially useful for the inspection of (parts of) the knowledge base before starting a refactoring.

References

1. Joachim Baumeister. *Agile Development of Diagnostic Knowledge Systems*. PhD thesis, University Würzburg, Germany, 2004.
2. Joachim Baumeister, Dietmar Seipel, and Frank Puppe. Using Automated Tests and Restructuring Methods for an Agile Development of Diagnostic Knowledge Systems. In *Proceedings of the 17th International Florida Artificial Intelligence Research Society Conference (FLAIRS-2004)*. AAAI, 2004.
3. Robin Boswell and Susan Craw. *Organizing Knowledge Refinement Operators, In: Validation and Verification of Knowledge Based Systems*, pages 149–161. Kluwer, Oslo, Norway, 1999.
4. Hans-Peter Buscher, Ch. Engler, A. Führer, S. Kirschke, and Frank Puppe. HepatoConsult: A Knowledge-Based Second Opinion and Documentation System. *Artificial Intelligence in Medicine*, 24(3):205–216, 2002.
5. Martin Fowler. *Refactoring. Improving the Design of Existing Code*. Addison-Wesley, 1999.
6. Erich Gamma, Richard Helm, Raplh Johnson, and John Vlissides. *Design Patterns. Elements of Reusable Object-Oriented Software*. Addison-Wesley, 1995.
7. Yolanda Gil and Marcelo Tallis. A Script-Based Approach to Modifying Knowledge Bases. In *Proceedings of the 14th National Conference on Artificial Intelligence and 9th Innovative Applications of Artificial Intelligence Conference (AAAI/IAAI)*, pages 377–383. AAAI, 1997.
8. Asunción Gómez-Pérez, Mariano Fernándes-López, and Oscar Corcho. *Ontological Engineering*. Springer Verlag, 2004.
9. Asunción Gómez-Pérez and Dolores Rojas-Amaya. Ontological Reengineering for Reuse. In *Proceedings of the 11th European Workshop on Knowledge Acquisition, Modeling and Management (EKAW 1999)*, pages 139–156, 1999.
10. Matthias Hüttig, Georg Buscher, Thomas Menzel, Wolfgang Scheppach, Frank Puppe, and Hans-Peter Buscher. A Diagnostic Expert System for Structured Reports, Quality Assessment, and Training of Residents in Sonography. *Medizinische Klinik*, 3:117–22, 2004.
11. Ioannis Iglezakis and Thomas Reinartz. Relations between Customer Requirements, Performance Measures, and General Case Properties for Case Base Maintenance. In *Proceedings of the 6th European Conference on Case-Based Reasoning (ECCBR 2002)*, LNAI 2416, pages 159–173, Aberdeen, Scotland, 2002. Springer Verlag.
12. Rainer Knauf, Ilka Philippow, Avelino J. Gonzalez, Klaus P. Jantke, and Dirk Salecker. System Refinement in Practice – Using a Formal Method to Modify Real-Life Knowledge. In *Proceedings of 15th International Florida Artificial Intelligence Research Society Conference 2002 Society (FLAIRS-2002)*, pages 216–220, Pensacola, FL, USA, 2002.
13. Karl-Werner Lorenz, Joachim Baumeister, Christian Greim, Norbert Roewer, and Frank Puppe. QualiTEE - An Intelligent Guidance and Diagnosis System for the Documentation of Transesophageal Echocardiography Examinations. In *Proceedings of the 14th Annual Meeting of the European Society for Computing and Technology in Anaesthesia and Intensive Care (ESCTAIC)*, Berlin, Germany, 2003.

14. William F. Opdyke. *Refactoring Object-Oriented Frameworks.* PhD thesis, University of Illinois, Urbana-Champaign, IL, USA, 1992.
15. Alun Preece and Rajjan Shinghal. Foundation and Application of Knowledge Base Verification. *International Journal of Intelligent Systems*, 9:683–702, 1994.
16. Frank Puppe. Knowledge Reuse among Diagnostic Problem-Solving Methods in the Shell-Kit D3. *International Journal of Human-Computer Studies*, 49:627–649, 1998.
17. Frank Puppe. Knowledge Formalization Patterns. In *Proceedings of PKAW 2000*, Sydney, Australia, 2000.
18. Thomas Reinartz, Ioannis Iglezakis, and Thomas Roth-Berghofer. On Quality Measures for Case Base Maintenance. In *Proceedings of the 5th European Workshop on Case-Based Reasoning (EWCBR 2000)*, pages 247–259, 2000.
19. Dietmar Seipel, Joachim Baumeister, and Marbod Hopfner. Declaratively Querying and Visualizing Knowledge Bases in XML. In *Proceedings of the 15th International Conference on Applications of Declarative Programming and Knowledge Management (INAP 2004)*, pages 140–151, 2004.

Managing Patient Record Instances Using DL-Enabled Formal Concept Analysis

Bo Hu, Srinandan Dasmahapatra, David Dupplaw,
Paul Lewis, and Nigel Shadbolt

IAM Group, ECS, University of Southampton, SO17 1BJ, UK
{bh, sd, dpd, phl, nrs}@ecs.soton.ac.uk

Abstract. In this paper we describe a general logic-enabled Formal
Concept Analysis (FCA) approach to manage patient record instances. In
particular, the conceptual model of the domain is represented as a breast
cancer imaging ontology using a Description Logic (DL)-based web ontology modelling language, DAML+OIL. Patient records are treated as
instances with regard to the ontology. We studied a knowledge base (KB)
with 1,500 anonymous cases (2,200 abnormality instances), whose routine management functionalities, e.g. instance retrieval, instance introduction, KB visualisation and navigation, are driven by a DL-enabled
FCA engine. We demonstrate that our approach is capable of conveying not only the syntactic but also the semantic information, presenting
direct visual correlations between logic formulae (intent) and instants
(extent) in the knowledge base and facilitating a user-friendly graphic
interface easing the knowledge management processes for people with
limited expertise on knowledge engineering.

1 Introduction

Knowledge management systems in the medical domain can fulfill a variety of
roles, from decision support systems for diagnostics to the storage, indexing
and retrieval of patient records. In a system that we are developing in order
to support the multi-disciplinary meetings wherein patient management decisions for the treatment of breast cancer are undertaken, we have implemented a
range of such knowledge management components, in an ontologically mediated
fashion. A multi-disciplinary meeting involves radiologists, histopathologists, cy-
topathologists, clinical nurses, surgeons and oncologists each contributing a facet
of expert judgement on the patient's condition. A rule of thumb in deciding on
a course of action at such a meeting is to go by the most pessimistic prognosis
from any of the specialists involved.

Radiologists specialise in reading X-ray mammograms and other imaging systems like magnetic resonance (MR) and ultrasound, picking out tell-tale signatures of malignancy. Histopathologists analyse stained slices of extracted (biop-
sied) tissue under a microscope and describes the histologist's view of the mi-
croscopic features. Clinicians and surgeons are aware of the patient, her history,
prior medical and treatment states and so on. To have an ontologically mediated

E. Motta et al. (Eds.): EKAW 2004, LNAI 3257, pp. 172–186, 2004.
© Springer-Verlag Berlin Heidelberg 2004

system, adequate descriptions of all these domains need to be captured, which is what we have undertaken in the project. However, even though all these facets as described by various medical specialists are stored away, indexed against the relevant domain ontologies, they have to be pulled together at the time of the multi-disciplinary meeting in a patient-centric fashion.

In this paper we describe our use of generalised Formal Concept Analysis (FCA) to provide a browsable mechanism for the presentation and retrieval of case notes for patients undergoing some regime of care for the treatment of breast cancer. In particular, we present details of how FCA can be DL-enabled in this application to manage and retrieve case notes. Such case notes are composed by inputs from different medical staff with regard to different facets of the diagnosis and treatment process and are introduced as instances based on the concept definitions in our Breast Cancer Imaging Ontology (BCIO).

BCIO is developed in description logics (DLs) which are typically designed from a top-down perspective, with logical constructors used to define concept descriptions out of atomic concepts. FCA, on the other hand, is characterised by a bottom-up fashion when manipulating instances. It allows us direct access to the members of the concept classes introduced in DLs, facilitating the browse and navigation functionalities that a DL-based system does not normally possess. This is achieved by extending traditional FCA approaches, which lack flexibility and support for other forms of knowledge except the "presence" and "absence" of a particular attribute, to a DL-enabled one that generalises the attributes to any DL-based formulae and the FCA lattice to the one based on more generic inferencing relationships.Further details of the definitions and the correspondence of our approach are presented in subsequent sections.

2 Background

In this section, terms and definitions in both FCA and DLs are introduced. Their differences are briefly discussed and a DL-enabled generalisation of FCA is presented.

2.1 Formal Concept Analysis

In Formal Concept Analysis (FCA) a data set is represented by a *formal context*, which is defined as a triple $(\mathbb{O}, \mathbb{A}, \mathbb{I})$ where $\mathbb{O}$ is a set of objects, $\mathbb{A}$ is a set of attributes, and $\mathbb{I}$ is the relation between $\mathbb{O}$ and $\mathbb{A}$, i.e. $\mathbb{I} \subseteq \mathbb{O} \times \mathbb{A}$. If $(o, a) \in \mathbb{I}$ where $o \in \mathbb{O}$ and $a \in \mathbb{A}$, we say o has attribute a. A *formal concept* $\mathbb{C}$ is a pair (O, A) where $O \subseteq \mathbb{O}$ is the *extent* of $\mathbb{C}$ and $A \subseteq \mathbb{A}$, is the *intent* of $\mathbb{C}$. If an operation $\cdot'$ is defined as:

$$O' = \{a \in \mathbb{A} \,|\, \forall o \in O : (o, a) \in \mathbb{I}\}$$
$$A' = \{o \in \mathbb{O} \,|\, \forall a \in A : (o, a) \in \mathbb{I}\}$$

(1)

a *formal concept* of a context $(\mathbb{O}, \mathbb{A}, \mathbb{I})$ satisfies:

$$O' = A \quad \text{and} \quad A' = O$$

In other words, the intent consists of exactly those attributes that the objects in the extent share; and the extent consists of exactly those objects sharing all the attributes in the intent [10].

A specialisation ordering is defined among the *formal concepts*. A *formal concept* (O_1, A_1) is more specific than another concept (O_2, A_2), i.e. $(O_1, A_1) \preceq (O_2, A_2)$, if $O_1 \subseteq O_2$—an equivalent relation is held between A_1 and A_2, i.e. $A_2 \subseteq A_1$. Such an ordering can be exploited to construct a lattice, $\mathfrak{L}(\mathbb{O}, \mathbb{A}, \mathbb{I})$, referred to as *concept lattice* of the *formal context* $(\mathbb{O}, \mathbb{A}, \mathbb{I})$.

2.2 Description Logics

Description Logics (DLs) are a family of knowledge representation and reasoning formalisms which have attracted substantial research recently, specially, after the DL-based ontology modelling languages (e.g. OWL [17]) are considered to be of crucial importance for the Semantic Web initiative [2]. DLs are based on the notions of concepts (i.e. unary predicates) and properties (i.e. binary relations). Using different constructors, complex concepts can be built up from atomic ones.

Let *CN* denote a concept name, C and D be arbitrary concepts, R be a role name, n be a non-negative integer and $\top$, $\bot$ denote the top and the bottom. A *concept definition* in DLs is either $CN \sqsubseteq C$ (partial definition) or $CN \doteq C$ (full definition). An interpretation $\mathcal{I}$ is a couple ($\Delta^{\mathcal{I}}$, $\cdot^{\mathcal{I}}$) where the nonempty set $\Delta^{\mathcal{I}}$ is the domain of $\mathcal{I}$ and the $\cdot^{\mathcal{I}}$ function maps each concept to a subset of $\Delta^{\mathcal{I}}$ while each role to a subset of $\Delta^{\mathcal{I}} \times \Delta^{\mathcal{I}}$. The interpretation of some DL-based constructors are illustrated in Table 1

The uniform syntax and unambiguous semantics of DLs lend themselves to powerful reasoning algorithms that can automatically classify the domain knowledge in hierarchical structures which can be cached to provide support for subsequent taxonomic reasoning.

Table 1. Syntax and semantics of DL-based constructors

Constructor	Syntax	Semantics (*Interpretation*)
Top (Universe)	$\top$	$\Delta^{\mathcal{I}}$
Bottom (Nothing)	$\bot$	$\emptyset$
Atomic Concept	CN	$CN^{\mathcal{I}} \subseteq \Delta^{\mathcal{I}}$
Conjunction	$C \sqcap D$	$C^{\mathcal{I}} \cap D^{\mathcal{I}}$
Disjunction	$C \sqcup D$	$C^{\mathcal{I}} \cup D^{\mathcal{I}}$
Negation	$\neg C$	$\Delta^{\mathcal{I}} \setminus C^{\mathcal{I}}$
Universal quantification	$\forall R.C$	$\{ c \in \Delta^{\mathcal{I}} \mid \forall d \in \Delta^{\mathcal{I}} : \langle c, d \rangle \in R^{\mathcal{I}} \rightarrow d \in C^{\mathcal{I}} \}$
Existential quantification	$\exists R.C$	$\{ c \in \Delta^{\mathcal{I}} \mid \exists d \in \Delta^{\mathcal{I}} : \langle c, d \rangle \in R^{\mathcal{I}} \wedge d \in C^{\mathcal{I}} \}$
Number Restrictions	$\geq n R.\top$	$\{ c \in \Delta^{\mathcal{I}} \mid \sharp \{ d \in \Delta^{\mathcal{I}} : \langle c, d \rangle \in R^{\mathcal{I}} \} \geq n \}$
	$\leq n R.\top$	$\{ c \in \Delta^{\mathcal{I}} \mid \sharp \{ d \in \Delta^{\mathcal{I}} : \langle c, d \rangle \in R^{\mathcal{I}} \} \leq n \}$
Atomic Role	RN	$RN^{\mathcal{I}} \subseteq \Delta^{\mathcal{I}} \times \Delta^{\mathcal{I}}$

There is a significant difference between FCA and DLs. FCA takes a bottom-up approach starting from a set of instances and attributes of a domain to derive the conceptual model. DLs, on the other hand, create the set of definitions independently of the instantiated cases and associated to a domain through interpretation. Note that confusion might arise as both FCA and DLs use the same term "concept" when modelling but with different meanings. In this paper, the FCA concept is referred to as *formal concept* while the DL concept as *concept* in order to distinguish both notions.

2.3 DL-Enabled Formal Concept Analysis

FCA has been extended in various forms [4, 6, 7, 9, 20]. Among them, Logic Concept Analysis (LCA) [7] is introduced as a logic generalisation of FCA, in which the set of attributes, $\mathbb{A}$, is replaced by a set of arbitrary logic formulae. In this paper FCA is further DL-enabled and applied to analysis of a DL ABox, which contains all instances that satisfy its concept definitions. The DL-enabled FCA is a specialisation of the one formally defined in Definition (1).

Definition 1. *A* generalised context $\mathbb{C}$ *is a triple* $(\mathbb{O}, \mathbb{F}, \mathbb{I})$ *where* $\mathbb{O}$ *is a set of objects,* $\mathbb{F}$ *a set of well-formed formulae with associated deduction rules, and* $\mathbb{I}$ *a relation between* $\mathbb{O}$ *and* $\mathbb{F}$ *that maps each* $o \in \mathbb{O}$ *a subset of* $f \subseteq \mathbb{F}$.

If $\bigvee$ is defined as a disjunctive operator on *formal concepts* and $\bigwedge$ a conjunctive operator, the *supremum* (*infimum*, respectively) of the *generalised context* is the $\overset{\circ}{\bigvee}$ disjunction ($\overset{\circ}{\bigwedge}$ conjunction, respectively) of all *formal concepts*. Meanwhile, $\models$ introduces an ordering on $\mathbb{F}$, e.g. *set inclusion* and *logic entailment*.

A *generalised lattice* $\mathfrak{L}(\mathbb{O}, \mathbb{F}, \mathbb{I})$ can be constructed based on the relation $C_i \overset{\circ}{\preceq} C_j$ if and only if $F_i \models F_j$ where $C_n = (O_n, F_n)$, $n \geq i, n \geq j$. The *supremum* and *infimum* are calculated as shown in Equation 2, where $\cup^x$ and $\cap^x$ are disjunctive and conjunctive operators defined in a particular reasoning system x, and *formal concept* $C_i = (O_i, F_i)$ ($i \in I$ is the total index of the lattice).

$$\overset{\circ}{\bigvee} C_i = ((\cup_{i \in I}^{x} F_i)', \cup_{i \in I}^{x} F_i)$$
$$\overset{\circ}{\bigwedge} C_i = ((\cap_{i \in I}^{x} F_i)', \cap_{i \in I}^{x} F_i) \tag{2}$$

For instance, let $O_t = \{t_1, t_2, t_3\}$ be a set of objects with numeric features, e.g. the size ranges of tumours, F contains a set of constants of rational numbers, a set of comparison operators $\{<, >, \leq, \geq, =\}$ which are interpreted in the normal sense, and $I = \{ t_1 \rightarrow (\leq_{55mm}, \geq_{45mm}), t_2 \rightarrow (\leq_{25mm}, \geq_{10mm}), t_3 \rightarrow (\leq_{70mm}, \geq_{30mm}) \}$; also associated with F are a disjunctive operator $\cup^{set}$ which isinterpreted as set union, a conjunctive operator $\cap^{set}$ interpreted as set intersection, and adeduction relation $\subseteq$ instantiating $\models$ interpreted as set inclusion. A *concept lattice* is constructed as the line diagram shown in Figure 1 with the top node corresponding to the union of all numeric ranges and the bottom node the intersection. Meanwhile, each *formal concept* in Figure 1 is labeled with its intent, the range of numeric values, and its extent, a subset of O_t.

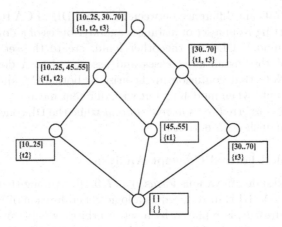

Fig. 1. Line Diagram of a numeric context

The great flexibility of the generalised FCA is demonstrated by its capability of analysing concrete domains and those based on first-order logic, e.g. description logic based formulae. If $\mathbb{F}$ in Definition 1 is replaced with a set of DL-based formulae and $\mathbb{I}$ is defined as $\mathbb{I}$: $o \mapsto f \models o \in (f)^{\mathcal{I}}$ where f is a subset of $\mathbb{F}$ and $\cdot^{\mathcal{I}}$ is the DL-based interpretation function, the mutant FCA is said to be DL-enabled. The DL-enabled FCA provides a correlation between intent and extent of an arbitrary "concept", based on which one can easily browse and navigate a DL-based knowledge base managing the instances with direct visual information. Moreover, FCA also serves as a knowledge discovery tool helping to identify "hidden (anonymous) concepts" that do not exist in the underlying conceptual model but are strongly suggested by the extent. Details of how FCA can help to identify new DL-based concepts are discussed in Section 3.2.

3   Managing Instances Using DL-Enabled FCA

The patient records dataset (denoted as Δ_{patient}) used in this paper consists of anonymous cases downloaded from the Digital Database for Screening Mammography (DDSM), University of South Florida (USF).

Each anonymous case contains verbal descriptions of the patient's background, e.g. age, metadata of the mammogram images, and abnormalities presenting on the images. They are mapped to a Breast Cancer Imaging Ontology [13] and rewritten as DL-based instances in RDF [16] format. For instance, a case file in USF data (Figure 2(a)) giving information concerning a particular abnormality is introduced as an instance, named 00011_right_cc_abnor_1, of concept Abnormality as shown in Figure 2(b). Note that an instance of Mass is also introduced to make complete the definition.

```
TOTAL_ABNORMALITIES 1
ABNORMALITY 1
LESION_TYPE MASS SHAPE IRREGULAR MARGINS SPICULATED
ASSESSMENT 5
SUBTLETY 5
PATHOLOGY MALIGNANT
```

(a) Fragment of USF case description

```
<rdf:RDF
    xmlns:rdf='http://www.w3.org/1999/02/22-rdf-syntax-ns#'
    xmlns:rdfs='http://www.w3.org/2000/01/rdf-schema#'
    ...
>

    <rdf:Description rdf:about='bcioNS#00011_right_cc_abnor_1'>
        <rdf:type rdf:resource='bcioNS#Abnormality'/>
        <NS2:is_finding rdf:resource='bcioNS#mass_00011_right_cc_abnor_1'/>
        <NS2:has_morph_feature rdf:resource='bcioNS#shape_mammo_irregular'/>
        <NS2:has_morph_feature rdf:resource='bcioNS#margin_mammo_spiculated'/>
        <NS2:has_overall_impression rdf:resource='bcioNS#assessment_definitely_malignant'/>
    </rdf:Description>

    <rdf:Description rdf:about='bcioNS:mass_00011_right_cc_abnor_1'>
        <rdf:type rdf:resource='bcioNS#Mass'/>
    </rdf:Description>

</rdf:RDF>
```

(b) Corresponding DL instance in RDF format

Fig. 2. Translating patient records into DL instances

3.1   Constructing Lattices

Due to the presence of concrete knowledge in some of the cases, e.g. the size of an abnormality or the age group a patient belongs to, lattice construction cannot solely rely on an abstract DL-based system. Two approaches can be adopted instead. If the concrete knowledge contains only linear equations and inequalities, DL-based systems extended with concrete domains, such as RACER [11], can be used to provide the deduction relation among different *formal concepts*. For more complicated concrete expressions and non-linear equations/inequalities with non-integer coefficients, instances may have to be *normalised* [12] to enable a separated reasoning for abstract and concrete knowledge using DL and constraint reasoning system respectively.

In our case, concrete knowledge is restricted to contain only numeric ranges (conjunction of linear inequations with rational or integer coefficients) when modelling patient records. Hence, for simplicity, RACER is used to help construct the lattice.

Unfolding Instances. By rewriting Δ_{patient} as an ABox $\mathcal{A}$ together with an acyclic TBox $\mathcal{T}$ containing BCIO, i.e. such that no atomic concepts appear on both sides of a concept introduction axiom, it is possible to unfold the righthand side of all instance introduction axioms and guarantee the termination of such an unfolding process. For instance, let d be an instance of concept D, i.e. $d_i : D_i \in$

Δ_{patient}, CN and RN be concept and role names appearing in D respectively, and (CN = C) $\in T$ and (RN = R) $\in T$. It is possible to thoroughly unfold d_i by recursively replacing defined concept names appearing on the righthand side of d_i : D_i and $\langle d_i, d_j \rangle$: R_k with definitions in T, i.e. d_i : $D_i[\frac{\text{RN}}{\text{R}}, \frac{\text{CN}}{\text{C}}]$ and $\langle d_i, d_j \rangle$: $R_k[\frac{\text{RN}}{\text{R}}]$ where $[\frac{x}{y}]$ defines the process of replacing all occurrences of x with y. Such a process terminates due to the acyclic nature of T and results in a finite set of DL-based formulae.

There are some prerequisites for the success of such an unfolding process. Firstly, all the DL concept definitions should be in their Negation-Normal Form (NNF), i.e. the negations are applied only to concept names. An NNF can be achieved by repetitively applying de Morgan's laws, e.g. $\neg \exists R.C = \forall R.\neg C$. Secondly, the unfolding of nested concepts is taken as given, i.e. the computational complexity is not considered in this paper. For certain knowledge bases, the space complexity of unfolding could be exponential, where suitable optimisation methods (e.g. methods applied when performing tableaux algorithms to DL-based reasoning) need to be adopted. Nevertheless, the application of USF data in this paper will not be effected as only a limited number of concepts need to be unfolded and no complex nested definition presents.

If all the unfolded definitions are fragmented at "$\sqcap$" and "$\sqcup$", we will have a set of formulae ($\mathbb{F}_{substring}$) that are substrings of the original concept definitions in T or instances introduced in $\mathcal{A}$. As a result, $\mathcal{A}$ can be transformed to a context $\mathbb{C}_{\mathcal{A}} = (\mathbb{O}_{\text{ind}}, 2^{\mathbb{F}_{substring}}, \mathbb{I}_{\text{ind}})$ where $\mathbb{O}_{\text{ind}}$ is a finite set of objects defined as instances in $\mathcal{A}$ and $\mathbb{I}_{\text{ind}}$ a mapping from the set of instances $\mathbb{O}_{\text{ind}}$ to the powerset of $\mathbb{F}_{substring}$ so that $(o, f) \in \mathbb{I} \mapsto o \in (f)^{\mathcal{I}}$ for $o \in \mathbb{O}$ and $f \in 2^{\mathbb{F}_{substring}}$. The $\cdot'$ operation defined in Equation 1 can be extended in a similar way as described in [7]:

$$O'_{\text{ind}} = \bigvee_{o \in O_{\text{ind}}} \{f \in 2^{\mathbb{F}_{substring}} | (o, f) \in \mathbb{I}\}$$

$$(f \subseteq 2^{\mathbb{F}_{substring}})' = \{o \in O_{\text{ind}} | o' \models_{\text{DL}} f\}$$

(3)

where $\models_{\text{DL}}$ is a DL-based deduction system, e.g. RACER.

For instance, one of the critical parts of the USF patient records is the information regarding abnormalities found on mammogram images. After unfolding, the formal context consists of a set of objects

$$\mathbb{O}^{\text{abnor}} = \{0011\_ \text{ right}\_ \text{ cc}\_ \text{ abnor}\_ 1, \ 0011\_ \text{ right}\_ \text{ mlo}\_ \text{ abnor}\_ 1,$$
$$0021\_ \text{ left\_cc\_abnor\_1}, \ 0011\_ \text{ left\_mlo\_abnor\_1},$$
$$0031\_ \text{ right\_cc\_abnor\_1},$$
$$\dots\}$$

a set of formulae

$$\mathbb{F}^{\text{abnor}}_{\text{substring}} = \{\exists \text{has\_morph\_feature.shape\_irregular},$$
$$\exists \text{has\_morph\_feature.margin\_spiculated},$$
$$\exists \text{has\_morph\_feature.margin\_ill\_defined},$$
$$\dots\}$$

and a set of mappings

$$\mathbb{I}^{\text{abnor}} = \{0011\_\text{right\_cc\_abnor\_1} \mapsto \exists\text{has\_morph\_feature.shape\_irregular},$$
$$0011\_\text{right\_cc\_abnor\_1} \mapsto \exists\text{has\_morph\_feature.margin\_spiculated},$$
$$0011\_\text{right\_mlo\_abnor\_1} \mapsto \exists\text{has\_morph\_feature.shape\_irregular},$$
$$0031\_\text{right\_mlo\_abnor\_1} \mapsto \exists\text{has\_morph\_feature.margin\_ill\_defined},$$
$$\dots\}$$

Labelling. Starting from a set of nodes each associated with a DL-based formulae $f \in \mathbb{F}_{\text{substring}}$, the lattice is constructed upwards by connecting formulae with the disjunctive operator and downwards with the conjunctive operator. The composite formula is used as the label of the corresponding node.

For instance, for formal context $\mathbb{C}_{\text{abnor}} = (\mathbb{O}^{\text{abnor}}, \mathbb{F}^{\text{abnor}}_{\text{substring}}, \mathbb{I}^{\text{abnor}})$, a lattice can be constructed from a set of simple DL-based formulae. A fragment of such a concept lattice is illustrated as a line diagram in Figure 3(a), where each node is labeled with the formulae that it is associated with and "extent-less" nodes are ignored for the sake of simplicity.

3.2   Discovering New Knowledge

As argued in [21], FCA has emerged as a knowledge management tool which not only provides an intriguing graphic user interface for navigating and retrieving but also gradually plays a significant role as a method for knowledge discovery, knowledge inference, bottom-up ontology merging, *etc.* With the DL-enabled FCA, new knowledge can be obtained and asserted in one of two different ways with the help of human experts.

While constructing a lattice "downwards" with the conjunctive operator, when the conjunction of two nodes has a non-empty extent, it may be worth considering introducing a new DL-based concept in $\mathcal{T}$ as the most common subsumee of the *formal concepts* represented by these two nodes, if such a concept has not already existed. For instance, let $f_1 = \exists\text{has-morphology-feature.Shape-Irregular}$ and $f_2 = \exists\text{has-morphology-feature.Margin-Spitulate}$, $(f_1' \sqcap^{\text{DL}} f_2')' \neq \emptyset$ with regard to $\mathcal{A}$ suggests a DL-based concept

$$\exists\text{has-morph-feature.shape\_irregular} \sqcap$$
$$\exists\text{has-morph-feature.margin\_spiculated}$$

may be worth considering as a particular type of abnormality. Further investigations of the specific domain reveal that a malignant lesion is normally associated with irregular shape and spiculated margin, and thus a concept might be introduced to indicate a highly suspicious lesion group.

In some cases, there may be nodes with null extent, i.e. $(f_n)' = \emptyset$. Two different situations have to be distinguished when an "extent-less" node is identified,

1. f_n is inconsistent with regard to the existing $\mathcal{T}$; or
2. $((f_n)', f_n)$ has null extent, i.e. $\forall o \in \mathcal{A} : o \notin (f_n)'$, based on closed world assumption.

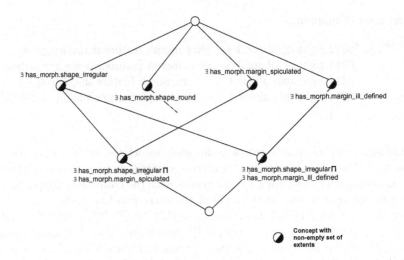

(a) Fragment of Line Diagram

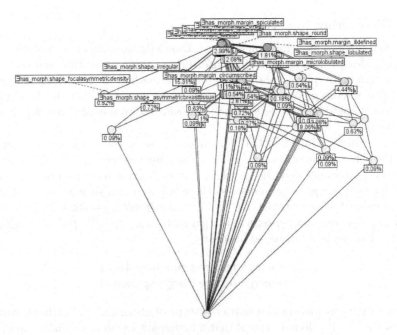

(b) Full Line Diagram

Fig. 3. Context $\mathbb{C}_{abnor}$

Human experts are expected to decide which case an "extent-less" node belongs to and take actions accordingly, e.g. classify $\mathcal{A}$ to isolate and remove inconsistent individuals or prune the line diagram and remove redundant nodes.

3.3   Navigating

To some extent, navigation encourages users to be more exploratory, allowing the users to actively get involved in the knowledge base and grasp concrete ideas of the structure of the knowledge base. Navigation follows the visualisation of the contents of a knowledge base, and there is extensive research on visualisation schemes in user interfaces [8, 14, 15, 18, 19] aiming to make the information intuitively laid out to enable comprehension. The visualisation can vary with the structure of a domain, and the constraints imposed by the knowledge representation structure underlying have to be accounted for in finding appropriate ways of rendering the necessary information in order to facilitate navigability. In [5], the authors argued that FCA has provided a straightforward and instructive interface for novice users, with the partial order easy to get used to. Our DL-enabled concept lattice retains all the merits of FCA lattices concerning browsing and navigating a knowledge base.

Meanwhile, for a large knowledge base, it is possible to adopt the nested line diagram approach to scale down the lattice while preserving all the necessary information [3]. With the aid of the ontology, two types of scaling down methods can be achieved, i.e. the structural and the semantic nesting. The structural nesting enables a line diagram to convey the joint context of two separated ones. As shown in Figure 4, by nesting a *shape* diagram–a line diagram only presenting information concerning shape descriptors–with a *margin* diagram, one can retrieve the extent of a concept determined by the conjunction of formulae of all paths proceeding up in diagrams from different nesting levels [3]. For instance, in Figure 4, a node residing inside one of the ovals in the top level diagram is marked. A further investigation shows this node corresponding to abnormality whose intent is restricted by both *shape* and *margin* descriptors as

$$\exists\text{has-morph-feature.margin\_microlobulated} \sqcap$$
$$\exists\text{has-morph-feature.margin\_circumscribed} \sqcap$$
$$\exists\text{has-morph-feature.shape\_lobulated}$$

with two corresponding instances (extent) in the knowledge base.

The semantic nesting intends to scale down the diagram in an ontology-driven semantic approach. BCIO can be separated into several relatively independent modules each representing a sub-context of the overall patient record formal context, e.g. image data, patient data, abnormality data, *etc.* Furthermore, for each of the modules, it is possible to define several levels of *context* based on the conceptual granularity thus determined. For instance, in Figure 5, image descriptors are grouped semantically into Shape_Descriptor, Margin_Descriptor, Distribution_Descriptor, *etc.* Since all *shape* descriptors (and other descriptors) are defined as instances of Shape_Descriptor concept (and other descriptor concepts) [13], the top level diagram can be constructed without considering the individual shape instances while a nested diagram can be used to present detailed information at the instance level accordingly. Such scaling preserves all the necessary information of $\mathbb{C}_{\text{abnor}}$ while reducing the complexity of the diagram. For instance, the marked node in Figure 5 presents the sub-context of all abnormalities defined with both *shape* and *margin* descriptors. When necessary, it is possible to semantically zoom in and retrieve the joint context, i.e. the context representing each individual shape and margin descriptors. Note that the nested contexts can be visualised using either a nested or a flat line diagram.

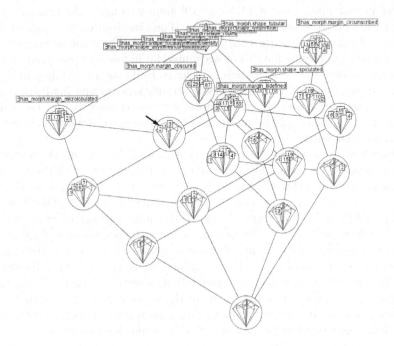

Fig. 4. Nested Line Diagram of $\mathbb{C}_{\text{abnor}}$

3.4   Retrieving Instances

Generally speaking, based on a DL-enabled concept lattice, two types of queries can be generated to retrieve instances from a knowledge base, i.e. extent-only querying and composite querying. Intuitively, extent-only querying is to locate and retrieve all the objects directly associated with a particular node in the concept lattice, while a composite query is more like a "shopping basket", which is a mixture of formulae associated with nodes and those added by the users.

Extent-only querying is a procedure combining navigating and retrieving. Let f_q be the query, starting from the top (bottom, respectively). Users traverse the lattice and locate the most desired combination of formulae along a path of the lattice adding formulae conjunctively (disjunctively) by moving downwards (upwards) to an adjacent node. If there is a node c with extent o_c and intent f_c in the lattice so that $f_q = f_c$, o_c will be retrieved as the answer to f_q. This is because each node in the concept lattice is associated with a set of DL-based formulae whose interpretation is the set of objects represented by the node.

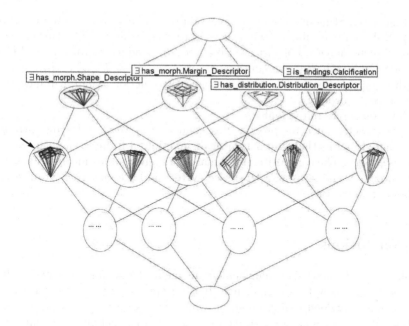

Fig. 5. Semantic Nested Line Diagram of $\mathbb{C}_{abnor}$

In contrast to extent-only querying, the "shopping basket" provides a method of interaction between human experts and computers. In the basket, users can dump in formulae randomly picked up from several different nodes and indicate whether a conjunctive or disjunctive relation is expected among these formulae. A lattice manipulating program will traverse the lattice upwards for disjunctive relations and downwards for conjunctive ones to find a node which has intent equivalent to the composite query. In some cases, DL-based systems are consulted to determine whether two sets of syntactically different formulae are semantically equivalent as different DL-based concept constructors do not necessary have different expressiveness [1]. An empty set may be returned to indicate that no object satisfies the composite f_q.

3.5 Populating and Updating

Because a concept lattice provides a direct and comprehensible correlation between terminological syntax in DLs and the objects mapped on to by the denotational semantics, it facilitates a populating method directly based on the line diagram. Populating and modifying a knowledge base can be considered as arbitrary combination of navigating actions. With DL-enabled FCA lattice, the following actions are likely to be supported:

Adding or removing objects from the extent of a concept represented by a node
  A DL-based reasoning system is needed to check whether $\mathcal{A}$ is still consistent
  after such changes. For instance, if object o_{ij} is added to (or removed from)
  node $C_i = (O_i, F_i)$, the consistency of $\mathcal{A} \cup \{o_{ij} \doteq F_i'\}$ $(\mathcal{A} \setminus \{o_{ij} \doteq F_i'\})$,
  where $o_{ij} \doteq F_i'$ is the DL-based instance introduction axiom, will have to be
  checked accordingly.
Adding composite individuals
  Similar to the querying process, users can select several nodes and introduce
  an individual as the conjunction or disjunction of formulae associated with
  these nodes. The composite individual is first checked for inconsistency with
  regard to $\mathcal{T}$ and $\mathcal{A}$ using a DL-based system and then inserted into the right
  level of the lattice.

4 Conclusions

Ontology-based knowledge management in medical domains presents itself as
an opportunity as well as a challenge. It is an opportunity as an ontology provides a shared understanding based on which successful communication can be
established. It is a challenge in the sense that as ontological modelling languages
become more and more sophisticated and automated inference enabled, it requires trained eyes to fully comprehend ontologies based on logics, such as DLs;
medical staff are not expected to possess such an ability. Hence, a user-friendly
and convenient method facilitating knowledge base visualisation and ontology
authoring by both laymen and experts is necessary.

In this paper, we adopt a DL-enabled generalised FCA approach to manage patient record instances. The conceptual structure is represented as the
breast cancer imaging ontology (BCIO) modelled using DAML+OIL. A knowledge base with 1,500 patient record instances (2,200 abnormalities instances) is
downloaded from the USF site and mapped upon to BCIO. Routine knowledge
base management, e.g. instance retrieval, update and visualisation, is driven by
a DL-enabled FCA engine. Compared to traditional FCA approaches, a DL-
enabled one is capable of conveying not only the syntactic but also semantic
information. It presents a direct visual correlation between the instances and
DL-based formulae via the relation between the extent and intent of a node.
With the aid of a line diagram labelled with well-formed DL-based formulae,
our approach supports a "see and use" fashion when populating and retrieving
instances. We expect users with limited training in knowledge representation
and artificial intelligence to be able to "shop" formulae from different nodes and
compose the desired one accordingly.

The unfolding process described in this paper treats complex nested universal
and existential quantifications as single line diagram building blocks. It helps to
reduce the overall computational complexity and the size of the diagram at the
price of possible duplicate entries and the readability of the diagram. For knowledge bases containing a large number of nested definitions, optimised unfolding
methods may be worth considering. The optimisation measures might include

the so-called "lazy-unfolding"[1] that unfolds concepts and constructs lattice on demand and/or the reuse of partial lattice.

The use of USF data studied in this paper is only to present the applicability of our approach to managing a logic based knowledge base. It is expected that when applied to hospital-based Breast Cancer Screening scheme with real patient records, vast amount of information will be available and subject to the study.

Acknowledgements

Research for this paper is funded by the British Engineering and Physical Sciences Research Council (EPSRC) under the MIAKT grant GR/R85150/01.

References

1. F. Baader, D. Calvanese, D. McGuinness, D. Nardi, and P. Patel-Schneider, editors. *The Description Logic Handbook: Theory, Implementation and Applications.* Cambridge University Press, 2003.
2. T. Berners-Lee, J. Hendler, and O. Lassila. The Semantic Web. *Scientific American*, pages 28–37, May 2001.
3. R. Cole and P. W. Eklund. Scalability in formal concept analysis. *Conputational Intelligence*, 15(1):11–27, 1999.
4. J. H. Correia and J. Klinger. Protoconcept Graphs: The Lattice of Conceptual Contents. In *Proceedings of International Conference on Formal Concept Analysis (ICFCA) 2004*, Sydney, Australia, 2004.
5. P. Eklund, J. Ducrou, and P. Brawn. Concept Lattices for Information Visualization: Can Novices Read Line-Diagrams? In *Second International Conference on Formal Concept Analysis, ICFCA*, number 2961 in Lecture Notes in Computer Science, pages 57–73, 2004.
6. Dau F. and J. Klinger. From Formal Concept Analysis to Contextual Logic. In *Proceedings of International Conference on Formal Concept Analysis (ICFCA) 2003*, Berlin, 2003.
7. S. Ferré and O. Ridoux. A logical generalization of formal concept analysis. In G. Mineau and B. editors Ganter, editors, *International Conference on Conceptual Structures*, 2000.
8. G.W. Furnas. The FISHEYE view: A new look at structured files. In *the Conference on Human Factors in Computing Systems*, pages 16–23, 1986.
9. B. Ganter and R. Wille. Contextual Attribute Logic. In *Proceedings of the 7th International Conference on Conceptual Structures: Standards and Practices*, number 1640 in Lecture Notes In Artificial Intelligence, pages 377–388, Berlin, 1999. Springer-Verlag.
10. B. Ganter and R. Wille. *Formal Concept Analysis — Mathematical Foundations.* Springer-Verlag, Berlin, 1999.
11. V. Haarslev and R. Möller. *RACER User's Guide and Reference Manual Version 1.6.* University of Hamburg, Computer Science Department, July 2001. Technical Report.

---

[1] Lazy-unfolding is widely adopted in DL-based reasoning systems.

12. B. Hu, I. Arana, and E. Compatangelo. Facilitating dl-based hybrid reasoning with *Inference Fusion. Jour. of Knowledge-Based Systems*, 16(5-6):253–260, 2003.

13. B. Hu, S. Dasmahapatra, P. Lewis, and S. Nigel. Ontology-based medical image annotation with description logics. In *The 15th IEEE International Conference on Tools with Artificial Intelligence*. IEEE Computer Society Press, 2003.

14. J. Lamping, R. Rao, and P. Pirolli. A Focus+Context Technique Based on Hyperbolic Geometry for Visualizing Large Hierarchies. In *Proc. ACM Conf. Human Factors in Computing Systems, CHI*, pages 401–408. ACM, 1995.

15. J.H. Larkin and A. Simon. Why a diagram is (sometimes) worth ten thousand words. *Cognitive Science*, 11(1):65–99, 1987.

16. O. Lassila and R.R. Swick. *Resource Description Framework (RDF) Model and Syntax Specification*. W3C, 22 February 1999.

17. D. L. McGuinness and F. van Harmelen. *OWL Web Ontology Language Overview*. W3C, 10 February 2003.

18. T. Munzner. H3: Laying out large directed graphs in 3D hyperbolic space. In *the IEEE Symposium on Information Visualization*, 1997.

19. D. Richards. Visualising knowledge based systems. In *the Third Workshop on Software Visualisation (SoftVis'99)*, 1999.

20. S. Rudolf. An FCA method for the extensional exploration of relational data. In B. Ganter and A. de Moor, editors, *Using Conceptual Structures–Contributions to ICCS 2003*. Shaker Verlag, 2003.

21. G. Stumme. Off to new shores: conceptual knowledge discovery and processing. *International Journal of Human-Computer Studies*, 59:287–325, 2003.

Medical Ontology and Virtual Staff
for a Health Network

Rose Dieng-Kuntz, David Minier, Frédéric Corby, Marek Ruzicka, Olivier Corby,
Laurent Alamarguy, and Phuc-Hiep Luong

INRIA, ACACIA Project, 2004, route des Lucioles, B.P. 93, 06902 Sophia Antipolis Cedex
{Rose.Dieng, Olivier.Corby, Marek.Ruzicka,
Laurent.Alamarguy}@sophia.inria.fr

Abstract. In the context of a care network, we describe our method for
reconstitution of a medical ontology via the translation of a medical database
(DB) towards RDF(S) language. Then we show how we extended this
ontology, among others through natural language processing of a textual
corpus. Then, we present the construction of a Virtual Staff, enabling a
cooperative diagnosis by some of the care network actors, by relying on this
medical ontology.

Keywords: ontologies, knowledge management, semantic web, cooperation,
medical application.

1 Context: Needs in a Care Network

The project *"Ligne de Vie" (Life Line)*, in collaboration with the Nautilus society and
the SPIM laboratory, aims at developing a knowledge management tool for a care
network [14]. In order to analyse the concrete needs of care network in general, we
had interviews with a physician and with a nurse. Specialised in a particular domain
or in a specific pathology, a care network is a health network gathering all the actors
intervening in the care or follow-up processes. The objective of the network is to ease
(a) communication and collaboration among these actors in spite of their physical
distance, (b) the regular follow-up of the patient et (c) the respect of best practices
inside the network. The patient must be guided towards relevant medical actors, that
must be informed about the patient's state and that may gather (sometimes virtually,
through synchronous or asynchronous communication tools) in order to work on the
patient's record. For example, cystic fibrosis demands daily cares throughout the
patient's life and requires several kinds of professionals : paediatricians, physicians,
gastro-enterologists, chest specialists, nurses, physiotherapists, psychologists,
dieticians, social workers, as well as the patient, his/her family, the school doctor or
the job doctor. The network must ease knowledge sharing about the patient record,
among all these actors from various competence domains, with a user-tailored
presentation of the information.

The ideas proposed by Nautilus SARL for launching the project Ligne de Vie stem
from fifteen years of experiences in health domain and from contacts with a network

E. Motta et al. (Eds.): EKAW 2004, LNAI 3257, pp. 187–202, 2004.
© Springer-Verlag Berlin Heidelberg 2004

dedicated to diabetes: Nautilus offers a software for management of electronic medical record, Episodus, relying on a problem-oriented vision of the patient record sand articulated around the notion of « Life Line » enabling to represent the life of the patient from his/her birth till his/her death with all the health problems encountered by this patient. As long as the patient still suffers from a problem, this problem remains open. When the patient gets completely cured from this problem, the problem is closed.

The technical choices of the project Ligne de Vie are motivated as follows:

- The need to build a *referential common to the network actors* led us naturally to rely on a medical ontology. Moreover, this ontology should help, through inferences, to improve information search on the documents shared or accessible by the network members.
- The need to take into account *actors from various competence domains* incited us to study *viewpoint modelling* [19] in the ontology, in the patient records, or in the presentation of the results to the user after his/her query.
- The need of cooperative work between the actors of a network led to the idea of our partner Nautilus to develop a software called *Virtual Staff* in order to enable the members of the network to *visualise their collective reasoning*: in order to diagnose the pathology of the patient (according to the symptoms expressed by the patient, the observations or analyses of the doctor and the already known health problems of this patient), or in order to determine the best possible therapeutic procedures. This virtual staff should offer to the users *a service of support to cooperative reasoning*, during the phases of elaboration of diagnosis or therapeutic decision and *a service of constitution of an organisational memory* [6] – the memory of decisions of the community constituted by the members of the care network.

This article focuses on the work of the Acacia team on the medical ontology and on the Virtual Staff: we will present our method for reconstituting the Nautilus ontology – this method rests on a translation from a medical DB towards the RDF(S) language; then we will show how we extended this ontology after analysis of a textual corpus. Then, we will describe the Virtual Staff based on this ontology. Last, we will conclude on the interest of this work and on our further work planned.

2 Reconstitution and Extensions of the Medical Ontology Nautilus

2.1 Role of the Ontology

In the project *Ligne de Vie*, the ontology aims at modelling some knowledge on general medicine or specialized medicine, on care networks and their actors : the ontology will represent the conceptual vocabulary common to the actors of a care network, and will be used in the Virtual Staff and for information search. This ontology will be the kernel of a medical *semantic Web dedicated to the care network*.

The medical community has long been sensitised to the need of modelling its knowledge and of making its terminologies explicit. Therefore, there exists several terminological or ontological resources in medical domain: GALEN [17] [18], MENELAS [23] [24], ON9 Library [8] [16], SNOMED RT [5] [21], UMLS [15] are ontologies/ontology libraries/thesauri/meta-thesauri that model a part of the medical domain. We could have relied on one of them but for reasons of collaboration, we had to use the Nautilus medical DB developed by our industrial partner.

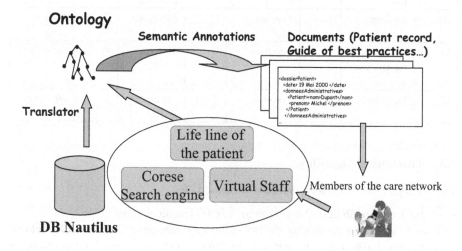

Fig. 1. Architecture of a Medical Semantic Web for a Care Network

In order to make the Nautilus ontology more understandable, it was important to represent it in a standard knowledge representation formalism: we chose RDF(S) [12] to which our semantic search engine CORESE [2] [3] [4] is dedicated. Therefore we developed   a translator from the Nautilus DB internal format towards RDF(S) language. Using a « reverse engineering » approach relying on the analysis of this DB coding principle, we decoded this DB in order to reconstitute a Nautilus ontology represented in RDF(S) so as to explore it and validate it via a semantic search engine, to annotate and search documents through this ontology, to guide the Virtual Staff, etc. Figure 1 shows the architecture of the medical semantic Web dedicated to a care network.

2.2 Discussion: DataBase vs Ontology

A preliminary question was the status of the Nautilus DB: could one regard it as an ontology? Some DB researchers assimilate a DB conceptual schema to an ontology. Admittedly, if one has available an explicit principle of how the concepts of an ontology are coded into the internal format of a DB, one can regard this DB as an implementation of the ontology. But it is important to represent the ontology explicitly in a form understandable by a human user, and in a knowledge representation formalism. We thus looked upon Nautilus as a medical ontology encoded in an internal format but without a representation readable by a human user. The reconstitution of the Nautilus ontology thus required the reconstitution of the hierarchy of concepts and of the set of relations implicit in the DB.

Table 1. Examples of characters coding the root concepts in the Nautilus DB

Code	Root Concept	Code	Root Concept	Code	Root Concept	Code	Root Concept
A	Anatomy	C	Foreign body	D	Physician	E	Patient's state
G	Diagnostic/ therapeutic gesture	N	Treatment	O	Material	P	Pathology
Q	Physiology	S	Symptom	T	Labotatory test	X	Histology

2.3   Translation Algorithm

The Nautilus DB is a Paradox database composed of:

- a table **Lexique.db** describing more than 36 000 medical terms,
- a file **Concept.txt** containing the list of the root concepts: **Anatomy, Physiology, Symptom, Pathology, Physician, Laboratory Test**, etc. Table 1 gives examples of characters coding such root concepts.
- a table **Savoir.db** describing the relations between the terms, with four types of relations: the ES specialisation relation (is-a), the E0 relation (non transitive is-a), the AT relation (located-on) and the ME relation (measured-with).

To each term appearing in **Lexique.db** corresponds a single, 6-characters long, code (e.g. **PABCF1**): the first character thus enables to find the associated concept root (for example, the character P corresponds to the root concept **Pathology**). The first 5 characters of the code associated to a term characterise the concept; the sixth character enables to distinguish the synonymous terms. For example, the terms « **abcès de derivation** » (**derivation abscess**) and « **abcès de fixation** » (**fixation abscess**) coded respectively **PABCF1** and **PABCF2** in the **Lexique.db** table are two synonymous terms naming the same concept, coded **PABCF** (**P** indicating that this concept is attached to the root concept **Pathology**). The translation algorithm enables to reconstitute in the concept hierarchy that the *Pathology* root concept has as direct or indirect subconcept a concept named by the synonymous terms « *derivation abscess* » and « *fixation abscess* ».

Using the **Concept.txt** file, the translator translates the root concepts into RDFS classes that are direct subclasses of the *ConceptNautilus* class. The codes of the **Lexique.db** table, without ES relation in the **Savoir.db** table, are also translated into RDFS classes that are direct subclasses the *ConceptNautilus* class.

The use of the **Savoir.db** table enables to gradually reconstitute the concept hierarchy by specifying the specialisation links between the concepts. If the **Savoir.db** table describes a relation ES between Code1 and Code2, the translator generates a *subClassOf* link between the concepts Concept1 and Concept2 (i.e. the RDFS classes generated by translation of Code1 and Code2): Concept1 becomes a subclass of Concept2 in the RDFS class hierarchy.

In the same way, the use of AT relations in the **Savoir.db** table makes it possible to determine the domain and range of the RDF property « *located-on* », and to generate the RDF triples *Concept1 located-on Concept2*.

Lastly, the use of the **Lexique.db** table which specifies the synonymous terms corresponding to the same code, makes it possible to represent through RDFS labels the various synonymous terms naming the concept associated with this code.

The whole translation algorithm is detailed in [14].

For the previous example, the translator will generate:

```
<lv:Concept rdf:ID="P">
   <rdfs:label xml:lang="fr">Pathologie</rdfs:label>
   <rdfs:subClassOf rdf:resource="#ConceptNautilus"/>
</lv:Concept>

 <lv:Concept rdf:ID="PABCF">
   <rdfs:label xml:lang="fr">abcès de
dérivation</rdfs:label>
     <rdfs:label xml:lang="fr">abcès de
fixation</rdfs:label>
     <rdfs:subClassOf rdf:resource="#P"/>
</lv:Concept>
```

Remark: The translation algorithm depends on the internal format of the Nautilus database but its principle is quite reusable for building an RDF(S) ontology from any DB, provided that the principle of coding of this DB is explicit enough for enabling such a reconstitution.

2.4 Verification and Validation of the Ontology

We distinguish on the one hand, *automatic checking* through automated processing performed by the *translation program*, and on the other hand, *human validation* by the doctors or by the ontologist through *visualisation and navigation in the ontology*.

Checking the Coherence of the Ontology

The translation program carries out some coherence tests, which enabled us to detect various errors in the initial Nautilus database: (a) relations inducing cycles for the specialisation relation; (b) specialisation relations between a concept and itself; (c) redundancies.

Some of these errors were modelling errors and others corresponded to non documented implementation tricks.

Validation of the Ontology with the CORESE Search Engine

The interest of the translation of the Nautilus DB is to enable to check the ontology, once represented in RDF(S). Indeed, the user can browse the ontology using CORESE, our semantic search engine dedicated to RDF(S) [2] [3] [4] Displaying the concepts via their labels instead of their code in the Nautilus DB makes the ontology more understandable for the doctors and its validation more friendly. CORESE interface could thus allow a team of doctors to visualise the ontology and to validate it by detecting the errors and by suggesting corrections.

By carrying out this validation within the Acacia team and with our Nautilus partner, we could detect several errors in the concept hierarchy. For example, in figure 2, we located several problems in the conceptualisation of pain:

- Problems of redundancy: two concepts represent the concept of *«douleur» (pain)* while one single concept would be sufficient.

- Structuring error: the concepts *douleur abdominale de type biliaire (abdominal pain of biliary type), douleur abdominale de type pancréatique (abdominal pain of pancreatic type), douleur abdominale de type ulcéreux (abdominal pain of ulcerous type)* should have been direct subconcepts of the concept *«douleur abdominale» (abdominal pain)*. It reveals that some ES relations had been forgotten in the **Savoir.db** table of the Nautilus DB.

- Mixture of several points of view in modelling: several viewpoints are mixed in the constitution of the hierarchy: some concepts characterise the pain by the part of the body concerned (e.g. *douleur abdominale (abdominal pain), douleur pelvienne (pelvic pain), douleur rénale (renal pain), douleur thoracique (thoracic pain)*) while others characterise it by its nature (e.g. *douleur exquise (exquisite pain), douleur fulgurante (fulgurating pain)...*).

Another advantage of CORESE search engine is to provide an environment to answer requests on the ontology - requests useful for the validation: since some concepts of the Nautilus ontology describe the anatomy, CORESE - which can find concepts via the terminology - can answer requests such as *« Which are the concepts having in their labels the word " abdominal " ? »*.

According to our partner, apart from the ontology validation, the queries of a doctor will rather relate to the ontology-based annotations on some medical documents or to the instances: e.g. *« Who are the patients whose medical record is annotated by a surgery for curing a pathology located on stomach? »*. The inferences of CORESE based on the ontology Nautilus will enable to find the record of a patient that were operated for a stomach cancer.

2.5   Extensions of the Nautilus Ontology

The Nautilus DB is used in the Episodus software for creating and editing the patient medical record. The concepts allowing to describe this patient record are thus useful when reasoning for diagnosis or for choice of the treatment. In the context of a tool aimed at supporting a care network, it seems interesting to extend the Nautilus ontology by concepts enabling to describe a care network and its actors, etc. For building these extensions, we rested on a corpus-based knowledge acquisition methodology [1] for semi-automatic acquisition relying on linguistic tools while being controlled by the expert and the knowledge engineer.

We thus constituted a corpus of documents on health networks: documents used for the preparation of the project *"Ligne de vie"*, documents found on the Web about health networks. Because of the disparate nature of these documents (scientific

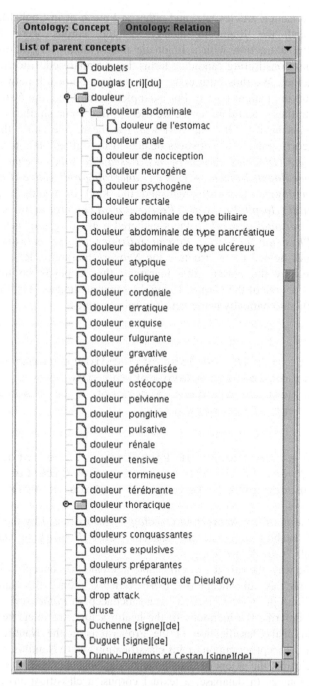

Fig. 2. Ill- formed hierarchy of *"douleur"* (pain)

articles, vulgarisation articles, etc, and either in French or in English), the discourse structuring and the linguistic quality of the corpus were heterogeneous. Terminological extraction with a linguistic tool, Nomino [7], allowed to extract noun syntagms constituting candidate terms that we analysed, filtered, structured or gathered together. We thus built concept hierarchies on health networks, on health centres and on the patient record. For example, for building the *Network* hierarchy obtained from these candidate terms, we tried to find some similarities between the candidate terms having *"Réseau" (Network)* as head. We could thus notice that some terms corresponded to networks dedicated to a given pathology (e.g. *Réseau de soin diabète (Diabetes care network), Réseau de soin en cancérologie (Care network in oncology), Réseau de soin en cancérologie digestive (Care network in digestive oncology)*, others distinguished the kind of health centres involved *(Réseau hôpital (Hospital network), Réseau libéral (Liberal network), Réseau ville hôpital (City hospital network)*, others gathered a given type of actors *(Réseau de médecins (Physician network), Réseau infirmier (Nurse network)...* All these linguistic clues helped us to structure the *Network* hierarchy. Resting on the only terms attested by the corpus, this hierarchy thus depends on the quality and completeness degree of the corpus. Using the same method as [11], this hierarchy is easy to enrich automatically using heuristic rules such as:

```
R1:
If the term X in the list of candidate terms starts
with the expression «Care Network in»
Then suggest to create the concept X as a subconcept of
the concept «Care Network».

R2:
If Y is a subconcept of Pathology in the ontology,
Then suggest to create the concept « Care Network in Y
» as subconcept of the concept « Care Network ».
```

Since the term *"Care Network in Oncology"* was extracted by the linguistic tool, the rule R1 enables to create the concept *"Care Network in Oncology"* as a subconcept of *"Care Network"*.

In the same way, the rule R2 would enable to create the concept *"Care Network in Cystic Fibrosis"* as subconcept of *"Care Network"*, since the Nautilus ontology includes the concept *"Cystic Fibrosis"* as a subconcept of *Pathology*.

Lastly, to describe the hierarchy of the health actors, we integrated a part of the Canadian National Classification of the Professions in the Nautilus ontology by relying on the concepts common to this classification and to Nautilus.

As a conclusion, the extended Nautilus ontology was obtained from heterogeneous information sources (a database, a textual corpus, a classification) and by several ontologists, with a risk of non homogeneity in its structuring, and a strong need of a validation by doctors. We will now show how this ontology is used in the Virtual Staff.

3 Representation and Use of the Virtual Staff

3.1 Objectives of the Virtual Staff

In the hospital, the unity of location and of time allows the doctors to meet as a staff in order to discuss about the decisions to take. In a care network, the Virtual Staff aims to be a collaborative work supporting tool, allowing the real time update and history of therapeutic decisions. As an electronic board where each one can note information readable by the other members of the team, it constitutes a discussion support that may be synchronous (if the participants take part to the discussion at the same time or in the same place) or asynchronous (if each one accesses it at the moment appropriate to him/her). Starting from the patient's health problems, the members of the team will formulate diagnostic hypotheses and proposals for a treatment. Via this Virtual Staff, the care team will connect the various elements of the patient record useful for the discussion, and thus will converge in an asynchronous way towards the definition of new health problems and of new therapeutic actions. The formulation of diagnostic hypotheses is a priori reserved to the medical actors, whereas the discussion on the treatment could sometimes imply non medical professionals (for example, a welfare officer could emit arguments against the choice of a heavy treatment incompatible with housing conditions of the patient).

3.2 Weed's SOAP Model

In Virtual Staff, the dependencies between the various diagnostic and therapeutic hypotheses can be represented through a graph using the concepts defined in the Nautilus ontology. The doctor will reason by linking the health problems to the symptoms, the clinical signs and the observations in order to propose care procedures.

The Virtual Staff can thus rest on the SOAP model (Subjective, Objective, Assessment, Plan) used by the medical community [22]. In this model:

- the S nodes describe current symptoms and clinical signs of the patient,
- the O nodes describe analyses or observations of the physician,
- the A nodes correspond to the diseases or health problems of the patient,
- and the P nodes correspond to the procedures or action plans set up in order to solve the health problems.

This SOAP model is used in the medical community to structure a patient record. Therefore, its use to structure the doctor's reasoning   - that relies on the same concepts - seems natural.

When a patient consults his/her doctor for new symptoms, the physician will create an instance of Virtual Staff. The system will then initialise a SOAP graph with all currently open pathologies and prescriptions for this patient (see fig. 3): the initial A and P nodes automatically added in the graph are the pathologies and the care procedures already existing and open in the patient's life line. The doctor can then reason in order to add, in case of need, new A nodes (i.e. new pathologies diagnosed) or new P nodes (i.e. new action plans) in order to diagnose and treat the new health problem of the patient.

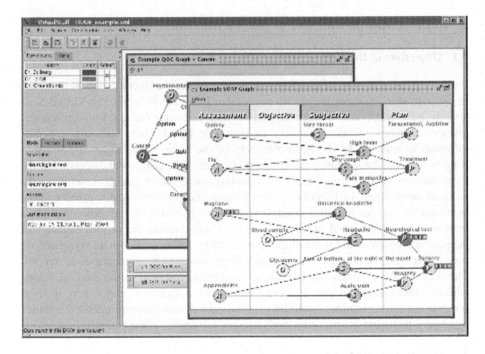

Fig. 3. Example of SOAP graph in the Virtual Staff

3.3   QOC Model (Question-Options-Criteria)

Sometimes, the doctor may need to visualise all the possible solutions and the arguments in their favour or against them. The QOC model (Question Options Criteria) [13], used by CSCW community for support to decision-making or for design rationale in a project, can then be useful. In this model, a question Q corresponds to a problem to solve. To solve the question Q, several Options are thought out, with, for each option, the criteria in its favour and the criteria against it: each option is thus connected positively or negatively to criteria. The QOC graph is reduced to a tree if no criterion is linked to several options.

Two types of questions are possible for the Virtual Staff:

- *Diagnosis of a pathology* (i.e. find the right A in the SOAP model): Which pathology explains the clinical signs of the patient?
- *Search of a prescription* (i.e. find the right P in the SOAP model): Which action plan will enable to treat the diagnosed pathology?

In the Virtual Staff, among the criteria to be satisfied, there are the patient's symptoms and the doctor's observations: for a question about the patient's pathology, each possible option will be linked by a positive influence link to the symptoms and observations compatible with this option, and by a negative link to the symptoms or observations rather incompatible with this pathology. The criteria will thus consist of

S or O nodes of the SOAP model but they may also sometimes correspond to A or P nodes, if some diseases are incompatible or if some care procedures are exclusive.

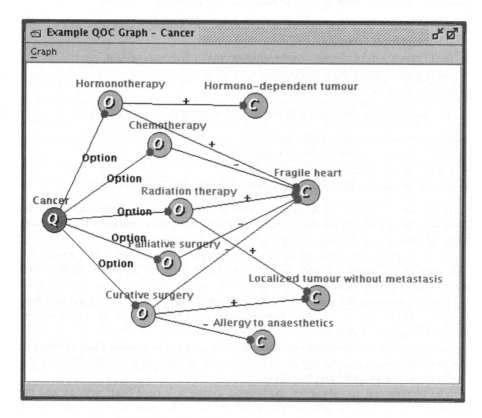

Fig. 4. QOC Graph for choice of a therapeutic protocol a cancer

For support to decision on a treatment to cure the diagnosed pathology, the options will be the various possible treatments, each one connected by a positive link to the criteria encouraging to choose it and by a negative link to the criteria inciting to reject it. For example, fig. 4 shows a QOC graph for choosing between an hormono-therapy, a chemotherapy, a radiotherapy, a palliative surgery and an eradicating surgery in order to treat a cancerous tumour, taking into account several criteria such as some characteristics of the tumour (e.g. hormono-dependent tumour, localised tumour without metastasis) or of the patient (e.g. fragile heart, allergy to anaesthesia).

3.4 Knowledge Representation for the Virtual Staff

In the Virtual Staff, we thus combine both models: SOAP to visualise the medical record and QOC in phase of decision to choose between pathologies or between action plans.

These graphs can be represented through conceptual graphs [20], built by using the concepts and relations of the Nautilus ontology. Due to the correspondence between conceptual graphs and RDF(S) language [2] 3] [4], SOAP or QOC graphs can also be represented in RDF(S). Using the Nautilus ontology, the system can propose a list of possible concepts to help the user to build the SOAP and QOC graphs:

- the S nodes will correspond to instances of selected concepts among the subconcepts of *Symptom*,
- the O nodes will be chosen among subconcepts of *Laboratory-Test*,
- the A nodes among those of *Pathology*,
- and the P nodes among those of *Treatment*.

The arcs between the nodes will correspond to relations among concepts:

- *Symptom has-for-cause Pathology;*
- *Pathology has-for-consequence Symptom;*
- *Pathology confirmed-by Laboratory-Test;*
- *Pathology treated-by Treatment; Symptom treated-by Treatment.*

In the same way, for QOC graphs aimed at determining the right pathology, the Options will be selected among the subconcepts of *Pathology*, and the Criteria among those of *Symptom, Laboratory-Test, Pathology* or *Treatment*.

To determine the right treatment, the Options will be selected among the subconcepts of *Treatment*, and the Criteria among those of *Symptom, Laboratory-Test, Pathology* or *Treatment*.

The arcs between the nodes of a QOC tree can be interpreted by « Question *has-solution* Option » or by « Option *has-argument-for* Criterion » or by « Option *has-argument-against* Criterion ».

To express certainty degrees on a diagnosis of disease or priority degrees between the possible treatments, the physician can indicate weights on some arcs between the nodes of SOAP or QOC graphs [14].

The incremental modifications performed during a Virtual Staff session and the final results of such a session are saved in an XML document in order to be exchanged with the Episodus software of our industrial partner.

Let us note that the Virtual Staff is not at all an expert system. It only allows the care team to visualise the reasoning and the decision-making process; the reasoning is carried out by the members of the network and the inferences based on the ontology enable the system to filter the choices offered to the user. The role of the QOC graph can be compared to a guide of best practices [10]. But the QOC graph relies on the specific data of the concerned patient and not on generic data. To the nodes or arcs of the SOAP and QOC graphs, one could associate medical documents such as guides of best practices: an argument on the choice of a given treatment could be connected by a hypertext link to a guide describing the criteria of selection of this treatment.

Remarks:
- If one integrates in the Nautilus ontology the list of symptoms associated to a pathology, a query to CORESE about all the pathologies possible for a given symptom of the patient could be useful for helping in the diagnosis of the disease while building the QOC graph.

- By the same way, if one integrates in Nautilus the possible treatments for each pathology, as described in a guide of best practices, CORESE will be able to suggest the list of the possible prescriptions for the QOC graph.
- If the Nautilus ontology is extended by the drugs and their side-effects or contra-indications, CORESE can suggest that a given drug may be cause of a given symptom or indicate a criterion against the choice of a given drug as a treatment of a pathology.

3.5 Virtual Staff Validation

The first version of the Virtual Staff was validated by our industrial partner, from two viewpoints: its functions and its interfaces. This evaluation led to several improvements of the graphical interface of the virtual staff: the new interface (see fig. 3 and 4) helps the user to really follow the reasoning guided by the SOAP model (each part of the graph is dedicated to nodes expressing either an Assessment or an Objective or a Subjective or a Plan) or by the QOC model (Question → Option → Criterion). Moreover, the parts of the SOAP and QOC graphs are visualised differently according to their creators: it is thus possible now to associate a colour to each participant in a given session so as to recognize, directly from the colour of the nodes or of the arcs, which physician or which member of the network argued about a given possible pathology or suggested a given treatment.

Our industrial partner will also ask actual physicians to handle the Virtual Staff in order to evaluate it from the viewpoint of a real end-user.

4 Conclusions

In this paper, we presented a translator of an ontology coded in an internal format of a database towards the RDF(S) language, in order to check and validate the ontology by visualising it via the CORESE engine, in a human-understandable form. The translation algorithm depends on the internal format of the database but the generic idea of building an ontology by decoding a database knowing its principle of coding, and then representing it in a standard formalism, is interesting for companies having DBs from which they wish to reconstitute an ontology.

Moreover this ontology was extended by using a knowledge acquisition method based on corpus analysis through a linguistic tool, as in [11] and by integrating an existing classification. This constitution of an ontology from heterogeneous sources (database, textual corpus, classification) could be compared with approaches such as the ONIONS method [8] [9].

We also specified and developed in JAVA a Virtual Staff, with:

- SOAP graphs describing the links between diagnostic and therapeutic hypotheses, symptoms and observations,
- and QOC graphs for support to decision-making.

The nodes of both kinds of graphs are typed by the concepts of the ontology.

Such a combination of these SOAP and QOC models with an ontology is original and illustrates the interest of an ontology to help the user to visualise a reasoning or a decision-making process.

The ontology and the Virtual Staff were validated by our Nautilus partner. As noticed earlier, the validation of the ontology through CORESE enabled to detect some errors in the initial ontology and the evaluation of the virtual staff led to strong improvements of its interfaces.

Notice that, even though the Virtual Staff was implemented with the Nautilus ontology (for collaboration reasons), it would be possible to adapt the Virtual Staff to another medical ontology such as UMLS meta-thesaurus.

As a further work, we plan several extensions and improvements of the Virtual Staff:

- *Extend the Nautilus ontology* as suggested in section 3.4; provided that such extensions are accepted by the physicians (cf. according to our industrial partner, it seems that some physicians do not appreciate to have "intelligent" suggestions from a system and prefer to choose and decide everything themselves).
- *Improve the cooperation of multiple users* through the Virtual Staff.

Last, our industrial partner will proceed to its evaluation by physicians taking part in an actual network (probably in diabetes).

Acknowledgements. We thank Ph Ameline the author of the Nautilus database who launched the project "Ligne de Vie", Pr P. Degoulet, Dr. Dericco, Mrs. Labelle and Mrs D. Sauquet, for our fruitful discussions, and the "Ministère de la Jeunesse, de l'Éducation Nationale et de la Recherche" for funding the project "Ligne de Vie".

References

1. Aussenac-Gilles, N., Biébow, B., Szulman, S.: Revisiting Ontology Design: a Methodology Based on Corpus Analysis. In R. Dieng, O. Corby eds, Knowledge Engineering and Knowledge Management: Methods, Models and Tools, Springer-Verlag, LNAI 1937, p. 172-188 October 2000.
2. Corby, O., Dieng, R., Hebert, C.: A Conceptual Graph Model for W3C Resource Description Framework. In B. Ganter, G. W. Mineau eds, Conceptual Structures: Theory, Tools, and Applications, Proc. of ICCS'2000, Springer-Verlag, LNAI 1867, Darmstadt, Germany, August 13-17, 2000, p. 468-482.
3. Corby, O., Faron-Zucker, C.: Corese : A Corporate Semantic Web Engine. In Workshop on Real World RDF and Semantic Web Applications - 11th International World Wide Web Conference 2002 Hawaii. May 2002. http:// paul.rutgers. edu/~kashyap/ workshop.html
4. Corby, O., Dieng-Kuntz, R., Faron-Zucker, C.: Querying the Semantic Web with the CORESE Search Engine. To appear in Proc. of the 3rd Prestigious Applications Intelligent Systems Conference (PAIS'2004) in conjunction with the 16th European Conference on Artificial Intelligence (ECAI'2004), Valencia (Spain), August 25-27th, 2004.
5. Côté, R. A, Rothwell, D. J., Palotay, J. L., Beckett, R. S., Brochu, L. (eds): The Systematized Nomenclature of Human and Veterinary Medicine: Snomed International. Northfield, Il: College Of American Pathologists. 1993.

6. Dieng-Kuntz, R., Matta, N. (eds): Knowledge Management and Organizational Memories, Kluwer Academic Publishers, July 2002.
7. Dumas, L., Plante, A., Plante, P.: ALN: Analyseur Linguistique de ALN, version 1.0. ATO, UQAM.
8. Gangemi, A., Pisanelli, D., Steve, G.: Ontology Integration: Experiences with Medical Terminologies, In N. Guarino ed, Formal Ontology in Information Systems, IOS Press, pp. 163-178, 1998.
9. Gangemi, A., Pisanelli, D., Steve, G.: An Overview of the ONIONS Project: Applying Ontologies to the Integration of Medical Terminologies. Data and Knowledge Engineering, 31(2):183-220, 1999.
10. Georg, G., Seroussi, B., Bouaud, J.: Dérivation d'une base de connaissances à partir d'une instance GEM d'un guide de bonnes pratiques médicales textuel. In R. Dieng-Kuntz ed, Actes des 14èmes Journées Francophones sur l'Ingénierie des Connaissances (IC'2003), Laval, Presses Universitaires de Grenoble, Juillet 2003.
11. Golebiowska, J., Dieng-Kuntz, R., Corby, O., Mousseau, D.: SAMOVAR : using ontologies and text-mining for building an automobile project memory, in R. Dieng-Kuntz & N. Matta eds, Knowledge Management and Organizational Memories, p. 89-102, Kluwer Academic Publishers, Boston, July 2002
12. Lassila, O., Swick R. R.: Resource Description Framework (RDF) Model and Syntax Specification. W3C Recomm., 22 Feb. 1999, http://www.w3.org/tr/rec-rdf-syntax/
13. Maclean, A., Young, R., Bellotti, V., Moran T.: Questions, Options, and Criteria: Elements of a Design Rationale for User Interfaces. Int. Journal of Human-Computer-Interaction, 6(3/4):201-250. 1991.
14. Minier, D., Corby, F., Dieng-Kuntz, R., Corby, O., Luong, P.-H., Alamarguy, L.: Rapport intermédiaire du contrat Ligne de Vie, Octobre 2003.
15. National Library of Medicine: UMLS Knowledge Source. 14th Edition, Jan. 2003 Doc. National Institute of Health – National Library of Medicine, Bethesda, Md, USA.
16. Pisanelli, D. M., Gangemi, A., Steve, G.: An Ontological Analysis of the UMLS Metathesaurus. Journal of the American Medical Inforlatiocs Association, 5:810-814, 1998.
17. Rector, A., Gangemi, A., Galeazzi, E., Glowinski, A., Rossi-Mori, A.: The Galen Model Schemata for Anatomy: Towards a Re-Usable Application- Independent Model of Medical Concepts. In P. Barahona, M. Veloso, J. Bryant (eds), Proceedings of Medical Informatics in Europe MIE 94, p. 229-233. 1994.
18. Rector, A., Rogers, J., Pole, P.: The Galen High Level Ontology. In J. Bender, J.P. Christensen, J.R. Scherrer & P. Mcnair (eds), Proceedings of Medical Informatics in Europe MIE 96, p. 174-178. Amsterdam: IOS Press. 1996.
19. Ribière, M., Dieng-Kuntz, R.: A Viewpoint Model for Cooperative Building of an Ontology, Conceptual Structures: Integration and Interfaces, Proc. of the 10th International Conference in Conceptual Structures (ICCS'2002), Springer-Verlag, LNCS 2393, U. Priss, D. Corbett, G. Angelova eds. p. 220-234, Borovetz, Bulgaria, July 15-19, 2002.
20. Sowa, J. F.: Conceptual Structures: Information Processing In Mind and Machine, Addison-Wesley, 1984.
21. Spackman, K., Campbell, K., Côté, R.: SNOMED RT: A Reference Terminology for Health Care. In D.R. Masys (ed.), The Emergence of Internetable Health Care. Systems That Really Work - Proceedings of the 1997 Amia Annual Symposium. Nashville. Tn, October 25-29, 1997. Philadelphia, Pa: Hanley & Belfus.
22. Weed, L. D.: The Problem Oriented Record as a Basic Tool in Medical Education, Patient Care and Clinical Research. Ann Clin Res 3(3):131-134. 1971.

23. Zweigenbaum P., Consortium Menelas: Menelas: Coding and Information Retrieval from Natural Language Patient Discharge Summaries. Advances in Health Telematics, p. 82-89, Amsterdam: IOS Press. 1995.
24. Zweigenbaum, P., Bachimont, B., Bouaud, J., Charlet, J., Boisvieux, J.-F.: Issues In the Structuring and Acquisition of an Ontology for Medical Language Understanding. Methods of Information In Medicine, 34(1/2), 15-24, (1995).

A Semantic Portal for the International Affairs Sector

Contreras J.[1], Benjamins V.R[1], Blázquez M[1], Losada S[1], Salla R[1], Sevilla, J[1],
Navarro D.[1], Casillas J.[1], Mompó A.[1], Patón D.[1],
Corcho O.[1], Tena P.[2], and Martos I[2]

[1]Intelligent Software Components, S.A.
www.isoco.com
{rbenjamins,jcontreras}@isoco.com
[2]Real Instituto Elcano
www.realinstitutoelcano.org
pilar.tena@r-i-elcano.org

Abstract. The Royal Institute Elcano[†] (Real Instituto Elcano) in Spain is a prestigious independent political institute whose mission is to comment on the political situation in the world focusing on its relation to Spain. As part of its dissemination strategy it operates a public website. The online content can be accessed by navigating through categories or by a keyword-based, full text search engine. The work described in this paper aims at improving access to the content. We describe an approach, tools and techniques that allow building a semantic portal, where access is based on the meaning of concepts and relations of the International Affairs domain. The approach comprises an automatic ontology-based annotator, a semantic search engine with a natural language interface, a web publication tool allowing semantic navigation, and a 3D visualization component. The semantic portal is currently being tested by the Institute.

1 Introduction

Worldwide there are several prestigious institutes that comment on the political situation in the world, such as the UK's Royal Institute for International Affairs (www.riia.org), the Dutch Institute for International Relations (www.clingendael.nl). In Spain, the Real Instituto Elcano (Royal Institute Elcano, www.realinstitutoelcano. org) is fulfilling this role. The institute provides several types of reports where they discuss the political situation in the world, with a focus on events relevant for Spain. The reports are organized in different categories, such as Economy, Defense, Society, Middle East, etc. In a special report - the "Barometer of the Royal Institute Elcano" - the Institute comments on how the rest of the world views Spain in the political arena. Access to the content is provided by categorical navigation and a traditional full text search engine. While full text search engines are helpful instruments for information retrieval (www.google.com is the champion), in domains where relations are

---

[†] Juan Sebastian Elcano was a famous Spanish sailor, a first seaman who ever made the complete circuit of the globe

E. Motta et al. (Eds.): EKAW 2004, LNAI 3257, pp. 203–215, 2004.
© Springer-Verlag Berlin Heidelberg 2004

important, those techniques fall short. For instance, a keyword-based search engine will have a hard time to find the answer to a question such as: "Governments of which countries have a favorable attitude toward the US-led armed intervention in Iraq?" since the crux of answering this question resides in "understanding" the relation "has-favourable-attitude-toward".

In this paper we describe a project whose aim was to provide semantic access to content available in the portal of the Elcano Institute. With semantics, we mean here meaning related to the domain of International Affairs. In other words, we aim to construct an island of the Semantic Web for the International Affairs sector.

In order to construct this Semantic Web Island, we use an approach, tools and techniques that are being developed in the context of several European and National R&D projects [1]. Components include:

- A domain ontology (in this case an ontology of International Affairs)
- An automatic annotator (metadata generator), called Knowledge Parser®
- A semantic search engine with a natural language interface, as well as a forms-based interface
- A publication tool for publishing semantic content on the web –Duontology®-, enabling semantic navigation including a 3D visualization tool

In Section 2, we describe the ontology of the International Relations domain. Section 3 details how we populate the ontology with instances, and how we establish relations between the current content of the Elcano Institute and the (instances of the) ontology. Then, in Section 4, we explain our approach (Duontology®) to publish the semantic content in a semantic web portal providing a semantic search engine. Section 5 concludes the paper.

2   An Ontology of International Affairs

2.1 Ontology

An ontology is a shared and common understanding of some domain that can be communicated across people and computers [6, 7, 3, and 8]. Ontologies can therefore be shared and reused among different applications [5]. An ontology can be defined as a formal, explicit specification of a shared conceptualization [6, 3]. "Conceptualization" refers to an abstract model of some phenomenon in the world by having identified the relevant concepts of that phenomenon. "Explicit" means that the type of concepts used, and the constraints on their use are explicitly defined. "Formal" refers to the fact that the ontology should be machine-readable. "Shared" reflects the notion that an ontology captures consensual knowledge, that is, it is not private to some individual, but accepted by a group. An ontology describes the subject matter using the notions of concepts, instances, relations, functions, and axioms. Concepts in the ontology are organized in taxonomies through which inheritance mechanisms can be applied. It is our experience that especially the social part for building a commonly agreed ontology is not easy [2].

2.2 An Ontology of International Affairs

Based on interviews with experts of the Elcano Institute, we used the CIA world factbook (www.cia.gov/cia/publications/factbook/) as the basis for the ontology of International Affairs. The CIA fact book is a large online repository with actual information on most countries of the world, along with relevant information in the fields of geography, politics, society, economics, etc.

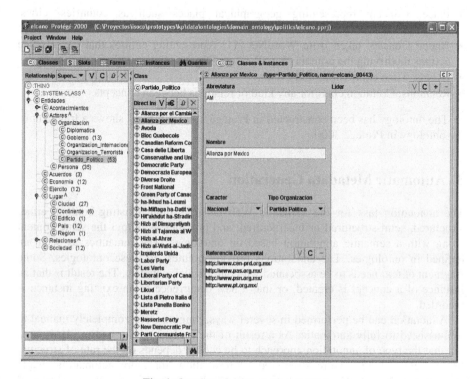

Fig. 1. Ontology for International Affairs

We have used the competency questions approach [10] to determine the scope and granularity of the domain ontology. Some examples of competency questions that we considered include:

```
What countries are participating on Iraq campaign?

Who is the head of the state of France?

What government type has Georgia?

How big is the population of Iceland?

Which are all European Union member countries?

Which are all agreements between Spain and Brazil subscribed
during Da Silva's govern?
```

An important design decision we took (based on [13]) was that relationships between concepts are modeled as first class objects. This decision was taken because often the relationships themselves have attributes that cannot be modeled by its involving concepts. Take for example, the relation "in_favour_of" between an agent (person, nation, government) and an event (war, boycott, treaty). This relation is qualified by a start and end date, which is not meaningful to agent nor event.

The ontology consists of several top level classes, some of which are:

- Place: Concept representing geographical places such as countries, cities, buildings, etc.
- Agent: Concept taken from WordNet [11] representing entities that can execute actions modifying the domain (e.g.: Persons, Organizations, etc.)
- Events: Time expressions and events
- Relations: Common class for any kind of relations between concepts.

The ontology has been constructed in Protégé 2000 [9]. Fig 1 shows a fragment of the ontology in Protégé 2000.

3   Automatic Metadata Generation

The annotation task for the Semantic Web takes as input existing content, either structured, semi-structured or unstructured, and provides as output the same content along with a semantic annotation based on ontologies. The semantics as such are defined in ontologies. The annotations provide pointers to these ontologies. Some fragment of text needs to be associated with ontological metadata. The result is that an instance of a concept is created, or that a new occurrence of an existing instance is recorded.

Annotation can be performed in several ways, ranging from completely manual to tool-assisted to fully automatic. As a result of the analysis performed in [4], it turns out that the type of annotation approach to be chosen depends on the rate of structure the content exhibits. More structured sources allow for more automation, while maintaining the quality of the annotations. As has been the experience of several researchers and practitioners, the annotation effort is a serious barrier to the Semantic Web [2].

Our approach for automatic metadata generation is based on a combination of several technologies from the information extraction research area: Natural Language Processing (NLP), Text Engineering (process strings: e.g.: using regular expressions), Document Structure Processing and Layout Processing. Such a combination of techniques allows processing each source with the most suitable and effective approach depending on its structure and content. For instance, for a highly structured table-based text the most effective approach would consists on structure processing with some help of layout and NLP techniques. For large descriptions where whole sentences are usual, the most appropriate approach would be mainly NLP processing.

We named our system Knowledge Parser® since it is able to parse content and extract knowledge from it. Following we explain in briefly how our Knowledge Parser works. Figure 2 illustrates the process executed in three main steps: Source Preprocessing, Information Identification and Ontology Population.

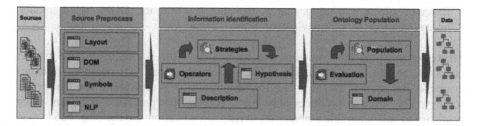

Fig. 2. Overview of the extraction and population process

3.1 Source Preprocessing

The Source Preprocess module (on the left-hand side) provides four different visions on the same source using four document access models:

- Document Object Model (DOM): This is used for HTML understanding of the source in term of allowing the system for navigation and tag processing
- Text Model: This model treats the source as a simple character string and allows using regular expression techniques.
- Layout Model: Provides a special model for the source assigning two dimension coordinates to each element.
- NLP Model: Provides access NLP information such as a list of proper names, verbal phrases, synonyms, etc.

3.2 Information Identification

The goal of the central Information Identification Module is the main control of the extraction activity. The result of this step is a hypothesis set about how the extracted information pieces fits into the domain ontology. It contains three key components:

- **Operators:** perform extraction actions on document access models provided in the first step.
- **Strategies:** build operator sequences according to user time and quality requirements
- **Source Description:** formal description of typical characteristics of sources (see below)

  In the following, we explain each of them in more detail.

Operators are software functionalities associated to each source access model that can perform some useful action for extraction purposes. We classify operators into three categories depending on their behavior:

1. Retrieval: perform text chunk extraction on some source access model (e.g.: all proper names extraction from the NLP source access model)
2. Check: checks some constraint on the extracted data (e.g.: whether two elements are in the same visual row in the Layout access model)

3. Execute: allows executing source elements (e.g.: in the DOM access model, executing a web form or navigating through a link)

Strategies are pluggable modules that according to the source description invoke operators. In the current version of the system there are two possible strategies available. For system usages where the response time is critical we use the greedy strategy. This strategy produces only one hypothesis per processed document using heuristics to solve possible ambiguities in data identification. On the other hand when quality of annotation is a priority and requirements on response time are less important we use a backtracking strategy. This strategy produces a whole set of hypothesis to be evaluated and populated into the domain ontology.

Source Description. In order to perform any strategy the system needs to understand what kind of information pieces are expected in the source. The **source description** is formalized in, a so called, wrapping ontology. The wrapping ontology contains the following elements:

- Document Types: Description of document types in the source. For instance the CIA World Factbook home page is described with its URL and some relation to country name pieces.
- Pieces: Are the basic elements of the retrieval process. They contain the searched information with which the ontology will be populated. Each piece has defined its possible data types (number, NLP phrase, string, etc.).
- Relations: Relation between pieces and documents are modeled here. For instance, there are two possible relations between two pieces:
  - Layout relation: (e.g.: IN ROW: Two pieces may lay in the same visual row in the documents, see Fig. 3)
  - Semantic relation: (e.g.: verbal predicate: Two pieces are related using a verbal phrase with the main verb: 'agree' or synonyms)

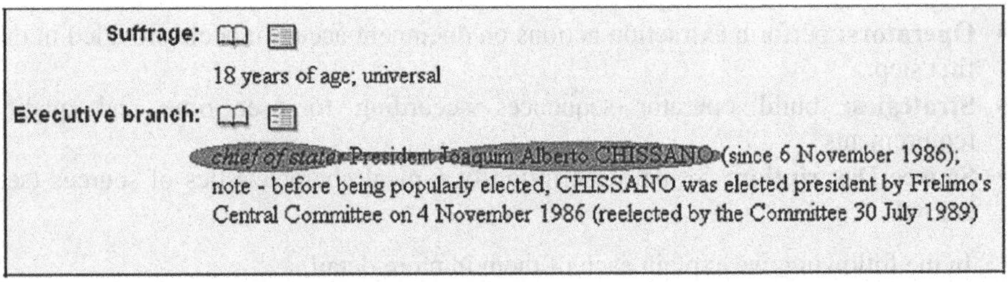

Fig. 3. Example of an IN ROW layout relation within the CIA World Factbook: Mozambique page

3.3 Ontology Population

The final stage of the overall process is to decide which hypothesis represents the extracted information to insert into the ontology. The Ontology Population Module (on the right-hand side at Fig. 2) is in charge of evaluating and sorting hypothesis for their insertion in the domain ontology. For evaluation purposes the module simulates insertions and calculates the cost according to the number of new instance creations, instance modifications or inconsistencies found (different values for the same instance). According to the Occam's razor principle only the lowest cost hypothesis is used for population. A low cost corresponds to an insertion with minimal modifications with respect to already existing instances. The result of this step, as well as the result of the whole system, is the augmented domain ontology including new instances and values.

3.4 Wrapping International Affairs Domain

In this particular application for the Elcano Institute, our Knowledge Parser fulfils two roles. The first one is the wrapping of the CIA World Factbook Web in order to populate the ontology with instances. From the CIA Factbook Web we extract information regarding countries such as their government composition, geographical data, political and commercial agreements, etc. We basically use a combination of the Layout Model and the NLP model. Once the ontology is populated with instances, we apply the Knowledge Parser to the documents provided by the Elcano institute. At this point, we are interested in identifying occurrences of instances. For example, if we found in the Factbook "Bush" as an instance of the "Head of State" concept of the ontology, then in the Elcano documents we want to find occurrences of these instances. That is, we want to recognize that when the parser finds "Bush", "George Bush" or "The president of the US", these are occurrences of .the instance "Bush".

Summarizing, in the Elcano application, we use the Knowlege Parser in a two-step approach. Of course, we could have populated the ontology directly by wrapping only the documents of the Elcano institute. However, it would be a pity not to use the CIA Factbook, which is a high-quality, up to date and free repository with relevant information. The state of the art is still that structured information is easier to wrap than unstructured information.

4 A Semantic Portal for International Relations

A semantic portal provides semantic access (as opposed to keyword-based access) to content. In our case semantic access is provided through:

- Semantic publishing and navigation
- Semantic search engine
- 3D Visualization

4.1 Semantic Publishing and Navigation

Experience has shown [14] that the knowledge base as modeled by domain experts and knowledge engineers is not always a good candidate to visualize it as is.

The main purpose for building ontologies is to provide semantically enhanced content for intelligent systems. The knowledge models are designed to offer the appropriate information to be exploited by the software. No visualization criteria are used to build an ontology and often the information is not suitable to be published as it is:

- Concepts may have too many attributes
- When relations are represented as independent concepts (first class objects) the navigation becomes tedious
- Concepts to be shown do not always correspond to modeled ones.

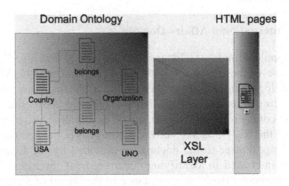

Fig. 4. Explicit visualization using direct translator

Therefore we felt a need for explicit visualization rules that allow the creation of views on the International Relations ontology, in order to visualize only the relevant information in a user friendly way. We introduced the concept of "visualization ontology", which makes explicit all visualization rules and allows an easy interface management. This ontology will contain concepts and instances (publication entities) as seen on the interface by the end user, and it will retrieve the attribute values from the International Relations ontology using a query. It does not duplicate the content of the original ontology, but links the content to publication entities using an ontology query language. This way one ontology that represents a particular domain can be visualized through different views.

The visualization ontology has two predefined concepts:

- Publication entity: Concept that encapsulates objects as they will be published in the portal. Any concept defined in the visualization ontology will inherit from it and should define these attributes
  - XSL style-sheet associated to the concept that translates its instances to final format (HTML, WAP, VoiceXML, etc.)
  - Query that retrieves all attribute values from the original ontology.
- Publication Slot: Each attribute that is going to appear on the web should inherit from this concept. Different facets describe how the attribute will appear on the page.
  - Web label: The label that will appear with the value
  - RDQL: reference to the query used to retrieve the attribute value

- Link: When the published value should perform some action on mouse click (link, email, button, etc...), the action is described here.

Portal elements are described as children of the Publication Entity and their instances are defined according to the languages the entity will be published in (labels in English, Spanish, etc.), or the channel (whether the transformation style-sheet is going to translate into HTML, WAP, or just XML.

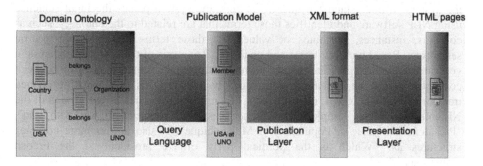

Fig. 5. Publication using specific visualization ontology (Duontology approach)

Back-office management is divided into two tasks:

- Content management on domain ontology: adding new instances or modifying the overall schema.
- Visualization management on publication ontology: modifying how information is shown (look and feel, layout, etc.)

Both tasks are performed using the Protégé 2000 editor, since both domain and publication models are defined in the RDF language.

4.2 Semantic Search Engine

We have developed a Semantic Search Engine for improving content access. Semantic search engines return instances that constitute answers to queries rather than documents containing searched strings as traditional keyword based engines would do. Semantic engines work with the meaning of the query terms. The meaning of each term is defined using the domain ontology.

The user can ask for a list of instances of a selected concept putting general constraints on attribute values. For instance, he or she can ask for all events that happened during 1991. Traditional engines would return all documents containing that number, including birth dates, names, etc. A Semantic engine returns instances of the concept "Event" whose duration includes the year 1991. For each instance there exists a link (called reference) to documents where that event is mentioned. The user is also able to make a compound query nesting concepts through their attributes, for example: all countries that have common border with Lithuania. An other way of searching is looking for relations. Since this ontology has been designed to model relations as first class concepts, the user can make a query about any relation between two states (e.g.: "All relations between Spain and France").

There are two kinds of interface for the search engine. The first is based on forms representing domain concepts and existing relations. The user chooses some concept and constructs a complex query putting values for attributes and/or nesting more concepts through relations.

The second type of interface accepts input written in natural language. The user can, if he or she prefers so, formulate a simple natural language query. It is the task of the system to understand the query. For this, the system parses the input sentence using NLP software and identifies those terms that are related to the ontology, such as concepts, instances, attributes or values (i.e those terms carry domain-specific semantics). Based on those terms and on the NLP analysis of the sentence, the system generates a domain-specific semantic representation of the sentence as a path between concepts, with some constraints introduced by values. This representation is then transformed into an RDQL query, which is then submitted. The current version of the NL interface allows simple sentences such as: "All countries in war with Iraq", "President of France", "Population of Mozambique". It also allows more complex structures as: "Which is the political party of the president of the French Government?"

4.3 3D Visualization

We have also developed a 3D generation module that allows navigating through the search result or ontology content. For that purposes we have implemented software that translates any given domain ontology, applying visualization rules, into the X3D [12] standard. The resulting scene shows instances in a three-dimensional net represented as geometrical bodies with an ad-hoc defined texture. The scene is highly interactive allowing users to move the focus position and interact with the object by clicking on them.

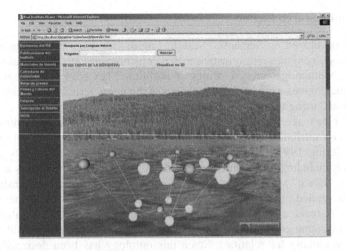

Fig. 6. 3D navigation on domain ontology

5 Related Work

Our Knowledge Parser is related to several other initiatives in the area of automatic annotation for the Semantic Web, including KIM [15], which is based on GATE [16], Annotea [17] of W3C., Amilcare [18] of the Open University (also based on GATE), and AeroDAML [19]. For an overview of those approaches and others, see [4]. All approaches use NLP as an important factor to extract semantic information. Our approach is innovative in the sense that it combines four different techniques for Information Extraction in a generic, scalable and open architecture. The state of the art of most of these approaches is still not mature enough (few commercial deployments) to provide concrete comparison in terms of performance and memory requirements.

6 Conclusions

In this paper, we presented an application of Semantic Web Technology for the International Affairs Sector. The application will be launched by the Royal Institute Elcano before Summer 2004 at www.realinstitutoelcano.org. Currently we are in the final testing phase (pre-deployment). The application allows visitors of the web site to access the Elcano's documents in a more intelligent manner through a semantic search engine, semantic navigation and 3D graphical navigation and interaction.

The ontology of International Relations is inspired by the CIA World Fact book, which is a large online up to date source with relevant information. Documents of the Elcano Institute are automatically associated to this ontology, thereby disclosing them semantically. Semantic access is made possible through a software we call Knowledge Parser®, which is capable of "understanding" digital text.

The Knowledge Parser® is a generic architecture currently integrating four different technologies relevant for information extraction from text: NLP, Text Engineering, Document Structure and Layout. Its input is digital content in more or less structured form, and the output is an ontological classification of the content (ontological annotation).

For this particular application, we have applied the Knowledge Parser® in a two-step bootstrapping approach. First, to automatically populate the International Relations Ontology with instances from the CIA World Fact Book, and secondly, to automatically find occurrences of the ontology instances in the Elcano documents.

In future work we plan to include content of other institutes of the same area, providing a semantic one-stop shop for access to information about International Affairs.

Acknowledgements

Part of this work has been funded by the European Commission in the context of the project Esperonto Services IST-2001- 34373, SWWS IST- 2001-37134, SEKT IST-

2003-506826 and by the Spanish government in the scope of the project: Buscador Semántico, Real Instituto Elcano (PROFIT 2003, TIC). The natural language software used in this application is licensed from Bitext (www.bitext.com). For ontology management we use JENA libraries from HP Labs (http://www.hpl.hp.com/semweb).

References

[1] Gómez-Pérez A, Fernández-López M, Corcho O (2003) Ontological Engineering. Springer-Verlag. London, UK.
[2] V. R. Benjamins, D. Fensel, S. Decker, and A. Gomez-Perez. (KA)2: Building ontologies for the internet: a mid term report. International Journal of Human-Computer Studies, 51(3):687–712, 1999.
[3] W. N. Borst. Construction of Engineering Ontologies. PhD thesis, University of Twente, Enschede, 1997.
[4] Contreras   et al. D31: Annotation Tools and Services, Esperonto Project: www.esperonto.net
[5] Farquhar, R. Fikes, and J. Rice. The ontolingua server: a tool for collaborative ontology construction. International Journal of Human-Computer Studies, 46(6):707–728, June 1997.
[6] T. R. Gruber. A translation approach to portable ontology specifications. Knowledge Acquisition, 5:199–220, 1993.
[7] N. Guarino. Formal ontology, conceptual analysis and knowledge representation. International Journal of Human-Computer Studies, 43(5/6):625–640, 1995. Special issue on The Role of Formal Ontology in the Information Technology.
[8] G. van Heijst, A. T. Schreiber, and B. J. Wielinga. Using explicit ontologies in KBS development. International Journal of Human-Computer Studies, 46(2/3):183–292, 1997.
[9] Protege 2000 tool: http://protege.stanford.edu
[10] M. Uschold and M. Gruninger. Ontologies: principles, methods, and applications. Knowledge Engineering Review, 11(2):93–155, 1996.
[11] WordNet: http://www.cogsci.princeton.edu/~wn/
[12] X3D http://www.web3d.org/x3d.html
[13] Benjamins, Contreras, et al, Cultural Heritage and the Semantic Web. In proceedings of First European Semantic Web Symposium, May 2004, Crete,
[14] Rubén Lara, Sung-Kook Han, Holger Lausen, Michael Stollberg, Ying Ding, Dieter Fensel: An Evaluation of Semantic Web Portals, IADIS Applied Computing International Conference 2004, Lisbon, Portugal, March 23-26, 2004
[15] Atanas Kiryakov, Borislav Popov, Damyan Ognyanoff, Dimitar Manov, Angel Kirilov, Miroslav Goranov Semantic Annotation, Indexing, and Retrieval 2nd International Semantic Web Conference (ISWC2003), 20-23 October 2003, Florida, USA. LNAI Vol. 2870, pp. 484-499, Springer-Verlag Berlin Heidelberg 2003
[16] H. Cunningham, D. Maynard, K. Bontcheva, V. Tablan. GATE: A Framework and Graphical Development Environment for Robust NLP Tools and Applications. Proceedings of the 40th Anniversary Meeting of the Association for Computational Linguistics (ACL'02). Philadelphia, July 2002
[17] José Kahan, Marja-Riitta Koivunen, Eric Prud'Hommeaux, and Ralph R. Swick, Annotea: An Open RDF Infrastructure for Shared Web Annotations, in Proc. of the WWW10 International Conference, Hong Kong, May 2001.

[18] Fabio Ciravegna: "(LP)2, an Adaptive Algorithm for Information Extraction from Web-related Texts" in Proceedings of the IJCAI-2001 Workshop on Adaptive Text Extraction and Mining, held in conjunction with the 17th International Conference on Artificial Intelligence (IJCAI-01), Seattle, August, 2001

[19] P. Kogut and W. Holmes, "AeroDAML: Applying Information Extraction to Generate DAML Annotations from Web Pages", in Proceedings of the First International Conference on Knowledge Capture (K-CAP 2001).

OntoWeaver-S: Supporting the Design of Knowledge Portals

Yuangui Lei, Enrico Motta, and John Domingue

Knowledge Media Institute, the Open University,
{y.lei,e.motta,j.b.domingue}@open.ac.uk

Abstract. This paper presents OntoWeaver-S, an ontology-based infrastructure for building knowledge portals. In particular, OntoWeaver-S is integrated with a comprehensive web service platform, IRS-II, for the publication, discovery, and execution of web services. In this way, OntoWeaver-S supports the access and provision of remote web services for knowledge portals. Moreover, it provides a set of comprehensive site ontologies to model and represent knowledge portals, and thus is able to offer high level support for the design and development process. Finally, OntoWeaver-S provides a set of powerful tools to support knowledge portals at design time as well as at run time.

1 Introduction

The semantic web [2] is the vision of next generation of the World Wide Web. It extends the current web by associating well-structured meaning with web resources. The major advantage of doing so is that it enables the information understandable and consumable not only for humans, but for computers as well. A substantial amount of efforts have been made for delivering the Semantic Web [19, 13, 15, 5, 21, 16]. In particular, a number of knowledge portals have been built, which allow users enjoying the benefits gained from the semantic web technology on information sharing and exchanging in specified communities. Examples include OntoWeb portal [19] (http://ontoweb.aifb.uni-karlsruhe.de/), Esperonto portal (http://www.esperonto. net) and KMi Semantic Portal (http://plainmoor.open.ac.uk/ksp). These knowledge portals typically employ a domain ontology as a share basis for information communication and information exchanging.   The typical functionalities provided by knowledge portals include:

- *Information provision*, which allows community users to submit information and make contributions to their communities.

- *Information presentation (or visualization)*, which visualizes the underlying data content coming from different sources.

- *Information querying*, which allows users to make queries over the underlying data sources.

E. Motta et al. (Eds.): EKAW 2004, LNAI 3257, pp. 216–230, 2004.
© Springer-Verlag Berlin Heidelberg 2004

Building such knowledge portals is a complex task. An ad-hoc development methodology often results in few re-usable components, costly and time consuming development processes, and poor performance on maintenance. In this context, a few approaches and tools have been developed [14, 8, 4, 18], which attempt to either automate the process of generating knowledge portals [4, 18] or facilitate and guide the activities involved in the design of knowledge portals [14, 8]. However, a number of requirements of knowledge portals have not been fully addressed in these frameworks:

- The need for accessing and providing remote web services. This requires the design frameworks of knowledge portals to be integrated with web service management platforms to allow end users to share their web services with others in their communities.
- The need for high-quality user interfaces. This calls for modelling languages with the expressive capability to describe sophisticated user interfaces and presentation styles, which provide appropriate facilities to allow end users to navigate and manipulate the back-end data sources and access remote web services.
- The ability to present personalized views of knowledge portals to individual users. This requires comprehensive customization support from the design frameworks.

OntoWeaver-S is an ontology-based application, which offers comprehensive support for the design and development of knowledge portals. In particular, it addresses the issues mentioned above by the following approaches:

- OntoWeaver-S extends OntoWeaver [9, 10, 11] by means of integrating the web service framework IRS-II [15] within the data-intensive web site design framework. In this way, OntoWeaver-S provides support for the target knowledge portals accessing and managing remote web services.
- OntoWeaver-S extends the OntoWeaver site view ontology to describe sophisticated site views of knowledge portals, including navigational structures and user interfaces, which allow the access to the back-end data sources and web services. In particular, web services can be specified within the site view components to allow the invocation of web services and the presentation of the web services results.
- OntoWeaver-S addresses the customization issues for knowledge portals by means of the inherited customization framework (from OntoWeaver).
- OntoWeaver-S offers a set of powerful tools for supporting knowledge portals at design time as well as at run time.

In this paper we focus on the support provided by OntoWeaver-S for the design and development of knowledge portals. We begin in section 2 by explaining the rationales of OntoWeaver-S. We then illustrate the OntoWeaver-S approach to modelling knowledge portals in section 3. Thereafter, in section 4 we discuss the customization support. In section 5 we describe the design-time support and the run-time support that the OntoWeaver-S tools provide for knowledge portals. In section 6 we describe the related work. Finally in section 7 we conclude our work and present the future work.

2 OntoWeaver-S Rationales

As shown in figure 1, OntoWeaver-S views a knowledge portal as a four-layer architecture: *a data layer, a site view layer, a presentation layer* and *a customization layer*. The data layer consists of data content that can be accessed and manipulated by means of accessing knowledge portals. It comprises *a domain ontology*, which serves as a share basis for knowledge exchanging, *structured semantic web content*, which represents instances of the domain ontology concepts, *unstructured conventional web content*, which is submitted by community users, and *remote web services*, which can be accessed through the user interfaces of knowledge portals. The site view layer defines sophisticated site views, which support the navigation within knowledge portals and the access to the data layer of knowledge portals. The presentation layer concerns the visual appearance and layout of knowledge portals. The customization layer describes customization requirements. It applies customization rules to the presentation layer, the site view layer, and the data layer to present customized views to individual users.

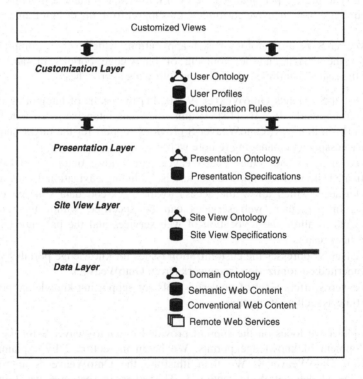

Fig. 1. The architecture of knowledge portals in OntoWeaver-S

OntoWeaver-S provides *a site view ontology, a presentation ontology, a customization framework,* and *a set of tools* to support the design and development of knowledge portals. Specifically, the site view ontology offers a set of comprehensive constructs to describe the site view layer; the presentation ontology allows the design of the presentation layer to be carried out at a high level of abstraction; and the customization framework offers high level support for the specification of customization requirements. Moreover, OntoWeaver-S is integrated with a comprehensive platform IRS-II to support the provision and access of remote web services for knowledge portals.

2.1 Integrating Web Services into Knowledge Portals

IRS-II is an implemented infrastructure, which has been developed in our lab, the Knowledge Media Institute (http://kmi.open.ac.uk). It supports the publication, discovery, and execution of semantic web services. The following informal specification shows the task description of a semantic web service, which answers requests for flights in accordance with the given user requirements.

Task Ontology: *flight-service*
Task Name: find-flights
Input Roles: from-place (type: city)
                to-place (type: city)
                depart-time (type: time-point)
                arrival-time (type: time-point)
                budget (type: amount-of-money)
Output Role: flights (type: Flight)

To invoke this semantic web service, a user (or an application) simply asks for the task to be achieved in terms of the task name *find-flights* and the task ontology name *flight-service,* the IRS-II *broker* then selects an appropriate problem solving method (*PSM*) and then uses *grounding information* to locate and invoke the corresponding web service – see [15] for a detailed description of IRS-II. In particular, the input roles carry parameters for executing the corresponding web service; the output roles store the service results. Please note that IRS-II only supports one output role at the moment. The data type of the output role can be primitive e.g. String and Integer, or non-primitive, e.g. being a domain class. When the data type of an output role is not primitive, IRS-II uses XML [24] to represent results. For example, IRS-II uses XML to represent the results of the web service find-flights, which are instances of the class *Flight* defined in the domain ontology of the semantic web service.

OntoWeaver-S employs IRS-II as a platform to integrate web services into knowledge portals. On the one hand, OntoWeaver-S relies on IRS-II to enable the access of remote web services, as IRS-II is able to locate and invoke remote web services and pass results back. On the other hand, OntoWeaver-S uses IRS-II as a platform to allow the provision of web services for knowledge portals.

Figure 2 shows the process of accessing remote web services in an OntoWeaver-S generated knowledge portal. OntoWeaver-S provides a run-time tool, called *Service Integrator*, to integrate IRS-II with knowledge portals. Specifically, the Service Integrator collects information from a knowledge portal, then calls the IRS-II server (by means of IRS-II APIs) to invoke the specified web service and gets results from IRS-II, and finally the Service Integrator passes the service results back to the knowledge portal. This process is invoked by end users when they submit information for accessing web services. Please see [12] for more details.

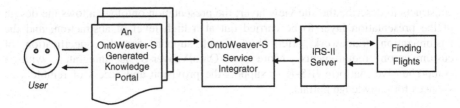

Fig. 2. The process of accessing web services in OntoWeaver-S generated knowledge portals

3 Modelling Knowledge Portals

As mentioned earlier, OntoWeaver-S offers a site view ontology to model the site view layer of knowledge portals. Figure 3 shows an overview of the site view ontology. It models a web site as a collection of logical resources; the logical resources describe web pages and are abstracted as compositions of resource components; and the resource components are described as compositions of a number of site view elements, e.g. output elements, input elements, command elements, and sub resource components.

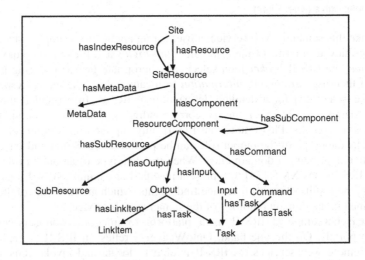

Fig. 3. An overview of the OntoWeaver-S site view ontology

The site view ontology offers *a set of navigational constructs* to facilitate the specification of complex navigational structures and *a set of user interface constructs* to allow for the composition of sophisticated user interfaces. The user interface constructs can be further classified into *atomic user interface constructs*, which describe atomic user interface elements that can not be further decomposed into other elements, and *composite user interface constructs*, which describe composite user interface elements.

On the one hand, these constructs can provide a fine grained level support for user interface composition. On the other hand, these constructs support the high level specification of access to semantic web services. Specifically, within the user interface constructs, remote web services are described in terms of *tasks*, *input roles* and *output roles*, which comply with the semantic representation approach employed in IRS-II. Please note that the concept of output role in OntoWeaver-S is slightly different from IRS-II when the data type of the output role of a web service is a class entity. As a class entity may have a number of slots, the output roles in OntoWeaver-S in this context refer to the slots of the result instances of the corresponding web service. For example, to present the results of the web service *find-flights*, the output roles specified in the user interface elements are slots of the class *Flight*.

3.1 Modelling Site Structures

By the term of site structure, we mean the coarse-grained level structure of an entire knowledge portal. A site structure comprises an index page node, which defines an entry point for the knowledge portal, a number of page nodes, which form the navigation space, and the URI of a domain ontology, which specifies the domain ontology for information sharing in the target knowledge portal. Like OntoWeaver, OntoWeaver-S relies on the construct *Site* to describe the components of web sites, *SiteResource* to define page nodes and *LinkItem* to express link relations between the page nodes. In particular, at the coarse-grained level, the detailed content of page nodes is not concerned. Each page node contains *a meta-data part* to describe its initial purpose and *a navigation component part* to hold links, which allow navigation from one page node to another. As the principle of specifying site structures in OntoWeaver-S remains the same with that in OntoWeaver, we will not detail the specification here. Please refer to [11] for details.

3.2 Modelling the Composition of Web Pages

Figure 4 shows a sample user interface, which visualizes the results of the web service *find-flights*. As illustrated in the figure, the user interface is composed of a number of static output elements and dynamic output elements. Like OntoWeaver, OntoWeaver-S abstracts the user interface of a web page as the composition of *resource components*. Each resource component is modelled as a composition of a number of sub elements. The sub elements can be composite elements, which in turn contain a number of elements. Thus, complex user interfaces can be easily composed.

3.3 Modelling Dynamic Features of Knowledge Portals

As mentioned earlier, the typical dynamic features of knowledge portals include i) *information visualization*, which publishes the dynamic data content coming from the underlying data sources or from remote web services; ii) *information provision*, which allows the provision of information for updating the underlying knowledge bases, iii) *web service access*, which allows end users to access web services, and iv) *information querying*, which allows end users to make queries over the back-end knowledge bases. OntoWeaver-S provides a set of user interface constructs to describe the user interfaces, which realize these dynamic features. Moreover, these user interface constructs can be easily adjusted to meet particular requirements of knowledge portals, as OntoWeaver-S provides fine-grained constructs to allow the declarative representation of user interface elements.

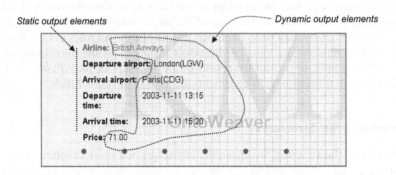

Static output elements   Dynamic output elements

Fig. 4. A user interface sample for visualizing the results of the web service *find-flights*

3.3.1 Information Visualization

Information visualization in knowledge portals presents dynamic information, which comes from the underlying knowledge bases, web resources or remote web services. OntoWeaver-S relies on the following constructs to enable the composition of the user interfaces for information visualization:

- *DynamicOutput*, which models basic user interface elements that present the dynamic value of the specified field of a given class entity or the dynamic value of the specified output role of a given web service. The construct *DynamicOutput* has a number of attributes: the attributes *hasTask* and *hasOutputRole* are used in the case of presenting dynamic values of web services; the attributes *hasClassEntity* and *hasSlotEntity* are used to specify values from the specified slot of a class entity.
- *OutputComponent*, which describes the composite user interface element for publishing the value of the specified slot of the given class entity or the value of the specified output role of the given web service. An output component typically comprises an output element, which presents explanations about the dynamic content, and a dynamic element, which displays the dynamic content.
- *DataComponent*, which abstracts user interface elements that visualize instances of a specified class entity or results of a specified web service. The user interface shown in figure 4 presents the result of the web service *find-flights*. As illustrated in the figure, the user interface comprises a number of static output elements explaining the meaning of the dynamic values and a number of dynamic output elements presenting dynamic values. The following RDF code illustrates the specification of the user interface (The prefix *'svo'* refers to the namespace of the site view ontology: xmlns:svo=*"http://kmi.open.ac.uk/people/yuangui/siteviewontology#"*).

```
<rdf:Description rdf:about="flights-result-page/datacomponent" >
  <rdf:type rdf:resource="&svo;DataComponent" />
  <svo:task rdf:resource="find-flights"/>
  <svo:outputComponent>
    ...
  </svo:outputCompoenent>
</rdf:Description>
...
<rdf:Description about="flights-result-page/datacomponent/airline/dynamicoutput" >
    <so:outputType>text</so:outputType>
    <so:task rdf:resource="find-flights" />
    <so:outputRole rdf:resource="find-flights/airline" />
</rdf:Descripltion>
```

3.3.2 Information Provision

The information provision is realized through knowledge acquisitions forms, which allow users to submit information to knowledge portals. The submitted information can be instances of the underlying domain ontology classes, web resources or information for invoking the specified service. Please note that in this context, the service can be a built-in service provided by OntoWeaver-S or a remote web service, which has been made available through IRS-II. In particular, a knowledge acquisition component can be used for information provision, information query and web services access. OntoWeaver-S proposes a set of constructs to model the composition of knowledge acquisition forms:

- *Input*, which abstracts the input fields for allowing end users specifying information for particular slots of the specified class entity or for particular input roles of the specified web service.
- *Command*, which describes the interface elements for submitting information. In particular, the specification of a command element indicates the associated service and the result page node, which intends to present results of the associated service.
- *InputComponent*, which describes the composite user interface elements for allowing the information provision for the specified slot of the given domain class entity or for the specified input role of the associated service. An input component typically contains an input element for presenting an input field and an output element for presenting an explanation about the input field.
- *KAComponent*, which models components that present forms for allowing end users to submit information to knowledge portals. The user interface of a knowledge acquisition component is composed by a number of output elements, which present explanations for input elements, a number of input elements, which present input fields, and a command element, which allows users to submit information. The purpose of the submitted information is indicated by the specified service. In the case of semantic web content provision, the associated service is the built-in knowledge acquisition service.

3.3.3 Web Service Access

As discussed above, the functionality of accessing remote web service can be realized through knowledge acquisition forms. In particular, for those web services, which have already been made available at the design time of knowledge portals, user interfaces for accessing them can be specified at design time. For those, which are made available later, the user interfaces can be generated automatically by mapping the semantic descriptions of web services to the provided user interface constructs.

Figure 5 shows an example user interface for accessing the remote web service *find-flights*, which answers requests for flights in accordance with the given user requirements. The user interface is made up of a number of input components, which present input fields and explanations about these input fields, and a command element, which allows end users to submit information and invoke the web service. The following code illustrates the composition of this user interface. In particular, the input elements define the connections between the input fields and the input roles of the specified web service. The command element specifies the web page, which is designed to visualize the results of the web service.

```
<rdf:Description about="find-flights-page/kacomponent" >
    <rdf:type rdf:resource="&svo;KAComponent"/>
    <svo:task rdf:resource="find-flights"/>
    <svo:inputComponent>
        <rdf:Bag>
            <rdf:li resource="find-flights-page/kacomponent/from-place"/>
            <rdf:li resource=" find-flights-page/kacomponent/to-place"/>
            ...
        </rdf:Bag>
    </svo:inputComponent>
    <svo:command rdf:resource="find-flights-page/kacomponent/command" />
</rdf:Description>
...
<!-- the specification of the command element -->
<rdf:Description about="find-flights-page/kacomponent/command" >
    <rdf:type rdf:resource="&svo;Command"/>
    <svo:commandText>Submit</svo:commandText>
    <svo:task rdf:resource="find-flights"/>
    <svo:resultPage rdf:resource="flights-result-page" />
</rdf:Description>

<!-- the specification of an input element -->
<rdf:Description about=" find-flights-page/kacomponent/from-place/input" >
    <svo:task rdf:resource="find-flights"/>
    <svo:inputRole rdf:resource="find-flights/param/from-place"/>
</rdf:Descripltion>
```

Regarding the web service provision, OntoWeaver-S relies on IRS-II to provide user interfaces for allowing the provision of web services.

3.3.4 Information Query

As discussed in section 3.3.2, the functionality of information query can also be achieved by knowledge acquisition forms, where the associated service is the built-in query service. At the moment, OntoWeaver-S only supports simple queries over the instances of the specified class entity. Later we plan to integrate powerful semantic query tools e.g. AquaLog [20] into OntoWeaver-S.

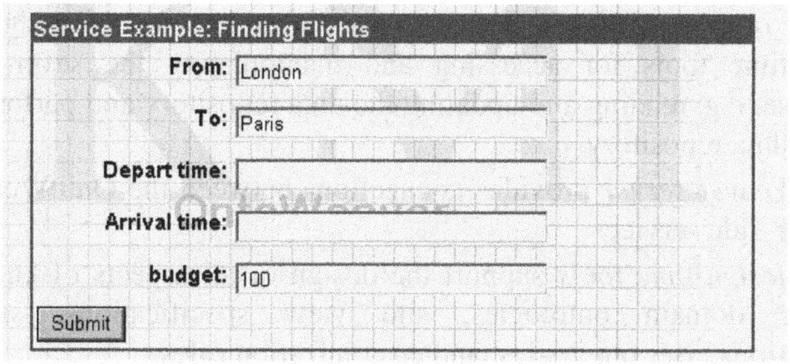

Fig. 5. An user interface example for accessing the web service *find-flights*

4 Customization Support

In the context of knowledge portals, customization support is one of the major requirements for design approaches, as it delivers personalized portals for individuals, which allow them to access data sources and web services in a way that reflects their personal requirements. In particular, at the user group specified level, different views are required for different user groups. For example, advanced users can add knowledge facts to portals for particular domain classes, while others can only access such information. This kind of customization is supported by the OntoWeaver-S modular architecture, which strictly separates the domain data model, the site view model and the presentation model. In particular, different site views can be constructed over the same domain model and different layouts and appearances can be specified for the same site view model.

The customization discussed above is static, i.e. being specified at the design time. Further support for dynamic (i.e. run time) customization, which personalizes web portals according to the contextual information of end users, should be provided as well. For example, the instances of domain classes can be ordered according to users' preferences. To support this kind of customization, OntoWeaver-S inherits the OntoWeaver customization framework, which allows rules to be specified at a high level of abstraction. In particular, the customization framework takes advantage of the declarative specifications of all aspects of knowledge portals, offers a customization rule model and a basic user model for specifying customization rules, and employs a customization engine to produce customized web pages for individual users. As the entire site model is available to customization, the OntoWeaver-S support for customization is not restricted. More information about the customization framework can be found in [10].

5 OntoWeaver-S Architecture

As shown in figure 6, the OntoWeaver-S architecture comprises the following components:

- *A knowledge warehouse* hosts ontologies, knowledge bases and specifications of knowledge portals, which are represented in RDFS [23] and RDF [22].

- *A number of server-side components* provide services for the design-time tools and the run-time tools for accessing and manipulating the sever-side knowledge warehouse, e.g. reading and updating the data repository and performing inferences over the data repository.
- *An OntoWeaver server* provides connections between the OntoWeaver-S tools and the server-side services.
- *A set of design-time tools* support the design of all aspects of knowledge portals, including domain ontologies, site view specifications, site presentation specifications, user ontologies, and customization rules.
- *A set of run-time tools* provide support for knowledge portals at run-time to achieve their functionalities.

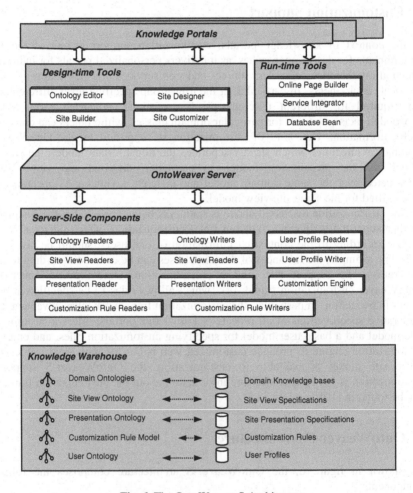

Fig. 6. The OntoWeaver-S Architecture

5.1 Design-Time Support

Designing knowledge portals in OntoWeaver-S can be achieved by means of *the Site Designer*, *the Site Builder*, and *the Site Customizer*. In particular, the Site designer offers visual facilities to allow the design of generic knowledge portals. As shown in figure 7, the Site Designer offers a site structure design pane (i.e. the left pane) to facilitate the construction of site structures, a page content design pane to allow the definition of user interface elements, a presentation style design pane to support the specification of presentation styles, and a layout design pane to facilitate the layout design.

The Site Builder compiles the specifications of knowledge portals into implementations. In particular, it augments the site view specification with the specified presentation model to produce a particular rendering of the target knowledge portal. The Site Customizer offers facilities for user group specified customization design, which allows creating different site views for different user groups, and rule specified customization design, which supports developers to specify customization rules. In addition, OntoWeaver-S provides an Ontology Editor to support the design of ontologies.

5.2 Run-Time Support

The run-time support that OntoWeaver-S provides includes i) retrieving and managing data stored in the back-end knowledge bases, ii) generating customized web pages on the fly according to the result of the customization engine, and iii) calling the IRS-II server to achieve the specified task with the input information and delivering the results back to knowledge portals.

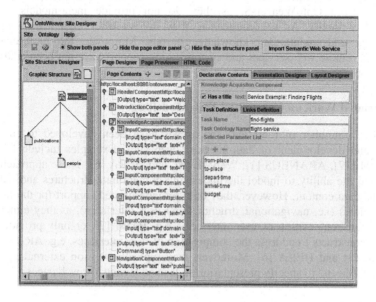

Fig. 7. A screenshot of the Site Designer

6 Related Work

6.1 Related Work on Building Knowledge Portals

OntoWebber [8] is an ontology-based tool for building and managing knowledge portals. It proposes a site ontology to model knowledge portals, and thus offers support for the creation and the management of knowledge portals. However, OntoWebber does not address the support for accessing remote web services. Moreover, the requirement of creating sophisticated user interfaces for knowledge portals has not been addressed appropriately. Specifically, the OntoWebber site ontology models site views at a coarse-grained level. For example, OntoWebber views that *a card* is a basic element to compose web pages. However, a card should consist of a number of components, e.g. texts, hyperlinks and images. Therefore, more fine-grained constructs should be proposed to allow cards to be composed and manipulated according to complex requirements.

SEAL [14] is another ontology-based approach, which addresses the design and development of knowledge portals. It employs an ontology for semantic integration of existing data sources as well as for knowledge portal presentation and management. The main functionalities the SEAL approach provides for knowledge portals include information access, information provision and information query. ODESeW [4] focuses on the automatic generation of knowledge portals from domain ontologies. It provides a number of functionalities for knowledge portals, including domain modelling, content provision, content visualization, content querying and web site administration. MetaLib [18] is a library portal solution, which relies on its Knowledge-base repository to enable the functionalities of library portals, including information querying and information visualization.

The SEAL approach, the ODESeW approach and the MetaLib approach are very different from OntoWeaver-S, as they do not provide meta-models to model knowledge portals. As a consequence, they do not offer high level support for specifying and maintaining knowledge portals. Moreover, the requirements on accessing remote web services and customization support have not been addressed in these approaches.

6.2 Related Work on Conceptual Web Modelling

Recently, a number of tools and approaches have been developed to address the design and development of data-intensive web sites. Examples include RMM [7], OOHDM [17], ARANEUS [1], WebML [3], and HERA [6]. These approaches have addressed the ability to model the underlying domain data structures and handle the dynamic data content. However, they only provide limited support for the modelling of site views (i.e. navigational structures and user interfaces), as they either do not address the composition of user interfaces, e.g. RMM [7], or only provide coarse-grained constructs to address the composition of user interfaces, e.g. ARANEUS [1], WebML [3] and HERA [6]. Moreover, they typically rely on external approaches (e.g. style sheets) to specify presentation styles and layouts for web pages.

7   Conclusions and Future Work

This paper has presented OntoWeaver-S, an ontology-based infrastructure for building knowledge portals. OntoWeaver-S distinguishes itself from other approaches in several ways. First, it offers a set of comprehensive functionalities for the target knowledge portals, including *information visualization*, which presents dynamic data content coming from the underlying knowledge bases or remote web services, *information provision*, which allows end users to submit knowledge facts to knowledge portals, *web service access*, which allows end users to access the remote web services, and *information querying*, which allows end users to make queries over the underlying knowledge bases. Second, it offers a set of ontologies to enable the high level support for the specification of all aspects of knowledge portals. Third, it addresses customization issues of knowledge portals by means of a customization framework. Finally, it offers a set of powerful tools for supporting knowledge portals at design time as well as at run time.

An OntoWeaver-S prototype system, including all the tools mentioned in this paper, has been implemented. In the future, we will focus on i) defining constraints validating the complex site specifications and provide tools helping developers to find and correct the specifications that are either with errors or being inconsistent in the entire site model, ii) enhancing the information querying functionality by integrating with an ontology-based questing-answering engine (e.g. AquaLog [20]), and iii) bringing the semantic layer of knowledge portals to end users for enabling semantic browsing, e.g. allowing users to browsing the semantic neighbourhood of particular entities.

References

1. P. Atzeni, G. Mecca, P. Merialdo, *Design and Maintenance of Data-Intensive Web Sites,* proceeding of the 6th int. Conference On Extending Database Technology (EDBT), Valencia, Spain, March 1998.
2. T. Berners-Lee, J. Hendler, and O. Lassila, *The Semantic Web*, Scientific American, 2001.
3. S. Ceri, P. Fratenali, A. Bongio. *Web Modelling Language (WebML): a modelling language for designing Web sites.* WWW9 Conference, Amsterdam, May 2000.
4. O. Corcho, A. Gomez-Perez, A. Lopez-Cima, V. Lopez-Garcia, and M. C. Suarez-Figueroa, *ODESeW. Automatic Generation of Knowledge Portals for Intranets and Extranets*, In Proceedings of the 2nd International Semantic Web Conference 2003 (ISWC 2003), 20-23 October 2003, Florida, USA.
5. J. B. Domingue, M. Dzbor, *Magpie: Browsing and Navigating on the Semantic Web*, In Proc. of the Conference on Intelligent User Interfaces, January 2004, Portugal.
6. F. Frasincar, G. J. Houben, *Hypermedia Presentation Adaptation on the Semantic Web.* Second International Conference, AH2002, Malaga, Spain, pp. 133-142.
7. T. Isakowitz, E.A. Stohr and P. Balasubramaninan, *RMM: A Methodology for Structured Hypermedia Design*, Communications of the ACM, August 1995.
8. Y. Jin, S. Decker, G. Wiederhold, *OntoWebber: Model-Driven Ontology-Based Web site Management*, Semantic Web Workshop, Stanford, California, July 2001.

9. Y. Lei, E. Motta, and J. Domingue, *An Ontology-Driven Approach to Web Site Generation and Maintenance,* In proceedings of 13th International Conference on Knowledge Engineering and Management, Sigüenza, Spain 1-4 October 2002, pp. 219-234.

10. Y. Lei, E. Motta and J. Domingue, *Design of Customized Web Applications with OntoWeaver*, in proceedings of the International Conference on Knowledge Capture, October, Florida, USA, 2003, pp 54-61.

11. Y. Lei, E. Motta and J. Domingue, Modelling Data-Intensive Web Sites With OntoWeaver, in proceedings of the international workshop on Web-based Information System Modelling (WISM 2004), Riga, Latvia, 2004.

12. Y. Lei, E. Motta and J. Domingue, OntoWeaver-S: Integrating Web Services into Data-Intensive Web Sites, in Proceedings of the WWW2004 workshop on Application Design, Development and Implementation Issues in the Semantic Web, New York, 2004.

13. F. Lima and D. Schwabe, *Application Modelling for the Semantic Web*, in Proceedings of the First Latin American Web Congress (LA-WEB 2003).

14. Maedche, S., R. Studer, Y. Sure, and R. Volz, *Seal --- Tying up information integration and Web site management by ontologies.* IEEE Data Engineering Bulletin, March 2002.

15. E. Motta, J. Domingue, L. Cabral, and M. Gaspari,   *IRS-II: A Framework and Infrastructure for Semantic Web Services*, in Proceedings of the 2nd International Semantic Web Conference 2003 (ISWC 2003), 20-23 October 2003, Florida, USA.

16. D. Quan, D. Huynh and D. R. Karger, *Haystack: A Platform for Authoring End User Semantic Web Applications*, in Proceedings of the 2nd International Semantic Web Conference 2003 (ISWC 2003), 20-23 October 2003, Florida, USA.

17. D. Schwabe and G. Rossi, *an Object Oriented Approach to Web-Based Application Design*, Theory and Practice of Object Systems 4(4), 1998, Wiley and Sons, New York, ISSN 1074-3224).

18. T. Sadeh and F. Walker, *Library Portals: toward the Semantic Web*, New Library World, volume 104 (1184/1185) pp 11-19.

19. P. Spyns et al., *OntoWeb - a Semantic Web Community Portal.* In Proc. Fourth International Conference on Practical Aspects of Knowledge Management (PAKM), December 2002, Vienna, Austria, 2002.

20. V. Lopez and E. Motta, *Ontology-driven Question Answering in AquaLog,* In Proceedings of 9th international conference on applications of natural language to information systems, Manchester, 2004.

21. R. Volz, D. Oberle, S. Staab, B. Motik, *KAON SERVER - A Semantic Web Management System*, in Alternate Track Proceedings of the Twelfth International World Wide Web Conference, WWW2003, Budapest, Hungary, 20-24 May 2003, ACM, 2003.

22. W3C, *Resource Description Framework (RDF) Model and Syntax*, available online at http://www.w3.org/TR/PR-rdf-syntax/.

23. W3C, *Resource Description Framework (RDF) Schema Specification 1.0*, available online at http://www.w3.org/TR/2000/CR-rdf-schema-20000327/.

24. W3C, *Extensible Markup Language (XML) 1.0, Second Edition*, available on line at http://www.w3.org/TR/2000/REC-xml-20001006.

Graph-Based Acquisition of Expressive Knowledge

Vinay Chaudhri[1], Kenneth Murray[1], John Pacheco[1],
Peter Clark[2], Bruce Porter[3], and Pat Hayes[4]

[1] SRI International, Menlo Park, California, USA
{chaudhri, murray, pacheco}@ai.sri.com
[2] Mathematics and Computing Technology,
Boeing Phantom Works, Seattle, Washington, USA
peter.e.clark@boeing.com
[3] Computer Science, University of Texas at Austin, Austin, Texas, USA
porter@cs.utexas.edu
[4] Institute for Human and Machine Cognition, Pensacola, FL, USA
phayes@ihmc.us

Abstract. Capturing and exploiting knowledge is at the heart of several important problems such as decision making, the semantic web, and intelligent agents. The captured knowledge must be accessible to subject matter experts so that the knowledge can be easily extended, queried, and debugged. In our previous work to meet this objective, we created a knowledge-authoring system based on graphical assembly from components that allowed acquisition of an interestingly broad class of axioms. In this paper, we explore the question: can we expand the axiom classes acquired by building on our existing graphical methods and still retain simplicity so that people with minimal training in knowledge representation can use it? Specifically, we present techniques used to capture ternary relations, classification rules, constraints, and if-then rules.

Keywords: authoring tools, knowledge-acquisition tools

Categories and Subject Descriptors.
    H.5.2 User Interfaces – *Graphical user interfaces (GUI)*
    I.2.4 Knowledge Representation Formalisms and Methods – *representation languages, predicate logic.*

1 Introduction

Our goal is to develop tools that enable domain experts to author knowledge bases (KBs) with minimal training in knowledge representation. This goal is important because significant KBs are central to many applications; domain experts lack knowledge-engineering skills, and knowledge engineers lack the domain expertise to replace them.

Previous work on this problem has resulted in a variety of KB editing tools, for example, frame-based editors, such as Protégé[1], OntoEdit[2], Ontosaurus[3], and

E. Motta et al. (Eds.): EKAW 2004, LNAI 3257, pp. 231–247, 2004.
© Springer-Verlag Berlin Heidelberg 2004

WebOnto[4]; [5] graphical KB editors, such as the GKB editor[6], the Visual Language (VL) for CLASSIC[7], and task-acquisition methods, such as EXPECT[8].

For the purpose of this paper, we will use the standard knowledge representation terminology of classes, slots, relations, individuals, subclass-of, [10, 11] etc. The work being reported here was done in the context of an object oriented knowledge representation and reasoning system called Knowledge Machine [12].

A common theme in the design of graphical editors such as the GKB-Editor[6] and VL by Gaines[7] has been to construct a graph in which each node represents a class, and labeled edges represent relations or constraints. This approach captures the taxonomic subset of a representation language well, but is limited to just that. In order to capture taxonomic knowledge, rules and their potential interactions, a substantially complex language is required. Using such a language can make it very difficult to work with and understand a knowledge base. Based on our experience in several projects, it is quite apparent that such knowledge bases are of great practical interest for building systems that can answer questions on a wide variety of topics[9]. Effectively addressing the knowledge capture for such knowledge bases requires a shift in the way we view knowledge bases that can be specified in the following two hypotheses:

1. Examples of concepts are a cognitively natural way to capture knowledge.
2. The user's view of the knowledge base should be of a collection of interrelated concepts.

The first hypothesis rules out designs that involve constructing a graph in which each node represents a class, or designs in which a user is presented with an explicitly quantified sentence. The second hypothesis rules out designs that support editing one rule at a time.

Even though the design changes suggested by these two hypotheses are subtle, they are a shift in the way knowledge is presented to a user, and a user's ability to comprehend that knowledge. The approach of viewing a knowledge base as a collection of interrelated concepts is not unique to SHAKEN. Existing graphical editors such as the GKB-Editor and VL also utilize this idea in their design. SHAKEN is, however, unique in using this view as the primary mode of knowledge capture.

In the context of the above two hypotheses, we have been building a knowledge base called the Component Library[13], and a graphical knowledge base editor called SHAKEN[14, 15]. The component library is built by knowledge engineers and contains domain independent classes such as Attach, Penetrate, Physical Object; predefined set of relations such as agent, object, location; and property values to help represent units and scales such as size, color, etc. SHAKEN presents a class to a user as a graph representing an example of the class, and the users construct new classes by connecting instances of the graphs representing existing classes using simple graph manipulation operations such as *add, connect, specialize, etc.*

To illustrate our approach, In Figure 1, we show a graph that captures the concept of Eucaryotic-Cell. Each node in this graph represents an individual, and each edge between two nodes a relationship between them. The class representing each node in the graph is constructed out of more general classes in the component library. For example, Eucaryotic cell is a specialization of Cell, which is constructed from the domain independent concept of Living Entity, which in turn is a Physical Object. In the design of the component library, the knowledge engineers specify pre-built definitions of domain independent concepts such as Physical Object which are inherited by the domain specific concepts shown here. In the component library, the knowledge engineers also specify which slots of a class a user should be usually asked for. This is indicated by a * next to the has-part relation.

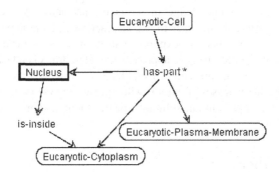

Fig. 1. Graph for the concept Eucaryotic-Cell

This graph is interpreted logically as follows: for every instance of Eucaryotic-Cell, there exists an instance of Nucleus, Eucaryotic-Cytoplasm, and Eucaryotic-Plasma Membrane, such that each is a part of the Eucaryotic-Cell and the Nucleus instance is inside the Eucaryotic Cytoplasm instance[14]. Thus each component description identifies a set of necessary conditions that must hold for each instance of the type of root individual.

If each node in the graph in Figure 1 was represented as a class, we would not have been able to assert the is-inside relationship between Nucleus and Eucaryotic Cytoplasm. This subtle difference is not obvious with a cursory look at Figure 1, and is a key differentiator between SHAKEN and previous graphical knowledge base editors.

We evaluated this system by having subject matter experts (SMEs) capture biology textbook knowledge[16]. These SMEs were first-year graduate students. We trained them with the system for about a week, and asked them to encode a section from a biology textbook. This evaluation revealed that (1) the parsimonious design of this knowledge entry tool was effective in capturing knowledge that supported answering an interestingly broad class of questions, but (2) there were several useful classes of axioms that SMEs wanted to state but the system was unable to handle. For example, consider the following pieces of knowledge.

1. The cell wall is between the nucleus and the virus.
2. If a cell has a nucleus, it is a Eucaryotic cell.
3. If a Christmas tree is taller than 10 feet, and you are in Palo Alto it costs an extra $50.

4. A tank division includes exactly one artillery brigade and at most two armored brigades.

The first example involves capturing ternary relations. The second example captures necessary and sufficient conditions for a class definition, and the fourth example captures constraints on a slot value[17]. The third example involves capturing rules. Taxonomic knowledge, as in the second and fourth examples, could be captured in prior tools such as VL[7]. Our approach differs, however, in its emphasis on expressing knowledge in terms of instances. We capture the same knowledge without forcing the user to use abstractions, in a context where examples are used to convey concepts and express relationships. This makes the knowledge capture cognitively simpler than the approach considered in Visual Language.

The evaluation results presented a challenge: How can we expand the basic design to support these classes of axioms while preserving the system's simplicity and ease of use? We next present our solutions, justify them, and present an evaluation of their use by SMEs.

2 N-Ary Relations

Traditional semantic network representations, and consequently the graphical editors supporting them, have been dominated primarily by binary relationships. Therefore, capturing knowledge that references relations of arity higher than two is a new challenge. In Figure 2, we illustrate how ternary relations are captured in our graphical description of an example of a class; in this example, the cell wall is in between the nucleus of the cell and the attacking virus. The *is-between* hyper-edge represents an atomic statement with a ternary predicate: as usual, the incoming arc indicates the first argument; the two outgoing arcs, from left to right, are the second and third arguments. The hyper edges are identified separately by showing them in bold italics.

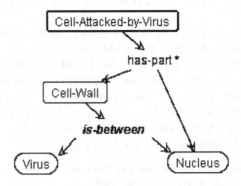

Fig. 2. Graphical presentation of a ternary relation

The *has-part* relation participates in two edges and represents two atomic statements that share a common first argument, indicated by the incoming arc. Each of the two outgoing arcs represents the second argument of the statement. Thus our approach to handling high-arity relations involves adopting a second display convention for representing statements with graph edges: the second argument is indicated by an outgoing arc from the bottom-left corner and the *nth* argument is denoted by an arc going from the bottom-right corner, with the remaining arguments indicated by the arcs emanating and spread equally between the bottom-left and the bottom-right corners. This approach gracefully expands the expressiveness of the basic graph formalism that traditionally uses binary edges.

3 Sufficient Conditions

We now consider axioms that define the sufficient conditions for an individual to be a member of a class. An example of such an axiom is *If a cell has a nucleus, it is a Eucaryotic cell.* We refer to such axioms as classification rules. SHAKEN enables a SME to capture a classification rule for a class A by selecting a subset of $A's$ necessary conditions as being sufficient to classify any instance of the direct super classes $B_1, ..., B_n$ of A as also being an instance of A.

While defining a class A, the first step is to define its super classes $B_1, ..., B_n$. This is accomplished using a form-based dialog through which the user gives a name to the class A, and specifies its super classes. We assume that the user has specified the super classes, and now they are ready to define the necessary and sufficient slot values.

The process for defining sufficient conditions requires a simple and intuitive extension to our existing interface[8]. First, the user selects a subset of the nodes in the graph to be treated as a group; the interface responds by displaying a rectangle that includes all selected nodes. Next, the user designates that the group of nodes defines a sufficient condition for that class, and the system synthesizes a classification axiom from the grouped nodes and edges.

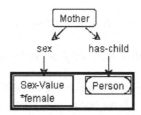

Fig. 3. Example class with sufficient condition

Figure 3 presents the graph describing an example of class Mother. This description also includes a sufficient condition indicated by the green rectangle around the nodes representing the individuals Sex-Value and Person. Since Figure 3 is an example of class Mother, the node Person is in fact an individual and should not be confused with a type constraint on the value of the slot has-child. Figure 4 shows a KIF[11] representation for the rule captured by the example description of this graph.

```
(implies
    (isa ?person Mother)
        (exists (?child ?sex-value)
            (and (isa ?child Person)
                 (isa ?sex-value Sex-Value)
                 (sex ?person ?sex-value)
                 (value ?sex-value *female)
                 (has-child ?person ?child)))))
(implies
    (and (isa ?person Person)
         (sex ?person ?sex-value)
            (value ?sex-value *female)
            (has-child ?person ?child))
         (isa ?person Mother))
```

Fig. 4. KIF for the class Mother

An alternative approach for capturing sufficient conditions could have been to introduce a new view on the example graph that exposes only sufficient properties. With such a design, there would have been no need to identify a subset of nodes that represent sufficient properties. We did not consider that approach in our initial design since one of our goals is that all knowledge capture should occur in the context of an example of a class.

4   Capturing Rules

Consider rules such as

If a terrain has a width that is less than 10 feet, then it has restricted trafficability for tanks.

If a Christmas tree is taller than 10 feet, and you are in Palo Alto it brings a premium of $50.

If it is raining or snowing, the person going out will wear a coat.

The kinds of rules shown above occur quite frequently. Sometimes, it is possible to force them into class definitions by defining more specific classes, such as a class representing Restricted Trafficability Terrain and Tall Christmas Trees, but very often, such classes are not natural, or too many, and a more direct encoding of rules is desired.

We capture this knowledge by introducing a *conditional edge*. For example, to specify the clothes worn, we simply state its value as a *Coat*, but we make this value conditional. The knowledge is stated in the context of an example instance of Go-out.

We illustrate this in Figure 5. The diamond indicates that the value of an edge is conditional. In the implemented system, the user can roll over the diamond and get a description of the condition. In the current version of the system, the conditions may be associated with only one edge. If a condition applies to multiple edges, it must be stated separately for each edge.

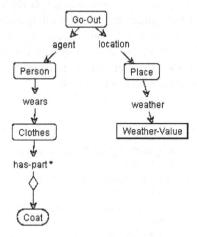

Fig. 5. Conditional rule that illustrates that if it is snowing, while going out, one should wear a coat

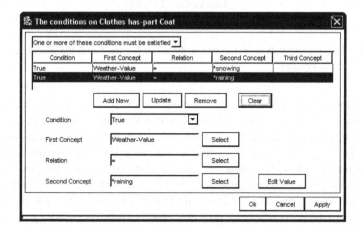

Fig. 6. Example slot-value condition

Figure 6 illustrates the authoring of a condition on an edge. The user will invoke this dialog when they need to author a piece of knowledge involving conditional knowledge. This relies on the assumption that the user has been trained to identify which tool is to be invoked when.

The dialogue of Figure 6 uses tables instead of a graphical method for capturing conditions. There is no deep reason for this other than the observation that it was straightforward to design a table-based interface in which a condition could be specified by pointing to the nodes in the graph, and that multiple conditions could be entered and edited. Therefore, for a value to be filled in the table, it must be a part of the graph. This works in practice because the graph representing an example of a class includes all related individuals that might participate in a condition. The table-based interface, by itself, is not novel, and is found in other knowledge base editors such as Protégé and GKB-Editor. Its use in conjunction with the example description of a class is novel in that when the user fills in various values in the table, they choose those values by pointing to the nodes in the graph.

```
(implies
   (isa ?action Go-Out)
      (exists (?person ?place ?weather ?clothes)
         (and (agent ?action ?person)
              (location ?action ?place)
              (wears ?person ?clothes)
              (weather ?place ?weather)
              (value ?weather ?weather-value)
                 (implies
                    (or
                       (equal ?weather-value *raining)
                       (equal ?weather-value *snowing))
                    (exists (?coat)
                       (has-part ?clothes ?coat))))))))
```

Fig. 7. KIF[11] representation of the graph shown in Figure 5 and the associated conditional rule as entered in Figure 6

Our support for capturing slot-value conditions is sufficiently expressive to author a large and useful subset of the SHAKEN Action Description Language (SADL), [18] however, to preserve simplicity we do impose restrictions. The conditions cannot be nested. For example, it is not possible to state an axiom that contains a conjunction and a disjunction: *If a Christmas tree is taller than 10 feet, and you are in Palo Alto or San Francisco, it costs an extra $50.* SADL is comparable to many other standard process languages, and is seamlessly integrated into our KM system. Its role is transparent to the users whenever they are authoring process knowledge.

5 Constraints

We consider only three types of constraints: type, numeric range, and cardinality constraints that apply to just one slot. We do not handle constraints that apply to multiple slots, or to several classes. The graph of Figure 8 specifies that a tank division includes an artillery brigade and two armored brigades and two Mechanized

Infantry Brigades; it does not indicate that there are no more than one artillery brigade and two armored brigades. It is often useful to denote what cannot be true in a domain by restricting the values of slots with constraints. In the current interface, we support two kinds of slot-value constraints: (1) *element constraints* apply to each distinct value of the slot, and (2) *set constraints* apply collectively to the set of known values for a slot. The element constraints we currently support include type constraints *must-be-a* and *mustnt-be-a*, and the set constraints we support include *exactly*, *at-least*, and *at-most*; see [12]for the semantics of these constraints.

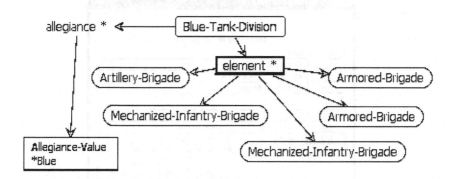

Fig. 8. Graph for Blue-Tank-Division

Figure 9 illustrates an example of the constraints that might appear on the destination (i.e., the second argument) of the *elements* edge for the class Blue-Tank-Division; we have adopted a tabular format for capturing constraints. The type of constraint (e.g., *must-be-a, mustnt-be-a, exactly*) is selected from a pull-down menu. The numeric values for constraints can be simply typed in the dialog box. The user can visualize the constraints that have been entered by right clicking on a slot label that has an option to display edge constraints.

Just like the condition editor, a SME would bring up this dialog when they need to state type or cardinality constraints about a class. This assumes that they have been trained to identify the constraints, and to invoke the constraint editor at an appropriate time.

An alternative way to model constraints would have been to display them on the same graph on which we are displaying the example of a class. We chose not to use that approach because the constraint information is conceptually a higher order information about the example, and we chose to not mix that with knowledge about the example itself.

The dialog of Figure 9 is fairly primitive in that it supports type, cardinality, and numeric constraints only. We implemented this set because our knowledge representation system [12] supports only those constraints. The basic design of Figure 9 can be generalized to a richer set of constraints, and in fact, many existing systems such as Protégé and the GKB-Editor support more elaborate interfaces for editing constraint information.

Figure 8 also illustrates another way a graph that represents an example of a class might differ from a graph that represents the class itself: A Blue-Tank-Division contains two instances of Armored-Brigade which are explicitly enumerated. Underneath these two nodes are two unique skolem individuals each representing a different Armored Brigade. We do not expose that level of detail to the users. The users can choose to distinguish between the two Armored-Brigades by assigning them a new label that is meaningful to them.

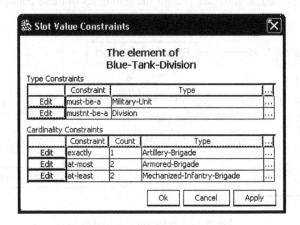

Fig. 9. Capturing Slot-Value Constraints

6 Evaluation

We have tested the extensions described here in two different application domains with different sets of users. Our claim in reporting the results of these studies here is that they give evidence that the capabilities proposed in the paper enable SMEs to capture knowledge. We do not claim that these are the best knowledge-capture capabilities possible, or that the results discussed next are a conclusive proof that these extensions will work with any set of users. We do not compare the version of the system with the extensions presented in the paper with the version that did not have those extensions, because the extensions represent new functionality which would not have been otherwise possible.

We tested the use of sufficient conditions during the fall of 2002 in the context of a military course of action (COA) analysis problem[19, 20]. We tested the slot value conditions, and constraint editing capabilities with domain exerts in physics, chemistry, and biology during January of 2004. We summarize here the highlights of these evaluations to substantiate the claim of this paper: we have effectively expanded the class of axioms captured by the interface and still retained its simplicity.

A military commander uses a COA to communicate to her subordinates one way to accomplish a mission. They then evaluate multiple competing COAs using appropriate comparison criteria and decide on one to build into a complete action plan for the mission. In the test the knowledge-capture task was to express the knowledge necessary to critique the COAs.

We retained two U.S. Army officers to conduct the evaluation. They used the necessary and sufficient conditions to specify the required combat power in given situations. During the evaluation, both SMEs quickly became adept at using the SHAKEN interface for capturing knowledge in the forms of class descriptions, and necessary and sufficient conditions. They collectively authored 56 additions to the critiquing knowledge (e.g., new classes or rules), including 13 new classes. An example of necessary and sufficient condition authored by the SMEs is suggested in the following piece of knowledge: When an aviation unit attacks an artillery unit, it is enough to have a combat power ratio of 0.3; SMEs captured this knowledge by defining the example of a class in which an aviation unit attacks an artillery unit. The sufficient conditions for such a class are that the agent is an aviation unit and the object is an artillery unit. Whenever an action is encountered that meets these sufficient conditions, it automatically gets classified as an instance of this class, and assigned a combat power ratio of 0.3. This example is illustrated in Figure 10 below.

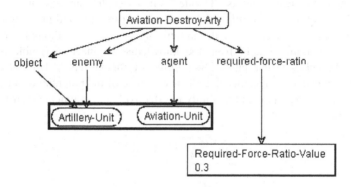

Fig. 10. Example of Classification Rule for an Aviation-Unit Attacking an Artillery-Unit

The evaluation showed that the SMEs successfully authored both new classes and new classification rules; however, there were a few problems observed in their attempts. We consider here two such examples. In one, the user meant to include two nodes while constructing a classification rule but selected, and thus included, only one node. In a second example, the user included four edges that failed to capture the intended classification rule; yet the desired rule could have been captured simply by including two nodes. This reflects a deficiency in the training that did not make it sufficiently clear that defining sufficient conditions requires including the relevant nodes. While many of the SME-authored sufficient conditions effectively captured the intended rule and supported useful inference, it is apparent that sometimes the SMEs did not clearly understand what classification rule resulted from the nodes or edges they selected.

In January 2004, we conducted a 1-day experiment with subject matter experts in physics, chemistry, and biology. The knowledge-authoring teams consisted of a domain expert, a usability expert, and a knowledge engineer. The domain expert was the knowledge author, the usability expert observed the kind of difficulties encountered by the SME, and the knowledge engineer answered questions and requests for assistance during the knowledge entry process. The first half of the experiment involved an intensive step-by-step training session, followed by an open-ended knowledge construction exercise.

In the open-ended exercise, the biology SME focused her knowledge authoring around the concept of Bacterial-Protein-Translation. Using a biology textbook to guide her knowledge entry, she constructed the graph shown in Figure 11. Central to the concept of protein translation is an iterative process where amino acids are linked together to form a polypeptide. In capturing this, the SME opted to write conditions to identify when the cycle of events should continue and when it should be terminated. In the figure below one can see that after the sub-event of "Recognition" there is a cycle of events: "Come-Together," "Catalyze," and "Slide." There are conditions, marked with diamonds, on the next-event edge between "Slide" and "Come-Together" and between "Slide" and "Divide." The condition, which is not shown in this view, states that if the destination of the slide event is a "Protein-Stop-Codon," then the next-event is "Divide," otherwise the next-event is a "Come-Together." This SME, with little to no prior training in logic and programming, with only a few hours of training on the system and a moderate, though certainly not insignificant, amount of help from the knowledge engineer, was able to capture expressive knowledge that pushed the limits of the system. This success with complicated concepts and advanced tools is evidence of the potential of the system to empower domain experts with the ability to effectively communicate their knowledge to the system.

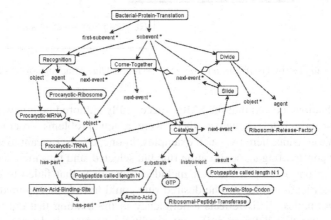

Fig. 11. Concept of Bacterial-Protein-Translation Authored by SME at January Experiment

The SME who created the above graph in the experiment had this to say about the experience, "When I first encountered the SHAKEN system, I anticipated that I would need a great deal of technical and programming knowledge in order to enter content information into the system. I was pleased to discover that once I learned a few rules and procedures, I was able to construct a reasonably detailed map of a multistep process. I did need some technical help navigating some of the more complex steps, but I think the end result was a workable map. It was very useful to have a library of specific terms already available in my content area, so I was able to assemble my map without having to define each noun and verb individually.

We have clearly expanded the class of axioms that can be captured using the system. An important and significant class of knowledge that remains to be captured involves following a detailed computational algorithm, for example, the procedure to compute the pH of a solution. Examples of knowledge that our designs are focusing on are equations and knowledge about how and when to apply them, policies, and a very limited set of visual programming tools trying to capture notions like iteration and decision making.

There are several other aspects of the knowledge capture problem that we have not explicitly considered in this paper. For example, the editing of taxonomies is supported by SHAKEN using a form based interface that is not particularly unique. SHAKEN does not, however, allow domain experts to create or edit relations. In the current system, this responsibility resides with the knowledge engineers. Before an SME starts to define concept descriptions, there are early phases of design in which the SME identifies relevant concepts, and breaks down the knowledge to be formalized into smaller chunks to be formalized [21]. The current SHAKEN system does not address the early phases of the knowledge capture process. As the knowledge capture is in progress, the user needs to be proactively supported, perhaps, by a mixed initiative dialog [22].

A possible question that arises based on the current experience is: whether graphs are a compelling way to capture knowledge? Even though there is success in using graphs for knowledge capture, the graphs as considered here are not a natural form that the knowledge occurs in the real world. The real world knowledge is found in form of text, diagrams, pictures, tables, formulas, etc. Given that we will not have an automatic translation from text to logic any time in the near future, the graphs offer a middle ground. The current work suggests that the graphs are a useful middle ground, but at the same time, we believe that they need to be complemented where more compelling visualizations such as tables or equations may apply. That is one of the topics for future extensions to SHAKEN.

7 Related Work

We will now compare our work with an earlier work on the VL system, since this system bears the most resemblance to SHAKEN and provides the most relevant framework for comparison. Both SHAKEN and VL [7] are motivated to support use by "non-programmers" (e.g., SMEs) and yet be formal and (unlike many of the early implementations of semantic networks as KRLs) precise.

The primary difference between VL and SHAKEN is that the knowledge entry in SHAKEN is driven by examples: that is, knowledge is captured by defining instances in an example of the concept being defined. This allows SHAKEN to capture more complex forms of axioms such as in Figure 1, 3, and 5 that cannot be captured using VL. Figure 1 shows the closest that VL can come to representing the knowledge of

Figure 1, however, the fact that the nucleus is inside the cytoplasm cannot be expressed since VL uses classes and not instances.

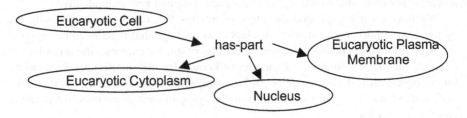

Fig. 12. Eucaryotic Cell as written in VL

Since SHAKEN graphs represent examples of classes, each node corresponds to an individual in the KB depicting an entity or event or property value, and each arc is directed and corresponds to a slot in the KB. In contrast, the VL includes several types of nodes (e.g., constraints and rules) that do not naturally correspond to the entities and events and property values in the domain being represented, as well as both directed and undirected arcs. Furthermore, arcs are unlabeled and the back-end denotation of each arc is substantially determined by the types of the nodes connected by the arc and whether or not the arc is directed. For example, in the graph from VL,

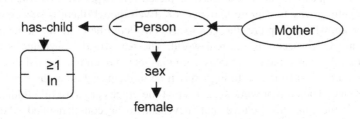

Fig. 13. Concept Mother as written in VL

Figure 13, represents the necessary and sufficient conditions for the class Mother that we considered earlier in Figure 3. The nodes in this graph, Mother, and Person are classes. The plain oval represents a defined class (e.g., Mother), and an oval with dashes on the side represents a primitive class (e.g., Person). The labels on the edges are relations. The values in the rounded box represent a constraint that the person has at least one child. The value of the slot sex is female. The advantage in the VL visualization is that it makes it explicit that Mother is a subclass of Person. The SHAKEN visualization leaves this information implicit because we do not explicitly represent classes in the graph. The fact that the super class of Mother is a Person is available when a user rolls the mouse over the Mother node. An apparent disadvantage of the VL representation that is based on our interpretation of the cited reference [7] is that if a defined class has some properties in addition to the defining properties, VL does not give a way to distinguish between the two. SHAKEN accomplishes this by providing the group node notation.

It is not possible to express in VL ternary relations or the complex rules considered in Figures 2 and 5. VL allows only rules that relate two classes. For example, consider another graph from VL, shown in Figure 14.

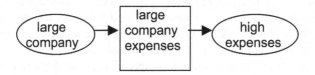

Fig. 14. Large Company Expenses rule as written in VL

This graph represents a rule named Large Company Expenses that applies to a Large Company, and asserts that its expenses are high. The same rule is expressed in SHAKEN as shown in Figure 15: We assert using the condition editor a conditional rule stating that if the size is large, the expenses must be high.

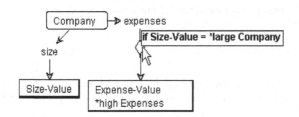

Fig. 15. Large Company Expenses rule as written in SHAKEN

The VL system uses a composition operation that allows the construction of large knowledge structures from smaller ones. The composition is achieved by grouping nodes with the same label together and defining a concept in terms of the outgoing arrows from the nodes. SHAKEN and VL approach are similar in that they both allow the visualization of knowledge as a collection of interrelated concepts.

Another distinctive aspect of our approach is that it is strongly dependent on the prior knowledge encoded in the library. The prior knowledge restricts the existing concepts that could be connected together, and also the relations with which they could be connected. Thus, unlike other graphical editors, the users do not draw arbitrary graphs: they have to use something that is already in the library.

We would like to compare the SHAKEN system to an alternative like Protégé[1]. Protégé is not designed with the intention of being primarily used by SMEs, and its interface can be customized to different domains.

8 Summary

We have motivated and presented several knowledge-authoring extensions to SHAKEN. These extensions support capturing a substantially greater variety of axiom classes than was previously possible. Hyper-edges enable capturing ternary (and higher) relations. Sufficient conditions as well as necessary conditions can be expressed in the graph structure. Slot-value conditions enable capturing important classes of problem-solving rules. Constraints limit the assertions that may be entered in the knowledge base. These pieces, defined functionally for the user, can be combined with one another to create robust and detailed knowledge. The extensions use an interface designed to increase the expressiveness of the acquirable knowledge while remaining faithful to our mandate of providing tools that support knowledge authoring by SMEs.

Acknowledgments

This research was supported by DARPA's Rapid Knowledge Formation project[23] under contract N66001-00-C-8018. We are grateful to Peter Yeh, Jim Blythe, Jihie Kim, Tomas Uribe, Yolanda Gil, Michael Eriksen, Chris DiGiano and the usability experts, and the many other members of our collaboration team.

References

1. Gennari, J., et al., The Evolution of Protege: An Environment for Knowledge-Based Systems Development. International Journal of Human-Computer Interaction, 2003. 58(1): p. 89-123.
2. Sure, Y., S. Staab, and J. Angele. OntoEdit: Guiding ontology development by methodology and inferencing. in International Conference on Ontologies, Databases and Applications of Semantics ODBASE 2002. 2002. University of California, Irvine, USA: Springer, LNCS.
3. Sowa, J., Knowledge Representation: Logical, Philophical, and Computational Foundations. 2000, Pacific Grove, CA: Brooks Cole Publishing Co.
4. Domingue, J., Tadzebao and WebOnto: Discussing, Browsing, and Editing Ontologies on the Web, in Proc. KAW'98. 1998
5. Aaronson, L., et al., Artifactory Research Resources. 2004, Artifactory research group at SRI http://www.ai.sri.com/artifactory/resources.html#Editors.
6. Paley, S. and P. Karp, GKB Editor User Manual. 1996.
7. Gaines, B.R., An Interactive Visual Language for Term Subsumption Languages, in IJCAI'91. 1991
8. Blythe, J., et al., An Integrated Environment for Knowledge Acquisition, in Int. Conf. on Intelligent User Interfaces. 2001. p. 13--20
9. Barker, K., et al., Halo Pilot Project. 2003, SRI International: Menlo Park. p. 35, http://www.ai.sri.com/pubs/full.php?id=990.
10. Chaudhri, V.K., et al., OKBC: A Programmatic Foundation for Knowledge Base Interoperability, in Proceedings of the AAAI-98. 1998: Madison, WI

11. Genesereth, M.R. and R.E. Fikes, Knowledge Interchange Format: Version 3.0 Reference Manual. Jun 1992(Logic-92-1).
12. Clark, P. and B. Porter, KM -- The Knowledge Machine: Reference Manual. 1999.
13. Barker, K., B. Porter, and P. Clark, A Library of Generic Concepts for Composing Knowledge Bases, in Proc. 1st Int Conf on Knowledge Capture (K-Cap'01). 2001. p. 14--21
14. Clark, P., et al., Knowledge Entry as the Graphical Assembly of Components, in Proc 1st Int Conf on Knowledge Capture (K-Cap'01). 2001. p. 22-29
15. Thomere, J., et al., A Web-based Ontology Browsing and Editing System, in Innovative Applications of Artificial Intelligence Conference. 2002. p. 927--934
16. Schrag, R., et al. Experimental Evaluation of Subject Matter Expert-oriented Knowledge Base Authoring Tools. in 2002 PerMIS Workshop. 2002. Gaithersburg, Maryland: National Institute of Standards and Technology.
17. Brachman, R. and J.G. Schmolze, An overview of the KL-ONE knowledge representation system. Cognitive Science, 1985. 9(2): p. 171-216.
18. Blythe   J.,   e.a.,   SADL: Shaken   Action   Description   Language.   2001 http://www.isi.edu/expect/rkf/sadl.html.
19. Barker, K., et al., A Knowledge Acquisition Tool for Course of Action Analysis, in Innovative Applications of Artificial Intelligence Conference. 2003. p. 34--50
20. Pool, M., J.F. K. Murray, M. Mehrotra, R. Schrag, J. Blythe, and H.C. J. Kim, P. Miraglia, T. Russ, and D. Schneider. Evaluation of Expert Knowledge Elicited for Critiquing Military Courses of Action. in Proceedings of the Second International Conference on Knowledge Capture (KCAP-03). 2003.
21. Boicu, M., et al. Mixed-initiative Control for Teaching and Learning in Disciple. in IJCAI-03 Workshop on Mixed-Initiative Intelligent Systems. 2003. Acapulco, Mexico.
22. Kim, J. and Y. Gil. Proactive Acquisition from Tutoring and Learning Principles. in AI in Education. 2003.
23. DARPA, The Rapid Knowledge Formation Project. 2000 http://reliant.teknowledge.com/RKF/.

Incremental Knowledge Acquisition for Improving Probabilistic Search Algorithms

J.P. Bekmann[1,2] and Achim Hoffmann[1]

[1] School of Computer Science and Engineering,
University of New South Wales, NSW 2052, Australia
[2] National ICT Australia (NICTA), A.T.P, NSW 1430, Australia

Abstract. A new incremental knowledge acquisition approach for the effective development of efficient problem solvers for combinatorial problems based on probabilistic search algorithms is proposed. The approach addresses the known problem of adapting probabilistic search algorithms, such as genetic algorithms or simulated annealing, by the introduction of domain knowledge. This is done by incrementally building a knowledge base that controls parts of the probabilistic algorithm, e.g. the fitness function and the mutation operators in a genetic algorithm.

The probabilistic search algorithm is monitored by a human who makes recommendations on search strategy based on individual solution candidates. It is assumed that the human has a reasonable intuition of the search problem. The human adds rules to a knowledge base describing how candidate solutions can be improved, or characteristics of candidate solutions which he/she feels are likely or unlikely to lead to good solutions. Our framework is inspired by the idea of (Nested) Ripple Down Rules where humans provide exception rules to rules already existing in the knowledge base using concrete examples of inappropriate performance of the existing knowledge base.

We present experiments on industrially relevant domains of channel routing as well as switchbox routing in VLSI design. We show very encouraging inital experimental results demonstrating that our approach can solve problems comparably well to other approaches. These other approaches use algorithms developed over decades, while we were able to develop an effective search procedure in a very short time. A brief discussion outlines our KA experience with these experiments.

1 Introduction

General purpose search algorithms attempting hard problems rely on the introduction of domain knowledge in order to make the search feasible. For a long time Genetic Algorithms (GA) have been considered to be general purpose search techniques which can be applied to all sorts of search problems. In practice, however, it usually proves to be rather difficult to adapt a general purpose GA design to a particular problem type at hand [1, 2]. To tailor the GA to a problem really well may easily take months of development.

Anecdotal accounts suggest that tailoring a general purpose probabilistic search technique, such as GA or simulated annealing, to suit a given problem

E. Motta et al. (Eds.): EKAW 2004, LNAI 3257, pp. 248–264, 2004.

can take months or even years while the implementation of the basic algorithm can be done in a matter of days.

Hence, it is critical to address the problem of tailoring general algorithms to suit a given problem. In genetic algorithms, there are a number of issues which need to be adjusted for a problem. They include general parameters, such as number of generations, population size, the problem encoding and the way offspring is generated (i.e. what kind of mutation, cross-over etc.).

In particular, for the way of how offspring are generated it appears that a knowledge acquisition approach can be used to address the problem as humans seem generally to have some idea of what kind of offspring might improve the chances of finding a (good) solution.

We pursued the idea that a knowledge acquisition approach could be used to develop a knowledge base that controls the generation of promising offspring. While the GA without a tailored knowledge base can be expected to find some sort of solution (often by far suboptimal), after sufficient computing time is given (often excessive), an incrementally developed knowledge base for improving the offspring generation lets us expect a gradual improvement in performance of the GA.

We chose an incremental knowledge acquisition process, inspired by Ripple Down Rules [5], as it seems usually possible for a human, who has some idea of how to find solutions for the problem at hand, to judge at least for extreme cases, which offspring should be ignored and what kind of offspring are promising compared to their parents.

The incremental knowledge acquisition approach we present in this paper allows the user to inspect individuals as they were generated by the existing GA process. If a generated individual is considered to be useless the probability of it being generated can be reduced by providing suitable characteristics of the kind of offspring that should be generated less often or not at all. Similarly, the probability of promising offspring to be generated can be increased in the same way. Furthermore, if the human wants to propose a particular way of constructing an offspring from a parent (or parents), the human can define a suitable operator that modifies the parent(s) accordingly. The applicability of such a newly introduced operator would again be controlled by a set of rules, which are organised in a Ripple Down Rules (RDR) structure.

Our incremental knowledge acquisition framework ensures that previously provided knowledge about the quality of individuals is largely maintained while additional knowledge is integrated into the knowledge base by only being applicable to those cases where the existing knowledge base did not judge in accordance with the human. In other words, the adverse interaction of multiple rules in a knowledge base is effectively avoided. Our work differs is some important aspects from traditional RDR in that conditions and rules in the knowledge base (KB) can be edited, and solutions can be found with an incomplete KB (specification that does not cover all possible cases).

Our framework HeurEAKA (Heuristic Evolutionary Algorithms using Knowledge Acquisition) allows the GA to run in conjunction with the current - initially empty - knowledge base on problem instances. The evolutionary process can be monitored by the human and individuals can be evaluated. If a particular individual is generated that appears undesirable or suboptimal, the human could enter a new rule that prevents such behaviour in future or provide an improved alternative action. The user might also add a rule which imposes a fitness penalty on such individuals. More generally, the user formulates rules based on characteristics of selected individuals, and these are applied in the general case by the GA.

We expect the application of KA to other GA problems to be promising whenever an expert has some kind of intuition of what differentiates good candidates from bad candidates, as well as being able to make at least a guess at how individual candidates may be improved. Given these considerations, we expect that our approach is applicable to most practical GA applications.

This paper is organised as follows: In the next section we present our knowledge acquisition framework HeurEAKA including a brief review of genetic algorithms. Section 3 presents a case study where our framework was applied to the problem of switchbox routing, an industrially relevant problem from the realm of VLSI design. It also briefly discusses earlier experiments with the problem of channel routing in VLSI design. The following sections, section 4 and section 5 discuss our results and the lessons learned so far. This is followed by the conclusions in section 6.

2   Our Incremental Knowledge Acquisition Framework HeurEAKA

The HeurEAKA framework naturally falls into a genetic algorithm and a knowledge acquisition component. The GA is essentially a general purpose genetic algorithm. The KA part comprises a knowledge base manager which controls modification of the KB as well as the evaluation of cases supplied by the GA. The KA module contains a *primitives interface* which allows customization for problem domain specific functionality. The framework is implemented with a graphical user interface, but also supports batch-style processing.

2.1   Genetic Algorithms

Evolutionary algorithms are loosely based on natural selection, applying these principles to search and optimisation. These include evolution strategy, evolutionary programming, genetic programming and genetic algorithms, which we concentrate our work on.

Basic GAs are relatively easy to implement. A solution candidate of the problem to be solved is encoded into a genome. A collection of genomes makes up a population of potential solutions. The GA performs a search through the solution space by modifying the population, guided by an evolutionary heuristic. When a suitable solution has been identified, the search terminates.

A genetic algorithm usually starts with a randomly initialized population of individuals, and searches through the solution space guided by a *fitness* value assigned to individuals in the population. Based on probabilistic operators for selection, mutation and crossover, the GA directs the search to promising areas. GAs have been applied to a wide variety of domains, and were found to be quite effective at solving otherwise intractable problems [3] .

GAs do suffer from a variety of problems, most notably the "black art" of tuning GA parameters such as population size, selection strategies, operator weightings, as well as being very sensitive to problem encoding and operator formulation [1, 4]. We aim to address some of these issues with an explicit formulation of domain knowledge using well suited KA techniques.

Genome encoding and manipulation is treated by the GA as opaque. All manipulations take place indirectly via the *primitives interface* (see Section 3.3).

In order to generate new individuals, the GA has to select parents from the current population and then generate offspring either by mutation and/or by crossover. Further, some individuals of the current generation should be selected for removal and replaced by newly generated individuals.

Offspring of selected parents are either created via a crossover copy operation or as a mutated copy. A parameter determines which operator will be applied. The crossover operator mimics natural evolutionary genetics and allows for recombination and distribution of successful solution sub-components in the population.

In order to select individuals either as a parent for a new individual or as a candidate to be removed from the population, the knowledge base is invoked to determine the fitness of an individual as explained below. In order to generate suitable offspring, another knowledge base is invoked which probabilistically selects mutation operators.

Fig. 1 illustrates the interaction between the GA and the KA module.

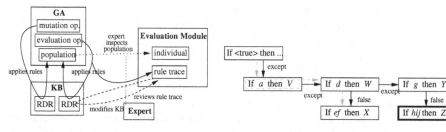

Fig. 1. The GA consults the KB when evaluating and mutating a genome. Picking an individual, the expert can iteratively review the corresponding rule trace and modify the KB. For compactness, the diagram only shows the refinement of the evaluation operators - in practice, the mutation operators are refined in the same way

Fig. 2. A simple RDR structure. The dashed line indicates the path taken & rule executed (V) for $a\overline{de}$, the bold box indicates how action Z would be added for $ad\overline{g}hij$

2.2 Knowledge Acquisition

Our knowledge acquisition approach for building the knowledge base for fitness determination and the knowledge base for selecting operators for offspring generation is based on the ideas of ripple down rules (RDR) [5]. RDR builds a rule base incrementally based on specific problem instances for which the user explains their choices. An extension of RDR allows hierarchical structuring of RDRs - "nested RDR" (NRDR) [6]. NRDR allows re-use of definitions in a KB, and the abstraction of concepts which make it easier to describe complex problems on the knowledge level and also allow for more compact knowledge bases for complex domains.

Ripple Down Rules Knowledge Base: We use single classification RDRs (SCRDRs) for both types of knowledge bases. A single classification RDR is a binary tree where the root node is also called the default node. To each node in the tree a rule is associated, with a condition part and a conclusion which is usually a class - in our case it is an operator application though. A node can have up to two children, one is attached to an *except* link and the other one is attached to the so-called if-not link. The condition of the default rule in the default node is always true and the conclusion is the default conclusion. When evaluating a tree on a case (the object to be classified), a *current conclusion* variable is maintained and initialised with the default conclusion. If a node's rule condition is satisfied, then its conclusion overwrites the *current conclusion* and the except-link, if it exists, is followed and the corresponding child node is evaluated. Otherwise, the if-not link is followed, if it exists, and the corresponding child node is evaluated. Once a node is reached such that there is no link to follow the *current conclusion* is returned as a result. Figure 2 shows a simple RDR tree structure. In bold is a rule that a user might have added for the case where conditions $ad\overline{g}hij$ hold, causing action Z to be executed, instead of W.

In typical RDR implementations, any KB modification would be by adding exception rules, using conditions which only apply to the current case for which the current knowledge base is inappropriate. By doing this, it is ensured that proper performance of the KB on previous cases is maintained.

Nesting RDRs allows the user to define multiple RDRs in a knowledge base, where one RDR rule may use another, nested RDR tree in its condition, and in HeurEAKA as an action. I.e. the nested RDR tree is evaluated in order to determine whether the condition is satisfied. A strict hierarchy of rules is required to avoid circular definitions etc.

For the purpose of controlling the Genetic Algorithm, in our approach all conclusions are actually actions that can be applied to the case, which is an individual genome. The rules are formulated using the Rule Specification Language as detailed below.

Fitness Knowledge Base: The user specifies a list of RDRs which are to be executed when the fitness of a genome is determined. The evaluation task can thus be broken into components as needed, each corresponding to a RDR. The evaluator executes each RDR in sequence.

Mutation Knowledge Base: For determining a specific mutation operator a list of RDRs provided by the user is consulted. Each RDR determines which specific operator would be applied for modifying an individual. Unlike for the evaluation, for mutation only one of the RDRs for execution will be picked probabilistically using weights supplied by the user.

Rule Specification Language (RSL): Conditions and actions for a rule are specified in a simple language based loosely on "C" syntax. It allows logical expressions in the condition of a rule, and a list of statements in the action section.

The RSL supports variables and loop structures. Domain specific variable types can be defined, as well as built-in primitive commands relevant to the problem domain. Section 3 gives examples of rule specification.

The Knowledge Acquisition Process in HeurEAKA: The knowledge acquisition process goes through a number of iterations as follows: on each individual the fitness KB is applied and a set of rules executed. The user can select some of the individuals that appear to be of interest and then review the rules that were involved in the creating of those individuals.

The genetic algorithm can be started, stopped and reset via a graphical user interface. A snapshot of the GA population is presented, from which the user can pick an individual for closer inspection. Figure 3 shows an example of the GA window, in this case applied in the problem domain of switchbox routing.

As shown in Fig. 4, an individual solution can be inspected. It was found necessary to have a good visualization and debugging interface to be able to productively create and test rules.

A user can step back, forward and review the application of RDR rules to the genome, and make modifications to the respective KB by adding exception rules. Figure 10 shows an example of how these would be entered.

Since the evaluation of a set of RDRs can cause a number of actions to be executed, it is necessary to allow the user to step through an execution history. Given non-deterministic elements of operator selection, the interactive debugger has to maintain complete state descriptions, i.e. genome data, variable instantiation and values used in random elements, to make it feasible for the user to recreate conditions for repeated testing.

If the user does not agree with the performance of a rule R in the knowledge base, there are two ways of addressing it: Either the addition of an exception rule to R can be made, or a modification of R is possible.

Modification of rules in the KB is not normally done with Ripple Down Rules, as it is assumed that every rule which is ever entered into the knowledge base has its reason to be there. Also, a modification of a rule may have undesirable side effects which are not necessarily easy to control.

While these are valid reasons for not modifying rules, our initial experiments suggest that it is sensible to modify rules at the beginning of building a knowledge

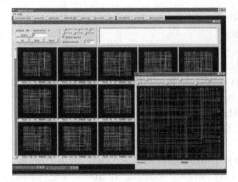
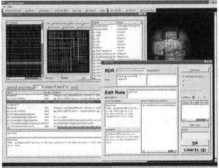

Fig. 3. Taken from an application of the HeurEAKA framework to the domain of switchbox routing: The GA window displays snapshots of the population at given intervals. The user can start, stop and step through evolution. An individual can be selected for closer inspection and evaluation, leading to Fig. 4

Fig. 4. The interactive screen allows the user to inspect the individual, step through rule application, and amend the KB as needed. More details in Fig. 10.(Note that these screenshots were included to convey an overall impression only)

base. In particular, for the definition of new actions for modifying genomes, it proved useful to have this option to modify rules.

In traditional RDR, the system can suggest conditions for new rules based on past cases and the conditions of rules that did not fire. In our current framework this is not supported for two reasons. Firstly, the rule attribute space is very large - it extends over expressions containing GA attributes, RSL variables and nested RDRs with parameters. Coming up with useful suggestions based on this large set is quite hard - one might consider machine learning methods for suggesting conditions. The second reason is that we are dealing with non-deterministic choices in the probabilistic algorithm. These choices are not reflected in the attributes tested by conditions, therefore past cases are not usually sufficient for determining how one arrived at a certain conclusion. Nonetheless, we hope that further work on methods for evaluating operator effectiveness might help in identifying useful rule construction strategies.

Indeed, it is part of our approach to be able to use a KB which is incomplete. i.e. Rules will not always be applied correctly since there is not always supervision by the user, also the selection of rules is left to chance, so there is no guarantee that an 'optimal' rule will be picked. Nonetheless, the heuristic search will be able to cope with an incomplete ruleset and still find useful solutions. The idea is that one provides generally useful operators and heuristic knowledge (e.g. in the form of operator weightings) and allow the genetic algorithm's search strategies and probabilistic selection to make up the rest of the algorithm.

User Interface: As mentioned previously, a good user interface is necessary for the productive development of rules. Visualisation of complex problems is a powerful way to elicit intuitive understanding from the user. Rules can be added easily and interactively, appearing in the same context as the visualisation. KB organization is handled transparently using RDR principles.

The user interface is re-usable for different problem domains. The only part that needs to be changed is the visualisation window. The GUI is implemented in Qt (a portable GUI toolkit by Trolltech), and the visualisation is wrapped in a single graphical widget object. This can readily be replaced by something that translates the genome into graphical format. Should the visualisation not be straightforward, requiring, e.g. interaction or animation, this can all be conveniently wrapped in this object. Along with the other modules in HeurEAKA, it should be relatively straightforward to apply to a new problem domain.

User Assistance: HeurEAKA provides some assistance to the user, helping to identify appropriate cases for modification of the KB:

A set of validation functions can be defined by the user, which are run on each individual during the execution of the GA. When a function identifies an appropriate individual, the GA is halted with an exception and provides a pointer to the individual along with a trace of all the rules applied in the last mutation operation. The user can then decide whether to further examine the individual. It is up to the user what he/she wants in the evaluation function, but we found it useful to include some general heuristic conditions which we found would indicate particularly bad characteristics, or even illegal solutions - allowing us to trace the origins of such individuals in the population.

Statistics are kept on rules involved in mutation operations. Changes in fitness are attributed to the rules that caused them, also the frequency of rule use in successful vs. unsuccessful individuals is tracked. These data help the user gain an overview of how useful particular parts of the KB are, and highlight problem areas that might need attention.

3 Case Study and Experiments

The following section provides an overview of two case studies done using Heur-EAKA. A detailed description of the features available is not possible due to space limitation. We present how our framework was applied to the problem domain of channel and switchbox routing, along with experimental results.

3.1 Domain Specifics

In order to demonstrate that genetic algorithms enhanced with knowledge acquisition can be used to develop algorithms for solving complex combinatorial problems, detailed channel routing as well as switchbox routing, both industrially relevant problems within the realm of VLSI design, were chosen to demonstrate the approach.

A channel routing problem (CRP) is given by a channel of a certain width. On both sides of the channel are connection points. Each connection point belongs to a certain electrical net and all connection points of the same net need to be physically connected with each other by routing a wire through the channel and, of course, without two nets crossing. The width of the channel determines how many wires can run in parallel through the channel. The length of the channel determines how many connection points on both sides of the channel there may be. Furthermore, the layout is done on a small number of different layers (e.g. 2 to 4 layers), to make a connection of all nets without crossing possible at all. It is possible to have a connection between two adjacent layers at any point in the channel. Such a connection is also called a *via*.

The switchbox routing problem is similar to the CRP, but does not deal with only a two-sided channel, but rather a rectangle with connections on all sides. Since wires can originate and terminate on the sides of a switchbox, and the width of a channel generally being fixed (due to the fixed wire terminals on either side), the SRP is more difficult to solve.

A solution to the CRP and SRP will be referred to as a *layout*. A KB contains rules for the manipulation of layout instances, these can be used as part of a heuristic algorithm capable of solving layouts in the general case.

Fig. 5. Switchbox and channel routing in a general VLSI layout problem

Fig. 6. An example of a switchbox solution containing 60 wires, 70 tracks and 100 columns

Fig. 7. A sample of a three layer channel routing layout with 150 columns (3 layer is easier than 2 layer)

Genome Encoding: A genome describes the layout of a CRP or SRP solution. This takes the form of a list of wires. The wires are numbered 0-w where w is the number of pin pairs that need to be connected, each connection being a wire. Each wire contains a sequential list of nodes. Each node has three coordinates corresponding to the row, column and layer number.

A layout is characterized by the number of columns and rows (tracks), how many pins (wire terminals) are to be found on the side of the channel / switchbox and what the pin configuration is. A problem instance used for the system would be given by the VLSI layout problem to be solved. Initially, a genome will usually not represent a valid solution as some wires are usually crossing. Only when all those crossings have been eliminated and not more than the prescribed number of layers are used would the fitness value of a genome reach a satisfactory level.

Genome Operations: Individuals in the GA are initialised with a random wire layout without regard to conflicts. The GA operates on a genome by crossover, mutation and evaluation.

The GA's crossover operation is currently not part of a knowledge base (Sect. 5 discusses this further). In crossover, two parents are duplicated giving two children. A set of wires is exchanged between the two children using 2 point crossover. This works by picking 2 random numbers, c_1 and c_2 (where $0 \leq c_1 \leq c_2 <$ *number of wires*). The set of wires numbered c_1 to c_2 are exchanged between the children.

Evaluation is done using the evaluation KB. Typically the user uses as a fitness criteria the number of layers and conflicts in a layout. The length of wires, number of vias and possible cross-talk (electronic interference occurring in parallel wires) are also useful fitness criteria.

The mutation KB contains rules designed to manipulate the layout, typically they would describe the resolution of a conflict identified using the *.findconflict* command (a primitive function returning a conflict found in the layout).

Primitives Interface and Rule Specification Language Extensions: Primitives relating to the layout problem are supplied. These include the types *wire* and *node*, as well as other layout-specific commands. High level operators are defined as NRDRs forming a useful vocabulary for intuitive descriptions on the knowledge level. Pre-defined primitive functions are also supported, these include, for example, *.maxlayers* (counts the number of layers found in a layout), *.countconflicts* (the number of conflicts found in a layout). Some describe aspects of the GA operation, for example *.ga.generation* and *.ga.popmaxfitness* (highest fitness in whole population).

Example of Rules Applied to the Switchbox Routing Problem: Initially, a KB is built up defining operators using primitives based on node and wire manipulation. These form the foundation for more high-level concepts which can be used intuitively by an expert.

Assuming we start with a KB with relatively high-level actions defined, e.g. *RaiseWholeWire*, *MoveVerticalSegmentRight*, *MoveHorizontalSegmentDown* and *MoveHorizontalSegmentUp*, we can show how a sequence of these actions could be applied by the GA to solve a conflict, as seen in Fig. 8.

When applied to another example, Fig. 9 shows that the same sequence is unlikely to find a solution, and the expert can amend the KB to suggest an alternative action. A little background information might be in order: when improving a genome, the KB has rules which identify a random conflict to be fixed. This will tag the nodes immediately preceding or at the conflict of the two conflicting wires - labeled here as *N1* and *N2*. 'Preceding' is defined in relation to the node ordering which starts at the bottom or left side of a channel/switchbox and ends at the terminating pin.

In this case, the user may find that *MoveVerticalSegmentRight* is undesirable, and formulate a rule with condition *is_Vertical(N1) && is_Horizontal(N2) && right_of(N2.next,N1)*, and action *MoveHorizontalSegmentUp(N1.prev)*. This rule would be added as an exception in the KB. The operators referenced here are defined as RDRs elsewhere in the KB, where *is_Vertical(N1)* returns true if the segment between *N1* and its succeeding node is vertical (change in row), *is_Horizontal(N2)* returns true if the segment between *N2* and its successor is horizontal (change in column). *right_of(N2.next,N1)* will return true if the node succeeding *N2* lies to the right of *N1*.

Figure 10 and Fig. 11 show how an expert would interact with the GUI to add the exception for the rule in Fig. 9.

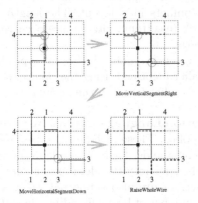

Fig. 8. Resolution of conflicts in a switch-box using 3 actions suggestions given by an expert. See Sect. 3.1. for a description

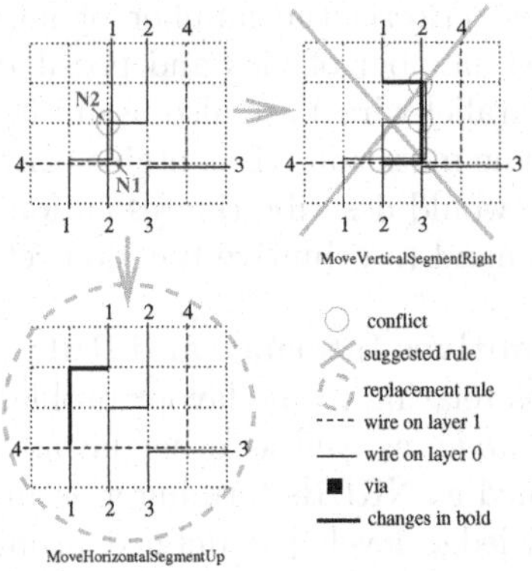

Fig. 9. An exception is created by the expert, replacing the first rule suggested by the KB, using the rule specified in Fig. 8. The tags N1 and N2 are explained in Sect3.1

3.2   Channel Routing Experiments

In order to test our approach and the implemented tool, a KB was created. Initial tests were done with a KB containing 2 RDRs and 10 rules, later tests were run with 50 RDRs and 167 rules. On average the KA process took approximately 10 minutes per rule.

We tested HeurEAKA with a "minimal" KB in order to approximate a GA with very little domain knowledge, the 10 rule KB mentioned above was our "small" KB. Both of these KBs were relative trivial to create. With this we showed that without any useful knowledge about how to go about trying to solve a layout problem, the GA was unable to find a solution. The graph in Fig.12 shows how they performed. Initially, we see a reduction in conflicts due to the GA selecting those randomly initialised layouts with the least number of conflicts. The crossover operator accounted for some improvement too, since it spread useful sub-components of solutions through the population. Once the easy part of the solution had been completed, both rule bases were ineffective

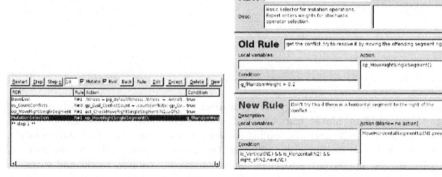

Fig. 10. The user is presented with a trace of rules selected for each mutation & evaluation step. When Nested RDRs are used, each RDR has a chosen rule

Fig. 11. An exception to the rule selected by the user in Fig.10 can be added

for resolving the more difficult conflicts. The mature KB was able to solve the problems.

Layer Restriction: Initial tests using the 167 rule KB were run for 3 layer layouts, with some found for up to 150 pins a side, an example is shown in Fig. 7. We decided to concentrate on 2 layer solutions as they are more comparable to other attempts at solving the CRP, and the theoretical limits are better understood for 2 layer layouts.

Channel Width/Number of Tracks: For testing purposes, random pin configurations where generated. In order to approximate real problems and also to control layout *density*, a heuristic ratio of long distance to short distance crossing connections was used. This ratio was around 1:3.

The *density* for a 2-layer problem is defined as the maximum over all positions p along the length of the channel as follows: the number of nets which have at least one connection point on the left as well as one connection point on the right of p. This determines the theoretical lower limit on tracks needed to solve the problem.

CRP problems tested included 30,50,70 and 80 columns, with densities and track numbers of 20/25, 24/35, 39/50, 44/70 respectively. Our experiments show that reasonable solutions can be found using our approach. The size of layouts and track sizes look comparable to those benchmarks used with other CRP algorithms [11] and [7] - many are in the 12-23 column range, some up to 129.

3.3 Switchbox Routing Experiments

In order to see how flexible the HeurEAKA approach is, we tried to use the existing KB on a slightly different problem. We made modifications in the prim-

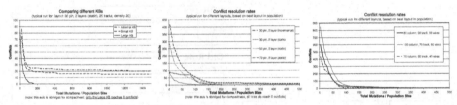

Fig. 12. Channel routing: Quasi random mutations "minimal" KB and a "small" KB are unable to solve the 30 pin layout problem. The more mature KB can solve it effectively

Fig. 13. Channel routing: Comparison of different conflict resolution rates, given different layout sizes and layer allocation strategies (static vs incremental)

Fig. 14. Switchbox routing: Comparison of different conflict resolution rates, given different number of colums, tracks and wires

itives module reflecting a different problem. We used a modified version of the KB developed for the CRP. Changing the primitives and adapting the KB from CRP to SRP took 2 days. Generally the SRP is more difficult to solve than the CRP. Track availability is far more restricted in the SRP since wire terminals are fixed on tracks (at the sides of the switchbox). Also, assumptions about terminals locations and wire orientation made in the CRP KB were not always valid for SRP. Nonetheless, it was found that due to the flexible nature of how HeurEAKA applies rules, it was possible to solve SRPs. In other words, in order to solve the CRP we encoded sufficient examples for solving problems that we generic enough to apply to the SRP. Also we are using a GA that is robust enough to recover from wrong operations and capable of functioning with incomplete operations.

Only two layer switchboxes were tested. Switchbox configurations were generated randomly with no restrictions on wire crossing distances. Solutions to switchbox layouts were found for (column number, track number, wire count): (30,20,20), (50,30,30), (70,50,40), (80,50,50), (100,70,60). Figure 14 shows conflict resolution rates for these switchboxes, and Fig. 6 shows an example of a switchbox solution.

The dimensions the SRPs solved compare favourably with the benchmarks tested in other attempts for do switchbox routing, notably when compared to those achieved by other GA approaches [8, 12].

4 Knowledge Acquisition Experience

A comprehensive KB was created, comprising 49 RDRs and 167 rules. Initial rules were low-level rules needed for the manipulation of nodes and wires. These were necessary for establishing sufficient operators to use in a knowledge level description. This work was fairly technical and required repeated editing and debugging to ensure operator correctness. Incorrect operators at the low level would often create invalid layouts (diagonal wires or vias, moved wire terminals) or undesirable wiring - double-backing, repeated nodes etc. In order to help the user, a validation module was run during a genome's evolution, and any invalid layouts would generate an exception. The offender could then be hand-analysed (the exception generates an execution trace).

After the low level rules were defined, the KA process became easier since most rules could be defined at a higher level of abstraction. Because this was a more intuitive abstraction level, it was easier to formulate rules and required less revision of conditions or actions. This part of the KB is primarily what the probabilistic algorithm makes use of: choosing from the different high level strategies in an attempt to resolve conflicts.

Using some of the simple rule statistics provided by HeurEAKA, it was possible to identify some dud rules, i.e. those that attracted excessive fitness penalties. In general it was felt that these statistics needed to be further developed to be really useful.

Another general strategy used for formulating rules was to let the GA run and wait for the population to converge to promising solutions. Once the population fitness rates had plateau'd, it was assumed current rules could suggest no better improvements. Individuals were pulled out of the population and rules added where the expert could suggest a strategy for improving on them.

5 Discussion

The experiments show that it is feasible to attempt solutions to complex problems using the HeurEAKA framework - in this case we applied it to the domain of detailed Channel Routing Problem (CRP) and the Switchbox Routing Problem (SRP). We were able to effectively perform KA using ripple-down rules based knowledge acquisition, which formed an effective KB for the GA.

The development of the problem specific components of HeurEAKA did require some effort in addition to KB construction, it would be commensurate with any other attempt at solving a CRP/SRP, since basic encoding and access of a layout is necessary. We argue that the additional effort usually spent on adapting and tuning GAs towards a problem domain is in excess of ours.

A number of studies have been made in the application of GAs to CRP and SRP, these make extensive use of domain knowledge by formulating either custom operators, or using existing known routing techniques [7, 8]. [7] show that the use of informed operators results in finding of better solutions for the CRP, which is what one would expect.

It is known that the development of a suitable representation, mutation and crossover operators for genetic algorithms is often quite difficult [1]. Instead of relying on the definition of operators through expert introspection and trial and error, we allow the user to formulate them by exploring example cases. There is an approach somewhat related in the use of case based reasoning for GA in VLSI design [9]. Here, however, previous cases are selected by an expert and only used for injection into a GA search, rather than formulation of operators.

It does not build on generalizations and expert insight learned from these cases, thus being far less powerful.

There is some controversy over the importance of mutation vs. crossover operators [2] in the successful design of GAs. In our current implementation, we have chosen to initially concentrate on KA for the mutation and evaluation operators.

It is worth investigating the use of KA for replacing the current crossover operator with a KB based one. Goldberg [2] explains that in selectorecombinative GAs, the design of crossover operators is very important for successful search. When choosing the operator one wants a good chance of preserving subsolutions when exchanging between two individuals. When designing a crossover operator, initially a user is likely to have very little prior knowledge in matching the crossover operator to the problem encoding [2]. With KA one can support the iterative refinement of the crossover operator in a similar way to our existing approach. We expect, however, that it will not be as easy for a user to create rules identifying good strategies for sub-component exchange as it is for incremental improvement of one genome (as is currently done for the mutation operator).

We have provided the user with useful tools in the formulation of a KB. The KA process was effective and supported by a good user interface. Helper functions providing some automated selection of cases which would be good candidates for formulation of new rules have been attempted. Extensions could include the ability to review new and exisiting rules against a case history, and better statistical measures relating their use in successful and unsuccessful evolutionary paths.

On average rules took approximately 10 minutes each to formulate, taking about 30 hours for the formulation of a viable knowledge base. The formulation of effective CRP and SRP algorithms has been the subject of much study and industry-standard algorithms took many years to develop [10]. In our case KA was done by a novice, using mainly intuition and being able to incrementally specify rules in a natural way on the knowledge level. Thus the effort and expertise required was significantly less than commercial routing solutions.

Direct comparison of our solution to existing benchmarks needs extension to supporting wire nets in the HeurEAKA tool. The results outlined in the previous sections look promising, and with the continued development of the KB, should produce even better results in the future.

The application of our framework in the well understood domain of CRP and SRP, enables us to benchmark our results against industrially used algorithms.

6   Conclusion

In this paper we have presented a framework for solving complex combinatorial problems based on incremental knowledge acquisition from a human expert. We outline how our approach makes it easier to tackle such problems than the conventional design of algorithms.

Given that the development of standard genetic algorithms still requires considerable effort in the formulation and tuning of operators, we introduce a method that is better suited to integrate domain knowledge. We used NRDR, an unconventional KA technique, by integrating it into the design process to provide an intuitive method of supporting an expert's development effort.

We have adapted the principles of RDR to apply them in probabilistic search algorithms. Considering the use of unusual RDR characteristics, our approach showed that they still allowed us to perform effectively.

We demonstrate our approach in the domain of detailed channel and switch-box routing. This shows that the approach achieves results comparable to conventional approaches developed with considerably more effort.

We also hope to extend the RDR techniques used to provide more automated support for rule formulation such as the automatic evaluation of proposed new rules on databases of genomes that were generated through previous genetic searches. Currently the process of identifying good candidate solutions for rule formulation requires a fair amount of interaction by the user. In future this process can be more automated by leveraging performance statistics of muta-tion operators, as well as the possible introduction of some machine learning techniques.

The knowledge base used in the experiments for CRP and SRP is sufficient to solve problems comparable to those used in other GA benchmarks. However, in future work we plan to extend our implementation to be able to tackle more challenging problems. If we can show the competitiveness of these solutions, we hope to apply the framework to problems in other domains.

References

1. Rothlauf, F.: Representations for Genetic and Evolutionary Algorithms. Springer Verlag (2002)
2. Goldberg, D.E.: The Design of Innovation: Lessons from and for Competent Ge-netic Algorithms. Volume 7, Kluwer Series on Genetic Algorithms and Evolution-ary Computation. Kluwer Academic Publishers (2002)
3. De Jong, K., Spears, W.: Using genetic algorithm to solve NP-complete problems. In Schaffer, J.D., ed.: Proc. of the Third Int. Conf. on Genetic Algorithms, San Mateo, CA, Morgan Kaufmann (1989) 124–132
4. Holland, J.: Adaptation in Natural and Artificial Systems. University of Michigan Press. (1975)
5. Compton, P., Jansen, R.: Knowledge in context: A strategy for expert system maintenance. In: 2nd Australian Joint Artificial Intelligence Conference. Volume 1. (1989) 292–306
6. Beydoun, G., Hoffmann, A.: Theoretical basis for hierarchical incremental knowl-edge acquisition. In: International Journal in Human-Computer Studies. (2001) 407–452
7. Gockel, N., Pudelko, G., Drechsler, R., Becker, B.: A hybrid genetic algorithm for the channel routing problem. In: International Symposium on Circuits and Systems, volume IV. (1996) 675–678

8. Lin, Y., Hsu, Y., Tsai, F.: Silk: A simulated evolution router. In: IEEE Transactions on CAD. Volume 8.10. (1989) 1108–1114
9. Liu, X.: Combining genetic algorithm and casebased reasoning for structure design (1996)
10. Lengauer, T.: Combinational Algorithms for Integrated Circuit Layout. B.G. Teubner/John Wiley & Sons (1990)
11. Lienig, J., Thulasiraman, K.: A new genetic algorithm for the channel routing problem. In: 7th International Conference on VLSI Design, Calcutta (1994) 133–136
12. Lienig, J.: Channel and switchbox routing with minimized crosstalk - a parallel genetic algorithm approach. In: the 10th International Conference on VLSI Design,Hyderabad (1997) 27–31

Parallel Knowledge Base Development
by Subject Matter Experts

Gheorghe Tecuci, Mihai Boicu, Dorin Marcu,
Bogdan Stanescu, Cristina Boicu, and Marcel Barbulescu

MSN 4A5, Learning Agents Center, George Mason
University, 4400 University Drive, Fairfax, VA 22030, USA
{tecuci, mboicu, dmarcu, bstanesc, ccascava}@gmu.edu,
mbarb@cs.gmu.edu, http://lac.gmu.edu,
tel: 1 703 993-1722, fax: 1 703 993-1710

Abstract. This paper presents an experiment of parallel knowledge base development by subject matter experts, performed as part of the DARPA's Rapid Knowledge Formation Program. It introduces the Disciple-RKF development environment used in this experiment and proposes design guidelines for systems that support authoring of problem solving knowledge by subject matter experts. Finally, it compares Disciple-RKF with the other development environments from the same DARPA program, providing further support for the proposed guidelines.

1 Introduction

Traditionally, a knowledge-based system is built by a knowledge engineer (KE) who needs to acquire the knowledge from a subject matter expert (SME) and to encode it into the knowledge base. This is a very difficult process because the SMEs express their knowledge informally, using natural language, visual representations, and common sense, often omitting many essential details they regard as being obvious. In order to properly understand an SME's problem solving knowledge and to represent it in a formal, precise, and "complete" knowledge base, the knowledge engineer needs to become himself/herself a kind of SME. Therefore this process is very difficult, error-prone, and time-consuming, being known as the knowledge acquisition bottleneck in system development.

One solution to this problem, pursued by the DARPA's Rapid Knowledge Formation program (2000-03), is the development of knowledge bases directly by SMEs, the central objective of this program being to enable distributed teams of SMEs to enter and modify knowledge directly and easily, without the need of prior knowledge engineering experience (http://cerberus.cyc.com/RKF/).

This paper presents an experiment of parallel knowledge base development by SMEs, and proposes guidelines for the design of systems that support authoring of

E. Motta et al. (Eds.): EKAW 2004, LNAI 3257, pp. 265–279, 2004.

problem solving knowledge by SMEs. It briefly introduces the Disciple-RKF integrated development environment used in this experiment, and discusses the main phases of the experiment. Finally, it compares Disciple-RKF with the other two systems developed in the DARPA's RKF program, KRAKEN and SHAKEN [6], which provide further experimental support for the proposed design guidelines.

2 Disciple-RKF Knowledge Base Development Environment

The Disciple approach is the result of 20 years of research on developing a theory and associated methodologies and tools for knowledge base development [8, 4, 9, 2, 3]. Disciple-RKF, the implementation of the most recent version of the Disciple approach, is an agent shell with a knowledge base structured into an object ontology that describes the entities from an application domain, and a set of task reduction and solution composition rules expressed with these objects. The main functional components of Disciple-RKF are:

- A problem solving component based on task reduction. It includes a mixed-initiative (step-by-step) problem solver that allows the user and the agent to collaborate in the problem solving process, and an autonomous problem solver. It also includes a modeling assistant that helps the user to express his/her contributions to the problem solving process.
- A learning component for acquiring and refining the knowledge of the agent, allowing a wide range of operations, from ontology import and user definition of knowledge base elements (through the use of editors and browsers), to ontology learning and rule learning.
- A knowledge base manager which controls the access and the updates to the knowledge base. Each module of Disciple-RKF accesses the knowledge base only through the functions of the knowledge base manager.
- A window-based graphical user interface.

   The development of the knowledge base of a Disciple-RKF agent is based on importing ontological knowledge from existing knowledge repositories, and on teaching the agent how to perform various tasks, in a way that resembles how an SME teaches a human apprentice. For instance, to teach the agent, the SME may formulate a specific problem and show the agent the reasoning steps to solve it, helping the agent to understand each of them. Each problem solving step represents an example from which the agent learns a general rule. As Disciple learns new rules from the SME, the interaction between the SME and Disciple evolves from a teacher-student interaction, toward an interaction where both collaborate in solving a problem. During this mixed-initiative problem solving phase, Disciple learns not only from the contributions of the SME, but also from its own successful or unsuccessful problem solving attempts, which lead to the refinement of the learned rules. This process is based on:

- *mixed-initiative problem solving*, where the SME and the agent solve problems in cooperation and the agent learns from the contributions of the SME;

– *integrated teaching and learning*, where the agent helps the SME to teach it (for instance, by asking relevant questions), and the SME helps the agent to learn (for instance, by providing examples, hints and explanations); and
– *multistrategy learning*, where the agent integrates different strategies, such as learning from examples, from explanations, and by analogy, to learn general concepts and rules.

3 Parallel Knowledge Base Development Experiment

A knowledge base development experiment with Disciple-RKF was conducted during the Military Applications of Artificial Intelligence (MAAI) course, taught at the US Army War College, in Spring 2003. This was a 10 week, 3 hours/week course, attended by 13 colonels and lieutenant colonels from different military services. The students, who had no prior knowledge engineering experience, were introduced to the Disciple approach, and used Disciple-RKF to jointly develop an agent for the determination of the centers of gravity (COG) of the opposing forces from a conflict. The concept of center of gravity is fundamental to military strategy, denoting the primary source of moral or physical strength, power or resistance of a force [7]. The most important objective of a force is to protect its own center of gravity, while attacking the center of gravity of its enemy.

Our approach to center of gravity determination, developed with the experts from the US Army War College, consists of two main phases: *identification* and *testing*. During the identification phase, center of gravity candidates from different elements of power of a force (such as government, military, people, economy) are identified. For instance, a strong leader is a center of gravity candidate with respect to the government of a force. Then, during the testing phase, each candidate is analyzed to determine whether it has all the critical capabilities that are necessary to be the center of gravity. For example, a leader needs to be protected, stay informed, communicate (with the government, the military, and the people), be influential (with the government, the military, and the people), be a driving force, have support (from the government, the military, and the people), and be irreplaceable. For each capability, one needs to determine the existence of the essential conditions, resources and means that are required by that capability to be fully operative, and which of these, if any, represent critical vulnerabilities. The testing of the critical capabilities is based on a general theory developed by Strange [7].

Figure 1 provides an overview of the performed experiment. Before starting the experiment, the Disciple-RKF agent was trained to identify leaders as center of gravity candidates. The knowledge base of this agent contained the definitions of 432 concepts and features, 29 tasks and 18 task reduction rules. However, the agent had no knowledge of how to test the identified candidates.

We then performed a joint domain analysis and ontology development with all the SMEs, by considering the example of testing whether Saddam Hussein, in the Iraq 2003 scenario, has all the required critical capabilities to be the center of gravity for Iraq. We determined which are the critical requirements for these capabilities to be operational, and which are the corresponding critical vulnerabilities, if any. Based on this domain analysis, we extended the ontology of Disciple-RKF with the definition of 37 new concepts and features identified with the help of the SMEs.

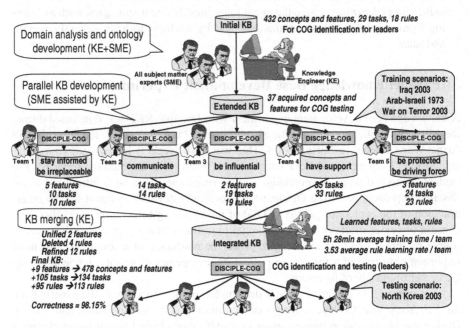

Fig. 1. Experiment of rapid knowledge base development by SMEs

The 13 SMEs were grouped into five teams (of 2 or 3 SMEs each), and each team was given a copy of the extended Disciple-RKF agent. After that, each team trained its agent to test whether a leader has one or two critical capabilities, as indicated in Figure 1. For instance, Team 1 trained its agent how to test whether a leader has the critical capabilities of staying informed and being irreplaceable. The training was done based on three scenarios (Iraq 2003, Arab-Israeli 1973, and War on Terror 2003), the SMEs teaching Disciple-RKF how to test each strategic leader from these scenarios. As a result of the training performed by the SMEs, the knowledge base of each Disciple-RKF agent was extended with new features, tasks, and rules, as indicated in Figure 1. For instance, the knowledge base of the agent trained by Team 1 was extended with 5 features, 10 tasks and 10 rules for testing whether a leader has the capabilities to stay informed and be irreplaceable. The average training time per team was 5 hours and 28 minutes, and the average rule learning rate per team was 3.53 rules/hour. This included the time spent in all the agent training activities (i.e., scenario specification, modeling SME's reasoning, task formalization, rule learning, problem solving, and rule refinement).

During each class the SMEs were introduced to the Disciple theory and tools corresponding to a particular agent training activity (e.g. scenario specification). The SMEs were supervised by knowledge engineers who were asked not to offer help, unless it was requested, and were not allowed to do SME's work. The SMEs were helped in the initial phases of learning to use a tool, after it was demonstrated by the course's instructor.

After the training of the 5 Disciple-RKF agents, their knowledge bases were merged by a knowledge engineer, who used the knowledge base merging tool of Disciple-RKF. The knowledge engineer also performed a general testing of the integrated knowledge base, in which we included 10 new features, 102 new tasks, and 99 new rules (all acquired in less than 6 hours). During this process two semantically equivalent features were unified, 4 rules were deleted, and 12 other rules were refined by the knowledge engineer. The other 8 features and 83 rules learned from the SMEs were not changed. Most of the modifications were done to remove rule redundancies, or to specialize overly general rules.

Next, each SME team tested the integrated agent on a new scenario (North Korea 2003), and was asked to judge the correctness of each reasoning step performed by the agent, but only for the capabilities for which that SME team performed the training of the agent. The result was a very high 98.15% correctness.

In addition to the above experiment, agent training experiments were also conducted during the Spring 2001 and Spring 2002 sessions of the MAAI course, which were attended by 25 military experts [12]. However, *the Spring 2003 experiment is the first one ever that also included the merging of the developed knowledge bases into a functional agent*, demonstrating a capability for rapid and parallel development of a knowledge base by SMEs, with limited assistance from knowledge engineers. One should also mention that this was also the only experiment of parallel knowledge base development and integration, performed in the DARPA's RKF program.

The design of this experiment provides the following general guideline for the parallel development of a knowledge base by the SMEs.

Guideline 1: *Structure the knowledge base development process as follows:*

1) Partition the application domain into sub-domains that are as independent as possible, and assign each partition to an SME.

2) Develop an object ontology for the entire domain (i.e., a hierarchical representation of the domain objects and their properties and relationships).

3) Develop the knowledge base for the top-level reasoning of the agent, allowing the agent to reduce any input problem solving task to a set of subtasks from the defined sub-domains.

4) Provide each SME with a copy of the agent, to author problem solving knowledge for his/her sub-domain. This will result in several parallel extensions of the object ontology, and in several sets of rules.

5) Integrate the knowledge bases of all the agents by merging all the extended ontologies into a shared ontology, and by keeping the developed rules in separate partitions. Any input problem solving task for the final agent is reduced to subtasks from different sub-domains. Then each subtask is solved using the rules learned from a single SME (or SME team).

6) Test the agent with the integrated knowledge base.

Notice that the SMEs needed to agree on a common ontology, but not on how to solve a given subtask, significantly simplifying the knowledge base integration process. The next sections discuss two of the most important phases of this process and their corresponding guidelines.

4   Modeling the Reasoning of an SME

In order to teach an agent how to solve problems, the SME has first to be able to make explicit the way he or she reasons. Our experience shows that *this is the single most difficult agent training activity for the SME.* In the following we will briefly describe the Disciple approach to this challenging problem, and then present several design guidelines that help simplifying it.

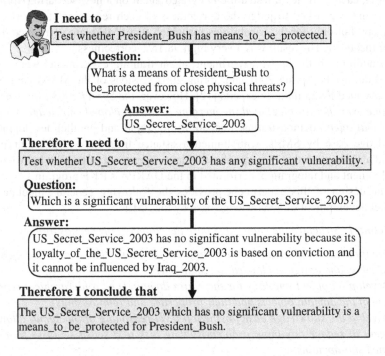

Fig. 2. A sequence of two task reduction steps

We have developed a very simple and intuitive modeling language in which the SME expresses the way he/she is solving a specific problem, using natural language, as if the SME would think aloud. The SME follows a task reduction paradigm, guided by questions and answers, successively reducing a complex problem solving task to simpler tasks, finding the solutions of the simplest tasks, and successively combining them into the solution of the initial task. The Disciple-RKF modeling language is illustrated in Figure 2 which includes a sequence of two reduction steps.

The question associated with the task from the top of Figure 2 considers some relevant piece of information for solving that task. The answer identifies that piece of information and leads the SME to reduce this task to a simpler task (or, in other cases, to several simpler tasks). Alternative questions correspond to alternative approaches to solve the current problem solving task. Several answers to a question correspond to several potential solutions. The modeling language includes many helpful guidelines for the SME, such as [3]:

Guideline 2: Ask small, incremental questions that are likely to have a single category of answer (but not necessarily a single answer). This usually means ask who, or what, or where, or what kind of, or is this or that etc., not complex questions such as who and what, or what and where.

Higher-level design guidelines, supported by our experiments, are briefly described below.

Guideline 3: Train the SMEs to express their reasoning using the problem solving paradigm of the knowledge base development environment.

In our experiment, the problem solving strategy of task reduction based on questions and answers was discussed and illustrated in action planning, course of action critiquing, and center of gravity identification. A general approach to center of gravity testing was also discussed, as presented at the beginning of section 3.

Guideline 4: Allow the SMEs to express their reasoning in natural language, but provide them with helpful and non-disruptive mechanisms for automatic identification of the knowledge base elements in their phrases.

For instance, Disciple-RKF includes a Modeling Assistant with an effective word completion capability. When the SME types a few characters of a phrase, such as, "means to be protected" (see Figure 2), the assistant proposes all the partially matching names from the knowledge base, ordered by their plausibility, to be used in the current context, including "means_to_be_protected." The SME selects this name only because it is simpler than typing it. However, now the system also partially "understands" the English sentence entered by the SME, which will significantly facilitate the follow-on process of language to knowledge transformation.

Guideline 5: Do not ask the SMEs to provide general problem solving rules. Ask them to express how to solve specific problems.

The modeling language and the associated Modeling Assistant help the SME to express how to solve a specific problem, thus providing examples of problem solving steps from which Disciple-RKF learns general rules, as will be discussed in section 5.

Guideline 6: Provide non-disruptive mechanisms for helping the SMEs to express their reasoning process.

For instance, at each step in the modeling process, the Modeling Assistant shows the SME both all the allowable user actions, and the recommended ones (such as "Copy and modify the current Task to define a Subtask"). Also, when possible, the Modeling Assistant automatically performs the selected action. Moreover, using analogical reasoning with previously learned rules, this assistant may suggest a partially instantiated pattern for the current question to be asked, or for the answer to the question.

The usefulness of this guideline is supported by the comparative analysis of the modeling process performed during the Spring 2002 agent training experiment (when the SMEs were not supported by the Modeling Assistant), and the modeling process performed during the Spring 2003 experiment (when the SMEs were helped by the Modeling Assistant). In Spring 2003, the modeling process was considered more natural, was faster and more correct, due to the support provided by the Modeling Assistant [2].

The 13 SMEs who participated in the Spring 2003 experiment (see Figure 1) evaluated the difficulty in modeling their own reasoning process, using the task reduction paradigm. For instance, on a 5-point scale (strongly agree, agree, neutral, disagree, strongly disagree), 8 of them strongly agreed, 2 agreed, 3 were neutral, and none disagreed with the statement *"The task reduction paradigm implemented in Disciple is a reasonable way of expressing in detail the logic involved in identifying and testing strategic COG candidates."* Moreover, 10 experts strongly agreed, 2 agreed, 1 was neutral, and none disagreed with the statement *"Subject matter experts that are not computer scientists can learn to express their reasoning process using the task reduction paradigm, with a reasonable amount of effort."*

5   Rule Learning

After the SME expresses his/her reasoning as a sequence of task reduction steps, as illustrated in Figure 2, the SME needs to help the agent to learn a general task reduction rule from each task reduction step. Rule learning is a mixed-initiative process between the SME (who knows why the reduction is correct and can help the agent to understand this) and the Disciple-RKF agent (that is able to generalize the task reduction example and its explanation into a general rule, by using the object ontology as a generalization language). This process is based on a communication protocol which takes into account that:

- it is easier for an SME to understand sentences in the formal language of the agent than it is to produce such formal sentences; and
- it is easier for the agent to generate formal sentences than it is to understand sentences in the natural language used by the SME.

Part of this process is illustrated in Figure 3. The left hand side of Figure 3 shows the task reduction example from the top part of Figure 2. This example is in natural language, except for the phrases with underscores which have already been recognized as representing elements from the Disciple's ontology, as discussed in the previous section. The right hand side of Figure 3 is the same task reduction example in a structured form. This structured form is generated by Disciple-RKF with the help of the SME. First Disciple-RKF proposes formalizations of the tasks from the example, by rephrasing the unstructured form of the task into a general task name (which does not contain any specific object), and one or several task features that identify the specific objects from the task. The SME can accept the formalization proposed by Disciple-RKF or, in rare cases, can modify it so that the task name is more understandable.

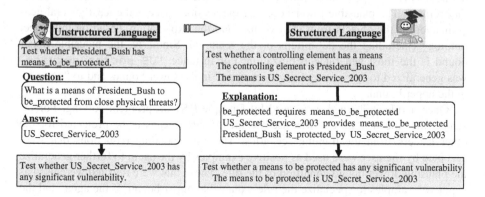

Fig. 3. Mixed-initiative language to knowledge translation

The natural language question and its answer from a task reduction step are intended to represent the SME's reason (or explanation) for performing that reduction. But they are in natural language and the SME has to help Disciple-RKF to "understand" them. The agent will use analogical reasoning with previously learned rules, as well as general heuristics, to hypothesize the meaning of the question-answer pair. It will generate plausible explanation fragments (ordered by their plausibility), and the SME will select those that best express this meaning. The SME may also help the agent to propose the right explanation pieces by proving hints, such as pointing to a relevant object that should be part of the explanation. Each explanation fragment proposed by the agent is a relationship (or a relationship chain) involving instances, concepts and constants from the task reduction step and from the knowledge base. For instance, the right hand side of Figure 3 shows the explanation fragments selected by the SME, from those proposed by the agent.

Once the explanations have been identified, the agent generates the task reduction rule shown in Figure 4. This rule has an informal structure, shown at the top of Figure 4, and a formal structure, shown at the bottom of Figure 4. Compare the informal structure of the learned rule with the example from the left hand side of Figure 3. As one can see, this rule is generated by simply turning the constants from the example into variables. Therefore, the informal structure of the rule preserves the natural language of the SME, and is used in agent-user communication. This rule should be interpreted as follows: If the task to be solved is T_1, I am asking the question Q, and if the answer is A, then I can reduce T_1 to T_{11}.

The formal structure of the learned rule, shown at the bottom of Figure 4, corresponds to the formalized version of the example from the right hand side of Figure 3. This formal structure is used in the actual problem solving process, and is interpreted as follows: If the task to be solved is FT_1, and the rule's applicability condition is satisfied, then I can reduce FT_1 to FT_{11}. Notice that both FT_1 and FT_{11} are formal task expressions. Moreover, instead of a single applicability condition, the rule in Figure 4 has a plausible version space for the exact condition, because the rule is only partially learned. This rule, generated from a single example and its explanation, will be further refined. The plausible lower bound of the version space is the least general generalization of the objects from the example and the explanation, based on the object ontology (including the definitions of the features). Similarly, the plausible upper bound is the most general generalization. For instance, "US_secret_service" was generalized to "protection_service" in the lower bound, and to "agent" in the upper bound.

Once a rule is learned, it is used by Disciple-RKF in problem solving. For instance, the rule in Figure 4 was used to identify the means to be protected for the other leaders from the training scenarios. The corresponding reductions that were accepted by the user were used as positive examples by the agent to further generalize the plausible lower bound condition of the rule. Those that were rejected were used as negative examples to specialize the rule's plausible upper bound. If the agent and the SME identified an explanation of why a reduction was wrong, then a corresponding "except-when" plausible version space condition was added to the rule. In the future, the rule will be applicable only if the except-when condition will not be satisfied. During this process, the agent may learn complex rules with quantificators and negation. More details on the learning methods used are given in [9, 2].

The high accuracy of the learned rules in the performed experiment (see Figure 1) shows that the above approach to rule learning from SMEs is very successful, leading to the learning of good quality rules, in a very short time, and from a small number of examples.

The performed experiments support the following guidelines for the design of systems that help SMEs to author problem solving knowledge.

Guideline 7: *Provide the SME with easy to use features for helping the agent to understand the natural language phrases of the SME.*

For instance, the SME helped Disciple-RKF to generate the correct meaning of the SME's phrases by pointing to relevant objects, or by guiding the refinement of abstract structures.

Guideline 8: *Implement mechanisms to automatically generalize the specific examples provided by the SMEs into general knowledge pieces.*

These mechanisms are illustrated by the rule learning process of Disciple-RKF.

Guideline 9: *Verify the general rules learned by asking the SME to judge the results of their applications in other cases, and use SME's critiques to automatically refine them.*

Because it is much easier for an SME to judge concrete cases than general pieces of knowledge, in our approach, the SME does not even see the rules, but only their application to specific situations.

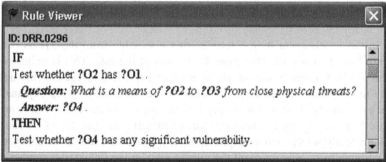

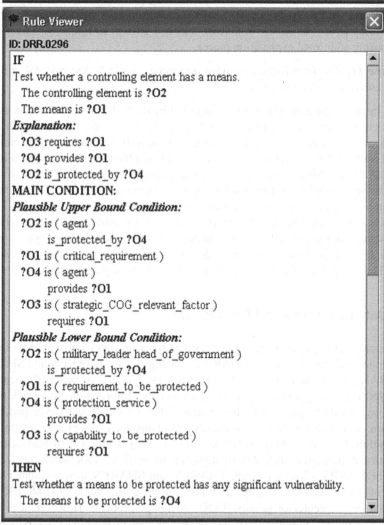

Fig. 4. A learned rule

Guideline 10: Implement mechanisms to automatically check the learned knowledge pieces, and to correct them by asking clarification questions about specific examples.

For instance, the agent may determine that a variable from the THEN part of a rule is not linked to any variable from the IF part of the rule. This is indicative of a rule which was learned based on an incomplete explanation, causing the agent to reinitiate the explanation generation process. Sometimes, the missing explanation is so obvious to the SME that it is simply ignored as, for instance, the following one: "US_2003 has_as_government government_of_US_2003." The agent will automatically select such an explanation, if it provides a link to an unconstrained variable. Sometimes, even when all the rule's variables are linked, the number of rule instances may still be very large. In such a case the agent will attempt to identify which variables are the least constrained, and will attempt to further constrain them, by proposing additional explanation pieces.

Guideline 11: The knowledge authoring approach should be incremental, allowing imperfections from the SME.

For instance, the explanation pieces selected by the SME do not need to constitute a complete explanation of a task reduction step. In such a case the learned rule will generate wrong reductions which will reveal to the SME what factors were not considered, and what new explanation pieces should be added. Another common imperfection is for the SME to select too many explanation pieces. This leads to a rule which is less general than it should be, but it is correct nevertheless. The agent may then automatically combine and generalize similar rules.

At the end of the Spring 2003 experiment, 7 SMEs strongly agreed, 4 agreed, 1 was neutral and 1 disagreed with the statement "*I think that a subject matter expert can use Disciple to build an agent, with limited assistance from a knowledge engineer*". This is a powerful experimental support for the Disciple approach.

6 Related Research and Conclusions

In addition to Disciple-RKF, two other systems for acquiring expert problem solving knowledge were developed in the DARPA's RKF program, KRAKEN and SHAKEN [6]. KRAKEN was developed by the Cycorp team, which also included researchers from Northwestern University, Stanford University, Information Science Institute, University of Edinburgh, Teknowledge, and SAIC. SHAKEN was developed by the SRI team, which also included researchers from University of Texas at Austin, Boeing, Stanford University, MIT, Northwestern University, University of Massachusetts, University of Western Florida, Information Science Institute, PSR, and Pragati.

In the DARPA's RKF program, KRAKEN and SHAKEN were evaluated on the course of action (COA) critiquing challenge problem [6], while Disciple-RKF was evaluated on the center of gravity (COG) challenge problem. However, a previous version of Disciple, Disciple-COA, developed as part of the DARPA's HPKB program, was also evaluated on the course of action critiquing problem, as discussed in [10, 11]. As opposed to Disciple-COA and Disciple-RKF, which use rule chaining, the course of action critiquing of both KRAKEN and SHAKEN is more limited, being based on a single rule, where the antecedent represents some characteristics of the course of action, and the consequent is a critique of the course of action. Therefore, the kind of problem solving knowledge acquired by Disciple was more complex than that acquired by KRAKEN and SHAKEN.

The approach taken by KRAKEN and SHAKEN to the authoring of problem solving knowledge from SMEs was radically different from that of Disciple-RKF. The philosophy behind both systems was to develop advanced tools that would allow the SMEs to directly author general problem solving rules. The main difference between the two systems was in the type of the rule editing tools used. KRAKEN used text-oriented tools, its key strategy for facilitating SME-authoring being natural language presentation and a knowledge-driven acquisition dialog with natural language understanding, supported by the large Cyc knowledge base [5]. Notice here the relationship with *Guideline 4* on the use of natural language.

SHAKEN provided the SME with a graph (concept map) editor to represent the antecedents and the consequent of a rule pattern. This graph editor facilitated the SME's use of the objects and relationships from the knowledge base of SHAKEN (as also suggested in the second part of *Guideline 4*). Such a graph was then automatically translated into a formal rule, so that the SMEs did not need to be trained in formal logic [1].

It is interesting to notice that the conclusions of the experiments performed with KRAKEN and SHAKEN indirectly support the Disciple approach to acquiring problem solving knowledge, and several of the design guidelines stated in the previous sections. For instance, one of these conclusions is: "For purposes of rule elicitation, the focus on a particular scenario rendered the initial rule articulation much more manageable for the SME. It would have been more difficult to articulate rules from more universally acceptable general principles initially" [6]. This justifies *Guideline 5* which is also based on the idea that it is easier for an SME to reason with specific scenarios.

However, "an unfortunate consequence of the scenario focus is that the SMEs occasionally tended to overly restrict a rule by including unnecessary details from a particular scenario" making necessary for the rule to be further generalized [6].

Moreover, sometimes the generalization performed by the SME was incorrect in the sense that it was not really a generalization of the studied scenario. The proposed solution to this problem is to have the rule "examined for generalization, either by a system tool, or in consultation with a knowledge engineer" [6]. Our experiments with Disciple have also revealed the SME's tendency to provide more specific explanations of the problem solving episodes considered, as stated in the explanations for *Guideline 11*. However, as opposed to SHAKEN and KRAKEN, the generalization of the examples is performed by the Disciple learning agent and not by the SME, and it is correct (with respect to the current ontology). Therefore *Guideline 8* suggests that the generalizations should be performed by the agent.

Because the SMEs cannot test the correctness of a rule by direct examination, these rules acquired by KRAKEN and SHAKEN were tested on the concrete scenarios that inspired them in the first place, allowing the SMEs to further improve the rules. This supports *Guideline 9* and the approach taken in Disciple-RKF where the SMEs do not even see the rules learned by the system, but only the results of their application. Moreover, a Disciple rule learned from a scenario is guaranteed to correctly work for that scenario.

A global conclusion of the developers of KRAKEN and SHAKEN is that "given representational subtleties, especially those associated with negation and quantification, fully automated elicitation of any arbitrary complex rule remains somewhat elusive" [6]. In essence, these experiments confirmed that it is difficult for an SME to formulate general rules, and these rules are very likely to be incomplete and only partially correct (which justifies *Guideline 5*).

On the contrary, Disciple-RKF agents successfully acquired a significant number of accurate problem solving rules from the SMEs because the Disciple approach requires the SMEs to do what they know best (i.e. to solve specific problems), and not to perform knowledge engineering tasks, which proved to be very difficult for them, even with the very powerful knowledge engineering tools offered by KRAKEN and SHAKEN.

Maybe the most significant factor in the comparison of Disciple-RKF and, in general, of the Disciple approach to acquiring and integrating problem solving knowledge from SMEs (on one hand), and the approaches illustrated by KRAKEN and SHAKEN (on the other hand), is that the Disciple team was the only team from the DARPA's RKF program that has successfully conducted a parallel knowledge base development and integration experiment.

The deployment and evaluation of Disciple-RKF have also revealed several limitations of this approach and have provided numerous ideas for improvement. For instance, while the subject matter expert has an increased role and independence in the agent development process, the knowledge engineer still has a critical role to play. The knowledge engineer has to assure the development of a fairly complete and correct object ontology. The knowledge engineer also has to develop a generic modeling of the expert's problem solving process based on the task reduction paradigm. Even guided by this generic modeling, and using natural language, the subject matter expert has difficulties in expressing his reasoning process. Therefore more work is needed to develop methods for helping the expert in this task, along the path opened by the Modeling Advisor.

The experimentations also revealed that the mixed-initiative reasoning methods of Disciple-RKF could be significantly empowered by developing the natural language processing capabilities of the system.

Finally, because the expert who teaches Disciple-RKF has no formal training in knowledge engineering or computer science, the knowledge pieces learned by the agent and the knowledge base itself will not be optimally represented, and will require periodic revisions by the knowledge engineer. Examples of encountered problems with the knowledge base are: semantic inconsistencies within a rule, proliferation of semantically equivalent tasks, and the violation of certain knowledge engineering principles. It is therefore necessary to develop mixed-initiative knowledge base reformulation and optimization methods to identify and correct such problems in the knowledge base.

Acknowledgments

This research was sponsored by DARPA, AFRL, AFMC, USAF, under agreement number F30602-00-2-0546, by the AFOSR under grant no. F49620-00-1-0072, and by the US Army War College. Several persons supported this effort, including Jerome Comello, William Cleckner, Murray Burke, William Rzepka, Douglass Campbell, David Brooks, and Christopher Fowler. We are also grateful to the anonymous reviewers for their insightful comments.

References

1. Barker, K., Blythe, J., Borchardt, G., Chaudhri, V.K., Clark, P.E., Cohen, P, Fitzgerald, J., Forbus, K., Gil, Y., Katz, B., Kim, J., King, G., Mishra, S., Morrison C., Murray, K., Otstott, C., Porter, B., Schrag, R.C., Uribe, T., Usher, J., Yeh, P.Z.: A Knowledge Acquisition Tool for Course of Action Analysis. In: Proc. of the 15th Innovative Applications of Artificial Intelligence Conference. AAAI Press, Menlo Park, California, USA (2003) 43-50

2. Boicu, M.: Modeling and Learning with Incomplete Knowledge, PhD dissertation. George Mason University, Fairfax, Virginia, USA (2002)

3. Bowman, M.: A Methodology for Modeling Expert Knowledge that Supports Teaching Based Development of Agents, PhD dissertation. George Mason University, Fairfax, Virginia, USA (2002)

4. Dybala, T.: Shared Expertise Model for Building Interactive Learning Agents, *Ph.D. Dissertation,* Department of Computer Science, George Mason University, Fairfax, Virginia (1996)

5. Lenat, D.B.: CYC: A Large-scale Investment in Knowledge Infrastructure. Communications of the ACM, 38(11), (1995) 33-38

6. Pool, M., Murray, K., Fitzgerald, J., Mehrotra, M., Schrag, R., Blythe J., Kim, J., Chalupsky, H., Miraglia, P., Russ, T., Schneider, D.: Evaluating Expert-Authored Rules for Military Reasoning. In: Proc. of the 2nd Int. Conf. on Know-ledge Capture. ACM Press, Florida, USA (2003) 69-104

7. Strange, J.: Centers of Gravity & Critical Vulnerabilities: Building on the Clausewitzian Foundation So That We Can All Speak the Same Language. Quantico, Virginia, USA, Marine Corps University (1996)

8. Tecuci, G.: DISCIPLE: A Theory, Methodology and System for Learning Expert Knowledge, *Thèse de Docteur en Science,* University of Paris-South (1988)

9. Tecuci, G.: Building Intelligent Agents: An Apprenticeship Multistrategy Learning Theory, Methodology, Tool and Case Studies. Academic Press, London (1998)

10. Tecuci G., Boicu M., Bowman M., Marcu D., Shyr P., and Cascaval C.: An Experiment in Agent Teaching by Subject Matter Experts. *International Journal of Human-Computer Studies,* 53 (2000) 583-610

11. Tecuci G., Boicu M., Bowman M., and Marcu D., with a commentary by Burke M.: An Innovative Application from the DARPA Knowledge Bases Programs: Rapid Development of a High Performance Knowledge Base for Course of Action Critiquing. *AI Magazine,* 22, 2. AAAI Press, Menlo Park, California (2001) 43-61

12. Tecuci G., Boicu, M., Marcu, D., Stanescu, B., Boicu, C., and Comello, J.: Training and Using Disciple Agents: A Case Study in the Military Center of Gravity Analysis Domain. AI Magazine 23(4) (2002) 51–68

Designing a Procedure for the Acquisition of Probability Constraints for Bayesian Networks

Eveline M. Helsper[1], Linda C. van der Gaag[1], and Floris Groenendaal[2]

[1] Institute of Information and Computing Sciences, Utrecht University,
P.O. Box 80.089, 3508 TB Utrecht, The Netherlands
{eveline,linda}@cs.uu.nl
[2] Department of Neonatology, University Medical Center Utrecht,
P.O. Box 85.090, 3508 AB Utrecht, The Netherlands
F.Groenendaal@azu.nl

Abstract. Among the various tasks involved in building a Bayesian network for a real-life application, the task of eliciting all probabilities required is generally considered the most daunting. We propose to simplify this task by first acquiring qualitative features of the probability distribution to be represented; these features can subsequently be taken as constraints on the precise probabilities to be obtained. We discuss the design of a procedure that guides the knowledge engineer in acquiring these qualitative features in an efficient way, based on an in-depth analysis of all viable combinations of features. In addition, we report on initial experiences with our procedure in the domain of neonatology.

1 Introduction

Bayesian networks are well established in artificial-intelligence research as intuitively appealing representations of knowledge, tailored to domains in which uncertainty is predominant [1]. A Bayesian network is a concise representation of a joint probability distribution, consisting of a graphical part and an associated numerical part. The graphical part of the network encodes the variables of importance in the domain being represented, along with their probabilistic interrelationships. The strengths of the relationships between the variables are quantified by conditional probability distributions. These distributions constitute the numerical part of the network.

Bayesian networks for real-life applications are often constructed with the help of a domain expert. Experience shows that, although it may require considerable effort, configuring the graphical part of the network is quite practicable. In fact, building the graphical part has parallels to designing a domain model for any knowledge-based system; well-known knowledge engineering techniques can therefore, to at least some extent, be employed for this purpose [2]. Obtaining all probabilities required for the numerical part of the network is generally considered a far harder task, however, especially if these probabilities have to be assessed by the domain expert [3]. The more interactions there are among the represented variables, moreover, the harder the task is.

E. Motta et al. (Eds.): EKAW 2004, LNAI 3257, pp. 280–292, 2004.

Given a well-constructed graphical part, we propose to simplify the task of obtaining all probabilities required for a Bayesian network in the making by first acquiring the probabilistic interactions among the represented variables in qualitative terms. The acquired qualitative features of the distribution being captured can subsequently be taken as constraints on the precise probabilities to be obtained [4, 5]. For the acquisition of the qualitative features, we designed a procedure based upon the concepts of qualitative influence and qualitative synergy [6]. Our procedure more specifically derives from an analysis of the fundamental properties of these concepts.

We conducted an in-depth study of the qualitative features that may hold for the conditional probability distributions for a variable and its possible causes. Our study revealed that the viable combinations of features constitute four classes [7]. We exploited these classes to design an efficient procedure for acquiring combinations of qualitative features for a Bayesian network in the making from a domain expert. Our procedure begins with the elicitation of knowledge to establish, for each variable and its causes, the class of the features that hold for its conditional probability distributions. As within each class various features are fixed, it serves to indicate the additional knowledge that needs to be acquired to fully specify the combination of features under study. By building upon the four classes, therefore, the procedure guides the knowledge engineer, step by step, in focusing further acquisition efforts.

We conducted an initial study of the use of our procedure with an intensive-care neonatologist to acquire probabilistic information for a real-life Bayesian network in the making. The results indicate that our procedure requires relatively little effort on the part of the expert. From our initial experiences, in fact, we feel that deriving an acquisition procedure from an analysis of the fundamental properties of the concepts used, has resulted in an efficient, dedicated procedure for one of the harder tasks in building Bayesian networks.

The paper is organised as follows. Sect. 2 briefly reviews Bayesian networks and the concepts of qualitative influence and qualitative synergy. Sect. 3 introduces the four classes of combinations of qualitative features. In Sect. 4, we present our procedure, and associated techniques, for acquiring qualitative features of conditional probability distributions from a domain expert. We report on an initial study of the use of our procedure in Sect. 5. The paper ends with our concluding observations in Sect. 6.

2   Bayesian Networks

A *Bayesian network* is a model of a joint probability distribution over a set of statistical variables [1]. The model includes a graphical structure in which each node represents a variable. For ease of exposition, we assume all statistical variables to be binary, taking one of the values *true* and *false*; we further assume that the two values are ordered by *true* > *false*. For abbreviation, we use a to denote that the variable A adopts the value *true* and $\bar{a}$ to denote $A = false$. The arcs in the graphical structure represent the presence of probabilistic influences

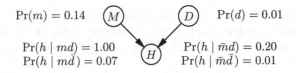

$\Pr(m) = 0.14$ ⓜ   ⓓ $\Pr(d) = 0.01$

$\Pr(h \mid md) = 1.00$
$\Pr(h \mid m\bar{d}) = 0.07$ Ⓗ
$\Pr(h \mid \bar{m}d) = 0.20$
$\Pr(h \mid \bar{m}\bar{d}) = 0.01$

Fig. 1. A fragment of a Bayesian network in neonatology

between the variables. An arc $B \to C$ between the two variables B and C indicates that there is a direct influence between them; B then is generally referred to as the *cause* of the *effect* C. The variable C with all its possible causes is termed a *causal mechanism*. We note that the term causal mechanism is used to denote *any* variable and its parents in the graphical structure, also if the influences involved are not strictly causal. Associated with the graphical part of the Bayesian network are numerical quantities from the modelled probability distribution: with each variable C are specified *conditional probability distributions* $\Pr(C \mid \pi(C))$, that describe the joint effect of values for the causes $\pi(C)$ of C, on the probabilities of C's values.

Fig. 1 depicts a fragment of a Bayesian network in the domain of neonatology. The fragment pertains to the possible causes of a hypoplastic, or underdeveloped, lung in premature newborns. The presence or absence of a hypoplastic lung is modelled by the variable H. One of its possible causes is a spontaneous, prolonged rupture of the foetal membranes and the subsequent lack of amniotic fluid; the variable M captures whether or not there has been such a rupture. The other possible cause of a hypoplastic lung is a diaphragmatic hernia. Such a hernia is a defect in the diaphragm through which the abdominal contents herniate and thereby reduce the space for the lung to develop; the presence or absence of the defect is modelled by the variable D. The conditional probabilities specified for the variable H indicate the likelihood of a hypoplastic lung occurring in a premature newborn. These probabilities show, for example, that a hypoplastic lung is very unlikely to result from another cause than the two mentioned above: the associated probability is just 0.01. The conditional probabilities further reveal that the presence of a diaphragmatic hernia is more likely to result in a hypoplastic lung in a newborn than a prolonged rupture of the foetal membranes; the associated probabilities equal 0.20 and 0.07, respectively. While the presence of either one of the two causes is not very likely to result in a hypoplastic lung, the presence of both causes is certain to give rise to the condition: the influences of the two causes on the likelihood of a hypoplastic lung serve to strengthen one another. We note that, while the graphical structure of a Bayesian network models the presence of probabilistic influences between the variables, the interactions among the influences are modelled in the associated probabilities only.

To provide for capturing probabilistic influences and the interactions among them in a qualitative way, we build upon the concepts of qualitative influence and synergy [6]. A *qualitative influence* between two statistical variables expresses how observing a value for the one variable affects the probability distribution for the other variable. For example, a *positive qualitative influence* of a variable B on a variable C expresses that observing the higher value for B makes the higher value for C more likely, regardless of any other influences on C, that is,

$$\Pr(c \mid bx) \geq \Pr(c \mid \bar{b}x)$$

for any combination of values x for the other causes of C than B. A *negative influence* and a *zero influence* are defined analogously, replacing the inequality $\geq$ in the above formula by $\leq$ and $=$, respectively. If the influence of B on C is positive for one combination of values x and negative for another combination, then it is said to be *ambiguous*. From the probabilities specified for the variable H in the network from Fig. 1, for example, we observe that $\Pr(h \mid md) \geq \Pr(h \mid m\bar{d})$ and $\Pr(h \mid \bar{m}d) \geq \Pr(h \mid \bar{m}\bar{d})$. We conclude that D exerts a positive qualitative influence on H, that is, the presence of a diaphragmatic hernia makes the occurrence of a hypoplastic lung more likely.

An *additive synergy* expresses how the values of two variables combine to yield a joint effect on the third variable. A *positive additive synergy* of the variables A and B on their common effect C, for example, expresses that the joint influence of A and B on C is greater than the sum of their separate influences, regardless of any other influences on C, that is,

$$\Pr(c \mid abx) + \Pr(c \mid \bar{a}\bar{b}x) \geq \Pr(c \mid a\bar{b}x) + \Pr(c \mid \bar{a}bx)$$

for any combination of values x for the other causes of C than A and B. Negative, zero and ambiguous additive synergies are defined analogously. From the probabilities specified in Fig. 1, for example, we have that $\Pr(h \mid md) + \Pr(h \mid \bar{m}\bar{d}) = 1.01$ and $\Pr(h \mid m\bar{d}) + \Pr(h \mid \bar{m}d) = 0.27$. We conclude that M and D show a positive additive synergy on D, that is, the joint influence of a prolonged rupture of the foetal membranes and a diaphragmatic hernia on the occurrence of a hypoplastic lung is larger than the sum of their separate influences.

Product synergies express how observing a value for a variable affects the probability distribution for another variable in view of a value for a third variable [8]. A *negative product synergy* of a variable A on a variable B (and vice versa) given the value c for their common effect C, for example, expresses that, given c, observing the higher value for A renders the higher value for B less likely; formally, the negative product synergy given c is defined as

$$\Pr(c \mid abx) \cdot \Pr(c \mid \bar{a}\bar{b}x) \leq \Pr(c \mid a\bar{b}x) \cdot \Pr(c \mid \bar{a}bx)$$

for any combination of values x for the other causes of C than A and B. *Positive, zero* and *ambiguous product synergies* again are defined analogously. From the probabilities specified for the variable H in Fig. 1, for example, we have that $\Pr(h \mid md) \cdot \Pr(h \mid \bar{m}\bar{d}) = 0.01$ and $\Pr(h \mid m\bar{d}) \cdot \Pr(h \mid \bar{m}d) = 0.014$, from which we conclude that M and D show a negative product synergy given h. A product synergy of the variable A on the variable B in essence describes the influence that is induced between them by the observation of a value for their common effect. From a negative product synergy of A on B given c, we then have that

$$\Pr(b \mid acy) \leq \Pr(b \mid \bar{a}cy)$$

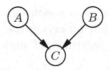

Fig. 2. A basic causal mechanism

for any combination of values y for all causes of B and C except A and B itself. From the negative product synergy that we found from Fig. 1, we thus have that, given the occurrence of a hypoplastic lung, the absence of a prolonged rupture of the foetal membranes makes the presence of a diaphragmatic hernia more likely.

3   Classes of Qualitative Features

In a Bayesian network, each causal mechanism has associated a *pattern of interaction* composed of qualitative influences and synergies. The pattern has a qualitative influence of each cause on the common effect. It further has an additive synergy for each pair of causes. For each such pair, moreover, it specifies two opposite product synergies, one for each value of the common effect. Not all combinations of qualitative features constitute viable patterns of interaction, however. To identify the viable patterns, we investigated the mechanism from Fig. 2 and studied the conditional probabilities for the presence of the effect C in detail [7]. Each ordering of these four probabilities gives rise to a specific pattern of interaction. By studying all possible orderings, we identified four classes of patterns, each resulting in a different type of combination of influences.

Class I includes all orderings of the four conditional probabilities under study in which the common effect is less likely to occur in the cases in which just one of the two causes is present than in the cases where both causes are either present or absent, or vice versa. These orderings give rise to an interaction pattern that specifies ambiguous influences of each cause separately; the additive synergy and the product synergy given the common effect both are positive, or negative alternatively. As an example, we consider

$$\Pr(c \mid ab) \geq \Pr(c \mid \bar{a}\bar{b}) \geq \Pr(c \mid \bar{a}b) \geq \Pr(c \mid a\bar{b})$$

We have that the influence of the cause A on the effect C is positive in the presence of B and negative in the absence of B. We conclude that the overall influence of A on C is ambiguous. A similar observation holds for the influence of B on C. We further find that the two causes exhibit a positive additive synergy on their common effect as well as a positive product synergy given c.

Class II includes all orderings of the four conditional probabilities under study in which the common effect is more likely to occur in the cases in which just one of the causes is present than in the case in which both causes are absent yet less likely to occur than in the case in which both causes are present, or vice versa. These orderings give rise to an interaction pattern that specifies positive influences of both causes on the common effect, or negative influences alternatively. The additive and product synergies are dependent upon the precise numbers for the four probabilities. As an example, we consider

$$\Pr(c \mid ab) \geq \Pr(c \mid \bar{a}b) \geq \Pr(c \mid a\bar{b}) \geq \Pr(c \mid \bar{a}\bar{b})$$

From the ordering, we find that both influences on C are positive.

Class *III* includes all orderings of the four conditional probabilities under study in which the common effect is more likely to occur in the two cases in which both causes are either present or absent than in the case in which just the one cause is present yet less likely than in the case in which just the other cause is present, or vice versa. These orderings give rise to an interaction pattern that specifies opposite non-ambiguous influences of the two causes separately. The orderings may again give rise to different additive synergies and different product synergies given the common effect. As an example, we consider

$$\Pr(c \mid \bar{a}b) \geq \Pr(c \mid ab) \geq \Pr(c \mid \bar{a}\bar{b}) \geq \Pr(c \mid a\bar{b})$$

From the ordering, we find that the variable A exerts a negative influence on C while the variable B exerts a positive influence on C.

Class *IV*, to conclude, comprises all orderings that give rise to an interaction pattern that specifies an ambiguous influence of one of the causes and a non-ambiguous influence of the other cause. The additive synergy and the product synergy given the common effect are both positive, or both negative alternatively. An example ordering of the four probabilities from this class is

$$\Pr(c \mid ab) \geq \Pr(c \mid \bar{a}b) \geq \Pr(c \mid \bar{a}\bar{b}) \geq \Pr(c \mid a\bar{b})$$

which gives rise to an ambiguous influence of A and a positive influence of B on the common effect C.

The four classes of orderings are defined for causal mechanisms composed of an effect and two possible causes. A mechanism that comprises three possible causes in essence is composed of three partial mechanisms, each consisting of the effect and two of its causes. The patterns of interaction for these partial mechanisms then combine into the overall pattern.

4   The Acquisition of Interaction Patterns

Obtaining all probabilities required for a Bayesian network is a demanding task. To simplify the task, we propose to first acquire qualitative patterns of interaction for the network's causal mechanisms. These patterns can subsequently be used as constraints on the precise probabilities to be obtained. For the acquisition of interaction patterns from a domain expert, we designed a dedicated procedure by building upon the classes of probability orderings that we identified before. As these classes include viable patterns of interaction only, we are guaranteed not to obtain any impossible ones. By not using the concepts of qualitative influence and synergy for the elicitation directly, moreover, we circumvent any misinterpretation by the domain expert of these concepts. Furthermore, intermediate elicitation results serve to restrict the possible patterns for a mechanism and, hence, the additional knowledge that needs to be acquired to fully specify the pattern under study. The procedure thus minimises the amount of knowledge to be elicited from the expert, and guides the knowledge engineer in the acquisition process. In this section, we present our basic acquisition procedure and propose elicitation techniques to be used with it.

4.1 A Procedure for Acquiring Interaction Patterns

Our basic procedure for acquiring interaction patterns for mechanisms involving two causes, is shown schematically in Fig. 3; the steps in which knowledge is elicited from a domain expert are distinguished from the various other steps performed by the knowledge engineer by a bold outline. Before discussing the procedure in some detail, we would like to note that it uses two clusters of classes to guide the acquisition. We observe that, for the two classes II and III, the qualitative influences involved follow directly from the largest and smallest probabilities of the effect being present. For the classes I and IV, a similar observation holds for the additive and product synergies. The procedure therefore distinguishes between the two clusters of classes $\{I, IV\}$ and $\{II, III\}$.

The first phase of our acquisition procedure serves to identify the cluster of classes that applies to the causal mechanism under study. To this end, knowledge is elicited about the cases in which the presence of the effect is the most likely and the least likely to occur, respectively. Based upon the obtained partial ordering of the probabilities involved, the knowledge engineer associates the appropriate cluster of classes with the mechanism. Now, if the associated cluster equals $\{I, IV\}$, then the additive and product synergies are uniquely defined and, hence, readily looked up by the knowledge engineer; no further elicitation efforts are required for this purpose. For example, if for the mechanism of Fig. 2, the probabilities $\Pr(c \mid ab)$ and $\Pr(c \mid a\bar{b})$ are indicated by the expert as being the largest and the smallest, respectively, among the four conditional probabilities involved, then the knowledge engineer associates the cluster of classes $\{I, IV\}$ with the mechanism. From the characterisations of the two classes and the order of the selected probabilities, it now follows directly that both the additive synergy and the product synergy given c, are positive. For establishing the qualitative influences, however, a total ordering of the probabilities is required. In the next phase of our procedure, therefore, such an ordering is elicited from the domain expert. Based upon the ordering obtained, the knowledge engineer associates the appropriate class with the mechanism under study and decides upon the qualitative influences. For example, if the expert gives the ordering $\Pr(c \mid ab) \geq \Pr(c \mid \bar{a}b) \geq \Pr(c \mid \bar{a}b) \geq \Pr(c \mid a\bar{b})$, then class I is associated with the mechanism. Since all orderings from class I give rise to ambiguous influences, the knowledge engineer now knows that the qualitative influences of the mechanism under study are ambiguous. Similar observations apply if class IV would have been associated with the mechanism.

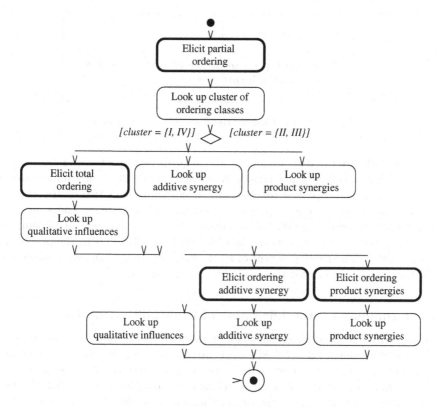

Fig. 3. The basic procedure for acquiring interaction patterns for causal mechanisms

In the first phase of our acquisition procedure, the cluster of classes {*II*, *III*} is readily distinguished from the cluster {*I*, *IV*} by the knowledge engineer through the largest and smallest probabilities indicated by the domain expert. The partial ordering obtained, moreover, allows the knowledge engineer to distinguish between the two classes *II* and *III*. For both classes, the qualitative influences of the mechanism under study are uniquely defined. In fact, there is no need to elicit a total ordering of the probabilities involved. The second phase of our procedure therefore focuses on the elicitation of additional knowledge that serves to identify the additive and product synergies of the mechanism. We will return to this elicitation task in further detail in Sect. 4.2. In summary, as soon as a cluster of classes is associated with a causal mechanism under study, some of the qualitative features of its pattern of interaction are fixed. The classes thus provide a means for readily distinguishing between features that can be looked up and features for which additional knowledge has to be elicited from the expert. We would like to note that the situations in which two or more probabilities appear to be equal are also covered by the procedure, albeit that one or more steps in the procedure may become redundant; the procedure can be easily extended to address these situations explicitly, however.

> A group of 100 patients with:
>
> Prolonged rupture of the foetal membranes: **yes**
> Diaphragmatic hernia: **yes**

Fig. 4. A case card for the domain of neonatology

To conclude, we briefly comment on the acquisition of patterns of interaction for mechanisms involving three causes. As we argued in Sect. 3, such a mechanism is composed of three partial mechanisms, each comprising two of the causes. For the acquisition, we build upon this fundamental observation and subdivide the mechanism into its partial mechanisms. For each partial mechanism, an appropriate pattern of interaction is established, basically by using the procedure outlined above. The three patterns of interaction obtained then are combined to yield the overall pattern for the mechanism under study.

4.2   Techniques for the Elicitation of Probability Orderings

Our procedure for acquiring patterns of interaction includes various steps in which the domain expert is asked to indicate an ordering for a number of conditional probabilities. Since reasoning in terms of frequencies is generally perceived as less demanding than reasoning in terms of probabilities [9], we use the frequency format for presenting the probabilities to be ordered to the expert. For the mechanism of Fig. 2, for example, the probabilities $\Pr(c \mid ab)$ and $\Pr(c \mid \bar{a}\bar{b})$ equal

$$\Pr(c \mid ab) = \frac{\text{number of cases in which } cab \text{ holds}}{\text{number of cases in which } ab \text{ holds}}$$

$$\Pr(c \mid \bar{a}\bar{b}) = \frac{\text{number of cases in which } c\bar{a}\bar{b} \text{ holds}}{\text{number of cases in which } \bar{a}\bar{b} \text{ holds}}$$

Since the precise numbers are not relevant for the ordering task, we take the number of cases in which ab holds to be equal to the number of cases in which $\bar{a}\bar{b}$ holds. Indicating an ordering for the probabilities $\Pr(c \mid ab)$ and $\Pr(c \mid \bar{a}\bar{b})$ now amounts to establishing which of the two groups of cases, in which ab and $\bar{a}\bar{b}$ holds, respectively, contains the largest number of cases in which also c holds. To support the domain expert in this task, the various groups of cases are presented on *case cards*. For convenience of comparison, the information on each card is represented in an easily surveyable manner. To make the ordering task more concrete, moreover, we randomly chose a fixed size for the various groups. An example case card for the domain of neonatology is shown in Fig. 4.

In the first phase of our acquisition procedure, a partial ordering of probabilities is to be obtained. For Fig. 2, for example, a partial ordering is required of the probabilities $\Pr(c \mid ab)$, $\Pr(c \mid a\bar{b})$, $\Pr(c \mid \bar{a}b)$ and $\Pr(c \mid \bar{a}\bar{b})$. A case card is constructed for each of the four groups of cases as described above; the resulting four case cards are presented to the expert, who is asked to select the group containing the largest number of cases in which c holds and the group having the smallest number of such cases.

After the expert has given the partial ordering, either a total ordering of the probabilities is required, or knowledge for establishing the additive and product synergies involved. For the first of these tasks, the same case cards are used as before. The domain expert is asked to assign an order to the four groups of cases, rather than to select specific groups. For establishing the additive synergy for Fig. 2, for example, information is to be obtained as to whether or not

$$\Pr(c \mid ab) + \Pr(c \mid \bar{a}\bar{b}) \geq \Pr(c \mid a\bar{b}) + \Pr(c \mid \bar{a}b)$$

In essence, the task involved for the domain expert again is an ordering task, in which the two sums of probabilities $\Pr(c \mid ab) + \Pr(c \mid \bar{a}\bar{b})$ and $\Pr(c \mid a\bar{b}) + \Pr(c \mid \bar{a}b)$ are to be compared. We visualise each sum by joining the two cards with the two groups of cases under study, to yield a compound group. The expert is then asked to assign an order to the two compound groups thus constructed.

For establishing the product synergies, we do not build upon their definition in terms of products of probabilities directly, since comparing products of fractions at a qualitative level is known to be very hard. Instead, we build upon the influence between two causes that is induced by the observation of a value for their common effect. For establishing for Fig. 2 the product synergy of A on B given c, for example, information is to be obtained as to whether or not

$$\Pr(b \mid acy) \geq \Pr(b \mid \bar{a}cy)$$

for any combination of values y for all causes of B other than A; note that since we consider mechanisms with two causes only, the effect C does not have any other causes to be taken into account. We refer to the combination of values y as the *context* of the influence. The domain expert in essence now has to perform a number of ordering tasks, one for each possible context y. We view the context as background knowledge and ask the expert to indicate an ordering for the probabilities $\Pr(b \mid ac)$ and $\Pr(b \mid \bar{a}c)$ for each such context, using case cards as before. For each separate ordering task, the context is visualised by a card, termed the *context bar*; this card is put over the two case cards to be ordered. An example context bar for the domain of neonatology is shown in Fig. 5. After obtaining the product synergy given c for each context, the overall synergy is established as defined in Sect. 2.

For the acquisition of interaction patterns for mechanisms with three causes, we subdivide such a mechanism into its partial mechanisms as described in Sect. 4.1. For each partial mechanism, an interaction pattern is established given each value of the third cause. The two patterns thus obtained are then combined to yield the overall pattern for the partial mechanism. The patterns of interaction for the three partial mechanisms are subsequently combined to yield the pattern for the entire mechanism. We would like to note that the probability orderings that are elicited from the domain expert for the different partial mechanisms

---

We only consider patients with
Sepsis: **yes**

Fig. 5. A context bar for the domain of neonatology

may be mutually inconsistent. If such an inconsistency arises, we propose to ask the expert to assign a total ordering to eight case cards, describing the eight conditional probabilities for the common effect of the mechanism under study.

5   Experiences with our Procedure

We used our procedure for acquiring the patterns of interaction for different parts of a Bayesian network in the making for the domain of neonatology. The network currently consists of some fifty causal mechanisms, a handful of which have been considered in the evaluation of our procedure. The graphical structure of the network has been developed with the help of an intensive-care neonatologist, who is the third author of the present paper. We acquired from the same expert, the knowledge for establishing the various qualitative influences and synergies. The knowledge engineers, who are the first two authors of the paper, divided the engineering tasks involved in conducting the knowledge acquisition session. The session was held in an office with a large empty table that provided sufficient space for the expert to rearrange the various cards used with our procedure.

In reviewing the experiences with the application of our acquisition procedure, we focus on the results obtained for the mechanism that pertains to a hypoplastic lung and its two causes, shown in Fig. 1. We would like to note that the four conditional probabilities indicated in the figure for the presence of a hypoplastic lung, were estimated from patient data available from the domain expert's home institute. For the elicitation of the pattern of interaction for the mechanism under study, we constructed four case cards, one for each combination of values for the two causes of a hypoplastic lung. In case knowledge had to be acquired for establishing the product synergies, two additional case cards were constructed, for the presence and for the absence of a diaphragmatic hernia, respectively; since the causes of a hypoplastic lung do not have any causes themselves in the network, no context bars were required.

We presented the expert with the first four case cards and asked him to select, from among the four groups, the group with the largest number of newborns with a hypoplastic lung and the group with the smallest such number. He indicated the group of newborns in whom both causes are present as the group with the highest occurrence of a hypoplastic lung; he further indicated the group of patients in whom both causes are absent as the group in which the fewest cases of an underdeveloped lung occur. Based on the partial ordering of the underlying probabilities, we associated class *II* with the mechanism. From the partial ordering, moreover, we established positive qualitative influences of the two causes separately. As prescribed by our procedure, further knowledge elicitation was focused on the two types of synergy. For the additive synergy, we constructed compound groups of patients, as described in the previous section. The expert initially indicated that the two compound groups of patients had equally many newborns with a hypoplastic lung; after some further consideration, however, he expressed that the compound group with the patients in whom just one of the causes is present, was likely to include more patients with a hypoplastic lung. The acquisition results further indicated the product synergy given the presence of a hypoplastic lung to be negative. We would like to note that from the expert a negative additive synergy was elicited, while the data indicated a positive one. The number of patients in the available data set in whom either one or both causes are present, is very small, however, as a consequence of which the probability estimates obtained may be strongly biased.

After the acquisition session, the domain expert mentioned that he found the task of ordering groups of patients to be quite easy in general. His observation was supported by the finding that he selected the groups with the highest and the lowest number of patients with a condition under study, within a second. The task of indicating an ordering for two compound groups of patients clearly was more demanding; the expert indicated that he tended to associate concrete numbers with the cards, in order to be able to compare the two groups involved. Still, the task was generally performed within 30 seconds.

To conclude, we would like to mention that some of the causal mechanisms under study included a medical intervention as one of its causes. During the acquisition session, the expert appeared to interpret the intervention as stating that *the intervention is called for* rather than as stating that *the intervention has been performed*. Afterwards the expert indicated that he found the co-occurrence of truly statistical events and interventions in a single mechanism to be confusing and counterintuitive.

6   Conclusions and Future Work

The task of obtaining all probabilities required for a Bayesian network, can be simplified by first establishing the qualitative pattern of interaction for each causal mechanism; these patterns can subsequently be used as constraints on the precise probabilities to be obtained. In this paper, we elaborated on this idea and designed a dedicated procedure for acquiring interaction patterns; in addition, we proposed various elicitation techniques to be used for interaction with a domain expert. Initial experiences with our procedure in the domain of neonatology indicated that it requires relatively little effort on the part of the expert. In the future, we intend to further develop our procedure, for example by explicitly providing for equal probabilities. Moreover, we plan to investigate methods for dealing with variables that capture interventions and to focus on the task of obtaining precise probabilities that meet the established constraints.

In designing our acquisition procedure, we built to a large extent on a profound study of the fundamental properties of the concepts of qualitative influence and synergy. We feel that designing an acquisition procedure from the results of such a study has proved beneficial and has in fact resulted in an efficient dedicated procedure for one of the harder tasks in building Bayesian networks.

References

1. F.V. Jensen. *Bayesian Networks and Decision Graphs*. Springer-Verlag, New York, 2001.
2. E.M. Helsper, L.C. van der Gaag. Building Bayesian networks through ontologies. In: F. van Harmelen, editor, *Proceedings of the 15th European Conference on Artificial Intelligence*. IOS Press, Amsterdam, 2002, pp. 680 – 684.
3. M.J. Druzdzel, L.C. van der Gaag. Building probabilistic networks: "Where do the numbers come from?" Guest editors' introduction. *IEEE Transactions on Knowledge and Data Engineering*, 2000, **12**, pp. 481 – 486.
4. M.J. Druzdzel, L.C. van der Gaag. Elicitation of probabilities for belief networks: combining qualitative and quantitative information. In: Ph. Besnard, S. Hank, editors, *Proceedings of the Eleventh Conference on Uncertainty in Artificial Intelligence*. Morgan Kaufmann Publishers, San Francisco, 1995, pp. 141 – 148.
5. S. Renooij, L.C. van der Gaag. From qualitative to quantitative probabilistic networks. In: A. Darwiche, N. Friedman, editors, *Proceedings of the Eighteenth Conference on Uncertainty in Artificial Intelligence*. Morgan Kaufmann Publishers, San Francisco, 2002, pp. 422 – 429.
6. M.P. Wellman. Fundamental concepts of qualitative probabilistic networks. *Artificial Intelligence*, 1990, **44**, pp. 257 – 303.
7. L.C. van der Gaag, E.M. Helsper. Defining classes of influences for the acquisition of probability constraints for Bayesian networks. In: *Proceedings of the 16th Conference on Artificial Intelligence*, 2004, to appear.
8. M. Henrion, M.J. Druzdzel. Qualitative propagation and scenario-based approaches to explanation in probabilistic reasoning. In: P.P. Bonissone, M. Henrion, L.N. Kanal, J.F. Lemmer, editors, *Uncertainty in Artificial Intelligence 6*. Elsevier, North-Holland, 1991, pp. 17 – 32.
9. G. Gigerenzer, U. Hoffrage. How to improve Bayesian reasoning without instruction: Frequency formats. *Psychological Review*, 1995, **102**, pp. 684 – 704.

Invented Predicates to Reduce Knowledge Acquisition[1]

Hendra Suryanto and Paul Compton

School of Computer Science and Engineering,
University of New South Wales,
Sydney, Australia
{hendras, compton}@cse.unsw.edu.au

Abstract. The aim of this study was to develop machine-learning techniques that would speed up knowledge acquisition from an expert. As the expert provided knowledge the system would generalize from this knowledge in order to reduce the need for later knowledge acquisition. This generalization should be completely hidden from the expert. We have developed such a learning technique based on Duce's intra-construction and absorption operators [1] and applied to Ripple-Down Rule (RDR) incremental knowledge acquisition [2]. Preliminary evaluation shows that knowledge acquisition can be reduced by up to 50%.

1 Ripple-Down Rules (RDR)

RDR were developed to deal with the problem that experts never give a comprehensive explanation for their decision making. Rather they justify that the conclusion is correct and the justification is created for and shaped by the context in which it is given [2]. The critical features of RDR are that:

- Knowledge is added to the knowledge base (KB) to deal with specific cases; cases for which the system has made an error.
- The KB gradually evolves over time, whilst in use dealing with real cases.
- The system rather than the knowledge engineer or expert organizes the structure of the KB.
- Any knowledge acquisition is validated so that the knowledge added provides an incremental addition to the system's knowledge and does not degrade previous knowledge.
- To add new knowledge, the expert only has to identify features in a case that distinguish it from other related cases retrieved by the system.

RDR systems have been implemented for a range of application areas and tasks. The first industrial demonstration of this approach was the PEIRS system, which provided clinical interpretations for reports of pathology testing [3]. The approach has also been extended to other tasks: multiple classification [4], control [5] heuristic search [6,7], document management using multiple classification [8], configuration

---

[1] This is a modified version of paper presented at the IJCAI 2003 Workshop on Mixed-Initiative Intelligent Systems

E. Motta et al. (Eds.): EKAW 2004, LNAI 3257, pp. 293–306, 2004.

[9] and resource allocation [10]. Generalized first-order RDR have also been proposed [11]. The level of evaluation in these studies varies, but overall they demonstrate very simple and highly efficient knowledge acquisition.

Pacific Knowledge Systems markets RDR systems for pathologists to build knowledge bases that provide clinical interpretations for chemical pathology reports. Pathologists at one PKS customer have so far developed 23 knowledge bases with about 10,000 rules in total which process about 14,000 patient reports per day (PKS, personal communication) . The reports are highly patient specific relating to past treatment and results etc, and have been shown to influence clinical management (unpublished results). The pathologists continue to introduce new knowledge bases in different domains and currently add about 500 rules per month. It takes about one minute to add a rule, regardless of knowledge base size and pathologists have a two day training course.

RDR systems have also been shown to converge and end up with similar sized KBs to those developed by machine learning techniques [12,13] and cannot be compressed much by simple reorganization [14]. The exception structure of RDR has also been found to be a useful representation for machine learning where it tends to produce more compact KBs than other representations [15]. Various machine learning RDR systems have been developed [16–20]. However, the machine learning systems related to RDR do not replace RDR intended for use by an expert. As always machine learning systems depend on well-classified examples in sufficient numbers. An expert building an RDR KB can provide a rule, and a working system will start to evolve, by classifying single cases. Experts can deal successfully with single rare cases and the commercial RDR pathology knowledge bases appear to have a wide range of subtle comments.

2 Aim

RDR reduce the need for knowledge engineering, but they do not remove it completely. In most domains the expert will prefer to construct rules about higher-level features rather than the actual raw data and some initial knowledge engineering is required to set up the appropriate feature extraction for the expert to use. In early RDR the expert then builds rules that go straight from these initial features to final conclusion; there is no intermediate structure.

This lack of internal structure has been a criticism of RDR in the knowledge acquisition community and much knowledge acquisition research can be characterized as providing frameworks for developing structure in knowledge bases. One of the landmarks in this Clancey's paper on heuristic classification [21], which observed that many classification systems could be characterized as having rules that produced coarse intermediate conclusions which were then refined into detailed final conclusions. A common criticism was that surely it was better to use heuristic classification than a simple flat classification system.

The partial response to these criticisms is that the flat structure makes it quick and easy to build and maintain RDR systems, more than compensating for the lack of structure. RDR were first developed to deal with the difficulty of adding rules to systems to a heuristic classification structure [22].

The ideal solution would be a system with intermediate conclusions but the same ease of knowledge acquisition. Intermediate conclusions that the expert can define were introduced into RDR [23,24] and are also used in the commercial RDR systems. However, this is unattractive as it shifts the expert task from simply identifying reasons for a conclusion, towards the knowledge engineering task of structuring knowledge. The expert needs to remember, or be assisted in remembering, intermediate concepts and how they have been defined and used in the KB. This is not a task that is required when an expert is identifying features in a case to justify their conclusion about the case; it is a task that arises from using a KB.

The aim of this work then is to develop a method of predicate invention that can be used in conjunction with RDR to automatically discover appropriate intermediate conclusions and use these where possible. The expert should simply identify features in a case to justify a conclusion in the normal RDR fashion; however, hidden from the expert the system should try to discover generalizations in the knowledge provided and use these to reduce the need for further knowledge. In essence the aim is to automate the generalization of heuristic classification.

3 Method

3.1 Predicate Invention

Matheus and Rendell [25] defined feature construction as the application of set of constructive operators to a set of existing resulting in the construction of one or more new features intended for use in describing the target concept. Bloedorn and Michalski [26] have investigated feature construction where operators are algebraic such as addition, subtraction, multiplication etc. are applied to pair of existing features. Zupan et al. [27] proposed a suboptimal heuristic algorithm to decompose existing functions (in the RDR context such functions are rules). This function decomposition is data-driven and uses the compactness and accuracy of the resulting rule set as a success measure. Sutton and Matheus [28] have investigated feature construction for learning higher polynomial functions from examples. ILP researchers take a further step in constructing first order predicates [29] and [30].

In our present study we have limited the constructive operators to the Boolean-operators AND and OR, dealing with the predefined features available in the KBS. This applies to RDR and to rule-based systems in general. We restricted the operators because our main concern was integration with knowledge acquisition to produce a heuristic-classification-like system.

The closest to our goals is the Duce system [1] which suggests possible higher level domain features to the expert. In our application the higher level features are hidden from the expert as our goal is to reduce the number of interactions with the expert. Duce employs six operators: interconstruction, intraconstruction, absorption, identification, dichotomisation and truncation. We use only the intraconstruction and absorption operators as shown in the following examples:

The application of the intraconstruction operator is as follows:

$$X \leftarrow B, C, D, E \tag{1}$$
$$X \leftarrow A, B, D, F \tag{2}$$

are replaced by:

$$X \leftarrow B, D, Z \tag{3}$$
$$Z \leftarrow C, E \tag{4}$$
$$Z \leftarrow A, F \tag{5}$$

where Z is an invented predicate or intermediate conclusion. The absorption operator is used as follows:

$$X \leftarrow A, B, C, D, E, \tag{6}$$
$$Y \leftarrow A, B, F \tag{7}$$

are replaced by:

$$X \leftarrow A, B, D, Z, \tag{8}$$
$$Y \leftarrow B, Z \tag{9}$$

using the new predicate Z from (4) and (5).

In summary as the expert adds rules the intraconstruction operator finds generalizations in those rules. Absorption then uses these generalizations to expand the scope of existing rules or new rules added. It is likely that at least some of the generalizations suggested are inappropriate and in Duce the expert is asked about the suitability of the generalizations. Since in our system we are trying to hide the generalizations from the expert, we require some sort of automated assessment of the suitability of a generalization. We still use the expert to reject generalizations that are inappropriate despite the automated assessment, but the expert does not see the generalization, as far as they are concerned the RDR system has simply made a wrong conclusion and a new rule is required.

3.2 Algorithm

The following algorithm describes how the Duce operators are integrated into RDR knowledge acquisition and in particular how generalizations are managed and their suitability assessed. The algorithm can almost certainly be improved on, but even with this simple algorithm significant improvement in knowledge acquisition is achieved. It should be noted that following steps all happen automatically except for 2 and 3 where a case is introduced into the system and the expert accept s the conclusion or rejects it and adds one or more rules.

1. Start with an existing KB which may be empty.
2. Process a case. If previous rules do not interpret this case correctly according to the expert, then go to step 3, otherwise repeat step 2 to process more cases.

3. The expert sdd some new rules to provide the correct conclusions for the case. (Note: we use a multiple classification system which provides multiple conclusions so that more than one may need to be corrected).

4. If the system did not interpret the case correctly because a generalized rule gave an incorrect conclusion, the invented predicate it used is moved from the heap of good predicates to the heap of bad predicates (see below). As well information about the generalized rule is stored to be used later in assessing the likely usefulness of new generalizations (See unlikely generalizations below)

5. Apply the intraconstruction operator to each new rule added and any previous rule that gives the same conclusion as the new rule. The result is a set of new invented predicates. For simplicity a predicate consists of only two disjunctions. The only negative impact of this is that we may require more cases to be seen and rules added to cover the same generalization – and be closer to a conventional RDR system. On the other hand we may reduce the number of inappropriate generalizations.

   • If any of the new predicates are the same as existing predicates in the good or bad heaps then they are deleted (see below).

6. Apply absorption

   • Apply the absorption operator to each new invented predicate and all previous rules resulting in some generalized rules.

   • Apply the absorption operator to each previous invented predicate (only from the good heap) and the new rule resulting in some generalized rules.

   • Delete any of the new generalized rules that have appear to be an unlikely generalization (see below).

7. Add the new predicates to the good heap. Test all predicates in the good heap against all the cases so far seen by the system. If the size of the heap is exceeded delete the predicates which cover the least number of cases. In these studies the size of the heap was set at 1000.

8. Store all the resulting rules in the KB.

Note that no rules, either if added by the expert or if generated or modified by intraconstruction or generalized by absorption are removed from the KB. That is, although an invented predicate may be moved from the good heap to the bad heap and not used for future generalization, it will remain in the knowledge base along with any previous rules that used it.

Unlikely Generalizations

We use a very simple measure to assess if a newly generalized rule is likely to be of use. The basic idea is that if a generalization is found to cause an error, then any of the pairs of conditions from the original rule and the invented predicates might be at fault – except of course pairs of conditions that occur in the original rules. For example if we take parts of the previous example

The invented predicates were:

$$Z \leftarrow C, E \tag{4}$$
$$Z \leftarrow A, F \tag{5}$$

The rule

$$Y \leftarrow A, B, F \tag{7}$$

was generalized to

$$Y \leftarrow B, Z \tag{9}$$

If rule 9 now gives an incorrect conclusion, then the error might be due to any combination of conditions from the original rule (7) and the invented predicate rules (4 & 5). The following is all possible pairs of conditions from these three rules, with each condition in a pair coming from a separate rule. Pairs of conditions that occur in the original rule (7) are deleted as they were originally specified by the expert.

AC, BC, FC, AE, BE, FE, ~~AA, BA, FA, BF, FF,~~

We maintain a list of all the 'bad pairs' that are seen over the life of the system. In step 6 above, we derive a similar list of pairs from each newly generalized rule. If more than a certain fraction of the rule's pairs occur in the list of bad pairs, the new rule is deemed to be an unlikely generalization and deleted. In the studies below a rule was deemed unlikely if more than 75% of its pairs occurred in the bad list.

4 Experimental Evaluation

Evaluation of machine learning only requires appropriate data sets. However, evaluation of knowledge acquisition requires the availability of an expert. Experts rarely have the time available for this, particularly if a proper scientific study is proposed with control studies and comparison. To provide some sort of evaluation of knowledge acquisition we have previously developed a system of using a simulated expert, which can be put to work processing large numbers of cases under a variety of experimental conditions [31] [13]. A simulated expert is a knowledge-based system that is built by machine learning using one of the standard datasets. The 'expertise' it can provide to the RDR system that is being built is a classification of a case and some sort of rule trace indicating the features in the case that led to the conclusion. Of course this is a very limited source of knowledge and a long way from the capability of a real expert, but it seems to be the only low cost way of getting some measure of the performance of a knowledge acquisition system.

We used J4.8[2] from the WEKA tool bench to generate simulated experts from cases. We used three levels of expertise

---

[2] J4.8 is a re-implementation of C4.5 in java.

- P uses all the conditions from the rule trace. However, for this case we add some more refinement rules to cover every case in data set correctly.

- G uses one less condition than in the rule trace (from P), selected randomly, unless this rule causes inconsistency for any seen cases.

- S uses all the conditions from the rule trace (from P) but adds another from the case selected randomly.

- W uses all the conditions from the rule trace J4.8 in default mode. This results in some errors in the data set. For this simulated expert, cases which have errors are removed from the data set before building the RDR KBS.

There is no particular merit in these different types of simulated expert; a range of 'expertise' is used simply to demonstrate that the results are not an artifact of using one particular expert. Note that RDR only asks a human expert to provide the conclusion for a case and to identify the features in the case that indicate that conclusion. The simulated experts above behave in exactly the same way, with varying degrees of expertise in identifying the features indicating a conclusion.

We used four data sets from the UC Irvine Data Repository: Car, Monk1, Dermatology and Nursery. Each simulation is run 5 times with the order of the data set randomized each time. We use the Mutiple classification (MCRDR) version of RDR [32]

1. We start with a set of cases.
2. We provide an expert able to classify the cases and identify features indicating the classification. (This could have been a human expert, but here the expert is a classifier built by applying J4.8 to all the cases in a training set. (See the differences between the P and W protocols above)
3. Create an empty MCRDR knowledge based system..
4. Take one case randomly from collection of cases; input this case to MCRDR. Compare the classification from the MCRDR with the class of this labeled case. If the classification is correct according to the expert repeat 4. If the classification is incorrect go to 5.
5. Pass the case to the (simulated) expert to provide a new rule. This rule is then passed to the learning generalization algorithm described above. (Although cases from the data sets have a single class, MCRDR may fire multiple rules and give multiple conclusions and the correction rule may have to be added to multiple places in the knowledge base)
6. Repeat 4

5 Results

The main results are shown in Table 1. In all cases there is a reduction in the number of rules the expert has to add. In the case of the Nursery and the Car data set the reduction in knowledge acquisition required is large. This is particularly to be expected for the Car data set which is a synthetic data set with a hierarchical structure [27].

Table 1. The number of knowledge acquisition sesions using generalisation compared to the number without generalisation. A knowledge acquisition session occurs when a case is misclassified and the knowledge base is corrected. Becuase MCRDR is used the expert may add one or more rules during the session. The different data sets and levels of expertise are shown. The errors are the standard deviation of the 5 randomised studies for each data set and level of expertise. P, G, S & W represent experts with different levels of expertise

DATA SET	WITH GENERALISATION	WITHOUT GENERALISATION	IMPROVEMENT
CAR P	49.4 ± 2.4	97.0 ± 0.0	49.0 %
CAR G	50.0 ± 3.7	87.0 ± 2.9	42.6 %
CAR S	127.8 ± 6.2	253.8 ± 7.1	49.6 %
CAR W	44.8 ± 3.0	70.0 ± 0.0	36.0 %
MONK1 P	14.0 ± 0.7	18.0 ± 0.0	22.0 %
MONK1 G	14.2 ± 1.9	19.2 ± 1.3	26.0 %
MONK1 S	33.2 ± 1.9	61.0 ± 4.7	46.0 %
MONK1 W	13.2 ± 1.1	18.0 ± 0.0	27.0 %
DERMATOLOGY P	49.8 ± 1.6	56.8 ± 1.6	13.4 %
DERMATOLOGY G	48.9 ± 1.6	56.6 ± 1.7	14.9 %
DERMATOLOGY S	72.4 ± 2.6	75.8 ± 4.4	4.5 %
DERMATOLOGY W	26.8 ± 1.1	28.0 ± 0.0	4.5 %
NURSERY P	43.2 ± 2.8	77.2 ± 1.3	44.0 %
NURSERY G	48.2 ± 1.5	56.6 ± 1.7	32.9 %
NURSERY S	69.8 ± 10.2	118.4 ± 5.1	41.0 %
NURSERY W	30.0 ± 3.0	47.0 ± 0.0	36.2 %

It should be noted that when generalization is used the expert also needs to add rules to correct errors from inappropriate generalization; despite this further requirement for rules to be added, there was still a decrease in the rules that had to be added. It can also be noted that different simulated expert policies do not effect the overall trend.

We conclude from this that one might expect similar (or better) improvements when a genuine human expert is used.

Figure 1, 2, 3 and 4 show the number of errors made against the total cases seen. The slope of the graph at any point can be taken as a reasonable approximation to the error rate, as it is in essence the error rate on unseen samples. Note that these graphs do not show all the dataset; they are truncated at a maximum of a 1000 cases seen. The P expert only is shown.

As is the general case with RDR, the error rate of knowledge acquisition process rapidly plateaus. It plateaus to a similar error rate to good batch learning systems applied to the same domain. It can be noted that machine learning error rates are rarely zero and [15] has observed that increasing the size of the training set generally changes the KB. The graphs here highlight that RDR allow the expert to keep on correcting errors if they wish.

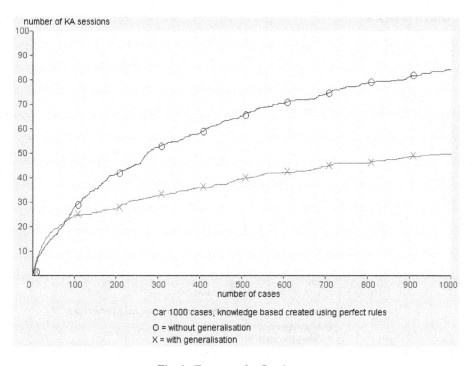

Fig. 1. Error rate for Car data set

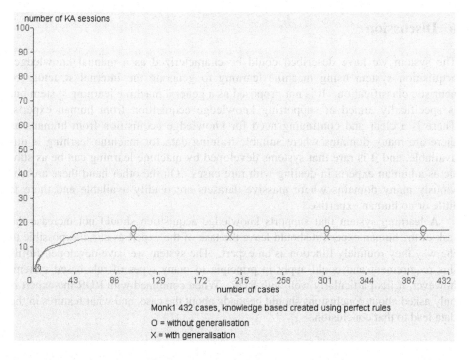

Fig. 2. Error rate for Monk1 data set

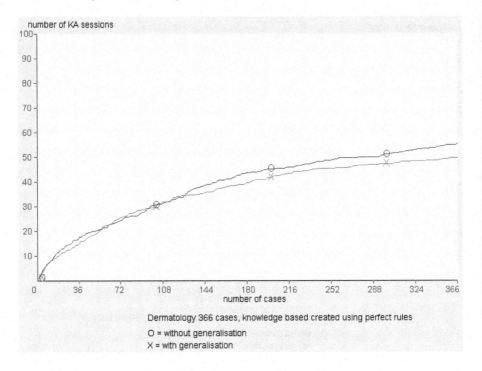

Fig. 3. Error rate for Dermatology data set

6 Discussion

The system we have described could be characterized as a manual knowledge-acquisition system using machine learning to generate the internal structure of heuristic classification. It is not proposed as a general machine learning system but is specifically aimed at supporting knowledge acquisition from human experts. There is a clear and continuing need for knowledge acquisition from humans as there are many domains where suitable training data for machine learning is unavailable, and it is rare that systems developed by machine learning can be as subtle as a human experts in dealing with rare cases. On the other hand there are obviously many domains where massive datasets are readily available and there is little or no human expertise.

A learning system that supports knowledge acquisition should not increase the task of the human expert; it should leave the task of the expert as close as possible to the way they routinely function as an expert. The system we have developed fulfils this requirement and could apply in principle to many types of rule-based system; however, it fits particularly well with RDR. When combined with RDR the expert is only asked about conclusions should be made about the case, and what features in the data lead to that conclusion.

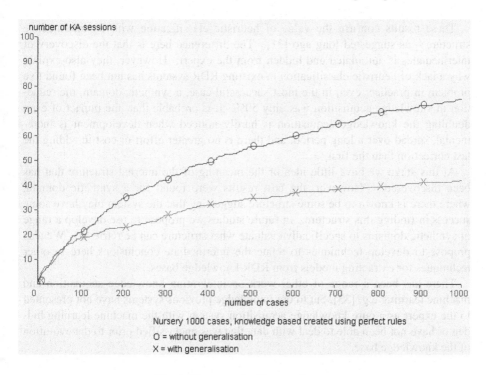

Fig. 4. Error rate for Nursery dataset

The decrease in the amount of knowledge acquisition required for two of the data sets suggests that it would be worthwhile testing the system with human experts. The results also show that in the other two domains there is no increase in the knowledge acquisition required. This is to be expected as cases where a generalization has been applied inappropriately, would not have been interpreted if there was no the generalization, and would require a rule anyway. This suggests that use of the system will not degrade knowledge acquisition in domains where there are no useful intermediate concepts; however there may be domains where it is preferable to give no conclusion rather than an incorrect conclusion, even though both are errors that require fixing.

We spent a considerable amount of time trying to come up with ways of automatically managing inappropriate overgeneralization, and selecting the best of the generalizations available. The heuristics we have eventually used are very simple and almost certainly better heuristics can be found; however, even with these heuristics, knowledge acquisition was reduced by close to 50% in the car domain. One obvious improvement would be to replace a generalization by its original rule if it made an error on the first case it processed; at present we add a refinement rule regardless of whether the error is on the first or a later case. We will explore other heuristics in future research and also look at extending the approach to other operators beyond Boolean.

These results confirm the value of heuristic classification with its intermediate structure – as suggested long ago [21]. The difference here is that the discovery of intermediates is automated and hidden from the expert. However, they also explain why a lack of heuristic classification in existing RDR systems has not been found to a problem in practice: even in the most successful case, a synthetic domain, the reduction in knowledge acquisition was only 50%. It is probable that the impact of even doubling the knowledge acquisition is hardly noticed when development is incremental, spread over a long period, and there is no greater effort or cost in adding the last correction than the first.

At this stage we have little idea of the meaning of the internal structure that has been discovered.   However, the best results were found for a synthetic domain, where there is known to be some structure suggesting that the system may have some success in finding this structure. In future studies we propose to use develop a range of synthetic domains to specifically evaluate what structure can be retrieved. We also propose to develop techniques to relate the intermediate conclusions here to other techniques for extracting models from RDR knowledge bases.

There has been a range of other work on integrating knowledge acquisition and machine learning e.g. [33], but to our knowledge previous systems have not presented to the expert as a pure knowledge acquisition system with the machine learning hidden or have not been able to deal with data that was unclassified prior to the evolution of the knowledge base.

Acknowledgements

This research is funded by the Australian Research Council and Smart Internet Technology CRC. We would like to thanks Rex Kwok for helpful discussions.

References

1. Muggleton, S. Duce, An oracle-based approach to constructive induction. Proceeding of the Tenth International Joint Conference on Artificial Intelligence.(1987) 287 - 292
2. Compton, P. and R. Jansen. A philosophical basis for knowledge acquisition. Knowledge Acquisition 2(1990) 241--257
3. Edwards, G., et al. PEIRS: a pathologist maintained expert system for the interpretation of chemical pathology reports. Pathology 25(1993) 27-34
4. Kang, B., P. Compton, and P. Preston. Multiple classification ripple down rules: Evaluation and possibilities. 9th AAAI-sponsored Banff Knowledge Acquisition for Knowledge Based Systems Workshop.(1995) 17.1--17.20
5. Shiraz, G. and C. Sammut. Combining knowledge acquisition and machine learning to control dynamic systems. 15th International Joint Conference on Artificial Intelligence, Nagoya Japan, Morgan Kaufmann.(1997) pp908-913
6. Beydoun, G. and A. Hoffmann. Acquisition of Search Knowledge. the 10th European Knowledge Acquisition Workshop.(1997) 1 -- 16

7. Beydoun, G. and A. Hoffmann. Building Problem Solvers Based on Search Control Knowledge. 11th Banff Knowledge Acquisition for Knowledge Base System Workshop, Calgary, SRDG publications,.(1998) ppShare1-1-Share1-16.
8. Kang, B., et al. A help desk system with intelligent interface. Applied Artificial Intelligence 11((7-8)): 611-631.(1997)
9. Compton, P., Ramadan, Z., Preston, P., Le-Gia, T., Chellen, V. and Mullholland, M. A trade-off between domain knowledge and problem solving method power. 11th Banff knowledge acquisition for knowledge-bases systems workshop, Banff, SRDG Publications, University of Calgary.(1998) SHARE 17,1-19
10. Richards, D. and P. Compton. SISYPHUS I Revisited: An Incremental Approach to Resource Allocation using Ripple Down Rules. 12th Workshop on Knowledge Acquisition, Modeling and Management, SRDG Publications, Banff, Canada, 16th-21st October (1999)
11. Drake, B. and G. Beydoun. Predicate logic-based incremental knowledge acquisition. Proceedings of the sixth Pacific International Knowledge Acquisition Workshop, P. Compton, A. Hoffmann, H. Motoda and T. Yamaguchi Sydney(2000) 71-88
12. Compton, P., P. Preston, and T. Yip. Local patching produces compact knowledge bases. The European Knowledge Acquisition Workshop, Springer-Verlag.(1994) 104--117
13. Kang, B., P. Compton, and P. Preston. Simulated Expert Evaluation of Multiple Classification Ripple Down Rules. 11th Banff knowledge acqustion for knowledge-based systems workshop, Banff, SRDG Publications, University of Calgary.(1998) EVAL 4, 1-19
14. Suryanto, H., D. Richards, and P. Compton. The automatic compression of Multiple Classification Ripple Down Rule Knowledged Based Systems: Preliminary Experiments. Knowledge-based Intelligence Information Engineering Systems, Adelaide, South Australia, IEEE.(1999) 203-206
15. Catlett, J. Ripple Down Rules as a Mediating Representation in Interactive Induction. Proceedings of the Second Japanese Knowledge Acquisition for Knowledge Based Systems Workshop, Kobe, Japan.(1992) 155-170
16. Gaines, B.R. and P.J. Compton. Induction of Ripple Down Rules. Fifth Australian Conference on Artificial Intelligence, Hobart.(1992)
17. Kivinen, J., H. Mannila, and E. Ukkonen. Learning Rules with Local Exceptions. European Conference on Computational Theory, Clarendon Press, Oxford.(1993) 35-46
18. Scheffer, T. Learning Rules with Nested Exceptions. International Workshop on Artificial Intelligence.(1995)
19. Siromoney, A. and R. Siromoney, Variations and Local Exception in Inductive Logic Programming, in Machine Intelligence - Applied Machine Intelligence, K. Furukawa, D. Michie, and S. Muggleton, Editors. 1993. p. 213 - 234.
20. Wada, T., et al. Integrating Inductive Learning and Knowledge Acquisition in the Ripple Down Rules Method. Proceeding of the 6th Pacific Knowledge Acquisition Workshop, Sydney, Australia(2000) 325-341
21. Clancey, W.J. Heuristic classification. Artificial Intelligence 27:. (1985) 289-350
22. Compton, P., et al., Maintaining an expert system, in Applications of Expert Systems, J.R. Quinlan, Editor. 1989, Addison Wesley: London. p. 366-385.
23. Beydoun, G. and H. A. Incremental Acquisition of Search Knowledge. International Journal of Human Computer Studies 52(3):(2000) 493-530
24. Compton, P. and D. Richards. Generalising Ripple-Down Rules. . Knowledge Engineering and Knowledge Management: Methods, Models, Tools, Eds. R. Dieng; O. Corby, Juan-les-Pins France, 2-6 Oct. Springer, Berlin,(2000) 380-386

25. Matheus, C.J. and L.A. Rendell. Constructive induction on decision trees. Proceed-ings of the Eleventh International Joint Conference on Artificial Intelligence Detroit, MI: Morgan Kaufmann,(1989) 645--650

26. Bloedorn, E. and M. R.S. Data Driven Constructive Induction in AQ17-PRE: A Method and Experiments. Proceedings of the Third International Conference on Tools for Artifi-ciall Intelligence, San Jose, CA, November 9-14(1991)

27. Zupan, B., et al. Machine Learning by Function Decompo-sition. Proceedings of the 14 th International Conference on Machine Learning.(1997) 421-429

28. Sutton, R.S. and C.J. Matheus. Learning polynomial functions by feature construction. Machine Learning: Proceedings of the Eighth Interna-tional Workshop, Evanston, IL: Morgan Kaufmann.(1991) 208-212

29. Srinivasan, A. and R.D. King. Feature construction with inductive logic program-ming: A study of quantitative predictions of biological activity aided by structural attributes. Induc-tive Logic Programming: Proceedings of the 6th International Workshop, Springer.(1996) 89--104

30. Flach, P.A. and N. Lavrac. The role of feature construction in inductive rule learning. Proceedings of the International Conference on Machine Learning 2000 workshop on At-tribute-Value and Relational Learning: crossing the boundaries, Stan-ford, USA, Luc De Raedt and Stefan Kramer.(2000) 1 -11,

31. Compton, P., P. Preston, and B. Kang. The Use of Simulated Experts in Evaluating Knowledge Acquisition. 9th AAAI-sponsored Banff Knowledge Acquisition for Knowl-edge Base System Workshop, Canada, Banff, Canada, University of Calgary.(1995) pp12.1-12.18

32. Kang, B. (1996). Validating Knowledge Acquisition: Multiple Classification Ripple Down Rules. School of Computer Science and Engineering. . Sydney, New South Wales University.

33. Tecuci, G. and Y. Kodratoff, Machine Learning and Knowledge Acquisition: Integrated Approaches. 1995: Academic Press.

Extending Semantic-Based Matchmaking via Concept Abduction and Contraction

Tommaso Di Noia[1], Eugenio Di Sciascio[1], and Francesco M. Donini[2]

[1] Politecnico di Bari, Via Re David, 200, I-70125, Bari, Italy
{t.dinoia,disciascio}@poliba.it
[2] Università della Tuscia, via San Carlo, 32, I-01100, Viterbo, Italy
donini@unitus.it

Abstract. Motivated by the need to extend features of semantic matchmaking between request and offer descriptions, a model is presented that exploits recently proposed non-standard inference services in Description Logics.

The model allows to manage negotiable and strict constraints of a request (equivalently of an offer) while performing a matchmaking process, even if both the request and the offer are incompatible –some part of one description is in conflict with the other– and some constraints in one description are not specified in the other one.

An algorithm is presented to compute both which part of the request should be retracted and which part of the offer has to be refined in order to make them completely satisfiable with each other.

1 Introduction

The problem of matching request and offer descriptions arises in several scenarios. Among them web-services discovery, e-marketplaces, personnel recruitment and job assignment, dating agencies. All these scenarios share a common purpose: given a request, find among available descriptions those best fulfilling it, or "'at worse'", when nothing better exists, those that fulfill at least some of the requirements.

Exact, or full, matches are usually rare and the true matchmaking process is aimed at providing one or more best available matches to be explored, in order to initiate a negotiation/transaction process. Non-exact matches should take into account both missing information – details that could be positively assessed in a second phase – and conflicting information – details that could leverage negotiation if the proposed match is worth enough pursuing. Obviously, when several matches are possible, a matchmaking service should rank them in a most-promising order, so as to maximize the probability of a successful match within the first trials.

Recently, motivated by the ongoing transformation of the "'unstructured'" Web in the Semantic, machine understandable one, Description Logics (DLs) have been investigated to model the matchmaking problem in various scenarios [39, 19, 35, 32, 33, 20, 6], which we discuss in the final Section. DLs formalization has several advantages; among them an open-world assumption can be made, incomplete information is admitted, and absence of information can be distinguished from negative information. In all proposals on matchmaking exploiting DLs formalization, constraints about an offer or a request are expressed as concepts O and R in a chosen DL. Then, a DL reasoner is used to

E. Motta et al. (Eds.): EKAW 2004, LNAI 3257, pp. 307–320, 2004.

check *(a)* satisfiability of the conjunction O ⊓ R — which corresponds to compatibility between the constraints of O and R — and *(b)* subsumption O ⊑ R — which corresponds to O fulfilling all requirements of R, and vice versa for R ⊑ O. However, when several offers $O_1, \ldots, O_n$ are compatible with a request R (or vice versa) a *ranking* of counteroffers should be provided, using some rational criterion, possibly based on the logical specification of $O_1, \ldots, O_n$ and R, and when unsatisfiability ensues a user might like to know which constraints in the request caused it.

Usually, DL approaches exclude the case when a request R is inconsistent with the concept describing an offer O, assuming that all requirements are strict ones. Nevertheless other approaches not based on DLs [36] are much more liberal on this subject, allowing a user to specify negotiable requirements — some of which could be bargained in favor of others. In practice, there can be cases when a request is expressed by a user as a description where some of the requirements are strict ones, while other might be more loose and negotiable.

In [18, 15] Concept Abduction and Concept Contraction have been proposed as nonstandard inference services in DL, to capture in a logical way the reasons why a counteroffer O_1 should be ranked better than a counteroffer O_2 for a given request R, and vice versa. In a nutshell, when a request is issued, Concept Contraction captures the possibility to relax some constraints of R when they are in conflict with an offer O — that is, when O ⊓ R is an unsatisfiable concept. Intuitively, relaxable constraints are negotiable preferences, that could be dropped if the offer O satisfies some more important requirements of R. On the other hand, Concept Abduction captures the reasoning mechanism – namely, making hypotheses – involved when some constraints required by R are not specified in O — that obviously in later stages of the request/offer interaction might turn out to be fulfilled or not.

Here we propose a model that exploits Concept Contraction and Abduction and is able to take into account also incompatible pairs O,R, which are usually discarded by a matchmaking facilitator, thus easing discovery of negotiation spaces. Based on the model an algorithm is devised, which computes both the part of the request that should be retracted and the part of the offer that should be refined in order to make them completely satisfiable with respect to other.

The remaining of the paper is so structured. Section 2 revises Description Logics basics and the logic adopted here. Then Section 3 describes the non-standard inference services for DL we use. In Section 4 our logical setting is motivated and presented. Then we show in Section 5 how Concept Abduction and Contraction can be exploited to deal with negotiable and strict requirements in an extended matchmaking scenario. A discussions on relevant related work closes the paper.

2 Description Logics

DLs are a family of logic formalisms for Knowledge Representation [9, 22, 3] whose basic syntax elements are

- *concept* names, *e.g.*, computer, CPU, device, software,
- *role* names, like hasSoftware, hasDevice
- *individuals*, like HPworkstationXW, IBMThinkPad, CompaqPresario.

More formally, a semantic *interpretation* is a pair $\mathcal{I} = (\Delta, \cdot^{\mathcal{I}})$, which consists of the *domain* Δ and the *interpretation function* $\cdot^{\mathcal{I}}$, which maps every concept to a subset of Δ, every role to a subset of $\Delta \times \Delta$, and every individual to an element of Δ. We assume that different individuals are mapped to different elements of Δ, *i.e.*, $a^{\mathcal{I}} \neq b^{\mathcal{I}}$ for individuals $a \neq b$. This restriction is usually called *Unique Name Assumption* (UNA).

Basic elements can be combined using *constructors* to form concept and role *expressions*, and each DL is identified by the operators set it is endowed with. Every DL allows one to form a *conjunction* of concepts, usually denoted as ⊓; some DL include also disjunction ⊔ and complement ¬ to close concept expressions under boolean operations. Expressive DLs [14] are built on the simple $\mathcal{AL}$ (Attributive Language) adding constructs in order to represent more expressive concepts.

Expressions are given a semantics by defining the interpretation function over each construct. For example, concept conjunction is interpreted as set intersection: $(C \sqcap D)^{\mathcal{I}} = C^{\mathcal{I}} \cap D^{\mathcal{I}}$, and also the other boolean connectives ⊔ and ¬, when present, are given the usual set-theoretic interpretation of union and complement. The interpretation of constructs involving quantification on roles needs to make domain elements explicit: for example, $(\forall R.C)^{\mathcal{I}} = \{d_1 \in \Delta \mid \forall d_2 \in \Delta : (d_1, d_2) \in R^{\mathcal{I}} \rightarrow d_2 \in C^{\mathcal{I}}\}$.

Concept expressions can be used in *inclusion assertions*, and *definitions*, which impose restrictions on possible interpretations according to the knowledge elicited for a given domain. Historically, sets of such inclusions are called TBox (Terminological Box). In simple DLs, only a concept name can appear on the left-hand side of an inclusion.

The semantics of inclusions and definitions is based on set containment: an interpretation $\mathcal{I}$ satisfies an inclusion $C \sqsubseteq D$ if $C^{\mathcal{I}} \subseteq D^{\mathcal{I}}$, and it satisfies a definition $C = D$ when $C^{\mathcal{I}} = D^{\mathcal{I}}$. A *model* of a TBox $\mathcal{T}$ is an interpretation satisfying all inclusions and definitions of $\mathcal{T}$.

Adding new constructors increases DL languages expressiveness. Nevertheless, it is a well known result [11] that this usually leads to an explosion in computational complexity of inference services. Hence a trade-off is necessary. In this paper we refer to an $\mathcal{ALN}$ (Attributive Language with unqualified Number restrictions) Description Logic and to *simple-TBox* modeled as set of axioms in which the left side can be only a concept name (both for inclusion and definition). Although limited, such a subset already allows a user to specify negotiable and strict constraints, to verify their consistency, and to hypothesize the feasibility of a negotiation process for a given offer, as we show in the following sections. In Table 1 we present the constructs of $\mathcal{ALN}$. Note that ontologies are usually designed as *simple-TBox* in order to express the relations among objects in the domain. Ontologies using the above logic can be easily modeled using languages for the Semantic Web. The strong relations between DLs and the above introduced languages for the Semantic Web [4] is clearly present in the definition of the OWL language, particularly in its sub-language OWL-DL where expressiveness is allowed, while trying to keep computational completeness and decidability. The subset of OWL-DL TAGs allowing to express an $\mathcal{ALN}$ DL is presented in Table 3. In the rest of the paper we will use DL syntax instead of OWL-DL syntax, because the former is more compact. Nevertheless all the examples and the simple ontology we use to model them, can be rewritten using OWL DL syntax.

Table 1. Syntax and semantics of the constructs of $\mathcal{ALN}$

name	syntax	semantics
top	$\top$	$\Delta^{\mathcal{I}}$
bottom	$\bot$	$\emptyset$
intersection	$C \sqcap D$	$C^{\mathcal{I}} \cap D^{\mathcal{I}}$
atomic negation	$\neg A$	$\Delta^{\mathcal{I}} \backslash A^{\mathcal{I}}$
universal quantification	$\forall R.C$	$\{d_1 \mid \forall d_2 : (d_1, d_2) \in R^{\mathcal{I}} \to d_2 \in C^{\mathcal{I}}\}$
number restrictions	$(\geq n\ R)$	$\{d_1 \mid \sharp\{d_2 \mid (d_1, d_2) \in R^{\mathcal{I}}\} \geq n\}$
	$(\leq n\ R)$	$\{d_1 \mid \sharp\{d_2 \mid (d_1, d_2) \in R^{\mathcal{I}}\} \leq n\}$

Table 2. Syntax and semantics of the TBox assertions

name	syntax	semantics
definition	$A = C$	$A^{\mathcal{I}} = C^{\mathcal{I}}$
inclusion	$A \sqsubseteq C$	$A^{\mathcal{I}} \subseteq C^{\mathcal{I}}$

Table 3. Correspondence between OWL and DL syntax

OWL syntax	DL syntax
$< owl : Thing/ >$	$\top$
$< owl : Nothing/ >$	$\bot$
$< owl : Class\,rdf : ID = "C"/ >$	C
$< owl : ObjectProperty\,rdf : ID = "R"/ >$	R
$< rdfs : subClassOf/ >$	$\sqsubseteq$
$< owl : equivalentClass/ >$	$\equiv$
$< owl : disjointWith/ >$	$\neg$
$< owl : intersectionOf/ >$	$\sqcap$
$< owl : allValuesFrom/ >$	$\forall$
$< owl : maxCardinality/ >$	$\leq$
$< owl : minCardinality/ >$	$\geq$

3 Non-standard Inferences for $\mathcal{ALN}$ DL

All DL systems provide subsumption and satisfiability as standard reasoning services.

1. *Concept Satisfiability*: given a TBox $\mathcal{T}$ and a concept C, does there exist at least one model of $\mathcal{T}$ assigning a non-empty extension to C?
2. *Subsumption*: given a TBox $\mathcal{T}$ and two concepts C and D, is C more general than D in any model of $\mathcal{T}$?

Although this two basic services are very useful in several scenarios, there are cases where there is the need to overcome subsumption and satisfiability.

In our matchmaking scenario –where obviously an open world assumption is made – if constraints in R are not specified in O, and then subsumption does not hold, it should be possible to hypothesize missed ones and ask to refine O giving information on them. On the other hand we may not will to discard an offer O with respect to a request R on the basis of the conjunction inconsistency, *i.e.*, where they present mutually conflicting features. A user may like to know both why they are in conflict and which are the features that are not compatible, in order to establish, in case, a negotiation process based on such characteristics.

The logical formalization of negotiable requirements can be based on Concept Contraction [15] — Contraction has been formalized by Gärdenfors' [25] as the first step in belief revision — and Concept Abduction [18].

In the following we highlight basic properties of these non-standard DL inferences, and we refer to [17] for a thorough presentation, in the framework of a tableaux-based approach.

Starting with the concepts O and R, if their conjunction $O \sqcap R$ is unsatisfiable in the TBox $\mathcal{T}$ representing the ontology, our aim is to retract requirements in R, G (for *Give up*), to obtain a concept K (for *Keep*) such that $K \sqcap O$ is satisfiable in $\mathcal{T}$.

Definition 1. *Let $\mathcal{L}$ be a DL, O, R, be two concepts in $\mathcal{L}$, and $\mathcal{T}$ be a set of axioms in $\mathcal{L}$, where both O and R are satisfiable in $\mathcal{T}$. A* Concept Contraction Problem *(CCP), identified by $\langle \mathcal{L}, R, O, \mathcal{T} \rangle$, is finding a pair of concepts $\langle G, K \rangle \in \mathcal{L} \times \mathcal{L}$ such that $\mathcal{T} \models R \equiv G \sqcap K$, and $K \sqcap O$ is satisfiable in $\mathcal{T}$. We call K a* contraction *of R according to O and $\mathcal{T}$.*

We use $\mathcal{Q}$ as a symbol for a CCP, and we denote with $SOLCCP(\mathcal{Q})$ the set of all solutions to a CCP $\mathcal{Q}$. We note that there is always the trivial solution $\langle G, K \rangle = \langle R, \top \rangle$ to a CCP. This solution corresponds to the most drastic contraction, that gives up everything of R. In our matchmaking framework, it models the (infrequent) situation in which, in front of some very appealing offer O, incompatible with the request, a user just gives up completely his/her specifications R in order to meet O.

On the other hand, when $O \sqcap R$ is satisfiable in $\mathcal{T}$, the " best" possible solution is $\langle \top, R \rangle$, that is, give up nothing — if possible. Since usually one wants to give up as few things as possible, some minimality in the contraction must be defined. We do not delve into details, and just mention that there exists an algorithm, *i.e.*, $solveCCP(O, R, \mathcal{T})$ [17] to compute a minimal G *i.e.*, with respect to a minimality criterion, (and a maximal K) for a given offer O with respect to a request R and a TBox $\mathcal{T}$.

Once contraction has been applied, and consistency between the offer and the request has been regained, there is still the problem with partial specifications, that is, it could be the case that the offer — though compatible — does not imply the request. Then, it is necessary to assess what should be hypothesized in the offer in order to initiate a transaction with the requester. This non-standard inference is named *Concept Abduction*, in analogy to Charles Peirce's Abduction [34, 31].

Definition 2. *Let $\mathcal{L}$ be a DL, O, R, be two concepts in $\mathcal{L}$, and $\mathcal{T}$ be a set of axioms in $\mathcal{L}$, where both O and R are satisfiable in $\mathcal{T}$. A* Concept Abduction Problem *(CAP), identified by $\langle \mathcal{L}, R, O, \mathcal{T} \rangle$, is finding a concept $H \in \mathcal{L}$ such that $\mathcal{T} \models O \sqcap H \sqsubseteq R$, and* *moreover* O ⊓ H *is satisfiable in* T. *We call* H *a hypothesis* about O according to D and T.

Also for Concept Abduction, there exist algorithms [18, 17] *i.e.,* $solveCAP(O, R, T)$ that can compute H for $\mathcal{ALN}$ concepts O, R and a simple TBox T. A numerical version $rankPotential(O, R, T)$ of the algorithm also exists [20], which computes the length of a Concept Abduction H, thus providing a score to the similarity between an offer and a request. An evolution of the above approach is presented in [13], where penalty functions are introduced managing user interest levels on both R and O features.

We note that Concept Contraction extends satisfiability — in particular, by providing new concepts G and K when a conjunction O ⊓ R is unsatisfiable — while Concept Abduction extends subsumption — in particular, by providing a new concept H when O is not subsumed by R.

4   DL Modeling of the Matchmaking Framework

Matchmaking systems are electronic intermediary systems that bring requests and offers together and usually provide various support services [23, 36, 37, 20]. Obviosly, other techniques, not logic-based have been used to model such systems. Nevertheless, using standard database techniques to model a matchmaking framework, we would be obliged to completely align the attributes of the offer and request in order to evaluate a match. If requests and offers are simple names or strings, the only possible match would be identity, resulting in an all-or-nothing approach to matchmaking. Vector-based techniques based on classical Information Retrieval can be used, too, thus reverting matchmaking to similarity between weighted vectors of terms. Although effective for fixed technical domains, such approaches miss the fact that offers and requests usually have some sort of structure in them. Our logical approach allows users to state only part of the information about their offers, and moreover, to state information at different abstract levels, leaving to the logic apparatus the burden of comparing specified characteristics. The logic apparatus we consider is based on a reference ontology, *i.e.*, a set of axioms (TBox), modeling implicit knowledge on the domain and a matchmaking service endowed with the non-standard services described in the previous section. We stress that every argument in what follows could be restated exchanging request with offer, depending on the actor who is actively starting the search. In the examples that follow we will use information modeled using the simplified ontology proposed in Figure 1, which models descriptions for a tiny computer marketplace. In a generic matchmaking framework, a concept describing a request, can be read as a set of constraints of the user needs. A description modeling explicit knowledge on a request Rrepresents a set of constraints on it. For example, the simple R = homePC ⊓ (≥ 1 hasOS) represents the following constraints: {homePC, (≥ 1 hasOS)}.

The idea is that the active requesting/offering user (or agent), models the previous set as the conjunction of two different ones. The first set accounts for negotiable features, *i.e.*, what the requester may accept to retract to initiate a transaction. The second set represents non-negotiable elements, the quota of Rthe requester is most interested in and then does not want in conflict with O; at least she/he may be willing to hypothesize some of them and, later in the process, request informations on the offer to the provider. In DL terms,

```
unix ⊑ ¬winX
linux ⊑ unix
CRTmonitor ⊑ ¬LCDmonitor
USBpen ⊑ removableDevice
AMD ⊑ ¬Intel
computer ⊑ (≥ 1 hasStorageDevice) ⊓ (≥ 1 hasComponent)
server ≡ computer ⊓ (≥ 2 hasCPU)
personalComputer ⊑ computer
personalComputer ⊑ ¬PDA
homePC ≡ personalComputer ⊓ (≥ 1 hasOS) ⊓ (≤ 1 hasOS) ⊓ (≤ 1 hasCPU)
```

Fig. 1. The toy ontology used as reference in examples

we model the non-negotiable and the negotiable constraints as a conjunction of concepts: negotiable constraints, from now on $\mathcal{NG}$ and non-negotiable, strict, constraints, from now on $\mathcal{ST}$. Basically, negotiable constraints express a continued interest in an agreement with a counterpart also when no potential match is available and on the basis of a relaxation of the constraint [36]. Obviously, if an element belongs to $\mathcal{NG}$ it cannot belong to $\mathcal{ST}$ i.e., if $(\geq 1\ \text{hasOS})$ is a negotiable constraint, then it cannot be also a non-negotiable one, otherwise an inconsistency ensues within the user specification. Such an inconsistency may be caused by the interplay between the ontology and the user's specifications about negotiable/non-negotiable constraints. For example, considering the previous description $\mathcal{NG} = \text{homePC}$ and $\mathcal{ST} = (\geq 1\ \text{hasOS})$, due to the ontology axiom related to homePC, one obtains $(\geq 1\ \text{hasOS})$ both in $\mathcal{NG}$ and $\mathcal{ST}$. Clearly an incoherent specification of what is negotiable and what is not. Scenarios as the one presented previously, can be managed using Concept Abduction and considering both $\mathcal{NG}$ and $\mathcal{ST}$ as conjunctions of $\mathcal{ALN}$ concepts. Solving the following **CAP**: $\mathcal{NG} \sqcap H_1 \sqsubseteq \mathcal{ST}$, if $H_1 = \mathcal{ST}$ then the whole $\mathcal{ST}$ has to be hypothesized to obtain a subsumption relation, i.e., nothing of both the explicit and implicit information in $\mathcal{NG}$ is in $\mathcal{ST}$. In our scenario if $H_1 \neq \mathcal{ST}$ the requester may be asked to reformulate her/his model of negotiable and not-negotiable information. Solving the **CAP** $H_1 \sqcap H_2 \sqsubseteq \mathcal{ST}$, H_2 represents the shared part between $\mathcal{ST}$ and $\mathcal{NG}$.

Notice that we model $\mathcal{NG}$ and $\mathcal{ST}$ after Rhas been formulated. Before the user composes R, nothing is known about $\mathcal{NG}$ and $\mathcal{ST}$. Our approach hence does not model a request like "I am looking for a personal computer possibly suited for domestic use and with necessarily an OS installed". The previous request already embeds negotiable and strict requirements in its specification. Its logical model can be built using a logic and an approach like the one proposed in [13].

Here, first we build the logical model of the request, e.g., "I am looking for a personal computer suited for domestic use and with an OS installed" (homePC ⊓ $(\geq 1\ \text{hasOS})$), and then the active user specifies $\mathcal{NG}$ and $\mathcal{ST}$. This remark is necessary to take into account the ontology concept hierarchy. In fact if the user is looking for ... ⊓ ∀hasOS.(linux⊓unix), due to the ontology axioms, actually s/he is looking for ... ⊓ ∀hasOS.linux. Then it is not correct to specify $\mathcal{ST} = \ldots \sqcap \forall\text{hasOS.linux}$ and $\mathcal{NG} = \ldots \sqcap \forall\text{hasOS.unix}$ or vice versa because of the subsumption relation between linux and unix.

5 Matchmaking Algorithm

In the following we show how, using both the notions of Concept Abduction and Contraction together with the logical formalization of negotiable constraints, the search of negotiation spaces within a matchmaking framework is feasible.

The basic assumption in this formalization is that an actor is willing to play an active role, *i.e.*, s/he may be willing to consider retracting on some of the constraints expressed in the initial description to leverage negotiation.

With reference to Figure 1, consider R = computer $\sqcap$ $\forall$hasCPU.Intel $\sqcap$ ($\geq$ 1hasCPU), with $\mathcal{NG}$ = $\forall$hasCPU.Intel and $\mathcal{ST}$ = computer $\sqcap$ ($\geq$ 1 hasCPU), and O = homePC $\sqcap$ $\forall$hasCPU.AMD. It is possible to verify that R $\sqcap$ O is unsatisfiable, due to CPU specification. A solution of the **CCP** $\langle \mathcal{ALN}, \mathsf{O}, \mathsf{R}, \mathcal{T} \rangle$ is the pair $\langle G, K \rangle$ where G = $\forall$hasCPU.Intel and K = computer $\sqcap$ ($\geq$ 1 hasCPU).

Note that the previous one is not "the" solution. In fact another solution pair is, for example, G = ($\geq$ 1 hasCPU) and K = computer $\sqcap$ $\forall$hasCPU.Intel. But a similar solution is not compatible with negotiable specification: the requester is not willing to retract on ($\geq$ 1 hasCPU).

To catch this possibility a minimality criterion for a **CCP** would be: "do not retract concepts belonging to $\mathcal{ST}$", *i.e.*, do not add to G concepts C so that $\mathcal{ST} \sqsubseteq C$. By definition $K \sqcap \mathsf{O}$ is satisfiable, hence, K potentially matches O.

Let us point out that, having R $\sqcap$ O unsatisfiable, if $\mathcal{ST} \sqcap \mathsf{O}$ is satisfiable, the unsatisfiability arises because of $\mathcal{NG}$ (or to the conjunction of elements $\mathcal{ST}$ and other elements in $\mathcal{NG}$). In spite of some conflicting constraints in O, there is at least a part of $\mathcal{ST}$ (that is the most important one from the user's point of view), which can be potentially satisfied by O, hypothesizing concepts not expressed there.

On the other hand if $\mathcal{ST}$ and O are unsatisfiable, there is no way to continue the matchmaking process, unless a reformulation of the request R or at least the negotiable preferences $\mathcal{NG}$. In the latter case suggestions on which part of $\mathcal{ST}$ has to be transformed into a negotiable constraint, can be made solving a a **CCP** $\langle \mathcal{L}, \mathcal{ST}, \mathsf{O}, \mathcal{T} \rangle$. The solution $\langle G, K \rangle$ can be interpreted as the part that must be set as negotiable (G), and the one remaining strict (K).

Actually, the above scenario keeps its significance also if we flip over R and O, *i.e.*, if we have an offer expressed as $\mathcal{ST}$ and $\mathcal{NG}$ by the active actor.

Notice that, if $\mathcal{NG}$ and $\mathcal{ST}$ are expressed in the demand R, a change in their specifications [see lines 7–15 in the algorithm below] requires recomputing previous matches. On the other hand, if $\mathcal{NG}$ and $\mathcal{ST}$ are expressed in the supplies Os, no recomputing is needed.

In a more formal way, we propose the following algorithm to cope with the extended matchmaking scenario. The algorithm executes calls to *solveCCP* and *solveCAP* and takes as inputs:

– R: description of the active actor (either a request or an offer), with R = $\mathcal{ST} \sqcap \mathcal{NG}$
– O: conversely defined description (with respect to the above item, either an offer or a request)
– $\mathcal{T}$: the ontology describing the marketplace domain

Algorithm $matchmaker(\mathsf{O}, \mathsf{R}, \mathcal{T})$
input $\mathcal{ALN}$ concepts O, R, where $\mathsf{R} = \mathcal{ST} \sqcap \mathcal{NG}$
output $\langle G, K, H_K \rangle$
begin algorithm
1:     **if** ($\mathsf{R} \sqcap \mathsf{O}$ is unsatisfiable)
2:       **if** ($\mathcal{ST} \sqcap \mathsf{O}$ is satisfiable){
3:          $\langle G, K \rangle = solveCCP(\mathsf{O}, \mathsf{R}, \mathcal{T})$;
4:          $H_K = solveCAP(\mathsf{O}, K, \mathcal{T})$;
5:          **return** $\langle G, K, H_K \rangle$;
6:       }
7:       **else**{
8:          Ask the active actor to change
            preferences on strict constraints ;
9:          **if** YES {
10:            $\langle G_{\mathcal{ST}}, K_{\mathcal{ST}} \rangle = solveCCP(\mathsf{O}, \mathcal{ST}, \mathcal{T})$;
11:            $\mathcal{ST}_{new} = K_{\mathcal{ST}}$;
12:            $\mathcal{NG}_{new} = \mathcal{NG} \sqcap G_{\mathcal{ST}}$;
13:            $\mathsf{R}_{new} = \mathcal{NG}_{new} \sqcap \mathcal{ST}_{new}$;
14:            **return** $matchmaker(\mathsf{O}, \mathsf{R}_{new}, \mathcal{T})$;
15:          }
16:          **else return** $\langle -, \bot, \bot \rangle$;
17:       }
18:     **else**{
19:       $H_D = solveCAP(\mathsf{O}, \mathsf{R}, \mathcal{T})$;
20:       **return** $\langle \top, \mathsf{R}, H_D \rangle$;
21:     }
end algorithm

The computational complexity of the above algorithm strictly depends on those of *solveCCP* and *solveCAP* [15, 17].

The algorithm *matchmaker* determines parameters useful to compare the relevance of a match between a request and several offers, returning the triple $\langle G, K, H_K \rangle$ of $\mathcal{ALN}$ concepts:

- G, represents the part to be retracted from R in order to obtain a compatible match
- K, what, in R, can be satisfied by O
- H_K, the hypothesis to be formulated to make R completely satisfied by O

The triple $\langle -, \bot, \bot \rangle$ is returned when the elements to give up in the transaction belong to $\mathcal{ST}$, *e.g.*, there are constraints the user does not want to retract on. $\langle -, \bot, \bot \rangle$ is a level of "unrecoverable" mismatch.

We would like to point out that it may look sufficient, at a first glance, $G = \mathsf{R}$. Nevertheless this result corresponds to the situation where $\mathcal{ST} = \top$, then $\mathcal{ST} \sqcap \mathsf{O}$ is still satisfiable and a *give up* is possible on the whole R. Notice that in row 3, *matchmaker* solves a ***CCP*** on O and R rather than on O and $\mathcal{NG}$. The rationale is easily understandable considering the example at the beginning of this section where the source of inconsistency is the conjunction of concepts both in $\mathcal{ST}$ and $\mathcal{NG}$ and the *give up* operation is on concepts subsuming $\mathcal{NG}$.

A global numerical parameter, evaluating how promising is a match, can be evaluated using $rankPotential$ [20], the numerical version of $solveCAP$, which allows to compute the length of of a Concept Abduction $|H|$. A function depending on $|G|$, $|K|$, $|H_K|$, the "length" of G, K and H_K, can hence evaluate a score for each match between a request and a set of offers.

5.1   A Simple Example

In order to better describe our approach we present hereafter a simple example scenario, which we build with reference to the ontology in Figure 1. Let us consider the following supply:

S. Single processor PC with at least Linux pre-installed. The offer includes an LCD monitor and a scanner.

> – $S =$ personalComputer $\sqcap$ $\forall$hasComponent.(LCDmonitor $\sqcap$ scanner)
> $\sqcap (\leq$ 1 hasCPU) $\sqcap$ $\forall$hasOS.linux $\sqcap$ ($\geq$ 1 hasOS)

and the request:

D. I'm looking for a PC for domestic use, with Unix, equipped with a CRT monitor and USB pen for data storing.

> – $D =$ homePC $\sqcap$ $\forall$hasOS.unix $\sqcap$ $\forall$hasComponent.CRTmonitor
> $\sqcap \forall$hasStorageDevice.USBpen

Within the above request let us consider:
I absolutely need a PC for domestic use with Unix.

> – $\mathcal{ST} =$ homePC $\sqcap$ $\forall$hasOS.unix

I would appreciate the CRT monitor and the USB pen.

> – $\mathcal{NG} =$ $\forall$hasComponent.CRTmonitor $\sqcap$ $\forall$hasStorageDevice.USBpen

S and D are not consistent with respect to the reference ontology, τ, due to the monitor specification.

The $matchmaker(S, D, \tau)$ returns:

$G =$ $\forall$hasComponent.CRTmonitor
$K =$ homePC $\sqcap$ $\forall$hasOS.unix $\sqcap$ $\forall$hasStorageDevice.USBpen
$H_K =$ ($\leq$ 1 hasOS) $\sqcap$ $\forall$hasStorageDevice.USBpen

6 Discussion

In this paper we proposed a model that, by exploiting Concept Contraction and Abduction allows to manage negotiable and strict constraints of a request (equivalently of an offer) while performing a matchmaking process, even if both the request and the offer are incompatible and some constraints in one description are not specified in the other one. An algorithm was presented able to compute both which part of the request should be retracted and which part of the offer should be refined to make a pair request - offer completely satisfiable.

In the remaining of this section we comment on similar approaches and discuss them. In [24] and [30] matchmaking was introduced, based on KQML, as an approach whereby potential producers / consumers could provide descriptions of their products/needs to be later unified by a matchmaker engine to identify potential matches. The proposed solutions to this challenging issue reverted to either a rule based approach using the Knowledge Interchange Format (KIF) [26] (the SHADE [30] prototype) or a free text comparison (the COINS [30] prototype). Approaches similar to the cited ones were deployed in SIMS [1], which used KQML and LOOM as description language and Info-Sleuth [29], which adopted KIF and the deductive database language LDL++. LOOM is also at the basis of the subsumption matching addressed in [27].

More recently there has been a growing interest towards matchmaking engines and techniques, with emphasis placed either on e-marketplaces or generic Web services. In [37] and [33] the LARKS language is proposed, specifically designed for agent advertisement. The matching process is a mixture of classical IR analysis of text and semantic match via Θ-subsumption. Nevertheless, a basic service of a semantic approach, such as inconsistency check, seems unavailable with this type of match.

First approaches based on subsumption services offered by DL reasoners were proposed in [21, 28, 39]. In [19, 20] properties that a matchmaker should have in a DL based framework, were described and motivated, and algorithms to classify and rank matches into classes were presented, *i.e.*, *Exact match:* all requested characteristics are available in the description examined; *Potential match:* some part of the request is not specified in the description examined; *Partial match:* some part of the request is in conflict with the description examined. The algorithms are modified versions of the structural subsumption algorithm originally proposed in [10] and compute a distance between each description w.r.t. a request in each class. Matchmaking of web-services described in DAML-S, providing a ranking of matches based on the DL-based approach of [19] is presented in [16]. An extension to the approach in [33] was proposed in [32] where two new levels for service profiles matching are introduced. Notice that there the *intersection satisfiable* level is introduced, whose definition is close to the one of *potential matching* proposed in [19], but no measure of similarity among intersection satisfiable concepts is given.

Semantic service discovery via matchmaking in the Bluetooth [8] framework has been investigated in [35]. Also here the issue of approximate matches, to be somehow ranked and proposed in the absence of exact matches, was discussed, but as in the previous papers no formal framework was given. Instead a logical formulation should allow to devise correct algorithms to classify and rank matches.

Matching in DLs has been widely treated in [5] although with no relation to match-making. In fact, in that work expressions denoting concepts are considered, with variables in expressions. Then a match is a substitution of variables with expressions that makes a concept expression equivalent to another.

Also in [7, 6] web services matchmaking was tackled. An approach was proposed, based on the Difference operator in DLs [38], followed by a set covering operation optimized using hypergraph techniques. The adopted DL is $\mathcal{L}_1$. Notice that performing a difference operation needs a subsumption relation between descriptions to be matched, which instead is not required to solve a Concept Contraction Problem. This strict condition may make Concept Difference hard to use in a matchmaking process, where descriptions overlap is usually a sufficient condition to start the process. Anyway, to the best of our knowledge there is no algorithm able to compute an exact Concept Difference in a DL endowed of the negation constructor. In [12] an algorithm is proposed for Difference on approximation of concepts.

At a first glance, also the Least Common Subsumer (lcs) [2] could be useful to model the problem of finding negotiation spaces in a matchmaking framework. In fact with lcs, given two concepts D and C, it is possible to compute the concept representing all the properties that D and C have in common. Nevertheless computing an lcs may lead to loss of information. For example having $O = \neg A \sqcap B$ and $R = A \sqcap C$, we obtain $lcs = \top$. There is no way to recover information of B in O and of C in R.

Acknowledgments

The authors acknowledge partial support of projects PON CNOSSO and MS3DI.

References

1. Y. Arens, C. A. Knoblock, and W. Shen. Query Reformulation for Dynamic Information Integration. *Journal of Intelligent Information Systems*, 6:99–130, 1996.
2. F. Baader. Least common subsumers and most specific concepts in a description logic with existential restrictions and terminological cycles. In *Proc. International Joint Conference on Artificial Intelligence (IJCAI2003)*, pages 319–324, 2003.
3. F. Baader, D. Calvanese, D. Mc Guinness, D. Nardi, and P. Patel-Schneider, editors. *The Description Logic Handbook*. Cambridge University Press, 2002.
4. F. Baader, I. Horrocks, and U. Sattler. Description logics as ontology languages for the semantic web. In D. Hutter and W. Stephan, editors, *Festschrift in honor of Jörg Siekmann*, Lecture Notes in Artificial Intelligence. Springer-Verlag, 2003.
5. F. Baader, R. Kusters, A. Borgida, and D. Mc Guinness. Matching in Description Logics. *Journal of Logic and Computation*, 9(3):411–447, 1999.
6. B. Benatallah, M.-S. Hacid, C. Rey, and F. Toumani. Request Rewriting-Based Web Service Discovery. In *International Semantic Web Conference*, volume 2870 of *Lecture Notes in Computer Science*, pages 242–257. Springer, 2003.
7. B. Benatallah, M.-S. Hacid, C. Rey, and F. Toumani. Semantic Reasoning for Web Services Discovery. In *Proc. of Workshop on E-Services and the Semantic Web at WWW 2003*, May 2003.
8. Bluetooth. http://www.bluetooth.com.

9. A. Borgida. Description Logics in Data Management. *IEEE Transactions on Knowledge and Data Engineering*, 7(5):671–682, 1995.

10. A. Borgida and P. F. Patel-Schneider. A Semantics and Complete Algorithm for Subsumption in the CLASSIC Description Logic. *Journal of Artificial Intelligence Research*, 1:277–308, 1994.

11. R. Brachman and H. Levesque. The tractability of subsumption in frame-based description languages. In *Proceedings of the Fourth National Conference on Artificial Intelligence (AAAI-84)*, pages 34–37. Morgan Kaufmann, Los Altos, 1984.

12. S. Brandt, R. Küsters, and A.-Y. Turhan. Approximation and difference in description logics. In *Proc. International Conference on Principles of Knowledge Representation and Reasoning (KR2002)*, pages 203–214. Morgan Kaufman, 2002.

13. A. Calì, D. Calvanese, S. Colucci, T. D. Noia, and F. Donini. A Logic-based Approach for Matching User Profiles. In *Proc. of KES'2004 Intl. Conf. on Knowledge-Based Intelligent Information and Engineering Systems*, 2004. To appear.

14. D. Calvanese and G. De Giacomo. Expressive description logics. In *The Description Logic Handbook: Theory, Implementation and Applications*, pages 178–218. 2003.

15. S. Colucci, T. Di Noia, E. Di Sciascio, F. Donini, and M. Mongiello. Concept Abduction and Contraction in Description Logics. In *Proceedings of the 16th International Workshop on Description Logics (DL'03)*, volume 81 of *CEUR Workshop Proceedings*, September 2003.

16. S. Colucci, T. Di Noia, E. Di Sciascio, F. Donini, and M. Mongiello. Logic Based Approach to web services discovery and matchmaking. In *Proceedings of the E-Services Workshop at ICEC'03*, September 2003.

17. S. Colucci, T. D. Noia, E. D. Sciascio, F. Donini, and M. Mongiello. Uniform Tableaux-Based Approach to Concept Abductiona and Contraction in ALN DL. In *Proceedings of the 17th International Workshop on Description Logics (DL'04)*, volume 104 of *CEUR Workshop Proceedings*, 2004.

18. T. Di Noia, E. Di Sciascio, F. Donini, and M. Mongiello. Abductive matchmaking using description logics. In *Proceedings of the Eighteenth International Joint Conference on Artificial Intelligence (IJCAI 2003)*, pages 337–342, Acapulco, Messico, August 9–15 2003. Morgan Kaufmann, Los Altos.

19. T. Di Noia, E. Di Sciascio, F. Donini, and M. Mongiello. Semantic matchmaking in a P-2-P electronic marketplace. In *Proc. Symposium on Applied Computing (SAC '03)*, pages 582–586. ACM, 2003.

20. T. Di Noia, E. Di Sciascio, F. Donini, and M. Mongiello. A system for principled Matchmaking in an electronic marketplace. In *Proc. International World Wide Web Conference (WWW '03)*, pages 321–330, Budapest, Hungary, May 20–24 2003. ACM, New York.

21. E. Di Sciascio, F. Donini, M. Mongiello, and G. Piscitelli. A Knowledge-Based System for Person-to-Person E-Commerce. In *Proceedings of the KI-2001 Workshop on Applications of Description Logics (ADL-2001)*, volume 44 of *CEUR Workshop Proceedings*, 2001.

22. F. M. Donini, M. Lenzerini, D. Nardi, and A. Schaerf. Reasoning in Description Logics. In G. Brewka, editor, *Principles of Knowledge Representation*, Studies in Logic, Language and Information, pages 193–238. CSLI Publications, 1996.

23. M. Dumas, B. Benatallah, N. Russell, and M. Spork. A Configurable Matchmaking Framework for Electronic Marketplaces. *Electronic Commerce Research and Appplications*, 3(1):95–106, 2004.

24. T. Finin, R. Fritzson, D. McKay, and R. McEntire. KQML as an Agent Communication Language. In *Proceedings of the Third International Conference on Information and Knowledge Management (CIKM'94)*, pages 456–463. ACM, 1994.

25. P. Gärdenfors. *Knowledge in Flux: Modeling the Dynamics of Epistemic States*. Bradford Books, MIT Press, Cambridge, MA, 1988.

26. M. R. Genesereth. Knowledge Interchange Format. In *Principles of Knowledge Representation and Reasoning: Proceedings of the 2nd International Conference*, pages 599–600, Cambridge, MA, 1991. Morgan Kaufmann, Los Altos.

27. Y. Gil and S. Ramachandran. PHOSPHORUS: a Task based Agent Matchmaker. In *Proc. International Conference on Autonomous Agents '01*, pages 110–111. ACM, 2001.

28. J. Gonzales-Castillo, D. Trastour, and C. Bartolini. Description Logics for Matchmaking of Services. In *Proceedings of the KI-2001 Workshop on Applications of Description Logics (ADL-2001)*, volume 44. CEUR Workshop Proceedings, 2001.

29. N. Jacobs and R. Shea. Carnot and Infosleuth – Database Technology and the Web. In *Proceedings of the ACM SIGMOD International Conference on Management of Data*, pages 443–444. ACM, 1995.

30. D. Kuokka and L. Harada. Integrating Information Via Matchmaking. *Journal of Intelligent Information Systems*, 6:261–279, 1996.

31. H. Levesque. A Knowledge-Level Account for Abduction. In *Proceedings of the Eleventh International Joint Conference on Artificial Intelligence (IJCAI'89)*, pages 1061–1067. Morgan Kaufmann, Los Altos, 1989.

32. L. Li and I. Horrocks. A Software Framework for Matchmaking Based on Semantic Web Technology. In *Proc. International World Wide Web Conference (WWW '03)*, pages 331–339, Budapest, Hungary, May 20–24 2003. ACM, New York.

33. M. Paolucci, T. Kawamura, T. Payne, and K. Sycara. Semantic Matching of Web Services Capabilities. In *The Semantic Web - ISWC 2002*, number 2342 in Lecture Notes in Computer Science, pages 333–347. Springer-Verlag, 2002.

34. C. . Peirce. Abduction and induction. In *Philosophical Writings of Peirce*, chapter 11. J. Buchler, 1955.

35. S.Avancha, A. Joshi, and T. Finin. Enhanced Service Discovery in Bluetooth. *IEEE Computer*, pages 96–99, 2002.

36. M. Ströbel and M. Stolze. A Matchmaking Component for the Discovery of Agreement and Negotiation Spaces in Electronic Markets. *Group Decision and Negotiation*, 11:165–181, 2002.

37. K. Sycara, S. Widoff, M. Klusch, and J. Lu. LARKS: Dynamic Matchmaking Among Heterogeneus Software Agents in Cyberspace. *Autonomous agents and multi-agent systems*, 5:173–203, 2002.

38. G. Teege. Making the difference: A subtraction operation for description logics. In *Proceedings of the Fourth International Conference on the Principles of Knowledge Representation and Reasoning (KR'94)*, pages 540–550. MK, 1994.

39. D. Trastour, C. Bartolini, and C. Priest. Semantic Web Support for the Business-to-Business E-Commerce Lifecycle. In *Proc. International World Wide Web Conference (WWW) '02*, pages 89–98. ACM, 2002.

Configuration of Web Services as Parametric Design

Annette ten Teije[1], Frank van Harmelen[2], and Bob Wielinga[3]

[1] Dept. of AI, Vrije Universiteit, Amsterdam
annette@cs.vu.nl
[2] Dept. of AI, Vrije Universiteit, Amsterdam
[3] Dept. of Social Science Informatics, SWI, University of Amsterdam

Abstract. The configuration of Web services is particularly hard given the heterogeneous, unreliable and open nature of the Web. Furthermore, such composite Web services are likely to be complex services, that will require adaptation for each specific use. Current approaches to Web service configuration are often based on pre/post-condition-style reasoning, resulting in a planning-style approach to service configuration, configuring a composite web service "from scratch" every time.

In this paper, we propose instead a knowledge-intensive brokering approach to the creation of composite Web services. In our approach, we describe a complex Web service as a fixed template, which must be configured for each specific use. Web service configuration can then be regarded as parametric design, in which the parameters of the fixed template have to be instantiated with appropriate component services. During the configuration process, we exploit detailed knowledge about the template and the components, to obtain the required composite web service.

We illustrate our proposal by applying it to a specific family of Web services, namely "heuristic classification services". We have implemented a prototype of our knowledge-intensive broker and describe its execution in a concrete scenario.

1 Introduction

Web services have raised much interest in various areas of Computer Science. In AI, the notion of *Semantic Web Services* has attracted much attention. According to [1]:

> "Semantic Web services build on Web service infrastructure to enable automatic discovery and invocation of existing services as well as *creation of new composite services* [...]".

In particular the configuration of Web services (the "creation of new composite services") has gained attention from AI researchers [2, 3]. This problem is particularly hard given the heterogeneous, unreliable and open nature of the Web. Furthermore, such composite Web services will be complex services, that will require adaptation for each specific use.

Current approaches to Web service configuration are often based on pre/post-condition-style reasoning. Given more or less semantic descriptions of elementary Web

E. Motta et al. (Eds.): EKAW 2004, LNAI 3257, pp. 321–336, 2004.
© Springer-Verlag Berlin Heidelberg 2004

services, and the required functionality of the composite Web service, they aim to try to construct a "plan" of how to compose the elementary services in order to obtain the required functionality. Techniques from the domain of planning are heavily being investigated for this purpose [4, 5].

This problem of creation of new composite web services is in principle equal to the old problem of generalised automatic programming. This problem is notoriously unsolved in general by any known techniques. There is no reason to belief that the Web service version of this problem will be any less resistant to a general solution.

In this paper, we propose instead a *knowledge intensive* approach to the creation of composite Web services. Following the general maxim of knowledge-based systems, problems that are in general hard (or even unsolvable) are perfectly solvable in the context of specialised knowledge for specific tasks and domains. In our approach, we describe a complex Web service as a fixed template, which must be configured for each specific use. Web service configuration can then be regarded as parametric design, in which the parameters of the fixed template have to be instantiated with appropriate component services. During the configuration process, we exploit detailed knowledge about the template and the components, to obtain the required composite web service.

Our approach is directly based on well-established work from Knowledge Engineering, and results obtained there in the 90's. Knowledge Engineering has extensively studied the notion of *reusable components* for knowledge-based systems, in particular reusable problem-solving methods: see [6, 7] for general reusability frameworks, and [8, 9] for example collections of reusable components. In essence, our contribution is nothing more than the insight that these results for the configuration of knowledge-based systems from reusable components can be directly brought to bear on the problem of configuring web-services. Indeed, we will propose to use exactly the same configuration method for web-services as has been used for the configuration of KBS components [10].

Whereas in other work the main metaphor is "Web service configuration = planning" (i.e. generalised reasoning based on only component specifications), our approach is based on the metaphor "Web service configuration = brokering" (i.e. reasoning with specialised knowledge in a narrow domain). A planner is assumed to be "domain free": it is supposed to work on any set of components, given simply their descriptions. A *broker* on the other hand (as in: a stock broker, a real-estate broker) exploits specific knowledge about the objects he is dealing with.

The idea of re-using preconfigured templates for Web service configuration also appears in other work: the notion of "generic procedures" in [11], the instantiation of predefined BPEL process models [12], and the coordination patterns from [13].

In the remainder of this paper, we describe how Web services advertise themselves as components to be used by a particular Web service broker, and how such a broker can be equipped with configuration knowledge on how to combine these web services.

In section 2 we describe our general parametric-design approach to Web service configuration. In sections 3 and 4 we illustrate our proposal by applying it to a specific family of Web services, namely "heuristic classification services". In section 5 we describe a specific implementation and execution of our approach.

2 Web Service Configuration as Parametric Design

In this section we will describe what parametric design is, why parametric design is a good basis for a Web service broker, and what descriptions of Web services are required to enable parametric-design reasoning by a broker, and finally we will describe a computational method for solving parametric design problems.

2.1 Parametric Design

Parametric Design is a method for designing objects which is a simplification of general configuration. As any design task, it takes as input the requirements to be met, and produces a design that satisfies these requirements. Parametric Design assumes that the objects-to-be-configured all have the same overall structure in the form of preconfigured templates. Variations on the configuration can only be obtained by choosing the values of given parameters within these templates.

The canonical example of Parametric Design is the design of elevators: every elevator has the same basic structure, namely a column, cable, cabin, counterweight, motor, etc, all in a fixed "template structure". Individual elevators differ only in the values for these parameters: the height of the column, the diameter of the cable, the capacity of the motor, etc. Elevator configuration can be reduced to simply choosing the right values for all these parameters [14].

In the case of web-service configuration, the "template" is a skeletal control structure, which determines how a number of component services will have to be composed. Each component service is then a possible value for one of the parameters within the overall template.

The advantages of Parametric Design in general are: (i) it is one of the easiest forms of configuration, (ii) it is well-studied in the literature [15], and (iii) computational methods are known and tractable (in section 2.2 we will describe one of these methods: propose-critique-modify). Advantages of parametric design for Web services configuration specifically are that the re-use of preconfigured templates avoids repeated multiple configurations of similar composite services for similar applications. These preconfigured templates are a way of "encoding" knowledge that can be used to obtain more sophisticated services than would be possible when configuring "from scratch" (in the sense of planning).

Parametric Design requires that the object-to-be-designed (in our case: a Web service) is described in terms of a fixed structure containing parameters with adjustable values. The following question must be answered before we can confidently apply Parametric Design to the problem of Web service configuration:

Question 1: can realistic classes of Web services be described in this way? This question will be tackled in section 3.

2.2 Propose-Critique-Modify

An existing reasoning method for parametric design is *Propose-Critique-Modify*, or PCM for short [15]. The PCM method consists of four steps:

The Propose Step. generates an initial partial or complete configuration. It proposes an instance of the general template used for representing the family of services.

The Verify Step. checks if the proposed configuration satisfies the required properties of the service. This checking can be done by both analytical pre/post-condition reasoning, and by running or simulating the service.

The Critique Step. If the verification step fails the critique step analyses the reasons for this failure: it indicates which parameters may have to be revised in order to repair these failures.

The Modify Step. determines alternative values for the parameters identified as culprits by the critique step. After executing the modification step, the PCM method continues again with a verify step. This loop is repeated until all required properties of the service are satisfied.

This method for solving configuration problems has a number of important characteristics: (i) it tries to *incrementally* improve a configuration: when the current candidate configuration does not meet all requirements, it is not thrown away, but instead it is modified in incremental steps. (ii) each of the four steps exploit specific domain knowledge about the objects-to-be-configured (in our case Web services in general, and classification-services in particular). Such domain knowledge is used to propose a good initial configuration, to analyse potential causes of failure, to identify possible modifications, etc. (iii) it does not solve a configuration problem from scratch, but exploits the structure of a predefined template.

The propose-critique-modify method for Parametric Design requires specific types of configuration knowledge to drive the different steps of the configuration process

Question 2: can this PCM-knowledge be identified for realistic classes of Web services? This question will be tackled in section 4.

3   Classification: An Example Family of Web Services

In this section we will illustrate our proposal by applying it to a specific family of Web services, namely "heuristic classification services". This is a good example because:
(i) They are of general applicability and value on the Web. They are used for example, on e-commerce web-sites, to classify products into categories based on their features (price, size, performance, etc) ; in web-site personalisation, to classify pages based on occurences of keywords, date-of-writing, picture-intensity, etc ; or to classify message in streams such as email or news. based on keyword occurrences, sender, date, size etc.
(ii) Heuristic classification services are complex services that require configuration. They must be adjusted to the presence of noise in the dataset, the degree of reliability of the classification rules, the required degree of soundness and completeness of the final classification, etc. All these properties must be taken into account during service configuration.
(iii) Classification is well-studied in the AI literature, so a sufficient body of theory is available as the basis for a configuration theory [16, 17].

The common definition of classification can be found in [18]:

"To classify something it to identify it as a member of a known class. Classification problems begin with data and identify classes as solutions. Knowledge is used to match elements of the data space to corresponding elements of the solutions space, whose elements are known in advance."

More formally,

$$Classification : Observations \times Knowledge \rightarrow Classes$$

where *Observations* is a set of ⟨*feature,value*⟩-pairs, and the *Knowledge* involved is a map of sets of ⟨*feature,value*⟩-pairs to *Classes*.

3.1   Template for Classification Services

We address question 1 above: can a realistic class of classification services be described in a single template? [19] does indeed present such a general template, on which the following structure from fig. 1 is based:

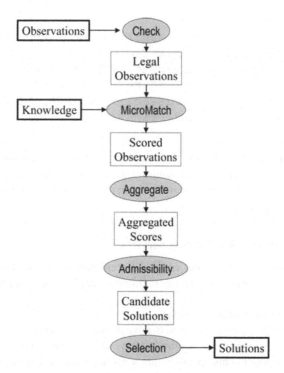

Fig. 1. Structure of classification services. The boxes with thick lines are input and output. The ovals are the parameters of the template for the family of classification services

First the observations have to be verified whether they are legal (**Check**). Each of these legal observations (⟨*feature,value*⟩-pairs) have to be scored on how they contribute to every possible solution in the solution space (MicroMatch). These individual scores are then aggregated (Aggregate). These aggregated scores are the basis for determining the candidate solutions (Admissibility). A final step (Selection) then selects among these candidate solutions the best final solutions.

This structure constitutes the overall template for classification services. Each box from fig. 1 is one parameter to configure in this fixed template.

We will now show that such a template structure can also be easily captured in current Web service description languages, such as OWL-S [20]. Any OWL-S description is conceptually divided into three sub-parts for specifying what a service does (the *profile*, used for advertising), how the service works internally (the *process model*) and how to interoperate with the service via messages (the *grounding*). We use the schematic notation for OWL-S introduced in [21]. I(.) and O(.) denote input- and output-arguments. We have used the capitals-only abbreviated version of the identifiers from figure 1 for typesetting reasons.

```
*Profile: PrClassification(I(O), I(K), O(S))
            (hasProc = CPClassification)

*ProcessModel
  CompositeProcess: CPClassification: sequence
  {AtomicProcess: APCheck(I(O), O(LO))
   AtomicProcess: APMicroMatch(I(LO), I(K), O(SO))
   AtomicProcess: APAggregate(I(SO), O(AS))
   AtomicProcess: APAdmissibility(I(AS), O(CS))
   AtomicProcess: APSelection(I(CS), O(S))
  }
```

Different forms of classification are made up of different values for the five "AtomicProcess" components (and their groundings as specific pieces of code). These AtomicProcess components are the parameters within the predefined template of the OWL-S description.

3.2   Components for Classification Services

We now give some example values of the different parameters, to illustrate the search space of the service-configuration process (more examples can be found in [22]):

Example values of the Check parameter:
• single-value: each feature is required to have at most one value.
• required-value: each feature is required to have at least one value.
• legal-feature-value(P): This specifies that a given predicate P must be true for each ⟨*feature,value*⟩-pair.

Example values of the MicroMatch parameter:
• MicroMatch-IEUM: Each feature can have the status inconsistent, explained, unexplained or missing. A feature is inconsistent w.r.t. a class if its value does not satisfy the feature condition of this class. A feature is explained w.r.t. a class if it is observed and

satisfies the feature condition of this class. A feature is missing w.r.t. a class if it is not observed yet the class has a feature condition for this feature. A feature is unexplained w.r.t. a class if it is observed yet the class does not have a feature condition for this feature. MicroMatch-IEUM computes for each feature for each class whether the feature is inconsistent, explained, unexplained or missing.

• MicroMatch-closeness: Compute for each feature per class how "close" the observed value is to the value prescribed for the class (e.g. giving a number in [-1,1], with 0 for unknown values).

*Example values of the **Aggregate** parameter:*
• Aggregate-IEUM: Collect per class the set of features that are inconsistent, explained, unexplained or missing and represent these in a 4-tuple $\langle I, E, U, M \rangle$, where I denotes the set of inconsistent features, etc.
• Aggregate-#-IEUM: Count per class the number of features that are inconsistent, explained, unexplained or missing and represent these in a 4-tuple $\langle |I|, |E|, |U|, |M| \rangle$.

*Example values of the **Admissibility** parameter:*
(The following are all taken from [18]).
• weak-coverage: Each $\langle feature, value \rangle$ pair in the observations has to be consistent with the feature specifications of the solution. In other words, a class c_1 is a solution if its set I denoting the inconsistent features of c_1 is empty ($I = \emptyset$).
• weak-relevant: Each $\langle feature, value \rangle$ pair in the observations has to be consistent with the feature specifications of the solution, and at least one feature is explained by the solution. A class c_1 is a solution if its set I denoting the inconsistent features of c_1 is empty ($I = \emptyset$), and its set E denoting the explained features is not empty ($|E| > 0$).
• strong-coverage: These are weak-coverage solutions with no unexplained features ($U = \emptyset$).
• explanative: These are weak-coverage solutions for which no feature specifications are missing ($M = \emptyset$).
• strong-explanative: These solutions satisfy both the requirements of strong-coverage and of explanative.

*Example values of the **Selection** parameter:*
• IEUM-size: Compute the minimal element under the lexicographic ordering on $\{|I|, -|E|, |U|, |M|\}$ using $<$. In other words: minimising inconsistent features, maximising explained features, and minimising unexplained and missing features (in order of importance).
• IE-size: As IEUM-size, but disregarding unexplained and missing features.
• Single-solution: Simply choose an arbitrary solution from the candidates.
• No-ranking: Return all candidate solutions, ie. there is no ranking at all, and all values are considered as "best" scores.

We have illustrated a number of instances of the parameters that can be used in the overall template for classification services. We now show that such parameter instances can be described in current Web service description languages (e.g. OWL-S). Below we give an example of a Check parameter.

```
*Profile: PrSingleValue(I(O), O(LO))
          (hasProc = APSingleValue)
          (serviceCategory = Check)
 *ProcesModel:
  AtomicProcess: APSingleValue(I(O), O(LO))
 *Grounding:
  GrSingleValue(APSingleValue--> single-value)
```

This describes an atomic service with a specific implementation (*grounding*). The service is registered to belong to the given serviceCategory Check. This allows the configuration process to discover that this specific component can be used to instantiate the AtomicProcess "APCheck" in the overall ProcessModel.

Summary: In summary, in this section we have shown that it is possible to develop a general structure (template) for a complex family of Web services (in our case for heuristic classification services), and that there exists a large variety of possible values for the individual components ("parameters") in this general template. This means that we can apply parametric design for constructing and adjusting classification Web services. We have also shown that both the the general structure and the individual components can be described in OWL-S.

4   PCM-Broker Knowledge

In the previous section, we have seen that indeed Web services can be represented in the form that is required for parametric design.

The question still remains if it is possible to identify the knowledge required for the propose-critique-modify method and each of its four steps (i.e. question 2 identified in section 2.2). We will now show that this is indeed the case, by giving parts of the PCM knowledge required to configure classification services. (Again, more examples can be found in [22]).

Example Propose knowledge for the Admissibility parameter:
• The following values for the Admissibility parameter are compatible with the value MicroMatch=MicroMatch-IEUM: weak-relevant, weak-coverage, strong-coverage and explanative.
• if many ⟨*feature,value*⟩ pairs are irrelevant, then do not use strong-coverage (because strong-coverage insists on an explanation for *all* observed features, including the irrelevant ones).

Example Propose knowledge for the Selection parameter:
• The following values for the Selection parameter are compatible with the value MicroMatch=MicroMatch-IEUM: IEUM-size, IE-size, no-ranking and single-solution.
• if not all observations are equally important, then do not use Selection=IEUM-size, since IEUM-size simply counts numbers of features in each category, given them all equal weight.

Example Critique knowledge for the Selection parameter:
- When the solution set is too small (e.g. empty) or too large (e.g. > 1), then adjust the Admissibility or the Selection parameter. *How* this adjustment should be done is part of the modify-knowledge for these parameters:

Example Modify knowledge for the Admissibility parameter:
- If the solution set has to increased (reduced) in size, then the value for the Admissibility parameter has to be moved down (up) in the following partial ordering:

$$\text{weak-coverage} \prec \text{weak-relevant}$$
$$\text{weak-coverage} \prec \text{strong-coverage} \prec \text{strong-explanative}$$
$$\text{weak-coverage} \prec \text{explanative} \quad\quad \prec \text{strong-explanative}$$

- If the configuration Admissibility=explanative gives no solutions, then choose Admissibility=strong-coverage. (This amounts to shifting from a conjunctive reading of class-definitions in terms of ⟨*feature,value*⟩ pairs to a disjunctive reading).

Example Modify knowledge for the Selection parameter:
- If the solution set has to be increased (reduced), then the value for the Selection parameter has to be moved down (up) in the following ordering:

$$\text{no-ranking} \prec \text{IE-size} \prec \text{IEUM-size} \prec \text{single-solution}$$

Conclusion: These examples affirmatively answer our question 2 from section 2.2. A PCM-broker requires knowledge about component-services in order to perform its task, and it has turned out to be possible to identify such knowledge for a realistic class of classification Web services.

This leaves open the question on how this knowledge is best represented in the broker. However, it should be clear that OWL-S is *not* the language in which this knowledge is expected to be stated. OWL-S is only used (1) to specify the general schema for the overal service to be configured (in the form of a `CompositeProcess`, and (2) to specify the seperate atomic services that can be used to fill out this general schema (in the form of a `AtomicProcess`). The implementation behind our example scenario in section 5 uses an ad-hoc Prolog representation for the brokering knowledge, but more principled representations can be found in the Knowledge Engineering literature

5   An Example Scenario

In section 3 we have already argued that classification services are used in many Web service scenario's (e-commerce, personalisation, alerting-services, etc.). To test our proposed brokering approach to Web service composition, we have chosen to configure the services needed to support Programme Chairs of major scientific conferences. Such services are available on commercial websites[1]. Currenlty, it is up to the programme

---

[1] e.g. `http://www.conferencereview.com/`

chair to configure the services offered by such sites. Ideally, such web-services should be configured in a (semi-)automatic scenario, which is what we will investigate in this section.

All scientific conferences are in essence similar, yet no two are exactly the same. Papers are always received, classified into areas, and allocated to reviewers, but the details of this process vary greatly: how many areas are available, how are they characterised, are papers allowed to fall under multiple areas, etc. This makes classification of conference papers a good example case for a parametric-design broker: a generally valid template, but with so much variation that a non-trivial configuration process is required.

In our experiment, we have emulated the paper-classification process for the ECAI 2002 conference. There were 605 submissions to ECAI 2002, each characterised by a set of author-supplied keywords, i.e. each keyword is a ⟨*feature,value*⟩-pair with value either 0 (keyword absent) or 1 (present). In total, 1990 keywords were given by authors. These had to be mapped onto 88 classes ("topic areas"): 15 broad classes which were further subdivided into 73 more specific classes. Of the 650 papers, 189 were classified by hand by the Programme Chair. These classifications can be considered as a golden standard.

Requirement 1: The classification service must classify each paper in at least one of the 15 major categories (since these reflected the structure of the programme committee).
Requirement 2: The service must reproduce the Chair's solution on the 189 handclassified papers.

Important characteristics of this domain are that:
Characteristic 1: The feature-values are often noisy (authors choose remarkably bad keywords to characterise their paper), and
Characteristic 2: It is hard to determine in advance what the required classification mechanism should be. Requiring all keywords of a paper to belong to a solution class might be too strict, resulting in many unclassified papers, and violating requirement 1. But requiring only a single keyword to appear might well be too liberal, causing violation of requirement 2. Again, these characteristics ensure that this domain is indeed suited for a dynamic configuration of the classification process.

We now discuss the iterative service-configuration process performed by our PCM broker. The scenario is summarised in the table below:

Iteration	Answers	Golden Standard	Modification
1	**0 (0%)**	0 (0%)	Admissibility
2	**93 (15%)**	16 (8%)	Admissibility
3	595 (98%)	**81 (45%)**	Selection
4	595 (98%)	**103 (54%)**	Selection
5	595 (98%)	**145 (76%)**	Selection
6	595 (98%)	**169 (89%)**	

• **Propose₁:** The broker generates an initial configuration. Based on the domain characteristics described above, a simple Check-parameter checks whether all features have at most one 0/1-value. The default-choice MicroMatch=MicroMatch-IEUM is taken, with the corresponding value Aggregate=Aggregate-IEUM. Of the values for the Admissibility parameter that are compatible with the chosen MicroMatch method, the broker initially takes the most conservative choice: Admissibility=explanative. The given requirements and domain characteristics do not strongly favour any particular value for the Selection parameter, so the broker chooses the default-value Selection=single-solution.

- **Verify$_1$:** The broker now determines that this initial choice is not very successful (see the first entry in the table): no papers are assigned to any class, violating both requirement 1 and 2.
- **Critique$_1$:** The broker now determines which parameter has to be adjusted. Increasing the number of solutions can be realised by adapting the Selection-criterion and by adapting the Admissibility-criterion.
- **Modify$_1$:** Since the number of solutions has to increase, it is attractive to adopt Admissibility=strong-coverage (switching from a conjunctive to a disjunctive reading of the class definitions in terms of keywords).
- **Verify$_2$:** This does indeed improve the results of the classification (2nd iteration in the table above), but not enough. Both requirements are still strongly violated.
- **Critique$_2$:** Again the broker decides to adjust the Admissibility-criterion.
- **Modify$_2$:** The next value that is one step weaker than the current choice is Admissibility=weak-coverage.
- **Verify$_3$:** Now requirement 1 is all but fulfilled, but requirement 2 still fails (iteration 3 in the table).
- **Critique$_3$:** An option to remove this failure is again to increase the set of solutions. Since the value Admissibility=weak-coverage cannot be reasonably weakened anymore, the broker decides to adapt the Selection-parameter.
- **Modify$_3$:** The next option down from the current value is Selection=IEUM-size.
- **Verify$_4$:** Although increasing, the Golden Standard is not yet achieved (only 45%).
- **Critique$_4$:** By the same reasoning as in *Critique$_3$*, the broker decides to further adjust the Selection-parameter.

After a repeated series of six of such cycles, the broker finally arrives at a web-configuration that satisfies requirements 1 and 2 to a sufficient degree.

A snapshot of part of the broker's searchspace for this scenario is displayed in figure 2: at some point in the brokering process, a particular service configuration consists of a certain set of components, say $\langle c_1, c_2, c_3, c_4, c_5, c_6 \rangle$, with each of the c_i being a value for the corresponding parameter in the template from figure 1. At that point, the verify step detects this configuration fails to satisfy requirement 1. An alternative path in this search space would be to notice that the other requirement is not satisfied. If all requirements had been satisfied, that would have lead to the current configuration $\langle c_1, c_2, c_3, c_4, c_5, c_6 \rangle$ as a terminal node in the search space. After noticing the failure to comply with requirement 1, a subsequent critique step determines the parameters that may be the culprit for this failure. Again, it is a matter of search strategy to decide which culprit to choose. Each of these choices leads to a subsequent modify step to repair the identified culprit. In our scenario, the broker decides to identify the Admissibility-criterion as the culprit. The modify step then has three options to adjust this Admissibility-criterion, and the broker chooses to select Admissibility=strong-coverage. This results in a new configuration, $\langle c_1, c_2, c_3, \text{strong-coverage}, c_5, c_6 \rangle$, which is then again subject to a verify step in the next iteration in this search space.

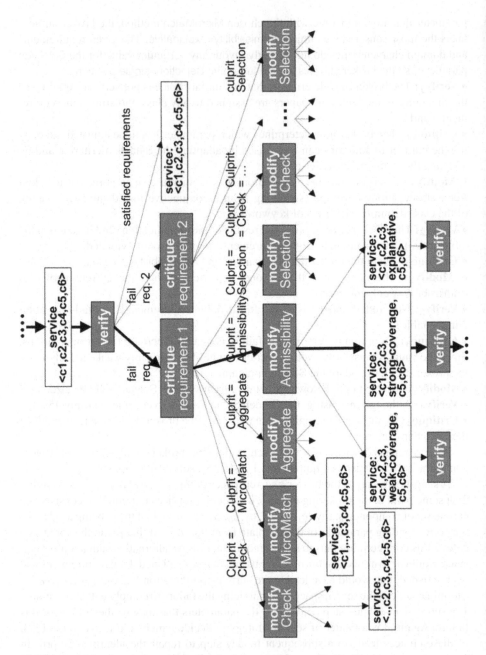

Fig. 2. Part of the search space of broker in the example scenario. Tuples $\langle c_1, c_2, c_3, c_4, c_5, c_6 \rangle$ in white boxes represent service configurations (ie *states* in the search space), while grey boxes represent steps of the propose-critique-modify method (ie *transitions* in the search space). The thick arrows indicate the path in the search space chosen by the broker in the example scenario, while thin arrows indicate possible alternatives in this search space

The entire scenario above is implemented in SWI-Prolog[2] The PCM-broker uses the template for classification services from figure 1, and a library of service-components much larger than those described in section 3, together with brokering knowledge as described in section 4.

The scenario from this section illustrates that indeed: (i) the broker configures a Web service by iteratively adjusting a fixed template of the service, and (ii) the broker uses extensive knowledge of the constituent services used to fill the parts of this template. This substantiates our metaphor in section 1 that our configuration process is "knowledge-intensive brokering", and not "generalised planning".

6   Limitations

As stated in the introduction, our approach to web-service configuration is based on earlier work on configuring reusable components of knowledge-based systems. Consequently, our proposal suffers from a number of limitations causes by mismatches between the old setting and the new one. We will now discuss some of these limitations.

The most obvious problem with our approach is the amount of high quality knowledge that the broker must be equipped with. This concerns both the general template (fig. 1) and the knowledge required to drive the propose-critique-modify steps (section 4). On the one hand, this meta-knowledge makes our approach to web-service configuration more computationally feasible then the generic planning approach, on the other hand the costs of acquiring this knowledge may well be prohibitive in a web-service scenario.

A second problem concerns that fact that candidate configurations are tested by actually executing them (the "verify"-step). In application domains where the service execution has irreversible effects in the real world, such multiple trials of a web-service would not be allowed (think for example what this would do to credit-card payments!). In such domains, the verification step must be done entirely through reasoning in the broker. Our previous experience in writing brokers ([10]) indicates that sufficiently strong verification knowledge will be very hard to obtain.

A final and more subtle problem concerns the fact that the current broker knowledge refers to individual web-service components by their name (see the examples in section 4). This is reasonable in a library-setting (as in the origins of our work in [10]), where the broker can be assumed to know which components are available. However, this is unrealistic in an open-world web-service scenario, where the broker cannot be assumed to know beforehand all the component services it has available for configuration. Ideally, new component services should be able to register themselves with the broker, declaring their type and properties, enabling the broker to include them in any informed choice it makes. This requires two changes over our current meta-knowledge: Firstly, the components must explicitly state their functional properties when they register themselves. Although principle in possible, current web-service languages like OWL-S do not provide any agreed-upon formalism for stating such functional properties [21]. Secondly, the broker must then use these properties to derive relations between components, such as the partial orderings in section 4, instead of having been given

---

[2] http://www.swi-prolog.org/

these relations explicitly, as is the case now. Of course, deriving such relations from the properties of the individual component-services would be a very hard reasoning task (and is currently done by the knowledge engineers that were building the broker (= us)).

7 Conclusion

In this paper, we have proposed an architecture for Web service brokers. The central idea is that a broker performs a parametric design task. This significantly reduces the complexity of the broker's task, for two reasons:

First, a broker no longer performs a completely open design task (as in more main-stream planning-style approaches to Web service configuration). Instead, the task of the broker is limited to choosing parameters within a fixed structure. This requires that the "Web service to be configured" can be described in terms of such a parameterised structure. For the case of classification Web services, we have shown that these can indeed be represented in this way, using current Web service description languages as OWL-S.

Secondly, viewing brokering as parametric design gives a reasoning model for the broker: propose-critique-modify (PCM) is a well-understood method for parametric design tasks, and can be exploited as the basis for the broker. PCM brokering offers the possibility of dynamically adapting the Web service on the basis of an assessment of the results of executing an earlier configuration. To this end, the required knowledge for the PCM method must be made available to the broker.

We have shown that for configuring heuristic classification tasks, this knowledge can be made sufficiently precise to be useable in an automated broker.

We have shown the feasibility of our approach by describing a specific broker that configures and adapts a classification service to be used for a realistic task, namely the classification of papers submitted to a large AI conference. In a number of iterations, our broker is able to increase the quality of the classification by successive reconfigurations.

We feel confident that this approach to Web service configuration is applicable in more than just our single example scenario (see for example our own work on diagnostic reasoners [10] and work by others on general task models [6]).

Our experience in realising the example scenario is that the main difficulty with the proposed approach lies in the identification of the knowledge for the critique and revise steps: if certain requirements are not met by the current service-configuration, which knowledge must be exploited to identify and repair the current configuration in order to improve its performance. Although we have now successfully met this challenge in two separate domains (diagnostic and classification reasoning), only further experiments can tell if our proposal is indeed generally applicable across a wide variety of Web services.

Acknowledgements. This research was partially supported by the European Commission through the IBROW project (IST-1999-19005). Enrico Motta designed and implemented the library of classification components. Anjo Anjewierden implemented the feature extraction module applied to ECAI manuscripts. The PCM implementation was based on an unpublished design of Guus Schreiber. Machiel Jansen provided useful insights in the nature of classification. Marta Sabou advised us on the use of OWL-S. We also thank three anonymous reviewers for their insightful suggestions on how to improve this paper.

References

1. M. Kiefer. Message to swsl-committee@daml.org, May 14, 2003.
2. Sirin, E., Hendler, J., Parsia, B.: Semi-automatic composition of web services using semantic descriptions. In: Web Services: Modeling, Architecture and Infrastructure workshop in conjunction with ICEIS2003. (2003)
3. Narayanan, S., McIlraith, S.: Simulation, verification and automated composition of web services. In: Proc. of the Eleventh International World Wide Web Conference, Honolulu (2002)
4. Wu, D., Sirin, E., Parsia, B., Hendler, J., Nau, D.: Automatic web services composition using SHOP2. In: Proceedings of Planning for Web Services Workshop in ICAPS 2003. (2003)
5. Sheshagiri, M., desJardins, M., Finin, T.: A planner for composing service described in daml-s. In: Proceedings Workshop on Planning for Web Services, International Conference on Automated Planning and Scheduling, Trento (2003)
6. Schreiber, G., Akkermans, H., Anjewierden, A., de Hoog, R., Shadbolt, N., de Velde, W.V., Wielinga., B.: Knowledge Engineering and Management: The CommonKADS Methodology. ISBN 0262193000. MIT Press (2000)
7. Chandrasekaran, B.: Generic tasks as building blocks for knowledge-based systems: The diagnosis and routine design examples. In: The Knowledge Engineering Review. ? (1988) 183–210
8. Benjamins, V.R.: Problem Solving Methods for Diagnosis. PhD thesis, University of Amsterdam, Amsterdam, The Netherlands (1993)
9. Valente, A., Benjamins, R., de Barros, L.N.: A library of system-derived problem-solving methods for planning. International Journal of Human Computer Studies 48 (1998) 417–447
10. ten Teije, A., van Harmelen, F., Schreiber, G., Wielinga, B.: Construction of problem-solving methods as parametric design. International Journal of Human-Computer Studies, Special issue on problem-solving methods 49 (1998)
11. McIlraith, S., Son, T.: Adapting golog for composition of semantic web services. In: Proc. of the International Conference on the Principles of Knowledge Representation and Reasoning (KRR'02). (2002) 482–496
12. Mandell, D., McIlraith, S.: Adapting bpel4ws for the semantic web: The bottom-up approach to web service interoperation. In D. Fensel, C.S., Mylopolis, J., eds.: Proceedings of the International Semantic Web Conference (ISWC). Volume 2870 of LNCS., Springer Verlag (2003) 227–241
13. van Splunter, S., Sabou, M., Brazier, F., Richards, D.: Configuring web service, using structurings and techniques from agent configuration. In: Proceedings of the 2003 IEEE/WIC International Conference on Web Intelligence (WI 2003), Halifax, Canada (2003)
14. Schreiber, A., Birmingham, W.: The sisyphus-vt initiative. International Journal of Human-Computer Studies, Special issue on VT 44 (3/4) (1996) 275–280
15. Brown, D., Chandrasekaran, B.: Design problem solving: knowledge structures and control strategies. Research notes in Artificial Intelligence (1989)
16. Clancey, W.: Heuristic classification. Artificial Intelligence 27 (1985) 289–350
17. Jansen, M.: Formal explorations of knowledge intensive tasks. PhD thesis, University of Amsterdam (SWI) (2003)

18. Stefik, M.: Introduction to knowledge systems. ISBN: 1-55860-166-X. Morgan Kaufmann Publishers (1995)
19. Motta, E., Lu, W.: A library of components for classification problem solving. In: Pacific Rim Knowledge Acquisition Workshop, Sydney, Australia (2000)
20. Ankolekar, A., Burstein, M., Hobbs, J., Lassila, O., Martin, D., McDermott, D., McIlraith, S., Narayanan, S., Paolucci, M., Payne, T., Sycara, K.: Daml-s: Semantic markup for web services. In Horrocks, I., Hendler, J., eds.: Proceedings of the International Semantic Web Conference (ISWC). Volume 2342 of LNCS., Sardinia, Springer (2002) 348–363
21. Sabou, M., Richards, D., van Splunter, S.: An experience report on using daml-s. In: Workshop on E-Services and the Semantic Web (ESSW '03), The Twelfth International World Wide Web Conference., Budapest, Hungary, (2003)
22. ten Teije, A., van Harmelen, F.: Ibrow deliverable wp4.1 & 4.2: Task & method adaptation (2003)

Knowledge Modelling for Deductive Web Mining

Vojtěch Svátek, Martin Labský, and Miroslav Vacura

Department of Information and Knowledge Engineering,
University of Economics, Prague, W. Churchill Sq. 4,
130 67 Praha 3, Czech Republic
phone: +420-224095462, fax: +420-224095400
{svatek,labsky}@vse.cz, vacuram@cuni.cz

Abstract. Knowledge-intensive methods that can altogether be characterised as deductive web mining (DWM) already act as supporting technology for building the semantic web. Reusable knowledge-level descriptions may further ease the deployment of DWM tools. We developed a multi-dimensional, ontology-based framework, and a collection of problem-solving methods, which enable to characterise DWM applications at an abstract level. We show that the heterogeneity and unboundedness of the web demands for some modifications of the problem-solving method paradigm used in the context of traditional artificial intelligence.

1 Introduction

The short history of knowledge modelling is usually viewed as consisting of three periods: first, with prevalent *problem-solving modelling* and stress on traditional AI applications (from the beginning of 80s to mid 90s), second, with growing interest in *domain ontologies* and expansion to more mundane computing environments (second half of 90s), and third, in which ontologies (and to lower degree, problem-solving models) are most often built and used in connection with the *semantic web* initiative (from about 2000). While the initial concept of semantic web assumed manual creation of knowledge annotations, most recent research efforts are aimed towards large-scale *automated* [8] or at least *semi-automated* [10] annotation of websites. This makes the rich variety of website *data structures* such as HTML trees or link topologies, as well as the *processes* of their analysis, primordial knowledge modelling targets. Knowledge models of website analysis applications and tools (in combination with ontologies of the respective problem domains) could facilitate their reuse and reconfiguration for novel tasks, and thus significantly contribute to the deployment of semantic web. However, 'universal' *problem-solving methods* (PSMs), e.g. those from CommonKADS [17], are not easy to use for this purpose. This is mainly due to the heterogeneity and unboundedness of the web space, which acts as 'case data' for knowledge-based reasoning. Instead, as starting point for our knowledge modelling effort, we propose a *multi-dimensional, ontology-based framework*, which enables to characterise apparently dissimilar website analysis applications at the

E. Motta et al. (Eds.): EKAW 2004, LNAI 3257, pp. 337–353, 2004.

knowledge level. The framework is further enriched with a collection of *more specialised PSMs*.

In section 2 we explain the notion of deductive web mining (DWM) and discuss its knowledge modelling challenges. In section 3 we briefly present the history of our own DWM project named *Rainbow*, as initial motivation for DWM knowledge modelling. In section 4 we describe the four-dimensional (TODD) model of DWM as main contribution of the paper. In section 5 we discuss the applicability of traditional PSMs on typical DWM tasks, and attempt to formulate a collection of PSMs custom-tailored for DWM. In section 6 we describe several existing DWM applications using the TODD model. Section 7 surveys some related projects, and section 8 wraps up the paper.

2   Deductive Web Mining and Its Knowledge-Level View

To our knowledge, there has been no concise term that would overarch various methods aiming at automated analysis (or, semantic annotation) of the web space. We therefore suggest a novel label, that of *Deductive Web Mining* (DWM). Our use of adjective 'deductive' is only meant as contrast to *inductive* web mining (i.e. Web Mining in the usual sense); it should thus not be rigorously identified with *deduction in formal logic*[1]. It is inspired by the notion of Deductive *Text* Mining introduced by Kodratoff [12] as synonym to Information Extraction and explained as 'finding instances of a predefined pattern in a set of texts'. Deductive Web Mining is however, in our interpretation, not just another word for Web Information Extraction. While Information Extraction from the web typically amounts to extraction (from another viewpoint, semantic annotation) of *texts* embedded in web pages, our notion of DWM covers all activities where *pre-existing patterns are matched with web data*, be they of textual, graphwise or, say, bitmap nature. DWM thus subsumes Web Information Extraction, and differs from Inductive Web Mining, which aims at discovery of *previously unseen, frequent* patterns in web data. This does not mean that the 'pre-existing patterns' in DWM have necessarily been hand-crafted: inductive learning of patterns (or analogous structures/models) is merely viewed as an activity separate from DWM ('reasoning').

The knowledge engineering research on problem-solving modelling during the 90s was quite systematic, and it is likely to have covered most typical *ways of reasoning* in knowledge-based applications, in a relatively domain-neutral fashion. The aspect in which DWM reasoning might differ is thus merely related to the nature of underlying *data*. Traditional PSMs typically deal with rather compact *objects* with a restricted number of *features*. This holds not only for 'System Analysis' tasks (referring e.g. to the CommonKADS library [17]) such as Diagnosis or Assessment, but also for 'System Synthesis' tasks, e.g. for input

---

[1] Web data structures are 'symptoms' of underlying 'causes' (intentions of website designers), i.e. the reasoning in DWM is rather *abductive*. Yet, some known variants of deduction, such as the *default logic*, might be highly relevant for DWM.

components in Planning or Scheduling. If larger structures appear, it is typically only as *static roles* (in KADS sense), and they are relatively *homogeneous*, such as causal networks in Diagnosis. In contrast, the World-Wide Web is a single but extremely *large structure*, consisting of an enormous number of *heterogeneous* and *intertwined* objects, such as pages, hyperlinks, HTML trees, blocks of free text, URLs or bitmap images. There is no clear notion of *object-feature relation*; instead, there are the (sometimes substitutable) notions of parthood and adjacency linking *pairs of objects*. Inference targeted on a single object may easily become infinite, and certainly comprises aspects of *recursion* (at the task-subtask level). As we show in section 5, the recursive nature of DWM may even question the strict dichotomy of (non-atomic) *tasks* and *atomic inferences*, imposed by KADS-style modelling.

3   Background: The *Rainbow* Project

The *Rainbow*[2] project represents a family of more-or-less independent web-mining projects undertaken by the same research group[3]. Their unifying principles are commitment to *web-service* (WSDL/SOAP) front-end and agreement on shared *upper-level ontology*. Furthermore, for each *application*, the developers involved also agree on a *domain* and share the source of training/testing *data*. Otherwise, the *formal principles* of analysis methods vary (from linguistic through statistical to e.g. graph theory), and so does the *representation of data*, also nicknamed as 'web view' (such as free text, HTML trees or link topology). In this way, the natural complementarity and/or supplementarity of information inferable from different types of web data can be exploited.

Three application areas have been attacked so far: recognition of web *pornography*, extraction of information about *companies* and extraction of product offers from *bicycle* catalogues. All applications can be characterised as DWM, mostly complemented with inductive learning of patterns. Different *pornography-recognition* services, specialised in image bitmap analysis, HTML structure analysis, link topology analysis, META tag analysis and URL analysis, have been executed more-or-less standalone. Empirical tests however proved that the synergy of different methods significantly improves recognition accuracy [22]. Very simple analysis of *company information* (at the level of single pages) was designed to be executed and integrated via a web browser plug-in, which displayed the structured list of extracted information in a side bar [19]. Finally, the application specialised in *bicycle offer extraction* is currently being sewn together, including (in addition to 'core' DWM tools)

---

[2] Stands for 'Reusable Architecture for INtelligent Brokering Of Web information access'. Beyond the acronym (shared with a host of other research projects), the name is motivated by the idea that multiple independent tools for analysis of web data should synergistically 'shed light' on the web content, in a similar way as the different colours of the rainbow join together to form the visible light.

[3] Knowledge engineering group at the University of Economics, Prague.

- *the full-text database engine AmphorA* [13], storing web pages as XHTML documents, in a native XML database, as source-data back-end,
- a simple *control procedure* (hard-coded in Java), calling individual DWM tools, and integrating and saving the results,
- the RDF repository *Sesame* [4] for storing the results corresponding to a 'bicycle-offer' ontology (RDF Schema), and, finally,
- an (HTML+JSP) *semantic query interface* with pre-fabricated templates, shielding the user from the underlying RDF query language[4] and enabling a simple form of navigational retrieval [20].

Results of experiments carried out with various DWM tools within the *Rainbow* project were summarised in [19], while [18] refers about synergistic evaluation of multiple tools in a 'company-profile-extraction' task. More information can be found at the project homepage http://rainbow.vse.cz. In the rest of the paper, we will use applications of *Rainbow* (beside other applications reported in the literature) to illustrate our knowledge modelling concepts.

4   The *TODD* Framework for Deductive Web Mining

Our framework should enable to position any DWM tool or service within a four-dimensional space. The dimensions of the space correspond to the following:

1. Abstract *task* accomplished by the tool. So far, we managed to characterise any concrete DWM task as instance of either:

   - *Classification* of a web object into one or more pre-defined classes.
   - *Retrieval* of one or more web objects.
   - *Extraction* of desired information content from (within) a web object.

   The *Classification* of an object takes as input its identifier and the list of classes under consideration. It returns one or more classes. The *Retrieval* of desired objects takes as input the (syntactic) *type* of object and *constraints* expressing its class membership as well as (part-of and adjacency) relations to other objects[5]. It outputs the *identifiers* (addresses based on URIs, XPath expressions and the like) of relevant objects[6]. The *Extraction* task takes as input the class of information to be extracted and the scope (i.e., an object)

---

[4] We currently use SeRQL, as generic language of *Sesame*, mainly because of its support for optional path expressions – a useful feature when dealing with incomplete information typically obtained via DWM.

[5] For example: "Retrieve (the XPath addresses of) those HTML tables from the given website that are immediately preceded with a possible 'Product Table Introduction Phrase' (containing e.g. the expression product*)".

[6] In the description of this as well as other tasks, we omit auxiliary information on output, such as numerical measures of relevance or uncertainty. These are also typically output by DWM applications, including those developed in *Rainbow*.

within which the extraction should take place[7]. It outputs some (possibly structured, and most often textual) *content*. In contrast to Retrieval, it does not provide the information about precise location from where the content was extracted[8].

2. Type of *object* to be classified or retrieved[9]. The types, such as Document, Hyperlink, or Phrase, represent an upper-level of abstraction of web objects; any class considered in a DWM application should be subclass of such type. This is facilitated by the fact that types correspond to classes of our Upper Web Ontology (see below). The basic assumption is that the type of object is always known, i.e. its assignment is not by itself subject of DWM.

3. *Data type and/or representation*[10], which can be e.g. full HTML code, plain text (without tags), HTML parse tree (with/without textual content), hyperlink topology (as directed graph), frequencies of various sub-objects or of their sequences (n-grams), image bitmaps or even URL addresses.

4. *Domain* to which the task is specific. In this paper, we will consider the domains addressed by our as well as other analysed applications: company sites with product information (incl. specialisations to bicycle offer and casting industry), pornography sites and sites of computer science departments (plus the associated domain of bibliography).

We thus denote the framework as '*task-object-data(type)-domain*' (TODD). Its dimensions are to high degree independent, e.g. *object type* is only partially correlated with *data type*. For example, a document may be classified based on its HTML code, URL, META tag content or position in topology. Similarly, a hyperlink can be classified based on its target URL or the HTML code of source document (e.g. the menu structure containing the respective <a> tag). Clearly, not all points of the 4-dimensional space are meaningful. For instance, a META tag content cannot directly be used to classify a hyperlink, since the relation of a META tag (being a special class of HTML document fragment) to a hyperlink is only intermediated by a whole HTML document.

Table 1 demonstrates how the four-dimensional space of the TODD model can be visualised, on the example of services implemented within the *Rainbow* applications mentioned in section 3. Rows correspond to *object types* and columns to *data/representation types*. The fields/columns are filled with corresponding *task acronyms* (hyphen-)followed with *domain acronyms*. The *task acronyms* are C for classification, R for retrieval and E for extraction (the last always pertaining to a whole column). The *domain acronyms* are Ge for general domain (universal web analysis), Po for pornography recognition, Co for general company

---

[7] For example: "Extract the occurrences of Company Name within the scope of given Company Website".

[8] This is of course merely a knowledge-level view, which does not discourage relevant DWM applications from remembering such information for technical purposes.

[9] Note that *extraction* aims at content and thus is not unambiguously associated with a particular object.

[10] We alternatively call this dimension 'web view', since the particular representation of data corresponds to a certain view of the complex structure of the web.

information extraction, and Bi for bicycle product information extraction. We omit potential columns that do not (yet) correspond to an implemented *Rainbow* service, such as HTML tree data type.

Table 1. *Rainbow* services in the TODD space

Data type / Object type	HTML code	Plain text	Frequen-cy	URL	Link topol-ogy	META tags	Image bitmap
Document collection					C-Po, R-Co		
Document			C-Po	C-Po, C-Co	C-Po	C-Po	
Document fragment	C-Po,						
Hyperlink				C-Co			
Phrase		C-Co					
Image							C-Ge, C-Po
Extraction	E-Bi	E-Co				E-Co	

The TODD framework by itself does not offer any added value to DWM application design until augmented with appropriate *ontologies*. As example we can take the *Rainbow* system of ontologies[11], which is indeed structured in correspondence to the dimensions of the TODD framework. First, the three *abstract tasks* are modelled in a *task ontology*, in terms of their inputs and outputs. Furthermore, the distinction of *data types* and *domains* suggests decomposition into four layers of ontologies. The upper two layers, *Upper Web Ontology* and *Partial Generic Web Models*, are domain–independent and therefore reusable by applications from all domains. The lower two layers, *Partial Domain Web Models* and *Domain Web Ontology* add information specific to a given domain (e.g. product information or pornography). In addition, the top-most and bottom-most layers, *Upper Web Ontology* and any *Domain Web Ontology*, cover all data/representation types, while the middle ones consist each of multiple partial models; each partial model is specific for one data type such as HTML code or link topology. The remaining dimension of the TODD model, *object type*, is reflected in the internal structure of the Upper Web Ontology (see the UML diagram at Fig. 1). The content of each of the four layers of the *Rainbow* system of ontologies as well as their mutual relations and their development process are described in [15]. The ontologies are not yet used for automated reasoning;

---

[11] Available in DAML+OIL at http://rainbow.vse.cz.

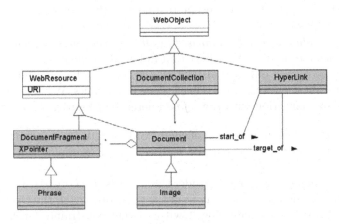

Fig. 1. Upper Web Ontology of *Rainbow*

they merely provide a basis for information exchange among the developers of *Rainbow* tools and applications. Precisely defined *object types and classes* allow for synergy of different tools in the reasoning phase, while precisely defined *data type/representation* is important for sharing training/testing data in the learning phase of individual tools.

5 Problem-Solving Methods of Deductive Web Mining

The textual descriptions of three core *tasks* introduced in the previous section only specify the *input* and *output* of these tasks, in a style analogous to CommonKADS [17]. A natural next step towards reusable knowledge models thus seems to be the identification of appropriate *problem-solving methods*, and their representation in the form of inference and task diagrams.

Among the three tasks, it is *Classification* that is most appropriate for comparison with existing PSM research. Classification problem solving was recently systematised by Motta&Lu [16]. Their taxonomy of classification problems is mainly derived from the presence (or absence) of a few key features:

1. *Whether the goal is to find one, all or the best solution.* This distinction can well be ported to the DWM context.
2. *Whether all observables are known at the beginning or are uncovered opportunistically (typically at some cost) during the problem solving process.* In DWM, the latter is typically the case (provided we interpret 'observables' as the web objects themselves); the cost is however only associated with download/analysis time, and its increase is smooth—unlike e.g. medical applications, where addition of a single examination may lead to abrupt increase of (financial or social) cost.
3. *Whether the solution space is structured according to a refinement hierarchy.* Presence of class hierarchy is quite typical in DWM; in the *Rainbow*

project, it is reflected in concept taxonomies that constitute our ontology, see Section 4.

4. *Whether solutions can be composed together or each presents a different, self-contained alternative.* We believe that in DWM, elementary classification will mostly be carried out over disjoint classes, but can be superposed by multi-way classification with non-exclusive class taxonomies. We discuss this option below, in connection with the *refine* inference of Heuristic Classification.

Let us now present a collection of eight PSMs for DWM. It is rather tentative, yet seems to cover a large part of realistic cases; examples will be given in section 6.

For *Classification*, we could consider three PSMs. *Look-up based Classification* amounts to picking the whole content of the given object (cf. the Overall Extraction PSM below), and comparing it with content constraints (such as look-up table), which yields the class; for example, a phrase is a Company Name if listed in business register. *Compact Classification* also corresponds to a single inference, it is however not based on simple content constraints but on some sort of computation (e.g. Bayesian classification), which is out of the scope of the knowledge modelling apparatus. Finally, *Structural Classification* corresponds to classification of an object based on the classes of related objects (sub–objects, super–objects and/or neighbours). It is thus decomposed to *retrieval* of related objects, their *individual classification*, and, finally, evaluation of *global classification patterns* for the current object. It is therefore *recursive*[12]: its 'inference structure' typically contains full-fledged (Direct) Retrieval and Classification tasks. We can also compare Structural Classification with the well-known Clancey's *Heuristic Classification* (HC) [6], consisting of *abstract, match* and *refine* inferences; note that HC was also chosen as the default PSM for classification by Motta&Lu [16], who defined all other models as its reductions. In (DWM) Structural Classification, the *abstract* inference is replaced with *classify* inferences applied on related (contained and/or adjacent) objects; this is due to the 'object-relation-object' (rather than 'object-feature-value') character of web data representation. The *match* inference from HC corresponds to 'evaluation of global classification patterns'. Finally, a *refinement* from general to case-specific solution might rather have the form of classification according to *multiple hierarchies* in DWM. The object is then assigned to the class that is defined as intersection of both original classes. For example, in the pornography application (section 6.1), an object classified as Image Gallery may also be independently classified as Scarce Text Fragment, which yields the class Porno Index.

For *Extraction*, there will be again three PSMs, rather analogous to those of Classification. *Overall Extraction* amounts to picking the whole content of the given object. *Compact Extraction* corresponds to a single inference based on

---

[12] The notion of recursion previously appeared in knowledge modelling literature, e.g. in the form of Systematic Refinement as form of classification [21]. Here, however, the problem is more severe, since a recursively processed data structure appears in a dynamic rather than static role (in the CommonKADS sense).

possibly complex computation, which directly returns the content of specific sub-object/s of the given 'scope' object. Finally, *Structural Extraction* corresponds to extraction of information from an object via focusing on its certain sub-objects. Such objects have first to be *retrieved*, then lower-grained *extraction* takes place, and, finally, multiple content items possibly have to be *integrated*. Structural Extraction is thus equally recursive as Structural Classification.

Finally, let us first introduce two PSMs for the *Retrieval* task. The upper inference structure[13] at Fig. 2 corresponds to Direct Retrieval and the lower

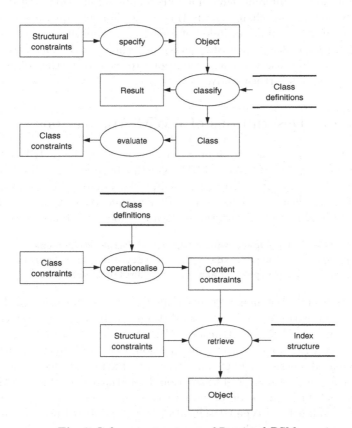

Fig. 2. Inference structures of Retrieval PSMs

one to Index-Based Retrieval, respectively. The names of inferences (in ovals) are mostly borrowed from the CommonKADS library [17], while the knowledge roles are more DWM-specific. In *Direct Retrieval*, potentially relevant objects are first retrieved based on structural (parthood and adjacency) constraints,

---

[13] We did not show inference structures for Classification and Extraction, due to limited space as well as due to incompatibility of their structural variants with the CommonKADS notation, see below.

and then classified. Objects whose classes satisfy the class constraints are the output of the method. In the absence of class constraints, the method reduces to the 'specify' inference. In *Index-based Retrieval*, the (abstract) class constraints are first operationalised so that they can be directly matched with the content of objects. Then the objects are retrieved in an index structure (which is considered as separate from the web space itself), possibly considering structural constraints (provided structural information is stored aside the core index).

An interesting issue related to the representation of above PSMs is the possible interaction of different 'time horizons' in one application; static roles may become dynamic when changing the time scale. For example, a typical DWM application may first build an index of a part of the website (or learn class definitions from a labelled subset of objects), and then use the index to efficiently retrieve objects (or use the class definitions to classify further objects). This interaction deserves further study.

6   Example Descriptions of DWM Applications

Let us now describe concrete applications in terms of the TODD framework, including the mapping of tasks to PSMs. For this purpose, we will use an ad hoc semi-formal language with Prolog-like syntax. Its building blocks are *decompositions* of tasks ('heads of clauses') to ordered sequences of subtasks ('bodies of clauses'). Individual task descriptions ('literals') look as follows, respectively:

```
Cla?(<obj_var>, <obj_type>, <data_type>, <domain>, <classes>)
Ret?(<obj_var>, <obj_type>, <data_type>, <domain>, <constraints>)
Ext?(<obj_var>, <obj_type>, <data_type>, <domain>, <content>)
```

The 'predicate' (task name) corresponds to the first dimension in the TODD framework. An extra letter is used to distinguish the PSMs introduced in the previous sections: ClaS for Structural Classification, ClaL for Look-up based Classification, ClaC for Compact Classification; RetD for Direct Retrieval, RetI for Index-based Retrieval; ExtS for Structural Extraction, ExtC for Compact Extraction and ExtO for Overall Extraction. From the nature of the PSMs follows that each ClaS task can be decomposed to a structure including (among other) one or more subtasks of type Classification; analogously, each ExtS task can be decomposed to a structure including one or more subtasks of type Extraction. In the examples, the 'unification' of a 'goal' with a 'clause head' is always unique; the representation is only 'folded' for better readability.

The remaining three TODD dimensions are reflected by the 'arguments' <obj_type>, <data_type> and <domain>. <obj_var> is variable referring to the 'current' object of the task instance: input object in the case of Classification and output object/s in the case of Retrieval. We use object variables (and object types) even for Extraction; however, here they only refer to the scope of extraction, not to a 'current' object as in Classification and Retrieval. <classes> is the list of classes distinguished in the classification task (beside named classes, we use the symbol @other for a 'complement' class). <constraints> is the list of logical expressions determining the set of objects to be retrieved; they correspond to the knowledge roles Class Constraints (class membership restrictions) and Structural Constraints (parthood/adjacency restrictions). Finally, <content> is the list of types of content information to be extracted. For simplicity, the language does not consider the cardinality of input and output.

We first describe the *Rainbow* applications: pornography-recognition application [22] and two variants of bicycle offer extraction [20]. Then we, for better coverage, attempt to describe three DWM methods from the literature: the company website classification method by Ester et al. [9], the information extraction application for foundry websites by Krötzch & Rösner [14], and the bootstrapping approach to website information extraction by Ciravegna et al. [5]. The common aspect of all of them is the effort to overcome the limitations of single resource and/or single representation in web mining. However, the symbol-level principles of the methods are different: the first relies on probabilistic reasoning, the second on a mix of domain-specific heuristics, and the third on shallow NLP augmented with knowledge reuse. Due to limited space, we sometimes slightly simplify the structure of applications, without affecting their core principles.

6.1 Pornography-Recognition Application

The upper level of the pornography-recognition process is an instantiation of the *Structural Classification* PSM as discussed in the previous section. In order to classify the whole website (i.e. document collection), symptomatic 'out-tree' topology structures are first sought; their sources (local hubs) can possibly be identified with 'index' pages with image miniatures. To verify that, the hub is examined for presence of 'nudity' PICS rating in META tags (Look-up Classification PSM), for presence of indicative strings in the URL, and its whole HTML code is searched for 'image gallery'-like structures with low proportion of text (which distinguishes pornography from regular image galleries). The analysis further concentrates on individual pages referenced by the hub, and attempts to identify a single dominant image at each of them. The images are then analysed by (bitmap) image analysis methods; in particular, the proportion of body colour and the central position of a dominant object are assessed. In the description, we omit the 'evaluation of global classification pattern' subtasks, for brevity; their inclusion would be straightforward.

```
ClaS(DC, DocCollection, _, Pornography, [PornoSite,@other]) :-
    RetD(D1, Document, topology, General, [D1 part-of DC, LocalHub(D1)]),
    ClaS(D1, Document, _, Pornography, [PornoIndex,@other]),
    RetD(D2, Document, topology, General, [D2 follows D1]),
    ClaS(D2, Document, _, Pornography, [PornoContentPage,@other]).
% classification of index page
ClaS(D, Document, _, Pornography, [PornoIndex,@other]) :-
    ClaL(D, Document, meta, Pornography, [PornoResource,@other]),
    ClaS(D, Document, url, Pornography, [PornoResource,@other]),
    RetD(DF, DocFragment, html-txt, General, [DF part-of D, ImgGallery(DF)]),
    ClaC(DF, DocFragment, freq, General, [ScarceTextFragment,@other]).
% classification of content page
```

```
ClaS(D, Document, _, Pornography, [PornoContentPage,@other]) :-
   ClaL(D, Document, meta, Pornography, [PornoResource,@other]),
   RetD(Im, Image, html-txt, General, [Im referenced-in D]),
   ClaC(Im, Image, image, Pornography, [PornoImage,@other]).
```

6.2   Bicycle Application

Navigational Data Access. The start-up scenario for extraction of user-oriented information from bicycle-selling sites is centred around *navigation-based* access to individual pages; for the time being, we use URL analysis (admittedly, a weak method only suitable for initial prototype) for this purpose. Subsequently, statistical extraction (Hidden Markov Models) is applied to obtain structured information (products, company address), while phrasal patterns are applied on the (presumably) free text describing the overall company profile. All Retrieval tasks (for navigation-based access to pages as well as at the level of phrases in the last subtask) are mapped on the Direct Retrieval PSM. Most Extraction tasks shown correspond to Structural Extraction. However, at the lowest level, company address is obtained via Compact Extraction, and company description (sentences) are obtained via Overall Extraction. Product information is still a Structural Extraction; if we decomposed it further (not shown in the code), it would however consist of Compact Extraction followed with integration of individual information (names, prices and the like) to a more complex structure.

The real application also includes other types of analysis (topology, META tags, images). We however omit them for brevity.

```
ExtS(DC, DocCollection, _, Bicycle, [products, comp_addr, comp_descr]) :-
   ExtS(DC, DocCollection, _, Bicycle, [products]).
   ExtS(DC, DocCollection, _, Company, [comp_descr]).
   ExtS(DC, DocCollection, _, Company, [comp_addr]).
% extraction of product information from catalogue pages
ExtS(DC, DocCollection, _, Bicycle, [products]) :-
   RetD(D, Document, url, Company, [D part-of DC, ProductCatalogue(D)]),
   ExtS(D, Document, html, Bicycle, [products]).
% extraction of company address from the contact page
ExtS(DC, DocCollection, _, Bicycle, [comp_addr]) :-
   RetD(D, Document, url, Company, [ContactPage(D)]),
   ExtC(D, Document, html, Company, [comp_addr]).
% extraction of general company profile from the profile page
ExtS(DC, DocCollection, _, Bicycle, [comp_descr]) :-
   RetD(D, Document, url, Company, [D part-of DC, ProfilePage(D)]),
   RetD(P1, Phrase, text, Company, [P1 part-of D, ProfilePhrase(P1)]),
   RetD(P2, Phrase, text, General, [Sentence(P2), P1 part-of P2]),
   ExtO(P2, Phrase, text, General, [comp_descr]).
```

Index-Based Data Access. Among alternative methods of page access, we are seriously considering the one taking advantage of the available full-text database engine (AmphorA), with its capability of term indexing combined with XML indexing. The parts of website suitable for detailed extraction can be efficiently detected via lexical indicators (e.g. phrases typically occurring nearby product catalogues): some sort of XML environment of the indicators can then be submitted to the extraction tool. Since the overall structure of the application is analogous to the previous one, we only show a fragment, in which Index-based Retrieval of indicative phrases plus Index-based Retrieval of 'mark-up environment' (in a native XML database storing the HTML trees) appears.

```
...
ExtS(DC, DocCollection, _, Bicycle, [products, ...]) :-
    RetI(P, Phrase, text, Company, [P part-of DC, ProductCataloguePhrase(P)]),
    RetI(DF, DocFragment, html-tree, General, [DF contains P]),
    ExtC(DF, DocFragment, html, Bicycle, [products]),
    ...
```

6.3   Website Mining by Ester et al.

The method is not knowledge-based: it relies on Bayesian classification of individual documents (wrt. topics) over the feature space of terms, and then again on Bayesian classification, this time of the whole website (i.e. document collection) over the feature space of individual document's topics. Hence, the overall task pattern amounts to Structural Classificationsimilar to the pornography-recognition task, while the embedded (Bayesian) classifications are Compact.

```
ClaS(DC, DocCollection, _, Company, TopicSet):-
    RetD(D, Document, topology, Company, [D part-of DC]),
    ClaC(D, Document, freq, Company, TopicSet),
    ClaC(DC, DocCollection, freq, Company, TopicSet).
```

6.4   Company Profile Extraction by Krötzch and Rösner

The overall scheme is similar to the bicycle application, except that product information is only extracted from tables (via heuristics), while phrasal patterns are used in a finer way, to extract not just sentences but names of either customers or quality certificates.

```
ExtS(DC, DocCollection, _, Foundry, [products, customers, certificates]):-
    RetD(D, Document, html, Company, [D part-of DC, InfoPage(D)]),
    ExtS(D, Document, _, Foundry, [products]),
    ExtS(D, Document, _, Company, [customers]),
    ExtS(D, Document, _, Company, [certificates]).
% product information extraction
ExtS(D, Document, _, Foundry, [products]) :-
    RetD(DF, DocFragment, html, General, [DF part-of D, ContentTable(DF)]),
    ExtS(DF, DocFragment, html, Foundry, [products]).
% customer information extraction
ExtS(D, Document, _, Company, [customers]) :-
    RetD(P1, Phrase, text, Company, [P1 part-of D, CustomerPhrase(P1)]),
    RetD(P2, Phrase, parse-tree, General, [P2 depends-on P1]),
    ExtO(P2, Phrase, text, General, [customers]),
```

```
% certificate extraction
ExtS(D, Document, _, Company, [certificates]) :-
    RetD(P1, Phrase, text, Company, [P1 part-of D, QualityPhrase(P1)]),
    RetD(P2, Phrase, parse-tree, General, [CertName(P2), P2 depends-on P1]),
    ExtO(P2, Phrase, text, General, [certificates]).
```

6.5   Bootstrapping Information Extraction by Ciravegna et al.

The approach described in [5] heavily relies on knowledge reuse, thanks to the well-known redundancy of WWW information. We only describe the most elaborated part of the method, targeted at extraction of person names (additionally, various personal data and paper titles are extracted for the persons in question). First, potential names are cropped from the website, and checked against binary classification tools such as context-based named-entity recognisers (Compact Classification), as well as against public search tools (namely, online bibliographies, homepage finders and general search engines) that produce the same binary classification (person name - yes/no) as by-product of offering information on papers or homepages (i.e. Index-based Retrieval). Furthermore, for the results of general web search, the page from the given site is labelled as homepage if the name occurs in a particular (typically, heading) tag. The seed names obtained are further extended by names co-occurring in a list or in the same column of a table. Finally, potential person names from anchors of intra-site hyperlinks are added.

```
ExtS(DC, DocCollection, _, CSDept, [names]) :-
    RetD(P1, Phrase, text, General, [P1 part-of DC, PotentPName(P1)]),
    % named entity recognition for person names
    ClaC(P1, Phrase, text, General, [PName,@other]),
    % use of public search tools over papers and homepages
    RetI(P2, Phrase, freq, Biblio, P1 part-of P2, PaperCitation(P2)]),
    RetI(D, Document, freq, General,
        [P1 part-of D, D part-of DC, PHomepage(D)]),
    RetD(DF1, DocFragment, freq, General,
        [Heading(DF1), DF1 part-of D, P1 part-of DF1),
    ExtO(P1, Phrase, text, General, [names]),
    % co-occurrence-based extraction
    RetD(DF2, DocFragment, html, General,
        [ListItem(DF2), DF2 part-of DC, P1 part-of DF2]),
    RetD(DF3, DocFragment, html, General,
        [ListItem(DF3), (DF3 below DF2; DF2 below DF3)]),
    ExtS(DF3, DocFragment, text, General, [names]),
    RetD(DF4, DocFragment, html, General,
        [TableField(DF4), DF4 part-of DC, P1 part-of DF4]),
    RetD(Q, DocFragment, html, General,
        [TableField(DF5), (DF5 below DF4; DF4 below DF5)]),
    ExtS(DF5, DocFragment, text, General, [names]),
    % extraction from links
```

```
RetD(DF5, DocFragment, html, General,
      [IntraSiteLinkElement(DF5), DF5 part-of DC]),
ExtS(DF5, DocFragment, text, General, [names]),
      ...
% extraction of potential person names from document fragments
ExtS(DF, DocFragment, text, General, [names]) :-
   RetD(P, Phrase, text, General,
         [DF contains P, PotentialPersonName(P)]),
   ExtO(P, Phrase, text, General, [names]).
```

7 Related Work

In the *IBrow* project [1], operational PSM libraries have been for developed for two areas of document search/analysis: Anjewierden [3] concentrated on *analysis of standalone documents* in terms of low-level formal and logical structure, and Abasolo et al. [2] dealt with information search in multiple external resources. Direct mining of websites was however not addressed; IBrow libraries thus do not cope with the problem of web heterogeneity and unboundedness, which motivated the development of the TODD framework. Partially related is also the *OntoWebber* project [11], in which a 'website ontology' was designed. It was however biased by its application on portal building (i.e. 'website synthesis'), and thus did not fully cover the needs of automated analysis; moreover, the problem-solving side of modelling was not explicitly addressed.

8 Conclusions and Future Work

We presented a general *ontology-based knowledge-level framework* for Deductive Web Mining (DWM), determined its role with respect to KADS-style problem-solving modelling, and endowed the core DWM tasks with corresponding *problem-solving methods*. Finally, we demonstrated the usability of the framework on several examples of our own as well as others' *applications*.

Although the TODD framework seems to be useful for communication of (semi-formal) application descriptions among humans, it is desirable to proceed to its fully operational exploitation. We plan to develop a meta-level tool on the top of our *Rainbow* architecture, which would enable *formal verification* and even *semi-automated composition* of DWM applications similar to those referenced in section 6. The experience (and possibly even the tangible results) of the IBrow project might help us in this effort. We plan to transform our models to the UPML language (developed in IBrow) so as to align them with the most recent PSM research achievements. The current research on *semantic web service composition*[14] is also highly relevant.

Finally, a natural next step to DWM modelling would be to cover Inductive Web Mining as well. In a sense, our 'library' thus would be extended (taking

---

[14] See e.g. http://swws.semanticweb.org.

analogy with KADS libraries [21], [17]) to cover not only System Analysis but also System Synthesis.

Acknowledgements

The research is partially supported by the grant no.201/03/1318 of the Czech Science Foundation. The authors would like to thank Annette ten Teije and Frank van Harmelen for invaluable comments on drafts of this paper.

References

1. IBROW homepage, http://www.swi.psy.uva.nl/projects/ibrow
2. Abasolo, C., Arcos, J.-L., Armengol, E., Gómez, M., López-Cobo, J.-M., López-Sánchez, M., López de Mantaras, R., Plaza, E., van Aart, C., Wielinga, B.: Libraries for Information Agents. IBROW Deliverable D4, online at http://www.swi.psy.uva.nl/projects/ibrow/docs/deliverables/deliverables.html.
3. Anjewierden, A.: A library of document analysis components, IBrow deliverable D2b. Online at http://www.swi.psy.uva.nl/projects/ibrow/docs/deliverables/deliverables.html.
4. Broekstra, J., Kampman, A., van Harmelen, F.: Sesame: An Architecture for Storing and Querying RDF and RDF Schema. In: ISWC 2002, Springer-Verlag, LNCS 2342.
5. Ciravegna, F., Dingli, A., Guthrie, D., Wilks, Y.: Integrating Information to Bootstrap Information Extraction from Web Sites. In: IJCAI'03 Workshop on Intelligent Information Integration, 2003.
6. Clancey, W. J.: Heuristic Classification. *Artificial Intelligence*, 27 - 3, 1985, 289-350.
7. Crubézy, M. Lu, W., Motta, E., Musen, M.A.: Configuring Configuring Online Problem-Solving Resources with the Internet Reasoning Service. *IEEE Intelligent Systems*, 2 (March-April):34-42, 2003.
8. Dill, S., Eiron, N., Gibson, D., Gruhl, D., Guha, R., Jhingran, A., Kanungo, T., Rajagopalan, S., Tomkins, A., Tomlin, J., Zien, J.: SemTag and Seeker: Bootstrapping the semantic web via automated semantic annotation. In: Proc. WWW2003, Budapest 2003.
9. Ester, M., Kriegel, H.P., Schubert, M.: Web Site Mining: a new way to spot Competitors, Customers and Suppliers in the World Wide Web. In: Proc. KDD 2002.
10. Handschuh, S., Staab, S., Ciravegna, F.: S-CREAM - Semi-automatic CREAtion of Metadata. In: Proc. EKAW-2002, LNCS, Springer, 2002.
11. Jin, Y., Decker, S., Wiederhold, G.: OntoWebber: Model-Driven Ontology-Based Web Site Management. In: 1st International Semantic Web Working Symposium (SWWS'01), Stanford University, Stanford, CA, July 29-Aug 1, 2001.
12. Kodratoff, Y.: Rating the Interest of Rules Induced from Data and within Texts In: Proc. DEXA 2001, IEEE Computer Science Press, 265-269, 2001.
13. Krátký, M., Pokorný, J., Snášel, V.: Indexing XML Data with UB-trees, in: ADBIS 2002, Research Communications, Bratislava 2002.
14. Krötzch, S., Rösner, D.: Ontology based Extraction of Company Profiles. In: Workshop DBFusion, Karlsruhe 2002.
15. Labský, M., Svátek, V.: Ontology Merging in Context of Web Analysis. In: Workshop DATESO03, TU Ostrava, 2003.

16. Motta, E., Lu, W.: A Library of Components for Classification Problem Solving. In: Proceedings of PKAW 2000: The 2000 Pacific Rim Knowledge Acquisition, Workshop, Sydney, Australia, December 11-13, 2000.
17. Schreiber, G., et al.: Knowledge Engineering and Management. The CommonKADS Methodology. MIT Press, 1999.
18. Svátek, V., Berka, P., Kavalec, M., Kosek, J., Vávra, V.: Discovering company descriptions on the web by multiway analysis. In: New Trends in Intelligent Information Processing and Web Mining (IIPWM'03), Zakopane 2003. Springer-Verlag, 'Advances in Soft Computing' series, 2003.
19. Svátek, V., Kosek, J., Labský, M., Bráza, J., Kavalec, M., Vacura, M., Vávra, V., Snášel, V.: Rainbow - Multiway Semantic Analysis of Websites. In: 2nd International DEXA Workshop on Web Semantics (WebS03), Prague 2003, IEEE Computer Society Press.
20. Šváb, O., Svátek, V., Kavalec, M., Labský, M.: Querying the RDF: Small Case Study in the Bicycle Sale Domain. In: Workshop on Databases, Texts, Specifications and Objects (DATESO'04), online at http://www.ceur-ws.org/Vol-98.
21. Tansley, D.S.W., Hayball, C.C.: KBS Analysis and Design. A KADS Developer's Handbook. Prentice Hall 1993.
22. Vacura, M.: Recognition of pornographic WWW documents on the Internet (in Czech), PhD Thesis, University of Economics, Prague, 2003.

On the Knowledge Level of an On-line Shop Assistant

Nenad Stojanovic and Rudi Studer

Institute AIFB, University of Karlsruhe, Germany
{nst,rst}@aifb.uni-karlsruhe.de

Abstract. Although several approaches have been proposed for modelling an on-line shop assistant, recent customer's analyses show that they miss some assistance in the buying process. The common problem is that the behaviour of an on-line shop assistant is modelled on the procedural level, i.e. like a workflow. In this paper we present an approach that models this behaviour on the knowledge level, i.e. it takes into account not only which actions (questions) a shop assistant will perform, but also which goals he wants to achieve by taking an action. As a generic reasoning pattern of such an e-shop agent we use the cover-and-differentiate problem-solving method, a method very successfully applied in various diagnosis and classification tasks. In that way, we can (i) model the question-answering process such that the minimal set of useful questions will be provided to a user, (ii) easily reinterpret and fine-tune shopping strategies that exist in other e-shop portals and (iii) design and integrate new methods into generic reasoning pattern. We present an evaluation study which illustrates these benefits.

1 Introduction

A lot of effort has been spent in the last decade in replicating real-world shopping experience in e-commerce sites. Particularly, a number of models have been proposed to describe a real-world customer-buying process [1], [2] and several recommendation strategies have been developed to represent the background knowledge and experience of a shop assistant [3]. Most of them introduce some plausible heuristics about a user's behaviour (e.g. a user should select the most preferable product among several alternatives) and in an intensive software engineering process they implement such a solution. However, the buying process can be considered as a decision-making process in which a user "searches", regarding a problem (formulated as an inquiry/query), for a solution (represented as a relevant product). Therefore, one can abstract particular e-commerce scenarios and consider the on-line shopping problem on the *knowledge level* [4]. In such a view the goal of problem solving is not just to select one of the possible actions, but rather to construct a model of part of the world that allows the problem-solver to conclude eventually that its goals have been achieved [5]. In other words, regarding the shopping domain, instead of interviewing an experienced shop assistant about concrete questions which should be given to a customer in a particular shopping situation (for a particular request of a user) [6], one should define a model regarding goals that a shop assistant would achieve by asking

E. Motta et al. (Eds.): EKAW 2004, LNAI 3257, pp. 354–370, 2004.
© Springer-Verlag Berlin Heidelberg 2004

such questions, i.e. why he would make a question. The more abstract (knowledgeable) model means more flexible, extendable problem solving. For example, above-mentioned models of customer-buying behaviour [1], [2] define (only) a heuristic/workflow how a shop assistant resolves a request in a particular situation. Such an approach does not support either easy evaluation (since the process is not defined on an abstract level) or the maintenance (in case a new method appears) of the system.

In this paper we present an approach to model the behaviour of an on-line shop assistant on the knowledge level, using generic problem solving methods (PSM) [7] [8]. Particularly, from the knowledge level point of view the problem-solving used in the e-shopping domain might be seen as a method that searches for a set of products relevant for a set of features (properties) given by a user and that refines that set (i.e. rules out some products) by introducing new features that are relevant for the user. It corresponds to the *cover and differentiate* PSM (in the rest of the text abbreviated as *c&d*) [9], very successfully applied in various diagnosis and classification tasks, in which the *cover-task* takes a set of symptoms and produces a set of explanations that seems applicable, whereas the *differentiate-task* tries to rule out elements of this set. More precisely, we use *c&d* as the model which underlines the problem solving process of a shop assistant, whereas the knowledge used for problem-solving in *c&d* is used as a guideline for the process of eliciting users needs. In that way we define the goal an on-line shop assistant would achieve by asking a user some questions, which enables us to generate more useful questions. Consequently, we can (i) model such a conversation with a user so that minimal and complete set of questions will be generated and (ii) design new support processes for on-line shopping (e.g. comparing a product with several alternate products) which will help an on-line shop assistant to "achieve" his goal in a more efficient manner. Moreover, we can show that some popular buying models can be easily interpreted using our generic problem-solving method.

This research relies on our work on interactive query refinement [10]. The corresponding system, called eShopAgent has been implemented in the KAON framework (kaon.semanticweb.org) and we set up a case study that compares navigating through the same product database using a traditional and our approach.

The paper is organised as follows: in the second section we describe our approach in details. Section 3 contains descriptions of the implementation and the evaluation of the approach. In Section 4 we present related works and in Section 5 we give concluding remarks.

2 Modelling e-Shopping Problem-Solving on the Knowledge Level

2.1 Knowledge Level

The knowledge level [4] provides the means to 'rationalise' the behaviour of a system from the standpoint of an external observer. This observer treats the system as a 'black box' but maintains that it acts 'as if' it possesses certain knowledge about the world and uses this knowledge in a perfectly rational way toward reaching its goals (*principle of rationality[1]*). There are three different perspectives on the knowledge level: *domain model* and *task model,* that talk in a precise and systematic way about domain knowledge and goals of the system, respectively and *problem-solving method,* that relates task and domain models in order to accomplish goals. In the meantime a lot of such generic inference patterns, called *problem-solving methods (PSM)* [8], have been identified: cover and differentiate for diagnosis [9], propose and revise [9] for parametric design, skeletal-plan-refinement for hierarchical planning etc.

2.2 E-Shopping as a Problem-Solving

As already mentioned in the introduction, a buying process can be considered as a problem solving process, in which a shop assistant tries to resolve a user's "problem" regarding shopping, i.e. a user selects several product's features for which a shop assistant tries to find the most relevant ones. In order to resolve the problem in the most efficient manner, a shop assistant narrows the searching space by eliciting some additional knowledge (e.g. more relevant product's features) from the user, by asking him directly or by observing his behaviour. Obviously, the quality of that elicitation process affects the quality of the buying process, e.g. a customer may feel distrust towards the shop assistant who posts irrelevant questions [1]. However, in most on-line shop systems the communication is initiated either by an anthropomorphic shopping agent for the given domain [6], who *transfers* his knowledge into the set of questions, or by an automatic analysis of product data, e.g. using some data-mining algorithms like ID3 [11]. The drawbacks of the first approach are well-known in the knowledge acquisition community: highly expensive hard-coding of the expert knowledge that disables its reusability in similar situations. In the second case the expert background knowledge is completely missing, such that the flexibility of the solution is lost.

Fortunately, from the knowledge level point of view the solution for an effective communication seems to be very simple: if we understand the rationale *why* a knowledge is needed, we can understand *what* knowledge should be elicited. Indeed, by analysing existing e-shop portals and their "conversations" with customers, we extracted the common behaviour (rationale) of different shop assistants, which we formulate in a simplified form like: in each action an e-shop assistant performs, he tries to eliminate as much as possible irrelevant products offered to a user. Consequently, in the elicitation process (e.g. by questioning) a shop assistant tries to acquire as much as possible "eliminating" knowledge - the knowledge that can be used for efficient elimination of products irrelevant for the current user. Finally, we can abstract this behaviour to a generic inference pattern, which (1) for a set of symptoms proposes a set of explanations and than (2) seek information to eliminate irrelevant explanations. By analysing available libraries of PSMs [8], we found a very suitable inference pattern - *cover and differentiate* PSM, developed for supporting diagnosis task [9].

---

[1] The agent will select an action that according to its knowledge leads to the achievement of one of his goals

2.3 Cover-and-Differentiate PSM

c&d is a role limiting method that implements a form of heuristic classification [12].
It resolves a problem by first proposing candidates that will cover or explain the
symptoms or complaints specified by the user and then seeking information that will
differentiate the candidates. The searching method is divided into a covering and a
differentiate task. These tasks are abstractly defined as follows: the cover task takes a
set of features (symptoms) and produces a set of candidates (explanations) that seen
applicable; the differentiate task tries to rule out elements of this set. In order to
achieve these goals each task uses corresponding knowledge (covering or
differentiating). Two constraints guide and confine search in the *c&d* method towards
its goal of producing a consistent explanation [9]: *exhaustivity* - if an symptom has at
least one potential explanation, the final diagnosis must include at least one of the
these potential explanations and *exclusivity* - each symptom can be explained only by
one final explanation.

In Fig.1. we present the structural decomposition of the method. This *c&d* process
is iterative, since some of the symptoms used to differentiate the candidates often
need to be explained in a subsequent skip.

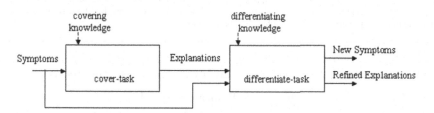

Fig. 1. The structure of the *c&d* PSM

The domain knowledge used in the method should be represented as a causal
network, which is the main source of the covering knowledge [9].

2.4 Using *c&d* for e-Shop Problem-Solving

If we consider a buying scenario as the process in which a shop assistant tries to find
suitable candidates (products) which satisfy (explain) a set of features a user prefers,
the mapping to the *c&d* domain is straightforward: features are symptoms and
products are explanations. Moreover, it has been shown that *c&d* can be applied for a
case-based assessments [13], where the task is to find the most specific decision in a
decision taxonomy that fits a specific case. This scenario is very similar to a buying
scenario. Both of above-mentioned constraints for *c&d* search are valid in the e-
shopping domain, since a user wants to find at least one relevant product and each
relevant product has to explain all requested features.

Therefore, from the structural point of view we can use *c&d* generic inference
patterns as the problem-solving method in a shopping portal. However, the main
problem is how to define covering and differentiating knowledge (relevant for *c&d*)
in the e-shopping problem solving.

2.4.1 Covering Knowledge

First of all, *c&d* requires a causal network as the covering knowledge, which is not a preferred knowledge representation paradigm in the shopping domain. Therefore we post minimal requirements on the structure of the domain knowledge in an e-shop scenario and try to prepare it for the *c&d* –based processing.

The most commonly used (knowledge) structure in the e-shopping domain can be interpreted as a light weight ontology about product's features, whereas the partial orders (taxonomy) between features are explicitly specified. The corresponding knowledge base contains a set of instances for a concrete domain (a product set). Table 1 (left column) illustrates a part of an ontology, related to the features of a car, which we consider in some examples through the paper. For example, a car can be a sport or a family car and has a colour and a luxury type.

Table 1. A part of an ontology about car

Ontology	Knowledge base
isA(Car, SportsCar) isA(Car, FamilyCar) has_colour(Car, Colour) has_luxury(Car, Luxury)	SportsCar(c1), has_colour(c1, blue) SportsCar(c2), has_luxury(c2, blue), has_luxury(c2, metallic) SportsCar(c3), has_luxury(c3, blue), has_luxury(c3, metallic), has_luxury(c3, automatic)

On the other hand, the nature of the causality in *c&d* can be expressed as:

If *cover*(S, E) then *cover*(S', E'),

where *cover*(S, E) means that a set of symptoms (S) can be explained with set of explanations (E), S and S' are sets of symptoms, E and E' are sets of explanations and S'⊆S and E⊆E'. In this case we consider that symptoms {S'\S} are caused by symptoms S.

According to the *c&d* interpretation of the e-shopping scenario, this condition can be rewritten as:

If *cover*(F, P) then *cover*(F', P'),

where F, F' are sets of features and P, P' are sets of products and F'⊆F and P⊆P' and *cover*(F, P) means that all products from P have all features from F. In such a causal case we consider that features {F'\F} are caused by features F. For the example given in Table1, one can conclude that the feature *metallic* is caused by the feature *blue*, since all cars that have feature *metallic* have the feature *blue* and not vice versa.

Therefore, we need a partial order between feature-products pairs in order to "simulate" a causal network for a whole product dataset. Comparing other e-shop applications this is a very important difference – we organize products in a causal network in the first place, whereas the most of other approaches uses a decision tree topology. In [14] we gave an overview of the advantages of using causal network topology comparing to decision trees. In the rest of this subsection we show how the causality between products' features can be derived from a product dataset.

Definition 1. A product dataset can be transformed into the structure $(\Phi, \Pi, cover)$, where:

- Φ is a set of all feature that exist in the given dataset. Features can be organized in the vocabulary V (see the definition 2).
- Π is the set of all products available in the given dataset
- $cover$ is a binary relation between a set of products and a set of features

We write $cover(f, p)$, meaning that a product p has a feature f.

Definition 2. A vocabulary on a set Φ of features is a structure:

$V := (\Phi, H)$, where H is the set of partial orders on Φ.
For the relations from the H holds:
$\forall p \in \Pi \forall f_1, f_2 \in \Phi \wedge \forall h \in H \ \ cover(f_1, p), \wedge h(f_1, f_2) \rightarrow cover(f_2, p)$

Definition 3. A product-feature pair (node) is a tuple, $N = (\Phi_x, \Pi_y)$ where:

- $\Phi_x \subseteq \Phi$, Φ_x is called a set of node_features ;
- $\Pi_y \subseteq \Pi$, Π_y is called a set of node_products; $\Pi_y = \{ p \in \Pi | (\forall f \in \Phi_x) \rightarrow cover(f, p) \}$.

In order to model causal knowledge we define two relations, equivalence and subsumption, on the set of nodes.

Definition 4. Structural equivalence ($=$) is a binary relation defined as:

$$(\Phi_{x1}, \Pi_{y1}) = (\Phi_{x2}, \Pi_{y2}) \leftrightarrow \Pi_{y1} = \Pi_{y2}, \text{ which can be written as } N_1 = N_2 \leftrightarrow \Pi_{y1} = \Pi_{y2} \tag{1}$$

Two nodes are structurally equivalent if their product sets are the same. Note that this relation is reflexive, symmetric and transitive.

Definition 5. Largest equivalent node (*len*) for the node $N_a = (\Phi_{xa}, \Pi_{ya})$ is a node

$$N_l = (\Phi_{xl}, \Pi_{yl}) \text{ such that: } \Phi_{xl} = \{ \bigcup \Phi_{xi} | \forall i \ N_i = N_l \} \text{ and } \Pi_{yl} = \Pi_{ya} \tag{2}$$

Definition 6. Structural subsumption (parent-child) is a binary relation defined as:

$$(\Phi_{x1}, \Pi_{y1}) < (\Phi_{x2}, \Pi_{y2}) \leftrightarrow \Pi_{y1} \subset \Pi_{y2}. \tag{3}$$

Two nodes are structurally subsumed if the product set of a node is subsumed by the product set of another. Note that this relation is symmetric and transitive.
For a node N_1 we define the *direct child* relation as follows:

$$N_2 <_{dir} N_1 \text{ iff } N_2 < N_1 \wedge \neg \exists N_i, N_2 < N_i < N_1 \tag{4}$$

In that case we call N_2 a direct_child of N_1.

Finally, the partial order "$<$" on the set of all nodes defines a lattice structure, which reflects the causality between features of products. In other words, it defines covering knowledge for *c&d* problem-solving in e-shopping domain. This covering knowledge is used in the cover-task of the problem-solving in order to find a set of relevant explanations (covering). Theoretically, the entire causal knowledge can be calculated using formal concept analysis FCA [15], since a set of all equivalent product-feature nodes corresponds to a formal concept. We omit here the mapping process. Since that FCA calculation can be very expensive and since we do not need the whole covering knowledge at once due to the iterative nature of the *c&d*, we can generate only a relevant portion of covering knowledge for a reasoning step. Indeed, the product-feature node N_x that contains the set of relevant products Π_x for a given set of features Φ_x (i.e. covering) can be very efficiently calculated: it is enough to find the most general largest equivalent node (*len*) whose node_features contains Φ_x, i.e.

$$N_x = len((\Phi_x, \Pi_x)).\tag{5}$$

Note that this transformation is not trivial, since it is possible that some features in a user's query are redundant or caused by some features not given in that query. For example, if a user selects the feature *metallic* ($\Phi_x = \{metallic\}$), the relevant node is ($\{metallic, blue\}, \{c_2, c_3\}$). It is important to notice that this procedure can be easily mapped into procedure for propagating symptoms through a causal network that is used in the original *c&d* method [16].

2.4.2 Differentiating Knowledge
The differentiate-task uses differentiating knowledge in order to eliminate some covering explanations generated in the cover-task. Obviously, the more explanations that are eliminated by using a differentiating knowledge, the more usability of that differentiating knowledge. In an ideal case, after applying this knowledge only one explanation should remain. In the *c&d* method such knowledge is elicited from experts in a highly interactive process of refining the knowledge base [9].

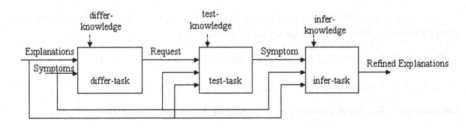

Fig. 2. The decomposition of the differentiate task of *c&d* PSM

Analogy to the *c&d* method, the differentiate-task in the e-shopping scenario consists of three subtasks represented in Fig. 2. The main problem is how to obtain the knowledge employed in these subtasks, which we discuss in next three subsections.

2.4.2.1 Differ Knowledge
This subtask finds out which new symptoms (features) should be tested (e.g. is the value of the symptom X equal Y). In a problem-solving system this task can be seen as the crucial one: a system seems to be more intelligent if it makes as less as possible tests/questions in order to conclude something.

From the knowledge level point of view, the realization of this subtask should be driven by the "principle of rationality" of the agent – in the case of a shop agent this is to eliminate as much as possible irrelevant candidates. In other words, the selection of the features for testing should be done in such a way that the results of tests would enable maximal restriction of the searching space. It is clear that the selection of features for testing has to be *fair* (*complete*) – each candidate (relevant product) has a chance to "survive". Moreover, it is clear that the number of tests should be *minimal*, since we can theoretically ask for the availability of each feature. In the e-shop domain the principle of the minimality is important due to a need to develop a buyer's information need incrementally, in the so called step-by-step manner. Briefly, on-line buyers often have a vague idea what to buy (due to the unfamiliarity with the content of the product database) or how to express their request (due to the unfamiliarity with the used vocabulary). In that case a shop assistant should ask only for features that do not imply another feature not yet considered by a user. For example, if all cars that are "metallic" have blue colour (by assuming that there are "non-metallic" blue cars) and a user does not yet set any of these features, then a "non-minimal" test is to ask: "Should the car be metallic?". An explanation is that in the case that the user does not want blue colour, the question about "metallic" feature is irrelevant. Moreover, since a shop agent tries to eliminate as much as possible products using a test, asking "Should the car be blue?" instead of the previous question, will cover all "blue-coloured" cars, inclusive all metallic cars.

A solution for this problem is to ask an expert which features should be tested in which situation. However, it can be a very expensive process and cannot guarantee a fair and minimal testing.

Another possibility is to reuse knowledge employed in the differ-task in the *c&d* method in e-shopping problem-solving. Basically, the *c&d* differ-knowledge compares *competing explanations* for a symptom directly, i.e. it compares each two explanations which cover the same set of symptoms. Therefore, for a set of initial symptoms *c&d* differ-knowledge calculates the set of competing explanations which cover all symptoms and then tries to eliminate some of them by asking for their availability [16]. We use the same idea: for a set of product's features Φ_{init} and the set of relevant products Π_{init} we calculate the set of possible competing features Φ_{com}, i.e. the set of features which can be found in relevant products. Using the notation introduced in the previous section, we can formalize this calculation as

$$\Phi_{com} = (\bigcup_{N_a <_{dir} N_l} \Phi_a) \backslash \Phi_{init} , \tag{6}$$

where N_l is the Largest equivalent node (*len*) for the node $(\Phi_{init}, \Pi_{init})$. Therefore, the calculation is based on considering the features found in direct_child nodes of the Largest equivalent node of the node $(\Phi_{init}, \Pi_{init})$.

Moreover, it can be shown that this strategy selects *minimal* set of features that ensures *complete* testing, i.e. each relevant and no irrelevant (regarding current user's need) product can be obtained/tested. Due to lack of space we omit here the proof.

2.4.2.2 Test Knowledge

The task of this knowledge is to perform tests on the features selected in the differ-task. In the simplest case a user is asked for the values of selected features. However, as we describe in Section 2.5, there are several methods that can be used to decide which products to eliminate. For example, several products can be compared, or the features of a product should be compared with each other. In all these tasks the test knowledge is used in order to perform tests in the most appropriate manner (from the user's point of view).

Note that our approach is based on testing feature-value pairs. It means that we do not ask a user to choose between all values of a feature in the case that some of these values depend on the values of some other features. For example, if the colour of a car can be red, green and blue, but all red cars are metallic, the system asks a user to select only between the green and blue colour and to decide if the car should be a metallic. In that way we ensure minimal testing. Note that most of the other methods for generating product catalogues do not treat such a kind of dependencies between features.

2.4.2.3 Infer Knowledge

This kind of knowledge enables the interpretation of test results in order to eliminate irrelevant results. Since the infer-task "understands" what is the goal of the whole method, it can interpret the test results differently depending on which strategy for elimination is selected. See Section 2.5 for more details.

2.5 Extending Original *c&d* PSM

The subtasks in a generic task can be seen as placeholders for various strategies that can be used for the same type of reasoning (i.e. for the same type of inputs and outputs and the same goal). In the previous section we describe the "default" strategy for reasoning about how to eliminate irrelevant products, which we borrow from the *c&d* method and its applications for diagnosis tasks. Since we assume (claim) that we find a generic reasoning pattern for "diagnostic" in the e-shopping domain, we should be able to map existing solutions for e-shopping into this pattern. Moreover, we should be able to process using the proposed framework all available information relevant for problem-solving in this domain. Finally, since we consider the problem from the knowledge level, we should be able to develop new services for more efficient e-shopping, which would be based on the proposed generic pattern. In the following we discuss these three challenges.

2.5.1 Mapping Existing Solutions

A popular strategy for eliciting the buyer's preferences in a shopping scenario is to propose the user several products and to ask him to select the most suitable or unsuitable one [1]. The buyer should also explain his decision. According to these answers the shop assistant selects new products for recommendation and repeats the procedure.

It is very easy to recognize the generic *cover and differentiate* pattern in this scenario: in the differ task several products are selected for comparison, in the test task they are compared and in the infer task these results are used for generating new relevant products that cover a user's need.

However, the problem we accounted in the "traditional" solutions is that they are performed on the symbolic level, so that they implement only a particular heuristic of a shop assistant, like [1]: in the case of proposing *exactly* three candidate products to a user, the first candidate is the product closest to the centre point[2] of the set of relevant products, the second one is positioned most distantly from the centre point and the third one is the product positioned most distantly from the second one.

It is clear that this heuristic cannot be directly reused in the case of arbitrary number of products that should be proposed to a user. The drawback is that the knowledge level analysis is missing: since it is not clear how the knowledge about comparison will be used, it is difficult to elicit this knowledge, i.e. to define a heuristic which products to compare in an arbitrary case.

On the other side, if we consider the comparison between products as a differ task in *c&d* (Section 2.4.2.1), then the goal is defined very clearly: select products for comparison in such a way that as much as possible information relevant for eliminating products can be obtained. In that case the selection of the n-products that should be proposed to a user is very simple regarding the lattice model presented in section 2.4.1: for the most general[3] node which covers features a user selected as relevant so far (see (5)), we should rank the directly subsumed nodes (i.e. direct_child nodes) according to the number of features and select the first n top ranked nodes. From each of these nodes we should pick-up one product, which is used as a representative of the entire node. More formally, if we assume that a user has selected so far the features Φ_{init} (i.e. his query is mapped into the node (Φ_{init}, Π_{init})), then the following function calculates the k clusters from each a product should be presented to the user:

$$how\_to\_user((\Phi_{init}, \Pi_{init}), k) =$$
$$\{n_x | n_x \in max(\{(\Phi_t, \Pi_t) | (\Phi_t, \Pi_t) <_{dir} len((\Phi_{init}, \Pi_{init}))\}, |\Phi_t|, k)\},$$

where $max(A, c, b)$ is the function that retrieves b-top ranked elements regarding the condition c of the set A and $|S|$ depicts the number of elements in the set S.

2.5.2 Interpreting Relevant Information

Beside using the explicit user feedback about the relevance of the retrieved results, preferences of a buyer can be derived from the so-called implicit relevance feedback [17], where each action of a buyer is captured as a relevant information about his preferences. For example, if a buyer selects a product in order to get more information about it, it is assumed that this product is somehow relevant for that buyer. By using the *c&d* method the information about a user's feedback can be interpreted as a type of differentiating knowledge, so-called *enabling connection knowledge* [9]. Briefly, for each connection (i.e. a link in the feature-product lattice) a symptom (feature) can be assigned, which defines an external condition when a causal connection can be established. Its task is to role out (eliminate) all connections which are not enabled in

---

[2] we do not discuss here how these parameters are calculated

[3] it means that this node is not subsumed by another node which covers the given set of features

a particular situation. In that way our approach can take into account a user's profile by generating questions to that user, of course only if such a profile exists.

The main problem is how to guess which features of that product the buyer actually likes and which are not so important for the buyer. However, similar to the discussion in previous subsection, the analysis on the knowledge level enables us to benefit maximally from a user's feedback: we interpret the feedback information such that as much as possible products will be eliminated. Due to lack of space we give here only an example and avoid the formalization of the solution. Let us assume that for a user's query three results are retrieved: p1 that has features (red, metallic, automatic), p2 with (green, metallic, non-automatic) and p3 with (blue, normal, automatic) and a user selects the first one. Using the e-shop agent "principle of rationality", the most relevant feature is the first one (colour) since in that case only one product remains relevant (p1). In the case of assuming that the user has selected the first product while the feature metallic is the most relevant feature for him, then two products can be considered as relevant (p1 and p2). A similar discussion is valid for the case of assuming that the feature automatic is the most relevant one. Moreover, a common-sense explanation why the colour is most relevant is also possible: by choosing the red colour, a user contrasted that value with two different ones. For the features metallic (and automatic) there is only one different value.

2.5.3 Developing New Services

The knowledge level analysis provides a consistent and abstract view on the problem solving. In the case of e-shopping that view looks like: do something such that as much as possible irrelevant products are eliminated. If we apply that principle on the situation that a user selected a product as very relevant (e.g. he is ready to buy it), we get a new service which can help a user to buy the most relevant product. Briefly, when a user selects a product for buying, we can try to eliminate that product by comparing it with some products that seem very interesting/relevant for the user, in order to be sure that selected product is exactly that one that the user needs. Interpretation using the *c&d* method looks like: relevant candidates are found in the differ task, the comparison is part of the test task and introducing a new product for buying is done in the infer task.

Although it sounds like a contradiction to the buying process, finding alternate products can be very useful service for a user. First, a lot of on-line buyers report the problem concerning the exhaustivity of their search when trying to buy a product: they are not sure that there is no better product for their need. Secondly, it is possible that a user made a constraint (e.g. the price is below 10000 EUR), which decreases the quality of other product's features very much (e.g. there is no car with an air conditioning system and a navigation system for that price). In the case that by relaxing that constraint slightly (e.g. the price is below 11000) a much better offer can be found (e.g. a car that has all for the user relevant features plus a navigation system and the metallic colour), the user should be informed about that offer. Our service can help a user in both situations. Due to lack of space we sketch here briefly the formalization of this procedure.

Definition 7. Structural-similarity (siblings relation ~) between nodes:

$$(\Phi_{x1},\Pi_{y1}) \sim (\Phi_{x2},\Pi_{y2}) \leftrightarrow$$

$$\exists(\Phi_{xi},\Pi_{yi}) \quad (\Phi_{x1},\Pi_{y1}) <_{dir} (\Phi_{xi},\Pi_{yi}) \wedge (\Phi_{x2},\Pi_{y2}) <_{dir} (\Phi_{xi},\Pi_{yi}) \wedge \neg((\Phi_{x1},\Pi_{y1}) = (\Phi_{x2},\Pi_{y2}))$$

Next, we define the function *Alternatives*(P_p, F, *level*), which finds all products from the neighbourhood of the node in which the user selected the product P_p, for which the feature F is in the offset *level* of the value for the product P_p. The system checks all products contained in sibling nodes which satisfy the offset of the selected feature (such a feature is known as a merchant characteristic). Formally,

Alternatives(P_p, F, *level*) =

$$\{P_{pi} \mid P_{pi} \subseteq \bigcup_{\forall(\Phi i,\Pi_{yi})(\Phi_{xi},\Pi_{yi}) <_{dir}(\Phi_{xp},\Pi_{yp}) \vee (\Phi_{xi},\Pi_{yi}) \sim (\Phi_{xp},\Pi_{yp})} P_{yi} \wedge |F(P_p) - F(P_{pi})| < level \} \quad ,$$

where (Φ_{xp},Π_{yp}) is the current node that contains the product P_p selected by the user.

3 Implementation and Evaluation

The research presented in this paper is a part of the Librarian Agent [18], a management system we have developed for the improvement of the search process in ontology-based information portals. The Librarian Agent is developed using the KAON ontology engineering framework.

The e-ShopAgent is an extension of the Query Management module (dedicated to the query refinement) of the Librarian Agent. It extends its functionality by enabling various modus for eliciting user's preferences, e.g. by comparing two products. The visualisation metaphor is taken from the Librarian Agent.

We comment very briefly the complexity of the approach. The most time-intensive operation is the calculation of the direct_child nodes of a given product-feature node (see Section 2.4.1). Since we map[4] all calculations regarding the product-feature nodes into calculating formal concepts [15] and their parameters, for basic manipulation with a concept lattice we use very efficient algorithms already developed in that community [19]. For example, the time complexity of the method for calculating direct_child nodes is proportional to ||O||.p, where p is the average number of children, which is usually proportional to the size of the cluster's intent (number of features) [20].

As we already stated, one very important advantage of using a knowledge level analysis is the possibility to reason about various features of the model of a system. In the information retrieval, where our problem statement can be placed, this is becoming increasingly important because conventional evaluating methods such as experimentally measuring precision and recall are sometimes insufficient.

Since the goal of our research is to model an efficient e-shopping support, our evaluation study concerns the comparison in the effectiveness (regarding searching) between a traditional e-shopping portal and a system based on the eShopAgent.

---

[4] Due to lack of space we do not represent this mapping. An approach can be found in [18]

Indeed, we compared searching for relevant products (holiday trips) in two tourist portals, the traditional one (http://demo.dwm.uni-hildesheim.de/ecommerce/) and semantic-driven one (kaon.semanticweb.org) that implements our approach. Both portals are based on the same product data. We avoid here the details about the structures of portals. We note only that the traditional portal is a very advanced one – it combines traditional Decision Tree approach with CBR techniques. The dataset contains a snapshot of offers acquired from a travel agency (about 5000 offers, each described with about 15 properties, like the place, price, ...). The semantic portal is based on an ontology that was derived from the given database schema using the approach described in [21].

We performed a classical user-drive study in which we wanted to prove the usefulness of the proposed approach. More clearly, we want to check the efficiency of the refinements that are provided by a portal to a user in a navigation step (we assume that a user makes a general query and than tries to specify it in several navigation steps, which forms a navigation session). We compared the navigation structure for 100 queries posted against both portals. The queries were selected by 10 participants (10 queries per a candidate) who actually have performed a search for a holiday trip. The participants were graduate students and no additional instructions were given to them. In order to ensure a fair comparison a half of tasks (searching), for each participant, was performed on each of portals.

We measured the *length of a navigation path*, the *duration of a navigation session* and the *confidence* of the user in the selected product. The confidence describes a user's sureness that his decision is the best possible one (i.e. that there is no a better product for his need). It is measured on the scale 1 - 4, whereas 4 means maximal confidence.

Note that user interfaces (GUI) in portals are different, but the structure of the information provided by portals is the same (list of refinements and list of products). We find that "syntax" differences in the GUI did not influence (strongly) the results of the experiment. The main difference is the "semantics" of the refinement process.

The results of the second experiment are presented in Table 2.

Table 2. Results from the second evaluation study

Method for navigation	Length of a path (average pro path)	Duration of a session (in sec.) (average)	Confidence
Traditional	3.7	35	3.2
e-ShopAgent	2.6	46	2.8

Discussion: We see that using our approach requires more navigation steps, what is, implicitly, desirable, since our approach tends to be a step-by-step refinement in which a user can develop his ill-defined information need incrementally. Not surprisingly, our approach took less time for a task and a user was more confident in the product selected in the semantic portal. This can be interpreted as the better quality of the questions provided by our approach, i.e. e-ShopAgent asks more questions but they seem to be carefully selected (more useful for a user), since a user did not spend much time in a navigation step. Finally, e-ShopAgent covers a large part of the searching space with such questions, so that a user is very confident with a selected product, i.e. he has feeling that lots of alternatives are taken into account in the navigation process. This is a very important feature in recommender applications – a user should to have trust in the recommendation process. Therefore, e-ShopAgent behaves more like an experienced human shop assistant, what was the goal of its designing, as we mentioned in Introduction.

Another advantage of using our approach is that it, due to dealing with a conceptual modelling point of view, provides a framework for the comparison between various e-shop (i.e. query refinement) approaches. Indeed, since we are dealing with the model of an application, it is possible to define several properties that can be proved formally, avoiding the subjectivity of users. We have defined four such parameters:

1. *Completeness of results in a step* – are all relevant products for a user's query found by the system?
2. *Soundness of results in a step* – are only relevant products for a user's query found by the system?
3. *Completeness of questions (query refinements) in a step* – are all relevant questions provided to the user in a refinement step?
4. *Minimality of questions* – are provided questions non-redundant?

If we consider the approach designed on the knowledge level as a gold standard (since it reasons about the refinement process and not suggest refinements in an ad-hoc manner), the process of the evaluation of an e-commerce portal can be very simplified: instead of using very intensive and very subjective user-based studies, it will be possible to measure its formal properties and compare with the gold standard. Note that for performing evaluation of formal parameters we need only several navigation paths, that can be produced automatically. Therefore we can build an objective, precise and not time-consuming evaluation. We work on a study that will prove this hypothesis.

Moreover, by comparing a traditional portal with a "gold" standard, we can locate the weakest points in it and try to improve these performances firstly. For example, regarding this evaluation study, we found out that a big problem in the considered traditional portal arises when a user does not select the destination for a trip, since the offers are fine clustered regarding the property "destination" and the traditional portal does not take such clustering into account. In that case a user misses a lot of offers that can be very relevant for his request.

4 Related Work

Due to nature of the work, we tried to present the main differences between our approach and related product catalog approaches directly after introducing our ideas, so that the analysis of the related work is somehow distributed through the paper. We give here only a short analysis of the work related to query refinement since our approach can treated in that way as well.

In [20] the authors described an approach, named REFINER, to combine Boolean information retrieval and the content-based navigation with concept lattices. For a Boolean query REFINER builds and displays a portion of the concept lattice associated with the documents being searched centred around the user's query. The cluster network displayed by the system shows the result of the query along with a set of minimal query refinements/enlargements. A similar approach is proposed in [22], by adding the size of the query result as an additional factor of the navigation. Moreover, the distance between queries in the lattice is used for similarity ranking. However, none of them put the concept lattice in a broader application context.

Regarding searching in product catalogues the most similar approach is presented in [23]. It is an extension of a mediator architecture that supports the relaxation or tightening of query constraints when no or too many results are retrieved from the catalogue. The query language is a type of Boolean queries suitable for the (web) form based querying against product catalogues. The query tightening is enabled when the cardinality of the resulted set has reached a predefined threshold and it is realized by selecting the most informative, not yet constrained product features. The information content of a feature is defined by measuring its entropy. However, this approach does not treat the problem of query refinement on the conceptual level, as our approach does.

Finally, our approach can be seen as a method for Interactive Query Refinement for the case of logic-based information retrieval. In that sense our recommendations can be treated as a combination of subject thesauri and co-occurrence term lists [24]. However, due to our scenario we extended existing methods for implicit relevance feedback.

5 Conclusion

In this paper we presented a general framework for modelling a buying process on the knowledge level, using the *cover and differentiate* problem solving method. We defined a reasoning pattern for an e-shop assistant, which models knowledge how to eliminate as much as possible irrelevant products using as less as possible questions in a refinement step. The role of a generic reasoning pattern in this scenario is not (only) to support reusability of a concrete solution, but to define the model in which all extensions of that reasoning pattern can be interpreted. For example, we have extended the differentiate task in the *c&d* PSM with several reasoning methods which occur frequently in the shopping domain and are not covered in the original *c&d* PSM. In a case study we illustrated one of very important advantages of the proposed approach: the possibility to compare product catalog applications on the conceptual level.

Acknowledgement

The research presented in this paper would not have been possible without our colleagues and students at the Institute AIFB and the FZI, University of Karlsruhe.

Research for this paper was partially financed by BMBF in the project "SemIPort" (08C5939) and EU in the project "KnowledgeWeb" (507482).

References

1. Shimazu, H.: ExpertClerk: Navigating Shoppers Buying Process with the Combination of Asking and Propossing, IJCAI 2001, Morgan Kaufmann, San Francisco, 2001. pp.1443-1448
2. Howard, J., Sheth, J.N.: The theory of buyer behaviour, Willy, 1994
3. Balabanovic, M., Shoham, Y.: Content-Based, Collaborative Recommendation. CACM 40 (3): 66-72, 1997
4. Newell, A: The knowledge level. Artificial Intelligence, 18:87-127, 1982.
5. Van de Velde, W.: Issues in Knowledge Level Modelling, David, J-M., Krivine, J-P., and Simmons, R. (Eds.) Second Generation Expert Systems, p211-231. Springer Verlag, Berlin, 1993
6. Berendt, B.: Using site semantics to analyze, visualize, and support navigation. Data Mining and Knowledge Discovery, 6, 37-59, 2002
7. Schreiber, A.Th., Wielinga, B.J., de Hoog, R., Akkermans, H., van de Velde, W.: CommonKADS: A Comprehensive Methodology for KBS Development. In: IEEE Expert, December 1994, 28-37.
8. Wielinga, B. J., Schreiber, A. Th., Breuker, J. A.: KADS: A modelling approach to knowledge engineering. Knowledge Acquisition, 4(1), Special issue `The KADS approach to knowledge engineering'., 1992
9. Marcus, S.: Automating Knowledge Acquisition for Expert Systems. Kluwer Academic Publishers, 1988
10. Stojanovic, N., Information-need Driven Query Refinement, The 2003 IEEE/WIC Conference on Web Intelligence (WI 2003), Halifax, Canada, IEEE Press
11. Sung, W.K., Yang, D., Yiu, S.M., Cheung, D.W., Ho, W.S., Lam, T.W., Lee, S.D.: Automatic Construction of Online Catalog Topologies, IEEE Transactions on Systems, Man and Cybernetics – Part C, IEEE Publication, V32, N4, 382-391, Nov., 2002.
12. Clancey, W.J.: The Knowledge Level Reinterpreted: Modeling How Systems Interact. In: MachineLearning 4, 1989, 285-291.
13. Duursma, C.: Role Limiting methods for the Concept Model Library KADS-II, ESPRIT Project P5248 http://arti.vub.ac.be/kads/CH/CH.html, 1993
14. Stojanovic, N.: On Using Query Neighbourhood for Better Navigation Through a Product Catalog: SMART Approach, IEEE International Conference on e-Technology, e-Commerce and e-Service, Taiwan, 2004
15. Ganter, B., Wille, R: Formal Concept Analysis: Mathematical Foundations, Springer Verlag, 1999.
16. Puppe, F.: Systematic Introduction to Expert Systems: Knowledge Representation and Problem-Solving Methods. Springer Verlag, Berlin, 1993.
17. Salton G., Buckley, C.: Improving retrieval performance by relevance feedback. Journal of the American Society for Information Science. 41(4): 288-297, 1990.
18. Stojanovic, N.: An Approach for Using Query Ambiguity for Query Refinement: The Librarian Agent Approach, 22nd International Conference on Conceptual Modeling (ER 2003), Chicago, Illinois, USA, Springer
19. Eklund, P., Groh, B., Stumme, G., Wille, R.: A Contextual-Logic Extension of TOSCANA, 8th ICCG, pp.453-467, LNAI 1867, Springer Verlag, 2000.

20. Carpineto, C., Romano, G.: Effective re formulation of boolean queries with concept lattices. In Flexible Query Answering Systems FQAS'98, pp. 277-291, Berlin Heidelberg, Springer-Verlag, 1998.
21. Stojanovic L., Stojanovic N., Volz R.: Migrating data-intensive Web Sites into the Semantic Web, ACM Symposium on Applied Computing SAC, Madrid, 2002.
22. Becker, P., Eklund, P.: Prospects for Document Retrieval using Formal Concept Analysis, Proceedings of the Sixth Australasian Document Computing Symposium, Coffs Harbour, Australia, December 7, 2001.
23. Ricci, F., Venturini, A., Cavada, D., Mirzadeh, N., Blaas, D., Nones, M.: Product Recommendation with Interactive Query Management and Twofold Similairty. In proceedings of the 5th International Conference on Case-Based Reasoning (ICCBR 2003), 2003
24. Schatz, B. R., Johnson, E.H., Cochrane, P.A., Chen, H.: Interactive Term Suggestion for Users of Digital Libraries: Using Subject Thesauri and Co-occurrence Lists for Information Retrieval. Digital Libraries 1996: pp. 126-133

A Customer Notification Agent for Financial Overdrawn Using Semantic Web Services

José Manuel López-Cobo, Silvestre Losada, Oscar Corcho,
Richard Benjamins, and Marcos Niño

Intelligent Software Components, S.A. (iSOCO),
C/ Francisca Delgado, 11 – 2. 28108 Alcobendas,
Madrid, Spain
{ozelin,slosada,ocorcho,rbenjamins,marcosn}@isoco.com

Abstract. In this paper, we present a Notification Agent designed and implemented using Semantic Web Services. The Notification Agent manages alerts when critical financial situations arise discovering and selecting multichannel notification services. This agent applies open research results on the Semantic Web Services technologies including on-the-fly composition based on a finite state machine and automatic discovery of semantic services. Financial Domain ontologies, based on IFX financial standard, have been constructed and extended for building agent systems using OWL and OWL-S standard (as well as other approaches like DL or f-Logic). This agent is going to be offered through integrated Online Aggregation systems in commercial financial organizations.

Keywords: Semantic Web Services, Ontologies, Composition, Intelligent Agent

1 Introduction

The objective of the distributed system described in this paper (the Customer Notification Agent) is to provide added value to customers of financial services. This added value consists in a fully customizable and configurable set of aggregations and estimation functionalities on account balance evolution, as well as SMS and email alerts (among others), which will allow customers to have more efficient information about his financial position.

This system reuses existing technology for aggregation available at our company (iSOCO GETsee ®), and migrates it to Semantic Web Services technology. The integrated use of Semantic Web technologies and Web Services allows us to describe and reason with pieces of code understandable for machines, discharging the sometimes tedious task of checking the online accounts to a software system. This system is able to engage with other commercial solutions for aggregation and to detect at run-time and raise alerts if some conditions are detected (for example, a possible overdrawn of a customer saving account, due to the future payment of an invoice).

E. Motta et al. (Eds.): EKAW 2004, LNAI 3257, pp. 371–385, 2004.

We have developed different ontologies to express the needed knowledge for this application. These ontologies are divided into three groups: general ontologies, which represent common sense knowledge reusable across domains; domain ontologies, which represent reusable knowledge in a specific domain; and application-dependent ontologies, which represent the application-dependent knowledge needed.

We have defined three high-level services for performing the task of the Customer Notification Agent. The *GETseeSWS Service* accesses the online accounts of the customer and the invoices associated with them, and calculates the balance for these accounts. The *NotificationService* notifies customers with different types of messages (discharging in 3rd party providers the execution of the actual notification) and finally, the *EstimationService* estimates, using different kinds of arithmetical functions, the expectable amount of an invoice for preventing an overdrawn situation.

One of the main innovations of our systems is the proposal of a finite state diagram to represent the composition of atomic processes into composite ones using conditions as a way to choose between different choices. Such an approach allows at run-time the discovery and invocation of services which comply with the conditions defined for the transition from one state to another. This allows describing a composite process at design-time by defining its behavior and leaving the selection of the specific service to the execution time. This is an innovation with respect to other approaches where the selection of the specific services is done also during the design time.

The paper is organized as follows. Section 2 describes a sample scenario where the Notification Agent can be used, showing the main actors and agents involved in the overall process and the steps usually followed by them. Section 3 describes the ontologies that we have developed, either from scratch or by reusing other ontologies or vocabularies already available elsewhere. Section 4 describes the Semantic Web services created for the system, which have been implemented using OWL-S, DL and f-Logic. Section 5 describes one of the main contributions of this paper, namely the proposal for service composition using finite state diagrams. Finally, section 6 provides some conclusions of our work and future lines of research.

2 Scenario Description

Let us suppose that we are working on the scenario presented in figure 1. In this scenario we have a customer with several banking accounts where he/she has different amounts of money. This customer has also contracts with some consumer goods companies such as a telephone company, and gas and electricity providers, among others.

Everyday, the Customer Notification Agent will detect whether any of the customer accounts is going to be in an overdrawn situation. Bank accounts may have different invoices associated from different consumer good companies. If the amount of the invoice is bigger than the amount of money of the account, there could be an overdrawn situation. To help the customer, the system calculates an estimation of the amount of every invoice expected for that account before its value date and notifies the customer if the balance of the saving account is less than the expected invoice amount. The system will choose any of the notification channels available for the customer and will notify him/her about the overdraw possibility.

As a specific example, let us suppose that our customer has 100 euros in one of his bank accounts, which have two invoice payments associated to it: electricity and gas. These invoices will be charged in two consecutive dates (April 3rd and 4th, 2004), with amounts equal to 60 and 50 euros each. Consequently, the costumer may have an overdrawn in case that he/she does not transfer money into this account. Bank transfers usually take two or three days to be actually done, so the bank transfer of 10 euros should be done before the end of March. This is a very simple example of the results expected from the Notification Agent.

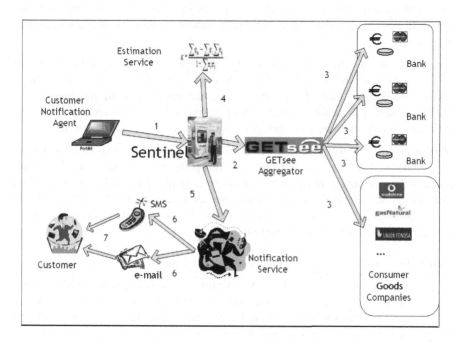

Fig. 1. Sample scenario diagram for the Notification Agent

In this scenario, the following actors are involved: the customer, the banks, and the consumer goods companies. And the following agents are involved: customer notification agent (CNA), Sentinel and some estimation services. Finally, the iSOCO GET-see® application is at the core of this scenario, in charge of the aggregation of data from bank accounts and consumer goods companies.

The following steps will be normally done:

Step 1: Everyday, the Customer Notification Agent dynamically configures and invokes the Sentinel Service. This agent has the entire customer's information needed for invoking the composed service (online username, password and other data). The update frequency of this agent can be customized.

Step 2: The Sentinel Service uses iSOCO GETsee® for collecting information from the customer's accounts.

Step 3: iSOCO GETsee® collects the amount balance of all the customer's accounts (of banks B1, B2, ..., Bn). In one (or more) of this accounts some consumer goods companies (E1, E2, ..., En) can charge invoices. The invoices have their notification and value dates. The frequency of those invoices is always the same (weekly, monthly, bimonthly, annually).

Step 4: For each invoice of consumer goods companies (E1, E2, ..., En) associated with the account, the Estimation Service estimates the probable amount at the end of the period, Ae (estimated amount) in terms of heuristics or mathematical models. Ae has a relationship with a consumer good company (Ee) and an account of a bank (ABe). If the Ae is less than the established threshold for the account, then an alert has to be raised.

Step 5: The Notification Service looks in a (de)centralized registry different ways to communicate with the user. It can find different services involving many different devices (phone calls using VoIP, SMS, electronic mail, telegram) and personal data (phone number, cell phone number, e-mail, postal address). The services discovered must have the ability to perform the action defined in the Notification Service.

Step 6: The invocation engine sorts in terms of cost, time to deliver, etc., the different possibilities and chooses the first service in this particular ranking. Some data mediation could be needed if terms of the ontology used differ from the one used by the Notification Service. If the service chosen has an irrecoverable mismatching of process or data, or some communication error occurs in the invocation, the service has to be able to choose another service and invoke it.

Step 7: The service chosen is invoked and the user is notified.

In summary, the objective of the Notification Agent is to provide added value to the user including a fully customizable and configurable set of aggregations and estimation functionalities on balance evolution as well as SMS and email alerts, allowing the customer to have more efficient information about his financial position in the incoming time period.

Several estimation functionalities allow calculating balance evolution on different accounts according to expected invoices and payments. The foreseen value of account balances will allow firing alert rules defined by the user and managed by the Notification Agent application. Those alerts could let him anticipate any trouble that could occur in his accounts or avoid missing any business opportunity.

3 Ontology Structure for the CNA

In this section we describe briefly the ontologies that model the domain presented in our scenario, and which will be used by the Semantic Web services developed for it and described in section 4. These ontologies have been implemented in OWL [3] using the Protégé-2000 ontology tool [5], with the OWL-plug-in [6]. A graphical outline of the main relationships between these ontologies is presented in figure 2.

According to the classifications of Van Heijst and colleagues [1] and of Mizoguchi and colleagues [2], we can distinguish the following types of ontologies:

- *General ontologies*, which represent common sense knowledge reusable across domains. In this group we can include our ontologies about users and notifications, which include basic concepts related to persons and their contact information, and our ontology about estimation parameters, which is based on statistical concepts.

- *Domain ontologies*, which represent reusable knowledge in a specific domain. In this group we can include our ontologies about financial products and financial services.

- *Application ontologies*, which represent the application-dependent knowledge needed. In this group we can include our ontologies about saving accounts and invoice payments, and our ontology about overdrawn situations. The reason why we classify them under this group does not mean that they might not be reusable in other ontology-based applications; instead it means that we have not designed them taking into account such objective.

We will first describe the general ontologies. The ontologies about users and notifications include basic concepts related to persons (users of information systems), such as name, surname, birth date, etc, and related to their contact information , such as email addresses, postal addresses, phone and fax numbers, etc. The same message can be sent in many different types of notifications, using the same or different physical devices. For instance, if you want to communicate with someone sending him a fax and an e- mail, the receiver will have two different communications, one in the facsimile device and the other in his e-mail inbox.

With regard to the ontology about estimation parameter, it describes the basic arithmetical functions that can be used, among others, to estimate the amount of the spending of an invoice (or whatever other numerical concept which has an historical evolution). This ontology considers parameters related to linear estimation factors, statistical information, heuristics, etc.

Regarding the domain ontologies defined, we have two different ones, as shown in figure 2: financial services and financial products. These ontologies are based on the IFX financial standard [12], so that they will be easier to reuse by other ontology-based applications.

The ontology about financial products contains the different types of products provided by a bank (loans, investment accounts, saving accounts, investment funds, etc.). In all of them the bank and the customer sign a contract where the bank stores or lend money from or to the customer. The most important characteristic to define a financial product is the *interestRate*, which can be positive or negative. When the interest rate is positive, the bank gives some money to the customer for having his or her money, and when this rate is negative, the customer pays some extra money for the money lent by the bank. Each financial product has their own specific attributes, and is related to the corresponding user(s) of the ontology about users. Each product can be owned by many holders and vice versa.

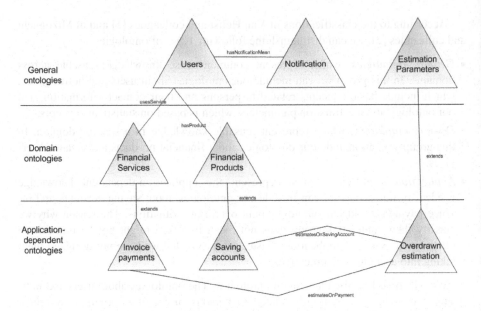

Fig. 2. Ontologies developed for the Customer Notification Agent for Financial Overdrawn

The ontology about financial services represents those services that banks can provide to their customers and which are not financial products. These financial services provide added value to the relationship between a bank and their customers. They include loyalty cards, paying invoices by direct debit, Internet connection advantages, information provision about stock markets, etc.

The application-dependent ontologies describe more specific concepts and relationships related to our system. One of these ontologies is the one related to invoice payment, which represents the service that the bank offers to their customers, allowing to charge directly to a saving account of the customer the payment of many different things (taxes, shopping, subscriptions, consumer goods companies consumes like gas, water or phone). The ontology related to saving accounts includes concepts related to the types of saving accounts that can be contracted with the banks with which we are working.

Finally, the last application-dependent ontology extends the general ontology about estimation parameters, focusing on the specific case of overdrawn situations like the ones presented in the previous section.

4   Discovery of Notification Semantic Web Services

The following top-level services are available, as shown in figure 3: GETsee Service, Notification Service and Estimation Service.

Besides, the figure shows how the GETsee Service is decomposed into five atomic services (openSession, getAccounts, getInvoices, getBalance, closeSession). These five services are annotated using the same ontology as the GETsee service (although this is not mandatory in our approach). Those atomic services invoke other services, which are annotated according to other ontologies. In these cases, data mediation is needed for the exchange of messages, although this is out of the scope of this paper. At last, the Notification Service looks for a service able to notify something to a person and finds at least two services (notification by SMS and notification by e-mail), which might be annotated according to other two more ontologies.

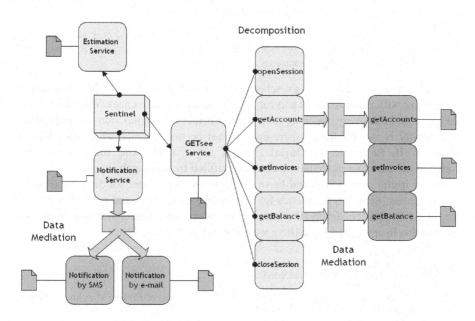

Fig. 3. A diagram of the Semantic Web services used for our notification scenario

As commented in the previous section, the Semantic Web services used in our scenario have been annotated with OWL-S, DL and f-Logic [4, 10]. OWL-S uses the class Service as a complete description of the content and behavior of a service. It has three differentiated parts. First of all, the Service Profile explains "what the service does". The Process Model describes "how the service works" and finally the Service Grounding maps the content and format of the messages needed to interact with the service. It provides a mapping from the semantic form of the messages exchanged as defined in the Process Model, to the syntactic form as defined in the WSDL input and output specifications.

For a further understanding about how is supposed to work the Discovery of Notification Services [17], we put the description (using DL) of two services (defined by their capabilities) and a Request from a User and depict how they will be matched.

Some domain-level facts:

```
Notification ⊑ Action
EmailNotification ⊑ Notification
⊤  ⊑  =1 from
```

Capabilities and a Request:

```
CapA ≡
EmailNotification   ⊓ ∃ from.User ⊓ ∃ to.User ⊓ ∀to.User ⊓
∃usedProvider.{ProviderA} ⊓ ∃sendingTime.Timestamp ⊓ ∃content.String ⊓
∀acknowledgement.=F ⊓ ∃cost. =5
CapB ≡
SMSNotification ⊓ ∃ from.User ⊓ ∃ to.CellphoneUser ⊓ ∀to.CellphoneUser
⊓ ∃ usedProvider.{ProviderB} ⊓ ∃ sendingTime.(Timestamp ⊓
≤currentTime+1week) ⊓ content.String ⊓ cost. =3
Req ≡
ElectronicNotification ⊓ ∃ from.{Userx} ⊓ ∃ to.{UserY} ⊓ ∃ to.{Userz} ⊓
=2to ⊓ ∀ usedProvider.Provider ⊓ ∃ sendTime ≤ 200406250900 ⊓ ∃ con-
tent.String ⊓ ∀ acknowledgment =T ⊓ ∀ cost ≤5
```

With respect to the ontology schema introduced above the DL-based discovery component will match requests and capabilities using DL inferences. The basic idea of the DL-based discovery matching is to check whether the conjunction of a request and a capability is satisfiable, i.e. there can at least be one instance which they have in common. If $Request ⊓ Capability_X ⊑ ⊥$ holds true there is no such common instance and the request cannot be fulfilled by this capability.

Other useful approach would be use f-Logic and a reasoner for describe capabilities and goals [8] and make queries for matchmake capabilities and goals. For the goal we model the postcondition (the state of the information space that is desired). We express this by a fact in f-logic (here we use the flora2 syntax, [16]).

```
myGoal:goal[
   postCondition->myNotification].
myNotification:notification[
   ntf_userToBeNotified -> johndoe,
   ntf_date -> d040606:date[dayOfMonth->5,monthOfYear->5,year->2004],
   paymentMethod -> creditCard,
   cost -> 0.2,
   ntf_body -> "Your Account Z will be in minus in 2 weeks",
   ntf_from -> sentinel].
johndoe:user[
   nif -> 123,
   name -> "John Doe",
   password -> "p",
   login -> "l",
   firstPreference -> jdMobile,
   contacts ->>
    {jdEmaill:eml_account[eml_account->"jon@doe.com"],
     jdMobile:phone[phn_number->"0123456", phn_type->mobile],
     jdHome:phone[phn_number->"6543210", phn_type->home]}].
sentinel:user[
   name -> "Sentinel System",
   contacts ->> {jdEmaill:eml_account[
      eml_account->"sentinel@isoco.com"]}].
```

The capability postcondition describes the state of the information space the service has after its execution. Here we use some prolog build in predicate e.g. '//' which is an integer division, but that might also be replaced by more declarative predicate names like "integerDivision(X,Y,Z)".

```
smsProvider[postcondition] :-
_AnyNotification:notificationSMS[
   phn_number -> _X:phone[phn_type->mobile],
```

```
       ntf_receiptAcknowledgement -> false,
       ntf_time -> Time:dateAndTime,
       content -> AnyMessage:message,
       payment -> Payment],
    is_charlist(
    AnyMessage.msg_body, AnyMessageLength)@prolog(),
    AnyMessageLength < 800,
    Tokens is '//'(AnyMessageLength,160)@prolog()+1,
    Cost is Tokens * 0.05,
    Payment.cost >= Cost,
    (Payment.paymentMode = creditCard; Payment.paymentMode = account),
    secondsBetween(currentDate,Time,X),    X < 5*60.
```

In the F-Logic approach for discovery we are checking if the capability entails the goal (capability ≤ goal). Current limitations with respect to available reasoners led to the current modeling, where we have the goal-postcondition as a fact (which may not be fully specified) and the capability-postcondition as a rule.

We would like to extend this approach on the one hand to overcome the limitations due to the modelling of the goal as fact (i.e. that makes it hard to express ranges and constraints) and on the other hand to extend it to other matching semantics (e.g. if the intersection is satisfiable like in the DL approach).

5   Composition Using Finite State Diagram

The functionality of the non-atomic processes could be decomposed in a structured (or not) set of atomic processes for performing the same task. This composition (or decomposition, viewed from the opposite side) can be specified by using control constructs such as *Sequence* and *If-then-else*. Such decomposition normally shows, among other things, how the various inputs of the process are accepted by particular subprocesses, and how its various outputs are returned by particular subprocesses.

A CompositeProcess must have a *composedOf* property by which is indicated the control structure of the composite, using a *ControlConstruct*

```
<rdf:Property rdf:ID="composedOf">
   <rdfs:domain rdf:resource="#CompositeProcess"/>
   <rdfs:range rdf:resource="#ControlConstruct"/>
</rdf:Property>
<owl:Class rdf:ID="ControlConstruct"/>
```

Each control construct, in turn, is associated with an additional property called *components* to indicate the ordering and conditional execution of the sub processes (or control constructs) from which it is composed. For instance, the control construct, *Sequence*, has a *components* property that ranges over a *ProcessComponentList* (a list whose items are restricted to be *ProcessComponents*, which are either processes or control constructs).

This property allows managing the control flow of the execution of a Composite-Process but, in counterpart, binds the ontologies used in the services to contain information about the data and control flow, and that is not always desirable, [13,14].

For that reason, in our system we have developed a mechanism to describe finite state machines (finite state diagrams). The situation calculus introduces first-order terms called *situations*, [15]. The intuition behind the situation calculus is that the world persists in one state until an *action* is performed that changes it to a new state. Time is discrete, one action occurs at a time, time durations do not matter, and actions are irreducible entities. Actions are conceptualized as objects in the universe of discourse, as are states of the world. Hence, states and actions are reified. All changes to the world are the result of *actions,* which correspond to our atomic processes. The situation that holds on entry to an action is different to that which holds on exit. The exit situation is said to be the *successor* of the entry situation. Sequences of actions combine to form histories that describe composite situations – in essence the state that holds at the end of the sequence. Given this interpretation we can clarify the meaning of preconditions. A precondition is a condition that must be true of the situation on entry to an atomic process. However, sometimes these preconditions cannot be computed in terms of the input that is in terms of the domain ontology. That kind of preconditions are also called *assumptions*.

So, speaking in terms of Semantic Web Services, each *state* can be seen as a situation, stable, after or before any *action*. The set of preconditions that must be true in this state are part of the preconditions of the atomic processes that make change that state. Following in this interpretation, transitions in the state diagram represent each atomic process needed for fulfill part of the goal, as is presented in figure 4.

At this very moment there are several efforts to describe preconditions, postconditions, effects and assumptions in the research area, but few consensus has been reached to determine a final good candidate (SWRL, F-Logic, OWL, DRS). In order to describe our current needs we define a naïve solution to model conditions. Of course, making use of the reuse, we can import references to other conditions expressed in other ontologies.

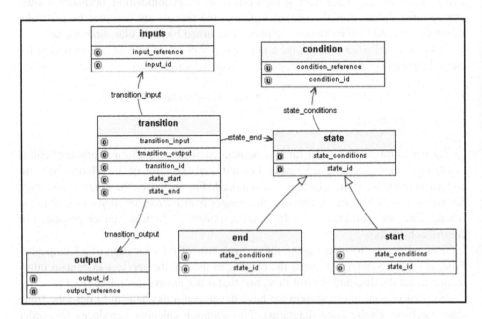

Fig. 4. Finite state diagram ontology

The class *Condition* represents conditions, that is, statements which can be true or false in a particular state of the world (depicted in the state diagram). These conditions could be expressed in the same way (in fact, they are exactly the same) that we use to describe conditions in Semantic Web Services. Conditions of a State are modeled as instances of this class (or subclasses defined by an Ontology designer). This class is defined as subclass of [...] Process.owl#Condition and [...] Process.owl#Effect defined in the OWL-S Process Ontology for model conditions and effects. Using this technique, expressing conditions in the state diagram in the same way as in the Services will favor any attempt to matchmake Services with Transitions.

```
<owl:Class rdf:ID="condition">
    <rdfs:subClassOf rdf:resource="Process.owl#Condition"/>
    <rdfs:subClassOf rdf:resource="Process.owl#Effect"/>
</owl:Class>
```

5.1 State

The class State models a state inside a state diagram. A state is represented as a node of the Graph which models a state machine. Each node is labeled with conditions, using the relationship *state_conditions*. Besides, each node is identified with a unique id, the slot *state_id*. A state in a Service Composition represents an intermediary step in the execution of two services.

The states (when we are talking of a concrete State Diagram) are represented as instances:

```
<state rdf:ID="estimated">
    <state_conditions rdf:resource="#logged_in"/>
</state>
```

5.2 Input and Output

The classes Input and Output defines the desired input and output of each transition. The specific inputs and outputs are modeled as subclasses of these classes. This is because the messages exchanged by the services (or viewed from the State Diagram point of view, the inputs needed for performing an action and the outputs derived from this actions) are, at last, classes or parts of some domain ontology. For a successful matchmaking it could be desirable Data Mediation for helping the Discovery Service to find services with similar inputs and outputs. The specific subclasses of Input and Output can be described in the same Ontology or they could inherit from other Ontologies (multiple inheritance) allowing to express the input and output of a Transaction in terms of the inputs and outputs of Services.

5.3 Transition

The class Transition models *actions* in a State Diagram. These actions are responsible for building a conversation in terms of the domain knowledge. From a stable situation (a state) and in presence of some conditions (which are true), some action is performed and some transition from the previous state to his successor is made. In a state diagram this transition is represented using an arrow from the starting state to the ending state. In a Composite Service framework, a Transition models the execution of an operation (in terms of Semantic Web Services this could be done by an Atomic Process or by another Composite Process).

The class Transition has the following attributes and relationships:

- State_start, State_end: They are the starting and ending state of the transition. They are instances of the class State. Each state is labeled with conditions which serve to refer to the preconditions and effect of the transition.
- Transition_input, Transition_output: Defines, in the domain ontology, the desired input and output for the transition. They references to subclasses of the class Input or Output (described before) or they could be a simple data type. This restriction makes mandatory the description of this ontology in OWL-full because OWL-DL doesn't allow this kind of description.

There are two special states labeled in a special way to denote what is the starting state and the ending state. Doing this, we always know what the first subgoal which can be achieved is and what is the final subgoal. With this information, some reasoning could be done forward or backward. To be able to transit from one state to another, The Discovery Service has to be able to find some Semantic Web Service with the same set of preconditions, effects, inputs and outputs which has the instance of Transition representing the transition between the states in the following terms:

- Preconditions: These conditions label the starting state.
- Effects: They are the conditions present on the ending state but missing in the starting state.
- Inputs: Define which part of the domain ontology need the service to be executed. Some data mediation could be needed if there are 3rd party services using other ontology.
- Outputs: Define which part of the domain ontology is the result of the execution of the service. Some data mediation could be needed if there are 3rd party services using other ontology.

For obtaining a more precise understanding of the relationship between the State Diagram and the Services (for the sake of matchmaking), see the figure 5.

This is the state diagram which models the functionality of Sentinel. It could be easily translated to the State Diagram Ontology, previously described. With this ontology and the description of the Service, an agent could accomplish the task described with the state machine. The agent will need to make some decision about what transition to take (i.e. what service has to execute) and some reasoner (with storage functionalities) will be needed to perform the control flow. Two instances of transitions can be seen below.

```
<transition rdf:ID="KB_044630_Individual_84">
    <state_end rdf:resource="#Logged"/>
    <state_start>
        <stateStart rdf:ID="initState"/>
    </state_start>
    <transition_id>GETseeSWSlogin</transition_id>
    <transition_input rdf:resource="#input_user"/>
    <transition_output rdf:resource="XMLSchema#boolean"/>
```

```
  </transition>
  <transition rdf:ID="KB_044630_Individual_92">
    <transition_input rdf:resource="#input_output_savingAccounts"/>
    <transition_input rdf:resource="#input_user"/>
    <transition_id>GETseeSWSgetinvoices</transition_id>
    <transition_output rdf:resource="#output_InvoicesPayments"/>
    <state_start rdf:resource="#AccountsLoaded"/>
    <state_end rdf:resource="#InvoicesLoaded"/>
  </transition>
```

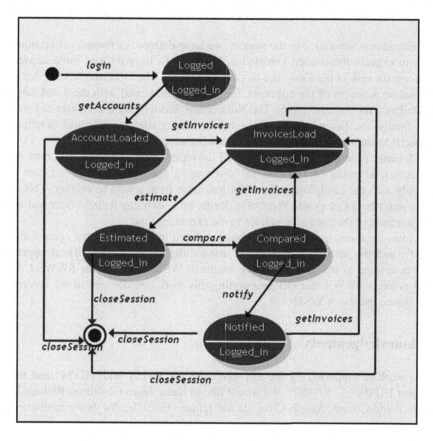

Fig. 5. Relationships between the state diagram and the Sentinel service

6 Conclusions

We have described the Customer Notification Agent which makes use of an aggregation system, developed by iSOCO, called GETsee. ISOCO GETsee® application is able to aggregate information coming from different sources. It can be financial information (saving accounts, credit cards, investment funds, etc.), different invoices from consumer goods companies, loyalty cards, insurance companies or e-mail accounts from different Web Portals.

The Customer Notification Agent focuses on the dynamic configuration of a system that generates notifications and suggestions for transactions to the customer related to conciliation between financial accounts and pending invoices.

Integration of applications is one of the most ambitious goals of the Semantic Web Services. The existence of different agents or legacy applications must not interfere in the shared use of information. Exploiting the advantages of semantic interoperability and loose-coupled services will allow us to interconnect different applications and integrate data and information through messages. So, the system to be built leans upon an existing iSOCO's commercial application and others agents or services built *ad hoc*.

For adding semantics to the system, we have defined, or reused, different ontologies to express the needed knowledge. Besides, we have defined three services for perform the task of the Customer Notification Agent. The GETseeSWS Service access the online accounts of the customer, the invoices associated with them and calculates the balance for these accounts. The Notification Service notifies the user any message and finally, the Estimation Service estimates, using some arithmetical functions, the expectable amount of an invoice for preventing an overdrawn situation.

A Finite state diagram has been used for representing the composition of Atomic Processes, allowing in run-time the discovering and invocation of services which comply with the conditions defined for transition from a state to another. This allows us to describe a Composite Process in design-time, defining its behaviour and leaving the selection of the particular service to the execution time.

Some open research issues have been explored in this work as the composition on-the-fly and the discovery of Services using different approaches. These approaches will contribute to the testing of the contents of WSMO [8] and the SWWS-CA [18]. The projects SWWS and DIP, supporting this work, are devoted to the contribution and dissemination of WSMO.

Acknowledgements

This work is supported by the IST project SWWS (IST-2001-37134) and the IST project DIP(FP6 – 507483). We would like to thank Jesús Contreras, Richard Benjamins, Pablo Gómez, Andrés Cirugeda and Ignacio González for their contributions.

References

1. van HeijstG, Schreiber ATh, Wielinga BJ (1997). *Using explicit ontologies in KBS development*.International Journal of Human-Computer Studies 45:183-192
2. Mizoguchi R, Vanwelkenhuysen J, Ikeda M (1995). *Task Ontology for reuse of problem solving knowledge*. In: Mars N (ed) Towards Very Large Knowledge Bases: Knowledge Building and Knowledge Sharing (KBKS'95). University of Twente, Schede, The Netherlands. IOS Press, Amsterdam, The Netherlands.
3. OWL. Web Ontology Language. http://www.w3.org/TR/2004/REC-owl- features-20040210/
4. OWL-S. OWL for Services. http://www.daml.org/services/owl-s/1.0/

5. Protégé 2000. Stanford Medical Informatics. http://protege.stanford.edu/
6. OWL Plugin: A Semantic Web Ontology Editor for Protégé. http://protege.stanford.edu/plugins/owl/
7. ezOWL Plugin for Protégé 2000. http://iweb.etri.re.kr/ezowl/plugin.html
8. WSMO. Web Service Modeling Framework. http://www.nextwebgeneration.org/projects/wsmo/
9. SWRL: A Semantic Web Rule Language Combining OWL and RuleML http://www.daml.org/2003/11/swrl/
10. Michael Kifer, Georg Lausen, James Wu , Logical Foundations of Object Oriented and Frame Based Languages. Journal of ACM 1995, vol. 42, p. 741-843
11. DRS: A Set of Conventions for Representing Logical Languages in RDF. Drew McDermott, January 2004. http://www.daml.org/services/owl-s/1.0/DRSguide.pdf
12. IFX. Interactive Financial eXchange. http://www.ifxforum.org
13. D. Berardi, F. De Rosa, L. De Santis, and M. Mecella. Finite state automata as conceptual model for e-services. In Proc. of the IDPT 2003 Conference, 2003. To appear.
14. S. Narayanan and S. McIlraith. Simulation, Verification and Automated Composition of Web Services. In *Proc. of WWW 2002*.
15. H. Levesque, F. Pirri, R. Reiter. Foundations of the Situation Calculus. Linköping Electronic Articles in Computer and Information Science, Vol 3, nr 18. http://www.ep.liu.se/ea/cis/1998/018. December 1998
16. *FLORA*-2: An Object-Oriented Knowledge Base Language. http://flora.sourceforge.net
17. S. Grimm, H. Lausen. Discussion document SWWS Service Description / Discovery. May 2004
18. C. Priest. SWWS-CA A Conceptual Architecture for Semantic Web Services. May 2004

Aggregating Web Services with Active Invocation and Ensembles of String Distance Metrics

Eddie Johnston and Nicholas Kushmerick

Computer Science Department, University College Dublin, Ireland
{eddie.johnston, nick}@ucd.ie

Abstract. The adoption of standards for exchanging information across the web could present a new world of opportunities for data integration and aggregation systems. Although Web Services simplify the discovery and access of information sources, the problem of semantic heterogeneity remains: how to find semantic correspondences within the data being integrated. In this paper, we propose OATS, a novel algorithm for schema matching that is specifically suited to Web Service data aggregation. We show how probing Web Services with a small set of related queries results in semantically correlated data instances which greatly simplifies the matching process, and demonstrate that the use of an ensemble of string distance metrics in matching data instances performs better than individual metrics. We also propose a method for adaptively combining distance metrics, and evaluate OATS on a large number of real-world Web Service operations.

1 Introduction

Emerging Web standards such as SOAP [w3.org/TR/soap], WSDL [w3.org/-TR/wsdl] and UDDI [uddi.org] promise a network of Web Services, interoperable networked computational components that can be invoked remotely using standard XML-based protocols. For example, major e-commerce companies such as Amazon and Google export Web Services that provide direct access to their content databases.

Data integration systems (e.g. [1, 2]) are an important class of applications that can benefit from Web Services. Data integration systems decompose complex user queries into subqueries that can be distributed to heterogeneous data sources, and integrate the resulting data into a coherent answer to the original query.

Clearly, the widespread adoption of Web Service protocols for submitting queries and obtaining results would greatly simplify the deployment of such systems. Complete data integration systems must solve a variety of sub-problems, including query decomposition, query optimization, monitoring query execution, and caching. But by far the deepest challenges involve semantic heterogeneity:

E. Motta et al. (Eds.): EKAW 2004, LNAI 3257, pp. 386–402, 2004.

How can the data integration system discover the semantics of the heterogeneous data being integrated?

This problem of semantic heterogeneity is usually formulated in terms of the well-known problem of database schema matching [3]. Schema matching is the problem of finding semantic correspondences between the elements of two or more data schemas. Specifically, two (heterogeneous) schemas are taken as input, and the output is a mapping between the semantically corresponding elements of the schemas.

We focus on schema matching for the purpose of aggregating data from Web Service operations. We envision a scenario in which an integration system has used some form of semantic metadata (e.g., UDDI or OWL-S [www.daml.org/services]) to identify a set of Web Services that can answer a given query. For example, given a user query for the weather forecast for the 98125 ZIP code, the integration system might identify operations o_1 and o_2 that can be queried with a ZIP code and that produce as output a weather forecast. However, the integration system does not understand the semantics of the data returned by each source. For example, suppose o_1 and o_2 return results of the form:

```
<fcast>                <prev>
    <hi>87</hi>            <haute>86</haute>
    <lo>56</lo>            <basse>57</basse>
    <wnd>NW 10</wnd>       <vent>N 11</vent>
</fcast>               </prev>
```

This simple example illustrates the focus of our research: how can a data integration system automatically aggregate such data into a single coherent structure such as:

```
<forecast>
    <high>87</high><high>86</high>
    <low>56</low><low>57</low>
    <wind>NW 10</wind><wind>N 11</wind>
</forecast>
```

Today, schema matching is primarily a time-consuming and error-prone manual process. Realistically, schema matching may never be fully automatable, but the development and improvement of tools to assist the process is essential given the rapidly growing number of data sources and applications.

Fig. 1 shows two real operation results that require aggregation. These documents are part of our test data, and represent a typical aggregation task. The first operation was invoked with an International Civil Aviation Organisation location code, and the second with a ZIP code for the same area, so the data

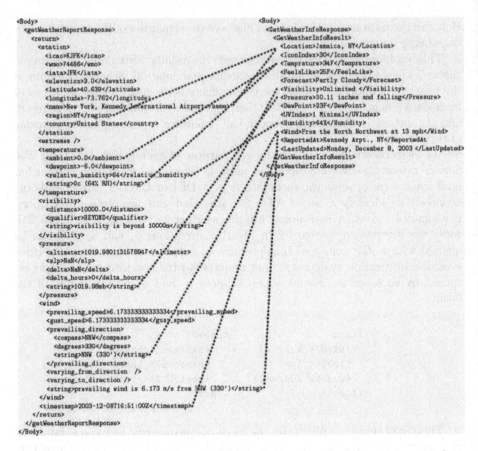

Fig. 1. A real-world example of Web Service aggregation. The left output comes from the Web Service http://live.capescience.com/wsdl/GlobalWeather.wsdl, the right output from http://www.ejse.com/WeatherService/Service.asmx?WSDL; both operations were queried for a weather forecast for Kennedy Airport, New York

instances correspond. An examination of the data highlights some of the difficulties that are encountered in schema matching:

- the size and structure of the input documents can be very different, and in many cases, there are only a small proportion of valid matching pairs.
- instance data can be used effectively to propose matching elements, but it can be difficult to obtain fully corresponding data (the reports above differed by four hours).
- in some cases, instance data can correspond, but additional knowledge is required to match it. In the operation outputs below, temperature

is given in degrees Celcius in one schema, but degrees Farenheit in the other.

Schema matching is challenging in many different ways. Because the schemas to be matched are usually created by different people, they will differ in structure and naming. The "related" schemas may well not overlap very much—elements of one schema S may form only a small subset of the schema element set T. Furthermore, an element of S may match more than one element of T, or match some combination of elements of T. Finally, schema matching is computationally expensive because the number of potential matches is exponential in the size of the schemas.

Because single clues cannot always be trusted, the semantics of each element must be inferred from a combination of features, including element names, data types, features of neighbouring elements, properties of the data, etc. For example, creating a match between two elements of S and T because they both have labels containing **phone** could result in a wrong match; in S, the **phone** element may correspond to some location's phone number, while in T, **phone** may contain a binary value indicating that a phone exists at some location, and this context can only be determined by looking at the datatypes and neighbours of the elements. Conversely, a match between a **mobile** element and **cell** elements should not be overlooked because while the elements' names are dissimilar, they match semantically.

In this paper, we propose a novel algorithm for schema mapping, OATS (Operation Aggregation Tool for Web Services) that is specifically suited to Web Service data aggregation. The novelty of our approach is two-fold. First, most schema matching algorithms that use instance data just take as input whatever data happens to be provided. In contrast (and inspired by the machine learning community's active learning algorithms [4]) our algorithm probes Web Service operations with a small set of related queries, which results in contextually similar data instances and greatly simplifies the matching process.

The second novel feature of OATS is the use of ensembles of distance metrics for matching instance data. For example, when comparing the **hi** and **haut** instance data, it makes sense to treat the data as numeric and measure the difference, but when comparing **wnd** and **vent** it would be more reliable to use Levenshtein edit distance [5]. Instead of using a single distance metric, we use a diverse set of metrics and adaptively combine their results (in the spirit of ensemble approaches to machine learning [6]). Furthermore, our algorithm can exploit training data to discover which distance metrics are most accurate for each semantic category.

In this paper, we make three contributions. First, we formulate the problem of Web Service data aggregation as a schema matching problem. Second, we describe OATS, a novel schema mapping algorithm specifically designed for the Web Services context. Finally, we empirically demonstrate that our approach is effective by describing experiments with 52 actual Web Service operations.

2   Related Work

The schema matching problem has been studied since the early 1980s resulting in many different approaches, each exploiting various features of the schemas and/or the instance data. Prior work can be classified according to whether it is schema vs. instance based, and whether it is structural vs. linguistic based. In our work, we focus on *instance* data using a *linguistic* matcher based on string-distance metrics such as the Levenshtein edit distance. Like most prior work, our OATS algorithm focuses on finding 1-1 mappings.

Schema-based matchers exploit any of the properties of the schema elements, such as their names, descriptions (if present), structure or constraints, while instance-based methods do the same for the data instances. Since there is generally more data available at the instance level than the schema level, data-intensive methods (such as those based on word frequencies) are usually more effective when applied to instance data. Nevertheless, most prior research on matching systems has focused on the schema level (see for example [7–10]). The OATS algorithm demonstrates that instance-based methods are well suited to scenarios such as Web Service aggregation where instance data can be actively requested.

Linguistic approaches use the text in element names and element instance data to find candidate matches. Any textual descriptions associated with the schemas can also be exploited by linguistic-based approaches. There are many ways of finding linguistic similarities between schemas: from finding exact string matches, to looking for common prefixes, suffixes, substrings, or even elements pronounced similarly. In contrast, structural approaches exploit the structure of schemas to be matched, proposing candidates based on similarities in the positions of elements and also of their neighbourhoods.

Many matching systems have both structural and linguistic components—two elements could be linguistically similar, but inspection of the other elements in the vicinity may suggest that the pair are not semantically related. For example, on first inspection, two elements with the label `population` having numerical data values may appear to be good match candidates, but when the elements' parents (`city` and `country`) are taken into account, it is clear that these elements don't match.

Our work has been influenced specifically by two prior research efforts: LSD [11] and ILA [12]. In LSD [11], similarities are computed at both the schema and the instance level. Here, Schema Matching is treated as a classification task where a mediated schema is first constructed and source elements classified into one of the elements of this schema. LSD employs a number of learner modules which are trained on the mediated schema and combined using a *meta learner*. The meta learner uses the training data to learn a weight for each classification label-learner combination, and combines each prediction accordingly. Because of the classification approach taken by LSD, training data must be employed.

ILA [12] learns models of relational Web information sources, where each model consists of a number of attributes and values. ILA learns the meaning of each attribute by explaining them in terms of the categories of its own internal model. That is, it maps between its own and the source's relational schemas. To do so, ILA probes the information source by querying with values from its model, and explains each field of the resulting string in terms of its internal model categories. Like OATS, ILA assumes that there is some overlap between its objects and the contents of each source.

3 Aggregating Web Services

In this section we formalise Web Services aggregation in a schema matching framework, and describe our OATS algorithm.

3.1 Web Services Aggregation as Schema Matching

One of the key features of Web Services is that they are platform-independent, and can be published, located, and invoked across the Web. This is made possible by requiring all communication with Web Services to conform to SOAP [w3.org/TR/soap], which is based on XML. When invoked, each Web Service operation returns an XML document consisting of metadata, schema elements and instance data. The structure and content of these documents is determined by the Web Service author when the operation is written, so even operations offering identical services will use different representations to encode their data.

In Web Service aggregation, the aim is to identify a set of Web Service operations that can answer a given query, invoke each of these operations with that query, and aggregate the elements from the XML documents that are returned. We refer to each XML tag as an element, and the text enclosed by opening and closing tags as instance data. Note that, like most schema matching systems, we do not attempt to match internal or empty elements (such as station or extremes in Fig. 1). In order to aggregate Web Service operation outputs, the semantically related elements among this heterogeneous XML data must be identified and grouped. Web Service aggregation can therefore be viewed as an instance of the schema matching problem.

A Web Service consists of one or more operations, each of which can be invoked with zero or more arguments. A major difference between traditional schema matching and our Web Service aggregation task is that we can exert some control over the instance data. Our OATS algorithm 'probes' each operation with arguments that correspond to the same real-world entity. For example, to aggregate operation o_1 that maps a ZIP code to its weather forecast, and operation o_2 that maps a latitude/longitude pair to its forecast, OATS could first select a specific location (eg, Seattle), and then query o_1 with

"98125" (a Seattle ZIP code), and query o_2 with "47.45N/122.30W" (Seattle's geocode).

Probing each operation with the related arguments should ensure that the instance data of related elements will closely correspond, increasing the accuracy of element matches. For example, invoking a set of weather forecast operations could result in data containing semantically related elements such as temp and high. If the operations are invoked with valid but unrelated arguments, there will likely be no correlation between the data instances of these elements—querying the operations with random locations may yield <temp>32</temp> and <high>-4</high>. On the other hand, if queried for the same location, the result may be <temp>10</temp> and <high>9</high>. This approach is inspired by the active learning scenario in machine learning (e.g., [4]), in which the learner constructs training examples that it guesses will lead to improved generalization. In contrast, prior work on machine learning for schema mapping adopts the standard supervised approch, in which the learner must rely on whatever training data happens to be provided.

As in ILA [12], this probe-based approach is based on the assumption that the operations overlap, i.e, there exists a set of real-world entities that are covered by all of the sources to be aggregated. For example, while two weather Web Services need not cover exactly the same locations in order to be aggregated, we do assume that there exists a set of locations covered by both.

We assume that the data integration system knows how to invoke the operations being aggregated. Specifically, we assume that the integration system can map the real-world probe entities to values for the operations' input parameters. While automatically performing this mapping is a separate issue beyond the scope of our research, we note that there are various methods of attaching explicit semantic metadata to Web Services (such as OWL-S [www.daml.org/services]), and [13, 14] investigate the automatic generation of such metadata.

3.2   The OATS Algorithm

As shown in Fig. 2, the input to the OATS algorithm is a set of Web Service operations, a set of probe objects, sufficient metadata about the operation so that each operation can be invoked on each probe, and a set of string distance metrics. The output of the OATS algorithm is a partition of the operations' elements into semantically equivalent classes.

One of the main features of our algorithm is the use of an ensemble of string distance metrics for matching elements based on string similarities. These metrics can be categorised as edit-based, token-based or hybrid metrics.

With edit-based metrics (such as the Levenshtein metric) the distance between two strings s and t is the cost of the best sequence of edit operations that converts s to t. Examples of edit operations are *delete*, *copy*, and *insert* a character. Some strings are likely to be duplicates, even if they aren't close in edit distance. With token based metrics, strings are split into token multisets S

Input:

- Web Service operations $O = \{o_1, o_2, \ldots, o_n\}$ and element sets $E = \{E_1, E_2, \ldots, E_n\}$, where operation o_i generates data with elements $E_i = \{e_1^i, e_2^i, \ldots\}$. (Let $E = \cup_i E_i$ be the set of all elements.)
- Probe objects $P = \{p_1, \ldots, p_m\}$.
- Invocation metadata $V = \{v_1, \ldots, v_n\}$, where v_i is a mapping from a probe $p_k \in P$ to the input parameters that will invoke o_i on p_k.[a]
- String distance metrics $D = \{d_1, d_2, \ldots\}$.

Output:

- A partition of the elements E.

Algorithm:

1. Query each operation o_i with $v_i(p_k)$ for each probe $p_k \in P$, and store the result in table T, where entry $T[i, j, k]$ holds the data for element $e_j^i \in E_i$ that result from invoking operation o_i with probe p_k.
2. For each pair $(e_j^i, e_{j'}^{i'}) \in E \times E$, compute an *ensemble distance* $D(e_j^i, e_{j'}^{i'})$ as follows:
   (a) For each distance metric $d_\ell \in D$, calculate the average (over the m probes) distance $\bar{d}_\ell$ between elements e_j^i and $e_{j'}^{i'}$. Normalize this average distance relative to the largest and smallest average over all element pairs. The result will be distances in the range [0-1], where 0 denotes the most similar pair of elements and 1 denotes the least similar pair.
   (b) Combine the normalized distances for each d_ℓ to get an ensemble distance $D(e_j^i, e_{j'}^{i'})$. In the standard OATS algorithm, this combination is simply an unweighted average. In the adaptive extension to OATS (Sec. 3.3), this combination is a weighted vote, where the weights are learned from the training data.
3. Cluster the elements in E using the ensemble distance $D(e_j^i, e_{j'}^{i'})$, terminating after a user-supplied threshold. Return the resulting clusters as groups of semantically related elements.

---

[a] In our implementation, the probes are encoded as a table of attribute/value pairs, and v_i is the subset of attributes needed for operation o_i.

Fig. 2. The OATS algorithm

and T, and similarity is generally a measure of the number of tokens that appear in both sets. Hybrid metrics are a combination of edit-based and token-based metrics. The SoftTFIDF metric for example, takes into account tokens in S that are *similar* to tokens in T as well as tokens that appear in both sets.

Some metrics are more useful than others, depending on the data being matched. For example, when looking for a match between the schema elements in Fig. 1, it makes more sense to use a token based matcher (e.g. TFIDF) for elements such as `<LastUpdated>Monday, December 8, 2003, at 12:51 PM Eastern Standard Time.</LastUpdated>`, and a character-level edit-distance metric (such as the Levenshtein metric) with elements such as `<Temprature>34F</Temprature>` [sic]. Furthermore, some of the distance metrics within these categories are more applicable to some data than to others. The Smith-Waterman distance metric [15] for instance, can discount mismatching text at the beginning and/or end of strings, so would have a natural advantage when looking for matches to strings such as phone numbers or latitudes which might only differ by their prefixes or suffixes.

The OATS algorithm calculate similarities based on the average similarities of an ensemble of distance metrics. Later, we describe an extension to OATS which assigns weights to distance metrics according to how well they correlate with a set of training data.

The algorithm proceeds as follows. Each of the n operations are invoked with the appropriate parameters for each of the m probe objects. The resulting nm XML documents are stored in a three-dimensional table T. The $T[i, \cdot, \cdot]$ entries of this table relate to operation $o_i \in O$, and the $T[\cdot, \cdot, k]$ entries relate to probe $p_k \in P$. Specifically, $T[i, j, k]$ stores the value returned for element $e_j^i \in E_i$ by operation o_i for probe p_k.

Each element is then compared with every other element. The distance between an element pair $(e_j^i, e_{j'}^{i'}) \in E \times E$ is calculated for each string distance metric $d_\ell \in D$, and these values are merged to provide an ensemble distance value for these elements. For each metric d_ℓ, the similarity $D(e_j^i, e_{j'}^{i'})$ between two elements $e_j^i \in E_i$ and $e_{j'}^{i'} \in E_{i'}$ is defined as follows:

$$D(e_j^i, e_{j'}^{i'}) = \frac{1}{|D|} \sum_\ell \frac{\bar{d}_\ell(e_j^i, e_{j'}^{i'}) - \min(\bar{d}_\ell)}{\max(\bar{d}_\ell) - \min(\bar{d}_\ell)},$$

$$\bar{d}_\ell(e_j^i, e_{j'}^{i'}) = \frac{1}{m} \sum_k d_\ell(T[i, j, k], T[i', j', k]),$$

$$\max(\bar{d}_\ell) = \max_{(e_j^i, e_{j'}^{i'})} \bar{d}_\ell(e_j^i, e_{j'}^{i'}),$$

$$\min(\bar{d}_\ell) = \min_{(e_j^i, e_{j'}^{i'})} \bar{d}_\ell(e_j^i, e_{j'}^{i'}).$$

By computing the average distance $\bar{d}_\ell$ over m related sets of element pairs, we are minimising the impact of any spurious instance data. For example, if we are calculating the distance between a `city` and `state` element with $m = 1$ probes, we could end up comparing the data instance `New York` with `New York` and getting a very low distance value for these elements (which is obviously misleading). Having more corresponding data pairs will decrease the chance of ambiguous data. This is inspired by the discrimination idea in ILA [12].

Before merging the distance metrics, they must be scaled in some way, as different metrics produce results in different scales (eg, Levenshtein distances are in the range $[-\infty,0]$, while TFIDF ranges over $[0,1]$). To do this we normalise the distances relative to the most similar and least similar pairs. As an example, suppose d_j returns a distance of 8 for the elements

getWeatherReportResponse.return.temperature.string

and

GetWeatherInfoResponse.GetWeatherInfoResult.Humidity

for some particular probe. If the most and least similar pairs for d_j have a distance of 1 and 23 respectively, then the normalized distance will be $\frac{(8-1)}{(23-1)}$.

To get the ensemble similarity $D(e^i_j, e^{i'}_{j'})$ for any pair we combine the normalized distances for each d_j. In the standard OATS algorithm, this combination is simply an unweighted average. We show in Section 3.3 how these weights can be 'tuned' for specific element-metric pairs.

Given the distances between each pair of elements, the final step of the OATS algorithm is to cluster the elements into semantically similar groups. This is done using the standard hierarchical agglomerative clustering (HAC) approach; Initially, each element is assigned to its own cluster. Next, the closest pair of clusters is found and these are merged into a single cluster. The previous step is repeated until some termination condition is satisfied, resulting in a set of semantically similar groups of elements. There are three ways to identify the closest pair of clusters: find the pair with the smallest minimum pairwise distance between the elements (single link), the pair with the smallest maximum pairwise distance (complete link), or the pair with the smallest average pairwise distance of elements of one cluster to elements of the other cluster (average link).

At some point in the clustering, all of the elements which are considered similar by our ensemble of distance metrics will be merged, and further iterations would only force together unrelated clusters. It is at this point that we should stop clustering. Our implementation relies on a user-specified termination threshold.

3.3 Learning Distance Metric Weights

Instead of giving an equal weight to each distance metric for all elements, it would make sense to treat some metrics as more important than others, depending on the characteristics of the data being compared. We have already given examples of cases where specific metrics are more suitable to particular data. We now show how we can exploit training data to automatically discover which distance metrics are most informative for which elements.

The key idea is that a good distance metric should have a small value between pairs of semantically related instances, while at the same time having a large value between pairs of semantically unrelated instances.

We assume access to a set of training data: a partition of some set of elements and their instance data. In our data aggregration scenario for example, this could correspond to a manually-generated partition of the elements of operations o_1 and o_2, and the goal is to aggregate data from a third related operation o_3.

Based on such training data, we define the *goodness* $G(d_j, C)$ of metric d_j for a non-singleton cluster C as follows.

1. Let $D_{\text{intra}}(d_j, C)$ be the average *intra*-cluster distance—i.e., the average distance between pairs of elements within C.
2. Let $D_{\text{inter}}(d_j, C)$ be the average *inter*-cluster distance—i.e., the average distance between an element in C and an element outside C.
3. Let $G'(d_j, C) = D_{\text{inter}}(d_j, C) - D_{\text{intra}}(d_j, C)$.
4. Finally, $G(d_j, C)$ is the extent to which $G'(d_j, C)$ exceeds the average over all clusters:
$$G(d_j, C) = \frac{G'(d_j, C)}{\frac{1}{c} \sum_{C'} G'(d_j, C')}$$

where c is the number of non-singleton clusters C' in the training data.

A distance metric d_j will have a score $G(d_j, C) > 1$ if it is "good" (better than average) at separating data from cluster C from data outside the cluster, while $G(d_j, C) < 1$ suggests that d_j is a bad metric for C.

Given these goodness values, we modify the OATS algorithm in two ways. The first approach (which we call "binary") gives a weight of 1 to metrics with $G > 1$, and gives weight 0 to (ie, ignores) metrics with $G < 1$. The second approach ("proportional"), assigns weights that are proportional to the goodness values.

4   Evaluation

4.1   Methodology

We evaluated our web service aggregation tool on three groups of semantically related web service operations: 31 operations providing information about geographical locations, 8 operations giving current weather information, and 13 operations giving current stock information.

To enable an objective evaluation, a reference partition was first created by hand for each of the three groups. The partitions generated by OATS were compared to these reference partitions.

In our evaluation, we used the method proposed by [13] to measure the similarity between two partitions. This method is based on the concepts of precision and recall used extensively in the information retrieval community. To calculate these values, each pair of elements in the predicted partition is allocated to one of four categories: a, clustered together (and should have been clustered together); b, not clustered together (but should have been clustered together); c, incorrectly clustered together; and d, correctly not clustered together. Precision is then computed as $P = \frac{a}{a+c}$, recall is $R = \frac{a}{a+b}$, and $F1 = \frac{2PR}{P+R}$.

Precision represents the number of returned clusters that are correct, while recall represents the number of correct clusters that are returned (a clustering with high precision but low recall, for instance, means that the majority of returned clusters are correct, but that many correct clusters remain undiscovered). The F1 value is a combination of precision and recall.

We ran a number of tests on each domain. Each of the tests was run using Average Link, Complete Link and Single Link clustering. We systematically vary the HAC termination threshold, from one extreme in which each element is placed in its own cluster, to the other extreme in which all elements are merged into one large cluster. Our methodology is similar to that of [16].

The ensemble of distance metrics was selected from Cohen's SecondString library [16]. We chose eight representative metrics, consisting of a variety of character-based, token-based and hybrid metrics. Specifically, our ensemble consisted of TFIDF, SlimTFIDF, Jaro, CharJaccard, Levenstein [sic], SmithWaterman, Level2Jaro and Level2JaroWinkler.

Each probe entity is constructed by hand and represented as a set of attribute/value pairs. Ideally, each of the probes will be 'recognised' by each of the Web Services, but this is not always the case. For instance, most weather-report Services will be able to return information given well known ICAO codes, but only some may be able to return data for other less well known ones. Invoking each operation a number of times with different probes increases the chance of obtaining meaningful data from the Web Services and the probability of creating correct matches. Apart from invoking the Web Services and examining the results, there is no way of knowing which probes will be most effective.

address	city	state	fullstate	zip	areacode	lat	long	icao
110 135th Avenue	New York	NY	New York	11430	718	40.38	-74.75	KJFK
101 Harborside Drive	Boston	MA	Massachusetts	02128	781	42.21	-71.00	KBOS
18740 Pacific Highway South	Seattle	WA	Washington	98188	206	47.44	-122.27	KSEA
9515 New Airport Drive	Austin	TX	Texas	78719	512	30.19	-97.67	KAUS

Fig. 3. The four probe objects for the zip and weather domains

Fig. 3 shows the four probes used for the weather and location information domains. We hand-crafted rules to match each of an operation's inputs to an attribute (ie, columns in Fig. 3). To invoke an operation, the probe objects (ie, rows in Fig. 3) are searched for the required attributes. Note that each operation may require different input data types: one location service may require a city name as input, another may require a ZIP code, and a third may require a geocode.

Our experimental data is available at www.smi.ucd.ie/RSWS.

4.2   Results

First, we show that by using an ensemble of different distance metrics, (each exploiting a different property of the data being compared), we achieve better results than using the metrics separately. Fig. 4 shows the F1 metric as a function of the HAC termination threshold, and the precision/recall curves, for our ensemble approach compared to the Levenshtein and TFIDF metrics alone (across the three domains). Lowering the HAC termination threshold increases precision at the expense of recall, and raising the threshold increases recall but lowers precision. The graphs in Fig. 4 show this tradeoff between precision and recall as the threshold is systematically varied.

While the maximum F1 is higher for the ensemble of matchers in only one case, the average F1 is higher in all three domains, meaning that the ensemble is much less sensitive to the tuning of the HAC termination threshold.

Next, we show that accuracy improves with additional probe queries, but that performance is beginning to level off after just a few probes. Fig. 5 shows the average (over all three domains) of the maximum and average (over all HAC termination thresholds) F1 score, as a function of the number of probe queries. Note that the difference between successive numbers of probes is starting to decrease (ie, the difference between one and two probes in greater than the difference between three and four). We have evaluated OATS with at most four probes, but we expect that the performance increase will rapidly slow beyond a relatively small number of probes.

Note that we did not carefully select the probe objects in order to maximize performance. Indeed, some of the operations returned missing elements for some probes. Our experiments suggest that the active invocation approach makes OATS robust to even a "bad" choice of probes.

We now compare the performance of OATS with our two methods (binary and proportional) for using the learned distance metric weights. These results are based on four probes.

We used two-fold cross validation, where the set of operations was split into two equal-sized subsets, S_{train} and S_{test}. We used just two folds due to the relatively small number of operations. S_{train} was clustered according to the ref-

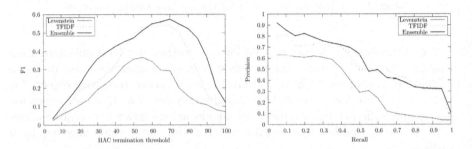

Fig. 4. Comparison of ensemble method against Levenshtein and TFIDF: F1 as a function of the HAC termination threshold (left), and precision/recall curve (right)

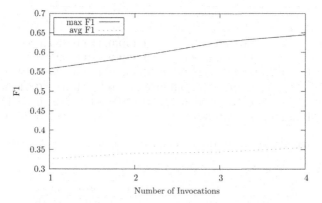

Fig. 5. F1 as a function of the number of probe queries

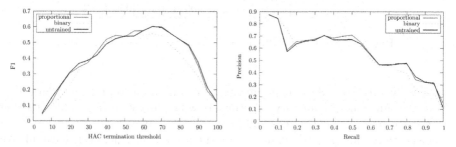

Fig. 6. Peformance of OATS: F1 as a function of the HAC termination threshold (left), and precision/recall curve (right)

erence clusters (i.e, all elements of the reference cluster that didn't appear in the training were discarded), and weights for each distance metric were learned. Clustering was then performed on the entire set of elements. Note that we clustered the training data along with the test data in the learning phase, but we did not initialize the clustering process with reference clusters for the training data prior to testing. We measured the performance of the clustering by calculating Precision and Recall for the elements of S_{test}.

Fig. 6 shows F1 as a function of the HAC termination threshold, and the precision/recall curves, for the binary and proportional learners and the original algorithm averaged across the three domains. Although neither of the learning methods increase the maximum F1, they do increase the average F1 in two-thirds of the cases (see the bold values in Fig. 7), suggesting that learning makes OATS somewhat less sensitive to the exact setting of the HAC termination threshold. All of the previous results were based on the average-link HAC algorithm; Fig. 7 also shows the performance of the single- and complete-link methods. The high maximum F1 illustrates how the majority of correct clusters were found by our algorithm, with most of these clusters being accurate, requiring only a small amount of manual rearranging.

		Stock			Weather			Location		
	Method	AL	CL	SL	AL	CL	SL	AL	CL	SL
	Proportional	**0.678**	**0.648**	0.701	**0.459**	**0.419**	**0.625**	0.885	0.826	0.772
max F1	Binary	**0.678**	**0.648**	0.701	**0.459**	**0.419**	**0.625**	0.885	0.826	0.772
	No Learning	**0.678**	**0.648**	**0.703**	**0.459**	**0.419**	**0.625**	**0.892**	**0.849**	**0.812**
	Proportional	0.410	0.387	**0.369**	0.272	**0.269**	**0.284**	**0.518**	**0.520**	**0.467**
ave F1	Binary	0.412	0.390	0.350	**0.274**	0.266	0.272	0.478	0.499	0.404
	No Learning	**0.415**	**0.391**	0.360	0.273	0.264	**0.284**	0.492	0.485	0.436

Fig. 7. Comparison of the average-, complete- and single-link clustering algorithms

F1	Method	Stock	Weather	Location
maximum F1	data only	0.571	0.460	0.904
	names & data	0.731	0.358	0.890
average F1	data only	0.357	0.262	0.448
	names & data	0.403	0.206	0.453

Fig. 8. Performance with element names as well as instance data

Finally, all of the above experiments were carried out on instance data only. We have run some preliminary experiments which apply our ensemble of string metrics to both element names and instance data. As can be seen in Fig. 8, in some domains this greatly enhances performance but in others it is harmful. We are currently investigating refinements of these experiments in order to extend OATS to element names and other schema data.

5 Summary and Future Work

We have shown how Web Service aggregation can be viewed as an instance of the schema matching problem in which instance data is particularly important. We have illustrated how actively probing Web Service operations with a very small number of inputs can result in related instance data which makes the matching task easier.

Our OATS algorithm uses an ensemble of string distance metrics to overcome the limitations of any particular metric. Our experiments demonstrate that this approach performs better than the application of individual metrics. We also proposed a method for adaptively combining distance metrics in relation to the characteristics of the data being compared. While this learning process was not always sucessful, in the majority of cases, F1 increased when learning was used.

Clearly, instance data alone is not sufficient for high-accuracy schema matching. We are currently exploring hybrid techniques that incorporate evidence from element names, structural comparisons etc. In our experiments, we used a simple ranking method for combining individual string metrics. We plan to examine the use of different techniques for aggregating the ensemble members.

As is reflected in our results, the ability to match schema elements is dependent on the quality of the elements data, which in this case is determined by the probe queries. We plan to examine the automatic selection of optimal probe queries, and methods of automatically mining useful probe queries.

One of the constraints of our aggregation system is that there must be an overlap between the sources, i.e all of the sources must "know about" the entity being queried. Ultimately, we would like our system to learn new objects from some information sources that could be used to probe other partially overlapping sources. We envisage a tool that, given a set of seed Web Services and probe queries, could find sets of related Web Services and learn new probe objects to query them with.

Acknowledgments. This research was supported by grants SFI/01/F.1/C015 from Science Foundation Ireland, and N00014-03-1-0274 from the US Office of Naval Research.

References

1. Wiederhold, G.: Value-added mediation in large-scale information systems. In: DS-6. (1995) 34–56
2. Levy, A.Y., Rajaraman, A., Ordille, J.J.: Query-answering algorithms for information agents. In: Proceedings of the Thirteenth National Conference on Artificial Intelligence and the Eighth Innovative Applications of Artificial Intelligence Conference, Menlo Park, AAAI Press / MIT Press (1996) 40–47
3. Rahm, E., Bernstein, P.: On matching schemas automatically. Technical report, Microsoft Research Technical Report (2001)
4. Lewis, D.D., Catlett, J.: Heterogeneous uncertainty sampling for supervised learning. In Cohen, W.W., Hirsh, H., eds.: Proceedings of ICML-94, 11th International Conference on Machine Learning, New Brunswick, US, Morgan Kaufmann Publishers, San Francisco, US (1994) 148–156
5. Levenshtein, V.I.: Binary codes capable of correcting spurious insertions and deletions of ones (original in russian). Russian Problemy Peredachi Informatsii **1** (1965) 12–25
6. Dietterich, T.: Ensemble methods in machine learning. In: Proc. 1st Int. Workshop on Multiple Classifier Systems. (2000)
7. Embley, D.W., Jackman, D., Xu, L.: Multifaceted exploitation of metadata for attribute match discovery in information integration. In: Workshop on Information Integration on the Web. (2001) 110–117
8. Popa, L., Velegrakis, Y., Miller, R.J., Hernandez, M.A., Fagin, R.: Translating web data. In: Proceedings of VLDB 2002, Hong Kong SAR, China. (2002) 598–609
9. Beneventano, D., Bergamaschi, S., Castano, S., Corni, A., Guidetti, R., Malvezzi, G., Melchiori, M., Vincini, M.: Information integration: The MOMIS project demonstration. In: The VLDB Journal. (2000) 611–614
10. Do, H., Rahm, E.: Coma - a system for flexible combination of schema matching approaches (2002)
11. Doan, A., Domingos, P., Halevy, A.: Learning to match the schemas of data sources: A multistrategy approach. Mach. Learn. **50** (2003) 279–301

12. Perkowitz, M., Etzioni, O.: Category translation: Learning to understand information on the internet. In: International Joint Conference on Artificial Intelligence, IJCAI-95, Montreal, Canada (1995) 930–938
13. Kushmerick, N., Heß, A.: Learning to attach semantic metadata to web services. In: Second International Semantic Web Conference (ISWC-03), Sanibel Island, Florida (2003)
14. Heß, A., Kushmerick, N.: Iterative ensemble classification for relational data: A case study of semantic web services. In: 15th European Conference on Machine Learning (ECML 2004). (2004)
15. Smith, T.F., Waterman, M.S.: Identification of common molecular subsequences. Journal of Molecular Biology **147** (1981) 195–197
16. Cohen, W.W., Ravikumar, P., Fienberg, S.E.: A comparison of string distance metrics for name-matching tasks. In: Proceedings of the IJCAI-2003 Workshop on Information Integration on the Web, Acapulco, Mexico (2003) 73–78

KATS: A Knowledge Acquisition Tool Based on Electronic Document Processing

Martin Molina and Gemma Blasco

Department of Artificial Intelligence, Universidad Politécnica de Madrid,
Campus de Montegancedo S/N 28660 Boadilla del Monte, Madrid, Spain
mmolina@fi.upm.es, gblasco@isys.dia.fi.upm.es

Abstract. This paper describes a particular knowledge acquisition tool for the construction and maintenance of the knowledge model of an intelligent system for emergency management in the field of hydrology. This tool has been developed following an innovative approach directed to end-users non familiarized in computer oriented terminology. According to this approach, the tool is conceived as a document processor specialized in a particular domain (hydrology) in such a way that the whole knowledge model is viewed by the user as an electronic document. The paper first describes the characteristics of the knowledge model of the intelligent system and summarizes the problems that we found during the development and maintenance of such type of model. Then, the paper describes the KATS tool, a software application that we have designed to help in this task to be used by users who are not experts in computer programming. Finally, the paper shows a comparison between KATS and other approaches for knowledge acquisition.

1 Introduction

Knowledge acquisition is a key issue in the development of intelligent systems. Despite that the advances in this field of knowledge acquisition the last years have significantly improved the way to perform this task with useful resources and tools, the current experience shows that there is still an important gap between the way end-users describe their expertise and the type of communication followed by existing tools. In particular, this issue has received recently special attention from AI researchers in the context of web-based applications. Thus, the need of knowledge development tools usable by non-experts in knowledge engineering has been recently underlined within the *semantic web* context as one of the challenges for the twenty-first century AI research [15].

In particular, this problem is especially significant when the complexity of the knowledge model of an intelligent system is high due to the presence of more than one complex tasks (e.g. diagnosis, prediction, configuration) each one with its particular knowledge organization. In this case, the difficulty of development and maintenance of the knowledge model increases because, among other reasons, it requires using different symbolic languages for representation of local knowledge bases and they present important dependences that need to be considered to guarantee the consistency of the global model.

E. Motta et al. (Eds.): EKAW 2004, LNAI 3257, pp. 403–418, 2004.

According to this need, this paper presents a contribution in this direction based on our recent experience in the development and maintenance of a complex real-world model for an intelligent system called SAIDA in the domain of emergency management in hydrology. This paper first describes a summary of the SAIDA system and its knowledge model to show the problems that we found in the development and maintenance of SAIDA models. Then, the paper describes a particular software tool called KATS (*Knowledge Acquisition Tool for SAIDA-Models*) that we designed to facilitate the development of hydrologic models for SAIDA. This tool presents an innovative approach that considers the knowledge model as an electronic document. The paper describes the characteristics of such a document and how it is processed by KATS to serve as knowledge model of SAIDA. Finally, the paper presents a comparison between KATS and other types of existing knowledge acquisition tools.

2   General View of the Knowledge Model for Decision Support

This section summarizes the characteristics of the knowledge model of the SAIDA system, which was developed to provide assistance in making decisions about hydraulic actions during floods. The SAIDA (Spanish acronym for Intelligent Agents Society for Decision-making during Floods) system is a computerized system based on artificial intelligence techniques that provides assistance in flash flood situations for basin control centers [8; 22; 20]. The system was developed in a project developed during more than three years promoted by the Spanish Ministry of the Environment with the purpose of having it installed and used in connection with the information hydrologic systems in several Spanish basins. SAIDA receives as input the available data provided by sensors about discharge, water level and rainfall at different locations in the river basin. The answers are produced with time constraints and the conclusions are justified at a reasonable level of abstraction given that the operator must take the final responsibility of decisions. SAIDA provides answers to the following types of questions: (1) what is happening? (2) what may happen in the future?, and (3) what can be done?. With SAIDA he operator can quickly understand the current situation, identify the main problems that have to be solved and is briefed on the actions that could be taken to reduce the problems and minimize the risks.

The design of the SAIDA knowledge base followed a *model-based* approach with which different problem-solving methods were used as building blocks to perform the different tasks. To implement such a model, the KSM environment was used [7] following and a methodology that use and extend some concepts that are present in methodologies such a CommonKADS [23]. SAIDA also followed a multiagent approach to facilitate the development of the complex knowledge base. Figure 2 shows the basic structure of the knowledge model of SAIDA according to the three main tasks provided by the system: (1) evaluation, (2) prediction and (3) recommendation. Each task is performed by the corresponding problem-solving methods (details can be found in [20]).

The distributed nature of the decisions and the spatial location of certain components makes very appropriate using the multiagent approach as a complementary design approach to organize the knowledge model. Within each type of agent, the knowledge bases were adequately organized and implemented by using additional modular approaches. According to different types of decisions, we identified four types of agents: (1) *hydraulic agents* that are responsible to give answers about the behavior of the physical process, (2) *problem detection agents*, responsible of evaluating the flood risk in a particular geographical area, (3) *reservoir management agents*, which contain criteria for exploitation strategy for each reservoir, and (4) *civil protection agents*, responsible to provide with resources of different types according to the needs of the problem detection agents. For each type of agent, there are several instances according to the geography of the river basin. The main three tasks (evaluation, prediction and recommendation) were distributed among the different agents, in such a way that they communicate partial results to complete their individual goals.

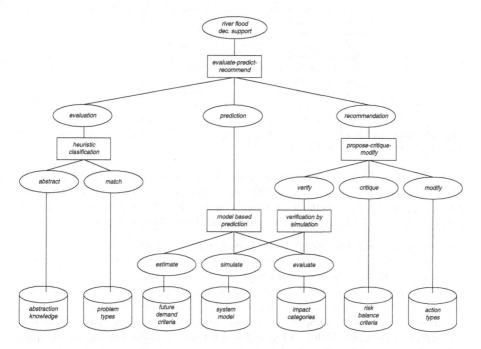

Fig. 1. The basic structure of the model for decision support in the field of emergency management during floods (circle = task, square = method, cylinder = type of knowledge base)

A model for a particular river basin is constructed formulating a set of knowledge bases. Figure 2 shows a summary of a complete model for the case of a river basin in Spain (the Júcar river basin). This includes a total of 23 agents, one for each specific decision point at certain location in the river basin depending on its nature (problem area, reservoir, river channel or protection). For each agent, there is a set of types of knowledge bases, each one with its particular language representation, with a total of 143 knowledge bases.

Agents	N. of agents	Knowledge Bases	Knowledge Representation	N. of KBs
Problem detection agents	15	Abstraction	Functional + temporal represent.	15
		Problem types	Frames with uncertainty degrees	15
		Future Demand	Rules	15
		Impact categories	Bayesian network	15
		Risk balance criteria	Rules	1
		Action types: agent relations	Horn Logic Clauses	15
Reservoir management agents	4	Abstraction	Functional + temporal represent.	4
		Problem types	Frames with uncertainty degrees	4
		Future Demand	Rules	4
		Impact categories	Bayesian nets	4
		Risk balance criteria	Rules	1
		Action types: discharge strategies	Rules	1
Hydraulic agents	2	Abstraction	Functional + temporal represent.	2
		System model: influence diagram	Temporal causal network	2
		System model: infiltration	Bayesian network	12
		System model: discharge	Bayesian network	12
		System model: reservoir discharge	Bayesian network	4
		System model: junction	Bayesian network	11
Protection agents	2	Action types: transport network	Rules	2
		Action types: population	Rules	2
		Action types: constructions	Rules	2
TOTAL	23 Ag.		TOTAL	143 KBs

Fig. 2. Summary of knowledge bases corresponding to a particular model for ariver basin in the case of the Júcar River Basin (East of Spain)

According to the previous description, the characteristics of a knowledge model for hydrologic decision presents a significant complexity, which is inherent to the physical phenomena in which the decision is based. The following list summarizes the problems reported by users that were responsible of model construction:

- *Dimension and Complexity.* The knowledge model presents a high level of complexity with different interrelated types of knowledge for different purposes (e.g., 143 KBs for the Júcar river model).
- *Heterogeneity of Symbolic Representation.* Each type of knowledge base has its own symbolic representation (frames, rules, uncertainty, temporal and spatial dimensions, etc.). Despite they are based on natural and declarative representation, this factor increases the difficulty of understanding the complete model.
- *Low Level of Certain Representations.* For certain types of knowledge, civil engineers use certain common sense usual in their professional area, but the corresponding knowledge base may use low level representations to represent such a knowledge with excessive detail about implicit terms that makes the model more artificial and difficult to understand.
- *Abstract Computer-Oriented Terminology.* The SAIDA model follows a general methodology based on the KSM tool. This introduces an additional terminology closer to information processing, different from hydrology, that sometimes is too abstract for end-users and increases the difficulty to understand the complete model.
- *Consistency Between Modules.* The model presents a distributed organization of knowledge, following a multiagent architecture and, for each agent there is a set of knowledge bases with different inference procedures. This modular organization makes easier to understand and validate parts of the whole model

but, still, sometimes it is difficult anticipate the dependencies between such modules in order to keep the global consistency.

- *False Idea of Procedural Representation.* The edition of the content of knowledge bases uses text processors with the corresponding language for each case. We found that this may give the false idea that the user writes a kind of procedure (following a conventional programming style) instead of a set of expertise criteria with a declarative approach with more freedom to add or remove sentences.

- *Different Procedures for Knowledge Acquisition.* Another problem is that the user must combine different non-integrated software tools to cope with different sources of knowledge. Thus, for example, certain knowledge can be manually represented using symbolic formalisms, but another type of knowledge can be learned with machine learning procedures.

- *Low Level of Guidance.* The user has the possibility of editing and modifying any part of the model with certain freedom. However, this freedom should be complemented with certain guidance in the model development, to suggest to the developer about what are the next steps to be done.

3   KATS: A Knowledge Acquisition Tool for SAIDA Models

In order to give an answer to the previous needs, we have designed and built a software tool called KATS that assists developers in the construction of hydrologic models for the SAIDA system. One of the most innovative characteristics of this tool is the user view of the knowledge model. We have applied the principles that we describe in [21]. According to them, the user perceives the whole knowledge model as an electronic document. This approach contrasts with the extended approach followed by knowledge acquisition tools that considers the user interface as a set of canned windows representing forms that must be filled by the user, together with a set of warning and help windows that supervise the process and guide the user. On the contrary, the basic idea in KATS is that when the user creates/maintains a knowledge model, she/he reads and writes a document in the same way that reads and writes a conventional document using standard text processors. A document is an entity very familiar to persons non specialized in computer science, so this a natural media to formulate the content of a model and it has been assumed and extended in the context of web-based applications with electronic features (hyper-links, multimedia, etc.).

The following sections analyze (1) the characteristics of the electronic document that describes to the complete knowledge model, and (2) the software tool that allows the user to consult and modify the electronic document.

3.1   The Electronic Document to Describe the Knowledge Model

The document is considered like a manual that describes problem solving methods for decision making procedures based on certain expertise. To satisfy the needs described in this paper, this document must accomplish the following three basic requirements:

- *Human Understandability.* The content of the document must be totally comprehensible by users non-experts in computer science. A way to guarantee this assumption is that the complete set of procedures described by the document should be able to be performed manually by a user specialized in the domain of the problem.

- *Computer Understandability.* The content of the document must be also comprehensible by computer programs that, based on this content, automatically perform the decision making procedures for which the knowledge based system has been designed.
- *Dynamic Content.* The content of the document must be able to be modified by the user. For this purpose, in a document we consider three types of parts: (1) *static*, that describe prefixed areas assumed by computer programs that manipulate the document, (2) *user*, dynamic areas that can be edited and modified by users, and (3) *automatic*, dynamic areas that are automatically generated by programs that process the information provided by the user.

In order to accomplish the requirement for human understandability, it is important that the document presents a structure with the different issues about the problem that need to be understood by persons. For this purpose, we consider the categories of knowledge established by knowledge engineering methodologies and tools (for instance, CommonKADS [23], KSM [7], etc.). In addition to that, we distribute the domain knowledge and we add complementary views at different levels of abstraction to facilitate global views of the model (a description of the general format can be found at [21]). To be complete, the content of the document includes both inference (problem-solving) and domain knowledge. Normally, with a few exceptions, the static areas correspond to user-oriented descriptions about inference procedures, the user-dynamic areas correspond to domain knowledge and the automatic-dynamic areas correspond with complementary and global views of domain knowledge. Figure 3 shows a general view of the electronic document and its different parts.

An important factor to make the document understandable by humans is that the type of symbolic formalism used to represent domain knowledge must be familiar to persons non-expert in computers. Thus, instead of including in the text descriptions of algorithms and/or low level symbolic representations, the document must follow natural representations such as text (natural language) descriptions, tables, mathematical notation, graphics, etc. typically used in the professional domain of the problem. In the particular case of the KATS tool we used a set of what we call *document representation resources* that include common communication elements and others more familiar to professionals of hydrology (figure 4). This set of resources are presented uniformly in the electronic document together with the static information.

3.2   The Software Tool for Document Processing

The knowledge acquisition tool is considered as a specialized electronic document processor, i.e. a text processor specialized in the domain of SAIDA (hydrology) that allows the user to write the knowledge base as an electronic document (figure 5). The tool provides the following services: (1) *user interaction* to present the document to the user (with the corresponding representation resources) with facilities to modify the content, (2) *consistency checking* to guarantee the consistency of the model applying

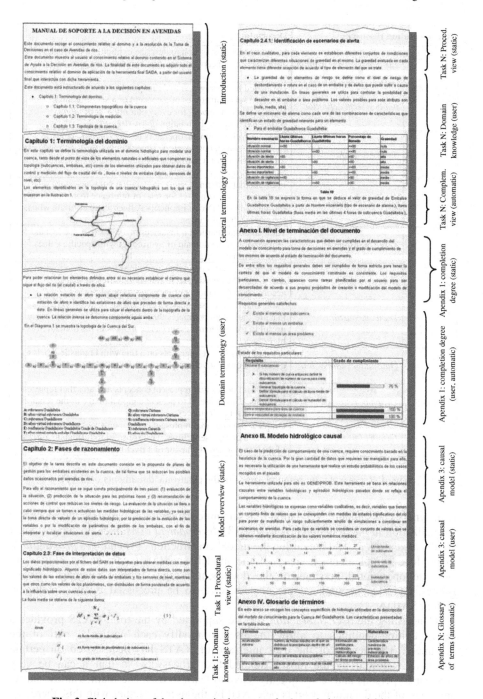

Fig. 3. Global view of the electronic document for knowledge acquisition

Representation resources		Descriptions
Paragraph	Explicit term description	Formatted text paragraph to describe explicitly a concept, an attribute of a concept or a relation between concepts.
	Implicit term definition	Formatted text paragraph to define implicitly a set of instances of a class, a set of attributes of a concept or a set of relations (for instance, there is a *path* for every pair *node-destination* connected through the relation *down-stream*).
Formula	Simple formula	Formula with arithmetic operators (+,-,/,*) and/or standard functions (sin(x), cos(x), etc.). The formula can be defined either for the attribute of a particular concept (specific) or for the attribute of a class (general).
	Iterative formula	Formula that is defined using an iteration (summatory , productory , etc) on a set (or sets) of reference that is explicitly formulated in a table or implicitly defined in an attribute whose content is a list of values.
Table	Table of instances	Table to define particular instances of a class (e.g. the instances of reservoir in the domain of hydrology) with specific values for certain attributes (e.g., volume of each particular reservoir, etc.).
	Decision table	Table that includes conditional relations to be used in logical decisions. The decision table can adopt different shapes according to the amount of elements to be presented.
	Table of causal relations	Table that shows a set of types of relations between variables that are causes and variables that are effects. This is especially useful to formulate bayesian causal models in the domain of hydrology.
Graphic	Qualitative number line	A set of consecutive segments on a line with linguistic labels to describe a qualitative interpretation of a quantitative dimension.
	Graph of relations	Graph with nodes that represent concepts and arcs that represent relations. This is useful to present a global image of the relations between a set of instances.
	Graph of processes	Graph with nodes that represent components and measure points, and arcs that represent flows. This is useful to formulate a model of the structure and behavior of a river basin.

Fig. 4. Representation resources used in the electronic documents of KATS

both syntax and semantic validation (the semantic validation is based on the processor specialization in the domain knowledge), (3) *development assistance*, to suggest what are the next steps to be done during the model construction , (4) *changes propagation*, to produce complementary views of the model, and (5) *document translation*, to generate operational versions of the document using symbolic languages (rules, frames, bayesian networks, logic clauses, etc.) to be processed by the intelligent system SAIDA.

Concerning the *user interaction* service supported by the tool, KATS provides a set of editing facilities to allow the user to modify each particular part of the document. The design of the user interface of KATS has been based on certain standards followed by the most extended text processors, so that it can be very familiar to persons and, consequently, easy to learn to use. The main window shows an image of the document as it is perceived by the user. Together with this, there is a set of editing facilities that are sensible to the part of the document to be modified.

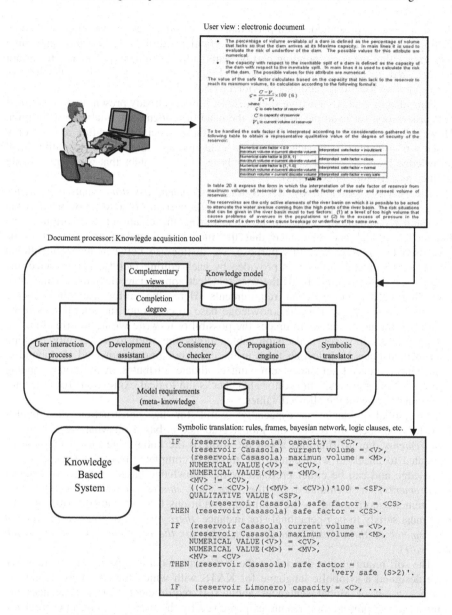

Fig. 5. Global view of the operation with the knowledge acquisition tool

Thus when the user desires to change a dynamic part of the document, she or he clicks directly on it and automatically a specialized editor window is presented. This particular window depends on the type of content in such a way that, for example, if a text paragraph for attributes is selected, an editor for attributes is presented. This editor allows to describe an attribute by selecting and completing prefixed natural language sentences. Similarly, if a decision table is selected, a specialized editor for decision tables is presented. Each particular type of presentation resource has its own editing facility. The window of each particular editing facility has the same appearance that the corresponding part presents in the document, together with certain buttons and resources for manipulation. Figure 6 shows examples of windows corresponding to editing facilities provided by KATS.

This idea of context-sensitive specialized editors is already present in conventional text processors, for example to modify the head of a document, a table or a formula. However, the KATS approach considers that these specialized editors are not only based on a syntax approach but their contents are interrelated to build local knowledge bases (e.g., a decision table only includes variables that where previously defined as attributes of concepts).

The services provided by KATS for *development assistance* and *consistency checking* are oriented to provide guidance to the user in order to know what is the next step (or remaining steps) to be done during the creation/modification of the knowledge model and guarantee that the model is complete and correct to be processed by SAIDA. For this purpose, we distinguish between local and global guidance. The local guidance is provided by each editing facility. For instance, the editor for a decision table helps the user to select appropriate elements for the table according certain construction requirements. Here, the editor uses the existing elements already present in the knowledge base to constraint the alternatives to be written by the user, which eliminates the possibility to write wrong information. For example, the editor for a decision table allows the user to write only existing concepts/attributes by selecting them in the corresponding menus, and also avoid to write autoreferenced sentences removing candidate attributes in the corresponding selection lists of menus. This editor also checks the logical expressions for attributes to be consistent with the allowed values.

The global guidance is especially useful for the construction of complex knowledge models. In KATS, the global guidance is based on what we call *model requirements*, i.e. affirmations about the form of the knowledge model that can be evaluated to check to what extend the model is complete. This is a kind of meta-knowledge and can be either prefixed by the knowledge based system (*hard model requirements*) or formulated by the user (*soft model requirements*). The hard requirements correspond to the minimum conditions that the model written by the user must satisfy to be operational (for instance, *there must be at least an instance of pluviometer* or *there must be a decision table for the attribute risk-level for each reservoir*).

The soft requirements depend on the particular model in a particular domain. We have designed a symbolic language for KATS with which the user may express in advance a set of global sentences about soft requirements. These sentences are referred to the presentation resources perceived by the user (e.g., concepts, decision tables, formula, diagrams, etc.). Figure 7 shows some examples of sentences (translated to English) that the user can write for this purpose. The KATS tool uses these sentences to inform to the user to what extend the model is complete. The sentences based on a quantitative reference (e.g. number of instances) allow to inform about the percentage of completion. The user may write this type of sentences with the help of a particular editor that presents the alternative options with the syntax details.

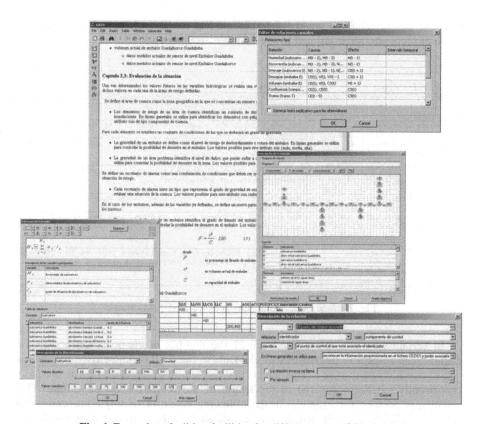

Fig. 6. Examples of editing facilities for different parts of the document

The service of *change propagation* provided by KATS is very useful for the construction and maintenance of complex knowledge models. With this service, when the user modifies certain part of the document, KATS automatically creates or changes other related parts of the document. Normally, these parts correspond to complementary views of the model that facilitate a better comprehension of the model. For example, the complementary views may correspond to a summary of certain elements that show a global view of certain part of the model. Other examples of complementary views are: cross references, glossaries of terms, etc.

Finally, the fifth service provided by KATS is *document translation*. In order to be operational (understandable by programs) the content of the document is translated by KATS to conventional symbolic structures to be manipulated by SAIDA. Thus, the changes in the document performed by the user with the help of KATS, modify the knowledge base of SAIDA and, consequently, its problem solving behavior. Basically, KATS translates the representation resources of the document in the following way: (1) paragraphs for term description, graphs for relations, number lines, tables of instances and paragraphs for instances are translated to hierarchies of classes, subclasses with attributes and values and also the set of agents (2) formulas and iterative formulas are translated to functional expressions with temporal extensions, (3) decision tables are translated to rules and frame-like patterns, (4) tables of causal relations are translated to models based on bayesian networks, (5) graph of processes are translated to a temporal causal network.

Format of sentence	Examples
Number of instances of <class> [greater than, less than, equal to] <number>	Number of instances of reservoir equal to 10
	Number of instances of pluviometer greater to 5
For every <class> where [<attribute> is <value>, <attribute> is known] a particular value for <attribute> must be known.	For every basin where number-of-curve is known a particular value for area must be known
	For every reservoir a particular value for objective-volume must be known
For every <class> there must be a qualitative interpretation for <attribute>	For every river-basin there must be a qualitative interpretation for average-rain
For every <class>, its <attribute> must be computed by [a formula, a decision table] [with the following attributes: <attribute-1>, …, <attribute-n>]	For every reservoir its objective-volume must be computed by a formula
	For every problem-area its risk-level must be computed by a decision table with the following attributes: flow-upstream of problem-area
The relation <relation> [between <classes>, between <class-1> and <class-2>] must be defined by a graph	The relation downstream-section between river-basin-component and measure-point must be defined by a graph

Fig. 7. Some examples of sentences for model requirement

In certain cases the correspondence of the number of elements defined in the document in respect to the number of elements in the SAIDA knowledge base is not one-to-one but one-to-many. This means that the length of the document is normally significantly smaller compared to the length of the SAIDA knowledge base. This situation is present, for example, in the following cases: (1) a single paragraph that defines implicitly a set of instances is translated into the corresponding number of instances, (2) a general formula that is defined with an iterative definition is translated into a set of formulas with the corresponding particularization, (3) the definition of a particular attribute for a physical magnitude (e.g., flow) is translated into several specific attributes corresponding to different views (with different time steps and different levels of abstraction), etc.

4   Discussion

This section presents a comparison of the existing approaches of knowledge acquisition tools with KATS. The comparison includes three types of the most advanced software tools for knowledge modeling: (1) method-based knowledge acquisition tools, (2) general knowledge modeling tools, and (3) ontology management tools.

The category of method-based knowledge acquisition tools includes a type of software tool that assists in the development of a knowledge-based system for a prefixed kind of task and problem-solving method. Examples of such tools are MORE [10] for diagnosis systems with the cover-and-differentiate method, or SALT [18] for design systems with the propose-and-revise method. This category also includes other more specific tools in certain domains such as SIRAH [1] for prediction tasks in hydrology. The advantages of method-based knowledge acquisition tools are derived from the fact that the organization of the knowledge is prefixed, so they have a good level of support for model construction and efficiency in the generation of the operational version. However the range of applicability is significant lower than other approaches. This category of tool is very similar to the case of KATS because KATS is a software tool oriented to help in building and maintaining the knowledge base of SAIDA which has a prefixed knowledge organization for a particular set of problem solving methods.

The main difference between KATS and the traditional approach of method-based knowledge acquisition tools is the user interface. With the second approach, normally, the user receives a kind of *data-base perception* of the knowledge model, i.e. a limited perception of the model mainly focused on domain knowledge that is presented as a kind of data base that is written with the help of prefixed windows. This approach is useful when the knowledge base presents low level of complexity. However when the complexity is higher (as it is the case of SAIDA that includes a number of problem-solving methods for different complex tasks, such as diagnosis, prediction and configuration, with different symbolic representations together with a multiagent organization) this approach does not guarantee that the user has an adequate uniform and global understanding and consequently an appropriate guidance to successfully create and maintain the models. On the contrary, the approach followed by KATS provides a *document perception* of the knowledge model, i.e. the model is presented as a document that brings together both inference and domain knowledge and could serves as complete documentation to perform manually the different tasks. This uniform and familiar way of presenting a knowledge model, with the corresponding editing facilities provided by KATS based on standards of text processors, make easier a complete understanding of the model.

The category of general knowledge modeling tools includes a type software tool that assists to the developer in the application of a modeling methodology. For example, MIKE [2] follows the KADS methodology [23] and allows a partial validation of the knowledge model using a computational language, KARL [12]. Other approaches such as KREST [17] or KSM [7] also follow a modeling methodology somehow similar to KADS but, in addition to that, they produce the final operational version using preprogrammed constructs. Another interesting approach derived from the EXPECT system, takes advantage of the explicit representation of problem-solving methods to guide the knowledge acquisition process [4]. The knowledge modeling tools are more general compared to the previous approach because the developer can formulate any kind of problem solving method. However they introduce certain abstract terminology that can be difficult to be understood by users non-programmers. Thus, the KATS tool is less general but is closer to the user language which is important when the complexity of the model is high. However, although the specific KATS tool is particular for hydrologic models, the principles of design followed in the construction of KATS are general and it can be reused for the development of other tools in different domains. In addition to that, certain components (such as the editing facilities) can be supported by programs whose code can be reused for the development of other tools.

The category of ontology management tools has been developed within the field of knowledge sharing and reuse, especially in the context of Internet. Examples of these tools are Protégé-2000 [13], WebOnto [9], OntoSaurus [16], Ontolingua/Chimaera [11], [19]. In general, these tools are easier to be operated by users who are not expert in programming, compared to the knowledge modeling tools. They also provide an interesting solution to the need of having certain professional common sense, by reusing standard ontologies that have been previously formulated in different domains. In addition to that, they provide certain advanced services that facilitate knowledge sharing such as cooperative construction, merging assistance or internationalization. However, they follow general standard knowledge representations (frames, relations, etc.) that can be limited in certain complex domains such as the case of hydrology presented in this paper. KATS, which is less general than these tools, uses more specific knowledge representations and inference procedures more appropriate for the tasks performed by SAIDA. In addition to that, KATS also is able to show the role that the different parts of the knowledge model plays in the model, which can be useful to better understand the model.

Besides the previous comparison with different types of knowledge acquisition tools, it is interesting to relate KATS with the concept of *semantic web* [3]. The semantic web approach is oriented to have electronic web documents that are not only understandable by persons by also by programs using standard *ontologies* [14] that establish certain common meaning about the potential content of documents. This idea is similar to KATS in the sense that both use the concept of document that should be understandable by humans and machines. However, the idea in semantic web establishes that programs are able to understand the *kind* of information in the document but not the information itself, for any kind of document. On the contrary, the approach followed by KATS, that is less general because it is limited to documents that represent knowledge models, *understands the content* of the document in the sense that certain parts of it are translated to symbolic representations that serve as knowledge bases of intelligent systems.

5 Conclusions

In summary, this paper presents the knowledge acquisition tool KATS that shows an innovative approach to improve knowledge acquisition and model maintenance of intelligent systems. In contrast to the traditional knowledge acquisition tools based on conventional user interfaces, we propose the idea of electronic document as basic media for knowledge acquisition. Under this approach, the knowledge acquisition tool is like an electronic document processor that allows the end user to read/write large and complex knowledge bases with automatic assistance (consistency checking, guidance, etc.).

KATS has been developed our group to serve as a knowledge acquisition tool to help users in building and maintaining the complex knowledge model of the SAIDA system. SAIDA is a decision-making tool that operates in the domain of emergency management in hydrology. SAIDA follows a knowledge-based multiagent approach with several symbolic representations and with, for example, 143 knowledge bases in a particular case. The first version of the KATS tool is now under evaluation by end-users specialized in the domain of hydrology.

It is important to note that the approach followed by KATS can be generalized to the construction of other knowledge acquisition tools in different domains. In particular, we are now applying this approach for the development of a new knowledge acquisition tool in the domain of transport management. For this purpose, we have reused not only the design concept of KATS but also certain programming libraries (for example, editing facilities for document representation resources).

Acknowledgements. The development of the SAIDA system was supported by the Ministry of Environment of Spain (*Dir. General de Obras Hidráulicas y Calidad de las Aguas*) with the participation of local public organizations from river basins (*Conf. Hidrográfica del Júcar* and *Conf. Hidrográfica del Sur de España.*). The development of the KATS tool was supported by the Ministry of Science and Technology of Spain.

References

1. Alonso M., Cuena J., Molina M."SIRAH: An Architecture for a Professional Intelligence", ECAI Conference 1990. (L.Carlucci Ed.) Pitman, 1990.
2. Angele J., Fensel D., Landes D., Neubert S., Studer R.: "Model-Based and Incremental Knowledge Engineering: The MIKE Approach" en Knowledge Oriented Software Design, J.Cuena (ed.). Elservier, 1993.
3. Barnes-Lee T, Hendler J. and Lassila O. "The Semantic Web." Scientific American, May 2001.
4. Blythe, J.; Kim J.; Ramachandran, S.; Gil Y.: "An Integrated Environment for Knowledge Acquisition". Proc. International Conference on Intelligent User Interfaces, 2001.
5. Brown D., Chandrasekaran B.: "Design Problem-solving: Knowledge Structures and Control Strategies", Morgan Kaufman, 1989.
6. Clancey W.J.: "Heuristic Classification". Artificial Intelligence, vol 27, pp. 289-350, 1985.
7. Cuena J., Molina M.: "The role of knowledge modelling techniques in software development: a general approach based on a knowledge management tool", International Journal of Human-Computer Studies No. 52. pp 385-421. Academic Press, 2000.
8. Cuena J., Molina M., "A Multiagent System for Emergency Management in Floods". En "Multiple Approaches to Intelligent Systems", 12th International Conference on Industrial Applications of Artificial Intelligence and Expert Systems, IEA/AIE-99. El Cairo, Egipto 1999.
9. Domingue, J.: "Tadzebao and WebOnto: Discussing, Browsing and Editing Ontologies on the Web", Proc. of the Eleventh Workshop on Knowledge Acquisition, Modeling and Management. Banff, Canada, 1998.
10. Eshelman L., Ehret D., McDermott J., Tan M.: "MOLE: a Tenacious Knowledge-Acquisition Tool". Academic Press Inc., London, 1987.
11. Farquhar A., Fikes R., Rice J.: "The Ontolingua Server: a Tool for Collaborative Ontology Construction", International Journal of Human-Computer Studies, 46, 707-727, 1997.
12. Fensel, D.; Angele, J.; Landes D.: "KARL: A Knowledge Acquisition and Representation Language". Proc. Expert Systems and their Applications, Avignon 1991.

13. Grosso W.E., Eriksson H., Fergerson R.W., Gennari J.H., Tu S.W., Musen M.A.: "Knowledge Modeling at the Millennium (The Design and Evolution of Protege-2000)". Twelfth Banff Workshop on Knowledge Acquisition, Modeling and Management. Banff, Alberta, 1999.
14. T. R. Gruber. "A translation approach to portable ontology specifications". Knowledge Acquisition, 6(2): 199-221, 1993.
15. Hendler J., Feigenbaum E.A.: "Knowledge Is Power: The Semantic Web Vision" in Web Intelligence: Research and Development, N.Zhong, Y.Yao, J.Liu, S.Ohsuga (eds.), Lecture Notes in Artificial Intelligence 2198, Springer, 2001.
16. ISX: http://www.isi.edu/isd/ontosaurus.html. ISX Corporation (1991). "LOOM Users Guide, Version 1.4".
17. Macintyre A.: "KREST User Manual 2.5". Wrije Universiteit Brussel, AI-lab. Brussels. 1993.
18. Marcus S., McDermott J.: "SALT: A Knowledge Acquisition Language for Propose-and-Revise Systems". Artificial Intelligence, Vol.39, No.1, 1989.
19. McGuinness D.L., Fikes R., Rice J., Wilder S.: "An Environment for Merging and Testing Large Ontologies". Proc. of the Seventh International Conference on Principles of Knowledge Representation and Reasoning, Breckenridge, Colorado, 2000.
20. Molina M., Blasco G: "A Multi-agent System for Emergency Decision Support". Proceedings of the Fourth International Conference Intelligent data Engineerging and automated Learning IDEAL 2003. LNCS, Springer.
21. Molina M., Blasco G.. "Using Electronic Documents for Knowledge Acquisition and Model Maintenance" Knowledge-Based Intelligent Information and Engineering Systems. Springer-Verlag. Lecture Notes in Artificial Intelligence 2774. Vol. II, pp. 1357-1364. Oxford, September 2003.
22. Molina M., Garrote L.: "Decision support for flash flood early warning using bayesian networks", Journal of Hydrology, (in press).
23. Schreiber G., Akkermans H., Anjewierden A., De Hoog R., Shadbolt N., Van de Velde W., Wielinga B.: "Knowledge engineering and management. The CommonKADS methodology" MIT Press, 2000.

SERSE: Searching for Digital Content in Esperonto

Valentina Tamma, Ian Blacoe, Ben Lithgow Smith, and Michael Wooldridge

Department of Computer Science, University of Liverpool,
Liverpool L69 3BX, United Kingdom
{V.A.M.Tamma, I.W.Blacoe, D.B.Lithgow-Smith,
M.J.Wooldridge}@csc.liv.ac.uk

Abstract. This paper presents SERSE, a multi-agent system that combines different technologies such as peer-to-peer, ontologies, and multi-agent technology in order to deal with the complexity of searching for digital content on the Semantic Web (SW). In SERSE, agents communicate and share responsibilities on a peer-to-peer basis. Peers are organised according to a *semantic overlay network*, where the neighbourhood is determined by the semantic proximity of the ontological definitions that are known to the agents. The integration of these technologies poses some problems. On the one hand, the more ontological knowledge the agents have, the better we can expect the system to perform. On the other hand, global knowledge would constitute a point of centralisation which might potentially degrade the performance of a P2P system. The paper identifies five requirements for efficiently searching SW content, and illustrates how the SERSE design addresses these requirements. The SERSE architecture is then presented, together with some experimental results that evaluate the performance of SERSE in response to changes in the size of semantic neighbourhood, ranging from strictly local knowledge (each agent knows about just one concept), to global knowledge (each agent has complete knowledge of the ontological definitions).

1 Introduction

Semantic web technology [15] is becoming increasingly popular because it promises to add value to the current web, without requiring any fundamental changes to the web infrastructure that is currently in place. The web of today is intended primarily for human consumption. In contrast, the Semantic Web (SW) is intended to be utilised and understood by software agents, and is based on machine-processable languages, which permit knowledge to be embedded within web pages. However, the transition from the current web to the semantic web is still slow, and a there is a need not only to provide technology to build semantic web resources from scratch, but also to make legacy web resources compliant with the semantic web.

This paper presents some results produced by the Esperonto project, that aims to *bridge the gap* between the current web and the semantic web. Esperonto provides its stakeholders with different types of knowledge services, and in particular we focus on Esperonto's *search and retrieval services*, which make it possible to retrieve digital content annotated by means of ontologies — explicit and machine sharable representations of the conceptualisation abstracting a phenomenon [22]. The Esperonto component responsible for searching and retrieving digital content is the *SEmantic Routing SystEm*

E. Motta et al. (Eds.): EKAW 2004, LNAI 3257, pp. 419–432, 2004.

(SERSE), a multi-agent system in which agents have equal capabilities and responsibilities, and which communicate on a peer-to-peer basis. Semantic descriptions of digital content are used to determine a *semantic overlay* on the network of peers, where the peers can communicate only with those peers who are within their *semantic neighbourhood* [12]. One critical issue in such a *semantically organised P2P* system is determining the ideal *size* of the semantic neighbourhood: the amount of ontological knowledge each peer must have to efficiently provide search and retrieval services. In the remainder of this paper, we describe the services offered by SERSE, illustrate its architecture from an agent perspective, and present some experimental results evaluating the performances of the system in relation to the ontological knowledge each of the peers has.

2   The Esperonto Architecture

The aim of the Esperonto project (www.esperonto.net) is to bridge the gap between the current web and the SW [9]. Esperonto offers three main type of knowledge services, provided by the components described below (see Figure 1 [8]).

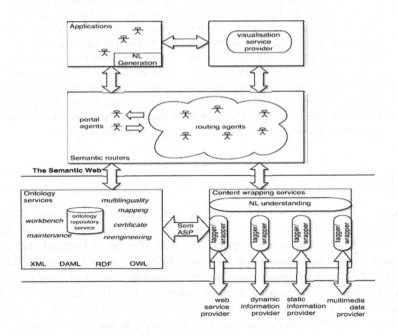

Fig. 1. The general architecture of the Esperonto system

Content Availability Services: One of the main obstacles that might prevent the wider takeup of SW technologies is the availability of SW content. In order to obtain critical mass, it is essential to make available web pages in which the semantics of the content is defined and made explicit in a machine processable language. Most of the current tools aim at reducing the burden of annotating web pages with semantic markup. However, these tools focus on *new* web pages, whose content is annotated while the page is written. Restricting the semantic web to new web content would imply discarding or ignoring the content represented in the current web: an unpractical and uneconomical choice. Esperonto provides *annotation services* to content providers, in the form of tools and techniques that enable them to publish their (existing and new) content on the SW.

Content availability services are provided by the SEMantic Annotation Service Provider (SemASP) [9], which has two main components: the *Ontology Server*, which provides the ontology services described below, and the *Annotation system*, which performs the annotation of different types of content. The Annotation System is comprised of two components: the *Annotation Server*, which is responsible for annotating resources with concepts described in ontologies in the ontology server, and the *Notification server*, which broadcasts notification messages concerning the annotation of new resources and the publication of new ontologies in the ontology server. The SemASP permits us to annotate static and dynamic content, multimedia content, and even web services.

Ontology Services: Ontology services are provided by the *Ontology server* component of the SemASP. The services offered are those related to the management and validation of multiple related ontologies and/or multiple versions of the same ontology. They include an ontology editor suite (WebODE) [11] which facilitates ontology construction, selection, and browsing, as well as translation into the common ontology and knowledge representation languages (such as DAML+OIL, OWL, Prolog, and Jess). The suite supports consistency checking, ontology versioning, and ontology maintenance. Knowledge sharing among different user communities is also supported, by means of ontology importing, alignment, and mapping services.

Search and Retrieval Services: Search and retrieval services are provided by the *Semantic Routing System* (SERSE), a peer-to-peer multi-agent system that deals with user queries. This component is responsible for query decomposition, answering, and aggregation. During the aggregation process, the retrieved web pages are also evaluated in order to avoid duplicate or incomplete data and to improve performance. In order to enable agents in SERSE to effectively search digital content in web pages, this content is *semantically indexed*: thus indexing is not based on keywords, but on the *concepts corresponding to the meaning of keywords*. The semantic indices are the mechanisms that permit the routing of queries to a competent agent on a P2P basis. A simple query is initially routed to an agent, which consults the indices to verify whether it can answer the query. If the agent cannot answer the query, or if it believes that the answer is incomplete, it routes the query to the agent with the closest interests. The decision about which agent has the closest interests is based on a measure of *semantic similarity* between concepts [25, 21].

3   The Principles of SERSE's Design

SERSE is the component in the Esperonto architecture that is concerned with creating and maintaining the infrastructure to search the SW for digital content. More precisely, SERSE searches for web resources that are instances of one or more concepts of the ontology(ies) used to annotate them. Unlike information retrieval systems, SERSE relies only on the annotations provided by the annotation server, rather than analyse the content of the web pages in order to find frequent terms. The infrastructure provided by SERSE includes the creation and management of the semantic indices used to index the resources, and the semantic routing mechanisms. We based the design of SERSE on what we considered as the desirable features that a system should exhibit in order to perform efficiently in a complex, distributed, open, large-scale, and dynamic environment such as the SW.

Searching the SW adds extra complexity to the task of searching the current web. Not only must a SW search system deal with a large number of distributed, heterogeneous resources, but these resources may reference many different ontologies, and in turn these ontologies may rely on many different ontology specification languages. Monolithic systems struggle to deal with such complexity: we believe that one solution to this increased complexity is decentralisation. We take the stance of the SW as a collection of "fragmented knowledge", where each fragment is composed of a group of similar concepts or a whole topic; resources referencing the same or similar concepts in their annotations belong to the "fragment", and neighbouring fragments store resources that reference concepts which have a high degree of semantic proximity. Decentralisation implies here that maintaining a central directory of topics would be cumbersome and unpractical. For this reason, searching for specific content in SERSE consists of determining the most efficient route from a starting topic S and a target topic T. The route is determined on the basis of the *semantic proximity* between fragments of knowledge. Indeed, the simplest approach would be to try a random direction – but this would give no guarantee to find T in a finite time. Alternatively, we can simply try to find an intermediate topic T', whose existence we are certain about, and that is closer to the topic we aim to reach. By using this approach we are sure to reach the right fragment of knowledge in a limited time (the sum of the times needed to reach each topic between S and T), and if a new fragment is discovered, we can compute the route to this fragment by finding the route to the topic closest to the new one, and then between these two.

To summarise, the design of SERSE was based on the search mechanism described above, and on a number of features, that should arguably be exhibited by a system searching for content on the SW:

1. Decentralisation;
2. Openness;
3. Autonomy and social ability;
4. Scalability;
5. Semantic based content retrieval;
6. Failure recovery;
7. Maintainability.

More precisely, this paper describes the implementation of the first prototype of the *Semantic Routing System* (SERSE). The SERSE prototype is implemented as a multi-agent system, whose agents share a core of equal capabilities and responsibilities, and which are capable of retrieving web resources based on the semantics of their annotations. The system is internally organised in a peer-to-peer fashion: Each router agent (described in

Section 4) is able to communicate only with its immediate neighbours, and the neighbourhood size is determined by the semantic proximity between the concepts known to the agents. No router agent can broadcast messages to the whole system, and no agent has global knowledge of the network: this ensures decentralisation.

In the first prototype, each router agent indexes instances of one concept only. This design decision was made to concentrate on the development of the main routing mechanism, and to approximate the behaviour of the system when dealing with very large ontologies (with thousands of concepts). The routing mechanism is based on the use of path length as semantic distance. We are currently in the process of developing a more complex type of distance that also takes into account the concept definitions and relations.

The prototype supports queries expressed in a language that allows users to select the concepts whose instances they are interested in. The concepts are those described in some ontology known to the system. At the moment, the system support the use of the most common logical connectives, excluding negation.

4 SERSE's Architecture

SERSE was implemented as a multi-agent system composed of five types of agents, which share to some degree a core of common capabilities and responsibilities, but which play different roles in the retrieval of digital content. The agents are described the subsection below.

SERSE was implemented using JADE [7], a FIPA-compliant middleware platform that manages the agent lifecycle. JADE is used to handle the transport aspects of agent communication: our implementation builds on JADE to provide a semantic overlay network, i.e., the *logical* organisation of the agents in a network of peers, which is based on the notion of semantic neighbourhood. Agents in SERSE have knowledge of a number of concepts forming the ontologies. These ontologies – expressed in OWL – are hosted on some web server. SERSE interacts with the web server in order to retrieve the ontology used for indexing the sources and for guiding the semantic routing. JADE provides two ways of referencing ontologies in agents communication. In SERSE we opted for the 'ad hoc' method, where the content of the ontology is returned to be parsed. We pass the ontology URI to JENA, a Java framework for writing Semantic Web applications developed by HP Labs [2]. JENA retrieves the ontology and performs the parsing, and the resulting representation is accessed through the JENA API.

SERSE also interacts with the *Notification Server* (which notifies the routing system of the annotation of new resources, returning a list with the URIs of the instances of those concepts used in the annotation).

Agents have the ability to send FIPA messages to the agents belonging to their immediate semantic neighbourhood. Although limited, these "social abilities" permit the agents to autonomously and dynamically determine the most appropriate agent, i.e., the agent that can retrieve instances of a concept that is identical or semantically closest to the queried concept, and to route them an unanswered query.

SERSE is composed of the following type of agents:

Portal Agent: The portal agent acts as the point of entry into the network of routers. It is responsible for triggering the routing process.

Notification Agent: The notification agent receives XML messages from the Notification Server and parses them. It can then resend the contents as an ACL message via the Portal Agent. The notification agent receives notifications of a new OWL ontology or of content acquisitions by the Annotation system. If the notification refers to a new ontology, the Notification Agent re-sends it to the Interface Agent. If the notification refers to instances of a new concept, the notification agent creates a new router for the concept. If the notification refers to instances of an existing concept, the notification agent re-sends the message into the router system to be routed to the correct index.

Router Agent: Router agents are created once the system receives a notification of content acquisition regarding a new concept. Each router agent is associated with a concept in an ontology and is capable of retrieving instances of this concept. The router agents access the instances to index by reading them directly from the RDF files created by the Annotation system. The locations of these files are reported to the router system by the Notification Server. The router agent also has a routing index, which contains the addresses of its semantic neighbours. When a router agent receives a query, it can either reply with a FIPA `inform-ref` message, whose content is the retrieved instances, or by sending a `query-ref`, which effectively re-routes the query to the agent with the least semantic distance. A router agent determines the semantic distance on the basis of the ontology, and in the current version of the prototype the semantic distance calculation is performed at run time. The concept for which the agent is responsible, and the set of concepts used to create the routing index are passed into the router agent as arguments when it is created.

Query Management Agent: The query management agent is the entry point for querying the system. It is intended to deal with the decomposition of complex queries and with the aggregation and validation of the results, but in the current implementation we support only the logical connectives AND and OR. The agent manages all the operations related to querying the system, including re-routing failed simple queries, sending multiple copies of queries in order to handle temporary unavailability, etc.

Interface Agent: The interface agent acts as interface between the agents on the JADE platform and the external applications using them. The interface itself is comprised of both the agent that creates a socket connection and exchanges messages between the Query Management Agent and external applications, and of an external interface object, that connects to the agent socket and provides a simple API for generating queries and handling the answers.

4.1 SERSE in Action

The work of SERSE begins when a user poses a query by means of the system interface, which allows users to formulate a query in terms of the ontology definitions known by the agents (in the first prototype, we consider one ontology only, but we are currently working to support multiple ontologies).

In order to receive queries, the system needs to be booted-up and initialised. We assume that the Notification Agent has been notified by the Notification Server the URI of the OWL ontology to use. We also assume that content availability messages were received by the *notification agent*, thus triggering the creation of the network of semantic routers.

When a query is generated by the *query management agent*, it forwards it to the *portal agent* which choses a random router and thus starts the routing process (in the second prototype, the portal agent will also be responsible for query decomposition and result aggregation). The portal agent sends a `query-ref` message to the selected *router agent* and the content of the message is the queried concept. The router agent consults its index to check whether it is able to access instances of the concepts. Instances are referenced by means of the URI they are accessible from. If the router agent can answer the query, it will reply back to the portal agent with an `inform-ref` whose content is the URIs of the instances of the queried concept.

If the router agent does not have reference to the queried concept in its index, it needs to forward the query to the neighbour that is *semantically closest* to the queried concept. The router agent computes the similarity between its neighbours and the queried concept, and then forwards the query to the router responsible for the closest concept to the queried one.

Figure 2 shows a screenshot of the user interface used to query the system; the URIs of the retrieved instances are shown in Figure 3.

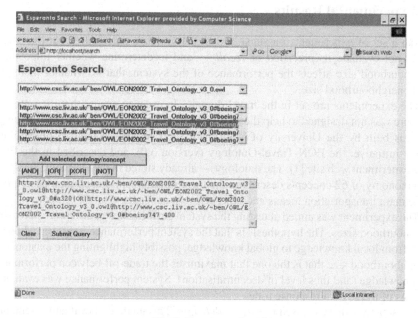

Fig. 2. Query user interface

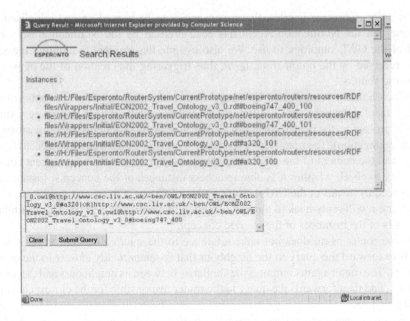

Fig. 3. Retrieved instances

5   Experimental Results

We ran a set of experiments on SERSE to test the system's *efficiency* — at this stage, we do not evaluate its *precision* or *recall* — and to determine whether imposing a neighbourhood size affects the performance of the system, that is, whether there is a "best" neighbourhood size.

The experiments are set in the travel domain. In order to ensure that the ontology structure was not designed to help the routing process in any way, we used an ontology that was built by the University of Madrid for the Ontoweb evaluation of ontology editors initiative: the EON-Travel-Ontology (version 3.0), and described in the EON 2002 experiment web site [1]. The ontology — already stored in the Ontology Server — is a taxonomy of 62 concepts describing the travelling domain, including a description of the main transportation means and other relevant concepts.

The experiment was aimed at testing the system performance at different, increasing neighbourhood sizes. The hypothesis is that the system performance improves when we range from local knowledge to global knowledge, possibly highlighting the existence of a neighbourhood size that is the one that maximises the trade-off between performance and knowledge (and thus level of decentralisation). System performance was evaluated in terms of the system response time.

The semantic distance used was the *path length*. This method of evaluating semantic similarity has occasionally been criticised for not being an accurate measure [20], and for not really taking into account the semantics of the concepts in the ontology. We made this choice for two main reasons: efficiency and ontological structure. The literature offers a number of similarity measures that can be used to evaluate similarity between concepts in an ontology, but none of them is widely accepted as being truly accurate, and most are computationally expensive and/or language sensitive. In our experiments we were interested in evaluating the response time of the system from the viewpoint of the routing mechanisms, and thus this choice of similarity measure permitted us to limit the burden of a heavy computation of the similarity measure, and to consider its cost negligible. Furthermore, the ontology chosen for the experiments is a simple taxonomy, and similarity measures that evaluate the degree of similarity of attributes and relationships (other than IS-A) become unreliable when used in simple taxonomies (concept hierarchies with no attribute description, and where concepts are related only through IS-A links).

We executed 500 queries over 50 runs of the experiment. For each run we picked at random the agent that originated the routing process, and we queried 10 concepts changing for each of the run the neighbourhood size, by varying the path length. In Table 1 we illustrate the ten concepts used in the queries.

Table 1. Queried concepts

Q1	hotel3star
Q2	boeing767
Q3	train
Q4	transportMean
Q5	seaTransportMean
Q6	boeingPlane
Q7	fokker
Q8	a320
Q9	taxi
Q10	city

By varying the path length, we increased the number of concepts in the neighbourhood, thus increasing the capabilities of an agent (in terms of the concepts it can deal with), and ultimately ranging from a purely decentralised P2P system, to one where the whole ontology becomes a centralisation point.

Figure 4 shows the trend in performance for each experiment run. The line illustrates the response time against the average neighbourhood size obtained by varying the path length.

We can make some observations on the results of the experiments. The best results in terms of system workload were obtained when the neighbourhood size was the whole ontology, or close to the whole ontology, even though this would imply that each agent maintains a copy of the whole ontology. This would have significant implications on the system maintenance time, since each time an ontology is modified each router must update its copy of the ontology. Ontology modifications might not occur often, but if we also take into account ontology versioning, these operations will affect the overall maintenance. From the experiment it emerges that a semantic neighbourhood that includes about 40 concepts (out of a possible 62) represents a good trade-off between agents

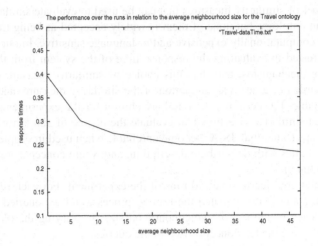

The performance over the runs in relation to the average neighbourhood size for the Travel ontology

Fig. 4. The performance of the system when using the Travel Ontology

knowledge and system performance (including maintenance time). A more accurate analysis of the system maintenance is presented in [24].

These results lead us to believe that *hybrid* [27] peer-to-peer systems (that is, P2P systems in which some functionalities remain centralised) offer better prospects for the provision of search and retrieval services on the semantic web. Indeed, best results referred to global knowledge defeats the hypothesis that a pure peer-to-peer system could be used to search the semantic web. Even in such small and controlled experiments we notice that the performance of the semantic routing mechanism improves when we range from equipping the routers with very localised knowledge (semantic neighbourhood = path length = 1) to equipping them with global knowledge (semantic neighbourhood = path length = 9), but it also proves the existence of a region in the space of the possible neighbourhood sizes that balances knowledge vs. performance. This evidence provides us with an objective starting point for building clusters of similar peers. The next challenge is therefore to reorganise the overlay network in a way such that we take advantage of the balance between the performance of the system and the size of the neighbourhood (that is, how much global knowledge) a router agent should have.

We also note that the growth of the neighbourhood size starts at a steady pace to later stabilise. This result depends on the ontology granularity. This lead us to stress the importance of using well engineered and well modelled ontologies for annotating digital content. Well engineered ontologies ensure that there is a good coverage of levels of abstraction in the classification of the concepts used to model the domain of interest. Well modelled ontologies guarantee that concepts are adequately described in term of attributes and relationships linking them. These can be used in more refined similarity measures, that although computationally expensive, are more accurate than the path-length.

6   Related Work

Approaches to the provision of search and retrieval services in the SW have been developed in disparate areas, from digital libraries to information retrieval. In the context of SERSE, we focus on peer-to-peer approaches for distributed knowledge management and intelligent information agents. In fact, SERSE can be seen as merging the two approaches, in that it creates a peer-to-peer system where the peers provide much of the functionalities characterising intelligent information agents.

Peer-to-peer systems are traditionally associated with file sharing and exchange applications, such as in Napster and Morpheus [3]. More recently, P2P systems have been used to reduce the complexity of distributed data and knowledge management applications [13, 10]. A typical example of such an application is EDUTELLA [19], a hybrid P2P architecture for sharing metadata, that implements an RDF-based metadata infrastructure for JXTA [4]. Nodes are organised into a set of thematic clusters, and a dedicated mediator performs semantic integration of source metadata in each cluster. The mediator receives queries concerning the sources and returns a list of candidate nodes that permit to access the information. Thematic clusters are obtained by superpeers that have semantic routing capabilities, however, there is little detail on the principles guiding the clustering of nodes and the impact of the cluster size on the system performance. In addition, the emphasis is more on RDF repositories of metadata rather than on the representation of semantic information in possibly heavyweight ontologies. Some other projects use "super-peers", which start the semantic routing process in the right direction.

Other approaches emphasise the use of semantics represented in ontologies. Among these there is the SWAP project [5]. In SWAP, each node is responsible for a single ontology: ontologies might represent different views of a same domain, multiple domains with overlapping concepts, or might be obtained by partitioning an upper level ontology. Knowledge sharing is obtained through ontology mapping and alignment, however mappings are not dynamically obtained.

Peer-to-Peer Semantic Web [6] builds on the research effort carried out at the LS-DIS Lab in the InfoQuilt project [17]. Peer-to-Peer Semantic Web aims at providing services to support distributed knowledge construction and knowledge sharing. Here the emphasis is on ontology services, such as the creation and advertisement of new ontologies and the discovery of ontology inter-relationship over a P2P infrastructure, and ontology driven content retrieval. However, the P2P architecture is not explicitly defined.

A similar approach, although not strictly peer-to-peer is the one based on the distributed annotations and queries [16]. This approach subdivides the architecture into societies, and concentrates on distributing the annotations among a society of agents who may share more or less close interests. The annotation dedicated society is concerned with the exploitation of annotations and offers the search and retrieval services. However, unlike SERSE, these agents are also responsible for managing archiving and managing the annotations.

There is a vast literature on intelligent information agents that is extremely relevant to SERSE, and especially the characterising features that constitute the notion of agency [26]. From this viewpoint SERSE can be classified among the cooperative information agents, such as RETSINA [23], InfoSleuth [14] and OBSERVER [18]. RETSINA is a matchmaker based information system where collaborative task execution is achieved through matching service providers and requesters over the web (and more recently, over the Semantic Web). We are currently exploring the possibility of adapting the similarity matching approach of RETSINA+LARKS in order to build the semantic neighbours.

InfoSleuth explicitly deals and reconciles multiple ontologies by means of specialised ontology agents that collectively maintain a knowledge base of the different ontologies used to specify requests, and return ontology information as requested. Finally, OBSERVER dynamically finds mappings between partially overlapping ontologies, therefore providing agents with a way to dynamically share knowledge. Many of these features are being studied for use in the second prototype of SERSE.

7   Conclusions

The paper has presented SERSE, the Esperonto component providing search and retrieval services. SERSE builds on peer to peer, ontologies, and multi-agent technology in order to deal with the complexity of searching for digital content on Semantic Web (SW). In SERSE, agents have knowledge of the ontological definitions used to annotate digital content and communicate on a peer-to-peer basis. Routing is determined by semantic proximity of the ontological definitions that are known to the agents (semantic neighbourhood).

We have illustrated and motivated the design of SERSE, and we have presented and evaluated its implementation. The evaluation has aimed at proving the hypothesis that in this kind of system the neighbourhood size affects the performance of the system in different ways: the more ontological definitions are known to the agents, the more easily the query can be routed to the most relevant peer. But, more ontological knowledge also causes a higher maintenance effort and a higher workload in terms of number of estimations of the semantic proximity. Our experiments prove that there is a region in the space of the neighbourhood sizes that represent a good trade-off between the number of concepts known to a router agent and the system performance. Therefore, we can reorganise our network of agents objectively on the basis of these findings. This means that the network does not need to have a global centralisation point but can be organised in a number of clusters, each offering different ontological expertise and whose size is determined by the number of concepts composing the ontology.

The results presented here concern the implementation of the first prototype. Future work is based on a more accurate evaluation of the semantic proximity between neighbours that uses ontology definitions and the ontology model itself (attributes and relationships).

Acknowledgements

The research described in this paper is funded by the IST project Esperonto. The authors would like to thank Floriana Grasso and all the members of the Esperonto consortium.

References

1. The EON 2002 experiment. http://km.aifb.uni-karlsruhe.de/eon2002/.
2. The jena website. http://www.hpl.hp.com/semweb/jena2.htm.
3. The morpheus website. http://musiccity.com.
4. Project jxta. http://www.jxta.org.
5. Semantic web and peer-to-peer. http://swap.semanticweb.org.
6. M. Arumugam, A. Sheth, and I.B. Arpinar. Towards peer-to-peer semantic web: A distributed environment for sharing semantic knowledge on the web. In *Proceedings of the International World Wide Web Conference 2002 (WWW2002)*, Honolulu, Hawaii, USA, May 2002.
7. F. Bellifemine, G. Caire, A. Poggi, and G. Rimassa. JADE a white paper. *EXP In search of innovation*, 3(3), September 2003.
8. V.R. Benjamins, J. Contreras, A. Gómez-Pérez, H. Uszkoreit, T. Declerck, D. Fensel, Y. Ding, M.J. Wooldridge, and V. Tamma. Esperonto application: Service provision of semantic annotation, aggregation, indexing, and routing of textual, multimedia and multilingual web content. In *Proc. of WIAMSI'03*, 2003.
9. V.R. Benjamins, J.Contreras, O. Corcho, and A. Gómez-Pérez. Six challenges for the semantic web. In *Proc. of the KR'02 Semantic Web workshop*, 2002.
10. S. Castano, A. Ferrara, S. Montanelli, E. Pagani, and G.P. Rossi. Ontology-addressable contents in p2p networks. In *Proc. of WWW'03 1st SemPGRID Workshop*, 2003.
11. O. Corcho, A. Gómez-Pérez, Angel López-Cima, and M.C. Suárez-Figueroa. ODESeW. automatic generation of knowledge portals for intranets and extranets. In *Proceedings of the 2nd International Semantic Web Conference, ISWC 2003*, LNCS. Springer, 2003.
12. A. Crespo and H. Garcia-Molina. Semantic overlay networks for p2p systems. Technical report, Computer Science, Stanford University, citeseer.nj.nec.com/garcia02semantic.html, October 2002.
13. M. Ehrig, P. Haase, R. Siebes, S. Staab, H. Stuckenschmidt, R. Studer, and C. Tempich. The SWAP data and metadata model for semantics-based peer-to-peer systems. In *Proceedings of MATES-2003: First German conference on multiagent technologies*, number 2831 in LNAI. Springer, 2003.
14. R.J. Bayardo *et al.* InfoSleuth: Agent-based semantic integration of information in open and dynamic environments. In *Proceedings of the ACM SIGMOD International Conference on Management of Data*, volume 26,2, pages 195–206, New York, 1997. ACM Press.
15. D. Fensel, J. Hendler, H. Lieberman, and W. Wahlster, editors. *Spinning the Semantic Web: Bringing the World Wide Web to its full potential*. The MIT Press: Cambridge, MA, 2003.
16. F. Gandon, L. Berthelot, and R. Dieng-Kuntz. A multi-agent platform for a corporate semantic wb. In *Proceedings of the First International Joint Conference on Autonomous Agents and Multiagent Systems*, pages 1025–1032, Bologna, Italy, 2002. ACM press.
17. T. Lima, A. Sheth, N. Ashish, M. Guntamadugu, S. Lakshminarayan, N. Palsena, and D. Singh. Digital library services supporting information integration over the web. In *Proceedings of WIIW 2001*, 2001.
18. E. Mena, A. Illarramendi, V. Kashyap, and A. Sheth. OBSERVER: An approach for query processing in global information systems based on interoperation across pre-existing ontologies. *Distributed and Parallel databases. An international journal*, 8(2):223–271, April 2000.
19. W. Nejdl, B. Wolf, C. Qu, S. Decker, M. Sintek, A. Naeve, M. Nilsson, M. Palmér, and T. Risch. EDUTELLA: A p2p networking infrastructure based on rdf. In *Proceedings of the International World Wide Web Conference 2002 (WWW2002)*, pages 604–615, Honolulu, Hawaii, USA, 2002.
20. P. Resnik. Semantic similarity in a taxonomy: An information-based measure and its application to problems of ambiguity in natural language. *Journal of Artificial Intelligence Research*, 11:95–130, 1999.

21. M.A. Rodríguez and M.J. Egenhofer. Determining semantic similarity among entity classes from different ontologies. *IEEE transactions on knowledge and data engineering*, 2002. in press.
22. R. Studer, V.R. Benjamins, and D. Fensel. Knowledge engineering, principles and methods. *Data and Knowledge Engineering*, 25(1-2):161–197, 1998.
23. K. Sycara, M. Klusch, S. Widoff, and J. Lu. Dynamic service matchmaking among agents in open information systems. *ACM SIGMOD Record. Special Issue on semantic interoperability in global information systems*, 1998.
24. V. Tamma, I. Blacoe, B. Lithgow Smith, and M. Wooldridge. SERSE: searching for semantic web content. In *Proceedings of the 16th European Conference on Artificial Intelligence, ECAI 2004*, 2004.
25. A. Tversky. Features of similarity. *Psychological Review*, 84(4):327–372, 1977.
26. M. Wooldridge and N.R. Jennings. Intelligent agents: Theory and practice. *Knowledge engineering review*, 10(2):115–152, 1995.
27. Beverly Yang and Hector Garcia-Molina. Comparing hybrid peer-to-peer systems. In *The VLDB Journal*, pages 561–570, sep 2001.

A Topic-Based Browser for Large Online Resources

Heiner Stuckenschmidt[1], Anita de Waard[2], Ravinder Bhogal[3], Christiaan Fluit[4], Arjohn Kampman[4], Jan van Buel[5], Erik van Mulligen[6,7], Jeen Broekstra[4], Ian Crowlesmith[5], Frank van Harmelen[1], and Tony Scerri[2]

[1]Vrije Universiteit Amsterdam, De Boelelaan 1081a, 1081HV Amsterdam
heiner@cs.vu.nl
[2]Advanced Technology Group, Elsevier, Amsterdam, NL / London, UK
[3]User-Centered Design Group, Elsevier, London, UK
[4]Aduna, Amersfoort, NL
[5]Bibliographic Databases, Elsevier, Amsterdam, NL
[6]Collexis B.V., Geldermalsen, NL
[7]Department of Medical Informatics, Erasmus University, Rotterdam, NL

Abstract. The exploration of large information spaces is a difficult task, especially if the user is not familiar with the terminology used to describe information. Conceptual models of a domain in terms of thesauri or ontologies can leverage this problem to some extend. In order to be useful, there is a need for interactive tools for exploring large information sets based on conceptual knowledge. We present a thesaurus based browser that supports a mixed-initiative exploration of large online resources that provides support for thesaurus-based search and topic-based exploration of query results. We motivate the chosen exploration strategy the browser functionality, present the results of user studies and discuss future improvements of the browser.

1 Introduction

The exploration of large information spaces is a difficult task. Users need to be supported by appropriate tools to access and present available information. Looking at the World Wide Web as the largest information space that is currently available to a large group of users, we recognize two main strategies for accessing information:

- Search engines provide keyword based methods to retrieve sets of relevant documents based on string matching techniques.
- Hyperlinks can be used to navigate between web pages in a way predefined by the developer of the particular web site.

Users typical employ an exploration strategy that combines these two techniques. Search engines are used to jump to a particular page that seems to be relevant to a query. From there on the information space connected to the page is

E. Motta et al. (Eds.): EKAW 2004, LNAI 3257, pp. 433–448, 2004.

explored by browsing existing hyperlinks. Both of these paradigms have serious drawbacks with respect to efficiency and precision of information access. Keyword based search engines suffer from the problem of ambiguity of terms used in the queries. Often the same keyword is used to describe different things leading to a low precision of the result or different words are used for the same thing lowering the recall. When using the browsing paradigm, exploration is limited to predefined paths that do not reflect the users view on relevance, but the one predefined by the information provider.

The problems mentioned above turn out to be the main bottleneck for efficient exploration of large information spaces, especially if the user is not familiar with the dominant terminology used. Current developments in the area of the semantic web aim at using explicit models of the terminology of a domain to improve information access (see e.g. [8]). Using conceptual structures has benefits with respect to searching as well as for browsing:

- The precision and recall of querying can be improved by normalizing the vocabulary used for indexing and for querying documents to a common set of terms.
- Navigation in the information space can be based on conceptual relations rather than existing links and the user can be given the choice of which relations to use.

We have developed a browser that uses conceptual knowledge in terms of a thesaurus to support the exploration of large information spaces. The browser is designed in such a way that it directly supports the mixed-initiative strategy employed by users and makes use of the conceptual knowledge to support searching as well as browsing. We applied the browser to large repositories of documents in the life science domain and performed user studies for assessing the benefits of our approach.

In the following, we briefly describe the DOPE[1] project in which the browser was developed and present the specific requirements for supporting the user in the exploration tasks we identified in the project. In section 2 we review the design rationales of the system we have developed in the DOPE project referring to results from empirical studies in the area of Information retrieval. Section 3 presents the browser we developed in order to meet the requirements. The results of a user study with real end users that confirm our claims about the adequacy of the approach are presented in section 4. We conclude with a summary of our results and some directions for future work.

2 The DOPE Project

Innovative science and technology institutes rely on the availability of complete and accurate information about new research and development. It is the business of information providers such as Elsevier to provide the required information in a cost-effective way. The semantic web will very likely provide an important

---

[1] Drug Ontology Project for Elsevier.

contribution to future scientific information solutions, since it facilitates easy and effective access to a large variety of data. With the unremitting growth of scientific information sources, the need for integrated access to such sources becomes even more urgent.

Thesauri have proven to be a key technology to effective information access as they provide a controlled vocabulary for indexing information, and thereby help to overcome some of the problems of free-text search by relating and grouping relevant terms in a specific domain. A number of thesauri have been developed in different domains of expertise. Examples from the area of medical information include MeSH [2] and Elsevier's life science thesaurus EMTREE [3].

These thesauri are used to access information sources (in particular document repositories) like EMBASE.com [4]. But currently there is no open architecture to allow access to these thesauri for querying other data sources. When we move from the centralized and controlled use of EMTREE inside Elsevier to a distributed setting, we need to improve the accessibility of the content by delivering it in a standardized representation using open data standards that allow for semantic qualifications, such as RDF.

Also, since the mental models and common terms for accessing data diverge between subject areas and communities, different ontologies will be developed and used, that need to coexist. An ideal architecture would therefore allow for the disclosure of distributed and heterogeneous data sources through different ontologies. The aim of the DOPE project (Drug Ontology Project for Elsevier) is to investigate the possibility of providing access to multiple information sources in the area of life science through a single interface

2.1   The Current Situation

Besides asking an information specialist at a company or academic institute to do a full literature or product review there is a tendency that researchers perform their own searches for relevant information. The two ways of searching used by the overwhelming majority of life science researchers (including Drug Discovery) are specialized Bibliographic resources and internet search engines.

Bibliographic Resources. PubMed[5] is an online repository produced by the National Centre for Biotechnology Information. The data searched through PubMed are the abstracts contained in MEDLINE, which contains over 12 million bibliographic citations and author abstracts from more than 4,600 biomedical journals. PubMed allows for fielded searches (e.g. search for Author name = Rat vs. Species = Rat).

Internet Search Engines. Scientists also use Google or other full-text web search engines such as Scirus (www.scirus.com) to search the web for information about

---

[2] http://www.nlm.nih.gov/mesh/meshhome.html

[3] http://www.elsevier.com/homepage/sah/spd/site/

[4] http://embase.com/

[5] http://www.ncbi.nlm.nih.gov/entrez/query.fcgi?db=PubMed

their specific topic. In this case, queries are usually one- or two keyword phrases that are so specific the records returned can be oversene by the searcher. A Google query of "MHC, peptide epitope" (one of the starting terms for one of our test users) retrieved 29,600 records.

Additionally, researchers search specific databases of either chemical compounds (one of the many drug databases available via the internet or the local intranet), genes (e.g. GenBank, http://www.ncbi.nlm.nih.gov/Genbank/, also published by NCBI) and proteins (e.g. SwissProt, http://www.ebi.ac.uk/swissprot/, produced by the European Bioinformatics Institute) as well as many proprietary, subject-specific or other data bases of compounds, nucleotides, proteins, genes, and other biochemical entities.

Integrating and sorting through the data of these user-driven searches is one of the main issues driving drug-discovery (there are entire conferences devoted to the subject of information integration in drug discovery,[6]. There is currently no one product that can index independent data sources to one or more thesauri and integrate the search over all of them.

2.2 Requirements for Tool Support

The quality of a system supporting the user in exploring large information spaces depends on many factors. Some of them are linked to human cognition, our way of thinking and our mental limitations. We will not discuss these general requirements but rather concentrate on the specific requirements that can be derived from the application in the context of the DOPE project. These requirements are mainly concerned with assisting the user in exploring the different document repositories linked to the browser based on terms from the thesaurus.

Some of the requirements directly arise from the nature of the application. First of all, the visualization has to support the use of conceptual knowledge, but not necessarily its creation or maintenance. A requirement the application area shares with the Web in general is the ability to deal with a high number of instances compared to a smaller conceptual model. At the current state of the DOPE project, the accessible information space contains about 10.5 million documents that are indexed using a thesaurus that contains about 50000 terms. It is quite obvious that we have to limit the the number of documents and terms presented to the user at the same time. Another requirement shared with the web is the fact that the assignment of documents to terms is not unique, because every document will be linked to many different terms in the thesaurus. Any system supporting the exploration of the documents will have to deal with a large amount of objects that are assigned to many different classes in the conceptual model.

From a functional point of view, the system has to support the user in navigating in the information space providing the following functions:

Query Formulation. query interfaces that contain a graphical presentation of the available knowledge (ontology), make the query formulation task much

---

[6] http://www.wbresearch.com/DDDII/agenda.html

easier as the user is already acquainted with the used terminology. The ideal situation would be that queries can be formulated visually.

Query Result Presentation. inadequate presentation of query answers shadows the performance of many search engines as the user is overwhelmed with results without being able to pick the part that is of interest for him. Graphical presentations can explain the relation of the answer to the original terms of the query.

Query Reformulation. Very often the user is not satisfied by the returned answer: there are either too many items or no items at all. Graphical presentation of results allows a user to perform:

- Query relaxation: in case of empty sets, by giving up some of the search terms and choosing the results that come closer to the original query.
- Query broadening: in the case of an empty answer set some terms can be replaced by their super-classes. thereby broadening the scope of the query.
- Query narrowing: if there are too many items, the query can be repeated with more specialized sub-classes of certain query terms, narrowing the scope of the query.

Visualizations should help the user in finding relevant information and in addition should make the formulation of queries easier by giving visual clues.

3   Design Rationales

Experimental research has a long tradition in the field of information retrieval and valuable insight has been gained in user behavior and the pros and cons of different retrieval techniques and visualizations. In the following we review existing results in information retrieval focussing on the role of interactive strategies for query refinement including the use of conceptual knowledge and techniques for visualizing search results in a structured way. We will further link previous results to design decisions we made when designing the DOPE browser that will be described in the next section.

3.1   Search Process

Different kinds of search processes can be identified that differ in their characteristics. These include monitoring, performing pre-defined search patterns and exploration of an largely unknown area [9]. Search tasks in the area of drug research largely fall in the last category which is the least structured one and requires special strategies [3]. Traditional information retrieval assumes a process model where the user poses a query to the system based on an existing information need, has the result retrieved and based on the result decides to stop or to reformulate the query in a way that promises to improve the result [10]. This is repeated until the 'perfect' answer is found (compare figure 1). It has been argued that this simple model is not adequate for complex search tasks [4]. This holds in particular for exploration tasks where the information need is not always well defined. As an alternative to the traditional model, the so-called berry-picking model has been proposed [11]. This model assumes that the information need changes during the search process as a result of partial results. In analogue to berry-picking the user takes some of the search results and moves on to a different topic area. This model is more adequate for the exploration task and has been adopted in our work. Figure 1 shows the corresponding process model underlying our work. It assumes that the user starts off with a query on a particular topic. Based on the result the user can either further explore the result set in order to get a better understanding of the results or re-scope the search by re-defining the information need and posing a new query to the system. This two level process provides the combination of search (retrieving potential results) and browsing (exploring the retrieved results).

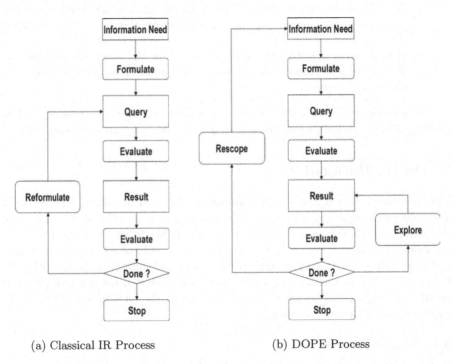

(a) Classical IR Process   (b) DOPE Process

Fig. 1. Process model for Information Search

It has been argued that people differ in their search behavior [5] which makes it difficult to provide adequate tool support for the exploration process. Results of a user study indicate however, that users normally prefer interactive methods where the system only performs parts of the search task provides feedback and lets the user decide about next steps [12]. This is a strong argument for an interactive exploration process, despite the fact that it has been shown that interactive methods fail to outperform completely automatic ones, mainly because users often have difficulties in choosing appropriate search terms [13]. It is therefore important to implement a method that leaves the user in control and supports him or her to combine different search strategies (querying and exploration) and to chose appropriate search terms [14]. Controlled vocabularies such as thesauri or ontologies play a key role in in this context [15].

3.2   User Support

As motivated above, the main task of an exploration tool is to assist the user in the different steps of the search process. In the process underlying our work, this mainly means supporting the user in formulating queries that scope the search and in exploring the result of this query.

Query Formulation. Considering the task of formulating the initial query, studies have shown that users normally start with quite short and simple queries [16]. It has also been shown that the use of Boolean operators in queries is problematic, because users tend to have an intuition about the meaning of these operators that is different from their logical interpretation used by the system [17]. We therefore abstain from providing a complex query formulation interface for this initial step and rather restrict it to the selection of a search term. As a consequence, supporting the user in the selection of this term is the main task in this first step. In a comparative study Chen and others have shown that term hierarchies provide better support for the user than methods that try to provide an overview of the existing information using term distribution maps and similar techniques [18]. In the DOPE context, we use the EMTREE thesaurus to suggest query terms: The user can browse the hierarchy and select a term or type in a free term that is matched against EMTREE and a corresponding term is proposed. EMTREE is also used to provide support for the re-scoping step. Results of Efthimiadis show that the most useful terms are the narrower terms from the hierarchy [19]. For re-scoping we therefore support the user in navigating the EMTREE hierarchy starting from the previous search term.

Result Exploration. The result of the search step is a collection of documents from different sources. As the number of these documents can be quite high, we have to support the user in exploring these documents. Research studies indicate that other terms occurring in the result documents provide valuable support for further structuring the result set [1]. We therefore extract relevant terms from these documents and offer them to the user as an exploration tool. Major problems have been reported with respect to linking individual results to the different terms used in querying. We address this problem using the principle of faceted queries where the query is split up according to different aspects and documents are explicitly linked to aspects rather than the query as a whole [20]. In our case, documents are explicitly linked to individual terms used for exploration. Different ways of representing these links have been proposed: The keyword in context method [7] extracts a relevant text passage from the document that contains the respective term and presents it to the user. TileBars [21] display the occurrence of different terms in different parts of the document and therefore also provide information about direct co-occurrences. The solution we have chosen is based on the visual representation of terms and documents in a network where documents are connected to terms they contain (compare [22, 2]). The advantage of this representation is that it provides an overview over the result set rather than individual information for each document. We argue that such an overview better supports the exploration task. The specific representation chosen here is based on earlier ideas on providing graphical representations of Boolean Queries [23]. We use the clustermap representation [24] developed by Aduna. The underlying concept of cluster maps is similar to the use of Venn diagrams for query formulation and result representation [25]. In our system, the use of restricted to the representation of conjunctions of search terms.

3.3 System and Interface Design

When developing a system that provides the user support mentioned above, we are facing several practical design decisions. From the point of view of this paper, the most relevant of these decisions are the ones concerned with the design of the user interface. It has been argued that monolithic interfaces that combine all the information in a single screen are preferably from a cognitive point of view, because otherwise the user quickly loses track of current state of the search process [6, 26]. We therefore chose to provide such an interface. The main disadvantage of this approach lies in the scalability. A single-window interface is naturally limited by the size of the screen and therefore does not scale arbitrarily. We approach this problem by introducing a number of thresholds that limit the amount of information shown at the same time:

- When matching a user-specified keyword with EMTREE we limit ourselves to showing maximally 100 potentially matching concepts.
- The result set consists of all matching documents with a minimum relevance (above 0.02), to a maximum of 500 documents.
- For supporting the exploration of the result set the 10 most relevant concepts from each document are chosen, with a minimum relevance of 0.5.

The first threshold is not a real limitation, because matches not in the first 100 are almost never relevant. The other thresholds are more critical. We rarely encountered less than 500 results for a query. This has been chosen based on technical considerations. As the amount of data influences the response time of the system, the challenge was to find an appropriate trade-off between amount of information and system performance. The current implementation is limited to 500 documents mainly because of high communication costs. Using improved communication protocols will enable us to retrieve more documents in future implementations. The relevance thresholds were determined empirically. They will have to be adjusted based on user feedback.

4   The DOPE Browser

In the presence of an information space of the size of the one used in DOPE, it is not enough to provide a technical infrastructure to query available sources.

The user will regularly be overwhelmed by the amount of results and will often not even know what to ask for. In order to address these common problems of information disclosure, we have to provide an intelligent interface that guides the user when exploring the information space and presents the results of a query in a structured way. In this section we describe the user interface of the DOPE system that is based on Aduna visualization technology and explain how to use it when searching for information. Further, we report the results of user studies carried out with potential end users.

4.1   The Browser Interface

We have designed and created a prototype of a user interface client called the "DOPE Browser". It gives users the ability to query and navigate a collection of documents using thesaurus-based techniques, while hiding much of the complexity of the back-end, such as the existence of multiple data sources, any thesaurus or ontology mapping that may take place, etc. In this system, the user sees a single virtual document collection made navigable using a single thesaurus (EMTREE). Typical document metadata such as e.g. title, authors and journal information is associated with each document. Due to this simplified view on the data, the user interface will be easily reusable on other data sets and thesauri.

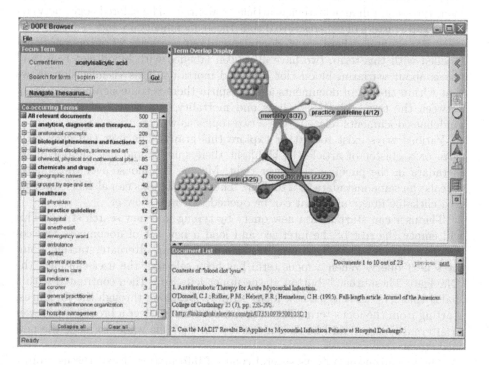

Fig. 2. The Browser Interface

Suppose a user wants to browse through the existing literature on aspirin. She can enter the string "aspirin" in the text field at the upper left part of the window. The system then consults Sesame for all concepts than can be related to this string. It responds with a dialog showing four possible EMTREE terms, asking the user to pick one. (This dialog is omitted when there is only one exact match with an EMTREE term.) We assume the user chooses the first term, "acetylsalicylic acid", which is the chemical name corresponding with the brand name, and is now the focus term.

The system consults Sesame again and retrieves the maximally 500 most relevant documents about "acetylsalicylic acid", their metadata fields (such as titles and authors) and the other most important terms with which these documents are indexed. The co-occurring terms are presented in the tree at the left hand side, grouped by their facet term (the most generic broader term, i.e. the root of the tree they belong to).

The user can now browse through the tree and check one or more checkboxes that appear behind the term names, to see their contents visualized at the right hand side.

Figure 2 shows the state of the interface after the user has checked the terms "mortality", "practice guideline", "blood clot lysis" and "warfarin". The visualization graph shows if and how their document sets overlap. Each sphere in the graph represents an individual document, with its color reflecting the document type, e.g. full article, review article or abstract. The colored edges between terms and clusters of spheres reveal that those documents are indexed with that term. For example, there are 25 documents about warfarin, 22 of them are only labelled with this term, two have also been labelled with blood clot lysis, and one is about warfarin, blood clot lysis and mortality. This visualization shows that within the set of documents about aspirin there is some significant overlap between the terms blood clot lysis and mortality, and that 4 of the practice guidelines documents relate to these two topics as well.

Various ways exist to further explore this graph. The user can click on a term or a cluster of articles to highlight their spheres and list the document metadata in the panel at the lower right. Moving the mouse over the spheres reveals the same metadata in a tool tip. The visualizations can also be exported to a clickable image map that can be opened in a web browser.

The user can start with a new query by typing in a new search string. This will empty the rest of the interface and load a new set of documents and co-occurring terms. The Thesaurus Browser provides an alternate starting point for a next query. When a focus term has been selected, the user can click the "Navigate Thesaurus..." button at the upper left. He is then confronted with a dialog that lets her select a new focus term, by browsing through the thesaurus, starting from the focus term. The user can iteratively select a broader, narrower or alternative term until he encounters a term that she wants to make the new focus term.

The visualization conveys several types of information. First, the user obviously sees document characteristics such as index terms and article types. Visualizing a set of terms shows all Boolean combinations, without the need for the user to express them all separately. Furthermore, the graph also shows within the scope of the selected set of documents how these terms relate, i.e. if they have some overlap and if so, which documents constitute that overlap. Consequently, the geometric distance between terms or between documents is an indication of their semantic distance: terms that share documents are located near one another, and so are documents with the same or similar term memberships.

5   User Studies

At a Drug Discovery conference held in the US in 2003, ten potential end users were given the prototype of DOPE and asked to conduct various tasks. The user group presented a mixture of academic users (6 users from 4th year student to professor) and industrial users, (4 users mainly in leading functions). Users were first given a brief overview of the prototype and were then asked to conduct tasks in the domain of their expertise. To make the results comparative, all users were given similar information and asked to follow the following steps:

1. Identify a search term
2. Explore the co-occurring terms
3. Explore the results with the use of visualization graph
4. Discussion to identify the potential benefits and issues of the prototype.

We will discuss the feedback we got from the users in the individual steps in the following.

5.1   Identifying a Search Term

The first step the users were asked to perform is the selection of an appropriate term to focus the search and to limit the results shown in the DOPE Browser. It turned out that in many cases the decision to enforce a focus term is too restrictive, as users often wanted to use more than one term for focussing. Another observation was, that users do not always want to start their search using a domain term from the thesaurus, but rather the name of an author or a journal. We conclude that the current prototype is rather suited for exploring the space of available information than for searching for a specific article which would normally require the possibility to define more search criteria. The following terms are examples of typical topics users looked for in the system:

 − Genomic
 − Glucagons
 − Kinase
 − Diabetes
 − Seroitonin
 − MHC, peptide epitope
 − COX-2 cyclo oxygenase
 − Hypertension

5.2   Exploring Co-occurring Terms

The general reaction of users to the use of co-occurring terms for narrowing down the search result was quite positive. Users indicated that the additional terms provide useful context information to refine their initial query. Most user liked the way of organizing the terms in a two level hierarchy, though there is a lack of support for finding a specific co-occurring term. Users mainly used terms from the second level. It turned out that users feel the need for using quite specific terms for narrowing down the query and there were complaints that often the co-occurring terms were too general given the quite specific focus term. We conclude that the use of co-occurring terms as a mechanism for narrowing down the search is useful approach, but that the selection and ordering of the terms for the interface needs more sophisticated solutions.

5.3   The Visualization Tool

In general, most users reacted very positively to the visualization and many referred to the graph as "this is what I'm thinking about" or "neat way of jumping between categories". The main two points that emerged from the study are that the visualization provides:

- Richer contextual information about the articles Many users inferred that using the graph helped them to see information that they would have otherwise missed enhancing serendipitous discovery.
- Simpler scanning of the articles. Most users commented that when they scan a list of articles they are looking for one or two keywords to appear in the article title; if the combination is more complex then it becomes increasingly cumbersome to scan the list effectively. The DOPE visualization tool acts as a reminder and map of their search criteria and alleviates cumbersome scanning.

There were three issues identified for improving the visualization:

Interpretation of the Subset Names. When users were asked what information they get from this graph, most referred to the terms as labels rather than the unions of the spheres.

Difficulty to Interpret Complex Term Overlaps. As with Venn diagrams, the complexity of representation increases rapidly after more than three terms are applied. Figure 3 above illustrates when the user has selected 4 terms and the visualization gets very complex. There is no immediate way to resolve this in the current visualization but one possibility may be to limit the terms displayed to alleviate from complexity.

Manipulation of the Graph. The selection and de-selection of the keywords is available only on the tree at the left hand side of the graph. However, most users were attempting to interact directly with the graph and to manipulate it in the process. This behavior indicates the need for supporting providing direct manipulation of the graph. In addition users were mainly scanning the titles with the rollover feature on the graph and they paid little attention to the list at the bottom frame.

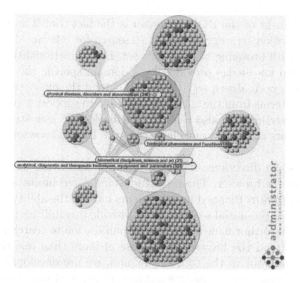

Fig. 3. The visualization where the user has selected 4 terms and a subset term

5.4   Discussion of Potential Benefits

Discussions with users about the potential benefits supported the observations made earlier, that the main benefit of the tool is the exploration of a large, mostly unknown information space rather than support for searching for concrete articles. Examples of beneficial applications that were mentioned by potential end users included filtering material for preparing lectures about a certain topic, and supporting graduate students in doing literature surveys. In this context the need for a "shopping basket" for collecting search results was mentioned. Monitoring focus changes in the research community was mentioned as an example of a more advanced potential application. This however would require an extension of the current system with mechanisms for filtering documents based on date of publication as well as advanced visualization strategies for changes that happen over time.

6   Conclusions

We discussed the benefits of using conceptual knowledge for supporting the exploration of large information spaces. We discussed requirements for an exploration tools. The requirements were defined based on user needs in the DOPE project on providing users thesaurus-based access to document repositories in the area of drug development. We reviewed existing tools for exploring RDF-based conceptual knowledge and concluded that these tools do not scale to large instance sets and do not provide sufficient support for formulating and manipulating queries. As our main contribution, we presented the DOPE browser, a topic based browser for large document sets that overcomes of the problems of existing tools.

The main benefit of the DOPE browser is the fact that it supports a mixed-initiative exploration strategy. It combines search for relevant documents based on a keyword with browsing of the result set. Both functionalities are improved using conceptual knowledge provided by a domain specific thesaurus. The thesaurus is used to normalize query terms and extend the query term with related terms. Further, terms from the thesaurus are used to support topic-based instead of link-based browsing. We also reported feedback from user studies. The result of the user studies confirmed our claim that the DOPE browser is a useful tool for exploration.

There are some directions of future work for improving and extending the functionality of the browser. The user studies indicated limitation of the search component of browser. Planned improvements include the ability to use a combination of terms in the initial search and to provide possibilities to use additional metadata such as author names and year of publication to search for documents. We currently extend the browser to the use of more than one thesaurus. In a case study carried out in the tourism domain, we are developing an extended version of the browser that combines a shared tourism ontology with local classifications used by different users. The connection between the different models is established by automatic classification of documents according to multiple term hierarchies.

Acknowledgments

This work was funded by the Elsevier Advanced Technology Group. The cluster map technology shown in this paper is owned and copyrighted by Aduna (formerly known as Aidministrator Nederland B.V.).

References

1. D. I-Iarman. Towards interactive query expansion. In *Proceedings of the ACM SIGIR Conference on Research and Development in Information Retrieval*, Grenoble, France, 1988.
2. Robert Korfhage. To see or not to see – is that the query? In *Proceedings of the 14th Annual International ACM/SIGIR Conference*, pages 134–141, Chicago, IL, 1991.
3. J.-A. Waterworth and M.-H. Chignell. A model of information exploration. *Hypermedia*, 3(1):35–58, 1991.
4. D. Ellis. A behavioural model for information retrieval system design. *Journal of Information Science*, 15:237–247, 1989.
5. Raya Fidel. Searchers' selection of search keys: Iii. searching styles. *Journal of the American Society for Information Science*, 42(7):515–527, 1991.
6. Patricia Billingsley. Taking panes: Issues in the design of windowing systems. In Martin Helander, editor, *andbook of HumanComputer Interaction*, pages 413–436. Springer Verlag, 1988.
7. Julian Kupiec, Jan Pedersen, and Francine Chen. A trainable document summarizer. In *Proceedings of the 18th Annual International ACM/SIGIR Conference*, pages 68–73, Seattle, WA, 1995.

8. Leslie Carr, Simon Kampa, Wendy Hall, Sean Bechhofer, and Carole Goble. Ontologies and hypertext. In Steffen Staab and Rudi Studer, editors, *Handbook on Ontologies*, volume XVI of *International Handbooks on Information Systems*. Springer Verlag, 2003.

9. V.L. O'Day and Robin Jeffries. Orienteering in an information landscape: how information seekers get from here to there. In *Proceedings of the INTERCHI'93*, Amsterdam, Netherlands, April 1993. IOS Press.

10. Ben Shneiderman, Donald Byrda, and W.-B. Croft. Sorting out searching: A userinterface framework for text searches. *Communications of the ACM*, 41(4):95–98, 1998.

11. M.-J. Bates. The design of browsing and berrypicking techniques for the online search interface. *Online Review*, 13(5):407–431, 1989.

12. J. Koenemann and N.J. Belkin. A case for interaction: A study of interactive information retrieval behavior and effectiveness. In *Proceedings of CHI 96 International conference on Human Computer Interaction*, pages 205–212, Vancouver, B.C., Canada, 1996.

13. Mark Magennis, J. Cornelis, and K. van Rijsbergen. The potential and actual effectiveness of interactive query expansion. In *ACM SIGIR Forum*, volume 31, pages 324–332, 1997.

14. G. Brajnik, S. Mizzaro, and C. Tasso. Evaluating user interfaces to information retrieval systems: a case study on user support. In *Proceedings of the 19th Annual International ACM/SIGIR Conference on Research and Development in Information Retrieval*, pages 128–136, Konstanz, Germany, 1996. Hartung-Gorre Verlag.

15. Raya Fidel. Searchers' selection of search keys: Ii. controlled vocabulary or free-text searching. *Journal of the American Society for Information Science*, 42(7):501–514, 1991.

16. P.-G. Anick. Adapting a fulltext information retrieval system to the computer troubleshooting domain. In *Proceedings of the Seventeenth Annual International ACM SIGIR Conference on Research and Development in Information Retrieval*, pages 349–358, 1994.

17. S.L. Greene, S.J. Devlin, P.E. Cannata, and L.M. Gomez. No ifs, ands, or ors: A study of database querying. *International Journal of ManMachine Studies*, 32(3):303–326, 1990.

18. Hsinchun Chen, R.-R. Sewell A.-L. Houston, and B.-R. Schatz. Internet browsing and searching: User evaluations of category map and concept space techniques. *Journal of the American Society for Information Science*, 49(7):582–608, 1998.

19. E.N. Efthimiadis. End-user's understanding of thesaural knowledge structures in interactive query expansion. In Hanne Albrechtsen and Susanne Oernager, editors, *Advances in Knowledge Organization. Proceedings of the Third International ISKO Conference*, volume 4, pages 295–303, Frankfurt am Main, 1994. Indeks Verlag.

20. Charles Meadow, Barbara Cerny, Christine Borgman, and Donald Case. Online access to knowledge: System design. *Journal of the American Society for Information Science*, 40(2):86–98, 1989.

21. Marti Hearst. Tilebars: Visualization of term distribution information in full text information access. In *Proceedings of the ACM SIGCHI Conference on Human Factors in Computing Systems*, pages 59–66, Denver, CO, May 1995.

22. Matthias Hemmje, Clemens Kunkel, and Alexander Willett. Lyberworld – a visualization user interface supporting fulltext retrieval. In *Proceedings of the 17th Annual International ACM/SIGIR Conference*, pages 249–259, Dublin, Ireland, July 1994.

448   H. Stuckenschmidt et al.

23. A. Michard. Graphical presentation of boolean expressions in a database query language: design notes and an ergonomic evaluation. *Behaviour and Information Technology*, 1(3):279–288, 1982.
24. Christiaan Fluit, Marta Sabou, and Frank van Harmelen. Ontology-based information visualisation. In V. Geroimenko and C. Chen, editors, *Visualizing the Semantic Web*. Springer Verlag, 2003.
25. Morten Hertzum and Erik Frokjaer. Browsing and querying in online documentation: A study of user interfaces and the interaction process. *ACM Transactions on ComputerHuman Interaction*, 3(2):136–161, 1996.
26. Ben Shneiderman. *Designing the user interface: strategies for effective humancomputer interaction*. AddisonWesley, Reading, MA, 1997.

Knowledge Formulation for AI Planning

T. L. McCluskey and R. M. Simpson

Department of Computing and Mathematical Sciences,
University of Huddersfield, UK
Queensgate Huddersfield HD1 3DH
Telephone 44 (0) 1484 422288, Fax 44 (0) 1484 421106
{t.l.mccluskey, r.m.simpson}@hud.ac.uk

Abstract. In this paper we present an overview of the principle components of GIPO, an environment to support knowledge acquisition for AI Planning. GIPO assists in the knowledge formulation of planning domains, and in prototyping planning problems within these domains. GIPO features mixed-initiative components such as generic type composition, an operator induction facility, and various plan animation and validation tools. We outline the basis of the main tools, and show how an engineer might use them to formulate a domain model. Throughout the paper we illustrate the formulation process using the *Hiking Domain*.

1 Introduction

In recent years AI planning technology has improved significantly in the complexity of problems that can be solved, and in the expressiveness of domain representation languages used. Real and potential applications (e.g. in space technology [19, 6], in information gathering [2], in travel plan generation [12], in Grid Computing [6], in e-commerce and e-work [5]) and community events such as the AIPS/ICAPS Planning Competition have moved the field on considerably in the last 10 years. Work in planning algorithms continues to keep a logical separation between planning engine and domain knowledge, but the problems of acquiring, constructing, validating and maintaining this kind knowledge are still considerable. In fact, in the planning area, the problem of knowledge engineering is still a barrier to making planning technology more accessible [16]. Planning domain description languages, of which PDDL [1, 8] is the most used, reflect the interests of plan engine builders in that they emphasise *expressiveness* (what can be represented) rather than *structure* (in what way things are expressed).

There are peculiarities of planning that clearly distinguish engineering planning knowledge from general expert knowledge. The ultimate use of the planning domain model is to be part of a system involved in the 'synthetic' task of plan construction. This distinguishes it from the more traditional diagnostic or classification problems familiar to knowledge based systems. Also, the knowledge elicited in planning is largely knowledge about actions and how objects are effected by actions. This knowledge has to be adequate in content to allow efficient automated reasoning and plan construction.

E. Motta et al. (Eds.): EKAW 2004, LNAI 3257, pp. 449–465, 2004.

With some exceptions (eg [3, 4] and other papers cited below), there is little research literature on planning domain knowledge acquisition. Not too many years ago tools for planning domain acquisition and validation amounted to little more than syntax checkers. 'Debugging' a planning application would naturally be linked to bug finding through dynamic testing, reflecting the 'knowledge-sparse' applications used to evaluate planners. The development of the two pioneering knowledge-based planning systems O-Plan and SIPE has led by necessity, to consideration of knowledge acquisition issues and resulted in dedicated tool support. The O-Plan system has for example its 'Common Process Editor' [24] and SIPE has its Act Editor [20]. These visualisation environments arose because of the obvious need in knowledge intensive applications of planning to assist the engineering process. They are quite specific to their respective planners, having been designed to help overcome problems encountered with domain construction in previous applications of these planning systems.

In this paper we describe a knowledge acquisition method supported by an experimental tools environment, GIPO, for engineering and prototyping planning applications. Like the research centred around application-oriented planners mentioned above, we are trying to develop a platform that can assist the acquisition of structurally complex domains; however our aim is to produce a system that can be used with a wide range of planning engines, and is transparent and portable enough to be used for research and experimentation.

GIPO (Graphical Interface for Planning with Objects) is an experimental GUI and tools environment for building planning domain models, providing help for those involved in knowledge acquisition and the domain modelling. It provides an interface that abstracts away much of the syntactic details of encoding domains, and embodies validation checks to help the user remove errors early in domain development. It integrates a range of planning tools - plan generators, a plan stepper, a plan animator, a random task generator and a reachability analysis tool. These help the user explore the domain encoding, eliminate errors, and determine the kind of planner that may be suitable to use with the domain. In theory, any planning engine that can input a domain model written via GIPO (and translated into the planner's input language) can be interfaced with it, thus creating an implementation of a working planner. We have developed 3 versions of GIPO that are aimed at (1) classical, hierarchical Strips-like domain models (2) HTN domain models (3) domains with processes and events. Beta versions of GIPO(1) and GIPO(2) are available from the GIPO web site *http://scom.hud.ac.uk/planform/GIPO*.

The contribution of this paper is that it draws together the main GIPO tools underlying a staged knowledge formulation method for the classical, hierarchical kind of domain model. The 3 phases of the method are shown in overview in Figure 1. These are:

- firstly, a static model of objects, relations, properties and constraints is derived from an informal statement of requirements. This is then augmented with local dynamic knowledge in the form of object behaviour. This step

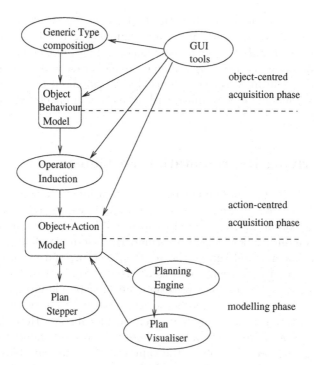

Fig. 1. An Overview of the Knowledge Engineering Process using GIPO

may involve and be informed by, the re-use of common design patterns of
planning domain structures [23].
- secondly, initial representations of the actions available to the planner are
  derived from the behaviour model and the initial requirements. This process
  may be assisted by the use of induction techniques to aid the acquisition of
  detailed operator descriptions [21].
- thirdly, the model is refined and debugged. This involves the integration of
  plan generation, plan visualisation, and planning domain model validation
  tools.

These steps and components combine to provide a tool assisted interface
for supporting planning domain knowledge acquisition which provides many opportunities to identify and remove both inconsistencies and inaccuracies in the
developing domain model. Additionally GIPO provides an opportunity to experiment with the encoding and planning engines available for dynamic testing.
GIPO has a public interface to facilitate the integration of third party planning
engines processing domains and problems expressed in PDDL. The translation
to to PDDL preserves the meaning of operators although hierarchical and state-
behaviour information may be lost.

In the next section we outline the underlying representation language for GIPO(1), and in section 3 introduce an example which will be used in the paper. In sections 4 and 5 we show how generic types and behaviour induction, respectively, can be used to help a domain modeller capture a domain in GIPO. In section 6 we outline a range of tools that can be used to validate the developing domain model, and we finish with a discussion of related work and some conclusions.

2   Underlying Representation Formalism

We briefly review the underlying representation language since this influences and underlies the KE process. The language family used is OCL_h [17, 15]. OCL_h a structured, formal language for the capture of both classical and hierarchical, HTN-like domains. Knowledge is captured by describing changes that the objects in the domain undergo as the result of actions and events. The domain definition is structured around classes of objects, the states that these objects may inhabit, and the possible transitions affected by planning operators. This object-transition metaphor underlies all the tools built into GIPO.

Objects involved in planning have their own local state. Here the state of the world is a vector of variable's values, where each variable holds the value of its own state. As the world 'evolves' the values of the state variables change. This differs from conventional wisdom in AI planning as represented by the standard domain description language PDDL. In OCL_h *the universe of potential states of objects are defined first, before operator definition*. This amounts to an exhaustive specification of what can be said about objects at each level in the class hierarchy. Of course, GIPO insulates the user from detailed syntax, displaying for example object class hierarchies graphically. Whereas the PDDL family is aimed at providing a minimumly adequate common language for communicating the physics of a domain, OCL_h provides a more natural, richer and partially graphical language for domain modelling. More natural because it is structured around the notion of *objects* and *object classes* and is richer because it captures constraints applying to the physics of the domain in addition to the bare physics of actions.

Either manually, or through automated tool support, we acquire for each class of object a set of "typical situations" that an object of that class may inhabit as a result of the planning process. We refer to the definitions of these "typical situations" as "substate classes". If one thinks of transitions of an object in the domain being modelled as arcs in a state-machine, then each substate class corresponds to a parameterised node in the state-machine. In a simple case, a class may have only one such substate class (node). For example, if it is enough to record only the position of a car in a domain model then all possible situations of the car may be recorded as simply "at(Car,Place)", where *Car* and *Place* range through all car and place objects respectively. On the other hand, in a hierarchical domain, an object such as a car may have relations and attributes inherited from different levels, where each level is modelled as a state-machine involving different substate classes.

The developed substate class definitions are then used in the definition of operators in our object-centred language, which are conceptualised as sets of parameterised *transitions*, written

$$(C, O, LHS \Rightarrow RHS)$$

where O is an object constant or variable belonging to class C, and LHS and RHS are substate classes. This means that O moves from a situation unifying with *LHS* to a situation unifying with *RHS*. Transitions can be necessary, conditional or null. Null transitions have an empty *RHS* implying that O must be in *LHS* and stays in that situation after operator execution. A necessary transition requires that there must be an object O that makes the required transition for the operator to be applicable. A conditional transition specifies that any object O in a state that unifies with *LHS* will make the transition to state *RHS*. OCL operators accordingly specify pre and post conditions for the objects participating in the application of an operator but in a way that requires the changes to objects to conform to the defined legal states for such objects.

The *OCL* family of languages additionally provides formalisms to capture problem specifications and to capture *static* knowledge, that is knowledge of *objects* within the domain that is not subject to change as a result of the application of domain operators/actions but may be referred to by the specification of such operators/actions.

3   Example Domain

GIPO has been used to build and model many domains since its first version in 2001. Here we will use a simple model of the *Hiking Domain* to exemplify the main features of the KA method. The reader can download more complex GIPO models from our web-site, including the transport logistics domains which contain several hundred static facts and objects in a hierarchy of 30 object classes.

Imagine you want to have a hiking holiday in the Lake District in North West England. You and your partner would like to walk round this area in a long clockwise circular route over several days. You walk in one direction, and do one "leg" each day. But not being very fit, you do not wish to carry your luggage and tent around with you. Instead you use two cars which you have to carry your tent/luggage and to carry you and your partner to the start/end of a leg, if necessary. Driving a car between any two points is allowed, but walking must be done with your partner and must start from the place where you left off. As you will be very tired when you have walked to the end of a leg, you must have your tent up already there and erected so you can sleep the night, before you set off again to do the next leg in the morning. Actions include walking, driving, moving and erecting tents, and sleeping. The requirement for the planner is to work out the logistics and generate plans for each day of the holiday.

The initial pre-formulation phase in the acquisition process is to examine the requirements of the problem, identify the main objects and actions, and make tentative decisions on the kind of planning problem involved. We are developing different flavours of GIPO to accommodate fundamental differences in the outcomes of this phase. For example, it might be considered necessary to model driving, walking, erecting tents, and sleeping as durative processes. If at this stage it was decided that we needed to model time, processes, events and actions explicitly in the domain, then we would use a particular version of GIPO equipped to handle these mechanisms [22]. However, assume we (at least initially) decide that we require to perform these actions in a sequential fashion, and that we are not concerned about how long they take to perform only the order that they must be performed in, then we can represent the actions as instantaneous and we have a "classical planning" problem.

4 Initial Domain Formulation: Generic Types and Generic Type Composition

The first phase of our GIPO-supported method is the formulation of a domain ontology augmented with a specification of object behaviour in the form of the typical state changes that objects go through. Any OCL_h formulation can be constructed manually via GIPO's GUI, but in this section we advocate the use of predefined "design patterns", which we call *Generic Types*. They can be used to help a domain author to develop a domain model using concepts at a higher level of abstraction than is provided by the underlying specification language. Traditional languages for the specification of planning domains, such as PDDL, or even the object-level OCL_h allow the authors of a new domain great freedom in their choice of representation of the domain details. This freedom is we contend for the most part unnecessary and provides an unwanted conceptual barrier to the development of effective domain definitions. In software engineering it is becoming common place to use "design patterns" to help structure the design and coding of applications. Within the AI planning community the notion of a "generic type" has been used to identify common structure across domains with a view to exploiting these similarities to improve plan generation processing speed [7, 13, 14]. In collaboration with Fox and Long [23] we have developed a fusion of these ideas to identify a set of structural elements that are capable of being used to help structure a wide range of potential planning domains. In this way we provide the domain engineer with a set of concepts at a higher level of generality to allow them to more easily identify the object behaviour of their domain. Broadly, a generic type then defines a class of classes of objects all subject to common transformations during plan execution. A generic type ranges over the types or classes of individual domains. The degree of commonality in the characterisation and transformations that these types or classes must share have been described in the literature in terms of parameterised state machines describing the patterns of transformations that the objects undergo. Within GIPO the domain engineer is presented with a range of templates, corresponding to the identified generic types, which she instantiates to create a first cut definition of the object behaviour of the domain.

4.1   Basic Generic Types

Perhaps the most useful of the "generic types" is that of a *mobile*. A *mobile* can initially be thought of as describing the types of objects that move on a map. They can very simply be characterised by the parameterised state machine shown in figure 2.

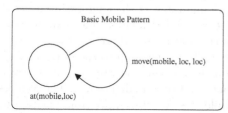
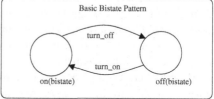

Fig. 2. Basic Mobile and Bistate Generic Types

In this one-state-machine the state is characterised by the property of the mobile object corresponding to its *locatedness* and the transition is identified by the action causing it to move. For this generic type to be applicable to a class in a particular domain there must be a type such that there is an action that changes the truth value of a n placed predicate $N >= 2$, typically the predicate *at*, where one argument identifies the class in question, *mobile*, and another a value *loc* which changes as a result of the application of the operator. In other words the value of *loc* differs in the pre- and post-conditions of the action in the reference to the *at* predicate. No other predicate referencing *mobiles* should change truth value in the same action definition in this most basic form of the mobile prototype. The naming of predicates and arguments may (and will) be different in different instances of the generic type. This is a very weak characterisation of a mobile, in that domains that describe actions that perform transformation on some property of the objects in question might fulfill the above requirements and hence be characterised as a mobile. We have identified a number of variations of the pattern that need to be distinguished from one another. In particular we identify cases where the class mobile must be associated with the class *driver* such that there needs to be an instance of a *driver* associated and co-located with the mobile to enable the mobile's *move* action to take place. The *move* action will also result in the driver changing location in step with the *mobile*. Other flavours of mobiles are associated with *portables* i.e. objects that can be "moved" in associations with mobiles. We also distinguish mobiles that consume or produce resources when they make a transition from one state to another.

A second common and very general *generic type* we call a *bistate*. A *bistate* defines a class *bistate* which is characterised by two one place predicates which we call *off* and *on* both referring to the same *bistate*. There is also a pair of actions that allow the bistate to "flip" from one state to the other. A bistate can be thought of in analogy to a switch than can be turned off and on, see Figure 2 Basic Bistate Pattern.

4.2   Generic Types in the Hiking Domain

In this section we use the example of the Hiking domain to illustrate the way in which generic types can be used as design patterns to support a more abstract view of the structure within a planning domain during the engineering process. Within the Hiking domain there are at least two candidates which can be identified as mobiles. There are the walkers themselves and there are the cars that are used to carry the tent from one overnight stop location to the next. Though both these candidates can be described as mobiles neither are adequately characterised by the simple pattern of a mobile illustrated in diagram 2. The walkers which we aggregate into *couples* are mobiles restricted to move from location to location as constrained by a directed graph linking the route locations, which is our *map* of the Lake District. The cars are also *mobiles* but are mobiles that require *drivers* and are used to carry passengers and the tent from overnight stop to overnight stop. The tent itself is a *bistate* which can be either *up* or *down* but is also a *portable* and as such can be *in* the car while being moved from location to location. Individual walkers are also characterised by more than one *generic type* pattern, as a couple they are mobiles, as individuals they are *drivers* or *portables* but are also *bistates* as they can "flip" between the states of being *fit*

Hiking Generic Types

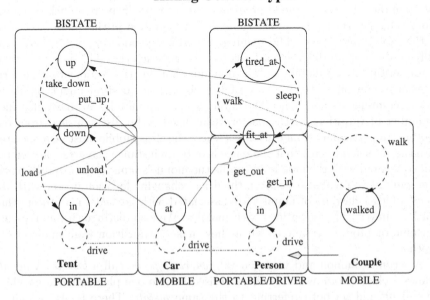

Fig. 3. Generic Types instantiated for the Hiking Domain

and *tired* as they successively walk and sleep. The generic types and the links between them are shown in diagram 3.

The GIPO Generic Type Editors. To enable the domain developer to use the identified generic types to structure a domain we have developed a series of dialogs which we have integrated into the *GIPO* domain development tool.

The dialogues allow the user to choose the relevant patterns and then tailor them to the problem in hand. In simple cases tailoring is simply a matter of naming the components of the pattern in an appropriate way. In more complex cases the user must add optional components to the pattern again by form filling and in the most complex cases ensure that domains using multiple patterns allow them to interact with each other in the correct way. This may involve unifying states from related patterns or associating common actions that facilitate transitions in multiple patterns.

The set of "generic type" dialogues form a domain editor in such a way that the user committing her choices in the editing dialogues will result in the formal domain model being automatically generated. We illustrate the process with snapshots taken from the "Pattern Manager" in figure 4 which is used to control the addition and editing of patterns known and instantiated within the domain. We also show the main dialog for defining the parameters of the "mobile" pattern in figure 5. At the end of this stage, GIPO will contain an initial formulation of the domain ontology including a characterisations of the states that objects in each class can inhabit.

5   Induction of Object Behaviour

The set of editors integrated into GIPO along with the use of generic type design patterns is adequate to develop fully working domain models. The process, however, requires considerable skill and familiarity with the differing A.I. planning

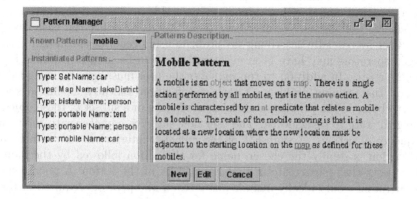

Fig. 4. The Pattern Manager

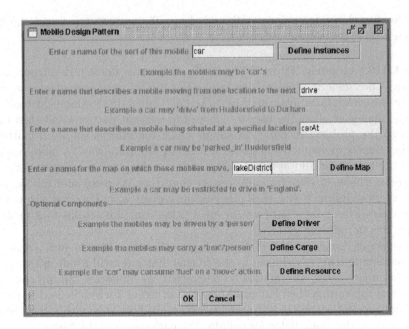

Fig. 5. The Mobile Dialog

paradigms to be successfully used. To lower the threshold of prior knowledge required to develop planning domain models we have developed an operator induction process, called *opmaker* in its GIPO integrated form, aimed at the knowledge engineer with good domain knowledge but weaker general knowledge of A.I. planning. *Opmaker* requires as input an initial structural description of the domain along with training data in the form of a well understood problem drawn from the domain accompanied with an action sequence adequate to solve the training problem. In particular we assume that the modeller has partially constructed her domain model and has reached the stage where there exists at least a partial model with a valid class hierarchy, predicate definitions and sub-state class definitions. We may have done this using either the base editors of GIPO or by partially describing the problem using generic type design patterns. Some operators may have been developed and will be used if available but are not necessary. In addition to run *opmaker* the user must specify, using the task editor, the training problem. A task specification allocates an initial state to every object in the problem and the desired state of a subset of these objects as the goal state to be achieved. The user now supplies *opmaker* with the training sequence of actions. A snapshot of the *opmaker* interface is shown in figure 6. An action is simply the chosen name for the action followed by the names of all objects that participate in that application of the action. A good sequence of operators would ideally include instances of all operators required in the domain, though this is not required by *opmaker* and the action set can be built up incrementally using different problem instances. For the Hiking domain a good

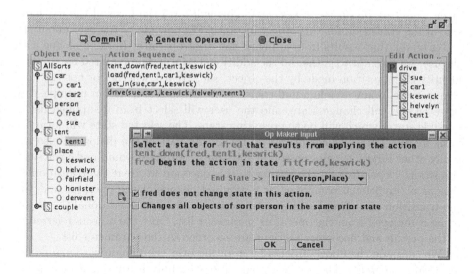

Fig. 6. A Screen Shot of *opmaker*

sequence would be one that enabled the couple to complete the first leg of the tour, and be rested and ready to start the next with their cars in the correct place. Such a sequence would include all the operators required. A fragment of the sequence is shown below.

```
putdown tent1 fred keswick
load fred tent1 car1 keswick
getin sue keswick car1
drive sue car1 keswick helvelyn tent1
```

The user is encouraged to think of each action in terms of a sentence describing what happens. For example in the last action we think of this as "Sue drives car1 from Keswick to Helvelyn taking the tent with her". We sketch the application of the algorithm for inducing the "drive" operator assuming that the earlier operators have been derived and that the specified start situation in the problem placed "Sue","Fred", the tent "tent1", and both cars in Keswick and that the tent was erected. Prior to reaching the point of the derivation of the *drive* operator we initialise the *worldstate* to that of all objects as described in the initial state of the chosen task and then as each operator is derived we advance the *worldstate* by applying the operator to change the states of the affected objects. In considering the *drive* operator we detect that this is the first application of the operator. Therefore to create the *drive* operator we generate a new operator skeleton and set the parameterised name of the operator to *drive(sue, car1, keswick, helvelyn, tent1)*. We then iterate over the dynamic objects in the parameterised name (these are the objects of classes for which substates have been defined). In this example it is all the objects excluding the two location arguments *keswick* and *helvelyn*. For the first object to be considered *sue* we find her state as stored in the *worldstate*, which for the operator sequence given would be $in(sue, car1, keswick)$. This will form the basis of the left hand side of the transition for this object instance. We now query the user about the states of *sue* that results from applying the *drive* operator. In the dialogue with the user we attempt to gather all the additional information required to correctly identify the transition made by the object, *sue*. We ask whether or not *sue* does change state, if not we add a null transition to the operator. In our example case however *sue* will change state, and the user will select from a supplied list of possible states which will be the resulting state. The selected state will form the basis for the *RHS* element of the transition. As part of the dialog we also ask if any other object of class person in the same prior state would make the same transition. Depending on the answer to this question we treat the transition either as a conditional change or as a required change of the operator and add the transition accordingly. When a transition is added as conditional the object name is removed from the operators parameter list. Only the objects referred to in the prevail and necessary sections are recorded in the parameter list.

We continue the above process by iterating over the remaining dynamic objects *car1* and *tent1* The result is that we have a fully instantiated instance of the *drive* operator. We generalise the operator by replacing the object names with variable names maintaining a one to one relationship between the object names and the variable names. Finally we apply the operator to the *worldstate* to advance the state ready for consideration of the next operator and our derivation of the operator *drive* is complete. Using this procedure the algorithm induces the following necessary transitions for objects of the sorts corresponding to *sue* and *car1*.

$$(person, Person0, [in(Person0, Car0, Place0)] \Rightarrow [in(Person0, Car0, Place1)])$$
$$(car, Car0, [at(Car0, Place0)] \Rightarrow [at(Car0, Place1)])$$

For *tent1* the conditional transition is as follows.

$$(tent, Tent0, [loaded(Tent0, B, Place0)] \Rightarrow [loaded(Tent0, B, Place1)])$$

The variables, starting with upper case letters, in the transitions above are all typed either explicitly in the transition or implicitly by their occurrence in the strongly typed predicates defining the transition.

After having been translated into PDDL by GIPO, the induced drive operator is as follows:

```
(:action drive
    :parameters ( ?x1 - person ?x2 - car
                  ?x3 - place ?x4 - place)
    :precondition (and (in ?x1 ?x2 ?x3)(at ?x2 ?x3))
    :effect (and (in ?x1 ?x2 ?x4)(not (in ?x1 ?x2 ?x3))
                 (at ?x2 ?x4)(not (at ?x2 ?x3))
                 (forall ( ?x5 - tent)
                     (when (loaded ?x5 ?x2 ?x3)
                         (and (loaded ?x5 ?x2 ?x4)
                             (not (loaded ?x5 ?x2 ?x3)))))))
```

The current version of *opmaker* allows existing operators to be used in the induction process and is capable of refining the operators to add additional features, such as new conditional clauses or static constraints. It is limited however in that the multiple uses must be consistent with one another it will not deal with conflicts. Operator refinement and use in inducing hierarchical operators is the subject of ongoing work [18].

6   Refining and Validating Domain Models

GIPO with its many graphical editors ensures that any domain model created within the system is at least syntactically correct, in terms of both the representation of the domain in OCL_h and their automatically generated translations into *PDDL*. Automatic validation of the domain is further enabled by the *type* system of OCL_h and the requirement that the static legal states of all dynamic objects are defined in the substate class definitions. As states have been explicitly enumerated operations can be checked to ensure that they do not violate the defined states. Defined tasks for the planning system can also be checked against these state definitions for legality. These static validation checks are capable of uncovering many potential errors within a domain model.

When the knowledge engineer has assembled a complete, statically validated model of the domain there is still the need to test it. Dynamic testing can be done by running the domain specification with a trusted planner against test problems. However, this is essentially "black box" testing and will provide little insight into problems when the desired output is not created. This problem is exacerbated when we take into account that the current generation of planning engines are not fully robust. To help overcome these limitations within the GIPO environment we provide a plan visualiser to allow the engineer to graphically view the output of successful plans generated by integrated planning engines. Perhaps more useful in GIPO is our *plan stepper* designed to allow the engineer to single step a hand crafted plan when the planning engine either fails to produce any plan or produces an unexpected plan. The attraction of single stepping a hand crafted plan is that it allows a separation in the testing process between validating that domain knowledge is adequate to support the desired plan and knowing that the planning engine is adequate to generate the plan. The plan visualiser and stepper both present plans at the level of objects, object states and the changes brought about to the objects by the application of actions.

In the *stepper* shown in figure 7 we see the emerging plan at a stage where the tent needs to be moved to the next overnight stop. The design engineer manually selects the operations to build the plan and instantiates the operation variables. Unfortunately in the case shown there is a mistake in the definition of the *drive* operation in that it fails to guarantee that objects loaded in the car move when the car moves. This can be seen by the engineer double clicking on the tent state following the drive operation and as we see in the pop-up window that the tent is at the wrong location, it should be in the same location as the car, namely "helvelyn". Also when the engineer next tries to unload the tent at the new destination the system generates an error message to indicate why that cannot be done. In this way the engineer can explore the adequacy of the domain specification.

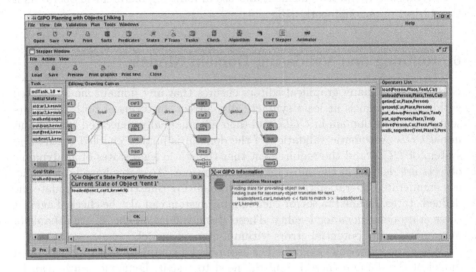

Fig. 7. A Screen Shot of the GIPO Stepper

7 Related Work

From a knowledge based system point of view, GIPO is a knowledge formulation tool that pre-supposes a common generic conceptual domain model for its range of applications. It assumes that domain knowledge is object-centred, and that actions (and events and processes) in the domain cause well-defined state changes to those objects. GIPO views a planning engine as a generic Problem Solving Method (PSM) - one that can output ordered action sets when input with some declarative goal or procedural abstract task. In this regard GIPO is similar to KBS tools that allow the user to select PSM components depending on the type of reasoning that best suits the derivation of solutions to problems.

As far as the authors are aware, no environments as sophisticated as GIPO have been built to help acquire knowledge in a form that can be used with a range of available planning engines. The environments that have been built for use in applications either tend to be aimed at specific AI planners, or are aimed at capturing more general knowledge. Several notable works in the knowledge acquisition literature such as EXPECT [9] and Protege [11] fall into the latter category. EXPECT is an extremely rich system that uses ontologies and knowledge acquisition scripts to generate and drive dialogues with users to acquire and maintain knowledge bases of a diverse nature. From the literature EXPECT is apparently not designed to interface to AI planning engines and hence enable the generation of plans, though it does allow reasoning about plans. One interesting analogue between GIPO and EXPECT is the use of what the latter calls 'interdependency knowledge'. In EXPECT's case, tools use the dependencies between the components of the developing knowledge base to guide user input to repair or input missing knowledge. In the case of GIPO, the static object knowledge, the dynamic object behaviour, and the operator/method definitions are compared against each other to ensure consistency and to identify bugs.

Part of our goal was to try and help bring the very sophisticated planning technology of the planning engines to a potentially wider user base. Our ambition falls some way between that of providing knowledge acquisition interfaces for specific planning engines and the goal of facilitating the gathering of knowledge for a broad spectrum of automated reasoning tasks. We are still exploring what sort of knowledge is needed for such sophisticated tasks and what automated help can be provided to assist end users gather the required knowledge. In the longer run it may be desirable to integrate the type of system we are creating with systems such as EXPECT or Protege as that would facilitate deployment of systems where complex planning is only one part of a broader knowledge based system. Until we have more experience in providing systems just to support the planning element we feel such integration would be too ambitious.

8   Conclusion

Knowledge acquisition and the validation of models of planning domains is notoriously difficult, due to the need to encode knowledge about actions and state change, as well as static and structural knowledge. We see GIPO as a prototype for a range of portable and planner-independent environments that will be used to ease these KA problems. Using high level tools such as the generic type adaptor, operator induction and plan stepping, domain experts with a limited knowledge of AI planning can build up domain models. Using GIPO's interface to state-of-the-art planners via the competition-standard PDDL language, domain experts can prototype planning applications using these planning engines and test them for their suitability to the application.

We have and continue to produce several flavours and versions of GIPO that can be used to formulate knowledge once the nature of the domain requirements are clear. Although implemented and tested, the tools described here are still being evaluated and are the subject of future development. Several hundred down-loads of GIPO have been recorded and we have a small user base around the world. A particularly promising direction is GIPO's use in teaching - it has been used successfully in a one year course in AI with undergraduate students. Particular avenues for future research and development include (a) the identification and build-up of a portable library of generic types for planning applications (b) upgrades of GIPO's automated acquisition tools to deal with domains involving continuous processes, actions and events.

Acknowledgements

This research was supported by the EPSRC grant no. GRM67421/01. Thanks go to our collaborators Ruth Aylett, Maria Fox and Derek Long. We are also grateful to members of our team at Huddersfield, including Weihong Zhao, Donghong Liu, Beth Richardson and Diane Kitchin.

References

1. AIPS-98 Planning Competition Committee. PDDL - The Planning Domain Definition Language. Technical Report CVC TR-98-003/DCS TR-1165, Yale Center for Computational Vision and Control, 1998.
2. G. Barish and C. A. Knoblock. Speculative Execution for Information Gathering Plans. In *The Sixth International Conference on Artificial Intelligence Planning Systems*, 2002.
3. R. Benjamins, L. Barros, and A. Valente. Constructing Planners through Problem-Solving Methods. In B. Gaines and M. Musen, editors, *Proceedings of the Tenth Knowledge Acquisition for Knowledge-Based Systems Workshop (KAW'96)*, 1996.
4. V.R. Benjamins and N. Shadbolt. Preface: Knowledge acquisition for planning. *Int. J. Hum.-Comput. Stud.*, 48:409–416, 1998.
5. S. Biundo, D. Barrajo, and T. L. McCluskey. Planning and Scheduling: A Technology for Improving Flexibility in e-Commerce and Electronic Work. In *Proceedings of e2002, The eBusiness and eWork Annual Conference, Prague The Czech Republic*, 2002.
6. J. Blythe, Eva Deelman, Yolanda Gil, Carl Kesselman, Amit Agarwal, Gaurang Mehta, and Karan Vahi. The Role of Planning in Grid Computing. In *Proceedings of the International Conference on Automated Planning and Scheduling, ICAPS 2003*, 2003.
7. M. Fox and D. Long. The Automatic Inference of State Invariants in TIM. *JAIR*, 9:367–421, 1997.
8. M. Fox and D. Long. PDDL2.1: An extension to PDDL for expressing temporal planning domains . In *Technical Report, Dept of Computer Science, University of Durham*, 2001.
9. Y. Gil, J. Blythe, J. Kim, and S. Ramachandran. Acquiring Procedural Knowledge in EXPECT. In *Proceedings of the AAAI 2000 Workshop on Representational Issues for Real-World Planning Systems*, 2000.
10. J. Hertzberg. On Building a Planning Tool Box. In M. Ghallab and A. Milani, editors, *New Directions in AI Planning*, pages 3–18. IOS Press, 1996.
11. John H. Gennari, Mark A. Musen, Ray W. Fergerson, William E. Grosso, Monica Crubzy, Henrik Eriksson, Natalya Fridman Noy, Samson W. Tu. The evolution of Protege: an environment for knowledge-based systems development. *Int. J. Hum.-Comput. Stud.*, 58, 2003.
12. C. Knoblock, S. Minton, J. L. Ambite, M. Muslea, J. Oh, and M. Frank. Mixed-Initiative, Multi-Source Information Assistants. In *Proceedings of WWW'01*, 2001.
13. D. Long and M. Fox. Automatic synthesis and use of generic types in planning. In *Proc. of 5th Conference on Artificial Intelligence Planning Systems (AIPS)*, pages 196–205. AAAI Press, 2000.
14. D. Long and M.Fox. Planning with generic types. Technical report, Invited talk at IJCAI'01 (Morgan-Kaufmann publication), 2001.

15. T. L. McCluskey. Object Transition Sequences: A New Form of Abstraction for HTN Planners. In *The Fifth International Conference on Artificial Intelligence Planning Systems*, 2000.

16. T. L. McCluskey, R. Aler, D. Borrajo, M.Garagnani, P.Haslum, P. Jarvis, I.Refanidis, and U. Scholz. Knowledge Engineering for Planning Roadmap. *http://scom.hud.ac.uk/planet/home*, 2003.

17. T. L. McCluskey and D. E. Kitchin. A Tool-Supported Approach to Engineering HTN Planning Models. In *Proceedings of 10th IEEE International Conference on Tools with Artificial Intelligence*, 1998.

18. T. L. McCluskey, N. E. Richardson, and R. M. Simpson. An Interactive Method for Inducing Operator Descriptions. In *The Sixth International Conference on Artificial Intelligence Planning Systems*, 2002.

19. N. Muscettola, P. P. Nayak, B. Pell, and B. C. Williams. Remote Agent: To Boldly Go Where No AI System Has Gone Before. *Artificial Intelligence*, 103(1-2):5–48, 1998.

20. K. Myers and D. Wilkins. The Act-Editor User's Guide: A Manual for Version2.2. SRI International, Artificial Intelligence Center, 1997.

21. N E Richardson. *an Operator Induction Tool supporting Knowledge Engineering in Planning*. PhD thesis, School of Computing and Mathematics, University of Huddersfield , forthcoming, 2004.

22. R. M. Simpson and T. L. McCluskey. Plan Authoring with Continuous Effects. In *Proceedings of the 22nd UK Planning and Scheduling Workshop (PLANSIG-2003), Glasgow, Scotland*, 2003.

23. R. M. Simpson, T. L. McCluskey, Maria Fox, and Derek Long. Generic Types as Design Patterns for Planning Domain specifications. In *Proceedings of the AIPS'02 Workshop on Knowledge Engineering Tools and Techniques for AI Planning*, 2002.

24. A. Tate, S. T. Polyak, and P. Jarvis. TF Method: An Initial Framework for Modelling and Analysing Planning Domains. Technical report, University of Edinburgh, 1998.

ConEditor: Tool to Input and Maintain Constraints

Suraj Ajit[1], Derek Sleeman[1], David W. Fowler[1], and David Knott[2]

[1]Department of Computing Science,
University of Aberdeen, Scotland, AB24 3UE, UK
{sajit,sleeman, dfowler}@csd.abdn.ac.uk
[2]Rolls Royce plc, Derby, UK
david.knott@rolls-royce.com

Abstract. We present a tool which helps domain experts capture and maintain constraints. The tool displays parts of an ontology (as classes, sub-classes and properties) in the form of a tree. A number of keywords and operators from a constraint language are also listed. The tool helps a user to create a constraint expression. Additionally, the tool has a facility which allows the user to input tabular data. The expressed constraints can be converted into a standard format, making them portable. It is planned to integrate this tool, ConEditor, with Designers' Workbench, a system that supports human designers.

1 Motivation

Designers in Rolls Royce, as in many large organizations, work in teams. Thus it is important when a group of designers are working on aspects of a common project that the subcomponent designed by one engineer is consistent with the overall specification, and with that designed by other members of the team. Additionally, all designs have to be consistent with the company's design rule book(s). Making sure that these various constraints are complied with is a complicated process, and so the AKT consortium has developed a Designers' Workbench [1], which seeks to support these activities. As noted above, the Designers' Workbench needs access to the various constraints, including those inherent in the company's design rule book(s). Currently, to capture this information, an engineer works with a knowledge engineer to identify the constraints, and it is then the task of the knowledge engineer to encode these, currently in Prolog, in the workbench's knowledge base. The purpose of ConEditor is to allow engineers (particularly those responsible for design standards) to capture and maintain these constraints themselves.

2 ConEditor

Here, we consider an example of a simple constraint and see how it can be input using ConEditor's GUI (Figure 1). A simple constraint expressed in Colan [2] is as follows:

Constrain each f in Concrete Feature
to have max_operating_temp (has_material (f)) >= operating_temp (f)

E. Motta et al. (Eds.): EKAW 2004, LNAI 3257, pp. 466–468, 2004.
© Springer-Verlag Berlin Heidelberg 2004

This constraint states that "For every instance of the class Concrete Feature, the value of the maximum operating temperature of its material must be greater than or equal to the environmental operating temperature." ConEditor's GUI mainly consists of five components, namely, keywords panel, taxonomy panel, central panel, tool bar and result panel. The **keywords panel** consists of a list of keywords, e.g. "Constrain each", "in", "to have". The **taxonomy panel** displays a taxonomy of classes, subclasses and properties, extracted from the domain ontology (ontology used by Designers' Workbench). The entities "Concrete Feature", "max_operating_temp", "has_material", "operating_temp" are selected from this panel. Clicking the "Add" button appends the selected entity to the result panel. The **central panel** lists operators, boolean values, function buttons and textfields (for entering constants). The **tool bar** displays the operators (arithmetic, relational and logical) and delimiters. The operator '>=' and the delimiters '(', ')' are chosen from the tool bar. The **result panel** consists of a text area, displaying the expression input by the user. These constraints input using ConEditor can then be converted into a standard format, Constraint Interchange Format (CIF) [3], making them portable.

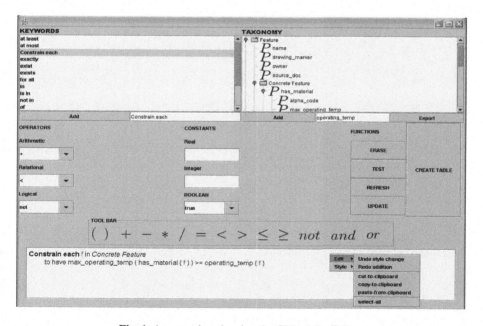

Fig. 1. A screenshot showing the GUI of ConEditor

References

1. D. Fowler, D. Sleeman, Gary Wills, Terry Lyon, David Knott, *Designers' Workbench*, Departmental Technical Report, University of Aberdeen, 2004.
2. N. Bassiliades, P. Gray, *CoLan: A Functional Constraint Language and its Implementation*, Data Knowledge Engineering, 14(3):203-249, 1995.

3. P. Gray, K. Hui, A. Preece, *An Expressive Constraint Language for Semantic Web Applications* in A.Preece & D.O'Leary (eds), E-Business and the Intelligent Web: Papers from the IJCAI-01 Workshop, AAAI Press, pp. 46-53, 2001.

Adaptive Link Services for the Semantic Web

Thanyalak Maneewatthana, Gary Wills, and Wendy Hall

School of Electronics and Computer Science,
University of Southampton, SO17 1BJ,
United Kingdom
Telephone: +44 (0)23 8059 3255, Fax: +44 (0) 23 8059 2865
{tm03r,gbw,wh}@ecs.soton.ac.uk

Abstract. There are shortcomings in using the Web to publish information which are information overload and lost in hyperspace. The aim of the research is investigating how the Semantic web, open hypermedia, and adaptive hypermedia can enhance the adaptation, interoperability and sharing of knowledge components of various hypermedia systems, especially in the medical discipline. It also investigates how to create and manage adaptive web services by using ontologies and semantic properties for adaptation. The adaptive link services for the semantic web is proposed.

1 Introduction

There are shortcomings in using the Web to publish information which are information overload and lost in hyperspace. Adaptive hypermedia systems can deliver personalized views of hypermedia document to users [Brusilovsky 2001]. The principles of the link service approach are that links are first class entities manipulated separately from hypermedia documents and stored independently in link databases. The advantages are that links can be created, added, edited without affected to the original document [Carr, *et al.* 2001]. The Semantic Web is developed to represent information which is understandable by human and machine processable [Berners-Lee, *et al.* 2001]. The Semantic Web can represent knowledge, including defining ontology as metadata of resources. Therefore, the ontology can be used with open hypermedia to create the links of resource or documents over the Web. In addition, adaptive hypermedia can be used with the Semantic Web and link services to produce the relevant information for a particular user's knowledge, background or experience.

2 Aim, Approach, Architecture

The aim of the research is investigating how the Semantic Web, open hypermedia, and adaptive hypermedia can enhance the adaptation, interoperability and sharing of knowledge components of various hypermedia systems, especially in the medical discipline. It also investigates how to create and manage adaptive web services by using ontologies and semantic properties for adaptation.

E. Motta et al. (Eds.): EKAW 2004, LNAI 3257, pp. 469–470, 2004.

The virtual orthopaedic European University provides tools for clinicians supporting the learning of information and clinical skills. Seven web services for specific purposes in the domain are implemented. There are library service, dynamic review journal service, surgical logbook service, virtual classroom service, discussion fora service, personal profile service, and, lastly, admin service. In addition, there are other web services for providing visualization documents to particular users' need and for maintaining user model.

In order to provide relevant information, including create and manage the content and structure of documents on the fly, suitable for particular users' needs, link services, the semantic web and adaptive hypermedia techniques are applied in the system. The system composes of ontology/knowledge based, composition engine, search/inference engine and rule based, and repository.

Ontology, represented in Web Ontology Language (OWL) and Resource Description Framework (RDF), is the backbone of the system. Most of the information is related by using ontology. Ontology is used to define specification of

1. User model: personal profile, history, preference, knowledge level.
2. Presentation model: is used for describing structure for presentation to users. It uses the Fundamental Open Hypermedia Model (FOHM) [Millard, *et al.* 2000].
3. Domain model: defines all the concepts and their relationships in a domain.
4. Metadata model: defines data about data.

Composition engine is used for creating and invoking services and transform the documents, using XSL/XSLT, to the users.

The Dynamic Link Resolution Service (DLRS) [Carr, *et al.* 2001], a link service, will generate on the fly the structure and annotated content of documents relevant to users' personal profile.

To handle adaptation, machine learning is used to form the models of user's situation. The stereotype and overlay techniques is also used.

To integrate the Semantic web technology, adaptive hypermedia and link services, the adaptive link services for the semantic web can generate the semantic augmented HTML documents which are relevant for particular users' needs.

References

[Berners-Lee, *et al.* 2001]   T. Berners-Lee, J. Hendler, and O. Lassila, "The Semantic Web," Scientific American, vol. 279, no. 5, pp. 35-43, 2001.

[Brusilovsky 2001]   P. Brusilovsky, "Adaptive Hypermedia," User Modeling and User Adapted Interaction, vol. 11, pp. 87-110, 2001.

[Carr, *et al.* 2001]   L. Carr, S. Bechhofer, C. Goble, and W. Hall, "Conceptual Linking: Ontology-based Open Hypermedia," presented at 10th World Wide Web Conference, Hong Kong, pp 334-342, 2001.

[Millard, *et al.* 2000]   D.E. Millard, L.A.V. Moreau, H.C. Davis and S. Reich "FOHM: A Fundamental Open Hypertext Model for Investigating Interoperability between Hypertext Domains," In proceedings of the '00 ACM Conference on Hypertext, San Antonio, TX (2000), pp. 93-102, 2001.

Using Case-Based Reasoning to Support Operational Knowledge Management

Giulio Valente[1] and Alessandro Rigallo[2]

[1] Dipartimento di Informatica, Università di Torino, Corso Svizzera 185; 10149
Torino; Italy valenteg@di.unito.it
[2] Telecom Italia Lab, Via G. Reiss Romoli 274; 10148 Torino; Italy
alessandro.rigallo@tilab.com

Introduction

Nowadays, companies like Telecom Italia have recognized that in order to remain competitive, they must efficiently and effectively create, locate, capture and share their operational knowledge (OK) in an innovative way. The OK is mainly based on individual competence and experience, namely some sets of procedures used by people to construct a genuine strategy tailored to the specificities of a given situation. In particular in the Asymmetric Digital Subscriber Line (ADSL) context, provisioning and assurance activities are critical services that allows differentiating Telecom Italia from its competitors. Technicians involved in the assurance and provisioning activities attempt to solve troubles related to the installation and maintenance of the ADSL components. Therefore, they usually access to technical documents, knowledge spread on different web-sites or call their colleagues for advice. However, in order to make faster and more efficiently and effectively provisioning and assurance activities, ADSL technicians need to share, fast access and manage update knowledge through a unique source. Therefore starting from our Operational Knowledge Management Framework (OKMF) [1] [1], we have developed an Operational Knowledge Management System (OKMS), called Remoter. It has a tree tier web-based architecture which groups different technologies (Document Management, Forum, CBR). In particular, this paper discuss our methodology involving CBR techniques in our OKMF.

Remoter: Involving CBR into OKMF. According to Davenport and Prusak [6], CBR systems have considerable success in the domains where rapid access to knowledge is at a premium. Moreover, unlike expert systems, which require that rules are well structured with no overlaps, case structure can reflect the fluid thinking that go in our minds. These are the main reasons because we chose CBR technology to develop Remoter. The most successful commercial application of CBR is conversational CBR (CCBR) [4]. At the end of a benchmark study, we chose to use eGain^{TM} Knowledge [3]. In order to involve eGain^{TM}

---

[1] Due to space constraints, in this paper we do not describe every OKMF phases and the relations to each others

E. Motta et al. (Eds.): EKAW 2004, LNAI 3257, pp. 471–473, 2004.

CCBR technology in our OKMF, we have adopted the followed methodology: a)we have divided the Knowledge Acquisition phase in three steeps: selecting the OK sources, structuring OK according to the CCBR formalism and storing it into a case base, validating the case base. We have identified three different OK sources: experts interviews, technical documents and existing ADSL web-sites. eGain^{TM} Knowledge provides to the knowledge engineer a very user-friendly interface, called eGain^{TM} Knowledge Author, which allows building step-by-step the case base. Therefore, starting from the OK sources, we planned the overall case base structure in term of case clusters, and associated links among them. Each case cluster has been identified by the symptoms of the problem to include. Then starting from the symptoms, we have recognized the underlying problems, and for each of them we have listed all possible solutions. Once we had the "top" (symptom/problem) and "bottom" (solutions) of the case cluster, we have created a consistent and efficient route between the problem and its solution. This route is composed by a list of question and answer pairs. Moreover, in order to get a consistent and efficient list of question and answer pairs we have followed some sample CCBR guidelines [4]. b)In order to perform the Knowledge Dissemination phase, Remoter exploit the eGain^{TM} Knowledge Self-Service component. It allows dissemination of OK by specifying queries or navigating the case base. The efficiency of CCBR Knowledge Dissemination phase has been increased by automatically deriving answers to the questions using the rule based reasoning facility provided by eGain^{TM}. c)eGain^{TM}, like most CCBR tools, act primarily as Knowledge Acquisition and Dissemination systems [5]. Therefore we have implemented an initial feedback mechanism in which the users can insert their new knowledge in form of text, document, audio file feedbacks. These feedbacks are knowledge proposals and are appended to each case they belong to. Then the knowledge manager will validate and integrate them into the overall set of cases stored in the case base.

Experiments. We have briefly shown the synergies between our OKMF and CBR techniques by describing a case study on the ADSL context of Telecom Italia, called Remoter. The Remoter OKMS has been field proved for the last six months of the 2003 in two Telecom territorial areas (TA) of Italy. Each TA had about 30 technicians which used Remoter with over 200 web-access in a day. At the beginning of the trials, Remoter's case base contained about 50 cases. After six months, thanks to the feedback mechanism, the case base is doubled.

References

1. G. Valente and A. Rigallo, *An Innovative Approach for Managing Competence: An Operational Knowledge Management Framework*, 1023-1029, LNCS 2773, Springer-Verlag, (2003).
2. E. Plaza and A. Aamodt, *Case-Based Reasoning: Foundational Issues, Methodological Variations, and System Approaches*, AI Communications, 39-59, **7(1)**, (1994).

3. Egain WEB Site, *http://www.egain.com*
4. D.W. Aha and L.A Breslow and H.Munoz-Avila, *Conversational Case-Based Reasoning*, Applied Intelligence, 9-32, **14**, Kluwer Academic, (2001).
5. B. Bartsch-Sporl and M. Lenz and A.Hubner, *Case-Based Reasoning - Survey and Future Directions*, Proc. of 5th Biannual German Conference on Knowledge-Based Systems, 67-89, 1999.
6. T.H. Davenport and L.Prusak, *Working Knowledge*, Harvard Business School Press, 1998, Boston.

A Hybrid Algorithm for
Alignment of Concept Hierarchies

Ryutaro Ichise[1,2], Masahiro Hamasaki[2], and
Hideaki Takeda[1,2]

[1] National Institute of Informatics,
Tokyo 101-8430, Japan
[2] The Graduate University for Advanced Studies,
Tokyo 101-8430, Japan
{ichise@,hamasaki@grad.,takeda@}nii.ac.jp

Abstract. Hierarchical categorization is a powerful and convenient method so that it is commonly used in various areas, such as ontologies. Although each hierarchy is useful, there are problems to manage multiple hierarchies. In this paper, we propose an alignment method between concept hierarchies by using the similarity of the categorization and the contents of the instance. By using this method, instances that exist in one hierarchy system but does not in the other can be located in a suitable position in the other. The experimental results show improved performance compared with the previous approaches.

Hierarchical categorization is a powerful and convenient method so that it is commonly used in various areas. Although each hierarchy is useful, there are problems to manage multiple hierarchies. Similarity-based integration (SBI) [2] is an effective method for solving this problem. By using this method, instances that exist in one hierarchy system but does not in the other can be located in a suitable position in the other. The main idea of SBI is to utilize only the similarity of categorizations across concept hierarchies. Namely, SBI does not analyze the contents of information assigned to the concept hierarchies. In this paper, we propose an extension of SBI which uses the contents in information instances.

In order to state our problem, we describe a model of the nature of concept hierarchies. Many information management systems for use with conceptual information like ontologies are managed via a system of hierarchical categorization. Such information management system is comprised of 2 elements, i.e, categories and information instances. The problem addressed in this paper is finding an appropriate category in the target concept hierarchy for each information instance in the source concept hierarchy. The important point of this approach is that the source concept hierarchy does not need to be adjusted to fit the target concept hierarchy. Thus, a user can apply our method while continuing to use whichever concept hierarchy they are accustomed to.

E. Motta et al. (Eds.): EKAW 2004, LNAI 3257, pp. 474–476, 2004.

A problem of SBI is that it is hard to learn an alignment rule when the destination category is in a lower category in the target concept hierarchy. In other words, the learned rules are likely to assign relatively general categories in the target concept hierarchy. In order to avoid this type of rules, we propose to combine a contents-based classification method after we apply the SBI algorithm. Since Naive Bayes (NB) [4] is very popular and easy to use, we adopt NB as the contents-based classification method. In order to apply the NB algorithm for hierarchical classification, we utilize the simple method of the *Pachinko Machine* NB. The Pachinko Machine classifies instances at internal nodes of the tree, and greedily selects sub-branches until it reaches a leaf [3]. This method is applied after the rule induced by SBI decides the starting category for the Pachinko Machine NB.

In order to evaluate this algorithm, we conducted experiments using the Yahoo! [5] and Google [1] directories as concept hierarchies, and the links (URLs) in each directory as information instances. We conducted ten-fold cross validations for the shared instances. The accuracy is measured for each depth of the Internet directories and is shown in Figure 1. The vertical axes show the accuracy

Yahoo!: Automotive   Google: Autos   Yahoo!: Photography Google: Photography

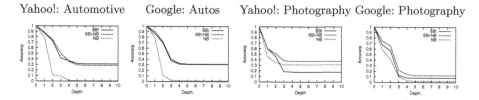

Fig. 1. Experimental Results

and horizontal axes show the depth of the concept hierarchies. The experimental domains of the graphs are integration into Yahoo!: Automotive, Google: Autos, Yahoo!: Photography, and Google: Photography, from left to right. We compared the proposed system called SBI-NB with the SBI system and the NB system. From the comparison of the results of both NB and SBI with SBI-NB, we can expect high accuracy when NB produces a good result. On the other hand, when the NB method has poor accuracy, our method has at least the same performance of SBI and does not have any side effect from NB. From this, we can conclude that our approach is a good method for integrating the approach of contents-based classification method and the approach of the similarity-based integration method.

In this paper, we propose a new method for aligning concept hierarchies as a new approach to utilizing information in multiple concept hierarchies. Our experimental results show improved performance compared with the previous approaches.

References

1. Google., http://directory.google.com/, 2003.
2. Ichise R., Takeda H. and Honiden S., Integrating Multiple Internet Directories by Instance-based Learning. In *Proc. of the 18th Int. Joint Conf. on AI*, 22–28, 2003.
3. McCallum A., et al., Improving text classification by shrinkage in a hierarchy of classes. In *Proc. of the 15th Int. Conf. on Machine Learning*, 359–367, 1998.
4. Mitchell. T., *Machine Learning*. McGraw-Hill, 1997.
5. Yahoo!, http://www.yahoo.com/, 2003.

Cultural Heritage Information on the Semantic Web

Efthimios C. Mavrikas[1,2], Nicolas Nicoloyannis[1], and Evangelia Kavakli[2]

[1] Université Lumière Lyon 2, Equipe de Recherche en Ingénierie des Connaissances,
Campus Porte des Alpes, Bât. L, 5 Avenue Pierre-Mendès-France, 69676 Bron, France
{nicolas.nicoloyannis}@univ-lyon2.fr
[2] University of the Aegean, Department of Cultural Technology and Communication,
Cultural Informatics Laboratory, Sapfous & Arionos Street, 81100 Mytilene, Greece
{tim, kavakli}@ct.aegean.gr

Abstract. In this paper, we outline an ontology-driven approach to the organisation, classification, and mining of cultural heritage documents on the Semantic Web. We propose its implementation as a person-machine system that uses Statistical NLP methods to extract cultural heritage information from texts contained in distributed information sources connected within a schema-based peer-to-peer network infrastructure.

1 Introduction

An expression of cultural heritage information has distinct characteristics of individuality, ethnicity and a position in the geopolitical and historical context. These characteristics form a body of knowledge which is not explicitly documented in text, but is implicitly recognised by a limited, expert audience. The transposition of such highly heterogeneous and localised information on the Internet in order to extend its audience, and encourage new interpretative positions and collaborative work [4], uncovers the need to formally express this knowledge in logical terms. Our approach places the formal logical, machine-readable expression of cultural heritage document semantics at the centre of a person-machine system which assists individual users and user groups in the task of integrating the meaning and utility of cultural heritage information, and forming value judgements. This system is being implemented by the first author in partial fulfilment of the requirements for the PhD degree of the Université Lumière Lyon 2 and the University of the Aegean, following a joint thesis supervision agreement between the two institutions (cotutelle de thèse).

2 Implementation Proposal

Ontology. The CIDOC Conceptual Reference Model (CRM) – a top-level ontology and proposed ISO standard [1] – provides a formal conceptualisation of the cultural heritage domain and the *semantic glue* for our implementation. The CIDOC CRM is expressed as an object-oriented semantic model and concentrates on the definition of

E. Motta et al. (Eds.): EKAW 2004, LNAI 3257, pp. 477–478, 2004.

properties rather than classes, which makes it a particularly suitable semantic support for the creation of relational metadata by document annotation. We use an RDFS conversion of the CIDOC CRM definition of 81 classes and 132 unique properties, and encode ontology instances in RDF and XML as relational metadata.

Communication. Project JXTA [5], an open-source network computing platform and generalised set of peer-to-peer protocols, is our basic communications toolkit. Project JXTA provides a framework for the development and testing of collaborative applications interconnecting highly heterogeneous peers in a ubiquitous and secure fashion. Based on this framework, the Edutella project has achieved the design of a schema-based peer-to-peer network infrastructure for the exchange of educational media, organised in a super-peer topology using the HyperCuP peer clustering algorithm [3]. Our implementation follows the ontology-based clustering approach introduced by the Edutella project to deploy a peer-to-peer network of distributed cultural heritage information sources, grouped together in concept clusters according to the instantiations of the CIDOC CRM by their document contents.

Document Analysis. There are two distinct document analysis tasks performed in support of the ontology-based clustering and querying of our distributed information sources: an information extraction (IE) task and a multi-document summarisation (MDS) task. The IE task execution processes the contents of each information source joining the peer-to-peer network and fills in template information for every newfound document, using templates derived from the CIDOC CRM class hierarchy and its associated DTD; the relational metadata obtained are used to structure the peer concept clusters, and populate inter-cluster and intra-cluster query routing tables. The MDS task execution mines the contents of each peer concept cluster, selects representative single-document summaries of the cluster main theme, and combines them into a multi-document summary; the final summary is a thematic label for the peer concept cluster and a browsing aid to the user. We are currently evaluating a number of adaptive IE algorithms [2], summarisers, and ontology-based document annotation tools for our implementation, using a NLP IDE and a balanced, representative corpus spanning the cultural heritage domain.

References

[1] M. Doerr, S. Stead, et al. Definition of the CIDOC CRM. http://cidoc.ics.forth.gr/
[2] Finn, N. Kushmerick. Active learning strategies for information extraction. In *Proceedings of the ECML/PKDD Workshop on ATEM*, Cavtat-Dubrovnik, Croatia, September 2003.
[3] W. Nejdl, et al. Super-peer-based routing and clustering strategies for RDF-based peer-to-peer networks. In *Proceedings of WWW2003*, Budapest, Hungary, May 2003.
[4] D.C. Papadopoulos, E.C. Mavrikas. Peer-to-peer ways to Cultural Heritage. In *Proceedings of CAA 2003*, Vienna, Austria, April 2003.
[5] Project JXTA. http://www.jxta.org/

Stepper: Annotation and Interactive Stepwise Transformation for Knowledge-Rich Documents

Marek Růžička and Vojtěch Svátek

Department of Information and Knowledge Engineering,
University of Economics, Prague, W. Churchill Sq. 4, 130 67 Praha 3, Czech Republic
{ruzicka,svatek}@vse.cz

Abstract. The *Stepper* system addresses a problem untackled by mainstream semantic annotation tools: extraction of formal content from documents that are unique, authoritative, and rich in ambiguously expressed knowledge. *Stepper* has been tested on medical guideline documents. It takes care of initial text mark-up as well as of subsequent rule-based transformation of the document across several user-definable levels.

1   State of the Art

Text annotation became hot topic in connection with *semantic web* [5]. Aside manual methods, adaptive information extraction [2] is exploited, especially when facing tremendous amounts of (rather knowledge-scarce) textual material in websites or newspaper articles. A separate family of tools has recently been developed for knowledge extraction from *medical guideline* documents. Each guideline document is unique, authoritative (endorsed by a board of clinical experts), rather concise but extremely rich in valuable knowledge—no part of the text can safely be skipped. These factors are definite obstacle to (at least, shallow) automated information extraction. Guidelines also differ from *legal* documents by lack of regularity in their language: concepts definitions are often ambiguous, background knowledge is missing and the writing style is extremely variable; direct mapping to a formal model is thus impossible. Therefore, guideline mark-up tools rely on human analysis, and only strive to ease the mapping from fragments of text to elements of formal models, with possibility of backward retrieval.

2   Functionality of *Stepper*

Our *Stepper* tool combines text *annotation* with subsequent rule-based (XML) *transformation* carried out over multiple user-defined levels (DTDs). Experiments on *medical guidelines*, using earlier versions of the tool, are described in [6, 8]. The latest version consists of interconnected environments for:

1. Free text semantic *mark-up*: delimitation of initial (XML) 'knowledge' blocks.
2. Interactive *step-by-step transformation* of XML structure and content by means of rules in an original language called *XKBT*; non-interactive XSLT [4] rules can also be used, via embedded XSLT processor.

E. Motta et al. (Eds.): EKAW 2004, LNAI 3257, pp. 479–480, 2004.

3. Convenient *editing* of XKBT rules (presumably done by domain expert).
4. Navigation along XLink references between source and target structures *across all transformation levels*: the whole chain (or tree) of predecessor and/or successor elements can be viewed at the same time.

The tool can be downloaded from http://euromise.vse.cz/stepper-en.

3   Related and Future Work

The stepwise character of *Stepper* is rather unique: other *annotation tools*, be they semantic-web ones [5] or medical-guideline ones (GMT [9], GEM-Cutter [1]), proceed in one step, except for *Uruz* (part of DeGeL [7]), which employs two steps. *Stepper* allows for unrestricted number of steps in order to bridge the gap between the text and ultimate formal knowledge base. In the *transformation* phase, *Stepper* encourages human analysis of document semantics: XKBT rules have multiple entry points for user interaction, while standard XSLT [4] can still be applied in non-interactive phases of transformation. *Stepper*-based transformation also shares some aspects with *Transmorpher* [3]; unfortunately, we could not make comparison due to inaccessibility of the *Transmorpher* site.

Stepper is undergoing continuous improvement. For the sake of medical guidelines modelling, we plan to incorporate clinical vocabulary management in the near future. Finally, we believe that the space of knowledge-rich and (to some extent) authoritative documents is not limited to medical guidelines: we also plan to experiment with documents from other domains, for example, with information system requirement specifications.

The research is partially supported by the project LN00B107 of the Ministry of Education of the Czech Republic.

References

1. GEM Cutter, available from http://ycmi.med.yale.edu/GEM
2. International Workshop on Adaptive Text Extraction and Mining within ECML/PKDD 2003, http://www.dcs.shef.ac.uk/~fabio/ATEM03.
3. Transmorpher, http://transmorpher.inrialpes.fr
4. Clark, J.: XSL Transformations (XSLT) Version 1.0, W3C, 1999. http://www.w3.org/TR/xslt.
5. Handschuh, S., Staab, S. (eds.). Annotation for the Semantic Web. IOS Press, 2003.
6. Růžička, M., Svátek, V.: Mark–up based analysis of narrative guidelines with the *Stepper* tool. In: Computer-based Support for Clinical Guidelines and Protocols, IOS Press 2004.
7. Shahar, Y. et al.: The Digital Electronic Guideline Library (DeGeL): A Hybrid Framework for Representation and Use of Clinical Guidelines. In: Computer-based Support for Clinical Guidelines and Protocols, IOS Press 2004.
8. Svátek, V., Růžička, M.: Step–by–Step Mark–Up of Medical Guideline Documents. *International Journal of Medical Informatics*, Vol. 70, No. 2-3, July 2003, 329–335.
9. Votruba, P., Miksch, S., Seyfang, A., Kosara, R.: Tracing the Formalization Steps of Textual Guidelines. In: Computer-based Support for Clinical Guidelines and Protocols, IOS Press 2004.

Knowledge Management and Interactive Learning

Nieves Pedreira[1], Julián Dorado[1], Juan Rabuñal[1], Alejandro Pazos[1], and Andrés Silva[2]

[1] RNASA-lab. Computer Science Faculty. University of A Coruña
{nieves,julian,juanra,apazos}@udc.es
[2] Computer Science Faculty. Polytechnic University of Madrid
asilva@fi.upm.es

Abstract. This work presents a proposal for an e-learning model that facilitate the learning process. Using a Knowledge Management System as support, learning is planned through action, which results in the execution of tasks based on computer games strategies. Both contents of the course and tasks are included into the Institutional Memory of System. The design of this Institutional Memory shows as a basis for the system. Intelligent agents will adapt the tasks to the level and preferences of the student.

1 Introduction

In this work, we try to engage two important aspects of learning: the acquisition of knowledge[1] and the motivation or interest in doing it. To cover the first point, we propose the use of a Knowledge Management System which, not only stores data or news, but makes the users part of the system itself and incorporates mechanisms to share tacit knowledge [2], such as meetings, pieces of advice, examples, and so on.

Relating to motivation, computer games, with their high level of interaction, incorporate interesting strategies to maintain a player involved for hours. We can remark the following ones: 1) the player knows the final aim, but not the intermediate steps; 2) trial and error makes the player learn to proceed helped by experience and improved dexterity; 3) errors and successful actions are immediately detected; 4) the rhythm of the game is self-regulated; 5) the Internet offers books and discussions with hints and suggestions; 6) the classical user manual is replaced by an interactive demo.

To apply these strategies into a learning system, the material should not be perceived as a boring obligation but rather as an interesting option. Contents should be represented not as an object of study but as necessary elements towards a series of objectives that will be discovered in the course of various actions.

2 Proposed Model

We propose a method to store and access the knowledge in a progressive way, so that the non-linear structure of the information and the active experience-based learning can be united. Instead of directly presenting the contents that are to be studied, we present tests that require the aimed knowledge. If the student cannot carry out these tests, they will be divided into easier subtests. The student disposes of a series of

E. Motta et al. (Eds.): EKAW 2004, LNAI 3257, pp. 481–482, 2004.
© Springer-Verlag Berlin Heidelberg 2004

helping tools: basic material, related subjects, examples, solutions proposed by other students, learned lessons, yellow pages and communication tools. In this way, the student gradually constructs his own knowledge through practice. Once he finds the solution to a problem, he will be confronted with more complicated tasks that require the previously acquired knowledge. In the course of the learning process, he will be able to increase the information stored in the system.

Our proposal incorporates the contents of the course and the interactive strategies into the Institutional Memory of the KMS. To design this Institutional Memory, we must first identify thematic units and the processes that the student should learn in each unit. After detailing these processes down to the most basic level of the course, the existing relations between the processes are charted in a Knowledge Map, which allows us to associate the knowledge elements to each process, and assign a pattern problem to each process and a series of real problems to each pattern problem.

Once the elements are organised, they must be included in the Knowledge Base. Since this information is quite diversified, one or several multimedia databases will be used. To implement the relations between contents, tasks and ability levels, we will use a global ontology that separates the conceptual structure from the storage structure. XML offer handy possibilities for its implementation and facilitates the interchange of information between the database and the user environment, a web based application. This integration is optimized by intelligent agents [3], which control the state of the system and the level of the student to offer the adequate information to his level and preferences.

The fact of being able to solve different tasks and having the access into information of different sources allows the learner to acquire the information by different means, so that his knowledge will be more complete and everlasting.

3 Summary

The proposed model incorporates the contents in the Institutional Memory of a KMS and uses an ontology to maintain the information and its categorisation independently. It also proposes learning through action, while guaranteeing that the acquired knowledge is used in the execution of tasks adapted to the level of the learner. The study is still in course and on going approximations with reduced prototypes show, by now, that the use of the environment allows the student to extend or improve his problem-solving methods and his abilities to apply known strategies to new problems.

References

1. Wiig, K. M., Knowledge Management Methods. Schema Press, Ltd., Arlington, 1995
2. Nonaka, I.; Takeuchi, H., The Knowledge Creating Company: How Japanese Companies Create the Dynamics of Innovation. Oxford University Press. New York, 1995
3. Gómez, A.; Juristo, N.; Montes, C.; Pazos, J., Ingeniería del Conocimiento. C. E. Ramón Areces, S.A. Madrid, 1997.

Ontology-Based Semantic Annotations for Biochip Domain

Khaled Khelif and Rose Dieng-Kuntz

INRIA, UR Sophia Antipolis project ACACIA,
2004, route des lucioles BP93, 06902 Sophia Antipolis Cedex, France
{khaled.khelif, rose.dieng}@sophia.inria.fr

Abstract. We propose a semi-automatic method using information extraction (IE) techniques for generating ontology-based annotations for scientific articles, useful for biologists working in the biochip domain.

1 Motivations

The documents published on the Web represent a very important source of knowledge which is essential for checking, validating and enriching a research work. It is the case of research in the domain of molecular biology and more particularly in the domain of biochip experiments. The biochip experiments provide a huge amount of information and it is difficult for the biologist to validate and interpret the obtained results. First, s/he has to search (using a classic search engine) documents which argue, confirm or invalidate his/her hypotheses, then s/he must analyse the documents found in order to identify relevant knowledge.

This task of IR can be facilitated by the semantic web techniques, and carried out by associating to each document a semantic annotation based on an ontology describing the domain. But, in spite of its advantages, creating a semantic annotation is a difficult and expensive process for biologists (time, people...) and an alternative to generate these annotations would be the automatic information extraction from texts. Within a collaboration project with IPMC biologists working on biochip experiments, we developed the MEAT-ANNOT tool for semi-automatic generation of ontology-based semantic annotations for scientific articles in the biochip domain.

2 Our Method

Starting from a text written by a biologist (e.g. scientific articles), our method allows the generation of a structured semantic annotation, based on a domain ontology, and describing the semantic contents of this text.

For the ontology, we chose the UMLS[1] semantic network which describes the biomedical domain: we considered the hierarchy of its types as a hierarchy of concepts and the terms of UMLS metathesaurus as instances of these concepts. Our method breaks up into the four following steps:

---

[1] http://www.nlm.nih.gov/research/umls/

E. Motta et al. (Eds.): EKAW 2004, LNAI 3257, pp. 483–484, 2004.
© Springer-Verlag Berlin Heidelberg 2004

- Term extraction : After tokenising and tagging texts with GATE [3], we used an extraction window of size four. For each candidate term, if it exists in UMLS, we process the following word otherwise we decrease the size of the window till zero;
- UMLS interrogation : For each candidate term extracted, we send a query to UMLS Knowledge Server; the answer received in XML format is parsed to obtain information about the term (its semantic type, its synonyms …);
- Relation extraction : In this step we used the linguistic tool Syntex [1] to reveal the potential relations between bio-medical concepts. Then, we used JAPE [3] to write information extraction grammar from texts processed by GATE. So, for each relation revealed by Syntex, we created manually an extraction grammar to extract from the corpus of articles all the instances of this relation;
- Annotation generation : An RDF annotation based on the UMLS ontology describing the validated information is generated automatically by our tool and associated to the studied article and stored in the directory containing the annotations of the other articles.

As an example, let us consider an article related to lung development and containing the sentence : "HGF plays an important role in lung development". Information extracted from this sentence is:

- HGF : instance of the "Amino Acid, Peptide, or Protein" concept of UMLS;
- Lung development : instance of the "Organ or Tissue Function" concept of UMLS;
- HGF play role lung development : instance of "play role" relationship.

And the RDF annotation describing this information is generated automatically. The base of RDF annotations can then be used by Corese search engine [2] for information retrieval among the scientific articles.

3 Conclusion

We presented a method that allows the generation of semantic annotations using ontology. Based not only on concept instances but also on relation instances, our method was validated by biologists who found the annotations quite relevant.

References

1. Bourigault D. & Fabre C., Approche linguistique pour l'analyse syntaxique de corpus. Cahiers de grammaire, Vol.25, pp.131-151. (2000)
2. Corby O. & Faron-Zucker C., Corese: A Corporate Semantic Web Engine. WWW11 Workshop on Real World RDF and Semantic Web Applications, Hawaii, 2002.
3. Cunningham H., Maynard D., Bontcheva K. & Tablan V., GATE: A Framework and Graphical Development Environment for Robust NLP Tools and Applications. ACL'02.

Toward a Library of Problem-Solving Methods on the Internet

Alvaro E. Arenas and Brian M. Matthews

CCLRC Rutherford Appleton Laboratory, OX11 0QX, UK
{A.E.Arenas, B.M.Matthews}@rl.ac.uk

Abstract. Problem-Solving Methods (PSMs) are software components that can be assembled with domain knowledge bases to create application systems. Researchers at CCLRC are developing a PSMs library, where each method is expressed as a web services described in the OWL-S language.

1 Introduction

The knowledge-engineering community has identified and developed Problem-Solving Methods (PSMs) for specific high-level tasks such as diagnosis, assessment, etc, and develop systems using them as components which are combined and instantiated into complete systems. Researchers at CCLRC are developing a PSMs library, where each method is expressed as a web services described in the OWL-S language. The library is part of a wider research objective that is applying knowledge-based methodologies for developing intelligent systems for the Web; indeed this research objective was identified in the well-known EU-NSF report on Research Challenges and Perspectives of the Semantic Web in 2002 [2].

In particular, we are utilising the library with the CommonKADS methodology [3]. By contrast to traditional web services discovery, tasks can be determined when modelling a system based on the involved knowledge as well as associated to particular PSMs. One case study we are analysing is the ITtalks Web Portal, which provides information about events in the IT area [1].

2 Modelling Problem-Solving Methods

Let us consider the *Assessment* PSM as described in CommonKADS. This method aims at finding a *decision category* for a *case* based on a set of domain-specific *norms*. For instance, determining the relevance of a talk can be seen as applying an assessment method, where the case corresponds to information about the talk to be qualified; the norms are the set of rules for qualifying a talk according to the user's profile and the importance of the speaker; and the decision category corresponds to the qualification of the talk.

We can represent PSMs as services using the mark-up language OWL-S. This has advantages associated to web services such as facilitating automatic composition and interoperability through their semantic description. We give the process description

E. Motta et al. (Eds.): EKAW 2004, LNAI 3257, pp. 485–486, 2004.

for the assessment method as a subclass of OWL-S Process. It receives two parameters: a *Case*, which corresponds to a list of things - domain-specific objects that constitute the case to be assessed; and *Norms*, which corresponds to a list of things denoting the norms (evaluation guide) to assess the case. The output is *Decision*, a thing indicating a decision category. We suppose classes have been defined for each parameter data type: Case, Norms and Decision. We also give classes to define the input and output parameters (i.e. the parameters as opposed to the parameter values). We give only *CaseInput* for brevity

```
<owl:Class rdf:ID="CaseInput>
   <rdfs:subClassOf rdf:resource="&process;Input">
    <rdfs:subClassOf>
       <owl:Restriction>
          <owl:onProperty rdf:resource="&process;parameterType"/>
          <owl:hasClass rdf:resource="#Case" />
       </owl:Restriction>
    </rdfs:subClassOf>
</owl:Class>
```

Let us now define the new *PSM Assessment*. It is a subclass of the generic atomic process class. For brevity, we show only the input of a Case.

```
<owl:Class rdf:ID="Assessment" >
   <rdfs:subClassOf rdf:resource="&process;AtomicProcess">
  <!-- one input is a Case -->
   <rdfs:subClassOf>
       <owl:Restriction>
          <owl:onProperty rdf:resource="&process;:hasInput" />
          <owl:someValuesFrom rdf:resource="#CaseInput" />
       </owl:Restriction>
    </rdfs:subClassOf>   …
</owl:Class>
```

In the case of task *Determine Talk Relevance*, the input *Case* corresponds to a list including two elements: the grade that the user has giving to the topic of the talk and the ranking of the speaker according to services such as CiteSeer. The input *Norms* corresponds to the rule for determining the relevance of the talk. The output category decision in this case is a real between 0 and 1 indicating the relevance of the talk.

References

1. R. Scott Cost et al. ITtalks: A Case Study in the Semantic Web and DAML+OIL. IEEE Intelligent Systems, pages 40–47, January/February 2002.
2. J. Euzenat. Research Challenges and Perspectives of the Semantic Web. Report of the EU-NSF Strategic Workshop, Sophia-Antipolis, France. 2002.
3. G. Schreiber *et al.* Knowledge Engineering and Management: The CommonKADS Methodology. The MIT Press, 2000.

Supporting Collaboration Through Semantic-Based Workflow and Constraint Solving

Yun-Heh Chen-Burger[1], Kit-Ying Hui[2]
Alun D. Preece[3], Peter M. D. Gray[3], and Austin Tate[1]

[1] AIAI, CISA, Informatics, The University of Edinburgh, UK
[2] School of Computing, The Robert Gordon University, UK
[3] Computing Science Department, University of Aberdeen, UK

Keywords: Virtual Organisation, Constraint Satisfaction, Business Process Modelling, IDEF3, Ontology, NIST PSL, Semantic Web, Semantic Grid.

1 Introduction

This paper describes our efforts to provide a collaborative problem solving architecture driven by semantic-based workflow orchestration and constraint problem solving. These technologies are based on shared ontologies that allows two systems of very different natures to communicate, perform specialised tasks and achieve common goals. We give an account of our approach for the workflow assisted collaboration with constraint solving capabilities. We found that systems built with semantic (web) based technologies is useful for collaboration and flexible to enhance the system with specialised capabilities. However, much care must be exercised before correct semantics may be exchanged and collaborations occur smoothly.

2 Workflow Collaboration with Constraint Solving Capabilities

Our work is illustrated in a demonstration example. Consider solving a PC configuration problem in a virtual organisation that builds PC based on customer's individual requirements. Different departments in the organisation are located dispersedly, each may have certain overlapping of domain knowledge with another but also has specific non-overlapping local expertise – that may be data and/or work procedure related. They need to collaborate with each other to achieve common organisational goals – i.e. to build customer-tailored PCs. Three technologies are involved: FBPML[1] to provide process modelling and workflow technologies, KRAFT system[2] to provide specialised support for constraint problem solving and I-X system[3] to provide a user front-end to manage workflow execution.

In this example, the domain knowledge in the PC configuration is divided and stored in different departments: Sales and Technical. This domain knowledge is based on two individual ontologies: marketing and technical. As the two departments collaborates in their operations, their ontologies are partially shared. This mimics real-life situations where specialised expertise centres are often geographically disperse yet collaboration

E. Motta et al. (Eds.): EKAW 2004, LNAI 3257, pp. 487–488, 2004.
© Springer-Verlag Berlin Heidelberg 2004

is required between them. The mapping of the underlying ontologies also provides a rich foundation for data that is being manipulated by workflow. In addition, domain knowledge are constrained using CIF (Constraint Interchange Format) that is RDF based. KRAFT based constraint language (Colan) and its counter part in FBPML are mapping into CIF and use CIF for communication between them.

In this experiment, two I-X Process Panels have been used to instantiate FBPML processes. It assists dynamic task execution, communication and collaboration with KRAFT System. The sales and technical units are each represented by the 'Edinburgh' and 'Aberdeen' I-X panels. The Edinburgh site needs to resolve a task that requires technical capabilities. The sales unit of Edinburgh passes this task to its technical counterpart in Aberdeen. As this problem may be resolved using Constraint Satisfaction Problem (CSP) solving technology, the Aberdeen site makes use of its local CSP solver, the KRAFT system, provided with the passed problem description from Edinburgh. After execution, the KRAFT system returns the solution (or acknowledge of failure) to the Aberdeen I-X panel, which returns the solution to the Edinburgh site. If a satisfactory solution was not found, the sales department may decide to find alternative answers through new enquiries.

3   Conclusions and Future Directions

Our work demonstrates a collaboration between two systems of very different natures: a workflow based (I-X and FBPML) and constraint solving systems (KRAFT). Our work has been successful in the defined task, but much mapping effort was needed in the earlier stages of the project as not all modelling concepts can be easily mapped, so practical solutions must be found. This echoes existing knowledge sharing and interoperability problems between any two or more potentially very different but partially overlapping systems that are well-known in the knowledge systems community. The ultimate goal of the Semantic Web is to provide ways of connecting arbitrary open systems to achieve non-trivial tasks using semantically rich knowledge. The *I-X-KRAFT "TIE"* is a small step towards this goal.

This work is supported under the Advanced Knowledge Technologies Interdisciplinary Research Collaboration, which is sponsored by the UK Engineering and Physical Sciences Research Council under grant number GR/N15764/01. The constraint fusing services were developed in the context of the KRAFT project, funded by the EPSRC and British Telecom. Kit Hui's work was performed while at The Aberdeen University as part of the AKT project.

References

1. Yun-Heh Chen-Burger and Jussi Stader. Formal support for adaptive workflow systems in a distributed environment. *Workflow Handbook 2003*, April 2003.
2. Kit-Ying Hui, Peter M. D. Gray, Graham J. L. Kemp, and Alun D. Preece. Constraints as mobile specifications in e-commerce applications. In *9th IFIP 2.6 Working Conference on Database Semantics (DS-9), Semantic Issues in e-Commerce Systems*, pages 357–379, 2001.
3. Austin Tate. I-X: Technology for intelligent systems. *www.i-x.info, AIAI, The University of Edinburgh*, 2002.

Towards a Knowledge-Aware Office Environment

Leslie Carr, Timothy Miles-Board, Gary Wills,
Arouna Woukeu, and Wendy Hall

Intelligence, Agents, Multimedia Group,
University of Southampton, UK
{lac,tmb,gbw,aw1,wh}@ecs.soton.ac.uk

We report the latest efforts of the Writing in the Context of Knowledge (WiCK) project[1] in investigating the use of Semantic Web technologies in a business-type environment, where authors create and re-use knowledge-rich documents. To date, we have integrated an established commercial off-the-shelf office production environment with knowledge Web services to assist authors in carrying out tasks in a business writing scenario.

Scenario. The task of writing a funding proposal is common in industrial and commercial environments; here, we consider a hypothetical funding proposal for a research project in an academic environment. The proposal is directed at the UK's Engineering and Physical Sciences Research Council (EPSRC), which has a well-defined procedure for submitting, reviewing, and selecting proposals for funding, and provides a standard form (the Je-SRP1) and comprehensive guidance notes on how to fill out the form, create the supplementary documentation (Case for Support), and submit it for consideration.

In order to properly model the Je-SRP1 form and Case for Support documents and the knowledge they contain, we define the following ontologies: *Research Ontology* stakeholders and activities participating in research — the researchers, their publications, research interests, conferences and journals; *Project Ontology* the activity of undertaking work — the ideas of work package, budget, personnel, milestones *etc.*; *Proposal Ontology* the objectives, beneficiaries, funding call, programme of activity *etc.*; *Subject Ontology* the area in which we wish to conduct research, the problems that we wish to address and the methods, systems and approaches which have been described in the literature.

Approach. Filling in the Je-SRP1 form is mainly a matter of choosing appropriate instances against the above ontologies from the knowledge-base. Creating the Case for Support document is more involved, however, as the author is required to construct a text, rather than enter data into clearly labelled spaces on a form. However the guidance notes indicate very clearly the kind of information that is expected in each part of the document. For example, *Provide a summary*

---

[1] http://wick.ecs.soton.ac.uk/

E. Motta et al. (Eds.): EKAW 2004, LNAI 3257, pp. 489–491, 2004.

of the results and conclusions of recent work in the technological/scientific area which is covered by the research proposal...: a simple query of the knowledge-base would provide a list of potentially relevant papers, but a more advanced reasoning agent would be required in order to assist the author in evaluating their relative significance.

WiCKOffice. Our development efforts to date have produced WiCKOffice, a Microsoft Office-based environment in which several services are available to authors. These services utilise knowledge managed by two knowledge-bases: the AKT Triplestore[2], which in this scenario provides a suitable Research ontology for our purposes, and a WiCK Triplestore which hosts the Project, Proposal, and Subject ontologies.

Knowledge. Fill-In and *Knowledge Recall* services are motivated by the need to provide timely and convenient access to knowledge, which would otherwise have to be manually "looked up" on the institutional intranet. The Knowledge Fill-In service assists the author in filling in the Je-SRP1 form. For example, the author is able to specify the (partial) name of the Principal Investigator and instruct the service to retrieve appropriate instances from the knowledge-base and fill in all the related fields on the form.

The author interacts with the Knowledge Recall service through the Microsoft Smart Tag interface. Recognised terms from the knowledge-base are highlighted in the document as the author types; by clicking on a recognised term, the author can access associated 'actions'. Our custom WiCKOffice Smart Tag makes different actions available according the author's current position in the Case for Support document. For example, if the author types "Wendy Hall" in the *Previous Research* section, options to insert a "potted" summary or browse Wendy Hall's previous research history are shown; typing "Wendy Hall" in the *References* section enables Wendy Hall's most recent/relevant publications to be automatically identified and inserted without having to resort to a manual search.

A third service, the *In-Line Guidelines* service, assists the writing process itself by providing direct access to the EPSRC guidance notes via the Microsoft Office Assistant interface. Two further services are currently under development: an *Augmented Experience* service provides the author with access to the "institutional memory" of previous research proposals, thereby augmenting their experience of writing proposals; an *Assisted Writing* service attempts to assist the author in making higher-level decisions about relevant content to include in the proposal by suggesting appropriate instances from the Subject ontology (for example, relevant projects, papers, resources).

Conclusion. In the context of a business writing scenario, WiCKOffice demonstrates that with a suitable set of ontologies and a supportive knowledge-aware environment, an author can be assisted in producing knowledge-rich documents.

---

[2] `http://triplestore.aktors.org/`

The knowledge-augmented document can then be intelligently processed in further ways, for example by the proposed Assisted Writing service. The completed documents are then used to update the knowledge-bases, asserting the new facts that the author has created.

Acknowledgements. EPSRC Knowledge Writing in Context GR/R91021/01// (a.k.a WiCK); EPSRC Advanced Knowledge Technologies IRC GR/N15764/01.

Computing Similarity Between XML Documents for XML Mining

Jung-Won Lee and Seung-Soo Park

Dept. of Computer Science and Engineering, Ewha Womans University,
11-1 Daehyun-dong, Sudaemun-ku, Seoul, Korea
{jungwony,sspark}@ewha.ac.kr

Abstract. The self-describing feature of XML offers both challenges and opportunities in document management and data mining. We propose new metric for computing similarity between XML documents for XML mining.

1 Introduction

We expect that many Web applications that process XML documents, such as grouping similar XML documents and searching for XML documents that match a sample XML document, will require techniques for clustering and classifying XML documents. It is intuitively obvious that if some of the rich semantics of XML can be taken into account, we should have a more powerful basis for XML mining. In this paper, we propose new metric for computing similarity between XML documents for XML mining and presents preliminary experimental results.

2 Pre-processing

It is essential to preprocess XML documents for quantitative determination of similarity between XML documents. The following is for preprocessing XML documents[1].

- *Structure Discovery*: The goal for discovering XML structures is to extract unique and minimized structures of XML documents. We formalize XML structures using finite automata and then apply a state-minimization algorithm to minimize them.
- *Identification of Similar Elements*: A lot of synonyms, compound words, or abbreviations may be used for defining XML elements in multiple documents. We generate extended-element vectors with synonym information for the elements in an XML document using WordNet.
- *Common Feature Extraction*: Among paths from minimized XML structures and elements with synonyms, we extract common paths between XML documents using sequential pattern mining algorithms.

---

[1] For further details of preprocessing for XML, see [1].

E. Motta et al. (Eds.): EKAW 2004, LNAI 3257, pp. 492–493, 2004.

3 Similarity Metric

To quantify similarity between XML structures, we define new similarity metric based on common paths. The key concept of the metric is to assign different weights to each element on the path. The more similar paths they share, the more weights it may be assigned.

$$\text{Similarity} = \frac{1}{T} \sum_{i=1}^{T} \frac{1}{2 \times L(PE_i) - 1} \sum_{k=1}^{L(PE_k)} V(E_k)$$

Here, T is a number of total paths of a base document, PE is a path expression, L(PE) is the total number of elements on PE, and E_k is k^{th} element of PE. $V(E_k)$ may have one value among 0, 1, or 2 according to the degree of match between elements of two documents.

4 Experimental Results

We collected 763 HTML pages from yahoo! site. There are 2 categories: charts, and messages. We randomly selected 100 HTML pages from the collection and translated them to XML documents with meaningful elements. We got preliminary results of similarity computation among all documents as the following.

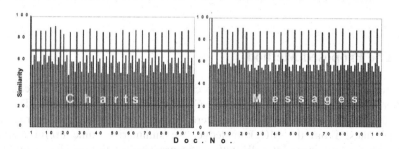

Fig. 1. Only documents that have similarity over threshold 70% are over the line. We confirmed that these documents were grouped into their categories correctly

5 Discussion

Although the dataset for experiment is small, our similarity metric provides high accuracy for XML document mining. We'll do more experiments with various and large datasets and then revise our metric for computing similarity.

References

1. J. W. Lee, K. Lee, and W. Kim.: Preparations for Semantics-based XML Mining. In Proc. of IEEE International Conference on Data Mining (ICDM). pages 345~352. Nov./Dec. 2001.

A CBR Driven Genetic Algorithm for
Microcalcification Cluster Detection

Bin Yao[1], Jianmin Jiang[1], and Yonghong Peng[2]

[1]EIMC Dept., [2]Computing Dept.,
University of Bradford, Bradford, UK
Postcode: BD7 1DP
{B.Yao,J.Jiang1,Y.H.Peng}@Bradford.ac.uk

Abstract. In this paper, we propose a CBR driven genetic algorithm to detect microcalcification clusters in digital mammograms towards computer-aided breast cancer screening. While being embedded inside the genetic algorithm, the CBR is performed as an "evaluator" and a "guide" in the proposed GA system. To form a base of cases, we adopted a competitive learning neural network to organize the MC feature vectors to construct the cases. Experiments are carried out under the DDSM database and the performances of the proposed algorithm are evaluated by the FROC curve, which show that the CBR driven genetic algorithm can achieve 98% accuracy at a low cost of false detection rate. Even in dense mammograms, the system can still detect the MCs correctly.

1 The Proposed Method

The aim of this proposed method is to correctly detect the microcalcification(MC) clusters in the mammogram through a CBR driven genetic algorithm. The idea is generated by the observation of the differences between the MC-present regions and normal ones. From the MC knowledge, we summarize some useful features to construct a modal of the MCs. With these features, we use the search capability of the GA to "find" the MCs in the images by properly constructing the chromosome. In order to use the existing knowledge to guide the GA to detect the MC cluster, CBR is employed and a case base including many feature vectors of different kinds of MCs is also created. The case-based reasoning simulates the procedure that people solves problems by exploitation of old information [1]. As a result, a flowchart of the proposed method can be summarised in Figure 1.

2 Experimental Results and Concluding Remarks

We obtain all our experimental data set from the Digital Database of Screening Mammography (DDSM) [2]. In line with medical imaging specifications, all the mammograms selected are of a pixel depth of 12 bits. To test the proposed algorithm, 288 images are cut from 188 mammograms in the cancer category, among which 188 of them are MC-presented images and the other 100 pieces are normal ones.

E. Motta et al. (Eds.): EKAW 2004, LNAI 3257, pp. 494–496, 2004.
© Springer-Verlag Berlin Heidelberg 2004

FROC curve is shown in Figure 2 which shows that the proposed GA algorithm achieves 98% accuracy at a cost of 0.25 false positive.

Finally, the authors wish to acknowledge the funding support from the Yorkshire Cancer Research.

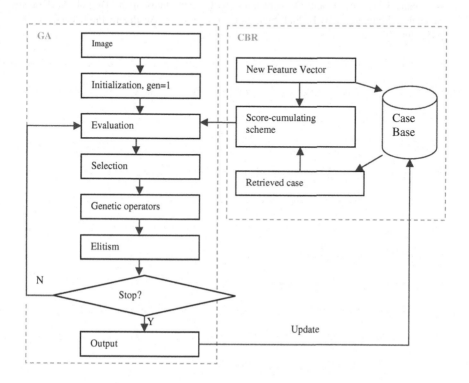

Fig. 1. Overview of the CBR driven genetic algorithm

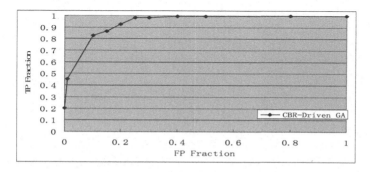

Fig. 2. FROC cure of the CBR-driven GA

References

1. CK Riesbeck and R. Schank : Inside Case-based Reasoning. Erlbaum, Northvale, NJ. (1989)
2. M. Heath, KW Bowyer and D. Kopans et al : Current status of the Digital Database for Screening Mammography.Digital Mammography, Kluwer Academic Publishers. (1998) p457-460

Ontology Enrichment Evaluation

Andreas Faatz and Ralf Steinmetz

Darmstadt University of Technology, Darmstadt, Germany
{Andreas.Faatz, Ralf.Steinmetz}@kom.tu-darmstadt.de

Abstract. Ontology enrichment algorithms propose new concepts to given concepts in a domain specific ontology. The paper is dedicated to the quality of ontology enrichment algorithms in terms of recall.

1 Definitions

An ontology is a set of concepts ordered by a subconcept relation. Moreover there exists a set of relation names together with a restriction for each one of them: the restriction expresses, which subconcepts of which superconcept are allowed at the i-th place of a relational tupel. We refer to Stumme and Maedche [SM01] for such an ontology definition.

Definition 1 (Ontology). *A (core-) ontology is a 4-tupel $\Omega := (B, \leq, R, \sigma)$, where B and R are finite sets, $\leq$ a transitive, reflexive and asymmetric Relation on $B \times B$ ($\leq \subseteq B \times B$), $\sigma : R \mapsto B^+$ a mapping, which maps each $r \in R$ to a pair $(B_1(r), B_2(r))$ with $B_1 \subseteq B$ and $B_2 \subseteq B$. We call the $b \in B$ concepts, $\leq$ the subconcept relation and the $r \in R$ semantic relation names. Furthermore there exists an abstract root concept $\top$ for all concepts in B: $\exists(\top \in B)\forall(b \in B) : b \leq \top$.*

In addition we define:

Definition 2 (Ontology Enrichment). *Let ξ be a text corpus, that means, a collection of written or spoken text documents, which are processable for natural language analysis. Let $B(\xi)$ a set of words and phrases from ξ. An ontology enrichment algorithm, is an algorithm which takes a given ξ and a given ontology Ω as input and produces for each $b \in B$ a set $P(b) \subseteq B(\xi)$ as output. We call $P(b)$ the set of propositions for b.*

Ontology enrichment methods can be found in [AL01] and [FS02].

2 Aspects Related to Recall

For a given $\Omega := \{B, \leq, R, \sigma\}$ we apply the general recall idea [BR99]. We remove existing concepts from a given ontology by chance. We collect the removed concepts in a set C which becomes the candidate set. C is independent from additional descriptors from the corpus. The idea of random choice of C can only be persuaded, if

$$\Omega' := \{B \setminus C, \leq, R', \sigma'\}, \tag{1}$$

E. Motta et al. (Eds.): EKAW 2004, LNAI 3257, pp. 497–498, 2004.
© Springer-Verlag Berlin Heidelberg 2004

where R' and σ' are restrictions of the relations and arities to remaining concepts in $B \setminus C$ is again an ontology. This holds because by transitivity of $\leq$ we may keep for instance a relation $k \leq m$, if $k \leq l \leq m$ was part of the original ontology. The restriction relation of the relation $\leq$ still remains transitive. Consequently we only have to claim $\top \notin C$.

Furthermore denote for $b_1, b_2 \in B$ by $d_\Omega(b_1, b_2)$ the shortest relational path along $\leq$ and its inversion $\geq$. Then we define our measure called 1-edge-recall for a given $c \in B$ as the ratio

$$\frac{|P(c) \cap \{b|d_\Omega(b, c) = 1\}|}{|\{b|d_\Omega(b, c) = 1\}|} \tag{2}$$

and more general n-edge-recall for a given $c \in B$ as the ratio

$$\frac{|P(c) \cap \{b|d_\Omega(b, c) \leq n\}|}{|\{b|d_\Omega(b, c) \leq n\}|} \tag{3}$$

Note that the n-edge-recall for $n > 1$ is not necessarily greater or equal than the n-edge-recall, as the denominator $\{b|d_\Omega(b, c) = n\}$ may grow faster than the corresponding enumerator.

By a variation on $|C|$ we can observe, if the enrichment algorithm is able to propose new concepts for more (greater $|C|$) or less (smaller $|C|$) complete ontologies.

In turn, the n-edge-recall motivates an enrichment quality measure, which computes the ratio of proposition failures with the aim of measuring recall. If

$$\frac{|P(c) \cap \{b|d_\Omega(b, c) > n\}|}{|\{b|d_\Omega(b, c) > n\}|} \tag{4}$$

is high, we obtain many propositions, which are actually out of scope and our precision decreases.

3   Conclusion

The recall measures shown in this paper exploit the given ontology structures, are independent from additional assumptions on candidates and can be extended to a proposition failure measure.

References

[AL01]   Eneko Aguirre, Mikel Lersundi: Extracción de relaciones léxico-semánticas a partir de palabras derivadas usando patrones de definición. Procesamiento del Language Natural 27, 2001

[BR99]   R. Baeza-Yates and B. Ribeiro-Neto: Modern Information Retrieval, Addison Wesley, 1999.

[FS02]   Andreas Faatz, Ralf Steinmetz: Ontology Enrichment with Texts from the WWW, Proceedings of the First International Workshop on Semantic Web Mining, European Conference on Machine Learning 2002, Helsinki 2002

[SM01]   Gerd Stumme, Alexander Mädche: FCA-MERGE: Bottom-Up Merging of Ontologies, Proceedings of the Seventeenth International Joint Conference on Artificial Intelligence, IJCAI 2001, Seattle, Washington, USA, August 4-10, 2001

KAFTIE: A New KA Framework for Building Sophisticated Information Extraction Systems

Son Bao Pham and Achim Hoffmann

School of Computer Science and Engineering,
University of New South Wales, Sydney 2052, Australia
{sonp,achim}@cse.unsw.edu.au

Keywords: Incremental Knowledge Acquisition, Natural language processing.

1 Introduction

The aim of our work is to develop a flexible and powerful Knowledge Acquisition framework that allows users to rapidly develop Natural Language Processing systems, including information extraction systems. Tasks on which we experimented with our framework are to identify concepts/terms of which positive or negative aspects are mentioned in scientific papers. The results so far are very promising as we managed to build systems with relative ease that achieve F-measures of around 84% on a corpus of scientific papers in the area of artificial intelligence.

In this short paper, we briefly sketch KAFTIE (Knowledge Acquisition Framework for Text classification and Information Extraction), an incremental knowledge acquisition framework that strongly supports the rapid prototyping of new NLP systems, that require classification of text segments and/or information extraction tasks. Our framework is inspired by the idea behind Ripple Down Rules [1] and allows for the incremental construction of large knowledge bases by providing one rule at a time. An expert just needs to monitor the system's performance on text and intervenes whenever the system does not perform as desired. The intervention will be based on a concrete text segment which the expert uses to specify rule conditions which are met by that text segment in order to formulate an exception rule to the rule that produced the undesirable system performances. Alternatively, the experts could modify an existing rule to cover the new case at hand provided the KB is still consistent.

2 KAFTIE

Rules in KAFTIE are stored in an exception structure as a Single Classification Ripple Down Rules tree. A rule is composed of a condition part and a conclusion part. A condition has an annotation pattern with annotation constraints. An annotation is an abstraction over string tokens. Conceptually, string tokens covered by annotations of the same type are considered to represent the same concept. An annotation also contains a list of feature value pairs.

E. Motta et al. (Eds.): EKAW 2004, LNAI 3257, pp. 499–501, 2004.
© Springer-Verlag Berlin Heidelberg 2004

The pattern is a regular expression over annotations. It can also post new annotations over matched phrases of the pattern's sub-components . The following is an example of a pattern which posts an annotation over the matched phrase:

({NP}{VG.voice == active}{NP}):MATCH

This pattern would match phrases starting with a NP annotation followed by a VG annotation (with feature *voice* having value *active*) followed by another NP annotation. When applying this pattern on a piece of text, MATCH annotations would be posted over phrases that match this pattern.

The rule's conclusion contains a classification and an annotation to be extracted. Since a rule's pattern can post annotations over components of the matched phrase, extracting those components is just a matter of selecting appropriate annotations.

Patterns are constructed using built-in annotations and custom annotations. Built-in annotations include annotations generated from our Shallow Parser module e.g. NP, VG.

3   Experimental Results

We have applied our framework KAFTIE to tackle two different tasks of recognizing sentences that contain positive and negative attributions of a concept/term as well as extracting the concept/term. These tasks are challenging as the analysis of positive and negative sentiments towards a concept requires deep understanding of the textual context, drawing on common sense, domain knowledge and linguistic knowledge. A concept could be mentioned with a positive or negative sentiment in a local context but not in a wider context. For example,

We do not think that X is very efficient.

If we just look at the phrase *X is very efficient*, we could say that X is of positive sentiment, but considering a wider context it is not.

A corpus was collected consisting of 140 machine learning papers and journals downloaded from citeseer, and converted from PDF into text. We randomly selected 16 documents of different authors and grouped them into 2 corpora. The first corpus has 3672 sentences from 9 documents and the second corpus contains 4713 sentences from 7documents.

For each of the two tasks of extracting positive and negative attributions of concepts/terms, we built a KB based on the first corpus and tested it on the second corpus. A sentence is deemed correctly suggested by the KB if the KB classifies the sentence to the right class and the concept/term of interest is also at least partly extracted.

The KBs for the tasks of extracting positive and negative attributions consist of 61 and 65 rules respectively. When tested on the second corpus, their precision are 74% and 86.4% respectively while their recall are 88% and 82% respectively.

4   Conclusion

Our experiments so far were very encouraging and showed that KAFTIE can be a very valuable support tool for the rapid development of advanced information extraction systems operating on complex texts as present in scientific papers.

The performance of the resulting information extraction systems, taking approximately 2 minutes of expert time per rule, has shown that the knowledge bases built using the framework achieved precisions of at least 74% and recalls up to 88% on an unseen corpus. It should be noted that all documents in the corpus are from different authors covering different topics. This suggests that it would be feasible to quickly build new knowledge bases for different tasks in new domains.

Reference

1. P. Compton and R. Jansen. A philosophical basis for knowledge acquisition. *Knowledge Acquisition*, 2:241–257, 1990.

From Text to Ontology: The Modelling of Economics Events

Alberto Méndez-Torreblanca[1,2] and Aurelio López-López[1]

[1] INAOE, Luis Enrique Erro No 1, Tonantzintla, Puebla, 72840 México
amendez@axtel.net and allopez@inaoep.mx
[2] Instituto Tecnológico de Puebla, Av. Tecnológico No 420,
Puebla,Puebla, 72220 México
amendez@itpuebla.edu.mx

Abstract. The construction of ontologies representing complex concepts, such as events, processes, and tasks, is a hard and complicated task. In this paper, we propose a method for modelling event ontologies from texts which was obtained from the lessons learned in the construction of an event ontology in the economics and financial domain.

1 Introduction

An ontology is an explicit specification of a conceptualization, where a conceptualization is an abstract, simplified view of the world that someone wants to represent for some purpose. Events are a part of the world that have to be represented. Similar challenging complex concepts are processes or tasks. The construction of ontologies representing such complex concepts is a hard and complicated task. In particular, modelling events is not an easy task. First, events represent something that happens at a given place and time, and they can not be represented as simple disconnected concepts. Second, the methodologies do not provide guidelines to identify or to model event concepts from texts; and third there are not currently many ontologies describing events that could help to identify or model new events. There are some previous works that only describe the necessary elements in an ontology of events and establish the basis for its construction; but none of them provide elements to identify event concepts from text [1] [2] [3]. Therefore, this paper proposes a method for modelling events from texts into an ontology.

2 Method Proposed

The experience learned in the construction of an ontology of events in the economic and financial led us to formulate a practical method that help to build, in a simple way, ontologies of events. The method consists of the following steps:

1. *Gather documents that report some event of interest.* There are different sources that can provide documents containing events, e.g. on-line news sites, available repositories in the web, or directly from organizations that generate them.

E. Motta et al. (Eds.): EKAW 2004, LNAI 3257, pp. 502–503, 2004.
© Springer-Verlag Berlin Heidelberg 2004

2. *Extract text fragments that describe some event from the documents gathered.* If there are several events in question, it is necessary to group the text fragments for the type of event that they describe.
3. *Identify events in the text fragments.* Key verbs are the trigger words used for the identification of events in the text fragments.
4. *Build a hierarchy of events.* A bottom-up approach is used in the construction of the hierarchy of events. It begins with the definition of the most specific events, i.e. the leaves or lowest level of the hierarchy, with a subsequent grouping of these events into more general events.
5. *Identify individual in events.* For each event identified, one has to identify the *individual* concepts or entities that participate in the event.
6. *Identify the roles played by each of the individual concepts.* The roles are non-taxonomical relations between the events and individuals.

The ontology of economic and financial events developed has three main elements: the events of interest, the participant entities or individuals. This ontology consists so far of 17 events, 32 individuals, 10 relations and 14 axioms. This ontology is currently employed by software agents for selection and classification of on-line news, in the direction of the semantic web [4].

3   Conclusions and Future Work

This method helps to enrich the current methodologies for building event ontologies, providing guidelines during the construction process. We are in the process of implementing the method to work in a semi-automatic way, using techniques from natural language processing.

Acknowledgements

This work was partially supported by Conacyt, Mexico through the scholarship granted to the first author and by research grant U39957-Y.

References

[1] Everett, J. O., *et al*: Making Ontologies Work for Resolving Redundancies Across Documents, In: Communications of the ACM, vol. 45, no. 2, pp. 55-60, (2002).
[2] OpenCyc.: OpenCyc.org, [Online],Available from: http://www.opencyc.org/ (2003), [15 April 2003].
[3] Domingue, J. and Motta, E.: A Knowledge-Based News Server Supporting Ontology-Driven Story Enrichment and Knowledge Retrieval. In: Proceedings of the 11th European Workshop on Knowledge Acquistion, Modelling, and Management (EKAW '99), Dagstahl Castle, Germany, 26-29 May, Springer-Verlag, (1999).
[4] Méndez-Torreblanca, A. and López-López, A.: An Ontology based Agent for Web Resource Pre-processing and Discovery. In: The Conference on Current Trends in Theory and Practice of Computer Science, Merin, Czech Republic, (2004).

Discovering Conceptual Web-Knowledge in Web Documents

Seung Yeol Yoo and Achim Hoffmann

School of Computer Science and Engineering,
University of New South Wales, Sydney
2052, NSW, Australia
{syy, achim}@cse.unsw.edu.au

1 Introduction

The Web provides virtually unlimited, but poorly organized information resources which cause the problem of information overload. It usually results from a query that does not indicate the intended senses of the query-words.

Our system, ContextExplicator, discovers the intended senses of query-words, articulated by the contexts (in the given documents) of the query-words. It incrementallyorganizes and visualizes the intended senses in a conceptual-lattice.

2 Related Work

The usage of context-terms, i.e. terms characterizing a word-sense, has shown good performance to disambiguate their word-senses in texts [2]. However, in [2], the occurrence-frequency of a term is counted without distinguishing the different senses of the term. The pre-defined senses of a query-term have been used for information retrieval or indexing, see e.g., [1]. However the senses of a term cannot be completely predefined, because new senses of terms are regularly created, as new objects and entire domains need to be described. Thus, discovering context-terms and their senses, and their relationships with each other in a document can support the construction of a conceptual lattice which classifies documents. Hereby, the user selects context-terms in the conceptual lattice to indicate the desired word-sense.

3 Context Explicator

The Conceptual Lattice works as a visual user-interface to incrementally display conceptual web-knowledge (relationships among concepts used across various web-documents). ContextExplicator constructs e.g. a conceptual lattice over the pre-classified 16 html-documents by Yahoo! for the term "java"(Figure 1). ContextExplicator used only the html-based free-texts to construct this conceptual lattice.

The relevance of a context-term to a sense is measured by two principles: 1) Maximizing the topical commonality among the intentions of the author who wrote

E. Motta et al. (Eds.): EKAW 2004, LNAI 3257, pp. 504–505, 2004.

the documents. 2) Minimizing the ambiguity of the author-intended word-sense and the query-intention of the user. These principles allow ContextExplicator to subclassifythe given documents.

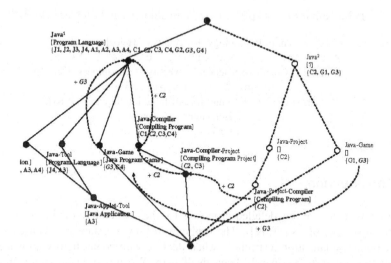

Fig. 1. Conceptual Lattice: Discovering context-terms of the query-word "java" over the given sample documents

Context-terms of query-words are called 1st-level context-terms. Context-terms of 1st-level context-terms are called 2nd-level context-terms. The resulting conceptual lattice does not depend on the order of selected context-term. This is achieved by including 2nd-level context-terms in the list of 1st-level context-terms, if the analysis of available documents supports that. I.e, if a 2nd-level context-term appears only in documents about a single word-sense of a query-term.

The novelty of our approach lies in extracting important context-terms and exploiting the newly discovered senses of those terms, in the process of automatic document categorization. By applying an iterative approach for discovering the context-terms of query-words, the user can refine their search criteria to view the refined categories of the available documents until the desired documents have been identified.

References

1. M. P. O. Christopher Stokoe and J. Tait. Word sense disambiguation in information retrieval revisited. In Proceedings of the 26th annual international ACM SIGIR conference on Research and development in information retrieval, pages 159 – 166. ACM, 2003.
2. D. B. Neill. Fully automatic word sense induction by semantic clustering. M.phil. in computer speech, Cambridge University, 2002.

Knowledge Mediation: A Procedure for the Cooperative Construction of Domain Ontologies

Felix-Robinson Aschoff[1], Franz Schmalhofer[2], and Ludger van Elst[3]

[1] Department of Psychology, University of Heidelberg, Germany
Felix-Robinson.Aschoff@urz.uni-heidelberg.de
[2] Institute of Cognitive Science, University of Osnabrueck, Germany
Franz.Schmalhofer@uos.de
[3] German Research Center for Artificial Intelligence (DFKI),
Kaiserslautern, Germany
elst@dfki.uni-kl.de

1 Introduction

Up to now, there are few detailed proposals for the cooperative (and distributed) construction of ontologies (cf. [2]). The problem of how to establish a consensus and a shared conceptualization, especially when dealing with contradictory knowledge and conflicting interests has hardly been dealt with. We propose and evaluate a three-phased knowledge mediation procedure which is especially conceived to integrate different perspectives and information needs into one consensual ontology.

2 The Knowledge Mediation Procedure

1) *Generation Phase:* Participants generate terms in a brainstorming session, using a middle-out approach as well as automatic thesaurus generation tools.
2) *Explication Phase:* Each participant *independently* explicates a taxonomy based on the collected terms and indicates the relevance of different parts of this proposal. Ontology mining techniques from texts (e.g. [4]) complement this phase.
3) *Integration Phase:* We adapted techniques from conflict mediation [3] to the requirements of ontology construction. While the knowledge mediator considers principles of ontology design, she usually does not interfere with the content of the ontology. She acts as a neutral person who can balance between the different perspectives and interests of ontology users. The mediator can use the following techniques:

Perspective Taking (Participants present the proposal of another participant to the group). *Balancing* (Everybody gets an equal chance to express ideas). *Summarizing* (Summarize reached agreements to structure the communication process). *Useful Questions* (Urge participants to explicate their viewpoints and the advantages or disadvantages of their proposals).

Neutral Knowledge Sources: Refer to the results from the ontology from text mining techniques and existing ontologies to settle disagreements.

E. Motta et al. (Eds.): EKAW 2004, LNAI 3257, pp. 506–508, 2004.

Analysis of Disagreement: Table 1 may help to understand reasons for disagreements.

Table 1. Possible disagreements during an ontology construction session (adapted from [5])

		term	
		same	different
refers to concept	same	**consensus** participants use terms and concepts in the same way	**correspondence** participants use different terms for the same concepts
	diff.	**conflict** participants use same terms for different concepts	**contrast** participants differ in terms and concepts

Participants agree on the resulting structure or conclude that no agreement is possible. A comprehensive documentation should be drawn up.

3 Experimental Evaluation

Method. 28 Cognitive Science students (University of Osnabrueck) who were matched into pairs were requested to agree about a common study programme after they had received contradictory programmes. In one condition students conducted the knowledge mediation procedure with a mediator, whereas in the other condition the pairs had an unassisted discussion. Recorded measures: speaking times, a qualitative category system, an analysis of resulting programmes, a questionnaire, a sorting task.

Results. The knowledge mediation procedure resulted in a more balanced negotiation (speaking times) and a more elaborated level of communication (qualitative categories). Stronger differences could presumably be found in real conflict situations, like company fusions. The evaluation showed the feasibility of the approach for distributed construction groups communicating via videoconference.

4 Conclusion

We proposed an ontology construction procedure for the integration of different *user* perspectives and contradictory information needs and showed benefits in an experimental evaluation. For more details see [1]. We conclude that an ontology construction process is not only an engineering task but more importantly also a social process where the relevant parties need to be involved before successful and durable solutions can be found.

References

1. Aschoff, F.-R.: Knowledge Mediation: A procedure for the cooperative construction of domain ontologies. Diploma Thesis, University of Heidelberg (2004)

2. Fernández-López, M. (Ed.): OntoWeb Deliverable 1.4. A survey on methodologies for developing, maintaining, evaluating and reengineering ontologies. Version 1.0. (2002) Available: http://onto web.aifb.uni-karlsruhe.de/About/Deliverables/ D1.4-v1.0.pdf
3. Haynes, J. M., Bastine, R., Link, G., Mecke, A.: Scheidung ohne Verlierer. Kösel, München (2002)
4. Maedche, A., Staab, S.: Mining ontologies from text. In: Proc. of International Conference on Knowledge Engineering and Knowledge Management (EKAW'2000). Juan-Les-Pins, France (2000)
5. Shaw, M. L. G., Gaines, B. R.: A methodology for recognizing conflict, correspondence, consensus and contrast in a knowledge acquisition system. Knowledge Acquisition 1:4 (1989) 341-363

A Framework to Improve Semantic Web Services Discovery and Integration in an E-Gov Knowledge Network

Denilson Sell[1], Liliana Cabral[2], Alexandre Gonçalves[1]
Enrico Motta[2], and Roberto Pacheco[1]

[1] Grupo Stela, UFSC, Lauro Linhares 2123, Bloco B, 2. andar Florianópolis,
88036-002, Brazil
{denilson, alexl, pacheco}@stela.ufsc.br
http://www.stela.ufsc.br
[2] Knowledge Media Institute, The Open University,
Walton Hall, Milton Keynes, MK7 6AA, UK
{l.s.cabral, e.motta}@open.ac.uk
http://www.kmi.open.ac.uk

Abstract. One of the major challenges in Semantic Web Service (SWS) technology is the improvement of the services matching process. This challenge is a critical issue to promote systems interoperability in the context of Scienti Network (SN), an international knowledge network in Science & Technology (S&T) [1]. We have been working on a framework to tackle this problem in the context of IRS-II SWS infrastructure. This framework (SeGOV), comprehends a set of ontologies to describe services in functional layers in order to allow their matching and improve their capabilities.

A considerable advance in services interoperability was obtained with the SWS advent. However, in the context of SN, SWS matching is still a challenge. In addition to the number of services (several hundreds), many of these services have similar descriptions despite accomplishing different tasks.

We have been working on a framework (SeGOV) to extend the IRS-II Task and PSM descriptions [2] contextualizing SWS capabilities according to main functionalities found in SN in order to improve the matching process. In SeGOV, SWS are described in three *Service Layers*: *Transactional* (describes operational services that perform support transactions such as data maintenance, login validation, etc), *Presentation* (describes the presentation instruments, such as portal functionalities, and how the data should be transformed to be displayed to users) and *Knowledge* (knowledge discovery applications). Each layer is described by an ontology written in OCML [2] comprehending the main operations found in SN and the relationships between SWS.

In addition, SeGOV comprehends three *Context Layers*, the *Domain Concepts* (description of concepts related to the S&T domain), the *Data Sources* (describes how the data is organized and stored to support maintenance and retrieval operations) and the *Information Units* (syntactic representation of the information units to support the exchange of messages and SWS grounding).

E. Motta et al. (Eds.): EKAW 2004, LNAI 3257, pp. 509–510, 2004.

510   D. Sell et al.

In the Fig. 1, we present a simplified description of the task *Find_Braz_CV_Task* and its relationships with several concepts distributed in the SeGOV layers. The relations between the concepts and this task support its matching according to its capabilities in a semi-automatic way similar to [3]. The relations with the *Context Layers* aim to support the matching according to the data manipulated by this task.

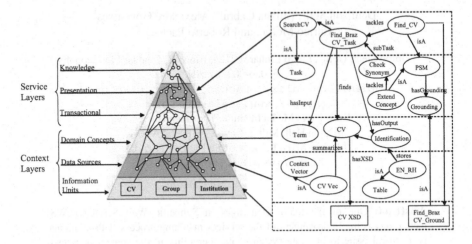

Fig. 1. Brief illustration of SWS description in SeGOV layers

We have been extending the user-guided composition process described in [3], by enabling the user to inform search arguments and presenting the list of related services, contextualizing the relationships between the data sources in which the arguments were found and the services related to each data source. Both *Service* and *Context Layers* have been designed to support the improvement of the services' capabilities as well. In addition, we are researching how to capture information about the context of user's interactions with SN in order to suggest services related to these interactions. Details about SeGOV ontologies and the improvement of SWS capabilities and matching process will be given in further papers.

Acknowledgements

This research is funded by CNPq, Brazil, and supported by KMi (Open University).

References

1. Pacheco, R. C. S.: Rede SCienti. In: VI Congreso Regional de Información in Ciencias de la Salud. Puebla. (2003)
2. Motta E., Domingue J., Cabral L., Gaspari M.: IRS-II: A Framework and Infrastructure for Semantic Web Services. In: Proceedings of 2nd. International Semantic Web Conference (ISWC2003), Florida, USA. (2003).
3. Sirin E., Hendler J., Parsia B.: Semi-automatic composition of web services using semantic descriptions. In: Web Services Workshop in Conjunction with ICEIS. (2003).

Knowledge Organisation and Information Retrieval with Galois Lattices

Laszlo Szathmary and Amedeo Napoli

LORIA UMR 7503, B.P. 239, 54506 Vandœuvre-lès-Nancy Cedex, France
{szathmar, napoli}@loria.fr

Abstract. We examine the application of Galois (or concept) lattices on different data sources in order to organise knowledge. This knowledge organisation can serve a number of purposes, e.g. knowledge management in an organisation, document retrieval on the Web, etc.

1 Introduction

In this paper[1] we investigate the application of Galois lattices on different data sources, e.g. web documents or bibliographical items, in order to organise knowledge that can be extracted from the data. We have made experiments within our research team for analysing the global work of the team, for finding interconnections between members, and for knowing the main/marginal works in the team, i.e. to carry out a diagnosis on the research work. This can be viewed as a classification task for organising data within a hierarchy of concepts, being part of a KM process whose objective is the analysis of the work within a research team.

In a research team, publications are one of the best ways to describe the interests of a person, and this is why we have chosen the team's bibliography. We have worked with BibTeX descriptions that provide metadata about a paper, e.g. title, authors, keywords, etc. To analyse the publications, we have used lattice-based classification, more precisely Galois lattice design guided by domain ontologies, as a data mining technique.

2 Ontologies in the KDD[2] Process

To explain and access knowledge about our team we needed some ontologies. Using ontologies within the KDD process we can ensure:

- Data cleaning. It allows mapping data to a single naming convention, and handling noise and errors in the data.
- Knowledge organisation (with Galois lattices). Formal concept analysis can be used as a classification method for data mining [1].

---

[1] This publication was made in the frame of the French-Hungarian research program Balaton (Balaton F-23/03).
[2] Knowledge Discovery in Databases.

E. Motta et al. (Eds.): EKAW 2004, LNAI 3257, pp. 511–512, 2004.

- Information retrieval. Query answering can be carried out on bibliographical items, for instance ranking them by their relevance with respect to a set of keywords [2].

3   Document Organisation Based on Galois Lattices

We have studied the relations between individuals (team members, X), publications (documents, Y) and keywords (Z) to find answers to the following questions:

1. Which persons have published together? Which are the concerned documents? For answering this question, the relation R_1 between individuals and publications has to be studied: $R_1(x \times y)$, where $x \in X$ (*individuals*) and $y \in Y$ (*documents*).
2. Which persons work on a common topic? What is this topic? For answering this question, the relation R_2 between individuals and keywords has to be studied: $R_2(x \times z)$, where $x \in X$ (*individuals*) and $z \in Z$ (*keywords*).
3. Which documents are written about a common topic? What is this topic? For answering this question, the relation R_3 between publications and keywords has to be studied: $R_3(y \times z)$, where $y \in Y$ (*documents*) and $z \in Z$ (*keywords*).

People, documents and keywords can also be considered as axes in a multidimensional system. In this system different lattices can be constructed on the planes defined by the axes, depending on the relation to be analysed.

4   Related Work

For our work we consider mainly two projects as reference works. First, SEAL (SEmantic PortAL) is a framework to build community web sites [3]. Second, the works of [2] on information retrieval using Galois lattices is similar to our classification task for organising, querying and visualising data in a concept hierarchy.

We have chosen these projects because one of our goals is to create a semantic portal for the team with integrated knowledge-discovery and ontological capabilities.

References

1. Ganter, B., Wille, R.: Formal concept analysis: mathematical foundations. Springer, Berlin/Heidelberg (1999)
2. Carpineto, C., Romano, G.: Order-Theoretical Ranking. Journal of the American Society for Information Science **51** (2000) 587–601
3. Maedche, A., Staab, S., Stojanovic, N., Studer, R., Sure, Y.: SEmantic PortAL - The SEAL Approach. In Fensel, D., Hendler, J., Lieberman, H., Wahlster, W., eds.: Spinning the Semantic Web. MIT Press, Cambridge, MA (2002)

Acquisition of Causal and Temporal Knowledge in Medical Domains. A Web-Based Approach*

J. Palma, M. Campos, J.M. Juarez, and A. Morales

Artificial Intelligence and Knowledge Engineering,
Faculty of Informatics, University of Murcia. Murcia 30100, Spain
jpalma@dif.um.es

Abstract. The highly specialized nature of medical domains has increased the demand of consultation of medical specialists to solve certain therapeutic and diagnostic problems. This problem requires the development of complex Knowledge Acquisition tools to build this Knowledge Base (KB). In this work, we present a KB System for medical domains which has shown the benefits of approaching the KB design from a wider perspective, allowing users to provide, query and browse knowledge.

1 The System Architecture: ACUDES

The complexity inherent to this knowledge models has increased the problems associated to the well-known knowledge acquisition (KA) bottleneck. We have designed ACUDES, a generic architecture for decision support systems for ICUs. ACUDES has been built to deal with the heterogeneous nature of the information regarding the patients' evolution. To this end we have paid special attention to KA issues through a web based KA tool. Due to the importance of temporal dimension of patients' evolution data in ICUs, patients' data are stored in a temporal data base, the Patients Temporal Data Base (PTDB). Temporal reasoning capabilities are also necessary to guarantee the temporal consistency of inserted data and to infer new temporal relations from data inserted. To this end, it is used the Fuzzy Temporal Information Management Engine (FuzzyTIME), a general purpose temporal reasoner that uses Fuzzy Temporal Constraint Networks (FTCN) [BMMP94] as underlying formalism for time representation and management. An Ontology Server, accessible through a web service interface, guarantee the semantic consistency of the information that flows through ACUDES modules.

In order to provide useful explanations about the patients' evolution, a model of the diseases in ICU is proposed, called Temporal Behavioural Model. Thus, explanations generation is carried out by: Temporal Behaviour Model (TBM), Causal and Temporal Knowledge Acquisition Tool (CATEKAT) and Diagnosis Agent. The key element in the TBM is the *Diagnostic Fuzzy Temporal Pattern* (DFTP). A DFTP captures the causal and temporal relations between a hypothesis and its effects. A pattern is composed of:

---

* This work is supported by the Spanish MCYT under the project *MEDICI: Outpatient monitoring for ischemic heart failure diagnosis and research. Tools for acquisition, visualization, integration and discovering of medical knowledge*, project number TIC2003-09400-C04-01

E. Motta et al. (Eds.): EKAW 2004, LNAI 3257, pp. 513–514, 2004.

the root hypothesis, zero or more IMPLIED HYPOTHESIS, and a non empty set of IMPLIED MANIFESTATION. Apart from the causal knowledge, the DFTP includes temporal and contextual knowledge.

2   Catekat

CATEKAT provides a set of wizards for assisting experts in the KA process. The complexity of the knowledge model underlying the definition of temporal patterns makes wizards necessary. Special attention has been paid to the specification of temporal information. But CATEKAT allows physicians not only to build the KB (descriptions of diseases), but also to browse and manage it, to conform a knowledge repository for the medical experience acquired during daily practice. Therefore, from the beginning of the design process, CATEKAT was approached with additional capabilities apart from those required for the KA tool for building KB. Among these extended capabilities, we include the possibility of cooperation among users in building, querying and browsing the KB. Moreover, in order to describe a disease, physicians can only interact with ACUDES in terms of those concepts defined in ICU domain ontology. This is a way of assuring the semantic consistency of knowledge inserted in the KB. Applying temporal reasoning techniques provided by FuzzyTIME, CATEKAT can also guarantee the temporal consistency of temporal knowledge provided by physicians.

The current web-based version of CATEKAT was conceived from the analysis of the evolution of previous versions, thus the main module in CATEKAT is the web based KA user interface. There are several requirements that characterize its design and implementation: a) a multi-user environment; b) role-aware; c) avoiding temporal inconsistencies; d) providing a cooperative platform; e) allowing the definition of projects related to different domains; and f) browsing and querying capabilities.

3   Conclusions and Future Works

This work addresses the development of a KA tool to overcome the problems associated to the KA bottleneck in the KBS development. In our application domain, causal and temporal knowledge can be captured by the TBM in which the temporal evolution of diseases can be represented. Another important advantage of CATEKAT is related with its reuse capability. As can be noted, CATEKAT can be easily reused in other domains. Currently, we are working in network computer security domain, in which network attacks can be viewed as a sequence of temporally related packet types.

Reference

[BMMP94] S. Barro, R. Marín, J. Mira, and A. R. Patón. A model and a language for the fuzzy representation and handling of time. *Fuzzy Sets and Systems*, 61:153–175, 1994.

Author Index

Lecture Notes in Artificial Intelligence (LNAI)

Vol. 3265: R.E. Frederking, K.B. Taylor (Eds.), Machine Translation: From Real Users to Research. XI, 392 pages. 2004.

Vol. 3264: G. Paliouras, Y. Sakakibara (Eds.), Grammatical Inference: Algorithms and Applications. XI, 291 pages. 2004.

Vol. 3257: E. Motta, N. Shadbolt, A. Stutt, N. Gibbins (Eds.), Engineering Knowledge in the Age of the Semantic Web. XVII, 517 pages. 2004.

Vol. 3249: B. Buchberger, J.A. Campbell (Eds.), Artificial Intelligence and Symbolic Computation. X, 285 pages. 2004.

Vol. 3245: E. Suzuki, S. Arikawa (Eds.), Discovery Science. XIV, 430 pages. 2004.

Vol. 3244: S. Ben-David, J. Case, A. Maruoka (Eds.), Algorithmic Learning Theory. XIV, 505 pages. 2004.

Vol. 3238: S. Biundo, T. Frühwirth, G. Palm (Eds.), KI 2004: Advances in Artificial Intelligence. XI, 467 pages. 2004.

Vol. 3229: J.J. Alferes, J. Leite (Eds.), Logics in Artificial Intelligence. XIV, 744 pages. 2004.

Vol. 3215: M.G.. Negoita, R.J. Howlett, L.C. Jain (Eds.), Knowledge-Based Intelligent Information and Engineering Systems. LVII, 906 pages. 2004.

Vol. 3214: M.G.. Negoita, R.J. Howlett, L.C. Jain (Eds.), Knowledge-Based Intelligent Information and Engineering Systems. LVIII, 1302 pages. 2004.

Vol. 3213: M.G.. Negoita, R.J. Howlett, L.C. Jain (Eds.), Knowledge-Based Intelligent Information and Engineering Systems. LVIII, 1280 pages. 2004.

Vol. 3209: B. Berendt, A. Hotho, D. Mladenic, M. van Someren, M. Spiliopoulou, G. Stumme (Eds.), Web Mining: From Web to Semantic Web. IX, 201 pages. 2004.

Vol. 3206: P. Sojka, I. Kopecek, K. Pala (Eds.), Text, Speech and Dialogue. XIII, 667 pages. 2004.

Vol. 3202: J.-F. Boulicaut, F. Esposito, F. Giannotti, D. Pedreschi (Eds.), Knowledge Discovery in Databases: PKDD 2004. XIX, 560 pages. 2004.

Vol. 3201: J.-F. Boulicaut, F. Esposito, F. Giannotti, D. Pedreschi (Eds.), Machine Learning: ECML 2004. XVIII, 580 pages. 2004.

Vol. 3194: R. Camacho, R. King, A. Srinivasan (Eds.), Inductive Logic Programming. XI, 361 pages. 2004.

Vol. 3192: C. Bussler, D. Fensel (Eds.), Artificial Intelligence: Methodology, Systems, and Applications. XIII, 522 pages. 2004.

Vol. 3191: M. Klusch, S. Ossowski, V. Kashyap, R. Unland (Eds.), Cooperative Information Agents VIII. XI, 303 pages. 2004.

Vol. 3187: G. Lindemann, J. Denzinger, I.J. Timm, R. Unland (Eds.), Multiagent System Technologies. XIII, 341 pages. 2004.

Vol. 3176: O. Bousquet, U. von Luxburg, G. Rätsch (Eds.), Advanced Lectures on Machine Learning. IX, 241 pages. 2004.

Vol. 3171: A.L.C. Bazzan, S. Labidi (Eds.), Advances in Artificial Intelligence – SBIA 2004. XVII, 548 pages. 2004.

Vol. 3159: U. Visser, Intelligent Information Integration for the Semantic Web. XIV, 150 pages. 2004.

Vol. 3157: C. Zhang, H. W. Guesgen, W.K. Yeap (Eds.), PRICAI 2004: Trends in Artificial Intelligence. XX, 1023 pages. 2004.

Vol. 3155: P. Funk, P.A. González Calero (Eds.), Advances in Case-Based Reasoning. XIII, 822 pages. 2004.

Vol. 3139: F. Iida, R. Pfeifer, L. Steels, Y. Kuniyoshi (Eds.), Embodied Artificial Intelligence. IX, 331 pages. 2004.

Vol. 3131: V. Torra, Y. Narukawa (Eds.), Modeling Decisions for Artificial Intelligence. XI, 327 pages. 2004.

Vol. 3127: K.E. Wolff, H.D. Pfeiffer, H.S. Delugach (Eds.), Conceptual Structures at Work. XI, 403 pages. 2004.

Vol. 3123: A. Belz, R. Evans, P. Piwek (Eds.), Natural Language Generation. X, 219 pages. 2004.

Vol. 3120: J. Shawe-Taylor, Y. Singer (Eds.), Learning Theory. X, 648 pages. 2004.

Vol. 3097: D. Basin, M. Rusinowitch (Eds.), Automated Reasoning. XII, 493 pages. 2004.

Vol. 3071: A. Omicini, P. Petta, J. Pitt (Eds.), Engineering Societies in the Agents World. XIII, 409 pages. 2004.

Vol. 3070: L. Rutkowski, J. Siekmann, R. Tadeusiewicz, L.A. Zadeh (Eds.), Artificial Intelligence and Soft Computing - ICAISC 2004. XXV, 1208 pages. 2004.

Vol. 3068: E. André, L. Dybkjær, W. Minker, P. Heisterkamp (Eds.), Affective Dialogue Systems. XII, 324 pages. 2004.

Vol. 3067: M. Dastani, J. Dix, A. El Fallah-Seghrouchni (Eds.), Programming Multi-Agent Systems. X, 221 pages. 2004.

Vol. 3066: S. Tsumoto, R. Słowiński, J. Komorowski, J.W. Grzymała-Busse (Eds.), Rough Sets and Current Trends in Computing. XX, 853 pages. 2004.

Vol. 3065: A. Lomuscio, D. Nute (Eds.), Deontic Logic in Computer Science. X, 275 pages. 2004.

Vol. 3060: A.Y. Tawfik, S.D. Goodwin (Eds.), Advances in Artificial Intelligence. XIII, 582 pages. 2004.

Vol. 3056: H. Dai, R. Srikant, C. Zhang (Eds.), Advances in Knowledge Discovery and Data Mining. XIX, 713 pages. 2004.

Vol. 3055: H. Christiansen, M.-S. Hacid, T. Andreasen, H.L. Larsen (Eds.), Flexible Query Answering Systems. X, 500 pages. 2004.

Vol. 3040: R. Conejo, M. Urretavizcaya, J.-L. Pérez-de-la-Cruz (Eds.), Current Topics in Artificial Intelligence. XIV, 689 pages. 2004.

Vol. 3035: M.A. Wimmer (Ed.), Knowledge Management in Electronic Government. XII, 326 pages. 2004.

Vol. 3034: J. Favela, E. Menasalvas, E. Chávez (Eds.), Advances in Web Intelligence. XIII, 227 pages. 2004.

Vol. 3030: P. Giorgini, B. Henderson-Sellers, M. Winikoff (Eds.), Agent-Oriented Information Systems. XIV, 207 pages. 2004.

Vol. 3029: B. Orchard, C. Yang, M. Ali (Eds.), Innovations in Applied Artificial Intelligence. XXI, 1272 pages. 2004.

Vol. 3025: G.A. Vouros, T. Panayiotopoulos (Eds.), Methods and Applications of Artificial Intelligence. XV, 546 pages. 2004.

Vol. 3020: D. Polani, B. Browning, A. Bonarini, K. Yoshida (Eds.), RoboCup 2003: Robot Soccer World Cup VII. XVI, 767 pages. 2004.

Vol. 3012: K. Kurumatani, S.-H. Chen, A. Ohuchi (Eds.), Multi-Agents for Mass User Support. X, 217 pages. 2004.

Vol. 3010: K.R. Apt, F. Fages, F. Rossi, P. Szeredi, J. Váncza (Eds.), Recent Advances in Constraints. VIII, 285 pages. 2004.

Vol. 2990: J. Leite, A. Omicini, L. Sterling, P. Torroni (Eds.), Declarative Agent Languages and Technologies. XII, 281 pages. 2004.

Vol. 2980: A. Blackwell, K. Marriott, A. Shimojima (Eds.), Diagrammatic Representation and Inference. XV, 448 pages. 2004.

Vol. 2977: G. Di Marzo Serugendo, A. Karageorgos, O.F. Rana, F. Zambonelli (Eds.), Engineering Self-Organising Systems. X, 299 pages. 2004.

Vol. 2972: R. Monroy, G. Arroyo-Figueroa, L.E. Sucar, H. Sossa (Eds.), MICAI 2004: Advances in Artificial Intelligence. XVII, 923 pages. 2004.

Vol. 2969: M. Nickles, M. Rovatsos, G. Weiss (Eds.), Agents and Computational Autonomy. X, 275 pages. 2004.

Vol. 2961: P. Eklund (Ed.), Concept Lattices. IX, 411 pages. 2004.

Vol. 2953: K. Konrad, Model Generation for Natural Language Interpretation and Analysis. XIII, 166 pages. 2004.

Vol. 2934: G. Lindemann, D. Moldt, M. Paolucci (Eds.), Regulated Agent-Based Social Systems. X, 301 pages. 2004.

Vol. 2930: F. Winkler (Ed.), Automated Deduction in Geometry. VII, 231 pages. 2004.

Vol. 2926: L. van Elst, V. Dignum, A. Abecker (Eds.), Agent-Mediated Knowledge Management. XI, 428 pages. 2004.

Vol. 2923: V. Lifschitz, I. Niemelä (Eds.), Logic Programming and Nonmonotonic Reasoning. IX, 365 pages. 2004.

Vol. 2915: A. Camurri, G. Volpe (Eds.), Gesture-Based Communication in Human-Computer Interaction. XIII, 558 pages. 2004.

Vol. 2913: T.M. Pinkston, V.K. Prasanna (Eds.), High Performance Computing - HiPC 2003. XX, 512 pages. 2003.

Vol. 2903: T.D. Gedeon, L.C.C. Fung (Eds.), AI 2003: Advances in Artificial Intelligence. XVI, 1075 pages. 2003.

Vol. 2902: F.M. Pires, S.P. Abreu (Eds.), Progress in Artificial Intelligence. XV, 504 pages. 2003.

Vol. 2892: F. Dau, The Logic System of Concept Graphs with Negation. XI, 213 pages. 2003.

Vol. 2891: J. Lee, M. Barley (Eds.), Intelligent Agents and Multi-Agent Systems. X, 215 pages. 2003.

Vol. 2882: D. Veit, Matchmaking in Electronic Markets. XV, 180 pages. 2003.

Vol. 2871: N. Zhong, Z.W. Raś, S. Tsumoto, E. Suzuki (Eds.), Foundations of Intelligent Systems. XV, 697 pages. 2003.

Vol. 2854: J. Hoffmann, Utilizing Problem Structure in Planing. XIII, 251 pages. 2003.

Vol. 2843: G. Grieser, Y. Tanaka, A. Yamamoto (Eds.), Discovery Science. XII, 504 pages. 2003.

Vol. 2842: R. Gavaldá, K.P. Jantke, E. Takimoto (Eds.), Algorithmic Learning Theory. XI, 313 pages. 2003.

Vol. 2838: N. Lavrač, D. Gamberger, L. Todorovski, H. Blockeel (Eds.), Knowledge Discovery in Databases: PKDD 2003. XVI, 508 pages. 2003.

Vol. 2837: N. Lavrač, D. Gamberger, L. Todorovski, H. Blockeel (Eds.), Machine Learning: ECML 2003. XVI, 504 pages. 2003.

Vol. 2835: T. Horváth, A. Yamamoto (Eds.), Inductive Logic Programming. X, 401 pages. 2003.

Vol. 2821: A. Günter, R. Kruse, B. Neumann (Eds.), KI 2003: Advances in Artificial Intelligence. XII, 662 pages. 2003.

Vol. 2807: V. Matoušek, P. Mautner (Eds.), Text, Speech and Dialogue. XIII, 426 pages. 2003.

Vol. 2801: W. Banzhaf, J. Ziegler, T. Christaller, P. Dittrich, J.T. Kim (Eds.), Advances in Artificial Life. XVI, 905 pages. 2003.

Vol. 2797: O.R. Zaïane, S.J. Simoff, C. Djeraba (Eds.), Mining Multimedia and Complex Data. XII, 281 pages. 2003.

Vol. 2792: T. Rist, R.S. Aylett, D. Ballin, J. Rickel (Eds.), Intelligent Virtual Agents. XV, 364 pages. 2003.

Vol. 2782: M. Klusch, A. Omicini, S. Ossowski, H. Laamanen (Eds.), Cooperative Information Agents VII. XI, 345 pages. 2003.

Vol. 2780: M. Dojat, E. Keravnou, P. Barahona (Eds.), Artificial Intelligence in Medicine. XIII, 388 pages. 2003.

Vol. 2777: B. Schölkopf, M.K. Warmuth (Eds.), Learning Theory and Kernel Machines. XIV, 746 pages. 2003.

Vol. 2752: G.A. Kaminka, P.U. Lima, R. Rojas (Eds.), RoboCup 2002: Robot Soccer World Cup VI. XVI, 498 pages. 2003.

Vol. 2741: F. Baader (Ed.), Automated Deduction – CADE-19. XII, 503 pages. 2003.

Vol. 2705: S. Renals, G. Grefenstette (Eds.), Text- and Speech-Triggered Information Access. VII, 197 pages. 2003.